AMERICAN EPOCH
A History of the
UNITED STATES
Since 1900

VOLUME II

AMERICAN EPOCH

Volume I: An Era of Economic Change, Reform,
and World Wars 1900–1945
Volume II: An Era of Total War and
Uncertain Peace 1938–1980

AMERICAN EPOCH

A History of the
UNITED STATES
Since 1900

Volume II: An Era of Total War and
Uncertain Peace   1938–1980

Arthur S. Link

George Henry Davis '86 Professor of American History and
Editor and Director of The Papers of Woodrow Wilson
Princeton University

William B. Catton

Professor Emeritus and Historian in Residence
Middlebury College

Fifth Edition

Alfred A. Knopf • New York

To David Wayne Hirst,
Friend and Colleague

E
741
L56
1980
V. 2

THIS IS A BORZOI BOOK
PUBLISHED BY ALFRED A. KNOPF, INC.

Fifth Edition
579864
Copyright © 1955 by Arthur S. Link
Copyright © 1963, 1967, 1973, 1974, 1980 by Arthur S. Link and William B. Catton

All rights reserved under International and Pan-American Copyright Conventions.
No part of this book may be reproduced in any form or by any means,
electronic or mechanical, including photocopying, without permission in writing
from the publisher.

All inquiries should be addressed to Alfred A. Knopf, Inc., 201 East 50th Street,
New York, N.Y. 10022.

Published in the United States by Alfred A. Knopf, Inc., New York, and
simultaneously in Canada by Random House of Canada Limited, Toronto.
Distributed by Random House, Inc., New York.

Library of Congress Cataloging in Publication Data
Link, Arthur Stanley.
An era of total war and uncertain peace, 1938-1980.
(Their American epoch, a history of the United States since 1900; v. 2)Includes
bibliography and index.
1. United States—History—1945-   2. World War, 1939-1945—United States. I.
Catton, William Bruce, 1926-   joint author. II. Title.
E741.L56 1980 vol. 2 973.9 80-12320
ISBN 0-394-32358-0 (Random House)

Book design by Lorraine Hohman
Cover design by Sol Schurman
Maps and charts by Theodore R. Miller

Manufactured in the United States of America

Published 1955; Second Edition 1963; Third Edition 1967; Fourth Edition 1973;
Fifth Edition 1980

Preface

The decision of the editors at Alfred A. Knopf to reset this fifth edition of *American Epoch* and publish it in a new format gave us an opportunity to review the fourth edition. The result is, we think, no routine revision. We have scrutinized the existing text in order to bring it into accord with the most recent interpretations and research. We have also updated the bibliography to mid-1979. The major revisions and additions, of course, involve events of the 1970s. Even though we are still close to these events, it is possible, on account of the available amount of documentary materials and relevant secondary works, to see them in something like historical perspective. Persons may well differ over details of the Vietnam war, but surely the present consensus concerning our involvement in that tragic conflict is not likely to change. We think that the lessons of the Watergate affair and the crisis of the presidency that culminated in Richard Nixon's resignation are also clear.

As we write this Preface, the American people are involved in an energy crisis, and the confront decisions that will affect their future for generations to come. We are not pessimistic about the future, although our conclusions and predictions about the merits of present policies must necessarily be tentative. *American Epoch* is fundamentally the story of a people who, for all their faults and mistakes, have faced dire problems of war, domestic conflict, and depression—and have overcome them. We are confident that after a difficult period of adjustment and reappraisal the nation will also come to satisfactory terms with the dire problems of today.

We are pleased to present this book anew and to note that it has now reached its twenty-fifth anniversary. We hope that it will prove as instructive to students in the future as it has been in the past.

We are grateful to David Follmer, Executive Editor of the College Department of Random House/Alfred A. Knopf, for his constant support and encouragement; to John Sturman of the College Department for seeing this volume through to publication; and to Lawrence Haas, a graduate student at Princeton University, for his help in updating the bibliography. The dedication is an attempt to express some small measure of our appreciation for a friendship and a professional association that have greatly enriched both of our lives for over a quarter of a century.

ARTHUR S. LINK
WILLIAM B. CATTON

Princeton, New Jersey
Middlebury, Vermont
October 23, 1979

Contents

Chapter 20   *The Second Road to War,*
                        1938–1941   *457*

1. From the Munich Crisis to the Outbreak of War   *458*
2. The Impact of the War upon the American People   *461*
3. The Menace of a Nazi Victory   *463*
4. The Great Debate   *465*
5. The Presidential Election of 1940 and the World Crisis   *467*
6. Lend-Lease: Implementing Nonbelligerency   *471*
7. The Invasion of Russia   *476*
8. The Atlantic Conference and the Brink of War   *477*
9. Futile Negotiations with Japan, 1938–1941   *480*
10. Pearl Harbor   *487*

Chapter 21   *The Second World War: The American*
                        Home Front   *492*

1. Manpower for War   *493*
2. Scientists Against Time   *495*
3. American Industry Goes to War   *497*
4. The Miracle of Production   *499*
5. The Greatest Tax Bill in History   *500*
6. Combating Inflation on the Home Front   *504*
7. Workers, Farmers, and the War Effort   *508*
8. Public Opinion, Civil Rights, and War   *512*
9. Blacks and the Home Front   *515*

Chapter 22   *The Second World War: Diplomatic and*
                Military Aspects   517

1. The Formation of the Grand Alliance   *517*
2. The Ebb Tide of Allied Military Fortunes   *520*
3. The Tide Begins to Turn   *525*
4. 1943: The United Nations on the Offensive   *529*
5. Planning for Victory and the Surrender of Italy   *533*
6. Slow Progress Toward Accord with Russia   *536*
7. The Allied Air Offensives in Europe, 1940–1945   *538*
8. Victory in Europe: To the Westwall   *539*
9. The Campaign and Election of 1944   *542*
10. Yalta: The High Tide of Allied Unity   *546*
11. Victory in Europe   *550*
12. Victory in the Pacific   *555*

Chapter 23   *The American Economy, 1940–1970*   *561*

1. The American People, 1940–1970   *561*
2. The American People: Income, Wealth, and Industry   *566*
3. The Further Technological Revolution   *573*
4. Industrial Pace Setters   *577*
5. Concentration and Competition in the American Economy   *583*
6. Organized Labor in the Postwar Era   *590*
7. Americans and Their "Mixed" Economy After Midcentury   *603*

Chapter 24   *Social and Cultural Trends,*
                1940–1970   *606*

1. The Affluent Society   *607*
2. The Turbulent Sixties   *615*
3. American Fiction, Drama, and Poetry   *622*
4. Crises and Changes in American Education   *631*
5. New Emphases in American Religion   *642*

Chapter 25   *Politics and Problems of the Truman*
                Era   *650*

1. Harry S Truman and the Progressive Movement   *651*
2. Demobilization, Reconversion, and a New Federal
      Structure   *653*
3. Truman's Struggles with Congress, 1945–1948   *658*
4. The Election of 1948   *661*
5. The Fair Deal: Revival of Progressivism   *665*
6. The Second Red Scare   *667*
7. Communism, the Courts, and Congress   *671*

Chapter 26   *Vain Struggles for a Brave New World,*
                1945-1949   *673*

1. The Brave New World   *674*
2. The Breakup of the Grand Alliance, 1945-1947   *679*
3. The Chinese Tragedy   *683*
4. The Decline of the Good Neighbor Policy   *688*
5. Beginnings of Containment: The Truman Doctrine   *691*
6. To Save Western Europe: The Marshall Plan   *694*
7. The Berlin Crisis and The North Atlantic Treaty   *697*

Chapter 27   *The Korean War and the Election of*
                1952   *702*

1. Prelude to the Korean Crisis   *702*
2. The Korean Crisis   *704*
3. The Korean War: First Phase   *706*
4. The Korean Crisis Threatens a Third World War   *709*
5. The Second "Great Debate" and the MacArthur Affair   *710*
6. Decision in Korea: Truce and Armistice   *714*
7. Challenges to Democratic Supremacy   *716*
8. The Campaign and Election of 1952   *717*

Chapter 28   *Politics and Problems of the Eisenhower*
                Era   *723*

1. The New Republican President   *724*
2. The Second Red Scare: Peak and Decline   *726*
3. The Anomaly of American Politics, 1953-1960   *731*
4. National Elections in the 1950s   *733*
5. Dynamic Conservatism: The Cabinet, Fiscal Policy, and Public
    Power   *738*
6. The Middle Road: Maintenance of the New Deal   *743*
7. Expansion of the New Deal: Education and Civil Rights   *749*
8. The Warren Court: Civil Rights and Civil Liberties   *751*
9. Blacks in the 1950s   *757*

Chapter 29   *The United States in a Turbulent World,*
                1953-1960   *766*

1. "New Look" in American Foreign and Defense Policies   *766*
2. America and the Soviet Union: Summit Diplomacy and Cold
    War   *773*
3. America and the Soviet Union: Nuclear Stalemate and the Quest
    for Disarmament   *776*

4. Europe and the United States in the 1950s   *780*
5. Recurrent Troubles in the Far East   *793*
6. The Middle East and Africa   *802*
7. The Western Hemisphere   *813*

Chapter 30   New Frontiers at Home and Abroad   818

1. The Election of 1960   *818*
2. The New Frontiersmen   *824*
3. Kennedy and Congress   *826*
4. The Black Revolt   *831*
5. The Cold War Continues   *834*
6. Trouble in Southeast Asia   *839*
7. Tragedy at Dallas   *843*

Chapter 31   The Great Society and the Vietnamese War   845

1. Johnson Takes the Helm   *846*
2. The Election of 1964   *848*
3. The Great Society   *851*
4. The Black Revolt Becomes Revolution   *857*
5. The Supreme Court in the 1960s   *865*
6. Continued Perplexities in a Changing World   *868*
7. War in Vietnam   *875*

Chapter 32   The Nixon Years, I: The First Term   882

1. The Election of 1968   *883*
2. The New Republican President   *891*
3. President and Congress, 1969–1972   *893*
4. The Supreme Court: Controversy and Change   *900*
5. Eagle Has Landed: Man Reaches the Moon   *908*
6. The Environment and the Consumer   *910*
7. Economic Stress   *913*
8. The Quest for Arms Control and Détente   *918*
9. Winding Down the War   *928*
10. The Election of 1972   *936*

Chapter 33   The Nixon Years, II: Watergate   948

1. The Second Term Begins   *948*
2. Background to Disaster, 1969–1972: Sabotage and Spying   *950*
3. Highway to Disaster, 1972–1973: Cover-Up   *953*

4. The White House Tapes   *955*
5. Spiro Agnew   *957*
6. Saturday Night Massacre, October 1973   *959*
7. Firestorm, October–December 1973   *963*
8. Battle Lines Drawn, January–April 1974   *966*
9. The April Transcripts   *968*
10. The White House Under Siege, May–July 1974   *970*
11. Downfall of a President   *972*
12. Resignation   *974*
13. Epilogue: Why Watergate?   *976*

Chapter 34   The Troubled Seventies   980

1. The President from Michigan   *981*
2. From Nixon to Ford: Legacy of Mistrust   *982*
3. Economic Troubles and Energy Crisis   *986*
4. Republican Response   *993*
5. GOP Foreign Policy: Shuttle Diplomacy and Congressional Power   *999*
6. GOP Foreign Policy: The Quest for Arms Control and Détente   *1003*
7. The Election of 1976   *1005*
8. The President from Georgia   *1011*
9. Toward New Accords: Panama and Middle East   *1013*
10. Toward New Accords: China and Russia   *1021*
11. Energy and the Economy: Democratic Response   *1024*
12. The Battle Against Inflation   *1028*
13. The Crisis of 1979   *1032*

Chapter 35   America in 1980: Dilemmas and Prospects   1035

1. The Question of Leadership   *1035*
2. The People and Their Heritage   *1038*
3. Race Relations   *1040*
4. The Prospect   *1041*

Suggested Additional Reading   i

Index   xxv

Maps

Election of 1940   *470*
Lend-Lease Supply Routes   *473*
The Coming of the War in the Atlantic, 1939–1941   *474*
The Coming of the War in the Pacific, 1939–1941   *481*
Axis Europe, 1941   *518*
The Tides of Japanese Expansion   *521*
Defensive Phase in the Southwest Pacific   *522*
Offensive-Defensive Phase in the Southwest Pacific   *526*
The War Against Germany in the East, 1941–1945   *530*
The Allied Offensives in the Pacific   *532*
The War Against Germany in the West, 1942–1945   *534*
The Normandy Landings and the Break-through   *541*
Election of 1944   *545*
Allied Offensives to the Rhine, 1944–1945   *552*
The War Against Japan: Final Phase, 1944–1945   *556*
Population Change, 1940–1970   *563*
Population Density, 1970   *565*
Election of 1948   *664*
Central and Eastern Europe: Territorial Changes, 1939–1947   *682*
Divided Germany and Austria; Berlin's Channels to the West   *698*
The Korean War, 1950–1953   *708*
Election of 1952   *721*
Election of 1956   *736*
Collective Defense Arrangements, 1961   *782*
European Common Market, 1979   *792*
Indochina, 1954   *796*
Taiwan, the Offshore Islands, and Adjacent Area   *799*
The Middle East, 1961; The Suez Crisis, 1956   *807*
Election of 1960   *823*
Election of 1964   *850*
Israel and the Suez, 1947, 1949, and 1967   *873*
Vietnam, 1966   *879*
Election of 1968   *890*
Election of 1972   *945*
Election of 1976   *1010*

Charts

American Public Opinion and the Issue of Intervention   *466*

Expansion of U.S. Armed Forces, 1941–1945   *493*

Expenditures of the United States Government, 1914–1952   *501*

Federal Expenditures and Receipts, 1939–1953   *502*

Corporate Profits, Taxes, and Dividends, 1940–1960   *503*

Wholesale Prices, 1920–1945   *505*

Personal Income, Consumption, and Saving, 1940–1961   *506*

Consumer Prices, 1940–1960   *507*

The American Labor Force, 1940–1950   *508*

Work Stoppages in the United States, 1935–1951   *511*

Merchant Ships Sunk by German Submarines, November 1941 to June
    1943   *523*

Gross National Product, 1940–1971   *567*

Business Expenditures on New Plant and Equipment,
    1940–1971   *568*

Hours and Earnings of Production Workers in Manufacturing,
    1940–1971   *571*

Industrial Production, 1940–1970   *574*

Research in the United States, 1941–1970   *576*

Value Added by Manufacture Per Production Worker, 1954 and
    1970   *578*

Nonagricultural Employees, by Occupation, 1940–1970   *591*

Corporate Pension Funds, 1950–1970   *597*

A Half Century of Public Welfare   *604*

A Nation of City Dwellers, 1970   *608*

American Public Education, 1940–1970   *632*

Federal Outlays for Education, 1955, 1965, and 1971   *635*

Organization Under the National Security Act, 1947   *657*

Organs of the United Nations   *676*

American Foreign Aid, 1945–1971   *696*

Foreign Trade, 1940–1970   *747*

The Federal Budget, 1955–1977   *856*

Median Family and Per Capita Income, 1975   *992*

Energy Consumption, 1940–1977   *995*

Immigration, 1951–1977   *1014*

Refugees Admitted, 1954–1977   *1015*

Employment and Unemployment in the United States,
    1950–1977   *1027*

Consumer Prices, 1960–1977   *1029*

AN ERA
OF
TOTAL WAR
AND
UNCERTAIN PEACE
1938–1980

In which the American people join in a victorious global struggle against the Axis powers, achieve international preeminence and unprecedented prosperity in the postwar years, and repeatedly find their power and security subjected to new threats and challenges in a constantly changing world.

20

The Second Road
to War,
1938–1941

Hitler brought Europe to the brink of war soon after his seizure of Austria in March 1938 by threatening to seize the German-speaking Sudeten provinces of Czechoslovakia. The British and French rejected Russian cooperation and submitted to Hitler's demands during this so-called Munich crisis. They thus postponed war but lost a powerful ally. Then Hitler's betrayal of his Munich pledges and attack against Poland in September 1939 caused the two western democracies to stand up and fight to prevent Nazi power from overwhelming all of Europe.

The policies demanded by the American people and followed by their government between September 1939 and June 1940 were certainly neither bold nor helpful to the western democracies. But it is easy to criticize in retrospect and to forget how divided and distraught the American people were in this time of crisis, and how the administration could not lead where Congress and the people would not follow. The important fact was that Americans, or a majority of them, rallied behind the president in bold if belated efforts once they understood the dimensions of the Nazi threat.

While the Washington government sought to help stem the Nazi tide in the West by measures short of war, it used stern diplomacy to turn back the rising tide of Japanese imperialism that threatened to engulf the Far East. At any time during the period from 1939 to December 1941 the American leaders could have come to terms with Japan—by accepting Japanese control of China and Japanese demands for leadership in the Orient. The supreme tragedy was that by 1941 the situation had passed beyond the point of reasonable solution. As compromise on any terms that did not violate everything the American people had stood for in the Far East seemed impossible by 1941, the two nations reached the point where diplomacy could not harmonize fundamentally divergent objectives.

In this chapter we will describe how the American government and people, haltingly at first, but boldly afterward, emerged from the chrysalis of isolation and assumed a position of decisive power in the affairs of mankind.

1. From the Munich Crisis to the Outbreak of War

After the annexation of Austria, Hitler began a campaign for incorporation of the German-speaking Sudeten provinces of Czechoslovakia into Greater Germany and made plans for a campaign in the East.

Prime Minister Chamberlain flew to Germany for a personal meeting with Hitler on September 15, 1938, where he learned that Germany would accept nothing less than outright cession of the Sudetenland. Chamberlain and the French premier, Edouard Daladier, knuckled under and agreed that Czechoslovakia must surrender to the führer's demands. The Czech leaders had no alternative but to submit. Then Hitler rejected Chamberlain's arrangement for the transfer of the disputed provinces, and it seemed that war was inevitable. Chamberlain in a last-ditch plea on September 27 suggested that Hitler, Daladier, Mussolini, and he meet personally to find a solution. The world was surprised when Hitler accepted and relieved when the four leaders met at Munich on September 29 and quickly agreed to a scheme for the dismemberment of the Czech republic.

Chamberlain and Daladier by a stroke of the pen confirmed Hitler's supremacy over his generals, who had opposed his recent reckless moves; made Germany absolutely dominant on the Continent; weakened the attractiveness of a western alignment for the Soviet leaders; and demonstrated their own incompetence as diplomats. All that they received in return was Hitler's unctuous promise that he would make no more territorial demands in Europe, respect Czech sovereignty, and settle all future disputes by peaceful negotiation.

Roosevelt had acted as an unhappy partner in appeasement by making several appeals to the European leaders for a peaceful settlement, but he was never guilty of believing that the Munich Pact offered any hope for real peace in Europe. On the contrary, he began to reorient his domestic and foreign policies soon afterward in preparation for the conflict that he was certain would ensue. He abandoned his "purge" of conservative Democrats, called a halt to the reform energies of the New Deal, and began a campaign for speedy rearmament in the autumn of 1938. Hitler announced an expansion of German military strength on October 9. Roosevelt countered two days later by announcing a $300 million increase in American spending for defense purposes and calling upon his military advisers to plan for huge increases in aircraft production. In his Annual Message to Congress and his Budget Message on January 4 and 5, 1939, he asked for $1.3 billion for the regular defense establishment and an additional $525 million, most of it for airplanes. These appeals fell upon receptive ears, for the Munich tragedy had opened the eyes of millions of Americans to the Nazi danger to world peace, while violent anti-Jewish pogroms in Germany in November 1938 had revealed anew the brutal character of the Nazi regime.[1] Thus Congress responded by increasing the military and naval budgets by nearly two-thirds and by authorizing the president to begin accumulating stockpiles of strategic raw materials for use if war occurred.

In addition, the administration intensified its campaign to strengthen the collective security system in the Western Hemisphere. This was now a more urgent and difficult task than during the early years of the Good Neighbor policy, for the German government had begun a tremendous economic and propaganda campaign aimed at establishing German hegemony in Latin America. Nazi agents had organized National Socialist parties among German immigrants in Brazil and Argentina, threatened economic reprisals against any Latin American nation that dared to cooperate with the United States, and engaged in wholesale military espionage under the cover of German steamship and air lines.

Roosevelt and Hull therefore determined to form a solid hemispheric anti-Nazi front at the Pan-American Conference that opened at Lima, Peru, on December 9, 1938. Hull, as chairman of the American delegation and chief advocate of hemispheric solidarity, had the cordial support of most Latin American governments. As during the conference in Buenos Aires two years before, however, the Argentine delegation seemed determined either to dominate or wreck the proceedings. Hull marshaled a nearly solid Latin American opinion and conducted patient negotiations with the president and foreign minister of Argentina. The result was unanimous approval of the Declaration of Lima on Christmas Eve. It reaffirmed

---

[1] It would be difficult to exaggerate the importance of the American reaction to this outbreak of terrorism against the Jews of Germany. Leaders of both parties joined in expressing the revulsion of the American people, while Roosevelt recalled Ambassador Hugh Wilson from Berlin in protest.

the twenty-one American republics' determination to resist jointly any Fascist or Nazi threat to the peace and security of the hemisphere.

Roosevelt's chief objective during the uneasy months following Munich was repeal or drastic amendment of the Neutrality Act of 1937. Hull was in constant communication with Key Pittman, chairman of the Senate foreign relations committee, urging him to take leadership in repealing the arms embargo, that "incitement to Hitler to go to war." But Pittman warned that a repeal measure could not pass, and Roosevelt and Hull momentarily gave up the fight and concentrated on measures for stronger defense.

The international situation suddenly deteriorated when Hitler sent his armies into Prague on March 15, 1939, and took control of what remained of unhappy Czechoslovakia. The dictator's cynical violation of an agreement upon which the ink was hardly dry caused such a profound revulsion of sentiment in Great Britain that Chamberlain was forced to abandon appeasement. The prime minister almost at once began negotiating treaties guaranteeing the independence and territorial integrity of countries believed to be next in Germany's line of march—Poland, Rumania, Greece, and Turkey.

Reaction in Washington to Hitler's latest move was nearly as violent as in London. Speaking for the president on March 17, Acting Secretary of State Sumner Welles condemned Germany's "wanton lawlessness" and use of "arbitrary force." On the same day the president decided not to recognize the destruction of Czechoslovakia and to continue to deal with the Czech minister in Washington. Accompanying this strong talk now went even stronger administration action to obtain revision of the neutrality statute. In order to win Senator Pittman's support, Roosevelt and Hull accepted a compromise measure—introduced by Pittman on March 20—that extended the cash-and-carry provision but amended it to include arms, ammunition, and other war materials.

The president ventured all his prestige in the fight to obtain either passage of the Pittman bill or outright repeal of the arms embargo, but the campaign was to no avail. Roosevelt called House leaders to the White House on May 19 and declared that repeal of the arms embargo might prevent war and would certainly make an Axis victory less likely if war occurred. But Congress would not budge; both houses decisively refused to approve measures of revision. Then the president invited Senate leaders to the White House on July 18 for a frank discussion of the European situation. All senators present but one thought that revision of the Neutrality Act was impossible, and Vice-President Garner turned to Roosevelt and said: "Well, Captain, we may as well face the facts. You haven't got the votes, and that's all there is to it." The president replied that he had done his best, and that the Senate would have to shoulder responsibility for refusing to take action to protect the nation's security.

2. *The Impact of the War upon the American People*

Leaders of Europe engaged in last-minute negotiations during the summer of 1939 in preparation for Armageddon. Chamberlain and Daladier by signing the Munich Pact had not only isolated Russia but had also intensified Russian suspicions that they were trying to turn Hitler eastward. The British and French premiers, once they had abandoned appeasement, appealed to the Kremlin to sign an alliance to contain nazism. The Russians demanded as their price a guarantee of the security of all eastern Europe and the Baltic states and acknowledgment of Russia's right in certain circumstances to occupy this broad zone stretching from Finland to Bulgaria.

While Chamberlain and Daladier were negotiating, Stalin and his new foreign minister, Vyacheslav Molotov, were simultaneously sounding out the possibilities of agreement with Germany. Hitler was glad to make temporary concessions to prevent Russia from joining his adversaries in the West. The upshot of these negotiations was the signing of a Nazi-Soviet treaty of nonaggression in Moscow on August 23, 1939. The published terms provided simply that Russia and Germany would refrain from attacking each other. The secret provisions provided that in the event of a territorial rearrangement in eastern Europe, Russia should have Finland, Estonia, Latvia, eastern Poland, and the Rumanian province of Bessarabia, while Germany might annex Lithuania[2] and western Poland.

Hitler was now protected against the danger of a two-front war and increased his demands on Poland. Chamberlain warned that Britain would go at once to Poland's aid if Germany attacked but offered to discuss the Polish question, and Roosevelt added a new appeal for peace. Hitler responded by sending his armies into Poland on September 1; two days later Britain and France declared war on the Reich. Thus the chips were finally down for a last play after four years of intolerable tension.

Most Americans had seen that war was inevitable and took the outbreak of hostilities in stride. The president issued an official proclamation of neutrality on September 5, 1939, and put the Neutrality Act into force,[3] as he was bound to do; but he did not ask the people to be impartial in thought as well as in deed, as Wilson had done in different circumstances in 1914.

The administration moved swiftly to strengthen the defenses of the Western Hemisphere by arranging for a conference of the foreign ministers of the American republics. They met at Panama City on September 23

---

[2]By subsequent negotiation Germany exchanged Lithuania for Polish territory.

[3]Thus the arms embargo went into effect, causing an immediate cancellation of Anglo-French war orders worth $79 million. Belligerents, however, were free to buy raw materials and food, although the Johnson Act prevented extension of credits to the British and French governments.

and agreed with surprising unanimity upon common neutrality regulations and mutual consultation in the event that a transfer of territory from one European power to another threatened the security of the New World. The most striking work of the conference was the adoption of the Declaration of Panama, marking out a broad zone 300 miles wide around the Americas, excluding Canada and European colonies, into which the belligerents were forbidden to carry the war. It was, actually, only a verbal prohibition and had no practical effect.

The president's primary objective, however, was still repeal of the arms embargo provision of the Neutrality Act. He called Congress into special session to plead earnestly for repeal on September 21. His main theme was maintenance of American neutrality, for he shared the prevalent view that Britain and France could defeat Germany if only they could obtain weapons of war. As if to prove that he believed that neutrality was desirable, he urged Congress to prohibit American ships from entering European war zones and to apply the cash-and-carry principle to all European purchases in the United States.

The request was modest and thoroughly neutral, but it stirred isolationists to frenzied activity. Senator Borah in a radio broadcast warned that lifting the arms embargo would be tantamount to taking sides in a war in which American interests were not involved. Pacifists, who argued that the only way to prevent war was to have nothing to do with the instruments of destruction, were joined by Communists, who charged that Britain and France were fighting to preserve imperialistic capitalism. On the other side, in support of the president, was ranged a powerful new combination of southern and eastern Democrats in Congress. They were joined in the country at large by such preparationist Republicans as Stimson and Frank Knox, a vast majority of the business interests and the metropolitan press, and a large segment of the intellectual leadership of the country. It was evident by the middle of October that the tide had turned in the president's favor. Meanwhile, Senator Pittman had drafted a new neutrality bill that lifed the arms embargo, applied the cash-and-carry principle, and forbade American ships to trade with belligerent countries and Americans to travel on belligerent ships. Pittman persuaded the foreign relations committee to report this measure favorably on September 28. Congress approved the Pittman bill after a month of debate, and the president signed it on November 4, 1939.

Meanwhile, Hitler's armies had overrun Poland before the French could mount an offensive on the western front, and the Russians had shocked the world by joining the Germans in devouring Poland. The Germans built their offensive power for a drive in the West during the following months, while the British and French acted as if the war could be won merely by waiting for the Nazi regime to collapse. This so-called phony war lulled Americans even more than the British and French into believing that the Germans could never win.

American attention was diverted from the western front by a Russian invasion of Finland in November and December 1939, which was mounted in order to protect Russia's northern flank against a potential German attack. A hot wave of anger swept over the American public, but the administration acted cautiously. Roosevelt indignantly denounced the "dreadful rape of Finland" and castigated the Soviet Union as "a dictatorship as absolute as any other dictatorship in the world." The State and Treasury departments instituted an effective moral embargo on the export of war supplies to the Soviets. But beyond this action the administration could not go. Roosevelt and Hull perceived that the marriage between Germany and Russia was incompatible, and they may well have understood the strategic reasons for the Russian attack against Finland.

3. The Menace of a Nazi Victory

The so-called phony war ended on April 9, 1940, when Hitler hurled his armies into Denmark and Norway, and German airplanes and *Panzer* (armored) divisions struck hard at Belgium, Holland, and northern France on May 10. Terror swept over the American people as this blitzkrieg (lightning war) developed. All Americans except a few diehard isolationists recognized that a Germany completely dominant in Europe would pose a dire threat to their peace and security. And now it was about to happen, the catastrophe that only a week before had seemed impossible. There was France, her dispirited armies reeling and scattering under the impact of Nazi power; there was the British expeditionary force, driven to the sea at Dunkirk and forced to execute a nearly impossible evacuation.

The immediate threat to American security was the possibility that Hitler might claim Iceland and Greenland, both of which commanded the American sea lanes to Britain, by virtue of his conquest of their mother country, Denmark. Roosevelt refused to order the occupation of Iceland but was obviously pleased when the British occupied it on May 10. Greenland, however, was too close to the United States and Canada to be ignored. Roosevelt declared on April 18 that the island enjoyed the protection of the Monroe Doctrine. Washington refused a request by Greenlanders that it assume a temporary protectorate. Instead, it furnished military supplies and established a Greenland Patrol by the Coast Guard.

Chamberlain resigned on May 10, 1940, the same day the Germans hurtled into the Low Countries, and Winston Spencer Churchill, long the chief British opponent of appeasement, took the helm as prime minister. He had nothing to offer the people of the empire but "blood, toil, tears, and sweat" and the hope of ultimate victory. Churchill sent a cable to Roosevelt when the blitzkrieg was in its fifth day in which he frankly acknowledged the likelihood of German conquest of Europe and asked the president to proclaim a state of nonbelligerency, lend Britain forty or fifty old destroyers, and supply several hundred aircraft and quantities of ammunition. Roosevelt had to reply that the moment for such action was not opportune since Congress would have to approve a transfer of the destroyers.

Roosevelt had determined even before he received Churchill's urgent plea to ask Congress to hasten the nation's armament campaign.[4] This he did in a special message on May 16, 1940, warning Americans that their own security would be gravely imperiled if an enemy should seize any outlying territory, and calling for production of 50,000 planes a year and large new expenditures for the armed forces. Moreover, after the Allied collapse on the western front, he asked Congress on May 31 for an additional $1 billion for defense and for authority to call the National Guard and reserve personnel into active service.

Meanwhile, Roosevelt had also been trying to bolster French morale and to dissuade Mussolini from joining Hitler. Mussolini was deaf to such appeals and rushed to join the Nazis in devouring the carcass of France on June 10. This act of aggression gave the president an opportunity to say in clear and ringing words what the United States would do. In an address at the University of Virginia on the same day that Italy entered the war, Roosevelt announced the end of American isolation and the beginning of a new phase of nonbelligerency. Hereafter the United States would "extend to the opponents of force the material resources of this nation."

This was the week in which France was tottering on the brink of ruin. German armies entered Paris on June 14. The government of Paul Reynaud, who had succeeded Daladier as premier on March 21, gave way on June 16 to a government headed by the aged Marshal Henri-Philippe Pétain. He surrendered to the Germans on June 22. The supreme moment of decision had now come for the president and his advisers. Hitler stood astride the Continent. Italian entry into the war seemed to presage early Axis control of the Mediterranean and North Africa. The British army was stripped of virtually all its heavy equipment after the Dunkirk evacuation. Churchill had warned in repeated messages that the British Isles might be overrun without immediate American assistance, and that a successor government might have to surrender the fleet in order to save the realm. Should the Roosevelt administration assume that the British were lost, abandon aid to them, and prepare to defend the Western Hemisphere? Or should it strip American defenses in the hope that the British could survive?

Not only isolationists but many "realistic" Americans demanded adherence to the former course. They were joined by the Joint Planners of the

---

[4]The War Department had made plans for increasing the army's strength to 500,000 men by July 1941, to 1 million by January 1942, and to nearly 2 million by July 1942; for production of 50,000 aircraft a year; and for manufacture of vast numbers of tanks and guns.

War and Navy departments, who warned on June 27, 1940, that Britain might not survive and urged the president to concentrate on American defenses. It was the kind of advice that military leaders, who think in terms of the worst contingencies, have to give. But Roosevelt decided to gamble on Britain. In this decision he had the support of his new secretaries of war and of the navy, Henry L. Stimson and Frank Knox, whom he had appointed on June 20 to gain Republican support for the defense effort. Roosevelt rejected Churchill's ambitious proposals for turning the United States into a gigantic arsenal for Britain, but he ordered the War and Navy departments to "scrape the bottom of the barrel" and turn over all available guns and ammunition to private firms for resale to Britain.[5] In addition, officials of the War, Navy, and Treasury departments conferred with a British Purchasing Mission and promised to deliver 14,375 aircraft by April 1942. Roosevelt's decision to gamble on British survival was the most momentous in his career to this time, for he acted in the certain knowledge that war with Germany was probable if Britain should go down.

4. The Great Debate

The fall of France and the seeming imminence of British defeat shocked the American people and stimulated much wild talk of an immediate German invasion of the Western Hemisphere. More significant was the way the threat of Nazi victory intensified the great debate over American foreign policy that had been in progress since the Munich crisis. Upon the outcome of this controversy would depend the fate of the world.

Hitler's destruction of Czechoslovakia had convinced a small but influential minority of Americans that the United States would live in deadly peril if nazism ever enveloped Europe. Soon after the outbreak of the war they formed the Non-Partisan Committee for Peace through Revision of the Neutrality Law, with William Allen White of Kansas as chairman. The Non-Partisan Committee had branches in thirty states by the end of October 1939. Its propaganda was a decisive factor in swinging public opinion behind repeal of the arms embargo provision. The committee quietly disbanded during the so-called phony war but reorganized on May 17, 1940, as the Committee to Defend America by Aiding the Allies. The committee had over 600 local branches within a few months and had taken leadership in a nationwide campaign to combat isolationism and stimulate public support for the government's policy of all aid short of war.

[5] Some 970,000 rifles, 200,500 revolvers, 87,500 machine guns, 895 75-mm guns, 316 mortars, and a huge quantity of ammunition were shipped to Britain from June to October 1940.

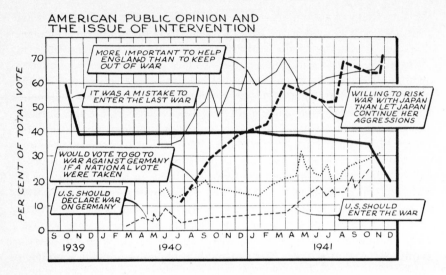

AMERICAN PUBLIC OPINION AND
THE ISSUE OF INTERVENTION

Reproduced by permission of Professor Hadley Cantril and the Public Opinion Research Project of Princeton University.

The committee's success was reflected in the transformation in public opinion that occurred during the summer of 1940. When polls revealed in July that probably a large majority favored aid to Britain, the committee next worked to generate public support for a transfer of destroyers to the British.[6] A Gallup poll in mid-August indicated that a majority of the people would approve if the president followed the committee's lead. In addition, White and other Republican leaders headed off an isolationist bloc in the Republican national convention and obtained a platform plank approving aid to "all peoples fighting for liberty."

It was inevitable that this movement to draw America closer to the war's orbit would not go unchallenged by isolationist leaders. Their ranks were considerably thinned by the fall of France, but they were still a powerful if incongruous group by the autumn of 1940. They included pro-Nazi spokesmen like Father Coughlin, Gerald L. K. Smith, and William Dudley Pelley. A large body of midwestern businessmen joined their ranks mainly out of hatred of the New Deal. Old progressives like senators Burton K. Wheeler and Gerald P. Nye still identified cooperation with England with the machinations of Wall Street. Many Protestant ministers and idealists had embraced a philosophy of nonresistance. The Hearst papers, the *Chicago Tribune*, the *New York Daily News*, the *Washington Times-Herald*, and other newspapers lent editorial support. Cooperating

[6]The president told White about the contemplated destroyer transfer at a conference on June 29, 1940, and won White's and the committee's support for the project.

also were the Socialists, led by Norman Thomas, who still thought of war in economic terms, and the Communists, who had become suddenly pro-Nazi after the signing of the Nazi-Soviet Non-Aggression Pact.

The leading isolationist organization was the America First Committee, incorporated in September 1940 with Robert E. Wood, chairman of the board of Sears, Roebuck and Company, as national chairman. The America First movement soon included thousands of patriotic Americans who sincerely believed that defense of the Western Hemisphere and noninter-vention in Europe's war were the only course of safety for the United States. But the America First Committee also had the support of all pro-Nazi groups in the country.

The debate between proponents of strong support for Britain and the noninterventionists did not end until Japanese bombs fell on Pearl Harbor, but it was evident that the former had won the battle for control of the American public mind long before this date. The polls showed the meta-morphosis that occurred. In September 1939 some 82 percent of persons queried thought that the Allies would win; by July 1940 only 43 percent were sure that Britain would win. More important, the proportion of Americans who believed that a German victory would menace their secu-rity increased from 43 percent in March 1940 to 69 percent in July 1940. All through the period 1939–1941 an overwhelming majority of Americans indicated a desire to avoid active participation in the war. The important fact was that this same majority approved strong assistance to Britain; and by the spring of 1941 a majority favored extending such aid even if it led to hostilities with Germany.

The president, administration leaders, and the Committee to Defend America played a significant role in this erosion of isolationist sentiments, but events in Europe and the Far East from 1939 to 1941 played an even more significant part. The American people, not wanting to defend obso-lete neutral rights or to engage in a second crusade for democracy, sup-ported the administration in a strong policy and accepted the risk of war. They were concerned only with defending their own security and free-dom. The tragedy was that it required the momentary triumph of Hitler and the near defeat of the British Empire to awaken Americans to the simple facts of international life.

5. *The Presidential Election of 1940 and the World Crisis*

Meanwhile, the crisis of the spring and summer had no less an impact upon the national conventions and presidential campaign of 1940 than upon popular attitudes regarding the American stake in an Allied victory.

It seemed certain at the beginning of the year that either Senator Robert A. Taft of Ohio, Senator Arthur H. Vandenberg of Michigan, or young Thomas E. Dewey of New York—all of them ardent noninterventionists at the time—would win the Republican presidential nomination. Almost at the last moment Wendell L. Willkie of Indiana, president of the Commonwealth & Southern Corporation and an old antagonist of the TVA, had entered the preconvention campaign. For all his big business connections, Willkie was a former Democrat who approved most of the New Deal reform measures. More important, he had long supported the president's program of aid to Britain. In more normal times Willkie would not have had a chance, but the Republican convention opened in Philadelphia on June 24 amid the panic created by the French surrender two days before. Willkie's managers were able to execute a miraculous whirlwind campaign in the fear and excitement of the time. They achieved his nomination on June 28 by marshaling the young progressive and internationalist element in the GOP. They won a second notable victory over the diehard isolationist bloc with adoption of a platform approving "prompt" and "realistic" defense and aid to victims of aggression.

The nomination of the rugged, popular Willkie—the first colorful Republican candidate since 1904—compelled President Roosevelt to come to some decision concerning the Democratic nomination. Roosevelt probably intended all along to run for a third term, for he made his nomination inevitable by refusing to support another candidate and by failing to discourage efforts in his own behalf. In any event, he sent a message on July 16 to the Democratic National Convention, which had opened in Chicago the day before, saying that he had no desire to remain in office and wanted the convention to be free to make a choice, but implying that he would accept the nomination if the convention insisted. Few of the party bosses wanted Roosevelt, but there was nothing that they could do except nominate him on the first ballot. The delegates rebelled, however, when the president insisted upon Secretary of Agriculture Henry A. Wallace as his running mate. Roosevelt's spokesman, Harry Hopkins, was able to force the Iowan upon an unwilling party only by using the most ruthless methods.

The president delivered his acceptance speech by radio to the convention early in the morning of July 19 and then did not make another campaign address until September 11. In the meantime he gave all his energies to more urgent problems: military, air, and naval expansion, which he obtained easily from Congress, and approval of the Burke-Wadsworth bill for selective service, which he won in September with Willkie's support.

There was danger at this time that the Nazis might seize the French islands in the Caribbean, Guadeloupe and Martinique. Washington first warned Berlin against trying any such stratagem; then it arranged for a conference of the Pan-American foreign ministers to meet at Havana on July 21, 1940, to consider countermeasures. Hull won unanimous approval on July 27 of a declaration that an attack on any American republic was an attack against all of them, as well as adoption of a convention providing that an Inter-American Commission for Territorial Administration should take temporary control of any European possessions in the New World about to be transferred to another sovereignty.

The most urgent necessity confronting the administration during this summer of campaign and crisis, however, was devising some means of transferring forty or fifty destroyers[7] to Britain for antisubmarine operations and assistance in defense of the British Isles against the invasion that Hitler planned for mid-September. The chief obstacle was an amendment to the naval appropriations bill that Congress had adopted on June 28. It forbade the president to transfer defense equipment to a foreign power unless the army chief of staff and the chief of naval operations first certified that the equipment was not essential to the national defense.

Roosevelt found a way out of this dilemma after the Nazis had begun a great air assault against Britain preparatory to the invasion. The upshot was an agreement signed in Washington on September 2, 1940. The United States gave fifty destroyers to the British government in return for a formal pledge that Britain would never surrender its fleet and ninety-nine-year leases on air and naval bases on British territory in Newfoundland, Bermuda, and the Caribbean. Because the agreement vastly enhanced the security of the Western Hemisphere, General George C. Marshall, army chief of staff, and Admiral Harold R. Stark, chief of naval operations, could in good conscience approve it, as the amendment of June 28 required. Churchill, however, rebelled at the idea of a deal and insisted upon giving outright the leases for American bases in Newfoundland and Bermuda. The destroyer-bases agreement meant the end of formal neutrality and marked the beginning of a period of limited American participation in the war. Henceforth the extent of that participation would bear a direct relation to German strength and British needs.

While Roosevelt was thus engaged, Wendell Willkie had undertaken a one-man campaign against a silent opponent. He was ebullient and confident during the early weeks in his strictures against Democratic inefficiency and a third term. He was fatally handicapped, however, by his own basic agreement with most of Roosevelt's domestic and foreign policies. Willkie apparently realized around the first of October that he might be defeated. In desperation, because he badly wanted to win, he jettisoned his progressive, internationalist advisers and accepted the counsel of the Old Guard professionals. They "begged Willkie to abandon this nonsense about a bipartisan foreign policy—to attack Roosevelt as a warmonger—to scare the American people with warnings that votes for Roosevelt meant wooden crosses for their sons and brothers and sweethearts."[8]

The more Willkie played upon the war issue the more his campaign

---

[7]They were to be supplied from a reserve of 172 destroyers built during the First World War, which the Navy Department had reconditioned and returned to service.

[8]Robert E. Sherwood, *Roosevelt and Hopkins, An Intimate History* (New York, 1948), p. 187.

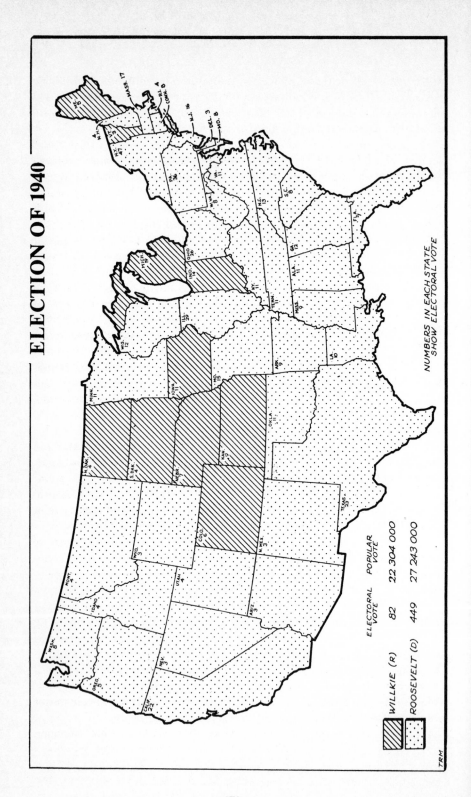

ELECTION OF 1940

NUMBERS IN EACH STATE
SHOW ELECTORAL VOTE

	ELECTORAL VOTE	POPULAR VOTE
WILLKIE (R)	82	22 304 000
ROOSEVELT (D)	449	27 243 000

caught fire, and Democratic managers throughout the country were appalled lest the rising antiwar tide sweep the Republican candidate into the White House. Worried Democrats begged Roosevelt to tell the country that he stood for peace. In response, the president reversed his field. He assured voters in a speech at Philadelphia on October 23 that he had made no secret agreement to involve the United States in the war, "or for any other purpose." He made a grand tour of New York City on October 28, climaxed by an evening address in Madison Square Garden. Reviewing his long efforts to strengthen the nation's defenses, he warned that Americans could keep war from their shores only by stopping aggression in Europe. He called this the "realistic" way to preserve the peace that all Americans desired.

The Madison Square Garden address was in the main a forthright enunciation, but it neither reversed the rising Willkie tide nor quieted the fears of Democratic politicians. On October 30 the president began a tour of New England, to be climaxed by a speech in Boston during the evening. He was inundated all during the day by telegrams warning that defeat impended unless he gave more explicit pledges to maintain peace. For once the great campaigner seemed unsure of himself. At the last minute he included the following promise in his Boston address: "I have said this before, but I shall say it again and again and again: Your boys are not going to be sent into any foreign wars. . . . The purpose of our defense is defense."

It was evident by the late evening of election day, November 5, that the president had won again, although the margin of his victory was considerably smaller than it had been in 1936. He received 27,243,000 popular and 449 electoral votes, as compared with 22,304,400 popular and 82 electoral votes for Willkie. In addition, the Democrats retained large majorities in both houses of Congress. The Socialist and Communist candidates, Norman Thomas and Earl Browder, received 100,264 and 48,579 popular votes, respectively.

6. Lend-Lease: Implementing Nonbelligerency

The chief concern of British and American leaders by the autumn of 1940 was the danger that the entire flow of American goods would be cut off as a result of the exhaustion of British dollar reserves. Out of their total dollar resources of $6.5 billion at the beginning of the war, the British had spent $4.5 billion in the United States by November 1940. By that date they were ready to place new orders for American airplanes, armored equipment for ten divisions, and cargo ships. But the Neutrality Act of 1939 required cash payment for all supplies, and the British were nearing the end of their ability to pay. Roosevelt and Treasury officials well knew that the entire system of American aid would soon collapse unless some solution was quickly found.

The president embarked upon a cruise of the Caribbean aboard the cruiser *Tuscaloosa* on December 2, 1940, when the crisis seemed darkest. A navy seaplane landed alongside the ship on the morning of December 9 and delivered a long letter from Churchill. The prime minister reviewed the naval and military situations and emphasized the grave danger of the growing submarine threat. That threat could be overcome, and Britain could mount air and land offensives, he wrote, only if American shipping and naval forces helped to keep the North Atlantic sea lanes open, and only if the British had enough American aircraft, especially heavy bombers, "to shatter the foundations of German military power." Moreover, Churchill went on, the time was approaching when Britain could no longer pay for shipping and other supplies. He was confident, he concluded, that the president could find the means to implement a common effort for victory.

Roosevelt pondered Churchill's message for two days and then acted swiftly. On December 17, the day after his return to Washington, he intimated to reporters the plan that had taken shape in his mind. Brushing aside suggestions that the United States either lend money to the British or else give them military supplies, he told a homely parable about a man who lent his neighbor a garden hose—without first demanding payment for it—in order to help put out the fire in his neighbor's house. Then, in a fireside chat on December 29, the president told the people frankly what he had in mind. Britain and the British fleet, he declared, stood between the New World and Nazi aggression. Britain asked for war materials, not for men. "We must be the great arsenal of democracy," he concluded. "I call upon our people with absolute confidence that our common cause will greatly succeed."

Public reaction was immediate and overwhelmingly favorable. Roosevelt reiterated the danger from Nazi aggression in his Annual Message on January 6, 1941, and asked Congress "for authority and for funds sufficient to manufacture additional munitions and war supplies of many kinds, to be turned over to those nations which are now in actual war with aggressor nations." These, he went on, would be paid for, not in dollars, but in goods and services at the end of the war. The president's measure, called the Lend-Lease bill, was drafted by Treasury officials during the first week in January 1941 and approved by administration and congressional leaders on January 9. It was introduced in Congress on the following day. The House approved the Lend-Lease bill on February 8; the Senate, on March 8. The president signed it on March 11, 1941, and promptly asked Congress for $7 billion for lend-lease production and export; Congress complied two weeks later.

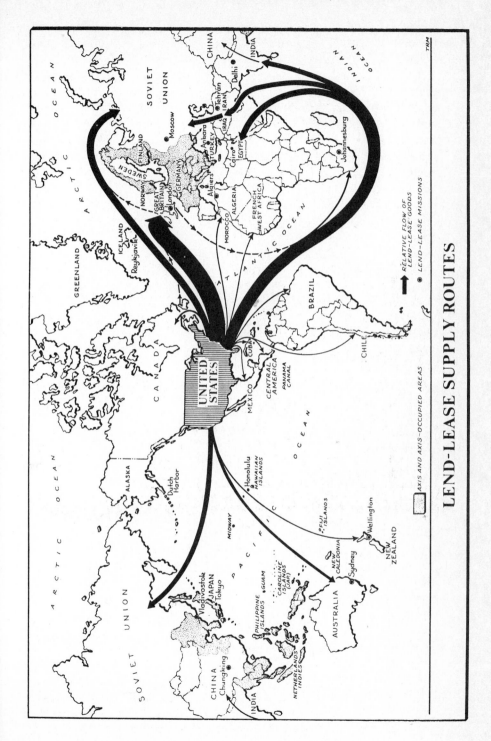

LEND-LEASE SUPPLY ROUTES

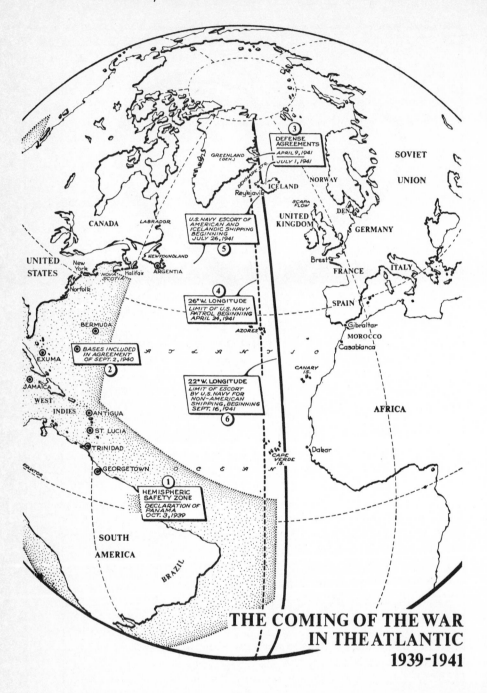

THE COMING OF THE WAR
IN THE ATLANTIC
1939-1941

No man could doubt what the enactment of the Lend-Lease Act signified. "Through this legislation," the president said on March 12, "our country has determined to do its full part in creating an adequate arsenal of democracy." Actually, Roosevelt's characterization was an understatement. Adoption of the Lend-Lease Act converted the United States from a friendly neutral, which sometimes helped more than the rules of traditional neutrality permitted, into a full-fledged nonbelligerent, committed to pour out all its resources if need be to enable Britain to bring Germany to her knees. If there had ever been any doubts before that the American people would falter or refrain from taking the risk of war, those doubts were now resolved.

Having committed itself to underwriting a British victory, the Washington government was not willing to watch Nazi submarines prevent the delivery of goods vital to German defeat. German depredations on British and neutral shipping from the beginning of the blitzkrieg to the end of 1940 had been staggering enough,[9] but the spring of 1941 witnessed an even more powerful German attack. The Nazis extended their war zone on March 25 to include Iceland and Denmark Strait between Greenland and Iceland and sent dozens of new submarines into the North Atlantic to hunt their prey in "wolf packs." They also used surface vessels in daring raids and threw a large part of their air force into the battle to choke off the stream of supplies flowing from American to British ports. The Germans destroyed 537,493 tons of merchant shipping in March 1941; 653,960 tons in April; and 500,063 tons in May. As Churchill repeatedly warned, the outcome of the Battle of the Atlantic might well determine the entire course of the war.

To the president, therefore, the choice did not seem to lie between action and inaction but rather among various means of participating in the Battle of the Atlantic. Consequently, on March 25 and April 2, 1941, he authorized American naval yards to repair British vessels; on March 28 he transferred ten Coast Guard cutters to the British fleet to assist in antisubmarine operations; on March 31 he had the Coast Guard seize thirty Axis and thirty-five Danish merchant ships in American ports. It was bold action, but it was not enough to clear the sea lanes. Secretary Stimson urged Roosevelt to order the navy to convoy British and Allied merchant ships all the way from American to British ports.

The president rejected Stimson's advice but decided on April 10 to extend the American Neutrality Patrol far out into the Atlantic—to longitude 25° west, a line between Brazil and the west coast of Africa in the south and slightly west of Iceland in the north. American naval vessels would search out, but not attack, Nazi submarines, and they would warn British vessels of the presence of U-boats within the area between the

[9]British, Allied, and neutral shipping losses totaled 3,139,190 tons from May through December 1940.

American coast and longitude 25° west.[10] In addition, the president issued a proclamation on April 10 removing the area of the Red Sea from the list of war zones forbidden to American ships.

Isolationists in Congress were meanwhile pressing the charge that Roosevelt had begun an undeclared naval war by ordering American vessels in the patrol area to convoy British ships and attack Nazi U-boats. A German submarine torpedoed an American freighter, *Robin Moor*, in the South Atlantic on May 21. The president had a fireside chat with the people six days later and told them what their navy was doing in the North Atlantic. He said that German control of the Atlantic would imperil American security, and he revealed that the Nazis were sinking ships twice as fast as British and American shipyards could replace them. The hope of victory, he continued, lay in increasing shipbuilding and in helping to reduce losses at sea. To accomplish the latter objective, he explained, "Our patrols are helping now to insure delivery of the needed supplies to Britain." He ended by warning that "all additional measures necessary to deliver the goods" would be taken, by calling upon industry and labor to redouble their efforts, and by declaring an unlimited state of national emergency.

7. The Invasion of Russia

An overwhelming majority of Americans had thought no better of the Russians than of the Nazis ever since the Soviet Union sealed its pact of friendship with Hitlerite Germany and then seized eastern Poland, absorbed the Baltic states, launched war against Finland, and afterward tore the province of Bessarabia from Rumania. This anti-Russian tension was increased during the period from August 1939 to June 1941 by efforts of American Communists to cripple defense production through strikes in airplane factories and otherwise to impair American solidarity. Congressional vexation at such subversion took form in the Smith Act in the spring of 1940. It made it unlawful for any group to advocate or teach the violent overthrow of government in the United States, or for any person to belong to such a group.

We now know that the Soviet leaders would have been prepared to come to agreement with Hitler for a division of Europe and the Middle East. Conversations between Hitler and Molotov in Berlin in November 1940 failed to bring agreement, but only because Hitler thought the Rus-

---

[10]This was the substance of orders issued by Roosevelt to Admiral Ernest J. King on April 19–21, 1941. The Navy began intensified patrol activities on April 24. Meanwhile, the State Department on April 9 concluded an agreement with the Danish minister in Washington, authorizing the United States to build naval and air bases on Greenland.

sians wanted too much. He was enraged by Russian demands and ordered preparations on December 18, 1940, for an invasion of Russia in the coming spring. Hitler launched his attack against the Soviet Union in the early morning hours of June 22, 1941. Washington reacted circumspectly, for the American public probably welcomed a showdown battle between the dictatorships, while Roosevelt's military advisers warned that Russia would collapse within three months and any aid given to the Soviet armies would only fall into Hitler's hands.

Meanwhile, Roosevelt used the breathing space afforded by the German attack to strengthen home defenses and the American position in the North Atlantic. The most urgent defense necessity in the early summer of 1941 was extension of the terms of service of the 900,000 men drafted in the preceding autumn. The defense effort would have practically collapsed if the men had been allowed to go home at the end of their one-year term. The president, therefore, permitted General Marshall to ask Congress on July 3 to extend the term of service and also to remove the provisions in the Selective Service Act of 1940 that prohibited sending draftees outside the Western Hemisphere. The Senate extended the term of service by six months on August 7, 1941. On the other hand, the struggle in the House of Representatives was bitter and long in doubt until that body approved extension by a vote of 203 to 202 on August 12.

While this controversy was in its first stage the president moved decisively to strengthen American control of the North Atlantic sea lanes. Negotiations among Roosevelt, Churchill, and the prime minister of Iceland culminated in the occupation of Iceland by American marines on July 7, 1941, and the inauguration of United States naval escorts for convoys of American and Icelandic ships between the Atlantic Coast and Iceland on July 26. Thus by one stroke the character of American operations in the North Atlantic was changed drastically. Henceforward the navy would not merely patrol the area between Iceland and the United States but would destroy "hostile forces" that threatened American and Icelandic shipping in that broad expanse of water.

8. *The Atlantic Conference and the Brink of War*

Harry Hopkins, lend-lease administrator and now Roosevelt's closet confidant, left Washington on July 13, 1941, for London to pave the way for a personal meeting between Roosevelt and Churchill. Roosevelt not only wanted to renew acquaintance with the "Former Naval Person"; he also wanted the military and naval leaders of both countries to coordinate plans for future operations. Churchill was delighted and agreed to come to a secret meeting "in some lonely bay or other" on August 9. Hopkins flew next to Moscow for conversations with Stalin and other Soviet leaders. From Stalin the American envoy heard the news that the Russian armies would withstand the first Nazi onslaught and take the offensive during the coming winter. Hopkins also learned that the Kremlin would welcome lend-lease aid and facilitate its delivery, and that the Russian government desired American entry into the war above all other things.

Hopkins was back in London in time to join Churchill and his party aboard the new battleship, *Prince of Wales*, for the journey to the rendez-vous with Roosevelt off Argentia, Newfoundland. The president arrived aboard the cruiser *Augusta*, and the two leaders met on the American vessel on the morning of August 9.[11] The British tried to obtain some commitment of American support if Japan attacked British possessions in the Far East. In this, as in all other matters discussed, Roosevelt and his advisers refused to make any promises of a military or naval character.

The most important work of the Argentia meeting was the approval, after some stiff argument about Britain's imperial policy, by Roosevelt and Churchill on August 12 of the joint declaration known as the Atlantic Charter. It was the product of careful thought and patient negotiation and recorded Anglo-American agreement on "certain common principles" on which the two governments based "their hopes for a better future for the world." These principles were no territorial aggrandizement, no territorial changes that did not accord with the wishes of the people involved, the right of all peoples to choose the form of government under which they lived, economic collaboration in the postwar world, and the right of all peoples to live in peace and in freedom from fear, want, and aggression.

News of the Argentia conference and the text of the Atlantic Charter were published in the press on August 15 and provoked isolationist editors and politicians to new outbursts. But the overwhelming majority of Americans believed Roosevelt's assurances that he had made no commitment to intervene actively and approved the Wilsonian aspirations embodied in the Atlantic Charter. Obviously, the preponderant majority continued to approve giving aid to Hitler's enemies and to hope that the United States would not have to enter the "shooting war." Roosevelt shared these sentiments. Like the great majority of his fellow countrymen, he continued to hope for peace while announcing objectives that could be attained only by full-fledged American participation in the war.

The president set about to provide greater assistance to Russia soon after his return from Argentia. This undertaking was made immensely difficult by the opposition of isolationists, the Catholic press, and many anti-Communist Americans. Even though he was uncertain of public and congressional reaction, Roosevelt began discussions that led to an Anglo-American-Soviet conference in Moscow in late September 1941 and an

[11]It was, incidentally, their second meeting. They had met casually in London on July 29, 1918.

Anglo-American promise to furnish $1 billion worth of aid to Russia before June 30, 1942. When Congress, while voting a new $6 billion appropriation for lend-lease production and export in October, rejected an amendment forbidding extension of aid to Russia, Roosevelt declared the Soviet Union eligible for lend-lease assistance on November 7.

More significant for the immediate future, however, was Roosevelt's decision further to relieve the British position in the North Atlantic. The president decided at Argentia to allow British and Allied vessels to join American convoys between the United States and Iceland. This was done unofficially before the end of August, although orders to this effect were not issued until September 13.

Roosevelt pondered the best way to break the news of this new policy to the people. Then a German submarine attacked the destroyer *Greer* south of Iceland on September 4, after the *Greer* had joined a British airplane in trailing the U-boat. The incident gave the president the "provocation" he needed to justify a change of policy. In a radio address on September 11, he declared in seeming seriousness that the attack on the *Greer* was part of a Nazi plan to control the Atlantic, in preparation for an assault upon the Western Hemisphere. The time for active defense had come, he added; hereafter American ships and planes would protect all ships within the area between the United States and Iceland. Moreover, he continued, he had ordered the army and navy to shoot on sight at all German and Italian war vessels in the American patrol area.

The president's speech was in effect a declaration of an undeclared naval war against Germany—the perhaps inevitable outcome of the adoption of the Lend-Lease Act and the American decision to get supplies through the troubled waters to Great Britain. Not only did a large majority of Congress and the public approve this forward step; the majority also approved when Roosevelt finally asked Congress on October 9, 1941, to revise the Neutrality Act of 1939. He requested permission to arm American merchantmen and indirectly suggested that Congress should permit American ships to enter war zones and belligerent ports. While debate on these proposals proceeded, a German submarine torpedoed the destroyer *Kearny* on the night of October 16-17, with the loss of eleven lives. The Senate on November 7 and the House on November 13 voted to allow merchantmen to arm and to pass through the war zone to British ports.

Meanwhile the undeclared naval war in the North Atlantic proceeded. A submarine sank the destroyer *Reuben James* with the loss of 115 lives on October 31, but there was no such general agitation for war as had followed German attacks on American ships in early 1917. The American people now clearly understood their immediate task—to deliver supplies to Britain and Russia regardless of the peril. They assumed that task not gladly, for they knew that it involved the risk of war, but with grim determination and still fervent hope that somehow they could avoid full-scale participation.

9. *Futile Negotiations with Japan, 1938–1941*

Relations between the United States and Japan were in a state of suspended hostility between the adjournment of the Brussels Conference of 1938 and the outbreak of the German-Polish crisis in the spring of 1939. During this period the military clique in the Tokyo government were pressing for an alliance with Germany to offset Soviet and American power. The Japanese army was also undertaking extensive military operations against Russian forces along the Manchurian border. The army's hopes for an alliance with the Nazis were momentarily blasted by the Nazi-Soviet Pact in August 1939; meanwhile, however, Japan undertook a diplomatic campaign to force the British to recognize Japanese conquests in China. The Chamberlain government surrendered to these demands on July 24, 1939, by recognizing that the Japanese army was supreme in the areas it occupied.

The announcement of this agreement galvanized Washington's determination to play a stronger role in the Far East. Therefore, the president sent to Tokyo on July 26 the necessary six months' notice of the possible abrogation of the Japanese-American Commercial Treaty of 1911. It was no idle warning but a stern threat that after January 26, 1940, the United States might deny Japan access to the source from which it obtained more than half the raw materials, especially iron, steel, and oil, for its war machine.

The threat of full-scale war with Russia and economic retaliation by the United States restrained the extreme militarists in Japan and prevented the imperial government from embarking upon new conquests following the outbreak of war in Europe. Instead, the Japanese ended the border conflict with Soviet forces in September and next launched a strenuous effort to liquidate the China Incident. Moreover, the Japanese opened negotiations with the State Department in December 1939 to prevent imposition of the threatened American embargo. These talks ended in a stalemate because neither government would recede on the basic issue of China. Washington simply reaffirmed its traditional position and declared that for the time being it would not end the export of American war supplies.

Japanese-American official relations were relatively quiescent during the early months of 1940, especially after a new moderate government under Admiral Mitsumasa Yonai came to power in Tokyo on January 14, 1940. In the United States, however, public opinion was moving strongly toward the application of an embargo. In fact, sentiment in Congress was so vociferous that administration leaders suppressed it only with difficulty.

THE COMING OF THE WAR
IN THE **PACIFIC, 1939-1941**

481

The State Department's policy of threatening economic retaliation might well have succeeded had not Germany's triumph in western Europe convinced the Japanese military leaders that the power of Britain, France, and the Netherlands was gone, and that henceforth they would have to deal only with the United States. Army leaders and expansionists were excited by the opportunity to seize or fall heir to French Indochina and the Netherlands East Indies and by the hope of an alliance with Germany. They caused the fall of the Yonai cabinet on July 16, 1940, and created a new government headed by Prince Fumimaro Konoye, with the boastful Yosuke Matsuoka as foreign minister and the ardent expansionist, General Hideki Tojo, as minister of war.

The new cabinet, as a first step toward achieving a "new order in Greater East Asia," demanded and after some negotiation obtained from the Vichy government the right to build airfields and station troops in northern Indochina. As a second and more important step, Konoye, Tojo, Matsuoka, and other leaders approved a program for future action on July 27 and September 4, 1940. It envisaged conquest of British, French, and Dutch Far Eastern possessions *if circumstances permitted* and a military alliance with Germany if Hitler approved these plans of conquest. The bargain was struck following the arrival of a new German ambassador in Tokyo on September 7. It was formally sealed in Berlin on September 27, 1940.[12]

Washington moved cautiously to apply such counterpressure as would not provoke an immediate Japanese thrust into the South Pacific. First, it applied an embargo on the export of aviation gasoline, lubricants, and prime scrap metal to Japan on July 26, 1940. Then, after the Japanese occupied northern Indochina, the American government announced extension of a new $25 million loan to China on September 25.[13] On the following day it decreed an embargo on the export of all types of scrap iron and steel. Following this action came a virtual embargo in December on the export of iron ore and pig iron, certain chemicals, certain machine tools, and other products. Churchill was encouraged to reopen the Burma Road, the chief supply route between Nationalist China and the outside world, on October 8, 1940.[14] The Japanese protested, but Washington's firm stand and rumors of Anglo-American naval cooperation in the Pa-

---

[12]This was the Tripartite Agreement, or Triple Alliance, in which Japan recognized German and Italian leadership in Europe, Germany and Italy recognized Japan's leadership in the establishment of a "new order" in Greater East Asia, and the three signatories agreed to cooperate militarily, politically, and economically "if one of the three Contracting Powers is attacked by a Power at present not involved in the European War or in the Chinese-Japanese conflict."

[13]Moreover, Roosevelt announced on November 30, 1940, after the Japanese had recognized a puppet Chinese government in Nanking, that the United States would extend a $100 million loan to Nationalist China. This assistance, incidentally, came in the nick of time to save Chiang Kai-shek's government at Chungking from collapse.

[14]The British had closed the Burma Road in response to Japanese threats on July 12, 1940.

cific[15] caused the Konoye government to beat a momentary diplomatic retreat.

The United States by a policy of implicit threatening had, therefore, prevented the Japanese from striking while Britain and America were in direst peril following the fall of France. Moreover, Japan was not yet prepared to engage the western democracies. There was still the danger that the Soviet Union would strike in the north if Japan turned southward; and there was still the faint hope that somehow the United States might be frightened into acquiescing in Japanese plans. In order to safeguard Japan's long exposed northern flank, Matsuoka made a pilgrimage to Berlin, Rome, and Moscow in March and April 1941. Hitler urged that Japan strike immediately at Singapore. Foreign Minister Joachim von Ribbentrop, intimating that a German-Russian conflict was no longer inconceivable, promised that Germany would attack Russia if the Soviets attacked Japan after she was involved in war with Britain and America. Matsuoka was pleased but not entirely satisfied by these assurances. His supreme objective—a pledge of Soviet neutrality—he obtained in Moscow on April 13, in a Neutrality Pact in which Japan and Russia promised to remain neutral if either power were attacked by one or more countries.

Meanwhile, Tokyo had begun secret discussions with Washington on the other side of the world in a desperate effort to see if any ground for accommodation existed. The background of these negotiations was somewhat odd. An American Catholic bishop and priest discussed the problem of Japanese-American relations with certain Japanese leaders in Tokyo in December 1940. In consequence Premier Konoye asked them to convey a startling message to President Roosevelt—that Japan would for all practical purposes nullify the Tripartite Pact, withdraw its troops from China, and discuss closer economic relations with the United States. The two Catholic emissaries delivered the message to the president in the latter part of January 1941. They were followed soon afterward by two unofficial Japanese representatives, who urged that Roosevelt and Konoye could come to a comprehensive agreement[16] in a personal meeting. After this,

[15]The Washington government, alarmed by the conclusion of the Tripartite Pact, also began in the late autumn of 1940 to consider joint British, American, and Dutch planning for defense of the western Pacific. Discussions between Washington and London culminated in elaborate Anglo-American staff meetings from January 27 to March 27, 1941, and in British-American-Dutch-Commonwealth staff discussions in Singapore in late April. During both conferences, known respectively as ABC-I and ADB, the American representatives refused to make political or military commitments. Instead, they simply joined potential allies in making tentative plans for common action in the event that a Japanese attack forced the United States into the war.

It should be added that the American conferees at the ADB Conference named certain circumstances—notably a Japanese attack on British and Dutch possessions—in which the United States would enter the war. General Marshall and Admiral Stark, however, refused to approve the ADB report because it contained this commitment.

[16]As elaborated in a proposal brought to the State Department on April 9 by a messenger from the imperial army, the Japanese proposed withdrawal of Japanese troops from China by agreement between China and Japan, reaffirmation of the Open Door policy, merger of the Chinese Nationalist regime with the Japanese puppet government in Nanking, resumption of normal economic relations between Japan and the United States, and an American loan to Japan.

they said, the emperor would dismiss Matsuoka. Hull doubted that Konoye could carry through, but he began discussions in March 1941 with
the new Japanese ambassador, Admiral Kichisaburo Nomura, who had
meanwhile been brought into the secret discussions. Hull did not reject
the Japanese proposal, which had been put into writing in language much
less promising between April 2 and April 5 as a "Draft Understanding."
The secretary of state simply countered on April 16 with a four-point
program that embodied traditional American demands concerning China
and disavowal of expansion by forceful means.

The Japanese leaders were encouraged by Nomura's report that Hull
was eager to negotiate and failed utterly to see the significance of the
secretary's four-point program because of the ambassador's incompetence.
Instead, they gained the impression that the "Draft Understanding" was
the American government's own proposal. A liaison conference in Tokyo
on April 21, 1941, decided to continue the discussions and to defer making
definite reply until the return of Matsuoka from Moscow. The foreign
minister was infuriated by the negotiations that had proceeded during his
absence. Japan's destiny, he argued, lay with Germany and in expansion;
he was certain that strength, not weakness, would prevent the United
States from interfering. He countered on May 7 with the suggestion that
Japan and the United States sign a neutrality pact. Hull at once rejected
the proposal as a carte blanche for Japanese seizure of British, French, and
Dutch Far Eastern possessions. Matsuoka next submitted to the State Department on May 12 a revised and remarkable proposal for a comprehensive understanding. It provided that the United States would cut off aid to
Britain, urge Chiang Kai-shek to come to terms with Japan, resume normal
trade relations with Japan, and end its ban on Japanese immigration.

Matsuoka's proposal was obviously unacceptable, but Roosevelt and
Hull agreed to continue the negotiations, chiefly to buy time in the hope
that moderates in the Tokyo government would depose the unruly foreign
minister. Hull, therefore, restated the American position on May 31 and
then again repeated it more fully on June 6 and 21. He proposed that the
Japanese agree that American aid to Britain was defensive in character
and that the Tripartite Pact would not apply if such aid led to a German-
American clash. At this moment, when it seemed that the opponents of
war with the United States might gain the upper hand in Tokyo, the
German attack on Russia removed the threat of Soviet interference and
encouraged the Japanese leaders to decide to occupy all of Indochina,
perhaps preparatory to an attack on Singapore.

The German assault on Russia also momentarily disrupted the desultory
Japanese-American talks then in progress. Matsuoka apparently wanted to
end the negotiations altogether and loudly demanded that Japan strike at
once at the Soviet Union. But he carried his arrogance too far and was
deposed on July 16 and replaced by the more moderate Admiral Teijiro
Toyoda. As Washingon knew from intercepted Japanese messages to Ber-

lin,[17] the cabinet shake-up did not mean any immediate change in Japanese policy. In fact, the imperial government presented a demand to Vichy on July 14 for the immediate occupation of land, air, and naval bases in southern Indochina by Japanese forces. It was the first step in a general program adopted at an imperial conference on July 2. Under its provisions Japan would attempt to conclude the China Incident, avoid war with the USSR for the time being, and advance southward (this provision was intentionally vague) even at the risk of war with the United States and Great Britain.

The Washington government reacted swiftly and violently. The United States, Hull told Nomura on July 23, 1941, could only conclude that the occupation of southern Indochina was the prelude to further Japanese conquests and could see no point in further discussions. On the following day, after Vichy had surrendered to the Japanese demands, the president received the Japanese ambassador, hinted that he was contemplating an embargo on the export of oil to Japan, and warned that a Japanese attack on the Dutch East Indies would result in serious consequences. On the other hand, Roosevelt continued, if Japan would withdraw from Indochina he would take leadership in a movement to neutralize that French colony and help Japan to find access to raw materials.

The president, however, was done with mere parleying. He impounded all Japanese funds in the United States, closed the Panama Canal to Japanese shipping, and called the Philippine militia into active service on July 26. On August 1 he forbade the export to Japan of a number of vital materials, including oil that could be refined into aviation gasoline, while the British and Dutch governments applied similar sanctions.

This decisive retaliation put Tokyo in the dilemma of having to choose between a modified retreat or a desperate war with the United States. Although some extremists welcomed the prospect of war, the naval leaders were reluctant to risk hostilities and warned that the empire would probably be defeated in a protracted conflict. The Cabinet, therefore, maneuvered to find a solution that would include both Japanese occupation of southern Indochina and peace with the United States. Premier Konoye proposed on August 7 that the president meet him in personal conference to discuss means to relieve the tension. Roosevelt gave his reply on August 17, after his return from the Atlantic Conference. If Japan made any further aggressive moves the United States would take all necessary steps to safeguard American security. However, if Japan sincerely desired to come to agreement along lines already laid down by the United States, then Washington would be willing to resume the exploratory discussions disrupted by the Japanese occupation of Indochina.

Faced squarely with the choice of war or agreement with the United States, Konoye now moved desperately to persuade the president to join

[17] Experts in the American government had earlier deciphered the Japanese diplomatic code.

him in a personal conference. Foreign Minister Toyoda reiterated Konoye's proposal to Ambassador Joseph C. Grew on August 18, while Konoye ordered a ship to stand in readiness to take him to the meeting. Then on August 28 Nomura presented the imperial government's reply to Roosevelt's note of August 17. Japan would withdraw its troops from Indochina as soon as the China Incident was settled; it would not undertake expansion southward or make war on the Soviet Union unless attacked; and it agreed that the principles set forth in the American note were "the prime requisites of a true peace." In a subsequent note of clarification dated September 4 the Japanese government made perhaps its most important offer, namely, that Japan would not feel bound by the Tripartite Pact to go to war if the United States became involved in a defensive war with Germany.

Roosevelt was so pleased by the Japanese response that he was ready to give immediate consent to the proposal for a meeting with Konoye. But Hull urged caution and insisted that the two governments agree upon the fundamental issue of China before the chiefs of state met. Despite warnings from Tokyo that only some bold stroke could restrain the war party, the president accepted the State Department's view that Japan would not attack and that a policy of continued firmness would force the imperial government to surrender. Thus Roosevelt replied on September 3 that he would be glad to confer with Konoye, but that basic differences, particularly on China, would have to be cleared up first.

The president's reply in the circumstances spelled the doom not only of the projected conference, but of peace as well. Whether the momentous decision was wise or foolish will be long debated by historians. Defenders of the administration have argued that agreement on important issues was impossible, and that in any event Konoye could not have forced the army to make the concessions necessary to preserve the peace. On the other hand, Roosevelt's antagonists have maintained that the administration rejected Konoye's invitation in order to goad Japan into attacking the United States. At least on the point of the administration's intentions the records are full and revealing. They indicate that the president and the State Department, far from desiring war, were convinced that the Japanese could not undertake hostilities and would retreat in the face of a firm American policy.

In view of the primacy of the Nazi danger and the likelihood that the United States would soon be drawn into the European war, American policy in the Far East might well have been directed at one objective only—maintenance of peace with Japan on any terms short of countenancing further Japanese aggressions in the southwestern Pacific. Such a policy might have necessitated unfreezing Japanese assets, lifting the embargo on export of oil and metals, and easing the pressure on Japan to withdraw immediately from China. There is considerable evidence that such concessions by the United States at this time—that is, early September 1941—

would have enormously strengthened the Japanese moderates and might have sufficed to preserve the status quo and gain precious time.

Roosevelt and Hull were influenced by a group of Sinophiles in the State Department into believing that Japan would not fight, and that it would not matter much if she did. Instead of making any concessions they continued to press demands for Japanese withdrawal from China, demands that were impossible in the circumstances. The time might have come when the United States and Britain could have forced a showdown on China without having to go to war.[18] But that time would be after the defeat of Germany, when the two democracies were invincible, not in the late summer of 1941, when they were weak, and when wisdom demanded a policy of delay.

10. Pearl Harbor

Events following the delivery of Roosevelt's reply of September 3 support the thesis that the effect of American policy was to strengthen the extremists and perhaps tip the balance in Tokyo in favor of the war party. An imperial conference met for a showdown on policy on September 6, soon after receipt of the president's reply. The army chief of staff urged immediate preparations, if not a decision, for war. The navy chief of general staff agreed that Japan might have to resort to hostilities to avoid economic destruction as a consequence of the American embargo. Emperor Hirohito, however, demanded that negotiations be continued in the hope of peaceful understanding. The imperial conference ended in agreement to continue military preparations, to be completed by the end of October, and to seek for the last time American acquiescence in the minimum Japanese program.[19]

Premier Konoye met secretly with Ambassador Grew during the evening of September 6, immediately after the imperial conference, and reit-

[18]From a sheerly strategic point of view, the continuation of the Sino-Japanese War served Anglo-American interests by keeping large Japanese forces occupied, draining Japanese resources, and deterring the Japanese from expanding into the southwestern Pacific. Perceiving the rather obvious fact that involvement in China in part prevented the Japanese from expanding northward, the Soviet leaders played a skillful game of preserving peace with Japan while at the same time sending a modicum of supplies to Nationalist China to make certain that the Japanese would have to continue their now useless war in China.

[19]This the imperial conference defined as (1) Anglo-American agreement to close the Burma Road, cease all aid to Nationalist China, and not obstruct a settlement of the China Incident by Japan; (2) Anglo-American agreement to make no offensive preparations in the Far East; and (3) Anglo-American agreement to resume normal trade relations with Japan and assist Japan in her negotiations with Siam and the Netherlands Indies. In return Japan would (1) agree not to use Indochina as a base for offensive operations except against China; (2) withdraw troops from Indochina after establishment of peace in the Far East; (3) guarantee the neutrality of the Philippines; (4) refrain from war against Russia unless attacked; and (5) agree to clarify Japanese obligations under the Tripartite Pact.

erated his desire for a personal meeting with Roosevelt. Konoye renewed his invitation on September 22, and Grew added a plea for acceptance. Hull replied on October 2, again declaring that the two governments must agree on fundmental issues, principally China, before a general conference could succeed. To Konoye, Washington's final refusal spelled the doom of his efforts to prevent war. He and the naval leaders tried to persuade the army chieftains that Japan could not defeat America and that they had to evacuate China as a prerequisite to peace. The army adamantly refused and insisted that there was no recourse but war. Then Konoye sent a special emissary to Washington to plead the absolute necessity for some kind of speedy agreement. Japan was even willing to evacuate China, the messenger told Welles on October 13.

But the situation in Tokyo was passing out of Konoye's control. The premier had a long conference with high military and naval officials on October 12 and argued in behalf of agreement to withdraw from China. But the war minister, General Tojo, instantly vetoed the proposal. Further discussions revealed that the premier and the army group had reached an impasse, and Konoye resigned on October 16. As his successor the emperor named Tojo himself, after the general had promised that he would continue negotiations.

The fall of the Konoye government only intensified the conflict in Tokyo between the army and the antiwar group. The emperor, supported by the navy, demanded reconsideration of the provisions for early military operations adopted by the imperial conference on September 6. Debate proceeded from mid-October through November 5. The new foreign minister, Shigenori Togo, tried to find a solution for the evacuation of China, but the army would not yield and insisted that war was preferable to the gradual economic ruin of the empire. Togo did persuade the army to agree to one last effort at compromise with the United States. The military chieftains agreed on November 5 but won the emperor's consent to preparations for immediate attack if the negotiations had yielded no agreement by about November 25. On November 5 the army and navy also issued war orders, to go into effect in early December if diplomacy had failed.

As a consequence negotiations proceeded anew in Washington between November 7 and December 7. The repetitious details need not be given here. It suffices to say that neither government retreated from its irrevocable position on the key issue of China, and that the American leaders continued the discussions mainly in the hope of deferring the conflict that they now thought was practically inevitable.

The utter hopelessness of the deadlock was further revealed after a special Japanese envoy, Saburu Kurusu, arrived at the White House on November 17. After talking with Roosevelt and Hull, Kurusu and Nomura were unable to persuade their government to agree to a stopgap proposal providing for immediate evacuation of southern Indochina, which the United States was willing to accept. Then Nomura on November 20 presented what was in fact Japan's final offer, actually, in Japanese eyes, an ultimatum. It was not entirely impossible as a basis for bargaining;[20] indeed, Foreign Minister Togo was confident that it would provide the basis for agreement.

Actually, Roosevelt had already drafted in his own hand a proposal for a temporary modus vivendi not entirely dissimilar from the Japanese proposal, except that the president's draft also provided for Japanese neutrality in the event of American hostilities in Europe. Thus the State Department, after receiving the Japanese note of November 20, drafted a counterproposal of its own, which was to run for three months. Its crucial provisions embodied mutual pledges against military action in the South Pacific, a Japanese promise to evacuate southern Indochina "forthwith," an American promise to restore normal trade relations with Japan, and a statement to the effect that the United States would "not look with disfavor upon the inauguration of conversations between the Government of China and the Government of Japan directed toward a peaceful settlement of their differences."

We will never know whether the American proposal could have saved the peace of the Pacific. Roosevelt and Hull decided not to submit the modus vivendi as a consequence of two events on November 25—receipt in Washington of news of the movement of Japanese troopships off Formosa, and the violent reaction of the British and Chinese governments to the proposed modus vivendi. The Chinese frankly warned that adoption of the modus vivendi would cause a collapse of their resistance. Receipt of a cable from Churchill on that same day evidently clinched Hull's decision to abandon the project. Hull called in Nomura and Kurusu on the following day, November 26, and formally rejected the Japanese proposal of November 20. He then proceeded to read the text of a draft "Mutual Declaration of Policy" and "Steps to be taken by the Government of the United States and by the Government of Japan." The mutual declaration was a reaffirmation of the principles that Hull had somewhat tediously enunciated many times. The proposed steps to be taken provided for Japanese evacuation not only of Indochina *but of China as well*, and for support of the Nationalist government by the Japanese.

In the circumstances, Hull's note came close to being an ultimatum. In any event, it spelled the doom of the negotiations. Its receipt in Tokyo on November 27 stunned the Japanese leaders, who concluded that it signified American insistence upon war. The Japanese deferred final decision until Nomura and Kurusu had conferred with President Roosevelt on No-

[20] It included (1) Japanese-American agreement not to invade any area in Southeast Asia and the South Seas, except for Indochina; (2) Japanese-American cooperation in guaranteeing mutual access to raw materials in the Netherlands Indies; (3) resumption of normal Japanese-American trade relationships; (4) American promise to put no obstacle in the way of Japan's attempts to make peace with China; (5) Japanese promise to withdraw from all of Indochina upon conclusion of a Sino-Japanese peace; and (6) Japanese promise to withdraw from southern to northern Indochina upon the conclusion of this agreement.

vember 27. When news of the president's refusal to consider any modus vivendi reached Tokyo, an imperial conference on December 1 decided on hostilities. To responsible Japanese leaders an uncertain war, which they really did not expect to win, seemed the only way to avoid slow economic strangulation or humiliating surrender that would spell Japan's end as a great power.

Meanwhile, Japanese preparations for probable conflict had been proceeding on the assumption that one must be prepared to fight if diplomacy fails. A carrier task force left the Kuriles on November 25 to attack the great American naval base at Pearl Harbor in Hawaii, while large army forces were poised in southern Indochina to strike at Malaya. The Washington leaders knew from intercepted messages only that the Japanese would attack somewhere soon. They recognized that an assault on the Philippines and Guam was possible, but they concluded that Tokyo would avoid such direct provocation to the United States. Thus the American government on the eve of war was more concerned with what to do in the event of a Japanese attack on Malaya and the Dutch East Indies than with immediate defense of American territory. When news of the movement of large Japanese forces against Malaya reached Washington on December 6, Roosevelt dispatched an urgent personal appeal to Hirohito, warning that the present tension could not last much longer and urging him to take some action to dispel the threat of war.

The Japanese reply to Hull's note of November 26 began to come to Washington over the wires in the afternoon of Saturday, December 6. The first sections, which were decoded by early evening, revealed Japan's rejection of the note; the final section, which announced termination of the negotiations, was in the president's hands by the morning of December 7. The attack on Pearl Harbor had already occurred, and first reports from the stricken base had reached Washington by the time that Nomura and Kurusu were able to deliver the message to Hull.

Meanwhile, American military and naval commanders in the Pacific had been duly but not strenuously warned on November 24 and 27 that surprise Japanese attacks were likely. Like their superiors in Washington, however, they expected the Japanese to strike at Malaya, not at them. The commanders in Hawaii, Admiral Husband E. Kimmel and General Walter C. Short, were unconcerned as what Roosevelt would call the "day of infamy" approached. Kimmel had concentrated virtually his entire fleet in Pearl Harbor; fearing sabotage, Short had disposed his airplanes and antiaircraft guns in such a manner as to make successful defense impossible. Neither commander had established an effective air patrol. Thus the carrier task force under Admiral Chuchi Nagumo approached Hawaii from the northwest undetected.

The first wave of Japanese airplanes attacked airfields at 7:55 A.M. on December 7, 1941, and then struck the fleet anchored in the harbor. A second wave followed at 8:50. The navy and marine corps were unable to get a single plane off the ground. An army fighter squadron at Haleiwa, which the Japanese overlooked, got a few planes into the air and destroyed several of the attackers. A few antiaircraft batteries were operating by the time of the second major assault. And several naval craft were able to get into action and attack Japanese submarines. Otherwise, the Japanese were unopposed and raked and bombed at will. When the last planes turned toward their carriers at about 9:45 the great American bastion in the Pacific was a smoking shambles. Practically every airplane on the island of Oahu was either destroyed or disabled. All eight battleships in Pearl Harbor were disabled—two of them, *Oklahoma* and *Arizona*, were destroyed or sunk. Three cruisers and three destroyers were heavily damaged or destroyed. And 2,323 men of both services were dead. The cost to the Japanese was twenty-nine airplanes, five midget submarines, and one fleet submarine.

First reports of the attack came to Washington at about two in the afternoon, while later news told of other Japanese attacks on the Philippines, Hong Kong, Wake Island, Midway Island, Siam, and Malaya, and of a Japanese declaration of war against the United States and Great Britain. After cabinet meetings in the afternoon and evening, the president called congressional leaders to the White House and reviewed dispatches he had received. He appeared before the two houses on the following day, December 8, excoriated the "unprovoked and dastardly attack by Japan," and asked Congress to recognize the obvious state of war that existed. It was done within an hour and with only one dissenting vote in the House of Representatives. Roosevelt had deliberately avoided mention of Germany and Italy in his war message, in order to leave the decision for full-fledged war for the time being to Hitler. The führer was delighted by the Pearl Harbor attack and responded to the Japanese request for a German declaration of war against the United States on December 11. Mussolini followed suit at once. The president and Congress reciprocated during the afternoon of the same day.

Shock and indignation surged through the American people as they heard the news of the Japanese attack over their radios on the afternoon of Pearl Harbor day. They did not know that their armed forces had suffered the most humiliating defeat in American history by a foreign foe, or the desperate circumstances that impelled the Japanese to undertake a suicidal war. The American people only thought that they had been treacherously attacked. And in their anger they forgot all the partisan quarrels and debates over foreign policy that had so long divided them and resolved with firm determination to win the war that the Japanese had begun. The agony of doubt was over; the issue was now fully joined. The American people had embarked not gladly upon a second crusade, but grimly upon a war for survival.

21

The Second World War: The American Home Front

Not since the dark days of the Revolution had the American people confronted so dire a military menace or so staggering a task as during the Second World War. Within a few months after Japanese bombs fell on Pearl Harbor, the ensign of the Rising Sun floated triumphantly over all the outposts and bastions of the far Pacific region, while Hitler and his armies stood poised to strike at the Middle East and join forces with the Japanese in India.

It was perhaps fortunate that the American people in December 1941 little knew how long the war would last and what the costs would be. However, they had certain advantages that made victory possible: courageous allies, unity unprecedented in American history, enormous resources and industrial capacity, superb political and military leadership, and, most important, determination to win. These factors combined from 1941 to 1945 to achieve miracles of production that made earlier American war efforts look small by comparison.

The astonishing thing, however, was the fact that Americans could engage in total war without submitting to the discipline of total war at home. To be sure, the war intensified certain social tensions and created new problems of adjustment; but the mass of Americans took the war in stride, without emotional excitement or hysteria.

1. *Manpower for War*

The adoption of the war resolutions found the United States in the midst of a sizable rearmament campaign, the momentum of which was daily increasing. Congress at once ordered the registration of all men between the ages of twenty (lowered to eighteen in 1942) and forty-four for war service and of men between forty-five and sixty-five for potential labor service. All told, draft boards registered some 31,000,000 men, of whom 9,867,707 were inducted into service. Including volunteers, a total of 15,145,115 men and women served in the armed services before the end of the war—10,420,000 in the army, 3,883,520 in the navy, 599,693 in the marines, and 241,902 in the Coast Guard.

Because the first offensive blows could be delivered from the air, the army air forces were authorized at the outset to increase their strength to 2.3 million men and were given highest priority on manpower and materials. When the Japanese attacked Pearl Harbor the AAF had 292,000 men and 9,000 planes (1,100 of which were fit for combat). When the Japanese

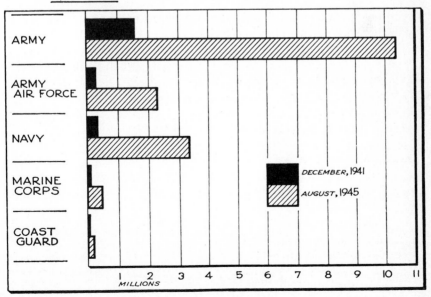

EXPANSION OF U.S. ARMED FORCES
1941-1945

surrendered in August 1945, the AAF enlisted 2.3 million men and women and had 72,000 planes in service.

Thanks to the wealth, technology, and industrial and agricultural capacity of his country, the American soldier was the best-paid, best-clothed, and by 1943 the best-equipped fighting man in the world. In that year, for example, Americans achieved not only a quantitative but also a decided qualitative superiority in fighter planes and bombers. Even in areas of research in which the Germans had a head start, such as atomic fission, American scientists and engineers had won decisive advantages by 1945. On the battlefield the best American weapons were the light semiautomatic Garand rifle and the multiple-driven truck. They combined to give a superiority in firepower and mobility that the Germans were never able to overcome in spite of general equality in machine guns, mortars, rocket-launched missiles, and artillery.[1]

In the meantime, the navy, marines, and Coast Guard had grown from relative weakness after Pearl Harbor to dimensions of gigantic strength at the time of the Japanese surrender. On December 7, 1941, the navy had a complement of 337,349 men, in addition to 66,048 in the Marine Corps and 25,336 in the Coast Guard. By the summer of 1945, the navy's manpower had increased to 3,408,347 officers and men, the Marine Corps' to 484,631, and the Coast Guard's to 170,480. Before Japanese bombs disabled or sank part of the Pacific Fleet at Pearl Harbor, the navy had in operation some 4,500 ships, including 17 battleships, 7 fleet carriers, 18 heavy and 19 light cruisers, 200 destroyers and torpedo boats, and 114 submarines. By the end of 1945 the navy had grown to more than 91,000 ships of all sizes, including 24 battleships, 2 large cruisers, 29 fleet carriers, 73 escort carriers, 23 heavy and 45 light cruisers, 489 destroyers and torpedo boats, 500 escort vessels, and 274 submarines.

Finally, there was mobilization of women for war service. The Women's Auxiliary Corps, which grew in size to 100,000, sent 17,000 WACs overseas; the navy's counterpart, the WAVEs, numbered about 86,000 at the end of the war. There was also the Coast Guard's SPARs and the Marine Corps' Women's Reserve. Working as stenographers, clerks, technicians, cryptographers, and the like, female contingents not only performed indispensable functions but released over 200,000 men for service on the battle fronts.

Measured in human costs, the price of victory in the Second World War came high to the American people—253,573 dead, 651,042 wounded, 114,204 prisoners, and 65,834 men missing. For the men who died, how-

---

[1] In certain categories, however, the Germans retained a marked advantage. The German 88-mm rifle, for example, was superior to the American 90-mm rifle. Use of a smokeless, flashless powder gave the German infantryman a great advantage over his American foe, who had to use powder that exposed his position every time he fired. Moreover, the American medium Sherman tank was no match from 1943 to 1945 for the heavy German Tiger and Panther tanks. Not until production of the heavy Pershing tank in the winter of 1944-1945 were American armored divisions able to meet German *Panzer* forces on equal terms.

ever, Americans and their allies exacted a fearful retribution. Germany and Italy suffered 373,600 dead and lost 8,108,983 prisoners to the Allies on the western front alone. The Japanese gave up 1,093,000 battle dead in areas outside China.

For their comparatively low death lists, Americans in large measure could thank the medical corps of the several services. Although American soldiers lived and fought in deserts and jungles as well as in the temperate zones, the death rate from nonbattle causes was no higher than the rate for similar groups at home. And for the sick and wounded there was extraordinary care, while use of sulfa drugs, penicillin, and whole blood brought such healing and relief from wounds and shock as would not have been possible a decade before. The result was to cut the rate of deaths from disease and battle wounds in half from the rate of the First World War.

2. *Scientists Against Time*

In the last analysis the war was won as much in the laboratory and on the testing ground as on the battlefield. American scientists at the outset of the war lagged far behind the Germans in research in atomic fission, jet propulsion, and rockets, and they were behind the British in work on jet propulsion, radar, and other electronic devices. Alarmed by the prospect of his country entering the war scientifically unprepared, Dr. Vannevar Bush, president of the Carnegie Institution of Washington, persuaded the president in June 1940 to establish the National Defense Research Committee (NDRC), with representatives from the defense departments, universities, and private industry. Then Roosevelt reorganized the government's research program in June 1941 by creating the Office of Scientific Research and Development (OSRD). Bush was director of the OSRD, with power to approve or veto all projects and to initiate research.

Bush and his colleagues had accomplished a full mobilization of scientific personnel and facilities by the autumn of 1941. Let us look briefly at some of the most significant results of this great effort—the development of radar and electronic devices, rockets for combat use, the proximity fuse, and, finally, the atomic bomb.

It was the British who first perfected radar and put it to large-scale use during the great German air assault of 1940–1941. Radar sets in patrol planes enabled the British and American navies to bring the German submarines under control.[2] Radar in fighters enabled the air forces to launch powerful night interceptors; in bombers, it provided a generally accurate bombsight. As the basis of a new method of fire-control, it gave eyes to guns as well as to airplanes and ships. The American armed services alone

[2]Perhaps even more effective in antisubmarine operations was so-called sonar, or underwater sound detection apparatus, developed by the NDRC in conjunction with the Harvard Underwater Sound Laboratory.

had received $3 billion worth of radar equipment and $71 million worth of Loran, a long-range navigational aid, by July 1945.

The outbreak of the war found research in the field of rocket warfare well advanced in Britain and Germany and practically nonexistent in the United States. But NDRC scientists had a sizable research program under way by the end of 1941. One of the first results was the "bazooka," a tube rocket-launcher perfected in 1942, which could be operated by two infantrymen and discharged a rocket powerful enough to destroy a tank. Subsequently, scientists developed an incredible variety of rocket-launchers and rockets for use in land combat and antiaircraft operations, by airplanes, and in ship-to-shore bombardments. What this meant in terms of increased firepower can perhaps best be illustrated by the fact that a single fighter plane carrying rockets could discharge a salvo as heavy as a destroyer's.

One of the most brilliant scientific achievements of the war was the development, exclusively by the OSRD, of the proximity fuse. It was a miniature radio set in the head of the shell that detonated it by proximity to the target. Proximity fuses were first used by the navy against Japanese aircraft in 1943. Fearing that the Germans would recover an unexploded shell and put the fuse into production, the Joint Chiefs of Staff did not allow the ground forces in Europe to use the new weapon until December 1944. Put into use against the Germans in their Ardennes counteroffensive (see pp. 550–551), the proximity fuse compounded the effectiveness of American artillery and proved devastating against German ground troops.

The mobilization of American scientists paid numerous other dividends—among them the development of more powerful explosives and fire bombs, of DDT and other weapons in the warfare against insects and vermin, of advanced techniques in the use of blood plasma and whole blood, of penicillin, and of new and deadly gases, which were never used. But the greatest triumph of American scientific and productive genius was the development of the atomic bomb. The perfection of this weapon marked a decisive turning point in history.

The Danish physicist Niels Bohr startled a group of American physicists assembled in Washington on January 26, 1939, by announcing that two Germans at the Kaiser Wilhelm Institute in Berlin had recently accomplished atomic fission in uranium. Nuclear physicists had long understood the structure of the atom and known that atomic fission was theoretically possible. But the deed had now been done, and the road was open for the development of a bomb more powerful and deadly than the world had ever dreamed of. The grave danger was that the Nazis would produce atomic bombs and literally conquer the world. Therefore, Enrico Fermi of Columbia University, Albert Einstein of the Institute for Advanced Study, and others persuaded the president to begin a small research program. It was not until 1940, however, that work began in earnest. By the summer of 1941 research at Columbia, California, and other universities had confirmed the possibilities of atomic fission through a chain reaction. The chief problem now was to find a fissionable element in sufficient quantity.

Earlier experiments had proved that the uranium isotope, U-235, was fissionable; but since U-235 was an infinitesimal part of uranium, the chances were remote of ever accumulating enough of the element to manufacture atomic bombs. This problem was solved by Dr. Ernest Lawrence of the University of California at Berkeley, who used a huge cyclotron, or "atom smasher," to convert the plentiful uranium element, U-238, into a new element, plutonium, which was as fissionable as U-235 and much easier to obtain in quantity.

The next objective became a chain reaction in uranium, that is, the almost simultaneous fission of the uranium atoms through a chain bombardment by neutrons. A group of physicists under the direction of Dr. Arthur H. Compton built the first atomic pile, or apparatus, under the stadium at Stagg Field of the University of Chicago. They produced the first controlled chain reaction on December 2, 1942. Production of an atomic bomb was now possible, provided a means of production could be devised. OSRD turned the problem over to the Manhattan District of the Army Engineer Corps, headed by General Leslie R. Groves, on May 1, 1943. Drawing upon the combined resources of the OSRD, universities, and private industries, Groves pushed the project with incredible speed. Work on the bomb itself was begun in the spring of 1943 at a laboratory built on a lonely mesa at Los Alamos, outside Santa Fe, New Mexico. Here a group of American, British, and European scientists under direction of Dr. J. Robert Oppenheimer worked night and day to perfect the bomb. They began the final assembly of the first atomic bomb on July 12, 1945, and tension mounted as the fateful day of testing drew near. Nearly $2 billion had been expended in an effort which yet might fail. The bomb was moved to the air base at Alamogordo and successfully detonated at 5:30 A.M. on July 16. A searing blast of light, many times brighter than the noonday sun, was followed by a deafening roar and a huge mushroom cloud; and relief mixed with a feeling of doom filled the minds of the men who watched the beginning of a new era in human history.

3. American Industry Goes to War

The story of how changing agencies mobilized the American economy for staggering tasks is a tale full of confusion and chaos, incompetence and momentary failure, political intrigue and personal vendetta, but withal one of superb achievement on many home fronts. Government and industry accomplished one of the economic miracles of modern times before it was too late—the production of a stream of goods that provided a high standard of living at home and also supplied the American armed forces with all and the British, French, and Russians with a large part of the resources and matériel for victory.

The task during the first period of industrial mobilization, from August

1939 until about the end of 1941, was the comparatively easy one of utilizing idle plants and men to supply the inchoate American armed forces and the British. The president in August 1939 established the War Resources Board, headed by Edward R. Stettinius, Jr., of the United States Steel Corporation, to advise the administration on industrial mobilization. It soon fell victim to labor and New Deal critics, who charged that it was dominated by Morgan and Du Pont interests.

This was, of course, the time of the so-called phony war, when Allied victory seemed assured and the necessity for total economic mobilization seemed remote. Nevertheless, the War Resources Board, before its dissolution in October 1939, prepared an industrial mobilization plan that envisaged dictatorial economic authority for a single administrator in the event that the United States entered the war. Roosevelt rejected this plan and asked the former chairman of Wilson's War Industries Board, Bernard M. Baruch, to prepare another. Baruch presented a plan that met all Roosevelt's objections to the earlier proposal and provided for gradual transition to a total war economy.

Roosevelt, for reasons still unknown, suppressed the Baruch plan and permitted the partial mobilization effort of 1939–1940 to drift aimlessly. The fall of France, however, galvanized the president into action, inadequate though it was. Calling for vast new defense appropriations and the production of 50,000 planes a year, he reestablished the Advisory Commission to the old and nearly defunct Council of National Defense on May 28, 1940. It was charged with responsibility for getting defense production into high gear. In addition, Congress on June 25 authorized the RFC to finance the building of defense plants and, in the Revenue Act of October 8, 1940, permitted businessmen to write off construction costs over a five-year period.

The Advisory Commission abdicated control over priorities to the Army-Navy Munitions Board and had lost all control of industrial mobilization by December 1940. Roosevelt still stubbornly refused to institute the kind of mobilization plan that Baruch had earlier suggested. Instead, on January 7, 1941, he established the Office of Production Management (OPM), headed by William S. Knudsen of the Advisory Commission and Sidney Hillman of the CIO. It was directed to cooperate with the president and defense secretaries in stimulating and controlling war production. In addition, an Office of Price Administration and Civilian Supply, established on April 11, would work to protect consumers' interests.

The OPM went to work to improve the priorities system, to coordinate British and American orders, and especially to help automobile manufacturers prepare for conversion to production of tanks and planes. The result was a gradual shift during the spring and summer of 1941 to a wartime economy. Shortages of electric power, aluminum, steel, railroad stock, and other materials became acute. The priorities system nearly broke down, and internal bickering and public criticism mounted. Roosevelt attempted another superficial reorganization. He suspended the OPM on August 28,

1941, but left an OPM Council. Then he created a Supplies Priorities and Allocation Board, headed by the Sears-Roebuck executive, Donald M. Nelson, and added other agencies, many of which overlapped in a confusing way. The central force in the new apparatus, however, was the Supplies Priorities and Allocations Board, for it had the power to determine and allocate requirements and supplies for the armed forces, the civilian economy, and the British and the Russians.

The president at last attempted to establish a comprehensive economic mobilization on January 16, 1942, by creating the War Production Board (WPB), under Donald Nelson, to take supreme command of the economic home front. Nelson was an excellent technician, but he failed to meet the test of leadership. He continued to allow the military departments to control priorities; consequently, he never established firm control over production. He permitted the great corporations to obtain a practical monopoly on war production, and this caused a near scandal when the facts were disclosed by a special Senate committee headed by Harry S. Truman of Missouri. Finally, he allowed industrial expansion to get out of hand and occur in the wrong areas.

American industry was booming by the autumn of 1942, but chaos threatened. Alarmed by the prospect, Roosevelt brought Justice James F. Byrnes to the White House as head of the new Office of Economic Stabilization on October 3 and gave him supreme command of the economic effort. One of Byrnes's first moves was to force adoption of a plan that established such complete control over allocation of steel, aluminum, and copper that the priorities difficulty vanished almost at once. Then Roosevelt in May 1943 created the Office of War Mobilization, a sort of high command with control over all aspects of the economy, with Byrnes as director or "assistant president." Representative Fred M. Vinson of Kentucky succeeded Byrnes as head of the Office of Economic Stabilization. The home front was at last well organized and under control.

4. The Miracle of Production

In spite of all its shortcomings, the American industrial mobilization did succeed far beyond any reasonable expectations. We can gain some understanding of the total achievement by considering the general performance of the American economy from 1939 through 1945. Measured by depression standards, 1939 was a relatively prosperous year. Gross national product stood at $91.3 billion—higher in real dollars than during the boom year of 1929. On the other hand, the gross national product had risen, in 1939 dollars, to $166.6 billion by 1945. Moreover, from 1939 to 1945 the index of manufacturing production increased 96 percent; agricultural production was up 22 percent; and transportation services increased 109 percent. Contrasted with the performance of the economy during the First

World War, when the total national output increased hardly at all, this was a remarkable achievement.

American war production in 1941 was a mere trickle, only $8.4 billion in value. It totaled $30.2 billion in value in 1942 and equaled that of Germany, Italy, and Japan combined. American factories by 1944 were producing twice the volume of the Axis partners. A few illustrations will give point to the generalizations. The American airplane industry employed 46,638 persons and produced 5,865 planes in 1939. At the peak of production in 1944, the industry employed more than 2.1 million persons and turned out 96,369 aircraft. All told, American factories from Pearl Harbor to the end of the war produced 274,941 military aircraft.

Production of merchant ships in the United States was an essential ingredient of Allied victory in the battle of supply. The construction of merchant shipping, which had totaled only 1 million tons in 1941, rose to a peak of over 19 million tons in 1943, and, as the need diminished, declined to nearly 16.5 million tons in 1944 and nearly 8 million tons from January through July of 1945. All told, from July 1, 1940, to August 1, 1945, American shipyards produced a total of more than 55.2 million tons of merchant shipping—a tonnage equal to two-thirds of the merchant marines of all Allied nations combined.

Perhaps the most remarkable miracle of production was the creation, almost overnight, of a new synthetic rubber industry. Japanese conquest of Malaya and the Netherlands East Indies deprived the United States of 90 percent of its natural rubber supply at a time when the total stockpile of rubber in the United States amounted to only 540,000 tons and normal consumption exceeded 600,000 tons annually. Total imports could not exceed 175,000 tons during 1942, and the rubber shortage threatened to hobble the entire war effort. On August 6, 1942, Roosevelt appointed a special committee headed by Bernard M. Baruch to investigate and recommend. The Baruch committee reported on September 10, warning that the war effort and civilian economy might collapse if a severe rubber shortage occurred and urging immediate construction of a vast industry to produce rubber synthetically from petroleum. Roosevelt acted at once, appointing William M. Jeffers, president of the Union Pacific Railroad, as rubber director in the WPB on September 15, 1942. Jeffers ruthlessly cut his way through the existing priorities system. By the end of 1943 he had brought into existence a synthetic rubber industry that produced 762,000 tons in 1944 and 820,000 tons in 1945.

5. The Greatest Tax Bill in History

Federal expenditures aggregated in excess of $321.2 billion from 1941 to 1945. Some 41 percent of the money for the war effort came from tax receipts, which totaled nearly $131 billion during the fiscal years

1941–1945. The balance was raised by borrowing, which in turn increased
the gross national debt from $49 billion in 1941 to $259 billion in mid-
1945.

Meanwhile, the administration and Congress had joined hands to revo-
lutionize the tax structure. On the one hand, the president, Congress, and
a vast majority of Americans, rich and poor alike, agreed that the few
should not profit from the sacrifices of the many, and that there should be
no new millionaires as a result of the defense and war efforts. On the other
hand, it became increasingly evident that it would be hopelessly inadequate to use the income tax as a tax principally on wealth, and that the
costs of the war would have to be borne in part also by the lower and
middle classes.

The administration's tax program evolved gradually in response to the
Treasury's need for funds and the necessity for curbing inflation. For example, Congress approved two revenue acts in 1940 that increased income and corporation taxes and imposed an excess profits tax graduated to
a maximum of 50 percent. Congress again increased old taxes in 1941 and
devised new means of finding revenue. Even so, the income tax still
touched only the small minority with upper middle- and upper-class incomes. The turning point came when the president presented his Budget
Message to Congress on January 5, 1942, proposing a $7 billion increase in
the tax burden. After months of agonizing delay, Congress responded with
the Revenue Act of 1942, approved October 21.

EXPENDITURES OF THE UNITED STATES GOVERNMENT,
1914–1952

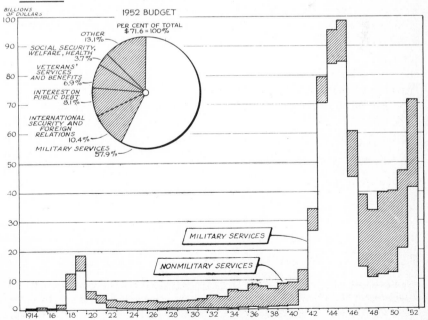

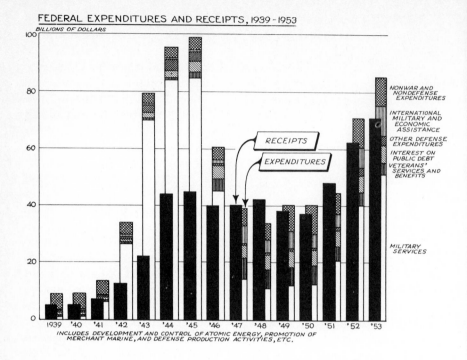

FEDERAL EXPENDITURES AND RECEIPTS, 1939-1953

INCLUDES DEVELOPMENT AND CONTROL OF ATOMIC ENERGY, PROMOTION OF MERCHANT MARINE, AND DEFENSE PRODUCTION ACTIVITIES, ETC.

It was, as the president said, "the greatest tax bill in American history," designed to raise more than $7 billion additional revenue annually, a sum exceeding total federal revenues in any peacetime year before 1941. The measure increased the combined corporate income tax to a maximum of 40 percent and raised the excess profits tax to a flat 90 percent. Moreover, it increased excise taxes and levied a host of new ones, and stiffly increased estate and gift taxes. The revolutionary feature of the Revenue Act of 1942, however, was its broadening of the income tax to tap low incomes as well as practically to confiscate large ones. Only 13 million persons had paid federal income taxes in 1941; in contrast, some 50 million persons were caught in the net cast in 1942.[3] The difficulty of collecting income taxes from 50 million persons by the conventional method of individual returns led to the adoption, in 1943, of a measure requiring employers to collect the tax by payroll deductions.

Meanwhile, personal incomes, governmental expenditures, and inflationary pressures continued to mount. The president therefore came back

[3] Specifically, the Revenue Act of 1942 lowered exemptions to $500 for single persons and $1,200 for married persons and increased the normal income tax from 4 to 6 percent. On top of this normal tax came a surtax ranging from 13 to 82 percent and a Victory tax of 5 percent, collected at the source on all incomes above $624 a year. The act of 1942 promised that part of the Victory tax would be refunded after the war, but Congress revoked this pledge in 1944. A married person with two dependents and a net income of $500,000 paid $344,476 in federal income taxes in 1941; he paid $439,931 under the act of 1942. A married person with two dependents and a net income of $3,000 paid $58 in the first instance and $267 in the second.

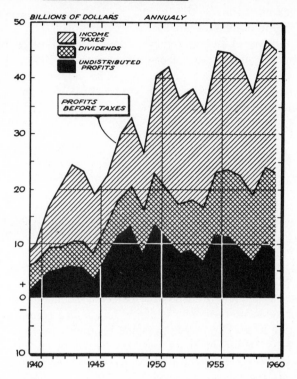

CORPORATE PROFITS, TAXES,
AND DIVIDENDS, 1940-1960

in his Budget Message of 1943 to demand an increase of $16 billion in the federal tax load. Treasury officials later lowered the request to $10.5 billion. Even so, congressional leaders rebelled and adopted a Revenue Act in early February 1944 that yielded additional revenue of only $2.2 billion, chiefly by increasing the excess profits tax to 95 percent and by heavy increases in excise taxes. The president replied on February 22 with a veto so stinging that his spokesman in the Senate, Alben W. Barkley of Kentucky, resigned his post as majority leader. The Senate Democratic caucus promptly and unanimously reelected Barkley, and an angry House and Senate overrode the veto by enormous majorities on February 24 and 25, 1944. From this time forward administration and congressional leaders were concerned not with increasing the tax burden, but with simplifying the withholding system and planning for the reconversion that would soon come with the end of the war.

In retrospect, perhaps the most significant aspect of the tax program from 1941 to 1945 was the way it reflected the nation's conviction that a war for survival should not become a war for the enrichment of the few. There could be no "swollen fortunes" when the federal income tax reached a maximum of 94 percent of total net income, to say nothing of state income and local property taxes. Indeed, the nation's top 5 percent of income receivers suffered their severest relative economic losses in the history of the country during this period. Their share of disposable income fell from 25.7 percent in 1940 to 15.9 percent in 1944. The relative status of the top 1 percent of income receivers declined even more. Their share of disposable income decreased from 11.5 percent in 1940 to 6.7 percent in 1944. And with an excess profits tax of 95 percent and corporation income taxes reaching a maximum of 50 percent there were few cases of swollen profits. Net corporation income was $9.4 billion in 1941 and 1942, increased slightly in 1943 and 1944, and fell back to $8.5 billion in 1945.

6. Combating Inflation on the Home Front

Aside from the mobilization of fighting men and the maintenance of a steady flow of materials to the battle fronts, perhaps the most important problem at home was prevention of a runaway inflation that would compound the costs of the war and increase the burdens of many classes. To state the problem in its simplest terms, inflationary pressures existed after 1941 because the volume of disposable personal income greatly exceeded the supply of goods and services available for civilian consumption at the prevailing price level. Disposable personal incomes rose from $92 billion in 1941 to $151 billion in 1945, but the supply of civilian goods and services, measured in constant dollars, rose from $77.6 billion to only $95.4 billion during the same period. The danger of inflation stalked the home front because of this inflationary gap.

The most obvious weapon against inflation and the first to be tried was control of prices and rents. It will be recalled that Roosevelt, while reorganizing the defense mobilization machinery, had established an Office of Price Administration and Civilian Supply (OPA), headed by Leon Henderson, to work in conjunction with the Office of Production Management. Without any real power, Henderson was helpless to control prices during 1941. Consequently, retail prices were rising at the rate of 2 percent a month by February 1942. The president pleaded for new authority, and Congress responded with the Emergency Price Control Act of 1942. It empowered the price administrator to fix maximum prices and rents in special areas and to pay subsidies to producers, if that was necessary to prevent price increases. On the other hand, the powerful farm bloc denied the price administrator authority to control agricultural prices until they reached 110 percent of parity.

The OPA during the next three months launched a two-pronged campaign—to stabilize prices piecemeal, and to establish a system of rationing for tires, automobiles, gasoline, and sugar and, somewhat later, for shoes, fuel oil, and coffee. Moreover, the OPA followed the president's lead on April 28 by issuing its first General Maximum Price Regulation. It froze

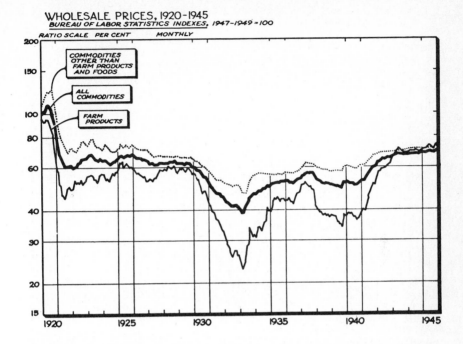

WHOLESALE PRICES, 1920-1945
BUREAU OF LABOR STATISTICS INDEXES, 1947-1949 = 100
RATIO SCALE　PER CENT　　MONTHLY

COMMODITIES OTHER THAN FARM PRODUCTS AND FOODS

ALL COMMODITIES

FARM PRODUCTS

most prices and rents at their level of March 1942. Events soon revealed large loopholes in the stabilization program. The most obvious was the ban on a ceiling for food prices until they reached an extraordinary level. As food prices continued their inexorable rise—they increased a total of 11 percent during 1942—organized labor redoubled its demands for pay increases that in turn would mean higher prices for manufactured products. Somehow, somewhere, the inflationary spiral had to be stopped, the president exclaimed in a special message on September 7, 1942. "I ask Congress to take . . . action by the first of October. . . . In the event that the Congress should fail to act, and act adequately, I shall accept the responsibility, and I will act."

Congress responded swiftly if grudgingly with the Anti-Inflation Act of October 2, 1942, empowering the president to stabilize wages, prices, and salaries at their levels on September 15. The president established the Office of Economic Stabilization on the following day, October 3, and forbade any further increase in wages and salaries without the approval of the stabilization director, James F. Byrnes. In addition, he froze agricultural prices at their level on September 15 and extended rent control to all areas of the country.

It was a heroic beginning, but even rougher storms lay ahead. The OPA administrator, Leon Henderson, had never been popular with Congress and the public. Roosevelt permitted him to resign in December 1942 and appointed Prentiss S. Brown, former senator frcm Michigan, in his stead.

PERSONAL INCOME, CONSUMPTION, AND SAVING, 1940-1961

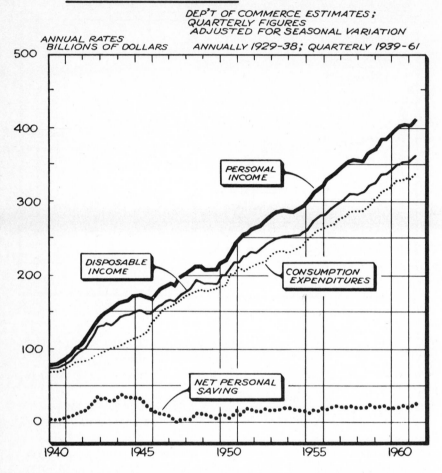

DEP'T OF COMMERCE ESTIMATES;
QUARTERLY FIGURES
ADJUSTED FOR SEASONAL VARIATION

ANNUAL RATES
BILLIONS OF DOLLARS   ANNUALLY 1929-38; QUARTERLY 1939-61

PERSONAL INCOME

DISPOSABLE INCOME

CONSUMPTION EXPENDITURES

NET PERSONAL SAVING

Unfortunately, business, farm, and labor groups took his appointment as a signal for an all-out campaign against stabilization. Congress tried to open a large hole in the dike in March 1943 by approving a bill to exclude subsidy and parity payments in determination of parity levels for agriculture. Roosevelt vetoed the measure on April 2, pointing out that it would increase the cost of living by more than 5 percent. At the same time, labor spokesmen were growing restive under a formula by which workers had been allowed a 15 percent wage increase in 1942, and were threatening to break the no-strike pledge they had given after Pearl Harbor.

It was a dangerous situation, but the president acted decisively on April 8 by ordering the stabilization agencies to "hold the line" against any further unwarranted price and wage increases. Nor was this all. When John L. Lewis called a general coal strike on May 1 in defiance of the hold

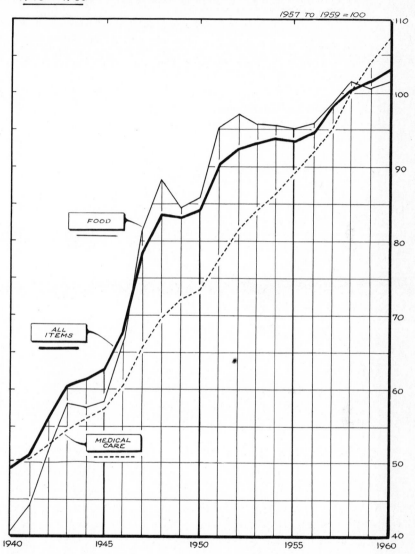

CONSUMER PRICES
1940 – 1960

the line order, the president seized the coal mines and virtually ordered miners back into the pits. Moreover, the OPA began an aggressive campaign to roll back food prices. It culminated in a 10 percent reduction in the retail prices of meat, coffee, and butter on May 7. The tide had turned, and the cost of living increased less than 1.5 percent between the spring of 1943 and the summer of 1945. The Consumer Price Index had increased by 28.3 percent during the entire period 1940–1945. This was a remarkable record in view of the power of organized pressure groups and inevitable public vexation at the inconveniences of direct controls.

7. *Workers, Farmers, and the War Effort*

The nearly insatiable demands of the American and Allied war machines solved the unemployment problem almost overnight, as the number of civilian workers increased from about 46.5 million to over 53 million from 1940 to the middle of 1945. The chief factor in this expansion was the addition of about 7 million workers from the reservoir of the unemployed. To all these workers the war boom brought such prosperity as they had

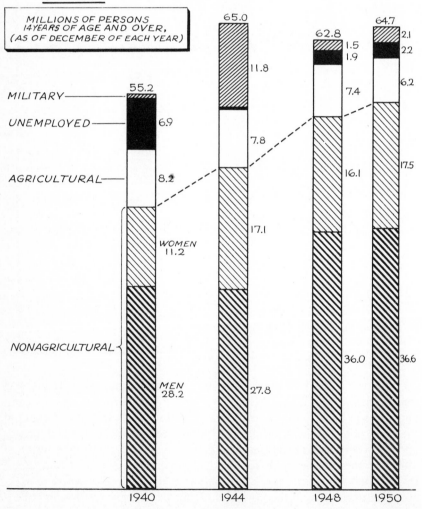

THE AMERICAN LABOR FORCE
1940-1950

MILLIONS OF PERSONS
14 YEARS OF AGE AND OVER,
(AS OF DECEMBER OF EACH YEAR)

never known before. The Consumer Price Index advanced 23.3 percent between 1941 and 1945, but weekly earnings of persons employed in manufacturing increased 70 percent.

It was no easy task to mobilize this huge labor force, restrain labor's natural desire for higher wages, and bridle irresponsible labor leaders. Indeed, the administration never did achieve comprehensive control over manpower resources. The president created the War Manpower Commission (WMC) in April 1942 and appointed former Governor Paul V. McNutt of Indiana to direct the flow of workers into war industries. The WMC gradually evolved coercive measures that prohibited workers in defense industries from leaving their jobs without approval of the United States Employment Service. This system worked reasonably well, but it did not solve the more important problem of recruiting new workers and shifting workers from nondefense to war industries. One solution, of course, was national service legislation to draft men for war work. The CIO and AF of L bitterly opposed such legislation, but the manpower shortage seemed so critical by the end of 1943 that the president finally came out in support of a national service act in his Annual Message in January 1944. The House approved a labor draft bill in December 1944, but Germany collapsed before the Senate could act on the measure.

Much more important and difficult was the task of preventing strikes and reconciling labor's natural desires for economic advancement and union security with the general objective of winning the war without runaway inflation. This gigantic and at times nearly impossible task was entrusted to the War Labor Board (WLB), created by the president on January 12, 1942. The WLB was established simply to settle labor disputes, but it soon discovered that mediation was impossible without a complete edifice of labor policy. Inevitably, therefore, the WLB emerged as a powerful policy-making body in the war economy.

To the leaders of organized labor the fundamental issue was protection of the right of collective bargaining. The WLB stood firm in defense of labor's rights under the Wagner Act, even the right to the closed shop when a majority of workers voted in favor of it. Moreover, it applied a compromise—the so-called maintenance of membership plan—that protected unions in rapidly expanding war plants.[4] Union membership expanded under its aegis to nearly 15 million by the end of the war.

The thorniest problems of wartime labor administration were inexorable demands for higher wages and strikes to enforce such demands. Here the issue lay not between labor and management, for management was usually eager to increase wages in order to hold and attract labor, but rather between the public interest and combined private interests. The WLB defended labor's right to enjoy a standard of living "compatible with

---

[4]Under this arrangement unions retained their membership and the right to bargain for all workers during the life of a bargaining contract. On the other hand, new workers coming into an industry or plant were not required to join the union as a condition of employment.

health and decency." It also endorsed union demands for equal pay for blacks and women and elimination of sectional differentials. On the other hand, it also asserted that workers should be content to maintain and not improve their standard of living during wartime. In theory most labor leaders concurred; the trouble was that they could never agree with the WLB on what that standard of living was. The rise in the cost of living during the early months of 1942 precipitated the first crisis. The WLB responded on July 16, 1942, with the so-called Little Steel formula. It granted most workers a 15 percent wage increase to offset a similar increase in the cost of living since January 1, 1941. But employers began to award pay increases that exceeded the Little Steel formula, and the president, under authority of the Stabilization Act of October 2, 1942, empowered the WLB to forbid increases that imperiled the stabilization program.

Meanwhile, the WLB's determination to hold the line on wages had driven a minority of labor to irresponsible action. The AF of L and CIO had given a no-strike pledge soon after Pearl Harbor and promised to "produce without interruption." Responsible labor leaders kept this promise for the most part, but a few reckless leaders and a minority of the rank and file accumulated a sorry record during the Second World War. All told, there were 14,731 work stoppages involving 6,744,000 workers and resulting in the loss of 36,301,000 man-days from December 8, 1941, through August 14, 1945. To cite only the bald record, however, would be to do injustice to the great majority of workers who remained faithful to the no-strike pledge. Most work stoppages were short-lived and occurred in defiance of union leadership. Moreover, they caused a loss of only one-ninth of 1 percent of total working time.

Even so, it was difficult for the mass of Americans to think in terms of averages when they saw workers in airplane factories and shipyards striking for higher pay or over union jurisdiction. Two major incidents—a coal strike and the near occurrence of a nationwide railroad strike in 1943—particularly alarmed the American people. John L. Lewis refused to appear before the WLB and called a general coal strike on May 1, 1943. The president seized the mines, but the miners struck again on June 11 because the WLB would not break the Little Steel formula and grant high wage increases. Miners returned to work when Roosevelt threatened to ask Congress to draft them, but Lewis forced the administration to surrender by threat of a third strike.[5]

Lewis's cynical defiance of federal authority was more than Congress would tolerate. In hot resentment it approved and reenacted over the president's veto on June 26, 1943, the Smith-Connally, or War Labor Disputes, Act. It empowered the president to seize any struck war plant. It also required unions to wait thirty days before striking, and to hold a secret vote of the workers before a strike was executed. More indicative of

[5]Under the agreement concluded between Lewis and Secretary of the Interior Ickes the miners received normal wage increases under the Little Steel formula. In addition, they received pay increases to compensate for reduced lunch periods and for time spent going to and from the pits.

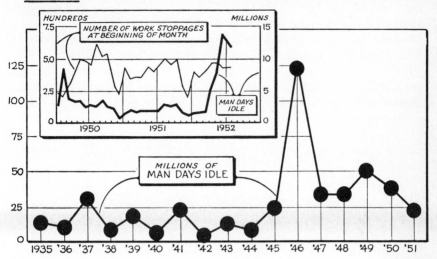

WORK STOPPAGES IN THE UNITED STATES, 1935–1951

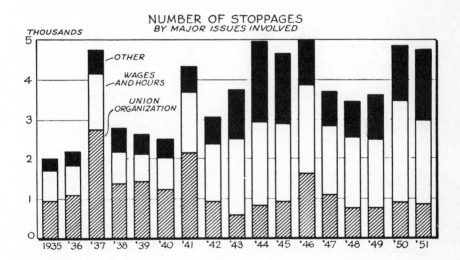

NUMBER OF STOPPAGES
BY MAJOR ISSUES INVOLVED

the rising antilabor sentiment was the enactment by many state legislatures of laws to prevent certain union practices and to subject unions to a measure of public regulation.[6]

For agriculture, the war boom brought new problems but also a stability and prosperity unknown since 1919. Net cash income from farming increased from $2,300,000,000 to $9,458,000,000 from 1940 to 1945, or by

[6]For example, these laws forbade the closed shop, mass picketing, secondary boycotts, and the like, and required unions to file financial reports and obtain licenses for labor organizers.

more than 300 percent. Two factors—increased production and higher prices, both of them stemming from vastly increased demands at home and abroad—made possible this return of agriculture to its long-sought position of parity in the American economy. Agricultural prices more than doubled between 1940 and 1945. During the same period, the index of all farm production rose from 108 to 123, while increases in food crops were even more spectacular. Incredible though it sounds, this expansion was accomplished in spite of a declining farm population and without any significant increase in acreage planted and harvested.[7]

8. Public Opinion, Civil Rights, and War

Never before had Americans gone to war with such determination and unity. Significant opposition to the war effort simply did not exist after the Pearl Harbor attack, mainly because Communists rallied to the defense and war efforts after the Germans attacked Russia. And because disloyalty was rare, there were no volunteer leagues of patriots, no committees of public safety, no high-powered propaganda campaigns and war madness. This is not to say that the government abandoned control over news and expressions of opinion,[8] or that it was not ready to act ruthlessly to suppress dangerous dissent. For example, the Justice Department at the president's command convened a special grand jury in Washington in July 1941 and laid before it and two succeeding grand juries voluminous evidence on the far-flung network of Nazi and Fascist organizations in the United States. The upshot was the indictment under the Smith Act of thirty leading seditionists for conspiring to establish a Nazi government in the United States and incite disloyalty among the armed forces. The trial proceeded for more than seven months in 1944 until the judge died, apparently a victim of the badgering of defense attorneys. The seditionists were in-

[7]The total number of agricultural workers declined from 11,671,000 in 1940 to 10,873,000 in 1945. On the other hand, the index of productivity in agriculture increased from 112 in 1940 to 136 in 1945 because of increased use of tractors, trucks, and other machinery. Two factors making possible larger yields without significant increases in acreage were a large expansion in the use of fertilizers and the spread of hybrid corn.

[8]Some kind of censorship was inevitable. The president entrusted censorship of war news to the War and Navy departments and the FBI on the day after the Pearl Harbor attack. Then, following passage by Congress of the first War Powers Act on December 18, 1941, the President established an Office of Censorship, with Byron Price, executive news director of the Associated Press, as director. Roosevelt next established the Office of War Information (OWI) on June 13, 1942, with Elmer Davis, veteran correspondent and commentator, in charge. The OWI happily never became a second Creel committee—the government's propaganda agency during the First World War. It produced motion pictures and published pamphlets and posters reminding Americans of their duty and depicting the dangers of an Axis victory. On the other hand, it did not spread manufactured atrocity stories—the truth was horrible enough—or attempt to engender hatred of the enemy. Indeed, such hatred, especially for the Japanese, already existed in full measure and was fanned by the radio, press, and motion pictures. The overseas branch of the OWI also broadcast daily programs to the Axis peoples.

dicted a second time in 1945, and government attorneys rushed to Germany to obtain new evidence. However, the Circuit Court of Appeals of the District of Columbia ended the fiasco in November 1946 by dismissing the indictment on the ground that the government's proceedings were a travesty of justice.

The government was scarcely more successful when it tried to imprison individual champions of nazism and opponents of the war. The critical test arose when the Justice Department invoked the Espionage Act of 1917 against a man named Hartzel, who published a diatribe against American participation in the war in 1942 and mailed copies to army officers. The Supreme Court, in *Hartzel* v. *United States*, 1944, made enforcement of the Espionage Act virtually impossible by declaring that the government had to prove specific intent to obstruct the war effort before it could obtain convictions under the law. Again, when the government obtained the conviction of twenty-four leaders of the German-American Bund for violating the Espionage Act, the court reversed the conviction on the ground of insufficient evidence of criminal intent.

Actually, the government knew that the assorted crackpots who made up the Bund and other pro-Nazi organizations were no menace, for the FBI had penetrated these groups and placed their leaders under surveillance. Espionage and sabotage, however, were different matters, and the Justice Department moved swiftly and sternly in dealing with them. The FBI broke a small Nazi espionage ring in 1938, destroyed the major Nazi network in 1941, and was prepared to move against potential spies and saboteurs on the eve of American entrance into the war. The FBI had taken more than 1,700 enemy aliens into custody within less than three days after the Pearl Harbor attack.[9] By such effective countermeasures the Justice Department completely destroyed the elaborate German intelligence and sabotage systems, with the results that not a single known act of sabotage was committed in the United States after December 7, 1941.

Deprived of its underground in America, the German high command resorted to audacious plans. It trained two teams of saboteurs—they were Germans who had lived in America and Americans citizens of German descent—and sent them by submarines in May 1942 to destroy the American aluminum industry and blow up bridges and railroad facilities. One team landed on Long Island, the other on the Florida coast. The eight invaders were captured almost immediately by the FBI, tried by a special military commission, sentenced to death, and executed on August 8.[10] The father of one of the saboteurs, Hans Haupt of Chicago, was also convicted of treason for hiding his son and given life imprisonment. Another German

[9] All told, the Justice Department arrested some 16,000 enemy aliens during the war, one-fourth of whom were imprisoned.

[10] The president commuted the sentences of two saboteurs who gave evidence to life imprisonment in one case and thirty years' imprisonment in the other.

American, Anthony Cramer, was convicted of treason for assisting one of the saboteurs.[11]

The one great blot on the administration's otherwise excellent civil liberties record during the war was the detention and forced removal of Japanese Americans from the West Coast to internment camps in the interior. It was the greatest single violation of civil rights in American history. The issue was not the arrest of Japanese subjects who were potential saboteurs, for they were rounded up immediately after the Pearl Harbor attack. It was the loyalty of some 41,000 Japanese ineligible to citizenship and 71,000 Nisei, or American citizens of Japanese ancestry. The general staff declared the West Coast a theater of war in the panic following December 7, 1941, and newspapers and political leaders in California began a widespread campaign for removal of all Japanese Americans, whether citizens or not. The demand was taken up in Washington by the congressional delegations from the Pacific Coast states, and was seconded by the commanding general on the West Coast, John L. De Witt. The president on February 19, 1942, authorized the army to take control. General De Witt soon afterward ordered removal of *all* Japanese Americans from an area comprising the western third of Washington and Oregon, the western half of California, and the southern quarter of Arizona. Some 110,000 Japanese and Nisei were ruthlessly ejected from their homes, herded into temporary stockades surrounded by barbed wire, and then transported to ten relocation centers established by the War Relocation Authority in western deserts and the swamplands of Arkansas. Eventually some 18,000 persons suspected of disloyalty were confined in a camp at Tule Lake, California, while the remainder were allowed to find new homes or go to colleges in the Midwest and East. Some 36,000 chose resettlement during the war.

The most disappointing aspect of the whole affair was the Supreme Court's refusal to vindicate the principle of civilian supremacy or defend elementary civil rights. A divided court, in *Korematsu* v. *United States*, December 1944, apologetically approved the evacuation on the ground that military leaders were justified in taking extreme measures against persons on account of race to protect national security, even though the situation was not serious enough to justify imposition of martial law. The

[11]The Supreme Court reversed Cramer's conviction in 1945 on the ground that the government had not proved that he gave aid and comfort to the enemy within the meaning of the treason clause. However, the Court upheld Haupt's conviction in 1947. Only one other person was tried for treason during the war. He was a Detroit Bundsman, Max Stephan, who was sentenced to death in 1942 for helping a German prisoner of war to escape. The president commuted his sentence to life imprisonment one day before the execution was to take place. However, the Justice Department obtained indictment of a number of turncoat Americans—among them Ezra Pound, the poet; Robert H. Best, a former foreign correspondent; Mildred Gillars, known to servicemen as "Axis Sally"; and Mrs. Iva d'Aquino, better known as "Tokyo Rose"—who broadcast for the Axis during the war. Most of them were apprehended at the end of hostilities, convicted of treason, and sentenced to long prison terms. Pound, however, was declared insane and incarcerated in St. Elizabeth's Hospital in Washington.

meaning of the decision was clear and foreboding: in future emergencies no American citizen would have any rights that the president and army were bound to respect when, *in their judgment*, the emergency justified drastic denial of civil rights.

9. Blacks and the Home Front

The Second World War was a time of unrest and new striving on America's troubled frontier of black-white relations. There were race riots, and national discriminations like continued segregation of nearly a million blacks in the armed services and separation of black and white blood in Red Cross blood banks. Racial tensions rose to the danger point in the South as blacks acquired a measure of financial independence and social self-respect. Yet, withal, Negroes emerged from the war with a larger measure of self-esteem and economic and political security than they had ever enjoyed.

The most dangerous racial tensions developed in industrial areas outside the South, as a result of the sudden immigration of nearly 1 million southern blacks in search of jobs and new social opportunities. There were numerous minor clashes in many cities, and New York escaped a major race riot in early 1944 only because of the quick action of its mayor and police force. Tensions flared into large-scale rioting in Detroit, home of Gerald L. K. Smith and other Negro-baiters. A fight between a black and a white man on June 20, 1943, led to other clashes. Soon mobs of whites were roaming the Negro section, killing and burning as they went. By the time that federal troops had restored order, twenty-five blacks and nine whites had been killed.

This was the dark side of an otherwise bright picture, for the Second World War was a time also of great advancement for American blacks. Blacks in the South enjoyed greater acceptance and security and larger political and economic opportunities than ever before. Lynching, long the extreme form of southern race control, became almost a historic phenomenon, as the number of Negroes thus put to death declined from five in 1942 to one in 1945. A distinguished body of southern leaders, black and white, met in Atlanta in 1944 and organized the Southern Regional Council to combat prejudice and misunderstanding by concerted action in communities and states. Equally significant was the growth during the war of an advanced equalitarian movement outside the South. Assuming the proportions almost of a crusade, this campaign against Jim Crow won many triumphs, the most important of which was a growing concern for civil rights by the major parties.

Negroes made greatest progress during the war, in both the North and the South, on the economic front. Of all groups they had suffered most during the depression and profited least from New Deal measures; nor did the defense boom of 1940–1941 bring relief, as employers stubbornly refused to hire black workers. The administration moved slowly, until A. Philip Randolph, president of the Brotherhood of Sleeping Car Porters, called upon 50,000 blacks to march on Washington to protest. Randolph called off the threatened march; but he did so only after Roosevelt had issued his notable Executive Order 8802 on June 25, 1941. It directed that blacks be admitted to job training programs, forbade discrimination in work on defense contracts, and established a Fair Employment Practices Committee to investigate charges of discrimination on account of race.

The FEPC made progress slowly and performed its most effective service during 1942 and 1943 by conducting hearings on discrimination in most of the large cities of the country. It set to work more vigorously when the president, in May 1943, reorganized the agency, expanded its budget, and directed that antidiscrimination clauses in contracts be enforced. Establishing fifteen regional offices, it heard some 8,000 complaints and conducted thirty public hearings from 1943 to 1946. The results were unexpectedly gratifying. Nearly 2 million Negroes were at work in aircraft factories, shipyards, steel mills, and other war plants in the South and elsewhere by the end of 1944.[12]

The millennium had not come for American blacks when the war ended. To men of good will, however, the steady enlargement of economic, social, and political opportunities for blacks during the war years was perhaps the most encouraging development on the American home front. Blacks in 1945 could look forward to a postwar era full not only of struggle but also of hope for a new era in which they might stand erect as free men and women and citizens of the great democracy.

[12]In addition, New York, New Jersey, and Indiana established Fair Employment Practices commissions, while many cities set up antidiscrimination boards.

22

The Second World War: Diplomatic and Military Aspects

The American people were destined to play a leading and decisive role in the military operations that brought victory for the United Nations in 1945. In this chapter we will follow the Allies on the long and tortuous road from near defeat to victory. Since the war was won not only in the factory and on the battlefield but around the conference table as well, we will also note how Roosevelt and Churchill forged the bonds of Anglo-American unity, drew the Russian leaders into close association, and gave such an effective demonstration of allied cooperation in wartime as the world had rarely seen before.

1. The Formation of the Grand Alliance

American and British leaders gathered in Washington soon after the Pearl Harbor attack to lay plans for combined conduct of the war. Liaison with the Russians would come later, as soon as circumstances permitted. Prime

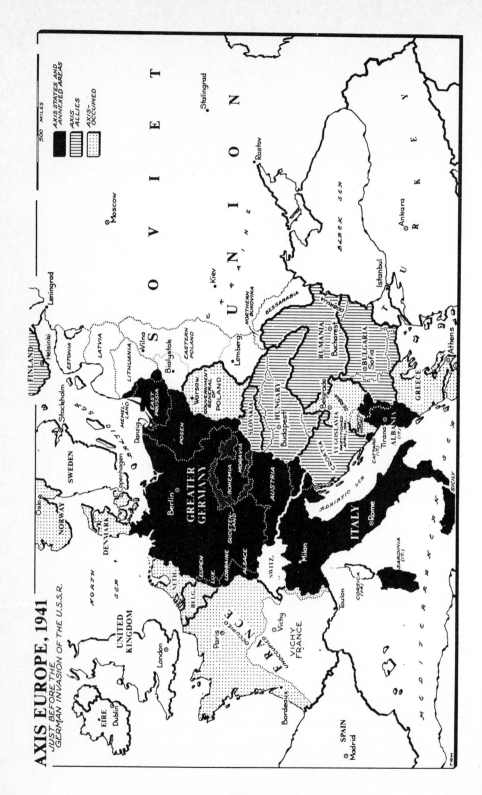

AXIS EUROPE, 1941

JUST BEFORE THE
GERMAN INVASION OF THE U.S.S.R.

500 MILES

AXIS STATES AND
ANNEXED AREAS

AXIS
ALLIES

AXIS-
OCCUPIED

518

Minister Winston Churchill arrived in Washington on December 22, 1941, for a week of conferences known by the code name of ARCADIA. These discussions continued on the military level until January 14, 1942. This was a time when Allied military fortunes were at their lowest ebb since the fall of France, but negotiations proceeded smoothly and yielded complete agreement on all important points: American production goals for 1942 and 1943, pooling of Anglo-American munitions and their disposal by a joint Munitions Assignment Board, and immediate establishment of a Combined Chiefs of Staff in Washington and a combined British, American, and Dutch command in the Pacific. ARCADIA's most important work was reaffirmation of the earlier staff decision to defeat Germany first since that nation was the stronger enemy and controlled industry and manpower superior to the Japanese. Therefore the Allies would launch their first major offensives against the Continent and conduct holding operations in the Pacific until Nazi power had been subdued.

On the diplomatic level, moreover, Roosevelt and Churchill worked in complete harmony for the formation of a grand coalition of the Allies. The fruit of their labor was the Declaration of the United Nations, signed at the White House on New Year's Day, 1942, by Roosevelt, Churchill, Maxim Litvinov for the USSR, and representatives of twenty-three other nations at war with the Axis. The signatory powers reaffirmed the principles set forth in the Atlantic Charter, pledged their full resources to the defeat of the Axis nations, and promised one another not to make a separate peace.

The most uncertain link in the new Allied chain was Russia. By hearty cooperation, the USSR could hasten victory and help lay the groundwork for postwar cooperation; by making a separate peace, on the other hand, Russia could postpone the hope of Allied victory perhaps indefinitely. The president's and the prime minister's most pressing diplomatic problem during early 1942 was Russian territorial ambitions in Europe and a Russian demand that Britain and the United States guarantee those ambitions in advance. The Kremlin presented the first installment of its demands during a visit of Foreign Secretary Anthony Eden to Moscow in December 1941. Stalin then requested Britain's immediate approval of Russia's absorption of the Baltic states and parts of Finland, Poland, and Rumania. He warned, moreover, that conclusion of a British-Soviet alliance would depend upon British endorsement of these territorial claims.

The issue came to a head when the Soviet foreign minister, Vyacheslav Molotov, arrived in London on May 20, 1942, to press Russian territorial and military demands. Churchill and Eden had been strengthened by a warning from Washington that the United States might publicly denounce any Anglo-Russian agreement conceding Stalin's ambitions. They stood firm and persuaded Molotov to sign, on May 26, a general twenty-year Treaty of Alliance that included no reference to boundaries.

2. *The Ebb Tide of Allied Military Fortunes*

Axis victories were so swift and far-reaching during the first six months of 1942 that it seemed that the United Nations might lose the war before they could begin fighting. The Japanese, following air attacks on British and American possessions on December 7, launched seaborne invasions of Hong Kong, Malaya, the Philippines, and lesser islands. They were free to roam and strike almost at will, for the once mighty Anglo-American Pacific naval power was nearly gone by the end of 1941. Guam fell on December 11, 1941; Wake Island, on December 23; Hong Kong, on Christmas Day. Meanwhile, Japanese forces pressed forward in conquest of Malaya, Burma, and the Philippines. Singapore, the great British naval base in the Far East, surrendered on February 15, 1942, to a Japanese force that came down from the north through Malaya. Most of Burma fell in March and April 1942, while Ceylon and India were threatened by a large Japanese naval force that momentarily controlled the Indian Ocean and the Bay of Bengal in April.

In the Philippines General Douglas MacArthur, with a force of 19,000 American regulars, 12,000 Philippine Scouts, and 100,000 soldiers of the new Philippine army, fought a desperate delaying action. When Japanese troops threatened Manila, MacArthur declared the capital an open city, moved to Corregidor, and withdrew his troops into Bataan Peninsula for a hopeless but gallant last stand. MacArthur was transferred to Australia on March 17, 1942. His successor, General Jonathan Wainwright, continued the fight from Corregidor and other forts off the tip of the peninsula and held out there until disease, starvation, and superior enemy forces made further resistance impossible. He surrendered May 6.

Meanwhile, large new Japanese forces were poised in Malaya and the Philippines by the end of December 1941 to strike at Borneo, the Celebes, New Guinea, and the Dutch East Indies. Only the small American Asiatic Fleet and a few Dutch and British cruisers stood athwart the path of Japanese conquest of the Indies. In the Battle of Macassar Strait, January 24, 1942, American destroyers executed a daring night attack against a Japanese convoy and forced it to turn back. But in the subsequent engagements, known as the Java Sea campaign, the Allies lost their entire naval force, except for four American destroyers. By the end of March 1942 the Japanese were in possession of the East Indies, had pushed into New Britain and the Solomon Islands, and were in position to strike at Port Moresby, the Allied base in southern New Guinea, and at Australia itself. In little more than three months they had gained control of a vast area extending from the Gilbert Islands in the Central Pacific west and south through the Solomons and New Guinea to Burma. India and Australia lay virtually undefended.

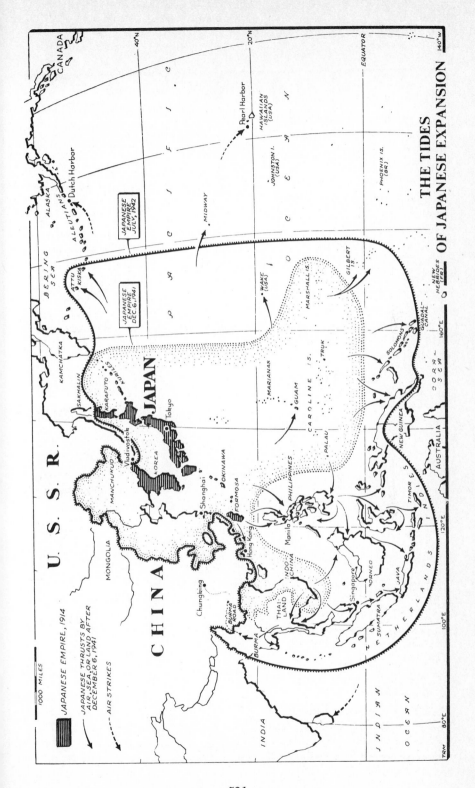

THE TIDES
OF JAPANESE EXPANSION

JAPANESE EMPIRE, 1914

JAPANESE THRUSTS BY
AIR, SEA OR LAND AFTER
DECEMBER 6, 1941

AIR STRIKES

1000 MILES

JAPANESE
EMPIRE
JULY, 1942

JAPANESE
EMPIRE
DEC. 6, 1941

CANADA

ALASKA

Dutch Harbor

ALEUTIANS

ATTU
KISKA

BERING SEA

KAMCHATKA

U. S. S. R.

SAKHALIN

KARAFUTO

KURILES

MONGOLIA

MANCHUKUO

Vladivostok

KOREA

JAPAN

Tokyo

CHINA

Chungking

Shanghai

OKINAWA

FORMOSA

Hong Kong

INDO-
CHINA

BURMA

THAI-
LAND

Singapore

SUMATRA

BORNEO

JAVA

NETHERLANDS

INDIES

TIMOR

PHILIPPINES

Manila

PALAU

CAROLINE IS.

TRUK

GUAM

MARIANAS

WAKE
(USA)

MARSHALL IS.

GILBERT
IS.

NEW GUINEA

AUSTRALIA

SOLOMONS

GUADAL-
CANAL

CORAL SEA

NEW
HEBRIDES
(FR)

PHOENIX IS.
(BR)

EQUATOR

MIDWAY

JOHNSTON I.
(USA)

HAWAIIAN
ISLANDS
(USA)

Pearl Harbor

PACIFIC OCEAN

INDIAN OCEAN

INDIA

40°N

20°N

20°N

140°W

160°E

120°E

100°E

80°E

TRM

521

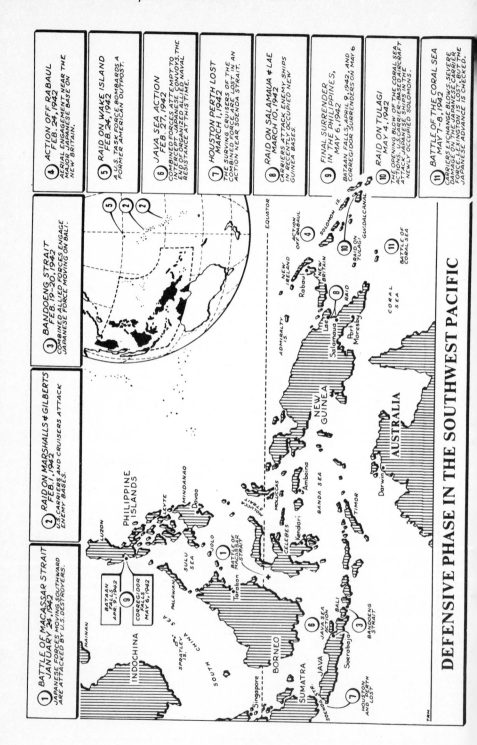

(1) BATTLE OF MACASSAR STRAIT
JANUARY 24, 1942
JAPANESE FORCES MOVING SOUTHWARD
ARE ATTACKED BY U.S. DESTROYERS.

(2) RAID ON MARSHALLS & GILBERTS
FEB. 1, 1942
U.S. CARRIERS AND CRUISERS ATTACK
ENEMY BASES.

(3) BANDOENG STRAIT
FEB. 19–20, 1942
COMBINED ALLIED FORCES ENGAGE
JAPANESE FORCE MOVING ON BALI.

(4) ACTION OFF RABAUL
FEB. 24, 1942
AERIAL ENGAGEMENT NEAR THE
MAJOR JAPANESE BASE ON
NEW BRITAIN.

(5) RAID ON WAKE ISLAND
FEB. 24, 1942
A U.S. TASK FORCE BOMBARDS A
FORMER AMERICAN OUTPOST.

(6) JAVA SEA ACTION
FEB. 27, 1942
COMBINED FORCES ATTEMPT TO
INTERCEPT JAPANESE CONVOYS. THE
END OF ORGANIZED ALLIED NAVAL
RESISTANCE AT THIS TIME.

(7) HOUSTON PERTH LOST
MARCH 1, 1942
THE SURVIVING CRUISERS OF THE
COMBINED FORCE ARE LOST IN AN
ACTION NEAR SOENDA STRAIT.

(8) RAID ON SALAMAUA & LAE
MARCH 10, 1942
CARRIERS ATTACK ENEMY SHIPS
IN RECENTLY OCCUPIED NEW
GUINEA BASES.

(9) FINAL SURRENDER
IN THE PHILIPPINES,
MAY 6, 1942
BATAAN FALLS APRIL 9, 1942, AND
CORREGIDOR SURRENDERS ON MAY 6

(10) RAID ON TULAGI
MAY 4, 1942
THE OPENING BLOW OF THE CORAL SEA
ACTIONS. U.S. CARRIER-BASED AIRCRAFT
ATTACK JAPANESE SHIPS IN THE
NEWLY OCCUPIED SOLOMONS.

(11) BATTLE OF THE CORAL SEA
MAY 7–8, 1942
CARRIERS EXCHANGE BLOWS. SEVERE
DAMAGE ON THE JAPANESE CARRIER
SHOKAKU AND THE LEXINGTON IS LOST. THE
JAPANESE ADVANCE IS CHECKED.

DEFENSIVE PHASE IN THE SOUTHWEST PACIFIC

Events almost as catastrophic for the Allies were transpiring in the Atlantic, on the eastern front in Russia, and in North Africa. German submarines came perilously close to winning the Battle of the Atlantic during 1942, when Allied and neutral shipping losses aggregated nearly 8 million tons. "The disaster of an indefinite prolongation of the war," to quote Churchill's phrase, threatened to upset Allied plans for military operations.

Meanwhile, the Germans had mounted a large offensive to drive through North Africa, cut the Suez Canal, and penetrate Arabia and the Middle East. General Erwin Rommel, the "Desert Fox," opened the campaign in Libya on May 26. The British, after several sharp defeats, retreated to El Alamein in Egypt, only seventy-five miles from Alexandria, to regroup and reinforce their shattered Eighth Army. The German lines were overextended by July 1, and Rommel's Afrika Korps was too exhausted to press the offensive.

These reversals during the spring and summer of 1942 had a nearly fatal impact on the Grand Alliance when the hard-pressed Russians demanded assistance in the form of a second front in the West. The issue first arose prominently when Molotov arrived in Washington on May 29, 1942, for

MERCHANT SHIPS SUNK
BY GERMAN SUBMARINES
NOVEMBER 1941 TO JUNE 1943

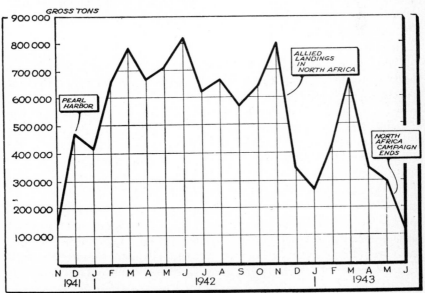

conferences mainly of a military nature with the president and his advisers. Stalin wanted, Molotov declared, an Anglo-American invasion of western Europe strong enough to draw forty German divisions from the eastern front. Without a second front in 1942, he continued, Germany might deal the USSR a mighty, crushing blow. "If you postpone your decision," he concluded in ominous words, "you will have eventually to bear the brunt of the war." Roosevelt turned to General Marshall for an answer. Marshall replied that there were enough men and supplies for the undertaking; the chief problem was to obtain adequate shipping for an expeditionary force without cutting off supplies to the Soviet Union.

Molotov returned to Moscow with a virtual promise that the United States would launch a cross-Channel invasion in 1942. The Germans drove deeper into southeastern Russia and penetrated the Caucasus, and the pressure from Moscow for relief in the West increased. At this point the president and his advisers began to consider the feasibility of an Anglo-American thrust at the northern coast of France, known by the code name SLEDGEHAMMER, as a means of averting total disaster in eastern Europe. This was the issue that dominated the conferences among Roosevelt, Churchill, and their chiefs of staff that began in Washington on June 21. Churchill stubbornly opposed any limited diversionary attempt. He admitted that the British would have six or eight divisions available for an invasion by September; they would participate if the Americans could guarantee the success of the undertaking. But were there not other ways, perhaps an invasion of North Africa, in which combined Anglo-American forces could attack more successfully? In the midst of these heated deliberations came news of Rommel's threatened drive into Egypt. It diverted the conferees' attention from the coast of France to the imperiled area, enabled Churchill to drive home his arguments for a North African invasion, and caused him to hurry home to face his critics in the House of Commons.

The president and his military staffs moved swiftly to bolster British defenses in Egypt during the last week of June 1942. But this crisis soon passed, and Roosevelt decided to have the issue of the second front determined once and for all. He sent Harry Hopkins, General Marshall, and Admiral Ernest J. King, American naval commander, to London on July 16. They joined General Dwight D. Eisenhower, now commander of the European theater of operations, and other Americans in London on July 18 for preliminary conferences. Marshall and Eisenhower were enthusiastic for an invasion of France, which they contemplated beginning on a limited scale until a large offensive could be mounted. But British staff officers refused to budge from their adamant opposition; and American naval officers agreed that a cross-Channel operation in September or October would be dangerous. Informed of the stalemate, Roosevelt replied that his spokesmen should now insist upon offensive operations somewhere, preferably in North Africa. When it seemed that the conferees would also postpone decision on GYMNAST, as the North African operation was then called, the president replied that plans must be made at once, and that landings in North Africa should occur no later than October 30, 1942. Churchill agreed, and there now remained only the task of preparing for TORCH—the new code name of the North African operation—and the unpleasant job of telling Stalin why his western Allies could not open a second front in France in 1942. All apprehensions about a premature second front were confirmed in August. A commando raid by a force of 5,000 men, mainly Canadians, against Dieppe, on the French coast, was a disaster with nearly 3,000 casualties inflicted by the strongly entrenched Germans.

3. *The Tide Begins to Turn*

Events of the autumn of 1942 began for the first time to bring some hope to the embattled United Nations. The American navy and marines finally stemmed the onrushing tide of Japanese conquest and began their slow and painful progress on the road to Tokyo. The Anglo-American Allies began a campaign in North Africa that ended the Nazi threat to the Middle East and culminated in an invasion of Sicily and Italy in 1943. The Russians finally held firm on the banks of the Volga and then began a counteroffensive that would not cease until Soviet armies had captured Berlin.

The American Pacific Fleet, commanded by Admiral Chester W. Nimitz, had regrouped and given warning even during the high tide of Japanese expansion. A spectacular blow came on April 18, 1942, when United States Army medium bombers under Colonel James Doolittle took off from the carrier *Hornet* to raid Tokyo. But the most decisive engagement during this defensive phase was the Battle of the Coral Sea, May 7 and 8, when planes from *Lexington* and *Yorktown* turned back a large Japanese force moving around the southeastern coast of New Guinea to attack Port Moresby.

The Japanese, shocked by the raid on Tokyo and unaware that the planes had come from a carrier, concluded that the Americans had launched the attack from one of the outlying islands in the Central Pacific. To avoid repetition of this air attack, they decided to extend their perimeter and sent a large armada and invasion force against Midway Island, an outpost guarding the Hawaiian Islands, in a bold bid to cut American communication lines in the Pacific and perhaps establish bases in the islands themselves. Warned of this attack by intercepted Japanese code

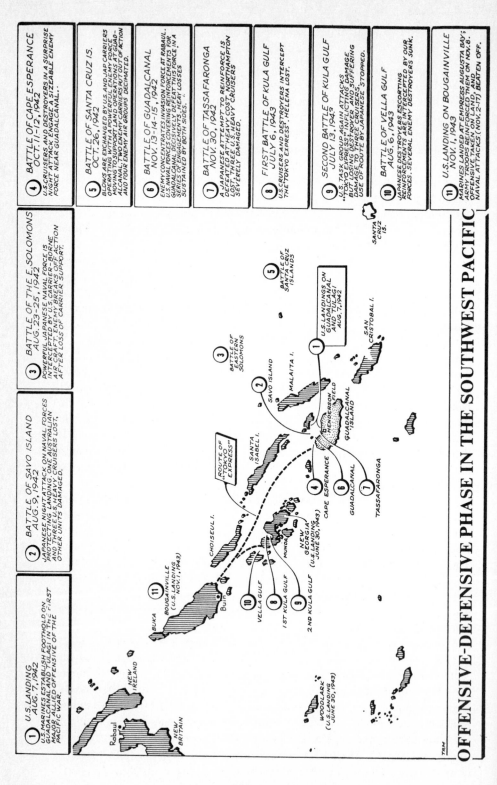

OFFENSIVE-DEFENSIVE PHASE IN THE SOUTHWEST PACIFIC

messages, Nimitz had moved his carriers and cruisers into the Central Pacific, and one of the most decisive battles of the Pacific war raged with incredible fury from June 3 to June 6. Dive bombers and B-17s from Midway joined with dive bombers and torpedo planes from *Enterprise, Hornet,* and *Yorktown* to sink four Japanese carriers, a heavy cruiser, and three destroyers, and to damage one heavy cruiser and two destroyers. In contrast, the Americans lost only *Yorktown* and a destroyer. The Battle of Midway not only removed the threat to the Hawaiian Islands but also restored the balance of naval power in the Pacific. It was, moreover, convincing proof of the importance of air power, for warships in this battle, as in the Battle of Coral Sea, did not exchange a single salvo during the engagement.

Now it was the Americans' turn to go on the offensive. The Japanese had recently moved into the southern Solomon Islands and were building an airfield on Guadalcanal, which imperiled the Allied position in the entire South Pacific and the line of communication to Australia. Assembling a large force of warships, transports, and marines in New Zealand, Admiral Robert L. Ghormley attacked Tulagi and Guadalcanal in the Solomons on August 7 and soon won control of Tulagi and the airfield on Guadalcanal. A Japanese cruiser and destroyer force surprised the Allies and sank four cruisers and damaged other ships in the Battle of Savo Island on August 8 in one of the most humiliating defeats ever suffered by the United States Navy. The Japanese did not know what damage they had done, and they withdrew without attacking the Allied transports. But they soon returned with troops, and the battle raged on Guadalcanal and for control of the air and seas in the area of the Solomons during the next six months. The issue was long in doubt, as the Japanese enjoyed an advantage in land-based aircraft from their base in Rabaul in New Britain Island. However, the American navy won control of the seas in a number of violent battles. Then American army forces, relieving the battle-weary First Marine Division, gradually overcame the enemy on Guadalcanal. The Japanese withdrew on the night of February 7-8, 1943.

In the meantime, Allied planners and diplomats had been at work preparing TORCH, the offensive in North Africa under General Eisenhower. The British Eighth Army opened an offensive against Rommel's forces at El Alamein on October 24, 1942, and three great Anglo-American convoys converged west of Gibraltar soon afterward. They struck simultaneously on November 8 at Oran and Algiers in Algeria and Casablanca on the Atlantic coast of French Morocco. They encountered heavy French resistance only around Casablanca. Marshal Henri-Philippe Pétain, head of the Vichy French government, severed diplomatic relations with the United States on November 9 and called upon his forces in North Africa to resist. But Pétain's deputy in North Africa, Admiral Jean Darlan, took control when the Germans invaded unoccupied France on November 11. He concluded an armistice agreement with the Allied supreme commander, General Eisenhower, that recognized Darlan's control and promised the cooperation of some 50,000 French colonial troops in North Africa.[1]

American and British policy toward France had diverged since 1940. Britain had given moral and material support to General Charles de Gaulle as the leader of the French forces carrying on outside France, and as representative to some extent of the growing underground resistance in France itself. The Americans, on the other hand, had regarded the de Gaullist movement as a minor military auxiliary. Roosevelt, in fact, was to continue to resist the political claims of de Gaulle's movement until after the liberation of France, when the support of the French people for the gallant general was unmistakable.

During the two weeks following the conclusion of the Darlan agreement, American and British units from Algiers engaged in a race with the Germans for control of Tunisia, then occupied by small French forces. The Germans reached the province in large numbers first and poured additional men, tanks, and planes into North Africa, and the ensuing campaign became a crucial test of strength. Fighting began in earnest on February 11, 1943. It mounted in intensity as General Sir Bernard Montgomery's British Eighth Army in the east and Eisenhower's combined armies in the west gradually closed the jaws of a gigantic vise on the Germans. The result was a complete Allied victory, signaled by German surrender on May 12, which cost the Axis fifteen divisions, and 349,206 men killed and captured, 250 tanks, over 2,300 airplanes, and 232 ships. In contrast, the Allies suffered 70,000 casualties in a campaign that seasoned their troops and opened the Mediterranean once again to Allied shipping.

In the meantime, Roosevelt, Churchill, their political advisers, and the American and British chiefs of staff had met at Casablanca for a full-dress conference in January 1943. When the conference opened on January 12, the chiefs of staff talked about operations to be launched after the Tunisian campaign had ended. These discussions continued after Roosevelt arrived on January 14. The upshot was a decision, agreed to reluctantly by the Americans (who preferred to concentrate upon an early second front in France), first, to invade Sicily in order to secure complete control of the Mediterranean and advanced air bases and, second, to defer the invasion of France at least until 1944. General Marshall argued strenuously for a cross-Channel invasion in 1943, but without success.

Roosevelt and Churchill also plunged into French politics at Casablanca. Darlan had been assassinated on December 24, 1942, and the de Gaull-

---

[1]Eisenhower's agreement with Darlan nearly cost him his post as supreme commander. The Americans had brought with them General Henri H. Giraud, who had escaped from German captivity, in the hope that he could command the loyalty of all French forces in North Africa. When Giraud failed to win that support, Eisenhower recognized Darlan because he was the de facto French chief of state. Nonetheless, liberal groups in the United States and Britain were outraged by what they charged was American collaboration with the worst reactionary elements in the Vichy regime.

ist Free French group in London and the supporters of General Giraud, Darlan's successor, were contending for the right to speak for the French nation. All that the president wanted was cooperation in the common cause of liberation, and agreement that the French people should decide the question of sovereignty after the war was over. Roosevelt and Churchill persuaded the austere and sensitive de Gaulle to come to Casablanca on January 22, meet with Giraud, and work out plans for future cooperation.

The work of the conference completed, Roosevelt and Churchill held a joint press conference at Casablanca on January 24 in which they reviewed their work and looked forward to victories ahead. But more important was Roosevelt's declaration, made after previous consultation with Churchill, that the Allies would insist upon the unconditional surrender of the Axis enemies. "It does not mean the destruction of the population of Germany, Italy, and Japan," he explained, "but it does mean the destruction of the philosophies in those countries which are based on conquest and the subjugation of other people." It was, as one critic afterward said, one of the "great mistakes of the war." It hardened the German popular will to resist and shut the door to negotiations by an anti-Hitler faction. Worse still, it virtually precluded a negotiated settlement of the Pacific war, the one conflict that might well have been terminated by negotiation.

4. 1943: The United Nations on the Offensive

The decisive turning point of the European war in 1942–1943 occurred when the Russians held Stalingrad from September to November 1942 against furious German attacks. Then the Russians launched a counteroffensive that destroyed or captured a large German army in the blazing city on February 2, 1943. From this point on, the Soviet armies pressed forward along the entire length of the eastern front. By October 1943 the Red armies had driven deep into the Ukraine and stood on the east bank of the Dnieper River, poised for a winter offensive that would drive through the Ukraine into Rumania.[2]

The year 1943 also witnessed the turning of the tide in the Battle of the Atlantic. The Germans had more than 100 U-boats constantly at sea by the spring of 1943. But the Anglo-American Allies had finally found the means of victory—aggressive offense through new methods of detection, air patrols both from land bases and escort carriers, and fast destroyers and destroyer escorts to protect the convoys. The turning point came from

[2]One factor in the Soviet victories was the increasing stream of lend-lease supplies from the United States. Supplies worth $4.25 billion went from the United States to Russia from October 1941 to January 1944. They included 7,800 planes, 4,700 tanks and tank destroyers, 70,000 trucks, and huge quantities of ammunition, food, and clothing.

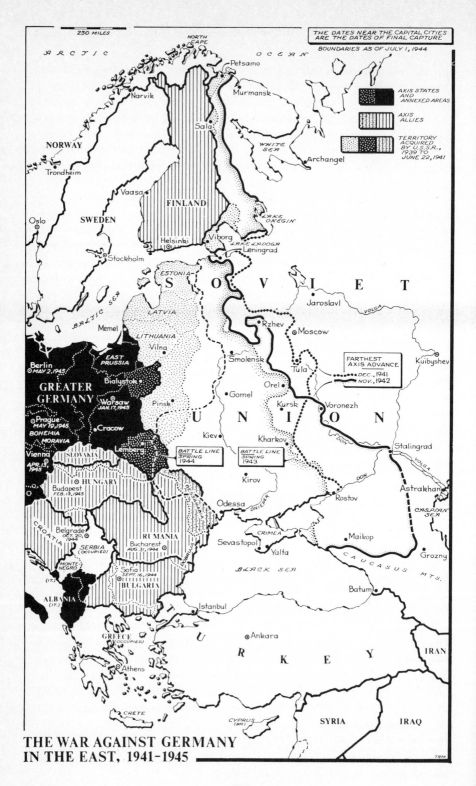

THE WAR AGAINST GERMANY
IN THE EAST, 1941-1945

March through May 1943, when U-boat sinkings in the Atlantic declined from 514,744 tons in March to 199,409 tons in May, and the number of submarines destroyed rose from 12 to 40. Allied shipping losses had declined to 29,297 tons by May 1944, and not a single Allied ship was torpedoed in the summer of 1944. And for decreasing results the Germans paid such a high price—237 submarines sunk in 1943, 241 in 1944, and 153 during the first four months of 1945—as to make their underseas campaign a useless drain on resources and manpower.

Allied power increased so swiftly in the Pacific from March 1943 to March 1944 that the two major commanders in the area, Admiral Nimitz and General MacArthur, were able not only to overwhelm or neutralize the Japanese bastions in the Central and South Pacific, but also to launch new offensives that pierced the outer perimeter of Japanese defenses.

The objective of the first great offensive was Rabaul in New Britain Island, the most important Japanese air and naval base in the Southwest Pacific area. The Allied attack was two-pronged. First came a tortuous drive up the New Guinea coast from Port Moresby to Hollandia by American and Australian ground forces, paratroops, and the American Fifth Air Force and Seventh Fleet—all under MacArthur's general command. The enemy had been cleared from the eastern part of New Guinea by February 1944. Meanwhile, American and New Zealand ground forces and strong air and naval forces under Admiral William F. Halsey began a drive through the central and northern Solomon Islands that carried to New Georgia on June 30, 1943, Bougainville on November 1, and Green Island on February 15, 1944. Finally, with the occupation of the Admiralty Islands north of New Guinea on February 29, Rabaul was cut off from communication with the Japanese base of Truk, and its encirclement was complete. Thereafter, Allied commanders were content to reduce Rabaul to impotence through aerial bombardment, without attempting to capture it.

While Allied forces under MacArthur were thus securing their hold on the South Pacific, the forces under Admiral Nimitz launched two major offensives in the Central Pacific that cracked the outer rim of Japanese defenses in that area. A new Central Pacific Force, including marine and army units, under the command of Admiral Raymond A. Spruance, attacked Tarawa and Makin islands in the Gilberts on November 20, 1943. Makin was lightly garrisoned and fell quickly to army troops; but the Second Marine Division that invaded Tarawa after an inadequate bombardment met fierce resistance from Japanese marines and had to fight for every inch of ground until the last defenders were wiped out on November 24. Striking next at the Marshall Islands, army and marine divisions rooted out Japanese defenders on Kwajalein, Roi, Namur, and Eniwetok between February 1 and 19, 1944. Next the American navy steamed into the enemy's interior defenses in daring raids against Truk on February 16

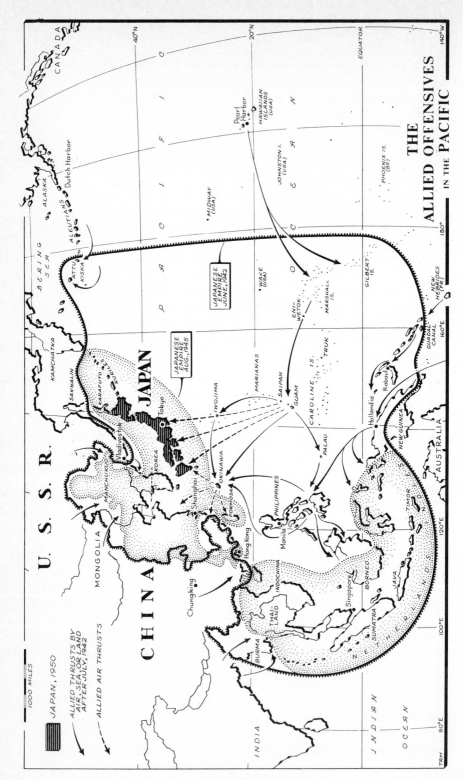

THE
ALLIED OFFENSIVES
IN THE PACIFIC

JAPAN, 1950

ALLIED THRUSTS BY
AIR, SEA, OR LAND
AFTER JULY, 1942

ALLIED AIR THRUSTS

1000 MILES

JAPANESE
EMPIRE
JUNE, 1942

JAPANESE
EMPIRE
AUG., 1945

CANADA

ALASKA

ALEUTIANS   Dutch Harbor

ATTU   KISKA

BERING SEA

KAMCHATKA

SAKHALIN

KARAFUTO

KURILES

U. S. S. R.

MANCHUKUO

Vladivostok

MONGOLIA

KOREA

JAPAN

Tokyo

Shanghai

C H I N A

Chungking

Hong Kong

INDOCHINA

BURMA

THAI-
LAND

SUMATRA

Singapore

N E T H E R L A N D S

BORNEO

JAVA

TIMOR

N. E. I.

INDIA

INDIAN OCEAN

MIDWAY
(USA)

Pearl
Harbor

HAWAIIAN
ISLANDS
(USA)

JOHNSTON I.
(USA)

PHOENIX IS.
(BR)

P A C I F I C

O C E A N

WAKE
(USA)

ENI-
WETOK

MARSHALL
IS.

GILBERT
IS.

TRUK

CAROLINE IS.

MARIANAS

SAIPAN

GUAM

PALAU

IWOJIMA

OKINAWA

FORMOSA

PHILIPPINES

Manila

NEW
HEBRIDES
(FR)

GUADAL-
CANAL

Rabaul

Hollandia

NEW GUINEA

AUSTRALIA

40°N   20°N   EQUATOR   140°W

180°

160°E

120°E

100°E

80°E

532

and against Saipan in the Marianas, only 1,350 miles from Tokyo, on February 21, 1944.

5. *Planning for Victory and the Surrender of Italy*

No sooner had the Anglo-American Allies taken the offensive than they began to look forward to victory and an uncertain postwar future. Roosevelt, Hull, and Hopkins began exploratory discussions in Washington with the British foreign secretary, Anthony Eden, in March 1943. The president was reluctant to approve Russia's absorption of the Baltic states and parts of Finland and Poland, but he agreed that there was probably nothing the United States and Britain could do to dislodge the Russians from territory that they had occupied. Roosevelt and Eden emphatically agreed that Germany should be completely disarmed and broken into a number of states. In addition, they talked in a general way about the organization of a postwar security agency, the United Nations.

Roosevelt and Hull were determined to avoid Wilson's mistake of ignoring congressional leaders and assiduously drew them into discussions of plans for a United Nations. There had been considerable debate in Congress and the press since Pearl Harbor looking toward American leadership in a postwar organization, and the public demand for strong American leadership in planning for the future was obviously overwhelming by the spring of 1943. The House on September 21 and the Senate on November 5 approved by large majorities the Fulbright and Connally resolutions pledging the United States to membership in an international organization, "with power adequate to establish and to maintain a just and lasting peace."

Meanwhile, Churchill and his advisers arrived in the United States on May 11, 1943, for another grand conference on war strategy known as TRIDENT. In brief, the conferees agreed that the British should seize the Azores Islands to provide new air and naval facilities;[3] approved plans for a tremendous increase in the aerial bombardment of Germany; instructed Eisenhower to plan for an invasion of Italy after the conquest of Sicily; set May 1, 1944, as the date for OVERLORD (the new code name for the invasion of France); and mapped plans for new offensive operations in the Pacific.

The war in the Mediterranean erupted again according to the Allied schedule soon after the TRIDENT conference. A huge Anglo-American ar-

[3] The British cabinet, however, won permission from the Portuguese government to establish these bases, and thus the projected invasion never came off.

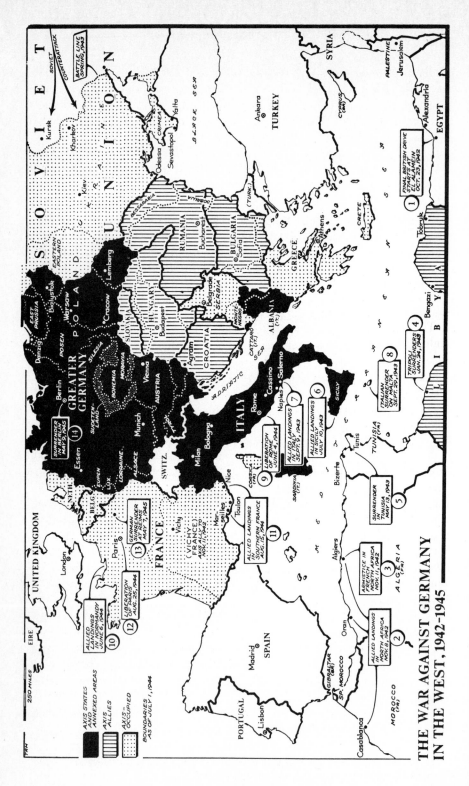

THE WAR AGAINST GERMANY
IN THE WEST, 1942–1945

Legend:
- AXIS STATES AND ANNEXED AREAS
- AXIS ALLIES
- AXIS-OCCUPIED
- BOUNDARIES AS OF JULY 1, 1944

250 MILES

Map labels (numbered boxes):
1. FINAL BRITISH DRIVE STARTS AT EL ALAMEIN OCT. 23, 1942
2. ALLIED LANDINGS IN NORTH AFRICA NOV. 8, 1942
3. ARMISTICE IN FRENCH NORTH AFRICA NOV. 11, 1942
4. TRIPOLI SURRENDERS JAN. 24, 1943
5. SURRENDER IN TUNISIA MAY 13, 1943
6. ALLIED LANDINGS IN SICILY JULY 10, 1943
7. ALLIED LANDINGS IN ITALY SEPT. 3, 1943
8. ITALIAN SURRENDER ON MALTA SEPT. 29, 1943
9. LIBERATION OF ROME JUNE 4, 1944
10. ALLIED LANDINGS IN NORMANDY JUNE 6, 1944
11. ALLIED LANDINGS IN SOUTHERN FRANCE AUG. 15, 1944
12. LIBERATION OF PARIS AUG. 25, 1944
13. GERMAN SURRENDER AT REIMS MAY 7, 1945
14. SURRENDER IN BERLIN MAY 9, 1945

SOVIET UNION · SOVIET COUNTERATTACK · BATTLE LINE SPRING, 1943

Geographic labels: EIRE, UNITED KINGDOM, London, NETH., BELG., LUX., EUPEN, FRANCE, (VICHY FRANCE) (AXIS ALLY TO NOV. 11, 1942), Paris, Vichy, Marseilles, Toulon, Nice, LORRAINE, ALSACE, SWITZ., GREATER GERMANY, Essen, Berlin, Munich, Vienna, AUSTRIA, SUDETENLAND, BOHEMIA, MORAVIA, SILESIA, EAST PRUSSIA, Danzig, POSEN, Bialystok, Warsaw, Cracow, GREATER POLAND, Lemberg, EASTERN POLAND, Kiev, Kharkov, Kursk, Odessa, Sevastopol, CRIMEA, Yalta, BESSARABIA, BUKOVINA, DOBRUDJA, RUMANIA, Bucharest, BULGARIA, Sofia, HUNGARY, Budapest, SLOVAKIA, CROATIA, Agram, SERBIA, Belgrade, MON.NEGRO, ALBANIA (IT.), CATTARO (IT.), GREECE, Athens, CRETE, TURKEY, Ankara, SYRIA, PALESTINE, Jerusalem, EGYPT, Alexandria, LIBYA, Tobruk, Bengazi, Tripoli, TUNISIA (FR.), Tunis, Bizerte, ALGERIA (FR.), Algiers, Oran, MOROCCO (FR.), Casablanca, SP. MOROCCO, GIBRALTAR (BR.), SPAIN, Madrid, PORTUGAL, Lisbon, ITALY, Rome, Cassino, Naples, Salerno, Bologna, Milan, SICILY, SARDINIA (IT.), CORSICA (FR.), BLACK SEA, ADRIATIC SEA, CYPRUS (BR.), MALTA (BR.)

ARN

mada disgorged 160,000 troops, 600 tanks, and 1,800 guns on the beaches of Sicily on July 10, 1943. The British Eighth Army under General Montgomery and the American Seventh Army, under General George S. Patton, had routed the Italian and German defenders and overrun the island by August 17. It was an important turning point, for a group of Italian conspirators persuaded King Victor Emmanuel to connive at the deposition and arrest of Mussolini on July 25[4] and formed a new government under Marshal Badoglio. He proceeded to open negotiations looking toward the surrender of Italy.

This sudden turn of events raised new perplexities for Roosevelt and Churchill—whether to negotiate with the Badoglio government, as Eisenhower and other Allied leaders requested, or to demand unconditional surrender in accordance with the Casablanca declaration. The situation was so uncertain that the president, the prime minister, and their respective entourages met in Quebec on August 17, 1943, for a conference known by the code name of QUADRANT.

The new Italian government made secret contact with the Allies. The Italians were eager to surrender but insisted that the Allies protect Rome, the king, and the government from the Germans, who had meanwhile taken control of most of Italy. Roosevelt and Churchill agreed to send an airborne division to capture the airfields around Rome, and the armistice was signed on September 3. By the time that preparations for an airborne assault on Rome were completed, however, the Germans had surrounded the city in force and seized the airfields.

Meanwhile, the British Eighth Army crossed the Straits of Messina on September 3 and began the invasion of the Italian mainland, known as operation AVALANCHE. A week later a British airborne division seized the large Italian naval base at Taranto, while the United States Fifth Army, under the command of General Mark Clark, landed in the Gulf of Salerno south of Naples. The Fifth Army occupied Naples on October 7 in spite of furious German counterattacks and pushed northward to the Volturno River. Meanwhile, British forces had cleared the central and eastern sections of the Italian boot. Allied forces had pushed to a winter line south of Cassino by January 1, 1944.

A long and bloody campaign for Italy still impended, but the Italian surrender and successful invasion of Italy yielded large dividends to the Anglo-American Allies. It brought the surrender of the Italian fleet and guaranteed complete Allied control of the Mediterranean. It gave the Allies advanced air bases from which to bomb the Balkans and Central Europe. It consumed some of Hitler's best divisions. Most important, it gave the British and Americans the incalculable advantage of being on the offensive.

[4]A German parachute force rescued Mussolini on September 12, 1943. He then established a new Fascist government at Lake Como under German protection.

6. Slow Progress Toward Accord with Russia

The QUADRANT conferees at Quebec turned to other urgent problems after approving final arrangements for the Italian surrender. They reaffirmed May 1, 1944, as the date for OVERLORD. Hull and Eden discussed postwar plans for Germany and approved the draft of a Four Power Declaration— to be submitted to the coming conference of foreign ministers in Moscow—pledging America, Britain, Russia, and China to work for establishment of an effective postwar security organization. The conference was over on August 24, and Churchill accompanied Roosevelt back to Washington and stayed with him intermittently during the next three weeks. During this time the Badoglio government surrendered, and the Allies began their invasion of the Italian mainland.

Soon afterward, Secretary Hull made the arduous air journey to Moscow for the conference of foreign ministers that opened in the Russian capital on October 18. Before this time no one in Washington or London knew what Russian postwar ambitions were, except for the territorial demands that Stalin had outlined to Eden in December 1941. Hull, Molotov, and Eden discussed immediate and postwar problems in Moscow from October 18 to 30, 1943, with so little disagreement that future accord seemed assured. They agreed, for example, upon a plan for the postwar treatment of Germany that the State Department had prepared and the president had tentatively approved. Indeed, Molotov declared that it expressed Stalin's views and had his complete endorsement.[5] They agreed, moreover, that Austria should be reconstituted an independent nation and regarded as a liberated and not an enemy state, while Hull persuaded Stalin and Molotov to sign the Four Power Declaration. In addition, at a state dinner on October 30 Stalin told Hull the welcome news that Russia would join the war against Japan after the defeat of Germany.

There were differences over Poland,[6] but the Moscow Conference was

[5] As this plan eventually became the cornerstone of Allied postwar policy toward Germany, it would be well to examine it in some detail. It called for the unconditional surrender of Germany by whatever government exercised power at the end of the war. An Inter-Allied Control Commission would supervise the surrender and occupation of Germany by Soviet, American, and British troops. During the occupation the Control Commission would undertake to destroy all vestiges of nazism and take necessary steps to encourage establishment of a democratic government and restore freedom of religion, speech, the press, and political activity. Moreover, Germany should be denied a standing army and general staff and prohibited from manufacturing any war materials or aircraft of any kind. The Hull plan was vague on future German boundaries, except to say that East Prussia should be separated from the Reich. Finally, Germany should be required to pay reparations in goods, equipment, and manpower, but not in money.

[6] The Kremlin had severed diplomatic relations with the Polish government-in-exile in London, because the Poles had demanded that the International Red Cross investigate a German charge that the Russians had murdered 8,000 to 10,000 Polish officers in 1939 and buried their bodies near Smolensk. Moreover, the Russians were beginning to deal with a group of Polish Communists in the Soviet Union. In Moscow, Hull urged the Russians to restore relations with the Polish government in London, but Molotov made it clear the Kremlin would deal only with a Polish government it could control.

nonetheless a resounding success. To be sure, no one in the West knew absolutely whether Russia would cooperate in the postwar era, but such cooperation now seemed at least possible. As one milestone along the road to Allied unity, the conference prepared the way for the next—a personal meeting of the Big Three.

Roosevelt had long wanted to meet with the Russian leader, and he had invited Stalin before the Moscow Conference to join him and Churchill at Ankara, Bagdad, or Basra in Iraq. Stalin replied that he would go only to Teheran, since he could maintain personal control over his high command from the Iranian capital. The president agreed and left Hampton Roads on the new battleship *Iowa* on November 13, 1943, for the long journey to Cairo. There he conferred with Churchill, Chiang Kai-shek, Lord Louis Mountbatten, Allied commander in Southeast Asia, and General Joseph W. Stilwell, American commander in the China area and adviser to Chiang, from November 23 to 27 on the situation in Burma and China. Most of these discussions revolved around an Allied drive in Burma to open supply lines to China, and a Chinese offensive in northern China.[7]

The president and his party next flew from Cairo to Teheran on November 27. For security reasons Roosevelt moved into a villa in the Russian compound on the next day. The Big Three thrashed over practically all outstanding military and political problems during the next four days. These included military operations in Italy and American plans for offensive operations in the Pacific, during discussions of which Stalin again promised that Russia would join the war against Japan after Germany's surrender.

The Russians were most concerned about OVERLORD and seemed desperately anxious to pin Roosevelt and Churchill to a definite time and place for the great invasion. Stalin pressed Roosevelt to name a supreme commander for OVERLORD and implied that he would believe that the operation would come off only after the president had named the commander. Roosevelt had long wanted General Marshall, for whom he had warm affection and respect, to have the honor of leading the liberation of Europe; but he wisely refused to follow the impulse to give Stalin an immediate answer. As it turned out, Roosevelt and his advisers concluded that Marshall could not be spared from his vital post in Washington. The president decided on his return from Teheran to name Eisenhower as supreme commander of OVERLORD.

The Big Three also discussed the future of Germany and plans for postwar collaboration. They now seemed to favor partition. Stalin empha-

[7]The Allies opened this campaign in December 1943, when General Stilwell's Chinese divisions moved from Ledo against Japanese forces in northern Burma, and British forces moved down the southwestern coast of Burma in January 1944. Japanese counterattacks against Chittagong and Imphal, both in India, were eventually repulsed but delayed British liberation of Rangoon and southern Burma until the spring of 1945. To the north, however, Stilwell's American and Chinese forces were more successful and assured completion of the new supply line to China, the Ledo Road. It was opened in January 1945.

sized the danger of future German resurgence and added that he did not think that the State Department plan submitted at the Moscow Conference was severe enough. Roosevelt outlined his plan for a future United Nations organization, which would assume responsibility for preventing wars and aggression. During all these conversations the utmost frankness and usually a spirit of cordiality prevailed. In fact, the president was convinced that he had broken through the wall of suspicion and distrust surrounding Stalin, won Russian trust and friendship, and laid the basis for fruitful collaboration in the future. His feeling was well expressed in the concluding sentences of the Declaration of Teheran, issued on December 1: "We came here with hope and determination. We leave here, friends in fact, in spirit, and in purpose."

The president said good-by to Stalin after a final dinner on December 2 and then went to Cairo for conferences with Churchill and Turkish leaders about Turkey's entrance into the war. In addition, Roosevelt and Churchill and the Combined Chiefs of Staff held conferences of tremendous military importance from December 4 to 6. Thus the end of the year 1943 found the Allies on the offensive on all fronts, Allied unity existing in fact as well as name, and Anglo-American leaders completing plans for final assaults against Germany and Japan.

7. The Allied Air Offensives in Europe, 1940-1945

Superiority in the air passed to the British after the failure of the German air blitz against England in 1940-1941. The RAF Bomber Command conducted a limited number of night raids against selected industrial and transportation targets in Germany from 1940 to early 1942. Results were so unsatisfactory that the new chief of the Bomber Command, Sir Arthur Harris, executed a complete change in British bombing tactics—from the target system to mass bombing of industrial areas in order to disrupt the German economy and lessen the will of the German people to fight. The first 1,000-plane RAF raid, against Cologne on May 30, signaled the beginning of the new campaign. It was followed in 1942 by others against centers in the Ruhr, Bremen, Hamburg, and other German cities. This was only a small beginning, for less than 50,000 tons of bombs fell on Axis Europe in 1942, and German war production and civilian morale were not visibly impaired.

Meanwhile, the United States Eighth Air Force had established bases in England in early 1942 and joined in the air war on August 17, 1942. The offensive power of the Eighth Air Force grew and was reinforced by the Ninth Air Force and the Fifteenth Air Force, and the Americans became a powerful factor in the air campaign during the summer of 1943. While the British continued their devastating night attacks, the Americans used their heavier armored Flying Fortresses and Liberators in daring daylight raids—until extremely heavy losses in a raid on Schweinfurt on October 14, 1943, convinced American commanders that further large daylight operations must await production of long-range fighters to protect the bombers. All told, American and British bombers dropped 206,188 tons of bombs on European targets in 1943.

A new phase in the air campaign began in February 1944. The arrival in England of substantial numbers of long-range American fighters made resumption of daylight raids possible. The introduction of radar bombsights had already greatly increased the accuracy of night bombing. And there was a use of increasingly heavy bombs and a rapid build-up of the Eighth and Fifteenth Air Forces. The Americans first began a systematic campaign to destroy the German aircraft industry. Then the attack shifted in March to French and Belgian marshaling yards, railroads, and bridges. And after the invasion of France, the American and British air forces began a coordinated and relentless round-the-clock assault upon German synthetic oil and chemical plants. Some 8,000 to 9,000 Allied planes turned to the task of paralyzing the German transportation system in February 1945. Finally, the air forces joined the advancing Allied armies in April in reducing the German nation to utter impotence and ruin.

The overall dimensions of the Anglo-American air effort in Europe stagger the imagination: 1,442,280 bomber and 2,686,799 fighter sorties, which dropped 2,697,473 tons of bombs on Germany and Nazi-occupied Europe, cost the Allies some 40,000 planes and 158,000 personnel. All told, Allied bombs dropped on Germany killed 305,000 persons and wounded 780,000 others, destroyed or damaged 5.5 million homes, and deprived 20 million persons of essential utilities. By the beginning of 1944, according to a poll taken by the Strategic Bombing Survey immediately after the war, some 77 percent of the German people were convinced that the war was lost; and by May 1945 most Germans had lost all will to continue the uneven struggle.

8. Victory in Europe: To the Westwall

General Dwight D. Eisenhower, supreme commander of the Allied Expeditionary Forces, arrived in London on January 15, 1944, with orders from Roosevelt and Churchill to "enter the continent of Europe and, in conjunction with the other Allied Nations, undertake operations aimed at the heart of Germany and the destruction of her armed forces." The Combined Chiefs of Staff and various technical staffs in Britain and America had been hard at work on OVERLORD since 1942. Planning for the actual invasion and subsequent operations proceeded apace in Eisenhower's London headquarters after mid-January 1944.

The appointed time, June 5, 1944,[8] for which the world had long waited now approached rapidly. The great invasion armada was delayed by a sudden storm and put out to sea early in the morning of June 6. The Germans expected the invasion to come in the Pas de Calais area, where the English Channel is narrowest. Instead, the Allies struck at five beaches along a sixty-mile stretch of the Cotentin Peninsula in Normandy. First there were furious air and naval bombardments of the invasion area and beaches. Next came the landing of three airborne divisions behind the German lines a few minutes after midnight on June 6. Finally, the seaborne troops hit the beaches at 7:30 in the morning. German resistance was generally light; but American invaders met a fierce defense on Omaha Beach and suffered heavy casualties.

The German commanders, field marshals Rommel and Karl von Rundstedt, mistook the Normandy invasion as a screen for a larger invasion in the Pas de Calais. They were not able to bring up their reserve divisions in time to prevent the Allies from securing and capturing a bridgehead in Normandy. Within two weeks after D day the Allies had landed more than 1 million troops with enormous quantities of supplies in a broad sector along the Normandy coast. They had also captured Cherbourg, Caen, and St. Lô, "eaten the guts out of the German defense," and were poised for a grand sweep through northern France.

The battle of the breakthrough began on July 25, with a lightninglike thrust by General Patton's Third Army into Brittany and a breakthrough to Avranches and Falaise by the American First Army and the British Second Army. Soon the battle for Normandy turned into the battle for France. The German Seventh Army in the area between Falaise and Argentan was under orders to stand firm. It was surrounded and partially destroyed or captured during a furious battle from August 19–23. The Allies completed the liberation of France in blitzkrieg fashion while the surviving German armies moved back to their Siegfried line. The American Seventh Army invaded southern France on August 15 and joined the race for the German frontier. Paris fell to French and American troops ten days later. By mid-September American and British armies had captured Brussels and Antwerp, occupied Luxembourg, and crossed the German border at Aachen.

The Allies were on the move on other fronts as well. They had tried vainly to break the German lines in southern Italy. Then they tried to turn the German flank on January 22, 1944, by landings at Anzio and Nettuno on the Italian western coast, only thirty-six miles from Rome. This effort failed. But the British Eighth Army and the American Fifth Army pushed

[8]The date for the launching of OVERLORD was postponed from May 1 to the more unfavorable first week in June 1944 because of a shortage of landing craft.

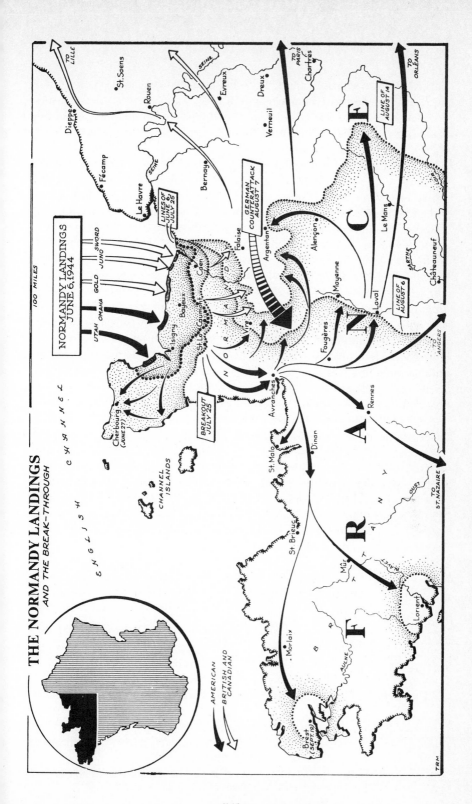

THE NORMANDY LANDINGS
AND THE BREAK-THROUGH

NORMANDY LANDINGS
JUNE 6, 1944

100 MILES

LINES OF
JUNE 6 &
JULY 25

BREAKOUT
JULY 25

GERMAN
COUNTER-ATTACK
AUGUST 7

LINE OF
AUGUST 14

LINE OF
AUGUST 6

AMERICAN

BRITISH AND
CANADIAN

ENGLISH   CHANNEL

CHANNEL
ISLANDS

UTAH OMAHA GOLD JUNO SWORD

N O R M A N D Y

F R A N C E

B R I T T A N Y

TO LILLE
St. Saens
Dieppe
Rouen
Fécamp
Le Havre
SEINE
SEINE
Bernay
Evreux
Dreux
Verneuil
Chartres
TO PARIS
TO ORLÉANS
Falaise
Caen
Bayeux
Isigny
St. Lô
Carentan
Cherbourg
(JUNE 27)
Vire
Argentan
Alençon
Le Mans
Mayenne
Fougères
Laval
Châteauneuf
SARTHE
LOIRE
TO
ANGERS
Avranches
St. Malo
Dinan
Rennes
St. Brieuc
Mur.
Morlaix
Brest
(SEPT. 19)
Lorient
OUST
TO
ST. NAZAIRE
AULNE
BLAVET

541

northward in the spring, joined the beleaguered divisions on the Anzio beachhead, and captured Rome on June 4, 1944. Under heavy Allied pressure and harassment, the Germans pulled back to their Gothic line, which ran across Italy some 150 miles north of Rome. There they managed to stabilize the fighting around September 1, 1944.

Meanwhile, the Russians, during the spring of 1944, began offensives along the entire eastern front fully as important in the Allied strategy as the Anglo-American sweep across France. One Russian drive on the northern sector forced Finland to sue for peace on August 25. The greatest Russian offensive, however, opened on June 23 to coincide with the Anglo-American drive in the West. Soviet armies captured the German stronghold of Vitebsk and then broke through to the Baltic on August 1. Five Russian armies in the central sector rolled into Poland, reached the Vistula River in late July, captured Warsaw on January 17, 1945, and reached the Oder River, only forty-five miles from Berlin, the following month. Farther to the south, two Red armies over-ran Rumania in August 1944. Then they marched into Bulgaria, captured Belgrade on October 20, and entered Budapest in February 1945.

It was obvious to almost everyone by the autumn of 1944 that the German military situation was hopeless. Germany was now a beleaguered fortress awaiting final destruction because her fanatical master preferred complete destruction to unconditional surrender. Some high German officers, foresee-ing inevitable ruin under Hitler's leadership, in cooperation with certain anti-Nazi groups perfected plans to take control of the German government and assassinate Hitler. Their agent left a time bomb in Hitler's headquarters on July 20, 1944. Thinking Hitler dead, the conspirators proceeded to take first steps to seize control of the army and government. Unfortunately, Hitler was only injured by the bomb's blast. With the support of loyal troops he rounded up the opposition, executed about 5,000 persons after drumhead trials, and sent another 10,000 enemies to concentration camps. In consequence, the war would proceed to its bitter end.

9. The Campaign and Election of 1944

Meanwhile, partisan politics had persisted in the United States. The Republi-cans made a hard fight to win control of Congress in 1942. They failed, but they made such sweeping gains in the elections on November 3 that a GOP victory in 1944 seemed at least possible.[9] Actually, what occurred in the fed-eral and state elections in November 1942 was not merely a Republican revival but also a strong conservative upsurge. The significance of the upheaval became apparent after the organization of the Seventy-eighth Con-gress in January 1943, when many southern Democrats joined Republicans to

---

[9] The Democrats elected 222 and the Republicans 209 members to the House—a Republican gain of 47 seats. The Republicans, moreover, gained 9 seats in the Senate.

form a majority coalition and seize control of legislative policy. This coalition gave the president aggressive support in all matters relating to the war and postwar policies. In domestic matters, however, they proceeded as fast as they could to destroy certain parts of the New Deal.

Politicians in both camps began preparations for the coming national conventions and presidential campaign while the conservative coalition and the president engaged in frequent verbal duels during the winter and spring of 1944. Wendell L. Willkie was still titular head of his party, but he had no support among party leaders and had become so closely identified with the Roosevelt administration as to lose his status as leader of the opposition. He withdrew from the preconvention campaign after suffering an impressive defeat in the Wisconsin presidential primary in April. Meanwhile, Willkie's chief rival, Governor Thomas E. Dewey of New York, was fast emerging as the new Republican leader. The presidential nomination went to him on the first ballot when the Republican national convention met in Chicago on June 26, with the vice-presidential nomination going to Governor John W. Bricker of Ohio. The convention adopted a platform that was aggressively internationalistic and essentially progressive in tone.[10]

There never was much doubt that the Democrats would nominate Roosevelt for a fourth term, and he was willing even though he had recently suffered cardiac failure, hypertension, and hypertensive heart disease. On July 11 the president announced that he would accept renomination, and his announcement settled the matter when the Democratic National Convention opened in Chicago on July 19.

In view of Roosevelt's precarious health and poor chances of serving out a fourth term, the crucial struggle revolved around the nomination of a vice-presidential candidate. This battle was bitter and created divisions in the party that persisted for years afterward. Vice-President Henry A. Wallace enjoyed the support of the advanced progressive wing and large elements in the CIO. But he was almost unanimously opposed by party bosses, southerners, and many moderates who suspected that he was temperamentally unfit for the presidency and hopelessly inept in political leadership. Roosevelt endorsed Wallace publicly but refused to insist upon his nomination. In fact, the president had apparently promised the succession to Byrnes and actually tried to obtain the nomination for the South Carolinian.

The president's plans, however, were upset on the eve of the convention by a newcomer in high Democratic councils, Sidney Hillman, a vice-president of the CIO and former co-director of the defense effort. Alarmed by the rising tide of antilabor sentiment and the failure of workers to go to the polls in 1942, Hillman organized the Political Action

---

[10]The Republican platform roundly condemned the Roosevelt administration's alleged inefficiency, waste, excessive centralization, and destruction of private enterprise. However, it made it clear that Republicans had no fundamental quarrel with Democrats on domestic issues by promising to strengthen the New Deal's labor, social security, and agricultural programs. All in all, it was the most significant endorsement of the Roosevelt policies yet written.

Committee (PAC) of the CIO in 1943. His purpose was not only to rally workers and progressives but also to win new bargaining power for labor within the Democratic party.

Hillman used his power in a spectacular way at the Democratic national convention. He virtually vetoed Byrnes's nomination by warning the president that the South Carolinian was unacceptable to labor and northern blacks. The president concluded that his assistant must give way to a compromise candidate. He therefore declared that either Senator Harry S. Truman or Justice William O. Douglas would be an agreeable running mate; and he agreed with Hillman that the PAC should shift its support from Wallace to Truman when it became obvious that Wallace could not be nominated. In any event, Roosevelt declared in his final instructions to National Chairman Robert E. Hannegan, the party managers must "clear it with Sidney," that is, must win Hillman's approval for any vice-presidential candidate.

The issue was actually settled during the three days before the Democratic convention opened in Chicago on July 19, 1944. Hillman declared that he would fight Byrnes's nomination to the bitter end, and the president on July 17 asked the South Carolinian to withdraw. Byrnes's withdrawal narrowed the field to Wallace, who still enjoyed the PAC's seeming support, and Truman, upon whom administration and party leaders had finally agreed. During the balloting for the vice-presidential nomination on July 19 and 20, Wallace led on the first ballot and Truman won on the third, as the leaders had planned. The convention had nominated the president on the first ballot a short time before. The Democratic platform promised continuation of progressive policies at home and vigorous American leadership abroad in the postwar era.

Dewey campaigned hard under tremendous handicaps during the ensuing summer and autumn. He was beaten before he started by smashing Allied victories in Europe and the Pacific, a general reluctance to change governments in the midst of the world crisis, and above all by his own general agreement with basic administration policies. This latter handicap forced him to make criticisms that could only sound captious. Dewey's chief advantage was Roosevelt's failing health and growing suspicion that perhaps the president was incapable of managing affairs of state. This suspicion increased after his address at Bremerton, Washington, during which he was halting and ineffective because he was suffering at this very time from an attack of angina pectoris. However, Roosevelt, his health substantially recovered, came back in a speech before the Teamsters' Union in Washington on September 23 that convinced millions of voters that he was still the champion campaigner. He followed this masterpiece with strenuous tours and speeches in Chicago, New York City, Wilmington, Delaware, and New England.

This aggressive campaign gave Roosevelt the initiative that he had seemingly lost. He also recovered lost ground by committing himself

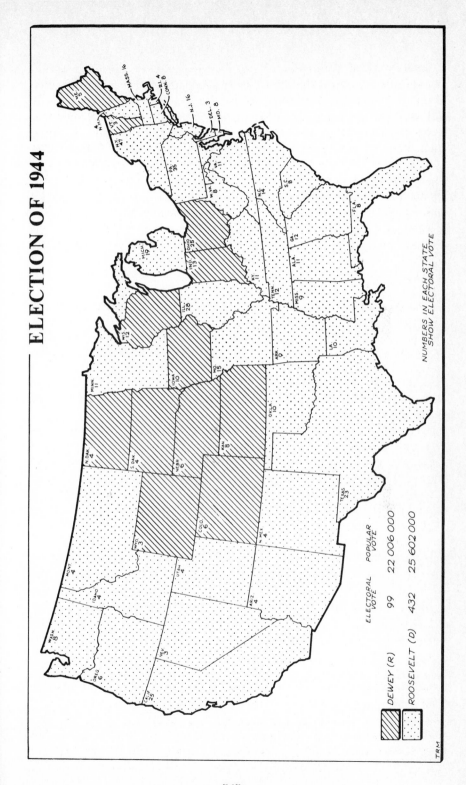

ELECTION OF 1944

NUMBERS IN EACH STATE
SHOW ELECTORAL VOTE

	ELECTORAL VOTE	POPULAR VOTE
DEWEY (R)	99	22 006 000
ROOSEVELT (D)	432	25 602 000

TRM

squarely to a full resumption of progressive policies in the postwar era. Almost as decisive was the PAC's success in getting workers to the polls. In the election on November 7, Roosevelt received 25,602,505 popular and 432 electoral votes; Dewey, 22,006,278 popular and 99 electoral votes. The Democrats lost one seat in the Senate, but they gained twenty seats in the House, all but four of them in the large cities, and captured governorships in Ohio, Massachusetts, Missouri, Idaho, and Washington. The most important outcome of the election was not the continuation of Democratic control but rather the fact that Americans of both parties were now irrevocably committed to assume the leadership in world affairs that they had so often rejected before 1941. For better or for worse, there could be no turning back on the high road to international responsibility.

10. Yalta: The High Tide of Allied Unity

The rapid progress of Allied and Russian armies raised the possibility that war in Europe might end before the three great powers had come to definitive agreement on plans for future collaboration. Indeed, there was little evidence that the American leaders yet knew even their own minds on the most important aspect of postwar planning, a policy for the control of Germany.[11] More disturbing, however, were signs of growing Allied dissension that threatened to split the Grand Alliance and prevent organization of a postwar United Nations. British, American, and Russian delegates met at Dumbarton Oaks in Washington in September 1944. They agreed on a basic structure for a United Nations but could not agree upon certain fundamental aspects of voting procedure. Following this the State Department and the British Foreign Office engaged in heated controversies over organization of a new Italian government and the methods and objectives of British intervention in Greece. The most dangerous potential source of trouble was Russian policy in eastern Europe, especially in Poland.

Roosevelt's thoughts inevitably turned toward another meeting of the Big Three to discuss matters that could be settled only on the high level. Churchill and Stalin were agreeable, although Stalin insisted that he could

[11]American confusion on this aspect of postwar policy was revealed during a heated controversy in the administration in the late summer of 1944 around the so-called Morgenthau Plan. Prepared by Harry Dexter White in the Treasury Department and presented by Secretary of the Treasury Henry Morgenthau, Jr., it proposed to give parts of Germany to Poland, Russia, Denmark, and France and to divide the remaining rump, strip it of all industrial capacity, and convert it into a large "goat pasture." Roosevelt approved it over the violent opposition of Hull and Secretary of War Stimson. Moreover, at a conference with Churchill in Quebec in September 1944, the president was so insistent that Churchill reluctantly agreed to consider the Morgenthau Plan as a basis for postwar German policy. Yet the president had dropped the plan altogether within six weeks.

not leave Russia because he was personally directing the Russian armies. The three leaders soon agreed upon Yalta in the Crimea as the place and early February 1945 as the time of the conference.

The Yalta meeting would obviously be the last Big Three conference before the surrender of Germany, and the president and the new secretary of state, Edward R. Stettinius, Jr.,[12] went to unusual effort, first, to formulate an American program and, second, to come to firm agreement with the British before the Big Three met. Stettinius took his staff to Marrakech in French Morocco for a briefing session from January 26 to 29, 1945. Then they went to Malta for conferences with Churchill and Eden on January 31 and February 1. Roosevelt arrived with his party aboard the cruiser *Quincy* on February 2, and it was soon evident that recent Anglo-American difficulties had not done fatal damage to his relationship with Churchill.

The Anglo-American-Russian conferees assembled at Yalta on February 3 and 4, 1945, for the opening of the conference called ARGONAUT on the latter day. The Big Three discussed almost every conceivable problem related to the future of Europe, Asia, and the United Nations from February 4 through 11. In addition, the foreign ministers and military and naval leaders of the three powers worked behind the scenes to smooth out minor differences and lay the groundwork for major understandings. Without following the conferees in their long deliberations, let us now summarize their major agreements and decisions.

GERMANY.   The discussions relating to Germany revolved around the questions of dismemberment, reparations, future Allied control, and French participation in the Inter-Allied Control Commission. The conferees approved dismemberment in principle and agreed to consider details in future negotiations. However, they agreed that northern East Prussia, including Königsberg, should go to Russia; that Poland should annex the southern half of East Prussia; that Russia should annex certain former eastern Polish provinces; and that Poland should receive territory in eastern Germany as compensation.[13] As for reparations, the Russians proposed exacting a total bill of $20 billion, half of which should be paid to the USSR. Roosevelt and Churchill would not approve any fixed sum. But they agreed to accept the Russian proposal as the basis for future negotiations and to establish a reparations commission with headquarters in Moscow. The Russians withdrew their objection to French participation in the

[12]Cordell Hull had resigned because of ill health on November 21, 1944, after thirteen and a half years as secretary of state.

[13]Roosevelt and Churchill refused to agree to a definite cession of this territory to Poland. However, the American and British leaders agreed at the Potsdam Conference in July 1945 that the Poles should occupy the region between the Oder-Neisse rivers and the old eastern German boundary, pending settlement of the boundary by a future peace conference. The Poles at once proceeded to incorporate the territory, expel the German population, and settle the region with Poles.

occupation of Germany, and Stalin agreed also that France should have a seat on the Control Commission. As the several occupation zones had already been drawn by the European Advisory Commission in London, there was no discussion of this matter at Yalta.

THE GOVERNMENTS OF POLAND AND EASTERN EUROPE.   The crucial question was Poland's political future. Stalin and Molotov said quite frankly that they would not tolerate a Polish regime unfriendly to the USSR. As they pointed out, the Germans had twice within twenty-five years used Poland as the corridor for attacks against Russia. They insisted that Britain and the United States recognize a provisional Polish government in Lublin that Russia had sponsored and recognized. Roosevelt and Churchill adamantly refused. Then Stalin suggested that the Lublin government be enlarged to include some of the leaders of the Polish government-in-exile that the western powers supported and which was now in London. Roosevelt and Churchill again refused. Stalin finally agreed that the Lublin government should be reorganized to include Polish democratic leaders at home and abroad, and that free elections should be held at an early date to determine the future government of the country. Roosevelt made it clear that the British and American ambassadors in Warsaw would judge whether this pledge had been honestly kept.

The three powers pledged themselves to assist the peoples of other so-called liberated countries of eastern Europe to establish, through free elections, democratic governments responsive to popular will.[14]

THE ORGANIZATION OF THE UNITED NATIONS.   The Russians conceded practically everything for which Americans had contended at the Dumbarton Oaks Conference in discussions at Yalta over organization of the United Nations. First, they accepted the American formula for voting in the Security Council.[15] Second, the Soviets withdrew their demand for sixteen votes in the General Assembly and received in return additional representatives and votes for the Ukraine and White Russia.[16] Third, Stalin

---

[14]It should be added that Churchill and Eden had had conferences with Stalin in Moscow over the future of the Balkans in October 1944. They agreed that during the coming months Russia should have predominance in Rumania and Bulgaria, that Britain should have predominance in Greece, and that the two countries would share responsibility in Yugoslavia and Hungary. Churchill tried to make it clear, however, that the arrangement provided merely a temporary modus vivendi to prevent a conflict of British and Russian forces during the period of German withdrawal and should not be construed to authorize interference in the domestic affairs of the Balkan states. In any event, the Yalta agreements superseded the Churchill-Stalin agreement.

[15]The main issue here was whether the permanent members of the Security Council, that is, the great powers, should have the right to veto consideration of disputes to which they were a party. The Americans fought against use of the veto in such circumstances and overcame Russian objections at Yalta. The right of the great powers to use the veto in all important matters was not involved, for Americans and Russians alike insisted upon having veto over any proposed action by the Security Council.

[16]In return, Stalin and Churchill agreed that the United States might have three votes in the General Assembly if it so desired.

agreed to Roosevelt's proposal that all nations at war with Germany by March 1, 1945, might become members of the United Nations.

THE FAR EAST.   By secret agreement between the Americans and Russians, which Churchill approved but did not help make, and which was not published until February 11, 1946, Stalin agreed to bring Russia into the war against Japan within two or three months after the surrender of Germany. In return, the president approved the transfer of the Kurile Islands from Japan to Russia, recognized Russian control of Outer Mongolia, and agreed that Russia should recover all rights and territory lost at the end of the Russo-Japanese War.[17] Finally, Stalin agreed to recognize Chinese sovereignty over Manchuria and to conclude a treaty of friendship and alliance with the Nationalist government of China.

Millions of words have since been spoken and written about the Yalta agreements. Critics have called them base appeasement of Russia, betrayal of Poland and eastern Europe to Soviet imperialism, and useless surrender to communism in the Far East—all by a mentally incompetent president who was hoodwinked by the wily Stalin. Defenders have replied that the agreements were necessary and realistic.

The charge that Roosevelt was mentally incompetent is most easily disposed of. Roosevelt was obviously tired at Yalta and exhausted afterward by the strain of the grueling sessions and of his long journeys. But there is no evidence that he was not in full possession of his mental faculties during the conference itself.[18] The consensus of historical judgment rather emphatically supports the conclusion that Roosevelt and Churchill achieved nearly everything that circumstances permitted. They undoubtedly knew the risks they were running in the agreements on Poland and eastern Europe. They knew also that they had no alternative but to accept a compromise and hope that the Russians would honor it. The Russians were already in eastern Europe. The United States and Britain might conceivably have driven them out, but neither the Anglo-American peoples nor soldiers would have tolerated even the suggestion of a long and bloody war to save Poland or Rumania from Communist domination. These were the two prime historical realities with which Roosevelt and Churchill had to reckon, and from which Stalin could benefit, at Yalta. The Anglo-American leaders obtained important concessions from Stalin in spite of their weak bargaining positions. Future conflicts with the Soviet

[17]This commitment involved (a) transfer of the southern half of Sakhalin from Japan to Russia; (b) internationalization of the port of Dairen and safeguarding of "the pre-eminent interests of the Soviet Union in this port"; (c) restoration of the Russian lease on Port Arthur as a naval base; and (d) joint Soviet-Chinese operation of the Chinese Eastern Railway and the South Manchurian Railway.

[18]It might be well in passing to mention the charge that Alger Hiss, who was a member of the State Department staff at Yalta, and who had been an agent for the Soviet spy ring in the 1930s, was the principal author of the Yalta agreements. It has never been demonstrated that Hiss had any influence in determining any important decisions at the conference.

Union developed not because the Russians honored the Yalta agreements, but precisely because they violated them.

We now know that Roosevelt concluded the secret Far Eastern agreement with Stalin because he and his military advisers believed that the Japanese would not surrender unconditionally without invasion and occupation. Moreover, no one yet knew whether the atomic bomb would explode or what damage it would do. Acting on the advice of his military advisers, Roosevelt made the agreement with Stalin, he thought, in order to prevent the death of perhaps 1 million American men in bloody campaigns in Japan and on the Asiatic mainland. To avert this catastrophe, the president virtually let Stalin name his own price for Soviet participation. Actually, Soviet Far Eastern policy was neither determined nor defined at Yalta. It is a fair assumption that the Russians would have entered the war against Japan and reestablished themselves as a major Far Eastern power whether the Americans liked it or not.[19]

Critics of the Yalta agreements tend to forget that the Russians, also, made substantial concessions. They agreed to participate in a United Nations that would certainly be controlled by the Anglo-American bloc; to give France a share in the control of Germany; and to respect the integrity of the peoples of eastern Europe. They seemed determined to act reasonably and to meet Churchill and Roosevelt halfway on all important issues. Roosevelt and Churchill, therefore, acted in the only manner that was historically possible. As Churchill put it, "Our hopeful assumptions were soon to be falsified. Still, they were the only ones possible at the time."

11. Victory in Europe

The British and American armies approached the Siegfried line in September 1944. Eisenhower made an effort to turn the northern flank of the German defenses by landing three airborne divisions to capture bridges across the Meuse, Waal, and Rhine rivers. This effort failed when the British First Airborne Division was unable to hold a bridge across the Rhine at Arnhem, and the Allies were denied the opportunity to make a rapid drive across the north German plain. Instead, they brought up reinforcements for a winter campaign through the heavy German defenses manned by armies now regrouped and strengthened.

While American and British armies were probing along the length of the Siegfried line, Hitler laid plans for one final gamble—a counteroffensive

---

[19]It might be added, also, that Chiang Kai-shek, who was not informed until much later of the details of the Far Eastern agreement, was delighted by the Russian promise of a treaty of alliance because he thought that it meant Soviet neutrality in the Nationalist government's war with the Chinese Communists.

through the weak center of the Allied lines in the Ardennes Forest. This he hoped would split the enemy's forces and carry to Liège and perhaps Antwerp. Bad weather in late November and early December enabled Von Rundstedt, the German commander, to bring up his forces in secret. They struck furiously in the Ardennes on December 16 and scored heavily until Allied counterattacks forced them to withdraw. The Battle of the Bulge, as the German offensive is commonly known, was over by January 1945. Hitler's gamble had cost him his last reserves of aircraft and some of his best divisions.

In fact, the German army in the west was so weakened by ruinous losses in the Ardennes counteroffensive that it could no longer prevent the Allied armies from advancing to the Rhine. Forces under Field Marshal Montgomery captured Cleves, in the north, on February 12. Cologne fell to the American First Army on March 6. Troops of the French First and the American Third and Seventh armies had cleared the Saar and Palatinate areas in the south by March 25. Meanwhile, American troops by an unbelievable stroke of good luck captured the Ludendorff Bridge across the Rhine at Remagen on March 7 before it could be demolished. They quickly established a bridgehead on the other side of the river.

Anglo-American armies were now poised along the Rhine for a final drive into the heart of Germany, and Russian armies were massed on the Oder River for an assault upon Berlin. But new tensions between the western democracies and Russia gave warning of troubled times ahead. For one thing, the Russians in February 1945 had imposed a Communist government on Rumania. Secondly, Anglo-American negotiations with a German general for surrender of German forces in Italy had caused Stalin to address a letter to Roosevelt virtually accusing him and Churchill of treacherously negotiating for surrender of all German forces in the west so that British and American armies could occupy Berlin before the Russians did.

Even more ominous were Russian actions in Poland. The Russians had not only refused to honor the Yalta agreement to reorganize the puppet Lublin government, but they had also refused to allow American and British observers to enter Poland and had proceeded to liquidate the leaders of the democratic parties in that unhappy country. It was plain that Stalin would tolerate no Polish government that he could not completely control; indeed, he admitted as much in correspondence with Churchill. The Polish dispute was nearing the point of open rupture by mid-March, but Roosevelt was now so weak that he had lost his grasp and could not take leadership in opposing Soviet violations of the Yalta agreements. Actually, Poland was irretrievably lost to Soviet domination, as Stalin's blunt replies to Churchill's vigorous protests revealed.

Poland was lost, but not yet Prague and Berlin, if the Allies resolved to act quickly and send their armies hurtling across Germany. Churchill perceived clearly enough that "Soviet Russia had become a mortal danger to

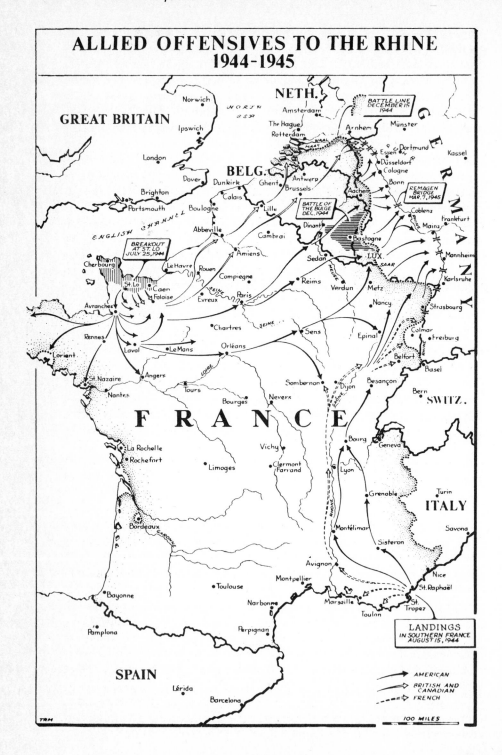

ALLIED OFFENSIVES TO THE RHINE
1944-1945

GREAT BRITAIN

NETH.

BELG.

LUX.

G E R M A N Y

FRANCE

SWITZ.

ITALY

SPAIN

NORTH SEA

ENGLISH CHANNEL

BATTLE LINE
DECEMBER 15
1944

REMAGEN
BRIDGE
MAR. 7, 1945

BREAKOUT
AT ST. LO
JULY 25, 1944

BATTLE OF
THE BULGE
DEC. 1944

LANDINGS
IN SOUTHERN FRANCE
AUGUST 15, 1944

Norwich
Ipswich
London
Dover
Brighton
Portsmouth
Boulogne
Calais
Dunkirk
Amsterdam
The Hague
Rotterdam
Arnhem
Münster
Dortmund
Essen
Düsseldorf
Cologne
Kassel
Aachen
Bonn
Antwerp
Brussels
Ghent
Lille
Coblenz
Frankfurt
Mainz
Abbeville
Cambrai
Dinant
Bastogne
Mannheim
Cherbourg
Le Havre
Rouen
Amiens
Sedan
Saar
Karlsruhe
St. Lo
Caen
Falaise
Compiegne
Paris
Reims
Verdun
Metz
Strasbourg
Avranches
Evreux
Seine
Nancy
Rennes
Chartres
Sens
Epinal
Colmar
Freiburg
Laval
Le Mans
Orléans
Sombernon
Dijon
Besançon
Belfort
Basel
Loriant
Angers
Tours
Bourges
Nevers
Geneva
Bern
St. Nazaire
Loire
Bourg
Nantes
Vichy
Clermont
Ferrand
Lyon
Grenoble
Turin
La Rochelle
Rochefort
Limoges
Rhone
Montélimar
Sisteron
Savona
Bordeaux
Garonne
Avignon
Montpellier
Nice
St. Raphaël
Bayonne
Toulouse
Narbonne
Marseille
St. Tropez
Toulon
Pamplona
Perpignan
Lérida
Barcelona
WAAL
MAAS
MEUSE
SAONE

AMERICAN
BRITISH AND
CANADIAN
FRENCH

100 MILES

the free world." He pleaded all through April and early May with his American colleagues to push as rapidly as possible toward the two central European capitals. Even more important, he proposed that the Allies stay in force on this forward eastern line until the Russians had honored earlier promises.[20]

The reasons for failure to attempt to seize strong outposts in Central Europe can best be seen in an account of military and political events. The combined Anglo-American armies began their crossing of the Rhine on March 24. Montgomery's forces in the north and Bradley's in the center had converged by April 1 to encircle the Ruhr and trap more than 250,000 German troops. General Montgomery was all for driving straight to Berlin. But Eisenhower, for what seemed to be sound military reasons, decided to "push his main force from the Kassel-Frankfurt area to the Elbe, split the German forces, cut off Berlin from the so-called 'National Redoubt' area [the Bavarian mountains, where Hitler was reputed to be preparing for a last stand], and then turn his forces directly to the north and to the south-west of the Elbe. These maneuvers would enable him to seize ports on the North Sea and the Baltic and also clean up the area to the south before the enemy could assemble a force there."[21]

Eisenhower relayed this decision to Stalin directly on March 28. Stalin approved, but Churchill was so distressed that he appealed personally to Roosevelt to join him in ordering the supreme commander to move against Berlin. "I deem it highly important," the prime minister wrote to Eisenhower on April 2, "that we should shake hands with the Russians as far to the east as possible." Eisenhower, however, argued that his plan was sound on military grounds; and he had the firm support of other American field generals. "I could see no political advantage accruing from the capture of Berlin that would offset the need for quick destruction of the German army on our front," Bradley wrote. "As soldiers we looked naïvely on the British inclination to complicate the war with political foresight and nonmilitary objectives."[22]

The vanguard of the American army reached the Elbe, only fifty-three miles from Berlin. The Russians were still on the banks of the Oder, thirty to forty miles from the German capital. Churchill now redoubled his pleading, but his voice was no longer heard in Washington. Roosevelt was tired and unable to stand any longer at the helm. He wanted rest and recovery, not a new quarrel with the Russians. He went to Warm Springs

[20]The Big Three at Yalta had approved the occupation zones drawn earlier by the European Advisory Commission, but Roosevelt and Churchill had made no agreement anywhere to stop their armies at any certain point. Churchill argued that Russian violations had already invalidated the Yalta agreements. He proposed to occupy as much of the Soviet zone of Germany and of Czechoslovakia as possible, and to stay there until the Russians lived up to the agreement on Poland and consented to a real integration of the occupation administration in Germany.

[21]Forrest C. Pogue, "The Decision to Halt at the Elbe," in K. R. Greenfield (ed.), *Command Decisions* (New York, 1959), p. 378.

[22]Omar N. Bradley, *A Soldier's Story* (New York, 1951), pp. 535–536.

early in April to renew his strength before opening the San Francisco Conference of the United Nations on April 25. On April 12 he complained of a terrific headache, lost consciousness, and died at 4:35 P.M. of a massive cerebral hemorrhage.

Roosevelt's growing weakness and death came at a fateful time in the history of the world. The new president, Harry S. Truman, had been utterly unprepared by his predecessor. Eisenhower had submitted a plan for further action to the Combined Chiefs of Staff on April 7. He proposed pushing through to the Elbe near Leipzig and then turning northward to the Baltic coast in order to prevent the Russians from occupying any part of the Danish peninsula. He added that he saw no point in making Berlin a military objective, but that he would cheerfully accept the decision of the Combined Chiefs of Staff on this matter. The military leaders did not discuss the question of Berlin. President Truman supported Eisenhower's proposal. Even Churchill agreed on April 19 that the Anglo-American forces were "not immediately in a position to force their way into Berlin." Eisenhower informed Stalin of his plan on April 21, adding that he intended to send forces not only northward but also southward into the Danube Valley. He sent General Patton into Bavaria on the following day.

Even at this date Eisenhower could have captured Prague with ease, and Churchill pleaded for action that "might make the whole difference to the postwar situation in Czechoslovakia." Eisenhower in response decided to send Patton into Prague and so informed the Soviet high command. But he called Patton back after receiving a vehement protest from Stalin. Thus while the Americans waited the Russians occupied Prague on May 9.

Meanwhile, Hitler remained in Berlin, confident that a miracle would yet save the Third Reich. He was heartened by Roosevelt's death and certain that the western Allies and Russia would soon turn against each other. But *Götterdämmerung* was near. Marshal Georgi K. Zhukov began a massive offensive across the Oder on April 15 that reached the suburbs of Berlin a week later. American and Russian troops met on the Elbe near Torgau on April 27. Italian partisans captured and shot Mussolini on the following day. Hitler married his mistress, Eva Braun, in his bunker in Berlin and appointed Admiral Karl Doenitz his successor on April 29. He committed suicide on the next day, and his body was burned in the garden of the Reichschancellery.

Nothing remained but to end the war as quickly as possible. Nearly 1 million German troops in northern Italy and Austria surrendered on May 2. Two days later German troops in northwest Germany, Holland, Schleswig-Holstein, and Denmark laid down their arms. Then Colonel General Alfred Jodl surrendered unconditionally the remnants of the German army, air force, and navy at Eisenhower's headquarters at Rheims at 2:41 A.M. on May 7. All hostilities ceased at midnight May 8, 1945.

12. Victory in the Pacific

American ground, naval, and air power in the Pacific was overwhelmingly preponderant by the early summer of 1944. The American navy was now five times stronger than the imperial fleet. The time had come to close in on the stronghold of the enemy's inner ring. Admiral Raymond A. Spruance with a huge force of ships, aircraft, and troops moved against the strongly held Marianas, about 1,350 miles south of Tokyo. After a bitter struggle, in which the Japanese fought fanatically, the three principal islands in the group, Saipan, Tinian, and Guam, fell before the overpowering assault. While Americans were invading Saipan a large Japanese force of 9 aircraft carriers, 5 battleships, and other ships sailed from the Philippines to intercept the invaders. Over 500 Japanese airplanes attacked and slightly damaged a battleship and 2 carriers on June 19, 1944. But the Japanese lost 402 airplanes and pilots, the core of their naval aviation. Pursuing American submarines and aircraft caught up with the Japanese fleet on June 20. On that date they sank 3 Japanese carriers and 2 destroyers and severely damaged 1 battleship, 4 carriers, and other craft in the first Battle of the Philippine Sea. American naval and ground forces then attacked the western Caroline Islands in September, overpowering fierce resistance on Peleliu, Angaur, and Ngesebus islands, and neutralizing the main Japanese garrisons on the islands of Babelthuap and Yap.

While Admiral Nimitz's forces were clearing the Central Pacific route to the Philippines, General MacArthur farther in the Southwest Pacific was making final preparations for an invasion of the islands. First came an Allied drive in April and May 1944 that cleared the northern coast of New Guinea; next, amphibious offensives against Wakde, Biak, Noemfoor, and other islands off the northwestern coast of New Guinea that cleared the lower approaches to the Philippines; finally, capture of Morotai Island in September, which put the Southwest Pacific forces within striking distance. As prelude to the great invasion, land-based bombers and planes from carriers of the Third Fleet scourged Japanese airfields and installations in Mindanao, Luzon, and Formosa during September and October. These operations practically destroyed Japanese air power in the area and disrupted Japanese sea communications. Then Americans returned on October 20 to redeem their pledge to liberate the Philippines—with an invasion of Leyte Island by the Sixth Army, the Seventh Fleet under Admiral Thomas C. Kinkaid, and the Third Fleet under Admiral Halsey.

The Japanese admirals well knew that American conquest of the Philippines would spell the doom of the empire, because it would cut communication between Japan and Indochina, Malaya, and the East Indies. They made one last desperate effort to destroy the American invaders in Leyte

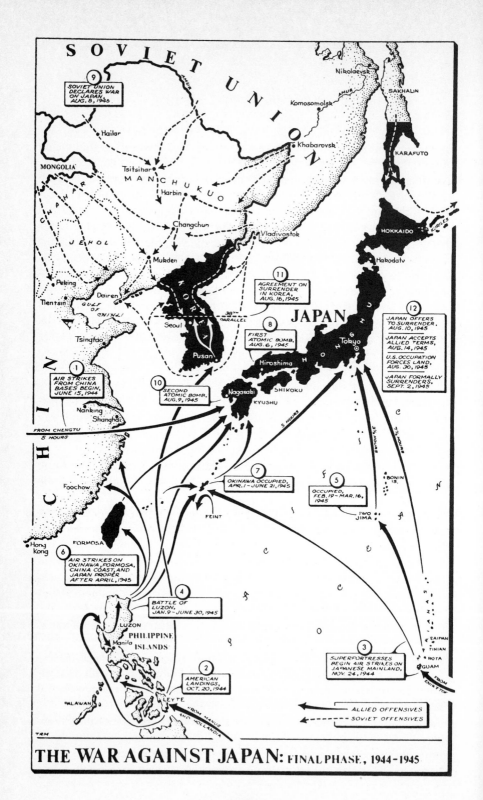

SOVIET UNION

Nikolaevsk

Komosomolsk

SAKHALIN

KARAFUTO

9
SOVIET
UNION
DECLARES WAR
ON JAPAN,
AUG. 8, 1945.

Hailar

Khabarovsk

MONGOLIA

Tsitsihar

MANCHUKUO

HOKKAIDO

Harbin

Hakodate

Changchun

Vladivostok

CHAHAR

JEHOL

Mukden

Peking

Dairen

KOREA

11
AGREEMENT ON
SURRENDER
IN KOREA,
AUG. 16, 1945.

JAPAN

Tientsin

GULF OF
CHIHLI

Seoul

38TH
PARALLEL

8
FIRST
ATOMIC BOMB,
AUG. 6, 1945.

Tokyo

12
JAPAN OFFERS
TO SURRENDER,
AUG. 10, 1945.

JAPAN ACCEPTS
ALLIED TERMS,
AUG. 14, 1945.

U.S. OCCUPATION
FORCES LAND,
AUG. 30, 1945.

JAPAN FORMALLY
SURRENDERS,
SEPT. 2, 1945.

Tsingtao

Pusan

Hiroshima

HONSHU

CHINA

1
AIR STRIKES
FROM CHINA
BASES BEGIN,
JUNE 15, 1944.

10
SECOND
ATOMIC BOMB,
AUG. 9, 1945.

Nagasaki

SHIKOKU

Nanking

KYUSHU

Shanghai

FROM CHENGTU
5 HOURS

5 HOURS

3½ HOURS

7½ HOURS

Foochow

7
OKINAWA OCCUPIED,
APR. 1 – JUNE 21, 1945.

5
OCCUPIED,
FEB. 19 – MAR. 16,
1945.

BONIN
IS.

FEINT

IWO
JIMA

FORMOSA

Hong
Kong

6
AIR STRIKES ON
OKINAWA, FORMOSA,
CHINA COAST, AND
JAPAN PROPER
AFTER APRIL, 1945.

4
BATTLE OF
LUZON,
JAN. 9 – JUNE 30, 1945.

LUZON

PHILIPPINE
ISLANDS

Manila

SAIPAN

TINIAN

ROTA

GUAM

3
SUPERFORTRESSES
BEGIN AIR STRIKES ON
JAPANESE MAINLAND,
NOV. 24, 1944.

FROM
ENIWETOK

2
AMERICAN
LANDINGS,
OCT. 20, 1944.

PALAWAN

LEYTE

FROM MANUS
AND HOLLANDIA

ALLIED OFFENSIVES
SOVIET OFFENSIVES

TRM

THE WAR AGAINST JAPAN: FINAL PHASE, 1944–1945

Gulf. The three naval engagements that ensued between October 24 and 25—the battle of Surigao Strait, the battle off Samar, and the battle off Cape Engaño, collectively known as the Battle for Leyte Gulf—ended disastrously for the Japanese. In this greatest naval battle in history the Japanese lost practically their entire fleet—three battleships, four carriers, nine cruisers, and eight destroyers.

The threat of Japanese naval intervention was forever ended, and MacArthur could now press forward with his overwhelming campaign in the Philippines. While the invasion of Leyte was at its height, he launched an attack against Mindoro in December and then attacked Luzon from Lingayen Gulf in early January 1945. Not until July 5, however, were the Japanese rooted out of the mountains of northern Luzon and out of Mindanao and dozens of smaller islands. All told, Japan lost over 400,000 men and 9,000 planes in the entire Philippines campaign.

The American conquest of the Marianas, western Carolines, and Philippines blasted the inner rim of Japanese defenses, cut communications between the home islands and Indochina, Malaya, and the East Indies, and reduced the Japanese navy to the size of a single task force. Equally important, it afforded advanced bases from which to bomb the homeland of the empire. Indeed, the air war against Japan had already begun in June 1944, when a force of large new B-29 Superfortresses of the Twentieth Air Force, operating from bases in China, attacked steel works in Kyushu. The Twentieth Air Force made subsequent raids on Japan and Manchuria, but its operations were limited because all its supplies and bombs had to be flown over the Himalayan Hump from India. A massive B-29 attack became possible only with the capture of Saipan in the Marianas. The capture of Iwo Jima later yielded bases for American fighter planes and fighter-bombers that joined in the increasing aerial assault. All told, American planes dropped about 160,000 tons of bombs on the Japanese home islands from November 1944, when the bombardment from the Marianas began, to September 1945, when the war ended.

Although the tonnage of bombs dropped on Japan was about one-ninth of that dropped on Germany, the physical destruction in Japan almost equaled that in Germany. American bombs killed 330,000 Japanese civilians and injured nearly 500,000; moreover, they destroyed 2,510,000 buildings and 40 percent of the built-up areas of sixty-six cities. The effects on the Japanese war economy were equally devastating. Air attacks by July 1945 had reduced the productive capacity of Japanese oil refineries by 83 percent, aircraft engine plants by 75 percent, electronics and communication equipment plants by 70 percent, and munitions factories by some 30 percent. For a nation with an industrial capacity only 10 percent that of its chief enemy, these losses were fatal.

Let us now turn back to the last phase of the relentless American drive by land and sea toward Japan. While MacArthur was bringing the Philippines campaign to its climax, marine divisions invaded Iwo Jima, 750 miles south of Japan, on February 19, 1945. The defenders had made the island virtually one vast pillbox. They fought so courageously that the Iwo Jima operation was the bloodiest in the history of the United States Marine Corps. However, the entire island, with its two airfields, was in American hands by March 16. Next came a larger attack, beginning April 1, by marine and army forces against Okinawa, a large island in the Ryukyus only 350 miles southwest of Japan. The Japanese and American leaders both knew that the fall of Okinawa would spell the early doom of the empire. The defenders, therefore, fought fanatically during the battle that raged from April 1 to June 21 and lost nearly 111,000 dead and 9,000 prisoners. The most spectacular aspect of the defense was the unrelenting and often effective Kamikaze, or suicide, attacks by Japanese aircraft against American warships and transports. All told, the Japanese lost some 4,000 aircraft, 3,500 of them in Kamikaze attacks, during the Battle of Okinawa.

By this time the main question was whether Japan would collapse internally before the Americans had launched their final invasion of the island empire. We have noted the terrible devastation wrought by the Superfortresses from Saipan. They were joined in February 1945 by thousands of planes of the Third Fleet and in April by fighter-bombers from Iwo Jima and Okinawa. American battleships and heavy cruisers joined in the attack in mid-July by shelling steel works, synthetic oil plants, and other industrial targets on the mainland and by heavy attacks upon Japanese shipping. But Japan was suffering most from a combined sea, air, and mine blockade that had reduced her once large merchant fleet to ineffectiveness and deprived her people of food and her industries of vital raw materials.[23]

Indeed, it had been evident to certain Japanese leaders since the autumn of 1943 that they were fighting a losing battle, and that the imperial government should seek peace, even at the cost of giving up China, Korea, and Formosa. On July 18, 1944, soon after the American invasion of the Marianas, a moderate group led principally by the naval chieftains forced Tojo to resign and establish a new cabinet under General Kuniaki Koiso. An important element in the new government, led by Navy Minister Mitsumasa Yonai and allied with officials in the imperial court, were determined to end the war as quickly as possible. The emperor threw his full support to the peace party in February 1945. After the invasion of Okinawa on April 8, he appointed Baron Kantaro Suzuki as premier and ordered him to end the war. Suzuki, however, did not control the army. It was determined to fight to the bitter end and threatened to revolt if the cabinet moved for peace. Thus the cabinet began secret discussions in

[23]Japan entered the war with 6 million tons of merchant shipping and constructed an additional 4.1 million tons between 1941 and 1945. Of this total of 10.1 million tons, the Japanese lost 8.9 million—54.7 percent to submarines, 16.3 percent to carrier-based planes, 14.5 percent to land-based planes, 9.3 percent to mines laid by B-29s, 4 percent to marine accidents, and less than 1 percent to surface gunfire.

May with the Russian ambassador, Jacob Malik, looking toward Russian mediation. In addition, the emperor appealed directly to the Soviet government in June and July to help arrange peace talks with the United States.

This was t ie situation when Truman, Churchill, Clement Attlee, soon to be Churchil s successor, and Stalin met at Potsdam on July 17, 1945, for the last conf rence of the Big Three. Truman almost certainly knew about the Japanese peace overtures even before the Potsdam Conference met; in any event, Stalin soon gave full information about them. The president was not inclined to take the overtures seriously. He did not trust the Japanese, and his military advisers believed that Japan would not surrender until Allied forces had invaded and occupied the islands. He therefore approved a discouraging Soviet reply to Tokyo.

Meanwhile, word had come to the American leaders at Postdam on July 16 that an atomic bomb had been exploded in New Mexico. Knowing that the bomb was a reality (there were materials on hand to assemble two additional bombs at once), and that its use might avert the necessity of a long and bloody campaign, Truman now concentrated on a public warning to Japan. It was the Potsdam Declaration issued on July 26 under Truman's, Churchill's, and Chiang Kai-shek's signatures. It promised stern justice to Japanese war criminals and enforcement of the Cairo Declaration stripping Japan of all conquests. But it also held out the hope of generous treatment of a Japan purged and reformed. "The alternative for Japan," it concluded, "is prompt and utter destruction."

The leaders of the Suzuki government in Tokyo agreed to accept the Potsdam Declaration but could not persuade the army leaders to surrender. When Suzuki declared on July 28, only for home consumption, that the Potsdam Declaration was "unworthy of public notice," President Truman and his advisers took this as a refusal and decided to use the atomic bomb.[24] The decision was made largely on military grounds. The Japanese were doomed, to be sure, but they still had large supplies of weapons and an army of 2 million in the home islands. An invasion would surely have succeeded only at great human costs on both sides.

Thus a lone B-29 flew over Hiroshima on August 6 and dropped the first atomic bomb used in warfare. It leveled 4.4 square miles of the city and killed between 70,000 and 80,000 persons. On the same day President Truman announced the news to the world and warned the Japanese that if they did not surrender they could expect "a rain of ruin from the air, the likes of which has never been seen on this earth." Still the Japanese army

---

[24]This decision to use the bomb if the Japanese refused to surrender was actually made at Potsdam on July 22, after intensive discussions among Truman, American military leaders, and Churchill, and after earlier discussions in the War Department and among the scientists involved in the Manhattan Project. Most of the scientists either opposed using the atomic bomb or else proposed dropping one on an uninhabited area as a demonstration and warning to the Japanese leaders.

refused to surrender. Then, on August 9, news came to Tokyo that Russia had entered the war,[25] and that the Americans had dropped a second atomic bomb on Nagasaki. When hurried conferences failed to yield agreement to accept the Potsdam ultimatum, the emperor made the decision for peace. The cabinet informed Washington on the following day that it accepted the Potsdam terms, provided that the status of the emperor would not be changed. The military and naval chieftains balked when Washington replied on August 11 that the emperor must be subject to the supreme commander of the Allied powers. But the emperor insisted, and the Suzuki government formally accepted the Allied demands on August 14. The emperor at once prepared records of an imperial rescript ordering his armed forces to surrender; and the cabinet, after suppressing an insurrection of army fanatics, sent emissaries to General MacArthur to arrange the details of surrender. A great Allied fleet entered Tokyo Bay on September 2. Soon afterward Foreign Minister Mamoru Shigemitsu and a representative of the imperial general staff signed articles of surrender on board the battleship *Missouri*. General MacArthur and representatives of the Allied powers accepted on behalf of their respective governments.

[25]The conferees at Potsdam had given careful attention to Russian plans for participation. American leaders still welcomed Russian intervention even though they were by no means as eager for it as they had been earlier.

23

The American Economy,

1940–1970

It is a forbidding task to relate in one chapter the swift emergence of the American people from the worst depression in their history to an unprecedented level of prosperity. Even more formidable is the attempt to describe the new economic society that Americans achieved after midcentury. In retrospect, we can see that the years 1940-1970 were, economically and socially, a discrete period characterized by unparalleled economic growth and all its attendant social dislocations. A new era began in the 1970s, particularly with the oil embargo of 1973—an era of worldwide economic disruptions and uncertainties. We will discuss these portentous developments in Chapters 32 and 34.

1. The American People, 1940-1970

A demographic change, beginning in the early forties and lasting more than fifteen years, dramatically reversed the declining birthrate of the previous two decades. With the advent of selective service and war in 1940-1941, the birthrate began to rise, declining only momentarily in 1944-1945 because of the absence of millions of men overseas. Then, as veterans returned to build homes and begin families, the birthrate resumed its rapid increase—from 19.4 per thousand in 1940, to 23.3 in 1946, and then up to 25.8 in 1947. Demographers were surprised when the postwar years witnessed no decline in the new high rate, but rather saw a leveling off within a range only slightly below the 1947 peak. After dropping to 24.1 in 1950, it hovered around 25.0 until 1957. Then a decline set in that continued until the end of the sixties. The rate dropped to 23.7 in 1960 and fell every year thereafter through 1968, when it reached a near-record low of 17.5. It rose to 18.2 in 1970.

The results were strikingly reflected in the census returns. The population of the United States expanded from about 132.6 million to almost 153.3 million between 1940 and 1950. No previous ten-year period had recorded so large a numerical gain, and the rate of increase of 14.5 percent was twice that of the thirties. Even more startling were the figures for the next decade. The census of 1960 reported a new record increase of 28 million Americans since 1950, a total population of nearly 180.7 million, and a rate of increase of 18.5 percent, highest since 1900-1910. Although the rate of increase for the sixties declined to 13.3 percent, the census of 1970 recorded a ten-year gain of over 24 million persons and a total population of 204.8 million—more than half again the figure for 1940.

Prosperity hardly accounts for the high birthrate in the period 1940-1957; the prosperous twenties and sixties both featured a falling birthrate. More important was a change in social values that took place during and after the Second World War—a growing conviction that families of three and four children were "normal" and desirable, in contrast to the socially correct family of one or two children in the twenties and thirties. A reverse trend set in during the sixties, however, as concern about the dangers of overpopulation led to pressure for smaller families and better birth-control practices. The percentage of families with three or more children rose steadily, from 14 in 1949 to a postwar high of 22.3 in 1964, and then declined slightly for the remainder of the decade, reaching 20.4 in 1970.[1]

Along with the increase in population went continued improvement in the health of the American people. Advances in the fields of medicine and surgery, better diet, expanding public health services, and an array of new

[1]Although the American population would obviously continue to grow, there was much uncertainty by 1970 as to the future rate of increase. The net reproduction rate, or intrinsic rate of natural increase, is a better index than the crude birthrate. The net rate during the thirties hovered around 981, which meant that the population was not in the long run reproducing itself. From 1944 to 1949, however, this rate was 1,385, and by the mid-fifties it had climbed past 1,700—far higher than any point since 1900. But the net rate declined markedly after 1960: from 1,715 in that year to 1,166 in 1968. On the basis of these varied trends, demographers were projecting national population figures for the year 2000 that ranged from 266 million to over 320 million.

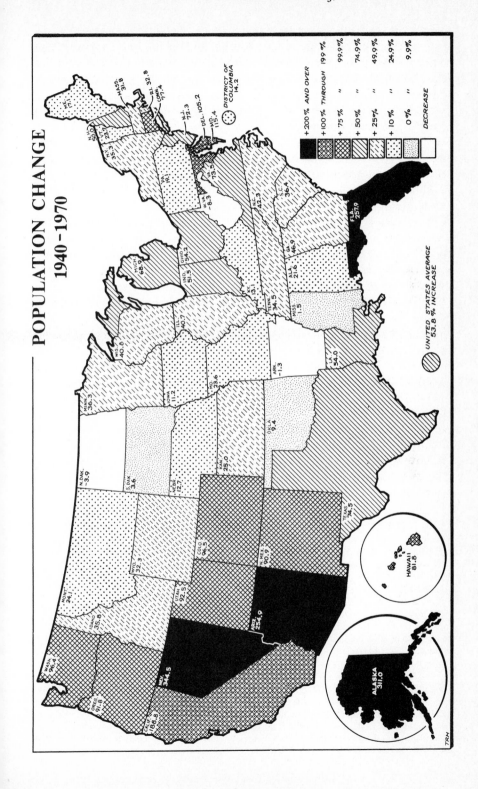

POPULATION CHANGE
1940–1970

+ 200 % AND OVER
+ 100% THROUGH 199 %   99.9%
+ 75 %   "   "   74.9%
+ 50 %   "   "   49.9%
+ 25%   "   "   24.9%
+ 10 %   "   "   9.9%
0 %   "   "
DECREASE

UNITED STATES AVERAGE
53.8 % INCREASE

DISTRICT OF
COLUMBIA
14.2

ME.
171.1

N.H.
50.1

VT.
23.7

MASS.
31.8

R.I. 32.8

CONN.
77.4

N.Y.
35.3

N.J.
72.3

DEL. 105.2

MD.
115.4

PA.
19.0

W.VA.
-8.3

VA.
73.5

OHIO
54.2

IND.
51.5

KY.
13.1

TENN.
34.5

N.C.
40.3

S.C.
36.1

GA.
46.9

ALA.
21.6

MISS.
1.5

FLA.
257.9

MICH.
68.9

ILL.
40.7

WIS.
40.8

MINN.
36.3

IOWA
11.2

MO.
23.6

ARK.
-1.3

LA.
54.0

N.DAK.
-3.9

S.DAK.
3.6

NEBR.
12.7

KAN.
25.0

OKLA.
9.4

TEXAS
34.5

COLO.
96.5

N. MEX.
90.9

ARIZ.
254.9

WYO.
32.3

UTAH
92.5

NEV.
314.5

MONT.
24.1

IDAHO
35.8

WASH.
96.1

OREG.
91.8

CALIF.
188.8

HAWAII
81.8

ALASKA
311.0

TRM

drugs—like sulfanilamide, penicillin, various antibiotics, and cortisone—all combined to render impotent many ancient enemies of mankind. Penicillin, for example, made possible the virtual eradication of venereal diseases.[2] Perfection of the famous Salk vaccine by the late fifties greatly reduced the ravages of poliomyelitis. The overall death rate decreased from 10.8 per thousand in 1940 to 9.6 in 1950 and held steady at about that figure for the next twenty years.[3]

One long-range trend in the racial composition of the American people—the slowly declining percentage of nonwhite to total population—was reversed after 1940. This was due primarily to a sharp drop in the death rate among nonwhite Americans, as rising educational and living standards and increased medical and health facilities enabled greater numbers to escape the diseases attendant upon poverty and ignorance. Between 1940 and 1970 the number of nonwhites nearly doubled, from 13.5 million to over 25.5 million—of whom about 22.7 million, or 89 percent, were black.[4] The ratio of nonwhites to total population rose from just over 10 to about 12.5 percent; the ratio of blacks, from 9.7 to 11.1 percent.

The percentage of foreign-born Americans continued to decline. Ninety-three of every one hundred Americans were native-born in 1950—the highest proportion yet recorded—and the number of foreign-born was lower than at any time since 1890. Fewer than 6 percent of the population in 1970 had been born outside the country. This figure would have been smaller still had not presidential and public pressure induced Congress to ease the immigration laws after 1945. By the War Brides Act of 1946 and the Displaced Persons Act of 1948, amended in 1950 to remove discriminations against southern and eastern Europeans, Congress permitted some 1.5 million quota immigrants to enter the country from 1946 to 1958, while 1 million nonquota arrivals came from elsewhere in the New World. The sixties witnessed the influx of 3.3 million newcomers, of whom more than half were nonquota immigrants.

Important internal changes also occurred after 1940. Prosperity stimu-

---

[2]Although the death rate from syphilis had declined to the vanishing point by the late sixties (0.3 per 100,000), the incidence of venereal disease began a startling upward climb in the late fifties that alarmed medical specialists. Reported civilian cases of gonorrhea had dropped from 313,000 in 1945 to 236,000 in 1955, then described a rising upward curve to 627,000 in 1971. The American Social Health Association, describing this as an epidemic situation, also reported in 1971 that over 500,000 persons were suffering from undetected syphilis.

[3]The Negro death rate declined from 13.8 in 1940 to 11.2 in 1960 and to 9.9 in 1969. This was only slightly above the national rate, as opposed to a Negro death rate 50 percent higher than the overall rate in 1900 and nearly 30 percent higher as recently as 1940. Average life expectancy for white males rose from 46 years in 1901, to 62 in 1940, to 66 in 1950, and then inched upward to almost 68 by 1970. Life expectancy for blacks had risen from 45.3 to 53.1 years between 1920 and 1940. It rose to 60.8 in 1950 and to 63.7 in 1955, where it remained until 1970.

[4]Other nonwhite groups registered spectacular gains in population. Between 1940 and 1970 the number of American Indians increased from 334,000 to 792,000; the number of Japanese, from 127,000 to 591,000; the number of Chinese, from 77,000 to 435,000; the number of Filipinos, from 46,000 to 343,000; and the "other" elements—Koreans, Aleuts, Eskimos, Hawaiians, Polynesians, Malayans—from 5,000 to 720,000. For these groups as a whole, the increase between 1940 and 1970 was from 589,000 to over 2.9 million.

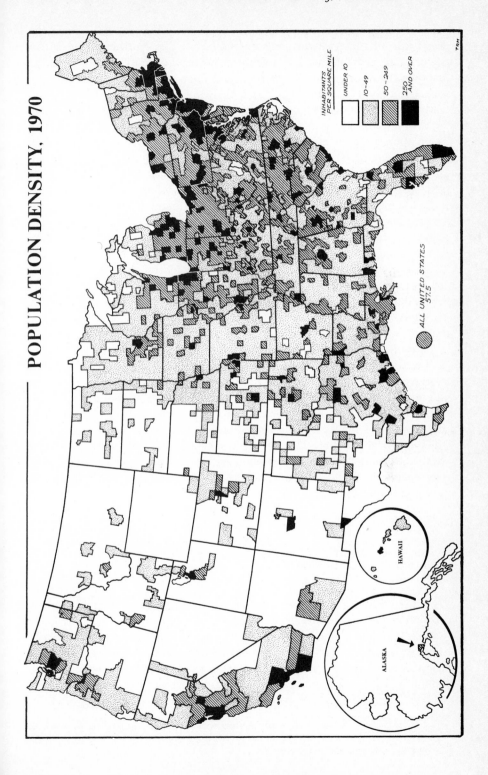

POPULATION DENSITY, 1970

INHABITANTS
PER SQUARE MILE

UNDER 10
10–49
50–249
250 AND OVER

ALL UNITED STATES
57.5

HAWAII

ALASKA

lated such astounding migrations as the country had not seen since the flood tide of the westward movement. While the Northeast, the Plains states, and parts of the South grew in population more slowly than the nation as a whole, other areas recorded huge gains. The South Atlantic states increased by over 75 percent, the Mountain states by 100 percent, and the Pacific states by an amazing 160 percent between 1940 and 1970.

Most importantly, people continued to move from country to city. Farm population shrank in absolute numbers from 30 million in 1940 to less than 10 million in 1970, while the percentage of Americans living in urban areas rose from 56 to 74. Urban growth also displayed an internal dimension of great significance: the rapid expansion of the suburbs. The so-called standard metropolitan statistical areas (central cities of 50,000 or more inhabitants together with their surrounding "urban fringe") contained a total population of 95 million in 1950. Of these, nearly 54 million lived in the central cities and over 40 million in the suburbs. While the central city population of these districts increased by about 10 million, or 18 percent, from 1950 to 1970, the suburban population shot up by fully 35 million, or 87 percent. By 1970 well over half of the nation's city dwellers—and three out of every eight Americans—had become suburbanites.

One other trend remains to be noted here, namely, acceleration of the movement of blacks from the South. The number living outside the South rose from just over 3 million in 1949 to almost 5 million in 1950, to over 7.5 million in 1960, and to 10.6 million in 1970. If the nonsouthern total is expanded to include Maryland, Delaware, and the District of Columbia, the number of blacks living outside the South in 1970 stood at nearly 12 million, or 54 percent. This reflected a truly awesome migration. Since 1940 the southern Negro population had increased by less than 15 percent, while the number residing elsewhere had multiplied more than three and a half times.

2. The American People: Income, Wealth, and Industry

The three decades after 1940 were, by and large, a time of unprecedented economic expansion. Recovery from the depression was already fairly complete before the great defense spending of 1941 opened a new era in American history. The gross national product, stimulated by the heavy volume of war production, increased from $227.2 billion in 1940 to $355.2 billion in 1945, while per capita disposable income[5] rose from $1,259 to $1,642. The GNP declined from its abnormal war peak to a level of about

[5]That is, income left after taxes and social security payments. Except where otherwise noted, all figures for GNP and per capita income in this section are in constant 1958 dollars, hence indicative of real rather than inflationary gains.

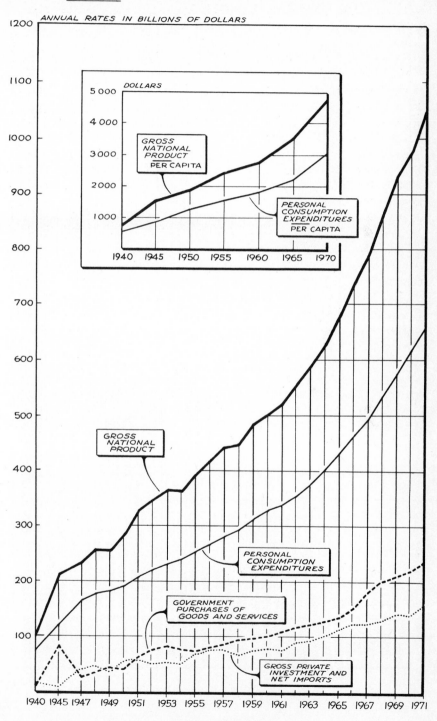

GROSS NATIONAL PRODUCT
1940–1971

ANNUAL RATES IN BILLIONS OF DOLLARS

DOLLARS

GROSS NATIONAL PRODUCT PER CAPITA

PERSONAL CONSUMPTION EXPENDITURES PER CAPITA

GROSS NATIONAL PRODUCT

PERSONAL CONSUMPTION EXPENDITURES

GOVERNMENT PURCHASES OF GOODS AND SERVICES

GROSS PRIVATE INVESTMENT AND NET IMPORTS

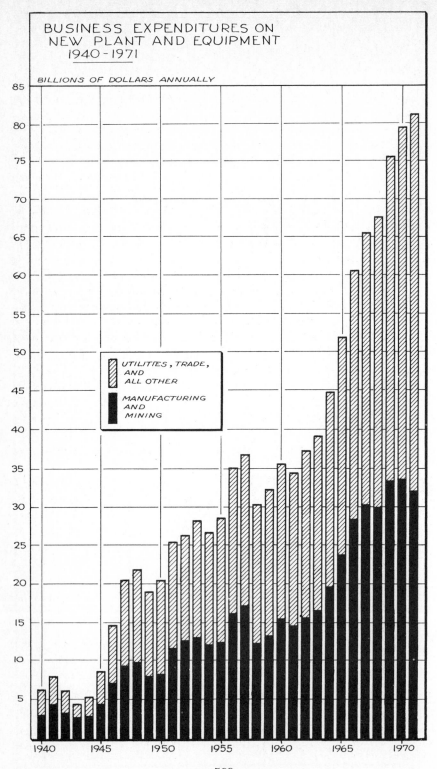

BUSINESS EXPENDITURES ON
NEW PLANT AND EQUIPMENT
1940 – 1971

BILLIONS OF DOLLARS ANNUALLY

UTILITIES, TRADE,
AND
ALL OTHER

MANUFACTURING
AND
MINING

$310 billion in 1946 and 1947, then rose steadily until the Korean War stimulated a new outburst of activity that took the figure to $412.8 billion in 1953. Further expansion in civilian production, together with a continued high level of defense spending, induced a seven-year rise to $487.7 billion in 1960. Per capita disposable income, after declining slightly in 1946-1947, rose steadily thereafter to $1,883 in 1960—an increase since 1940, in real dollars, of 50 percent. Indices rose even faster during the sixties. The GNP topped $727 billion in 1969, then fell slightly to $724.1 billion in 1970 as a recession halted the long upward trend. Per capita disposable income went up 37.5 percent during this prosperous decade, reaching $2,579 in 1970.[6]

To be sure, inflation posed a threat all during these years. It first developed during the war as disposable income grew faster than the supply of civilian goods. It reached critical proportions in 1946-1947, when the federal price control program collapsed and a series of strikes pushed prices higher. The general consumer price index (1957-1959 = 100) rose from 62.7 in 1945 to 83.8 in 1948. Prices leveled off in 1949, but the Korean War induced a second wave of inflation and forced the price index to a peak of 93.2 in 1953. For the next two years prices held steady, only to begin another slow climb in 1956 that brought the index to an all-time high of 103.1 in 1960. The rise continued, reaching 109.9 in 1965. Then prices took off on the worst inflationary spiral in twenty years. The index hit 113.1 in 1966, 121.3 in 1968, and 135.5 in 1970. The dollar was now worth less than half what it had been in 1945, and it had lost a third of its value in ten years.

In spite of inflation and attendant hardships, these were years of unparalleled prosperity for most Americans. While population increased about 50 percent, the GNP more than trebled and real per capita disposable income doubled. The civilian labor force grew from 52.8 million to 82.7 million persons; the number of business firms, from 3.2 million to over 8.3 million.

The foregoing generalizations fail to indicate the relative shifts in income distribution that occurred after 1940. Nowhere did these shifts have a more dramatic impact than in agriculture. Farmers experienced great prosperity during the war, as net income per farm rose (in constant 1960 dollars) from $1,714 in 1940 to $3,302 in 1945, and on to a peak of $3,677 in 1946. A steep downward plunge followed. Net income fell to $2,916 in 1950 and continued down to $2,487 in 1955, a 33 percent drop in nine years. The farmer's economic situation began to improve in the late fifties.

---

[6]The tonic of prosperity affected almost every segment of the economy and spurred, from 1946 through 1970, an investment of over $956 billion in new plant and equipment and nearly $117 billion in farm equipment and construction. It also stimulated the building of some 31 million nonfarm private homes and apartment houses (at a cost of over $478 billion) and the building of thousands of schools, hospitals, highways, and other public nonmilitary facilities (at a total cost of over $377 billion).

Net income rose to nearly $3,000 in 1958, held steady for a few years, then traced a sharper upward climb through the sixties—from $2,962 in 1960 to over $3,900 in 1965, and on to $4,500 in 1970, a real income 25 percent higher than the 1946 peak.[7]

But this prosperity was for survivors only, and they were remarkably few in number. The precipitate drop in agricultural income in the decade 1946-1955, at a time when other incomes were rising, touched off a migration from the farm that assumed the proportions of a mass exodus. It continued unabated even after farm income hit bottom in the mid-fifties; the improvement after 1958 was achieved by the inexorable process of squeezing more and more individuals out of farming altogether. Farm population shrank by two-thirds between 1947 and 1970, from 27.1 million to 9.7 million. The number of farms fell by over half, to less than 3 million. In 1947 one American in six still lived on a farm; by 1970, less than one in twenty.[8] And as we shall note in a later section, prosperity was distributed with gross unevenness among the farms that survived.

In contrast were the steady economic gains recorded by most workers in industry, mining, transport, construction, and other fields. The net spendable *real* income of an average worker with three dependents increased 80 percent from 1940 to 1970. Although unemployment, like inflation, remained a chronic problem after 1945, the *rate* of unemployment seldom touched unsatisfactory levels and never came close to the disastrous figures of the depression decade. During most of the period it hovered between 3 and 5 percent, rising above 5.5 percent during the recessions of 1948-1949, 1954-1955, and 1958-1960. It rose again in 1970-1971, approaching 6 percent and coinciding unhappily with soaring prices. Technological advances, which effected a 75 percent increase in output per man-hour between 1950 and 1970, helped explain the persistence of unemployment even in an expanding economy.

What was the economic condition of the American people in 1970, after thirty years of almost uninterrupted expansion and prosperity? The answer

[7]The chief cause of agrarian distress after 1945 was not declining prices, which were maintained above or only moderately below the parity level by federal support, but steadily rising costs. Increased expenses, in terms of equipment, labor, and taxes, reduced the farmer's net share of his gross income from almost 50 percent in 1946 to 30 percent in 1960 and after. The parity ratio fluctuated above 100 every year from 1945 to 1952, dropped to 92 in 1953, and declined steadily for the balance of the decade to 80 in 1960. It fell at a slower rate during the sixties, reaching 75 in 1970.

[8]The squeeze took place entirely on the smaller units. Of 6.1 million farms in 1940, some 5.4 million, or 88 percent, were under 260 acres in size; nearly 3.6 million, or almost 60 percent, were under 100 acres. By 1969, of 2.7 million remaining farms, only 1.9 million (70 percent) were under 260 acres and 1.1 million (about 40 percent) under 100 acres. In contrast, farms 260 acres and larger showed an absolute as well as a percentage increase: from 724,000, or 12 percent of all farms, in 1940, to 786,000, or 29 percent, in 1969. Even more pronounced was the increase in farms 500 acres and larger, from 265,000 in 1940 to 367,000 in 1969. Only one farm in twenty-five exceeded 500 acres at the outset of the Second World War; one farm in seven was in that category thirty years later.

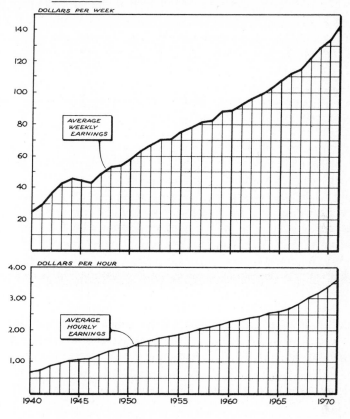

HOURS AND EARNINGS OF
PRODUCTION WORKERS IN MANUFACTURING
1940 – 1971

one gives depends in large measure upon the goals he sets for a democratic society. Most Americans want an expanding economy that affords a rising standard of living for the masses without destroying the incentives to talent and industry. In terms of income distribution, the nation moved closer to this democratic goal after 1940. The seemingly inexorable tide of concentration of wealth in fewer and fewer hands was checked: the percentage of aggregate income received by the top 5 percent of American families declined from 25.7 in 1940 to 14.7 in 1969. The following table (see p. 572) indicates shifts in income distribution, as well as the rising general income level, since 1941.

To be sure, Americans had not achieved the millennium by 1970. Nearly 25 million of them, or one-eighth of the population, were officially defined as being below the poverty level in 1969; 8 percent of white families and 20 percent of nonwhite families still earned less than $3,000 a year. Inflation bore cruelly upon the unemployed, the poor, and people

Money Income: Percent Distribution of Families by Income Level, 1941-1969

	1941	1947	1955	1960	1965	1969
Under $1,000	31.0	10.8	7.7	5.0	2.9	1.6
$ 1,000-$ 2,000	30.0	16.6	9.9	8.0	6.0	3.1
$ 2,000-$ 3,000	21.0	22.0	11.0	8.7	7.2	4.6
$ 3,000-$ 4,000	9.0	19.7	14.6	9.8	7.7	5.3
$ 4,000-$ 5,000	4.0	11.6	15.4	10.5	7.9	5.4
$ 5,000-$ 6,000		7.7	12.7	12.9	9.3	5.9
$ 6,000-$ 7,000			9.5	10.8	9.5	6.4
$ 7,000-$10,000	5.0	8.9	12.9	20.0	24.2	21.7
$10,000-$15,000			4.8	10.6	17.7	26.7
Over $15,000		2.7	1.4	3.7	7.6	19.2

with fixed incomes. Certain groups and regions had received a dispropor-
tionately small share of the great postwar prosperity. Yet the fact remains
that a large majority of Americans were no longer living in poverty or near
subsistence by 1970. The following contrast allows for inflation: whereas
only 19 percent of American families earned more than $5,000 in 1947,
almost 46 percent exceeded $10,000 in 1969. These figures help to cali-
brate one of the mightiest economic and social revolutions of modern
times.[9]

Moreover, it was a revolution in which, for the first time, a substantial
number of black Americans participated. Though the gap in average and
median economic achievement between whites and nonwhites remained
much too large in 1970, Negroes had moved measurably closer to a decent

[9]Some important qualifiers should be noted, however. For one thing, the shift in income distribution took place almost entirely during and right after the war: the share of aggregate income held
by the top 20 percent of families and unrelated individuals held quite steady from 1950 to 1970.
Secondly, the standards of material consumption—in terms of goods and services that became the
normal expectation for most families—rose so much faster than annual income after midcentury
that millions who were far from the arbitrary poverty line still faced considerable and growing
strain because their level of consumption tended to stay well ahead of their wages.

One authority concluded that families earning less than $10,000 a year in 1970—over half the
total—were under this kind of economic stress and could hardly be called "affluent" by the
changed standards of the late twentieth century. The truth of this observation was evidenced in
two ways: by the growing numbers of people (over 4 million in 1970) who held two or more jobs,
and by the rising percentage of families (over 40 percent in 1970) in which both the husband and
the wife worked. Affluence for many Americans was more apparent than real, and in millions of
homes it was dearly bought.

Furthermore, the figures measuring unemployment and defining poverty in 1970 were probably much too low. Figures of the Census Bureau and the Bureau of Labor Statistics revealed that
recent unemployment data omitted large numbers of men and women who had become so
discouraged that they had quit looking for work, and even larger numbers who held part-time
jobs but wanted, and could not find, full-time employment. The inner cities—not merely the
ghettos—also contained hundreds of thousands of people whose full-time jobs simply did not pay
enough to enable them to make ends meet. BLS computations suggested that the official poverty
line income of $4,000 was far too low; in many cities a more realistic figure that would provide a
minimally decent standard of living for a family of four was around $7,000. By this measurement,
some 33 percent of all families and as many as 40 to 60 percent of inner-city families were still
below the poverty level in the seventies.

place in the economic order. Over 80 percent of nonwhite families received less than $3,000 a year in 1947; only 20 percent were in that depressed category in 1969. Whereas a bare 3 percent of nonwhite families earned more than $6,000 in 1947, fully 51 percent surpassed that figure in 1969. The percentage of nonwhites officially classed as below the poverty level fell from 56.2 in 1959 to 31.1 ten years later. Median income for nonwhite families rose from $2,848 (54 percent of the white figure) in 1950 to $6,191 (63 percent of the white figure) in 1969.[10]

Not only were blacks working more and earning more than in any previous period, but larger numbers of them had acquired better kinds of jobs. In 1948, only 9 percent of nonwhite workers (as opposed to 39 percent of white workers) had white-collar jobs, and 70 percent were in menial or relatively unskilled occupations: blue-collar positions, farm and day labor, private household service. Only 2.4 percent were classified as professionals in 1948; only 4.4 percent were clerks or salesworkers; only 5.3 percent were craftsmen or foremen.

The figures for 1970 present gratifying contrasts. Nearly 28 percent of nonwhite workers were in white-collar categories, including 9.1 percent in the professions and over 15 percent in clerical and sales work. Eight percent had become craftsmen and foremen, whereas less than 45 percent remained in menial and unskilled jobs, including private household work. Over half of the nation's blacks had moved into professional, white-collar, or other relatively skilled occupations, at wage and salary levels that no longer mocked comparison with the national average.

3. The Further Technological Revolution

An expanding revolution in technology was largely responsible for American economic progress after 1940. It increased productivity in mines and factories and on farms, emancipated the housewife from numerous drudgeries, and destroyed unskilled labor's ancient slavery to the pick and shovel. It created new industries and inventions that made Jules Verne look like a prophet. We have already discussed the principal factors in the technological revolution of the period 1900-1940: increasing horsepower per worker, application of the principles of scientific management, the assembly line technique, use of interchangeable parts, and development of new inventions and processes. These were also components of the further revolution after 1940; the chief differences were in degree and speed.

[10]The nonwhite unemployment rate in 1955 was 100 percent greater than the national rate; in 1971 it was 63 percent greater. Three of every four nonwhite farmers were tenants in 1940, but by 1969 this figure had dropped to 20 percent; in absolute numbers nonwhite tenancy had declined from 507,000 to 21,000.

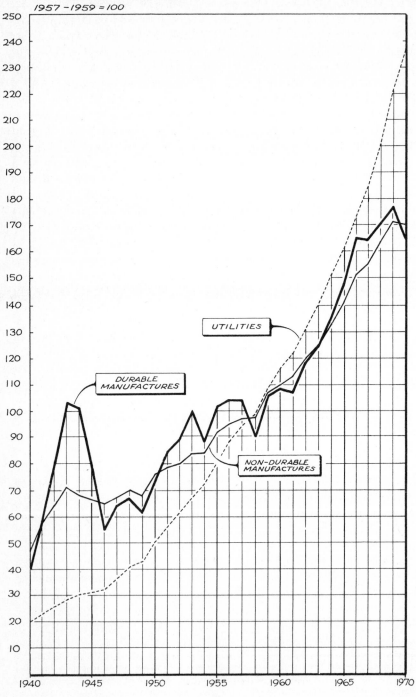

INDUSTRIAL PRODUCTION
1940-1970
BY MAJOR DIVISIONS
1957-1959 = 100

UTILITIES

DURABLE
MANUFACTURES

NON-DURABLE
MANUFACTURES

If the measure of technological advance is horsepower, then the extent of the new revolution was startling indeed. Energy developed from water power increased by over 300 percent and from mineral fuels by nearly 150 percent between 1940 and 1970. Production of electric power increased ninefold, from 180 billion to 1,638 billion kilowatt-hours. Total horsepower—including autos and trucks, factory and farm machinery, electric central stations, railroads, aircraft, and ships—rose incredibly, from 2.8 billion to over 20.4 billion. Horsepower per worker went up 400 percent.

Techniques of scientific management and mass production were applied more extensively than ever before. Further use of the assembly line and interchangeable parts had slowed during the depression but increased markedly during the war and after. New electronic measuring devices enabled machine tools to produce engines of almost perfect quality and virtually eliminated the need for hand tooling. More and more human effort in shop, office, and factory gave way to electronic equipment that automated entire processes by regulating and coordinating the activity in a continuous, integrated operation.

Industrial research, after a modest development during and after the First World War, became a vitally important enterprise. The government entered the field decisively with the creation of the National Defense Research Committee and the Office of Scientific Research and Development in 1940-1941. The number of scientists employed in research rose from 87,000 to 199,000 between 1941 and 1945; expenditures increased from $900 million to $1.5 billion. Both public and private research expanded by leaps and bounds after the war. By 1969, some 312,000 scientists in colleges and universities, government, and private industry—over 40 percent of all the scientists in the country—were engaged in research and development projects representing expenditures of over $26 billion.

The pervasive impact of this revolution is at once obvious and impossible to measure fully. We can, however, partially measure one of its principal results, the increase in the productivity of labor. During the thirties productivity in industry increased about 20 percent. The index of industrial production went up 300 percent from 1940 to 1969, and output per man-hour in manufacturing doubled. Output per man-hour in agriculture, which was static during the thirties, rose by a startling 430 percent between 1940 and 1970, as horse and mule gave way to truck and tractor, while new inventions like the corn picker, the cotton picker, the pickup baler, and the forage harvester displaced hundreds of thousands of hired hands and tenants.[11]

[11] The mechanization of agriculture proceeded at a prodigious rate after 1940. The number of trucks tripled, reaching an average of better than one truck per farm by 1970. The number of tractors also tripled, with an average by 1970 of better than three for every two farms. The number of grain combines increased from 190,000 (1 per 32 farms) to 850,000 (1 per 4); corn pickers, from 110,000 (1 per 55 farms) to 620,000 (1 per 5); pickup balers, from 42,000 in 1945 (1 per 140 farms) to 795,000 (1 per 4); forage harvesters, from 20,000 in 1945 (1 per 290 farms) to 331,000 (1 per 9).

RESEARCH IN THE UNITED STATES
1941 – 1970   *(SELECTED YEARS)*

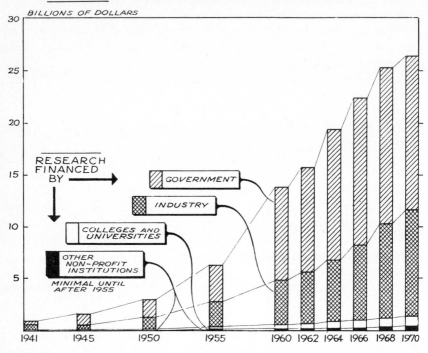

BILLIONS OF DOLLARS

RESEARCH
FINANCED
BY

GOVERNMENT

INDUSTRY

COLLEGES AND
UNIVERSITIES

OTHER
NON-PROFIT
INSTITUTIONS

*MINIMAL UNTIL
AFTER 1955*

1941   1945   1950   1955   1960 1962 1964 1966 1968 1970

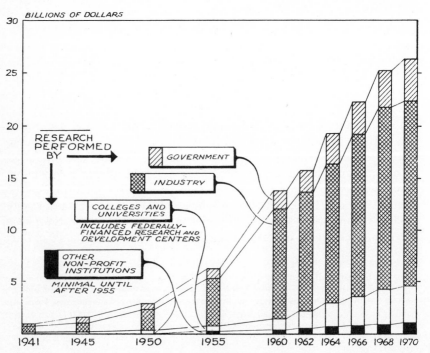

BILLIONS OF DOLLARS

RESEARCH
PERFORMED
BY

GOVERNMENT

INDUSTRY

COLLEGES AND
UNIVERSITIES

*INCLUDES FEDERALLY-
FINANCED RESEARCH AND
DEVELOPMENT CENTERS*

OTHER
NON-PROFIT
INSTITUTIONS

*MINIMAL UNTIL
AFTER 1955*

1941   1945   1950   1955   1960 1962 1964 1966 1968 1970

4. Industrial Pace Setters

This was also a time of marked change in the pattern of industrial production, as illustrated by the table below.

These statistics convey a sense of the shifts in production, but they only begin to tell the story. They fail to indicate, for example, such important developments as the rapid growth of industry in the South—which accounted for a bare 12 percent (or about $3 billion) of the value added by manufacture in the United States in 1939 and fully 23 percent (or over $70 billion) by 1968. These statistics also obscure the dynamic growth of certain segments of the economy. The rise of the automobile, chemical, radio, aviation, and motion picture industries had begun a profound revolution in American life in the twenties. That revolution, proceeding unevenly in the depressed thirties, virtually exploded after 1945 as mass production and technological advance multiplied their effects.

THE AUTOMOBILE.   The auto continued to enjoy its preeminence as the most important single factor in the American economy. Production of cars and trucks had declined from a peak of 5.3 million in 1929 to 1.4 million

The Ten Leading American Industries, 1939 and 1969

Rank	Industry	Value Added by Manufacturing (In Millions of Dollars)
	1939	
1.	Food and kindred products	$3,485
2.	Primary metal industries	2,169
3.	Machinery, except electrical	2,037
4.	Chemicals and allied products	1,819
5.	Textile mill products	1,818
6.	Transportation equipment, including automobiles	1,773
7.	Printing and publishing	1,765
8.	Fabricated metal products	1,401
9.	Apparel	1,386
10.	Electrical machinery	941
	1969	
1.	Transportation equipment, including automobiles	$35,068
2.	Machinery, except electrical	31,983
3.	Food and kindred products	30,120
4.	Electrical machinery	28,275
5.	Chemicals and allied products	27,177
6.	Primary metal industries	22,714
7.	Fabricated metal products	20,841
8.	Printing and publishing	16,615
9.	Apparel	11,639
10.	Paper and allied products	11,284

VALUE ADDED BY MANUFACTURE PER PRODUCTION WORKER 1954 AND 1970

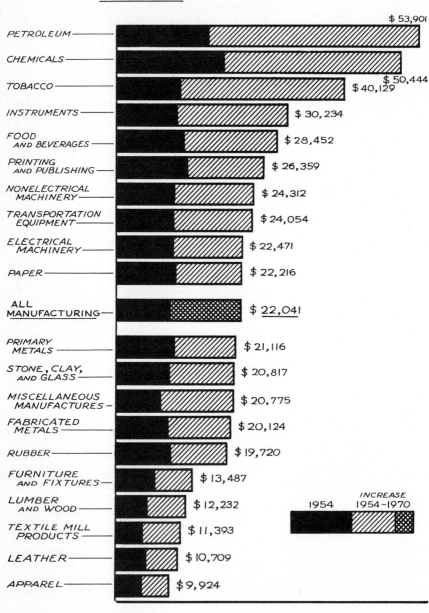

PETROLEUM — $ 53,901
CHEMICALS — $ 50,444
TOBACCO — $ 40,129
INSTRUMENTS — $ 30,234
FOOD AND BEVERAGES — $ 28,452
PRINTING AND PUBLISHING — $ 26,359
NONELECTRICAL MACHINERY — $ 24,312
TRANSPORTATION EQUIPMENT — $ 24,054
ELECTRICAL MACHINERY — $ 22,471
PAPER — $ 22,216
ALL MANUFACTURING — $ 22,041
PRIMARY METALS — $ 21,116
STONE, CLAY, AND GLASS — $ 20,817
MISCELLANEOUS MANUFACTURES — $ 20,775
FABRICATED METALS — $ 20,124
RUBBER — $ 19,720
FURNITURE AND FIXTURES — $ 13,487
LUMBER AND WOOD — $ 12,232
TEXTILE MILL PRODUCTS — $ 11,393
LEATHER — $ 10,709
APPAREL — $ 9,924

1954   INCREASE 1954–1970

in 1932, returned to nearly 5 million in 1937, and then ceased almost altogether durii g the war. New production records were set after 1945 in response to pent-up consumer demand, culminating in the manufacture of over 8 million cars and trucks in 1950. Annual factory sales averaged nearly 7 million throughout the fifties and over 9 million during the sixties. While the number of buses and trucks increased from 5 million to over 19 million between 1940 and 1970, the number of automobiles shot up from 27.5 million, or one car for every five Americans, to nearly 90 million, or almost one for every two. Filling stations, garages, motels, highway construction and maintenance (nearly $15 billion in 1969 alone), and the petroleum industry expanded and flourished accordingly.[12]

As the automobile multiplied, it became larger, more powerful, and gaudier. Automatic transmission became standard equipment on most models after the war and combined with power steering, power brakes, and high-horsepower engines to make the American car easier to drive, faster accelerating, and more lethal than ever before. In the fifties, it blossomed spectacularly in a burst of chromium ornamentation, two- and three-tone color combinations, soaring tailfins, enormous red tail lights, and other eye-catching features.

Two types of reaction set in. First, increasing numbers of Americans discovered that the smaller, more economical, less ostentatious European and Japanese cars had much to recommend them. As foreign makes like Volkswagen, Peugeot, Volvo, Fiat, Triumph, Toyota, and others gained popularity here in the sixties, Detroit responded with smaller and cheaper models of its own. But foreign cars proved to be more than a passing fancy, and their share of the American market grew rapidly: imports were 1 percent of domestic production in 1955, 10 percent in 1960, 20 percent in 1967, and over 30 percent by 1970. Their effect on automotive design had been salutary.

More important, a vocal minority began to challenge the priorities that had induced designers to stress horsepower and chromium at the expense of safety. Spearhead of this movement was a young graduate of Princeton and the Harvard Law School, Ralph Nader, whose scathing indictment of the automobile industry, *Unsafe at Any Speed*, appeared in 1965 and won nationwide attention. Detroit first tried to ignore the book, and one company hired detectives to investigate Nader. But public concern soon forced both Congress and the industry to respond positively. Hearings conducted by Senator Abraham Ribicoff of Connecticut culminated in

[12] A few statistics will illustrate the importance of the industries that serve the automobile owner. In 1969 the manufacturers of tires and tubes employed 103,000 workers, who added $2.3 billion in value by manufacture. In 1967 there were 105,000 automotive dealers employing 906,000 persons, with sales of $55.6 billion; 139,000 auto repair garages employing 316,000 persons, with sales of $7 billion; 216,000 gas stations employing 575,000 persons, with sales of $22.7 billion; 31,000 wholesale vehicle and equipment establishments employing 341,000 persons, with sales of $46.1 billion; 12,000 trailer parks and 42,000 motels and motor hotels employing 222,000 persons, with receipts of $2.7 billion.

1966 in highway and traffic safety acts, setting federal standards that were to be applied to all cars beginning in 1968. Detroit added several innovations—seat belts, padded dashboards, collapsible steering columns, flasher lights, and so on—which became standard equipment after 1968 under the new federal safety law. The auto companies, still smarting under the lash of Nader's charges, periodically recalled hundreds of thousands of cars for repair of possible defects.

The auto's mindless dominance faced an even broader challenge. Mounting concern in the sixties over environmental quality soon identified the millions of internal combustion engines on American streets and highways as a prime source of pollution. California, whose smog and traffic-clogged freeways were notorious, led the way with an exhaust-emission control law in 1965. This statute became the basis for a federal requirement as part of several Motor Vehicle Safety Standards established in 1967. Critics now charged that uncontrolled pandering to the desires of the American motorist was bringing blight and ruin to city and country alike, wastefully consuming precious resources, and endlessly proliferating superhighways, parking lots, junkyards, noise, and noxious fumes. It remained to be seen, however, whether the safety and antipollution campaigns would have much effect upon the nation's sustained love affair with its automobiles. As of 1970, the auto was still levying an annual toll of fifty thousand lives, millions of injuries, hundreds of millions of dollars in damages, and, many thought, imperiling the quality and viability of American life.[13]

THE AGE OF CHEMICALS.   Another major development of this period was the growth of the chemical industry and its spawning of new and related industries. With sales estimated at $58 billion in 1970, chemicals and allied products had become "a great, yeasty force at the center of the economy," representing a sizable portion of American industrial output.

Initial impetus came during the First World War as domestic manufacturers and the federal government, cut off from German supplies, began large-scale production of organic chemicals, dyes, and nitrogen. American producers, benefiting from tariff protection and confiscated German patents, turned out a product worth $3.2 billion by 1929 and nearly $4 billion ten years later. They had thus far concentrated upon products like rayon and organic chemicals for industrial, farm, and medicinal uses. But the manufacture of nylon, a synthetic yarn derived chemically from coal, air, and water, by Du Pont in 1939 heralded a new chemical age. The industry grew enormously, employing nearly 900,000 workers and adding over $27

[13]Urban planners insisted that unrestricted use of the automobile was bringing paralysis and decay to the central core of every American city. Experiments in one-way streets, fringe parking, downtown malls for pedestrians only, tax relief and other subsidies for commuter railroads, and new rapid transit projects were among the remedies being tried after midcentury. But such efforts had little apparent effect upon the chronic, stifling traffic snarls in most metropolitan areas.

billion in value by manufacture in 1969. Volume of production had increased elevenfold since 1939. Much of this growth stemmed from the rapid rise of a whole complex of new industries—plastics, synthetic rubber, synthetic fibers, detergents, drugs, insecticides—built upon chemical processes and production.

ELECTRICITY AND ELECTRONICS.   The great increase in the output of electric power after 1940 was a prime force in the new technological revolution. Two relatively new industries—appliances and electronics—vitalized the economy after midcentury as the automobile industry had done in the twenties, and affected American life as profoundly. A host of new appliances—air conditioners, electric blankets, dehumidifiers, automatic washing machines and clothes dryers, home freezers, dishwashers, waste disposal units, power lawn mowers, and many others—came on the market after 1945 in an unending stream.[14] Equally startling was the meteoric rise of the electronics industry. Taken all in all, electronics was undoubtedly the most important technological development of the age. The industry produced mainly radios and communications equipment during the thirties, and its product value barely exceeded $500 million in 1939. Revolutionary advances during and after the war culminated in a product value of nearly $15 billion by 1969.

One prime mover in the electronics field was television, which became one of the fastest-growing industries of the postwar era. Production increased from 7,000 sets in 1947 to 6 million in 1952 and remained at that level throughout the fifties and sixties. By 1971 American homes contained over 63 million black-and-white and 27 million color television sets, or about three for every two families. Television stations grew from 10 in 1946 to 673 in 1969; television revenues increased from $658,000 to $2.8 billion.

Even more significant was the development of the electronic computer, which ushered in a radical new phase of the technological revolution. A mere 200 computers were in use in the United States in 1954, an estimated 100,000 by 1970. Sales of computer and data-processing equipment to industry set new records for twenty straight years, topping $7.8 billion in 1969.

A growing array of complex new devices and systems amplified the computer's effectiveness. As its capabilities increased, the tasks that lent themselves to "computerization" multiplied. Only a few can be mentioned here. In manufacturing, computers could be employed in the mak-

---

[14] By 1971, nearly 64 million American homes (99.8 percent) had electric refrigerators; 59 million (92 percent) had automatic washing machines; 28.6 million (45 percent) had clothes dryers; 26 million (40 percent) had air conditioners; 20 million (31 percent) had home freezers; 17 million (26.5 percent) had dishwashers; and 16.3 million (25.5 percent) had food waste units. Annual sales of power lawn mowers rose from 2.7 million in 1955 to over 5.5 million in the late sixties.

ing of consumer goods like food and clothing, the fabrication and assembly of heavy industrial equipment, and the processing of chemical products. They could be used in cost accounting, market research, production scheduling, test grading, hospital diagnosis, legal research, criminal identification, and engineering designs. Train, highway, and air traffic were capable of direction and control by electronic systems. The electric utility, oil, steel, metals, and publishing industries began using computers for everything from monitoring operations at power stations to measuring oil well pressure and flow, from processing and evaluating research data to preparing bills and printing books.[15]

AEROSPACE.   Rapid technological change also made possible man's nearly complete conquest of the air. Larger and faster piston-engined planes contributed to a steady increase in air travel after 1945, but the big advance came with the successful adaptation of the jet engine to commercial aircraft in 1958. The sleek jetliners soon dominated the industry and flew travelers at speeds averaging three and four times faster than the best achievements of the prewar carriers. Advances in electronics enabled pilots to fly as easily at night as in daytime and to land safely even when the ceiling was zero. Air travel at home and overseas became commonplace, posing an almost fatal threat to passenger trains and ocean liners. In 1970, some forty-seven scheduled air carriers flew routes at home and abroad totaling 436,000 miles, carried 169 million passengers a total of 131 billion miles, employed over 300,000 persons, and collected $8.5 billion in revenues.

At the same time, the exploding electronics industry pushed man's frontiers into outer space, developed rockets and missiles of incredible speed and complexity, took Americans to the moon in 1969 (see pp. 908–910), and gave rise to another major new industry: aerospace. The aerospace companies, makers of commercial and military aircraft, missiles, rockets, and all manner of space vehicles and equipment, grew in size and scope at an almost inconceivable rate. First topping the $1 billion mark in sales in 1948, aerospace became a giant in the sixties: "the largest and most technically complex manufacturing industry in the United States," surpassing $30 billion in sales in 1968 and employing over 1 million persons, nearly half of whom were engineers and scientists.

NEW FUELS.   The period also recorded a greatly increased use of fuel oils and natural gas. While residential consumption of coal declined from

---

[15]An "electronic arm" was demonstrated in Massachusetts in 1968. An above-the-elbow amputee could literally "think" his artificial limb into action: when the brain ordered the arm muscles to contract, the arm stump generated electrical impulses which were sent through tiny electronic components. These in turn drove an electric motor that manipulated the artificial limb and its double-hook hand. The whole mechanism was contained in a fiberglass casing that looked like a normal arm.

85 million tons in 1940 to less than 13 million in 1969, the value of fuel oil sold to home and business users increased from $125.9 million in 1939 to over $3 billion in 1967. The value of natural gas consumed in homes, offices, and factories increased from $872 million in 1940 to nearly $10.8 billion in 1969; the number of users rose from 10 million to 41 million. The demand for natural gas greatly stimulated the construction of pipelines and transformed the gas utilities industry into a giant after 1945. It had assets of over $43 billion in 1969, an increase since 1940 of 800 percent, and utilized nearly 900,000 miles of gas mains and pipelines.

5. Concentration and Competition in the American Economy

It would little profit a democratic society if economic growth were accompanied by inexorable concentration of wealth and ownership in fewer and fewer hands. Did capitalism inevitably tend toward monopoly, restricted production at high prices, and centralization of economic and political power? An older trend toward concentration, stimulated by the great merger movement of the twenties, had virtually ceased during the depression decade. It is more difficult to generalize about this subject after 1940. The return of prosperity brought a marked renewal of concentration and merger activity, yet a substantial degree of competition was maintained in many areas.

We have already noted that in agriculture, traditionally the most competitive sector, the number of marginal and smaller units shrank rapidly after midcentury. The lion's share of agricultural profits, meanwhile, went to a small number of well-entrenched, highly mechanized commercial farms.[16] The successful farmer, operating through a complex network of cooperative associations that corresponded in purpose and function to the corporation, had become a modern businessman; his "rugged individualism" had disappeared.[17]

Manufacturing is more complicated and difficult to describe. In general,

[16]In 1969, more than 36 percent of the nation's farms had annual sales of less than $2,500 each; the aggregate gross income for all these units was $2.5 billion, or 4.5 percent of the national total. Another 30 percent of all farms (800,000 units) each had annual sales of between $2,500 and $10,000; the aggregate gross income for these units was $4.8 billion, or 8.5 percent of the national total. In sum, the bottom two-thirds of the nation's farms accounted for 13 percent of national gross farm income. The top one-fifth—those with annual sales exceeding $20,000—had an aggregate gross income of more than $40 billion, or 71 percent of the national total.

[17]Some 7,800 farm marketing and supply cooperatives, with total membership of 6.4 million, did an estimated business of $17 billion in 1969. There were also hundreds of land bank associations, rural credit unions and electric cooperatives, mutual irrigation companies, dairy-herd improvement associations, and other organizations.

it can be said that there was no clear trend toward greater market concentration in American industry after 1940. Among manufacturers of producer goods—items sold to other manufacturers or to service industries—the trend was toward less rather than more concentration, while the reverse held true in the consumer goods industries.[18] Although there were thirty-three industries in 1966 in which the top four firms produced 75 percent or more of the total output, this high level of concentration represented only 9 percent of all manufacturing industries and 14 percent of the value of shipments. In fully two-thirds of the 382 industries classified by the census in 1966, the share of output controlled by the top four firms was less than 50 percent. Nor did domination by a small number of large concerns necessarily mean an absence of competition. Even in the merger-filled sixties it remained true, as one expert concluded, that "the great bulk of manufacturing is carried on in industries which are quite competitively structured."[19]

The same was true, by and large, of the service and distributive trades, which accounted for one-fourth of the total national income and were generally more competitive than manufacturing industries. Yet there were some important exceptions. In the hotel and retail food businesses, for example, a few large chains absorbed many smaller rivals and exercised increasing dominance. And the number of mergers in services and trades rose even more rapidly than in manufacturing.

Moreover, a new and portentous movement toward greater *aggregate* concentration took shape after 1950, as more and more assets fell into the hands of a few giant corporations. In 1909, after the burst of merger activity at the turn of the century, the one hundred largest manufacturing concerns controlled about 18 percent of all manufacturing assets in the United States. In 1929, after the merger movement of the twenties, the one hundred largest firms controlled nearly 40 percent of such assets. This figure remained unchanged between 1929 and 1947, as depression and greater antitrust efforts halted centralizing tendencies. But a new merger movement developed after the war, picked up speed in the fifties, and accelerated so sharply in the sixties that it surpassed even the heyday of the late twenties.[20]

The share of manufacturing assets held by the 100 largest companies increased accordingly, from 39.3 percent in 1947 to almost 50 percent in

---

[18]Of 81 consumer goods industries, the share produced by the top 4 firms between 1948 and 1966 registered an increase in 47 industries, remained about the same in 16, and decreased in 18. Of 131 producer goods industries, on the other hand, concentration increased in 41, remained the same in 31, and decreased in 60. Of the 18 producer goods industries with the highest concentration (including such items as computers, aircraft engines, transformers, explosives, and copper), 13 showed a decline in market concentration between 1947 and 1963.

[19]Willard F. Mueller, *A Primer on Monopoly and Competition* (New York, 1970), pp. 35–36.

[20]This trend is illustrated in the table on the following page.

Period	No. of Concerns Absorbed by Larger Companies	Period	No. of Concerns Absorbed by Larger Companies
1920–1924	2,235	1945–1949	1,505
1925–1929	4,853	1950–1954	1,424
1930–1934	1,687	1955–1959	3,365
1935–1939	577	1960–1964	4,366
1940–1944	906	1965–1969	8,213

1970; the share held by the 200 largest rose from 47.2 percent to over 60 percent.[21] To put it another way, there were about 203,000 manufacturing corporations in the United States in 1970, of which 609, or three-tenths of 1 percent, each had assets exceeding $100 million. These supercorporations controlled 75 percent of all manufacturing assets and made 82 percent of all net profits. And the 102 giants at the very top of this pyramid—those with assets of $1 billion or more—controlled 48 percent of such assets and made 53 percent of the net profits.

As corporations assumed such mammoth dimensions, two familiar devices—interlocking directorates and corporate joint ventures—enjoyed a resurgence. Using figures reminiscent of Louis Brandeis and the Pujo Committee fifty years earlier, a congressional staff report in 1965 showed that the 20 largest industrial companies in the United States had officer and director interlocks with 498 other industrial corporations, 235 financial institutions, 95 insurance companies, and 32 other firms.[22] The joint venture, in which two "parent" companies set up a new aggregation, became increasingly popular. Since many "parents" produced identical or related products, joint ventures often represented a union of direct competitors.

The concentration movement also involved banking, reversing a fifty-year trend toward lessened control by banks over nonfinancial businesses. More and more corporations and other institutions established pension funds after 1945. Typically placed in trust with commercial banks, these funds grew from $25 billion in 1955 to over $100 billion in 1967. Such banks, their holdings further swelled by assets of individuals and estates, managed investments with a total market value of $250 billion in 1967. Nearly two-thirds of this huge sum was invested in corporate stocks, and most of it was held by 49 of the 3,100 banks that had trust departments. These 49 banks, individually, held 5 percent or more of the stock—enough

[21]In 1967, these 200 giants accounted for 30 percent of all manufacturing employees, 40 percent of manufacturing payrolls, 43 percent of total value of shipments, and 51 percent of new capital expenditures. In the period 1948–1968 the top 200 corporations acquired some 3,864 other companies with total assets exceeding $50 billion.

[22]For example, General Motors was interlocked with 63 companies with combined assets of over $65 billion; the 89 companies interlocked with United States Steel had combined assets exceeding $100 billion.

to exercise a commanding voice—in 5,270 corporations. And they acted as sole trustee for about 80 percent of the funds they managed. They affirmed their interest by placing directors on 6,591 other corporate boards in 1967.[23]

Another concentrative device that brought back memories of J. P. Morgan and Samuel Insull—the holding company—also flourished in the sixties. Banks as well as railroads experimented with it. Although most banks were prohibited from entering manufacturing, insurance, and other nonbanking fields, no such restriction applied to holding companies. So-called one-bank holding companies (prevented by law from controlling more than a single bank) were formed to make varied acquisitions. In the period 1967-1969, 34 of the 100 largest commercial banks, with total deposits exceeding $100 billion, formed holding companies and invested in railroads, insurance, mutual funds, hospitals, and manufacturing. Predictions were difficult for so recent a trend, but the potential for concentration was high because of the vast financial resources of the banks. Several major railroads also formed holding companies to acquire diversified holdings.

This reflected a larger phenomenon that gave the merger movement of the sixties a distinctive and perplexing cast: the so-called conglomerate. Prior to midcentury, most mergers had been either horizontal (firms engaged in the same activity) or vertical (firms with a buyer-seller relationship). As the postwar movement gained momentum, these conventional types were overshadowed by combinations involving companies that had no such connection. Conglomerates were of three varieties, merging either firms that produced the same commodity but sold it in different markets, firms that produced similar but not competitive items (such as a detergent and a bleach), or firms in totally unconnected fields. One of the largest of the new conglomerate giants was International Telephone & Telegraph, which acquired 120 diverse businesses with combined assets of over $2 billion in the sixties and had, by 1968, some 150 affiliates in 57 countries.

A few figures suggest the growing predominance of the conglomerate form. Whereas only 37 percent of the more than 800 industrial mergers in the period 1948-1951 were conglomerates, they constituted 89 percent of the 2,500 industrial mergers recorded in 1968. The ultimate effect remained unclear, but a well-planned conglomerate enterprise possessed huge advantages—the ability to mobilize resources and obtain advertising discounts, reciprocal buying and selling opportunities, and so on—over competitors confined to a single activity.

---

[23]The Morgan Guaranty Trust Company of New York held 5 percent or more of the stock of 270 companies with total assets of over $100 billion and had interlocking directorships with 233 companies. Morgan Guaranty Trust and Chase Manhattan brought an entire industry under the shadow of centralized control: between them, these two huge New York banks held 5 percent or more of the stock of the seven largest American airlines.

Despite the variety and scope of these new concentrative elements, recent history suggested that countervailing forces would continue to aid in preserving a measure of competition. To begin with, statistics indicated that the imperatives of modern technology—research, innovation, economies of scale, and the like—were *not* working inexorably, in and of themselves, in the direction of monopoly or excessive concentration.[24] Expansion, too, seemed to have a salutary effect: the fastest-growing industries in the period 1947-1966 tended to experience decreases rather than increases in concentration.

Most important, the federal government continued to play a vital role. Transformed after 1929 into the most powerful economic force in the nation, the government took control of the money supply and interest rates out of the hands of private bankers. It emerged as the single greatest spender, with decisive influence over contracts and prices. It entered the capital markets through the Reconstruction Finance Corporation, the Export-Import Bank, and other agencies. It broke the aluminum monopoly and destroyed the utility holding company empires, assumed a large share of responsibility for industrial research, and became a producer of electricity, synthetic rubber, and atomic energy. It encouraged business enterprise through tax depreciation and depletion allowances and other forms of subsidy.

In addition, the antitrust campaign launched by the Roosevelt administration in 1938 (see Vol. I, p. 410) was followed by a major shift in judicial opinion concerning restraint of trade. The Supreme Court had ruled, in a series of decisions from 1911 to 1927, that a corporation was not illegal under the Sherman law merely because it was large. This doctrine gave way in 1945 when Justice Learned Hand of the Court of Appeals delivered a verdict in *United States* v. *Aluminum Company of America*.[25] The government had asked for Alcoa's dissolution on the grounds that the company, because it controlled 90 percent of the production of bar aluminum and had used illegal methods to maintain this control, was ipso facto a monopoly. Affirming the allegations of unfair trade practices, Hand defined Alcoa as a monopoly because its market preponderance gave it the benefits of a monopoly.

The Supreme Court rendered an even more significant decision in *American Tobacco Company* v. *United States* in 1946. The antitrust division had brought suit in 1940 against the American, R. J. Reynolds, and Liggett & Myers tobacco companies, alleging that they had conspired to control the price of leaf tobacco and cigarettes. The government proved

---

[24]For a persuasively argued contrary view, see John K. Galbraith, *The New Industrial State* (Boston, 1967).

[25]The Supreme Court had failed to obtain a quorum to hear the case and allowed Justice Hand to render the decision.

that identical prices had been paid and charged but failed to prove conspiracy. The justices, sustaining the lower court's conviction, brushed aside the companies' pleas that they had not conspired and declared that the crime of monopoly lay as much in *possession* of power to suppress competition and fix prices as in *commission* of illegal acts. Collusion, the court added, did not have to be proved if it could be reasonably inferred from market conditions.

The decision in the *Tobacco* case finally conferred a power antitrust officials had sought since Taft's administration—namely, the ability to strike at oligopolies as well as monopolies. Washington now possessed effective recourse against the most common oligopolistic practice, collusion to maintain prices. The government also scored a legal triumph in the successful culmination of its long battle against another instrument for the elimination of price competition, the basing-point system.[26]

Congress took a hand in 1950 with the passage of the Celler-Kefauver Act, which plugged an old loophole in the Clayton law by prohibiting the purchase of the assets of one corporation by another when such purchase *might* lessen competition or *tended* to create a monopoly. Government could now take action against mergers before, rather than after, competition had actually been restricted, if a threat seemed to exist. Thus strengthened, the antitrust division and Federal Trade Commission issued over two hundred merger complaints in the period 1950–1966 and challenged some eight hundred mergers, with especial attention to those involving the largest corporations.

Though antitrust fervor declined in the fifties, the Eisenhower administration did maintain some momentum. The Justice Department had instituted over five hundred suits under the Sherman Act in the decade 1939–1948 (more than during the entire preceding forty-eight-year history of the law). It brought over four hundred suits during the fifties, together with fifty-two more under the Clayton Act, and won some notable victories. It blocked the merger of the Bethlehem Steel and Youngstown Sheet & Tube companies and brought twenty-nine manufacturers of electrical equipment to trial in 1960 for conspiring to rig prices, forcing them to plead no contest.[27] The FTC also remained active, particularly in battling against deceptive advertising, although it tended to condone policies that had been condemned earlier as restraints of trade.

---

[26]This system, invalidated by the Supreme Court in a series of decisions from 1945 to 1948, involved adding freight charges from a certain base point to the place where the sale was made, regardless of where the product was manufactured. A good example was the "Pittsburgh plus" system of determining the price of steel products. Buyers of steel in Chicago had to pay freight charges from Pittsburgh, even though the shipment had actually been produced in nearby Gary, Indiana.

[27]Seven vice-presidents of General Electric, Westinghouse, and other concerns went to jail for short terms in 1961. The defendants paid over $1.9 million in fines and reportedly paid treble damages exceeding $500 million.

Antitrust activity increased somewhat in the sixties. The Justice Department brought nearly four hundred and fifty suits under the Sherman and Clayton acts in the period 1960–1966. The FTC expanded its efforts, initiating some seven hundred antimonopoly cases and enlarging its campaign against deceptive advertising. In the interests of equity, harmony, and clarity, antitrust officials encouraged voluntary compliance and adopted guidance and industrywide enforcement programs in an effort to remove the ambiguities and discriminatory features of a case-by-case approach. The Justice Department applied the Sherman Act to a vital new industry in 1969 by charging the International Business Machines Corporation with attempting to monopolize the digital computer market.

The Supreme Court continued to adhere to the Alcoa doctrine of 1945, namely, that possession of power to control the market could be as illegal as the actual exercise of that power. A landmark decision reinforcing this doctrine was *United States* v. *E. I. Du Pont de Nemours & Company*, 1957. Du Pont had purchased 23 percent of the stock of the General Motors Corporation in 1917. The court, in compelling Du Pont to part with its GM shares, laid down three propositions of far-reaching import. It applied the antitrust laws to vertical mergers, required the government to prove only that mergers foreclosed a "substantial share" of the market, and tied the legality of mergers to conditions prevailing when suit was brought as well as when the merger took place.

Extensive though it was, the government's writ ran less clearly in the burgeoning, ill-defined realm of the conglomerate. Public policy remained hesitant during the sixties, although judicial opinion twice found existing statutes relevant to conglomerate practices. The Supreme Court ruled in 1965 that the Consolidated Foods Corporation had violated the Clayton Act in acquiring another firm because the takeover resulted in a reciprocal selling advantage, which the Court termed "an irrelevant and alien factor intruding . . . into the choice among competing products." And in 1967 it ruled that Procter & Gamble's acquisition of the Clorox Chemical Company had violated the Celler-Kefauver Act, again because the new conglomerate's advantages threatened the competitive structure of the liquid bleach industry.

Governmental response to the need for further guidelines began in 1969. The FTC required large corporations to report full details of projected mergers at least sixty days prior to their consummation, including enough information to permit an assessment of possible effects on competition. Congress studied ways of tightening the tax laws as a deterrent to excessive merger activity. And finally, both House and Senate antitrust committees initiated hearings on conglomerate mergers in order to determine whether new legislation was necessary. Many experts believed that the challenge to competition posed by the current merger movement demanded not merely vigilant antitrust activity but a far higher level of public awareness and support.

6. *Organized Labor in the Postwar Era*

The years after 1945 were a time of tumult, change, and challenge for American labor. They were also a time of achievement and growth as unions finally won security and equality of bargaining power, while membership rose from 14.6 million in 1945 to over 18 million a decade later. Strong unions became firmly established in all major fields of manufacturing, mining, transportation, and construction.

The struggle to secure these advances began at once. Labor entered the postwar era in a testy mood—resentful of a stabilization program that had supposedly deprived workers of deserved pay raises, fearful of inflation and large-scale unemployment during reconversion, and determined to hold and enlarge wartime gains. A wave of strikes began soon after the Japanese surrender. Nearly 2 million workers in various industries were out simultaneously by January 1946—including 180,000 electrical workers, 200,000 auto workers, and 750,000 steelworkers all demanding a 30 percent wage increase. In contrast to the mid-thirties, these postwar strikes were mild affairs; both sides eschewed violence and appealed to the public for support. When presidential fact-finding boards recommended wage increases of 19½¢ an hour, General Motors and the steel and electrical companies compromised on 18½¢, thereby setting the pattern for most other agreements.

Meanwhile, bigger eruptions began to occur in the coal and railroad industries. John L. Lewis, president of the United Mine Workers, demanded not only the 18½¢ increase but also a number of fringe benefits. When the operators refused, miners throughout the country left the pits in April 1946, and the government seized the mines soon afterward. Lewis achieved most of his goals in the ensuing settlement, but in October he demanded shorter hours and another wage increase and threatened a second strike. Negotiations failed and the miners struck, returning to work after a federal judge convicted Lewis and his union of contempt in December for defying a temporary injunction. Yet Lewis won a new contract conceding all his demands when the mines were returned to their owners in June 1947.

The country also faced a nationwide rail strike, called by the Engineers and Trainmen after lengthy negotiations over wages and work rules had failed. The president seized the railroads on May 17, 1946, and offered a compromise settlement that most unions accepted. The Engineers and Trainmen, however, would not yield, and walked out on May 23. With total paralysis imminent, President Truman asked Congress on May 25 for drastic, almost dictatorial, power after the strikers had ignored his appeal.[28] Union leaders gave in at the last minute, and the crisis ended.

---

[28]Specifically, Truman requested the power to declare a state of emergency whenever a strike imperiling the national safety occurred in a vital industry under federal control. Workers who persisted in striking would lose all employment and seniority benefits and would be drafted into

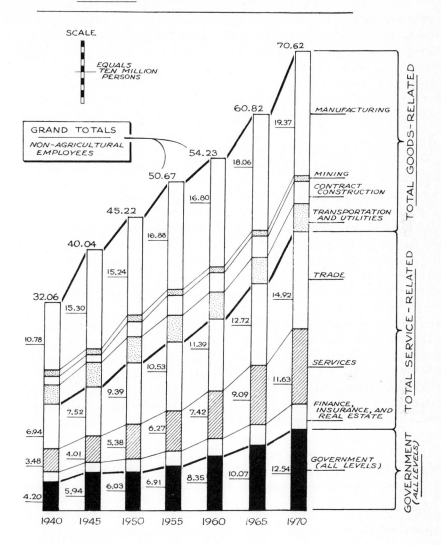

NON-AGRICULTURAL EMPLOYEES BY OCCUPATION *(MILLIONS OF PERSONS)* 1940-1970

SCALE

EQUALS TEN MILLION PERSONS

GRAND TOTALS
NON-AGRICULTURAL EMPLOYEES

TOTAL GOODS-RELATED

MANUFACTURING

MINING
CONTRACT CONSTRUCTION
TRANSPORTATION AND UTILITIES

TOTAL SERVICE-RELATED

TRADE

SERVICES

FINANCE, INSURANCE, AND REAL ESTATE

GOVERNMENT (ALL LEVELS)

70.62
60.82   19.37
54.23   18.06
50.67   16.80
45.22   16.88
40.04   15.24
32.06   15.30
10.78
           14.92
           12.72
11.39
10.53
9.39
7.52
           11.63
6.94   9.09
5.38
4.01   7.42
3.48
6.27
4.20   5.94   6.03   6.91   8.35   10.07   12.54

1940   1945   1950   1955   1960   1965   1970

Labor and management squared off again in the autumn of 1946, price increases having wiped out the previous year's wage gains. There were many small strikes but no big ones; most unions tried persuasion and appeals to public opinion. Negotiations tended to be protracted but not

the army, while union leaders faced fine and imprisonment. The House approved a measure embodying these demands, but the Senate refused to act once the danger had passed.

bitter. The break came in April 1947, when the automobile and steel companies set the pattern by conceding a 15¢ raise. These peaceful settlements marked a turning point. Other rounds of wage increases occurred, but management was willing to grant raises so long as they could be passed on to consumers in the form of higher prices. The number of workers involved in strikes declined from a high of 4.6 million in 1946 to 1.9 million in 1948. And with returning peace came a new spirit of mutual accommodation and epochal innovations in collective bargaining contracts.[29]

The Korean War stimulated further wage demands and a new wave of strikes. Congress made a gesture toward stabilization in August 1950 with the Defense Production Act empowering the president to establish price and wage controls. But the president's authority was so circumscribed that his stabilization boards could do little more than oversee and approve price and wage increases. Truman himself moved boldly, seizing the steel plants in April 1952 in order to avert a nationwide steel strike. He withdrew in June when the Supreme Court ruled the seizure illegal in the absence of statutory authority, and a fifty-four-day strike followed.

Although labor enhanced its power and became an established institution after 1945, it also lost heavily in popular support. Labor leaders themselves were primarily responsible for this. Undemocratic procedures, refusal to accept responsibility for fulfillment of contracts, efforts to break the wartime stabilization program, and failure to move decisively against featherbedding and racketeering all contributed to a change in public sentiment. Big labor, irresponsible and uncontrolled, now seemed as grave a problem as uncontrolled and irresponsible big business.

This new sentiment was reflected in Congress, where a coalition of conservative Democrats and Republicans drafted legislation designed to curb labor's power and rectify the alleged imbalance in labor's favor that

---

[29] A contract between General Motors and the United Auto Workers in 1948 contained two of the most important innovations: the escalator clause, providing for a revision of wage rates every three months according to a schedule based upon the price index; and the annual improvement provision, calling for 2 to 2.5 percent annual wage increases so as to give workers the benefit of increases in productivity.

The breakthrough for welfare provisions came in 1949 when the steelworkers won pensions and health insurance in lieu of a wage increase. By 1969 more than 29 million workers were covered by pension plans to supplement the Social Security system, and perhaps as many enjoyed the benefits of medical and life insurance purchased by their employers.

Another milestone was reached in 1955, when the UAW signed contracts with the auto, farm machinery, and aircraft manufacturers providing for a guaranteed annual wage (or supplementary unemployment benefits, as the device came to be called). It provided for company payments to its unemployed workers, in sufficient amount, when added to state unemployment compensation, to guarantee those workers a fixed percentage of their normal annual wage. The steel, rubber, aluminum, and maritime workers obtained supplementary unemployment benefits on the UAW model in 1957.

had been established by the Wagner Act.[30] They moved quickly to revise the New Deal statute when their strength was augmented by the Republican sweep in the elections of 1946. The Hartley bill, approved by the House in April 1947, was sweeping, severe, and vindictive—an obvious effort to break the labor movement. Antilabor forces in the Senate, led by Robert A. Taft of Ohio, were also determined to reduce union power, but they could not win approval for their most ambitious objectives, notably the prohibition of industry-wide bargaining.

The Taft-Hartley, or labor-management relations, bill of June 1947 represented a compromise. It outlawed the closed shop and certain "unfair" union practices—namely, refusal to bargain in good faith, secondary boycotts, jurisdictional strikes, exaction of pay for work not performed, and the like. It permitted employers to sue unions for breach of contract, petition the National Labor Relations Board for elections to determine the bargaining agents, and speak out during organizational campaigns. It provided for "cooling-off" periods and use of the injunction by the president in strikes imperiling the national health or safety. Finally, it required unions to submit annual financial reports to the secretary of labor, forbade union contributions to political parties, and prohibited certification of unions until their officers had filed affidavits that they were not Communists.

The Taft-Hartley Act engendered fierce controversy and dire predictions that appear unwarranted in retrospect. Labor leaders denounced the measure and fought vainly for over twenty years to effect its repeal. President Truman, in his unsuccessful veto message on June 20, 1947, declared that the act contained "seeds of discord which would plague this nation for years to come." And yet, although experts later found fault with its emergency provisions, no succeeding Congress could be persuaded to repeal or weaken the law. The public obviously wanted to retain a firm statutory check on organized labor. Union power did not in fact diminish after 1947, and management generally displayed a more cooperative attitude than before.

Labor's biggest achievement in the fifties was the merger of the American Federation of Labor and the Congress of Industrial Organizations into a single federation. Ably guided by the two new presidents, dynamic Walter P. Reuther of the CIO and burly, tenacious George Meany, who had succeeded the late William Green as AFL president in 1952, a joint unity

---

[30]Although Truman vetoed a bill in 1946 outlawing secondary boycotts and union interference with interstate commerce and allowing employers to sue unions for breach of contract, he did approve measures in 1946–1947 to outlaw a number of allegedly unfair union practices involving featherbedding and racketeering. More than thirty states enacted laws in 1947 prohibiting secondary boycotts, jurisdictional strikes, and strikes in vital industries.

committee announced full agreement in early 1955. AFL and CIO executive bodies quickly ratified the proposed new constitution, and both memberships gave overwhelming endorsement at their December conventions. The AFL-CIO came officially into being in December 1955, with Meany as president and Reuther as vice-president. Nearly 90 percent of America's 17.8 million organized workers were now members of a single, massive federation.

Labor moved ahead confidently. Unions obtained new rounds of moderate wage increases. The adoption of pension plans, paid vacations, and other fringe benefits proceeded apace. On the whole, labor and management met at the bargaining table in a mutual spirit of restraint, accommodation, and good will. Recurrent strikes still excited public attention, but most disputes were settled by negotiation, mediation, and arbitration. The AFL-CIO stepped up its political pressure for broader social security coverage, a higher minimum wage, more public housing, and related issues, and could point to legislative progress in many areas (see pp. 748–749).

Despite these gains, a variety of problems beset organized labor after midcentury. The most notorious was that of corruption, fraud, and dishonesty in the affairs of certain unions. Swollen membership, high wages, the union shop, and growing pension funds created opportunities for illegality, and a few union leaders succumbed to these temptations. Racketeers and other criminal elements had long been involved with vulnerable bodies like the International Longshoremen's Association. Labor leaders tried to reform or expel the racket-ridden unions, and the AFL-CIO intensified these efforts after the merger. But success in some areas was matched by failure in others, and the government soon took active notice. A Senate committee under the chairmanship of John L. McClellan of Arkansas began lengthy investigations into union affairs in 1957. A sordid tale of malfeasance, crime, violence, and questionable practices emerged from the reams of testimony.

The McClellan committee's most shocking disclosures involved the International Brotherhood of Teamsters, the nation's largest and strongest union. High Teamster officials, it was revealed, had indulged systematically in misuse of union funds, rigged elections, extortion, association with racketeers, and acts of terrorism and violence. Teamster president David Beck, deeply implicated, finally had to resign in the face of indictment and ultimate conviction upon charges of tax evasion and grand larceny. He was succeeded in December 1957 by his brash, tough-minded lieutenant, James R. Hoffa. When the AFL-CIO voted to oust the Teamsters, Hoffa welcomed the rupture and boasted that his union possessed the power to break the AFL-CIO and become the dominant American labor organization.

Public anger reinforced congressional desire for remedial legislation. The attempt to frame a bill that would correct real abuses, however, became entangled with larger questions. The elections of 1958 injected the issue into politics. Conservatives sought to combine an anticorruption bill with broader antilabor provisions, while liberals opposed any such expansion of the issue. The only measure that survived partisan wrangling to become law in 1958—the Douglas-Kennedy-Ives Act, requiring detailed disclosure of employee welfare and pension plans—was inadequate. Congress took another year to produce a stronger bill that majorities in both houses could accept: the Labor-Management Reporting and Disclosure, or Landrum-Griffin, Act of September 1959. Its anticorruption provisions were accompanied by a broadening of the Taft-Hartley Act's boycott and picketing clauses.[31]

Labor also experienced a halt in the twenty-year growth trend in union membership. The number of organized workers had increased, under the spur of New Deal legislation and wartime prosperity, from 3.7 million in 1935 to almost 15 million in 1945. Thereafter, membership expanded slowly but steadily to a peak of 18.5 million in 1956. By 1958, however, the figure had declined to around 18 million, where it hovered for ten years. The great period of expansion had ended.

Prosperity and technology were largely responsible for this. To be sure, traditional antiunion sentiment in the South impeded progress there. But even in industries and areas where unions were well entrenched, nonunion workers now showed less interest in joining—chiefly because the higher wages and increased benefits won by unions since 1940 had perforce been extended to unorganized workers as well. Of even greater import was the steady shift in the American labor force from blue-collar to white-collar occupations, where the task of unionization was harder. While new clerical and professional jobs multiplied in the expanding sectors of trade, finance, and government, technological advances sharply reduced the number of unskilled and semiskilled workers in manufacturing, mining, and transport.[32]

---

[31] The Landrum-Griffin Act extended the definition of a secondary boycott, which the Taft-Hartley Act had outlawed, to include coercing an employer to prevent his doing business with another employer. It also defined picketing against a company where another union was lawfully recognized as an unfair labor practice and allowed the states to assume jurisdiction when the NLRB refused to act in a labor dispute.

The anticorruption provisions sought to safeguard democratic procedures in union elections, subjected union officials found guilty of misusing funds to fine and imprisonment, made forcible interference with members' rights a federal crime, and prohibited certain types of criminal offenders from holding union office for five years after their release from prison.

[32] A few figures will reveal the extent of these changes. In 1940 over 48 percent of the nonfarm labor force was in the blue-collar category (exclusive of service workers, who formed an additional 14 percent), while not quite 38 percent were white-collar. By 1970 the blue-collar percentage had dwindled to 37, service workers constituted 13 percent, while fully half of the nonfarm workers had white-collar occupations.

Labor, while approving the greater efficiency and lessened drudgery that automation and mechanization made possible, felt that the too-rapid spread of such devices worked undue hardship upon employees whose jobs were thereby affected. As these concerns grew, questions of work rules and featherbedding[33] joined wages and fringe benefits as key items in labor disputes. Management claimed the right to cut labor costs by installing automative devices as it saw fit, while unions demanded job protection and employer responsibility for relocating and retraining displaced workers.[34]

One of the largest and costliest strikes in American history—the great steel strike of 1959—was fought over the issue of work rules. The dispute grew out of protracted negotiations between the companies and the United Steelworkers over a new wage contract. Management, seeking to avoid another round of increases, denied labor's claim that profits were high enough to afford the proposed advance without raising prices. Before a compromise could be reached, the companies demanded modification of existing work rules, and union resistance stiffened; wages were negotiable, but work rules were not. When talks broke down completely in July, 500,000 workers, in factories producing 85 percent of the nation's steel, banked furnaces and walked out.

Subsequent efforts to break the impasse were in vain. Neither side would budge, and the strike became a vast endurance contest, which, though unmarred by the violence that had attended the historic steel struggles of 1892, 1919, and 1937, was nevertheless waged with equal determination and even greater persistence. The entire economy began to feel the effects as steel supplies dwindled to zero by the end of the summer. Industries dependent on steel had to cut back production and lay off some 250,000 workers.

As the strike moved into its fourth month, public concern and economic

---

[33] *Work rules* has to do with defining, grading, and classifying all jobs in a given plant, a matter over which unions wish full jurisdiction so as to protect members from arbitrary layoffs. *Featherbedding* is the term for maintaining workers on the payroll, at union insistence, even after their jobs have been or could be eliminated.

[34] Automation had its greatest impact in mining and transport. Mechanical processes revolutionized—and saved—the American coal industry after 1940. Despite the challenge of rival fuels, coal was able to retain a substantial share of the market by drastically cutting production costs, especially payrolls. The figures are dramatic: while coal production increased from 512 million tons in 1940 to 571 million tons in 1969, or 10 percent, the number of miners decreased from 530,000 to 144,000, or nearly 73 percent. Output per man-hour had increased 250 percent.

Automation also affected longshoremen and transport workers. Huge box cargo containers that could be transferred from ship to truck or train without breaking bulk effected vast savings in time and labor costs at dockside. Technological advances enabled the railroads to carry 10 percent more traffic in 1969 than in 1945 with 60 percent fewer employees; the carriers eliminated over 800,000 jobs in that twenty-five-year period without decreasing their aggregate carrying capacity.

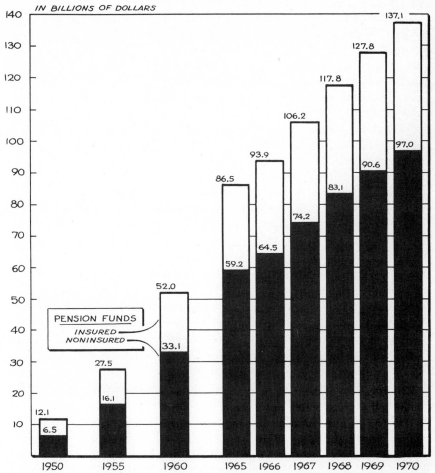

CORPORATE PENSION FUNDS
1950-1970

BOOK VALUE OF ASSETS AT END OF YEAR

IN BILLIONS OF DOLLARS

PENSION FUNDS
INSURED
NONINSURED

stagnation made governmental action imperative.[35] President Eisenhower invoked the emergency provisions of the Taft-Hartley Act on October 9. When a presidential board reported ten days later that it could find no

[35] All attempts at persuasion had failed. The Department of Labor published a report showing that both wages and prices in the steel industry had risen more since 1945 than in most sectors; labor and management each hailed this as supporting its position. Eisenhower pleaded for "intensive, uninterrupted, good faith bargaining," offered to name a nongovernmental fact-finding board if both sides requested it (the companies refused), and conferred separately with union and industry spokesmen at the White House to get them to renew the talks. They did so on October 2, but to no avail.

basis for a settlement, Eisenhower ordered the Department of Justice to seek an eighty-day injunction against the union. The district court in Pittsburgh issued one on October 20 and the Supreme Court sustained it on November 7, 1959.

The steelworkers returned to the plants, but the dispute had not been settled. While the economy slowly recovered, the union announced its intention to resume the strike when the injunction expired. This expiration date neared with the two sides still far from agreement, and only a last-minute intervention by Vice-President Nixon and Secretary of Labor James P. Mitchell averted a resumption. Nixon persuaded the reluctant steel companies that a second strike would only result in an enforced governmental settlement and stringent legislation pleasing to no one. The companies came to terms in January 1960 and acceded to most of the union's demands. In addition to raising wages and pension and insurance payments, the industry agreed to maintain existing work rules and cooperate in establishing joint committees under neutral chairmen to study human relations and work conditions.

Work rules and job protection remained major issues in collective bargaining during the sixties. More and more contracts featured innovations and programs designed to cushion the impact of technological unemployment.[36] Seeking a constructive role for government, President Kennedy appointed an advisory committee on labor-management policy in 1961. It termed automation and technological advance essential but stipulated that such gains had to be achieved without sacrifice of human values and that governmental as well as private action would be necessary. In line with these recommendations, the Manpower Development and Retraining Act of March 1962 established a three-year program, based on federal expenditures of $435 million and matching state funds, to assess manpower needs and help fill them by retraining unemployed or underemployed workers. Over 118,000 persons were enrolled in training programs under this act by 1966.

The government found itself even more directly involved when work-rules negotiations in the railroad industry broke down. Nowhere else was this problem more acute. The railway unions, with thousands of jobs already eliminated and thousands more threatened, were determined to protect their membership against further layoffs. Yet management, with dwindling profit margins in the face of effective competition by rival modes, saw labor-saving devices as the key to survival. After midcentury

[36]Working closely with management, the auto workers, steelworkers, and meat cutters blazed new trails and widened old ones in the search for greater job security. Some contracts enlarged existing supplementary unemployment benefits. Others embodied "technological adjustment pay"; work-spreading devices such as shorter work weeks, sabbatical vacations, and early retirement programs; protection against reduced earnings in the event of plant shutdowns; transfer assistance plans; and, in one steel company, an arrangement for distributing a portion of automation-induced savings among employees.

the dispute centered on the size of train crews and particularly on the jobs of some forty thousand railway firemen, whom the companies claimed were no longer needed now that steam locomotives had given way to diesels. The brotherhoods fought all proposals that would eliminate firemen's jobs or reduce the size of train crews from standards set decades before.

Over twenty years of controversy ensued, punctuated by strikes and strike threats, deadlocked negotiations, lawsuits, and innumerable governmental efforts to produce agreement. Yet not all the king's horses nor all the king's men—neither court decisions, emergency legislation, pressure and cajolery from four consecutive presidents, nor endless panels of expert mediators and arbitrators—proved able to resolve the question.

An arbitration board in 1963 tried to establish the principle of attrition, whereby unnecessary jobs would be abolished as incumbents died, retired, quit, or were discharged for cause. The courts upheld this award in 1964; by 1966 the railroads had eliminated some eighteen thousand firemen's jobs and reached similar attrition agreements with many nonoperating railway unions. Yet the dispute persisted. The Firemen's Union, as soon as the two-year arbitration award of 1964 expired, brought pressure upon the roads to cease eliminating these jobs; lawsuits and strikes forced some lines to comply, and many firemen's positions were restored in the late sixties. The United Transportation Union (UTU), formed in 1969 by a merger of four of the five operating brotherhoods, continued to press the firemen's claim. A new round of emergency actions in 1970 averted a rail tieup but failed to produce agreement. Although carriers and unions reached accord on a few disputed work rules in 1971, the question of train-crew size remained as insoluble as that of the firemen.

For labor as a whole, changing economic conditions in the mid-sixties shifted the emphasis back to wages and fringe benefits. From 1961 to 1965, with prices relatively stable and unemployment high, unions worried more about job protection. Thereafter, an expanding war in Vietnam combined with other inflationary pressures to drive prices upward while unemployment declined to the lowest levels in fifteen years. Wage demands grew more aggressive immediately.

The Kennedy administration, anxious to hold inflation down, had sought to curb the wage-price spiral by setting so-called guideposts for industry and labor to follow in negotiating contracts. On the theory that wage increases would not be inflationary if they did not exceed the general rate of increase in industrial productivity, the government estimated the latter figure at 3 percent and set the guidepost there. For a time it seemed to work: wage increases averaged close to 3 percent from 1962 to 1965.

But exceptions to the guidepost, however much a higher wage boost might be justified for a particular industry, proved contagious; one union was rarely content with a 3 percent raise when another secured 4 or 5 percent. Management tended to pass these larger increases along to the consumer. Thus set in motion, the upward spiral moved with a vengeance after 1965 despite appeals and warnings from Washington. The guidepost became a shambles. Average first-year wage-and-benefit increases reached 4.8 percent in 1966, 5.6 percent in 1967, 7.2 percent in 1968, 10.9 percent in 1969, and 13.2 percent in 1970. Prices more than kept pace—real wages declined slightly from 1966 to 1970—while labor, management, and government exchanged angry accusations.

Growing stubbornness at the bargaining table resulted in the highest number of strikes since the turbulent period right after the Second World War.[37] This new militance did not improve labor's public image. Many Americans, perhaps unfairly, tended to blame inflation on alleged union greed, while urban dwellers increasingly resented the inconvenience and disruption that attended many strikes.

The years following the merger, in fact, had been a disappointment for organized labor. Contrary to optimistic predictions, the AFL-CIO had lost rather than gained momentum in its efforts to recruit new members, organize new industries, and eliminate corruption and racial discrimination within unions.[38] Union membership fell slightly during the decade 1954–1964, despite a 15 percent increase in the civilian labor force. Whereas one nonfarm worker in three belonged to a union in 1954, this ratio had declined by 1968 to barely one in four. Corruption remained a

[37]The following table shows changes in the incidence of industrial unrest in the United States during the years 1945–1970.

Period	Work Stoppages (Annual Average)	Workers Involved (Annual Average)	Man-Days of Idleness (Annual Average)
1945–1953	4,500	3,000,000	47,000,000
1954–1960	3,700	1,800,000	30,340,000
1961–1965	3,600	1,360,000	19,000,000
1966–1970	5,100	2,600,000	45,000,000

[38]The AFL-CIO battled hard against racial discrimination. Its constitution contained an outright ban, and it consistently supported federal civil rights legislation and state fair employment laws. Backed by court decisions and clauses in the Taft-Hartley, Landrum-Griffin, and 1964 Civil Rights acts, all of which brought unions under more prohibitions against discriminatory practices, labor could justly claim that much progress had been made. Yet many locals remained entrenched strongholds of prejudice, resisting all efforts of national leaders to require fairer treatment and easier access for nonwhite workers.

Statistics are incomplete and inconclusive. The Equal Employment Opportunity Commission released figures in 1971 showing that among some 3,500 reporting unions, with a total membership of 2.6 million, the percentage of blacks was 9.2—heavily concentrated, however, in the laborers' and service unions and a few old standbys such as the Steelworkers, Meat Cutters, and Bricklayers. Most of the railway and building trades unions contained a negligible number of nonwhites.

problem, notably among Teamster and Mine Worker leadership.[39] Critics accused labor's high command of complacency, drift, and unimaginative policies; Walter Reuther became so dissatisfied with what he regarded as conservative and inadequate leadership that he and his United Auto Workers withdrew from the AFL-CIO altogether in 1968.[40] While democracy in many unions gained ground under the protective clauses of the Landrum-Griffin Act, the results were hardly millennial. "A candid appraisal compels the conclusion that the rank and file has contributed to most of the widely condemned union shortcomings: racial discrimination, excessive wage demands, featherbedding, and—in many instances—irresponsible strikes."[41]

Yet labor did make some important gains during the sixties. One new procedure that won at least partial acceptance was so-called multiunion or coalition bargaining, whereby all the unions involved with a given corporation or industry negotiated as a bloc. Management had several objections to this concept, which also ran the risk of invalidation as contrary to existing law. But labor had long resented the bargaining advantages held by big multiplant corporations in negotiating piecemeal with each union that had members on its payroll. The AFL-CIO formed a Collective Bargaining Committee in 1965 in an effort to coordinate union negotiations.

Their prime target was the General Electric Company, long noted for its alleged paternalistic and unyielding approach to collective bargaining. Labor won a partial victory in 1966 when the International Union of Electrical Workers, which represented some 90,000 of GE's 150,000 unionized employees, negotiated its GE wage contract in collaboration with ten other unions. But White House mediators, seeking to avert a strike, had induced this settlement, and a real showdown over coalition bargaining had to await negotiation of the next three-year contract in 1969.

The result was one of the hardest-fought strikes in recent history. The company, true to established policy, presented what it called a "full, fair and final" offer and stuck to it without budging. Labor's Collective Bar-

[39]After years of litigation, the controversial Hoffa went to prison in 1967, convicted of tampering with jury members and misusing union funds. The unchastened Teamsters enthusiastically re-elected him in 1966 *after* his conviction, establishing a special new office of general vice-president and electing Hoffa's close confederate, Frank Fitzsimmons, to this post so that leadership and policy would remain unchanged after Hoffa went to prison. He virtually ran the union from his cell for the balance of the decade.

Violence and scandal also rocked the United Mine Workers, beginning with the brutal murder of Joseph Yablonski and his family in 1970 shortly after he had suffered defeat in a close contest with W. A. (Tony) Boyle for presidency of the union. Boyle, whom Yablonski had charged with corruption during their battle for leadership, was ousted in 1971 as trustee of the UMW's Welfare Fund and convicted in 1972 on thirteen counts of conspiracy and illegal use of union funds.

[40]The UAW and the Teamsters, America's two largest unions, formed the Alliance for Labor Action in 1969 and spoke confidently of new organizing campaigns, but their impetus was badly weakened by Reuther's tragic death in an airplane crash in Michigan in May 1970.

[41]Derek C. Bok and John T. Dunlop, "How Trade Union Policy Is Made," *Monthly Labor Review* (February 1970), p. 18.

gaining Committee, meanwhile, kept the various unions and locals informed and coordinated at every stage. The strike began in October 1969, with George Meany promising that the "GE strikers will have every bit of support they need from the entire AFL-CIO until the hour of victory." Victory did not come until spring, after months of walking wintry picket lines in dozens of plants across the nation. The strike was reinforced by a nationwide boycott of GE products proclaimed by the AFL-CIO in November. Notwithstanding the company's massive publicity campaign, the unions held their ranks intact and finally won most of their demands after federal mediators entered the picture in January 1970 and helped produce a settlement. Multiunion bargaining had scored a de facto triumph.

Even more important, labor began making progress in areas hitherto on the periphery of union activity. White-collar workers, traditionally hostile or indifferent to unionization, showed new interest in the sixties as inflation and automation pinched harder. Not more than one-eighth of American white-collar workers were union members in 1970, but the percentage was growing, especially among trade and service employees.

Another breakthrough occurred in 1968 when AFL-CIO efforts made headway in a campaign to win better conditions, higher pay, and union recognition for the agricultural workers in California's grape, vegetable, and citrus regions. After years of negotiations, strikes, boycotts, and deadlock, Cesar Chavez's United Farm Workers won wage increases, fringe benefits, grievance procedures, and, ultimately, full recognition from several major producers in 1970-1971.

Labor's most dramatic gains occurred in the public sector. Resentful of lagging wage levels and reactionary or sluggish official responses, government workers stepped up their demands and sought progress through organization. Executive orders from Presidents Kennedy in 1962 and Nixon in 1969 encouraged unionization among federal employees and established procedures and guidelines. By 1970, moreover, some thirty-eight states had sanctioned the right of public workers to organize and bargain collectively. Thus encouraged, government employees joined unions at a rapid rate. While union membership in the private sector increased by about 5 percent between 1960 and 1968, the number of unionized public workers doubled, surpassing 2 million.[42]

This upsurge took place at all levels and in all areas of public employment: among United States postal workers and government clerks, school teachers and other state employees, and the entire range of municipal services, including fire fighters, policemen, and sanitation, hospital, transit, and utility workers. Moreover, public employees, emboldened by the suc-

---

[42]Federal workers were 50 percent unionized by 1970, state and local workers about 10 percent. The latter figure, however, does not include the large membership of professional bodies like the National Education Association and the American Nurses Association, which began behaving more and more like unions during the sixties. The adherence or cooperation of professionals who had hitherto scorned union membership promised to give the labor movement a new scope and thrust.

cesses of other groups and catching the spirit of the times, resorted increasingly to the militant tactics of confrontation, demonstration, slowdown, and—despite federal and state laws and hallowed traditions to the contrary—outright strikes. Some public unions, notably New York City's aggressive Transit Workers, had resorted to strikes in the forties. Such activity declined markedly after midcentury but began to crop up with growing frequency after 1964.[43] Highlighted by a thirty-six-day teachers' strike in New York City and a dramatic strike and mass march by underpaid Memphis sanitation workers in 1968, the trend culminated in an unprecedented phenomenon: a strike by the postal workers' unions against the federal government itself in 1970.[44]

Organized labor had clearly found new frontiers on which to recapture its momentum. It remained to be seen, however, whether the hoped-for gains—new members, revitalized leadership, fairer compensation, and better conditions for hitherto neglected groups—would outweigh the negative consequences feared by many: more inflation, higher taxes, increasing disruption of public services, and a crescendo of militancy, disorder, and mutual distrust.

7. Americans and Their "Mixed" Economy After Midcentury

What sort of definition best suits this modern American economy? Neither a socialistic pattern nor the terms of conventional capitalism can be made to fit. In actuality, it was neither capitalistic nor socialistic, competitive nor monopolistic. It was a "mixed" economy, a combination of various elements. Manufacturers, bankers, and businessmen still retained control over many major decisions. Yet their control was restrained or shared by other bodies—federal and state governments, labor unions, farm groups, and organized consumers. It was indubitably a "free" economy, yet hardly in the traditional sense; a variety of public and private organizations, rather than the market, set prices on many items. Labor and management, often assisted by government, jointly determined policies concerning wages and hours. America was not a welfare state in the European sense,

[43]Whereas in 1958 there were only 15 government work stoppages involving 1,720 workers and 7,500 man-days of idleness, in 1968 there were 254 such stoppages involving over 200,000 workers and 2.5 million man-days of idleness.

[44]Though laws against strikes by public employees remained on the statute books, actual enforcement against thousands of striking workers proved more difficult than settlement of the disputes—usually after negotiations and along lines barely distinguishable from practices in private industry. President Nixon put troops to work sorting and distributing mail in New York City during the postal strike of 1970, but the government came to terms with the postal workers in April—granting across-the-board and retroactive wage increases, faster movement up the salary scale, and collective bargaining rights (with impasses to be resolved by binding arbitration rather than by strikes). The Post Office was reorganized as a public corporation in an effort to increase efficiency and reduce costs.

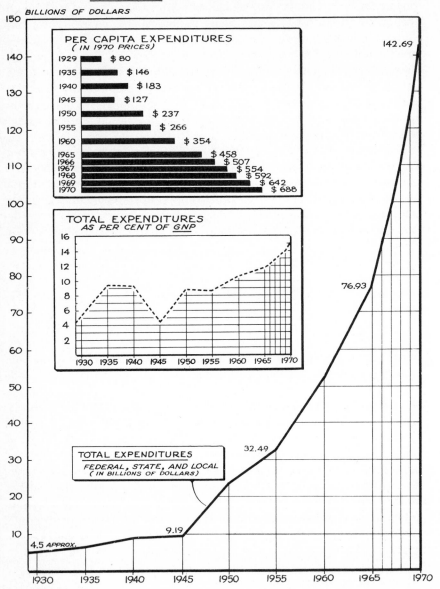

A HALF CENTURY OF
PUBLIC WELFARE *(FISCAL YEARS)*

BILLIONS OF DOLLARS

PER CAPITA EXPENDITURES
(IN 1970 PRICES)

1929	$ 80
1935	$ 146
1940	$ 183
1945	$ 127
1950	$ 237
1955	$ 266
1960	$ 354
1965	$ 458
1966	$ 507
1967	$ 554
1968	$ 592
1969	$ 642
1970	$ 688

TOTAL EXPENDITURES
AS PER CENT OF GNP

TOTAL EXPENDITURES
*FEDERAL, STATE, AND LOCAL
(IN BILLIONS OF DOLLARS)*

142.69

76.93

32.49

9.19

4.5 APPROX.

yet it sponsored far-reaching programs of social security and assistance to the poor.

In brief, New Deal reforms and other changes wrought by depression and war had transformed a monolithic economic order dominated by business-financial elements into a virtually new structure of what one economist called great countervailing forces—industry, finance, labor, agriculture—each struggling for a larger share of the national income, each appealing to the political power. Americans might not understand all its subtleties, but most regarded their complex system as far superior to the one that had prevailed before 1929.

In the sixties, however, the system came under sharp and growing critical scrutiny. Many charged that preoccupation with economic growth and material goods had created gross inequities and imbalances, and that emphasis upon quantitative expansion and a bigger GNP was not merely slighting but positively endangering the quality of life. Much of this concern reflected a new awareness of environmental problems, which we shall examine in later chapters (see pp. 854-855, 910-913). Others held that the accelerating pace of change demanded a reordering of many cherished economic assumptions and values; such, in part, was the message of Peter Drucker in *The Age of Discontinuity* (1968) and Alvin Toffler in *Future Shock* (1970).

Some writers, including several on the so-called New Left, were so alienated by an allegedly unjust and oppressive capitalist system that they stressed denunciation at the expense of objectivity or dispassionate analysis. But not all radicals could be so easily dismissed. One of the most thoughtful was Michael Harrington, who did much to awaken the public to the persistence of poverty amidst general affluence in *The Other America* (1962). In *The Accidental Century* (1965) and *Socialism* (1972), Harrington advocated a form of democratic socialism as the only way of arresting what he regarded as a decadent and ruinous system of planlessly exploiting technology in the interest of private profit.

Prominent economists like Robert L. Heilbroner and John K. Galbraith were only slightly less concerned. Heilbroner, in *The Limits of American Capitalism* (1965), wondered whether problems arising from the inequitable distribution of wealth could be properly solved while business values remained dominant. He predicted that the imperatives of science and technology would eventually erode capitalist values just as emergent capitalism had undermined the feudal system centuries before. And in the revised edition of *The Affluent Society* (1969), Galbraith deplored the emphasis upon private production and called for new expenditures and comprehensive planning in such relatively "starved" sectors as education, housing, and other public services, together with a new approach to questions of money, taxation, work, and leisure.

It became apparent by 1970 that behind or beside the articulate critics marched a growing number of other Americans, representing every economic, political, and social stratum, who had come to feel that the system was not working as well as it ought. Exactly what sort of new directions might emerge from the welter of criticism and vague discontent remained in doubt. But the pace of change virtually precluded the possibility that the mixed economy of the fifties and sixties could withstand substantial revision in years to come, as we will see in Chapter 34.

24

～～≫≫✿≪≪～～

Social and Cultural Trends,

1940–1970

$\mathbf{T}$he American people underwent a bewildering variety of experiences in the three decades after 1940—total war and limited wars, global responsibility marked by recurrent international crises and overhung with the threat of nuclear holocaust, and a steadily expanding prosperity that made a wider range of goods and services accessible to a higher percentage of the population than human history had ever recorded. This unprecedented affluence, generated by a mammoth industrial system and an exploding technology, appeared to be bringing the American democratic dream to the verge of fulfillment. It also created vast new problems, magnified old ones, jabbed every aspect of life with the persistent, quickening finger of change, and virtually remade American society within a single generation. Some insight into the meaning and scope of this gigantic experience can be gained by exploring a few of its social and cultural ramifications, for each facet in its way reflected the whole.

1. The Affluent Society

Mobility, both geographic and social, had always been a prominent feature of American life, but the period after 1940 made preceding generations seem sluggish by comparison. Never before had so many Americans been so continually and variously on the move. First came the defense and war crises of 1940-1945, dispersing millions of men and women to all corners of the globe and drawing millions of others out of their native communities (and often out of poverty as well) to work in war industries the country over. Veterans redistributed themselves at a rapid pace after 1945 in search of jobs or educational opportunities as the economy swung back into peacetime production. The readjustments, dislocations, and tensions resulting from all of this movement were considerable, but on the whole society withstood the strain remarkably well. And the lingering provincialism that had hitherto survived the processes of urbanization and industrialization now receded into the most remote corners and exercised far less influence on prevailing American attitudes.

Mobility and the tempo of life continued to quicken in the postwar decades. Some 20 percent of the population, on an average, changed their place of residence each year. The dictates of cold war diplomacy and related foreign entanglements made military service, with its attendant uprooting and travel, a normal phase of life for legions of young Americans. Millions of families left the farm during these years, never to return. Millions of impoverished blacks left the rural South for the urban North and West—or, in many instances, for fast-growing southern industrial centers. New opportunities in the electronics, chemical, aerospace, defense, and other industries periodically relocated countless thousands of young executives, engineers, scientists, and technicians; other thousands of housing and highway construction workers followed the busy contractors here and there across a continent whose outstanding symbol had become the bulldozer.

Mobility for millions of Americans, as we have noted, meant moving from the central city to the suburbs. Satellite communities had been multiplying in size and number in the United States ever since horsecars, then trolleys, and finally automobiles had made commuting possible for more and more people. But the great suburban thrust that began after 1945 dwarfed these earlier movements and must surely rank in importance and scope with the westward and urban migrations of the nineteenth century. When the contracting firm of Levitt & Sons demonstrated, first on Long Island and then near Philadelphia around midcentury, that modern mass-production and prefabricating techniques could produce quantities of small one-family homes at a price within the grasp of many blue-collar

A NATION OF CITY DWELLERS, 1970

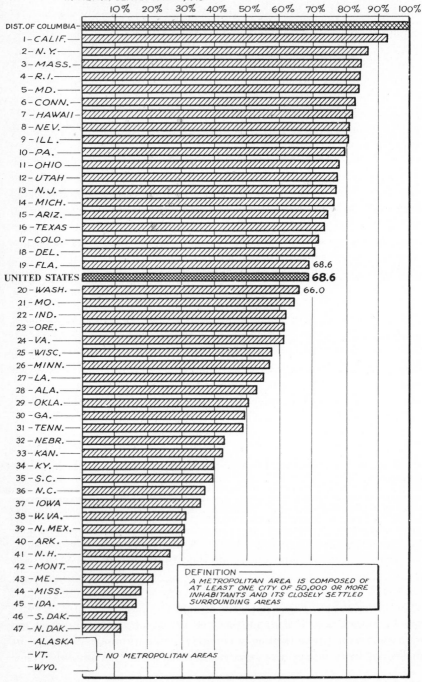

PER CENT OF STATE POPULATION
IN METROPOLITAN AREAS, 1970

10% 20% 30% 40% 50% 60% 70% 80% 90% 100%

DIST. OF COLUMBIA—

1 – CALIF. —

2 – N. Y. —

3 – MASS. —

4 – R. I. —

5 – MD. —

6 – CONN. —

7 – HAWAII —

8 – NEV. —

9 – ILL. —

10 – PA. —

11 – OHIO —

12 – UTAH —

13 – N. J. —

14 – MICH. —

15 – ARIZ. —

16 – TEXAS —

17 – COLO. —

18 – DEL. —

19 – FLA. —   68.6

UNITED STATES   **68.6**

20 – WASH. —   66.0

21 – MO. —

22 – IND. —

23 – ORE. —

24 – VA. —

25 – WISC. —

26 – MINN. —

27 – LA. —

28 – ALA. —

29 – OKLA. —

30 – GA. —

31 – TENN. —

32 – NEBR. —

33 – KAN. —

34 – KY. —

35 – S. C. —

36 – N. C. —

37 – IOWA —

38 – W. VA. —

39 – N. MEX. —

40 – ARK. —

41 – N. H. —

42 – MONT. —

43 – ME. —

44 – MISS. —

45 – IDA. —

46 – S. DAK. —

47 – N. DAK. —

– ALASKA

– VT.   — NO METROPOLITAN AREAS

– WYO.

DEFINITION ——
A METROPOLITAN AREA IS COMPOSED OF
AT LEAST ONE CITY OF 50,000 OR MORE
INHABITANTS AND ITS CLOSELY SETTLED
SURROUNDING AREAS

workers and young married couples, the pattern for a new mass migration had been set. Everywhere along the fringes of cities large communities of single-family homes or garden-apartment developments mushroomed. Older suburbs grew apace. "Levittown" and "megalopolis" passed into the language, and suburbia soon became the dominant version of the American way of life.

It was deceptively easy to stereotype the sprawling postwar suburbs. One image portrayed plush, wealthy, homogeneous communities inhabited by white, Protestant businessmen who lived shallow, sinful lives and commuted to work in gray flannel suits. Another image featured serried ranks of identical housing units each surrounded with its postage-stamp lawn and wire fence and clusters of small children. To many urban intellectuals (and not a few disillusioned suburbanites), life in suburbia seemed to embody a dreary, sterile sameness, rotating endlessly through a materialistic cycle whose chief components were the station wagon, the shopping center, and the television set. Books laying bare the shortcomings of such an existence were widely read during the fifties.

Like most stereotypes, these contained elements of truth. Yet, again like most stereotypes, they oversimplified, distorted, and largely missed the point. To begin with, there was much more diversity both within and among suburban communities, in terms of median income, political affiliation, ethnic and racial composition, and so forth, than the stereotypes suggested. Moreover, neither drawbacks nor criticism could alter the fact that the great majority found real satisfaction in suburbia. Postwar America, coming off a twenty-year drought in residential construction induced by depression and war and with a rampant "baby boom" under way, was starved for housing. Cheaply constructed and barren though many of the suburban tracts might be, the new homes were a distinct improvement over the tenements and other aging urban dwellings from which most suburbanites had moved.

And these eager migrants were seeking not merely new facilities and more space but a sense of proprietorship and community. Here they resembled the westward-moving pioneers of the previous century; as one observer has noted, "the suburban movement replicated the essential American experience by which the dependent Easterner became the free-holding Westerner."[1] Nearly 63 percent of the nation's housing units were owner-occupied in 1970, as compared with less than 44 percent in 1940. The pattern of "voluntary association" that Alexis de Tocqueville had seen as a major ingredient of life in Jacksonian America throve anew in the postwar suburbs. Outlets for social action flourished—neighborhood schools and PTAs, community churches and church groups, junior chambers of commerce and other business associations, local labor unions and

[1] William L. O'Neill, ed., *American Society Since 1945* (Chicago, 1969), p. 18.

professional societies, chapters of fraternal and benevolent orders, community chest and United Fund and other charitable organizations, boy and girl scout troops and Little League baseball, and grass-roots political units that ranged from Young Republicans and Americans for Democratic Action to nonpartisan groups like the League of Women Voters. Whatever its shortcomings, suburban life offered more variety, activity, and fulfillment than hostile urban critics generally realized.

For many Americans, affluence meant not merely a home in the suburbs but more leisure time. Typically, they "went at" leisure with the same fierce energy that characterized their approach to work, home, and community; higher incomes and longer paid vacations for larger numbers of people changed the pattern of life but did not slacken its tempo. Areas and industries that catered to recreational pursuits flourished spectacularly. Each year more visitors jammed national and state parks, forests, campgrounds, and historic spots. European charter flights and guided tours, Caribbean cruises, and cross-country motor trips became relatively commonplace experiences. The great population gains after 1940 in states like New Mexico, Arizona, Colorado, Nevada, California, and Florida were traceable primarily to good climate and a varied assortment of parks, mountain and ski resorts, ocean beaches, and lush night clubs and casinos. Year-round sunshine and warmth made vast, permanent meccas for invalids and retired persons out of California, Florida, and the Southwest—a reflection of the fact that the number of Americans aged sixty-five and over increased from 9 million in 1940 to 20 million in 1970.

The making and servicing of pleasure boats, vacation homes, camping equipment, sporting goods, and hunting and fishing gear became multimillion-dollar businesses. The recording and photographic equipment industries offered a proliferating array of complex equipment to growing numbers of enthusiasts. Makers of food and accessories for America's hordes of dogs, cats, and other pets enjoyed unprecedented profits. The mass search for new diversions brought such hitherto esoteric activities as surfing, scuba and sky diving, and snowmobiling into vogue.

The "average" American family, with a rising income and standard of living, thus faced a bewildering range of choices as to how to allocate its time, energy, and money. The effects of all this abundance and mobility on family life were considerable but difficult to assess. The divorce rate, which had averaged about one-sixth of the marriage rate during the twenties and thirties, rose to an abnormal peak of some 30 percent in 1945 as many hasty wartime marriages dissolved. The ratio of divorce to marriage then dropped to one in four and held quite steady at about that level until the late sixties, when it began a sharp rise that reached an all-time high in 1970 of one divorce for every three marriages. Traditionalists bewailed the prevalence of divorce, but the steadiness of the rate during most of this period—though admittedly high by prewar standards—suggests that the family structure was not fatally imperiled, and that a new belief in the wisdom of dissolving unhappy marriages had come to prevail over moral and religious sanctions.

In any event, family life was subject to many new stresses and influences. An increasingly automated and sophisticated economic system meant, among other things, a sharp and continued decrease in the kinds of unskilled and semiskilled job opportunities that had formerly absorbed much of the teenage population. As a result, a large and growing subculture of relatively affluent, relatively idle, and often restless young people had emerged by midcentury. Teenagers tended to seek their own heroes, fads, life-styles, and forms of diversion; the frictions thus generated both within families and in society at large were marked.

Another factor that altered older social and family patterns in a variety of subtle ways after 1940 was a steady rise in the number and percentage of women at work. Over 14 million women, constituting 25 percent of the civilian labor force, were employed in 1940; thirty years later these figures had risen to 31.5 million and 37.5 percent.[2] The sharpest increase, moreover, took place among married women. Of the female population aged fourteen and over, the percentage with jobs rose from 27 in 1940 to nearly 43 in 1970. Whereas the percentage of single women with jobs rose from 48 to 53 and that of widows and divorcees from 32 to 36 during those years, the percentage of working married women shot up from 14.7, or one in seven, to almost 41, or two out of five.

Nor was this startling increase confined to new brides and older women whose children had grown up. Of the 20 million American families in 1950 with a "male head" (to use the census terminology) and one or more children under eighteen, some 18 percent, or 3.6 million, had working mothers. Of 25.4 million such families in 1970, fully 40 percent, or over 10 million, included working mothers. Women's attitudes toward marriage, the home, and their place in society could not help but be affected by this growing fund of experience in the labor force; the eagerness with which many of them had accepted traditional roles as full-time housewives and mothers of big families in the immediate postwar years was subject to steady erosion.

Growing affluence engendered a variety of social attitudes and moods. An uneasy but widespread complacency marked the 1950s, and some of it,

---

[2] There were big increases in the number of working women in nearly every category of nonagricultural employment. Between 1950 and 1970 the number of women professional and technical workers rose from 1.1 million to 4.3 million; of clerical and salesworkers, from over 6 million to over 12 million; of serviceworkers, from 3.9 million to 6.4 million; of blue-collar operatives, from 3.3 million to 4.5 million. What these new employees learned about wage and salary differentials between males and females, in every job category, contributed no little to the force behind the Women's Liberation movement of the sixties.

at least, was justified. Both the absolute number and the relative proportion of Americans living in or near poverty were declining rapidly. The nation was making real progress toward the equitable distribution of wealth and achievement of middle-class norms to which it had long aspired. Moreover, this upward-leveling strengthened American egalitarian impulses (at least for a time) and eroded older attitudes and practices toward ethnic, racial, and religious minorities formerly outside the mainstream of social life. A postwar drive to bring democratic practice into line with democratic ideals, drawing upon lessons learned during the depression and Second World War, received direction and support from most leaders in church, school, press, labor, law, and government. It was a many-sided crusade, operating most spectacularly in the troubled area of black-white relations (see pp. 751–753, 757–765).

Although continued flare-ups and ugly recrudescences of racial and other tensions offered persistent reminders that America yet had a long distance to travel, the fact remained that traditional prejudices—against Jews, Catholics, southern and eastern Europeans, Hispanic-Americans, blacks, Indians, Orientals—had declined noticeably in the period after 1940. Both outright bigotry and the quieter, more polite forms of intolerance went on the defensive for the first time and stayed there, with the nation's intellectual leadership forthrightly arrayed against them.

Complacency also had its blinder side. The growing majority of persons who now enjoyed middle-class incomes and suburban homes were often so absorbed in their new way of life that they misread or failed to notice the persistence and growth of certain grave problems. With poverty on the wane, it was rather blithely assumed that this process would continue until virtually everyone had escaped it. Unfortunately, the millions who had not yet done so, or who were hopelessly mired by a lack of the necessary skills and opportunities, tended to be invisible—and silent. Suburban commuters rarely noticed the teeming urban slums; cross-country motorists seldom went near the isolated rural backwaters where squalor reigned supreme. Only a few neglected critics knew the alarming extent to which urban decay and environmental deterioration had kept grim pace with America's economic growth.

Affluence bred complacency on certain subjects but could not dispel, and indeed often exacerbated, a range of other fears and worries. Richer and more powerful by far than ever before, the American people never came close to recapturing the buoyant confidence of earlier years. Realization of what the mushroom clouds over Hiroshima and Nagasaki in 1945 portended for future world conflicts kept a tight rein on optimism. Memories of the Great Depression proved indelible, and most older Americans remained haunted by the fear that their new-found prosperity would be swept away.

Gloom deriving from such sources was pervasive but implicit, lurking covertly on the fringes of the American consciousness.[3] The fears that found most frequent expression during the fifties were of a different sort. Various insecurities having persuaded them that their prosperous system was a fragile and precarious thing, the affluent majority were wont to detect dire menace from enemies within and without. Some of the problems thus decried were real enough, but the reaction was usually out of all proportion to the threat.

Fear of communism and Communist subversion, for example, became virtually a national obsession. Concern over Soviet power and intentions after 1945 helped account for it, but the excesses of the second Red scare are best understood in terms of a chronic American tendency to suspect that their way of life is being subverted by an internal conspiracy of evil-doers. The search for Communists spurred as fierce and sustained an attack on dissent, nonconformity, and civil liberties as the nation had ever experienced (see pp. 667–672, 726–730).

Americans found another menace in organized crime, which flourished in the postwar years and threatened the integrity of many businesses, labor unions, and municipal governments. Criminals and racketeers proved far more active and numerous in the United States than did Communists, although popular notions of the power and wealth of crime syndicates were undoubtedly much exaggerated.[4] The evidence was disquieting enough, to be sure. Senate committees headed by Estes Kefauver of Tennessee and John McClellan of Arkansas investigated criminal activity during the fifties. Disclosures revealed that syndicates, using techniques learned during prohibition, were extending the scope of their operations. Profits from traditional criminal ventures—bootlegging, gambling, narcotics, loan-sharking, "numbers"—were channeled into promising new areas: wartime black markets, liquor and real estate agencies, brokerage firms, vending machines, the garment industry, bakeries, laundries, and several others. Racketeers enlarged their influence in certain labor unions, exploiting both workers and employers by a system of corruption, extortion, and violence (see p. 594). The arrest of some sixty criminal leaders from all over the country at a "gangland meeting" in Appalachin, New York, in 1957 further publicized the extent of the problem.

---

[3] Sometimes, of course, these fears became explicit and overt, as in the agitation over radioactive fallout in the late fifties and the "bomb-shelter scare" that accompanied tense confrontations between the United States and Russia in the early sixties. Talk of depression cropped up with each slight downturn of the economy or the stock market.

[4] Ramsey Clark, in *Crime in America* (New York, 1970), argued persuasively that organized crime was not nearly so powerful or wealthy as most estimates claimed. Assistant attorney general during the Kennedy administration and United States attorney general under Lyndon Johnson, Clark stated flatly that organized crime touched less than one-tenth of 1 percent of American business, and that recent estimates of syndicate income ($26 billion gross, $6–7 billion net) were "exaggerated beyond reason."

An alarmed public responded in several ways. Crime investigations and campaigns to oust corrupt politicians were launched in many cities and states. The federal government, particularly during the tenure of Attorney General Robert F. Kennedy and his successors in the sixties, advocated more stringent crime legislation.[5] A National Crime Commission appointed by President Johnson issued a comprehensive report in 1967.

In that same year the Justice Department, impressed by the cross-purposes, jurisdictional problems, and lack of coordination that attended anticrime effort, developed the concept of the federal strike force. Composed of teams of lawyers and experts from those federal agencies (Customs, Secret Service, Narcotics Bureau, Internal Revenue, Alcohol and Tobacco Tax Division) that dealt with various aspects of criminal activity, a strike force would move into a city where organized crime was established. After investigating and gathering evidence, it would work closely with state and local police and FBI agents in a concerted effort to make arrests and obtain indictments.

The strike forces proved highly successful. Operating in Buffalo, Detroit, Chicago, New York, Miami, Philadelphia, and other centers of organized criminal activity, the forces struck hard and telling blows at the most powerful of the syndicates, the so-called Mafia or La Cosa Nostra. Federal indictments, a negligible 19 in 1960, had risen to nearly 700 by 1964 as Justice Department and FBI agents stepped up their efforts. Strike forces enabled the government to indict over 2,000 criminal suspects in 1967–1968.[6]

Americans also worried a good deal over the growth of juvenile delinquency. Wartime dislocations, overcrowded schools, the rapidly changing character of urban and suburban neighborhoods, racial and ethnic tensions, and fewer unskilled and part-time jobs all contributed to this prob-

---

[5]Congress passed laws in 1961 prohibiting interstate wire services from sending gambling information and forbidding gamblers and illegal narcotics dealers to use the mails and interstate transportation facilities for business purposes. The Omnibus Crime Control and Safe Streets Act of 1968 included a controversial provision that legalized wire-tapping and electronic surveillance under specified conditions. The Organized Crime Act of 1970 added new agents to the FBI for the purpose of obtaining evidence against crime syndicates and contained a variety of other anticrime provisions.

[6]It was during Ramsay Clark's attorney-generalship (1965–1969) that the strike forces were conceived and put into action, and he was so impressed with their efforts that he could pronounce La Cosa Nostra "on the ropes" in 1970. But he added a strong word of caution. Despite improvements in law enforcement procedures, he maintained that organized crime in America would continue to survive as long as the conditions on which it flourished persisted. These included, in Clark's judgment, too many understaffed, underpaid, inadequately trained local police departments and continued crowding of vulnerable and powerless people into slums. Organized crime owed its existence to America's tendency to outlaw certain things that society believed to be morally wrong but wanted anyway—gambling, prostitution, narcotics, money at usurious interest. Enough people wanted these things badly enough as to provide a market that only criminal organizations could supply, and this situation—as the prohibition experience of the twenties could attest—put law enforcement at a hopeless disadvantage.

lem. Teenage gangs roamed the streets, making lurid headlines with their violent pitched battles and assaults on persons and property. The number of youths arrested for such crimes as theft, manslaughter, rape, and even homicide mounted ominously. Crime and vandalism on the part of affluent suburban youngsters also registered increases. With drug addiction among young people also apparently on the rise, anxious observers spoke fearfully of a maladjusted and rebellious generation. As later events would reveal, these were early symptoms of much larger problems that society had not yet really noticed.

Indeed, a later perspective virtually compels the conclusion that society during the fifties spent most of its time looking in the wrong direction for things to worry about. Complacency and the Red scare having combined to reduce dissent to a polite and almost apologetic minimum, criticism too often focused on external enemies or safe targets—Communists, mobsters, (many of whom, it was darkly noted, were of foreign antecedents), delinquent youths. Some critics also attacked Madison Avenue, symbol and headquarters of the advertising industry, for the insidious influence it allegedly exercised upon the American consumer.

From here it was an easy step to the position of asking whether, after all, so much affluence might not be bad for people. Had an excess of materialism produced moral decay? Critics began to speak of a loss of national purpose and weakened or misplaced values. The defection of a few American prisoners to China after the Korean War and the rigging of television quiz shows a few years later were cited as evidence of this. College youths were constantly accused, by older persons and by one another, of apathy. Traditional American individualism and the adventurous spirit that had once subdued a continent had allegedly given way to security-conscious, "other-directed" organization men. The Eisenhower administration was sufficiently moved by this kind of talk to appoint a distinguished Committee on National Goals, to help the nation rediscover where it ought to be going.

2. *The Turbulent Sixties*

Decades provide misleading and artificial benchmarks for measuring social change. Yet few Americans who lived through both the fifties and sixties would deny that the latter were startlingly different; not even the prosperous twenties and depressed thirties afford greater contrasts. The 1960s were so full of contradiction and controversy that the historian, at this close range, despairs of bringing them into balanced perspective in a few short pages. Yet the attempt is worth making. While these years, like all "periods," are part of history's seamless web and reflect a full measure of continuity with what had gone before, nothing in previous American experience offers anything quite like them.

Economic growth and technological change provided continuity between the fifties and the sixties; it was the social responses and adjustments that stood in such striking contrast. The tone of midcentury America was set by the dominant white middle class; other groups were either emulating it, patiently awaiting their chance to, or simply out of sight. A pragmatic "consensus" of social values and assumptions was hailed as a historic, continuing source of the nation's strength. Taken all in all (the ugly, divisive Red scare alone excepted), the fifties were quiet, relatively stable and harmonious, uncritically complacent, and not a little dull.

The sixties were dramatically, almost brutally, the exact opposite. Complacency broke on the rock of problems that could no longer be ignored, while consensus gave way to a crescendo of dissent, diversity, bitter strife, soul-searching criticism, and extravagant nonconformity. White middle-class dominance faced a multiple challenge. Tensions mounted, exploding periodically into violence; malaise grew and spread until it verged upon the prevailing national mood. It was an age of disillusionment and anger and fear, a "slum of a decade," as one social commentator called it. And yet, withal, it was a time of experimentation, new-found commitment, reevaluation, and irrepressible vitality.

No definitive explanation is possible, but two or three contributory factors can be noted. Some credit must go to John F. Kennedy, whose vague but urgent summons to "do for your country" and "get America moving again" touched a responsive chord during and after the 1960 campaign. Kennedy's youth, energy, style, and magnetic personality had an inspirational and galvanic effect.

The changing climate of opinion owed even more to the civil rights movement, which began to gather force during the late fifties (see pp. 757-765). The nation's most inspiring examples of moral commitment and courage in those complacent years were set by dedicated black leaders, and their dedication proved contagious. America's idealism and social conscience were stirred, rekindling an interest in reform. This stirring took place with especial force among college students, whose almost inexhaustible fund of causes in the late sixties began building with this one.

The black community also responded. As black racial pride, hope, frustration, anger, and self-awareness mounted, often finding expression in belligerent demonstrations and riotous outbreaks, society made some important discoveries. The poor were quiet and invisible no longer; the appalling nature and extent of the nation's urban problems began coming into focus at last. Black militance produced a counterreaction among nervous whites, and a consequent increase in racial tensions. But perhaps most importantly, the black man's dawning assertiveness and pride proved contagious too. Groups of every sort—whether their common denominator was ethnic origin, race, religion, sex, or age—became more conscious of their identity, reassessed their status and condition, and confronted the rest of society with new demands.

Television, too, deserves mention. Its impact was varied and incalculable, yet impossible to ignore. The ubiquitous tube, present in nearly every American home by 1960, had a way of bringing today's headline, today's crisis, and today's violence into the living room with inimitable force. Apathy could hardly withstand such exposure; the immediacy and urgency of many of the world's problems were literally brought home to millions by the electronics medium.

Television also brought today's product into the living room, offered with every blandishment an imaginative advertising industry could provide. The affluent consumer society undoubtedly consumed faster as a result; as one observer noted, "the consumer economy depended on advertising, which in turn leaned heavily on the pleasure principle. This had been true for fifty years at least, but not until television did it work really well."[7] Young people, on the other hand, could become variously disillusioned and alienated as they discovered that television programs and commercials offered an image of life that bore little resemblance to reality. And even the poorest of slum homes usually contained a TV set: it was the one glittering, lighted window to a better world that most such homes possessed. Both the "revolution of rising expectations" and the frustrated anger that surged out of the ghettos in the sixties owed much to what poor people knew to be available that they did not have.

Key events contributed their share to the rising social ferment. The note of torment and tragedy that hovers over this tumultuous decade is largely attributable to these events and their repercussions. For it was, as much as anything, an age of violence—harsh, recurrent, often purposeless violence, vicariously experienced as never before by almost everyone.[8] The civil rights movement met murderous resistance here and there in the deep South. Assassins' bullets took the lives of a president, a presidential candidate, a revered black leader, and two or three other figures of national prominence between 1963 and 1968. Destructive ghetto riots erupted in scores of cities in 1965 and after. Crimes like murder, rape, assault, and armed robbery appeared to be rising dangerously. By the end of the decade mob action seemed to have become endemic on college campuses, at political conventions, and in city streets. And finally there was the war in Vietnam—undoubtedly the cause of more unrelieved anguish, turmoil, and bitterness among the American people than any other single event in the nation's history.

[7]William L. O'Neill, *Coming Apart: An Informal History of America in the 1960s* (Chicago, 1971), p. 270.

[8]Millions of viewers, glued to their TV sets in the aftermath of President Kennedy's assassination in November 1963, literally watched a "live" murder when Jack Ruby shot Lee Harvey Oswald, Kennedy's alleged killer, before the cameras as police escorted him from a Dallas jail.

We shall discuss these events more fully later. Of importance here are the cumulative psychic and social wounds inflicted by this parade of violence. When it was joined by other evidence of trouble— decaying urban centers, polluted air and water, dwindling natural resources, rising inflation, ineradicable poverty—a growing number began to question the system that had allowed all of this to happen. Fractured leadership and racial antagonism beset the civil rights movement after 1965. Confidence in the ability of government to cure the nation's ills waned when the Kennedy-Johnson reform programs seemed to have little tangible impact and then became sidetracked by the war (see pp. 855-857).

Disaffection came in all shapes and sizes, increasing visibly in degree and extent during the latter half of the decade and adding greatly to the social strains besetting the American people. A few angry youths, black and white, resorted to extremism and revolutionary action. They demonstrated earnestly and often violently against the war or the police or the establishment or the grievance of the day; the radical fringe among this element occasionally employed dynamite and arson and similar destructive devices.

A more widespread manifestation of dissent was a semirebellious "counterculture" that emerged in the mid-sixties. It was prefigured in the fifties by a handful of bohemians, the so-called beatniks, who consciously rejected "straight" society in favor of allegedly simpler and freer lives and moral standards, seasoned with drugs and dashes of Zen Buddhism. The vogue of folk music among young people in the early sixties was another antecedent phase of the movement. With their two principal nuclei in Manhattan's East Village and the Haight-Ashbury district of San Francisco, the "hippies" or "flower children" groped for a new way of life and displayed their rejection of conventional society in every word and deed. Though never numerous, these devoutly disaffected young people attracted enough notoriety and enough assorted camp-followers and imitators as to impress their habits, style, and outlook upon a large minority of the nation's youth—and especially upon many among that important and growing minority that attended college.

A few of the strands in this varicolored tapestry are worth brief mention, if only to show what the dissidents disliked about the rest of society (and vice versa). In general, they were opposed to materialism, war, the establishment, and "middle-class morality." They emphasized peace, love for one's fellow man, and living closer to nature. They claimed that fewer inhibitions in matters of dress, speech, and morality, together with certain pleasures they had found, offered a degree of liberation and self-discovery unattainable in the overorganized, materialistic modern world.

These pleasures included rock music and the various things that electronics could do to it, several expressive new dances inspired by rock music's infectious beat, multimedia happenings featuring pop art exhibits and strobe lights and rock groups and tape recordings—and, of course, drugs. Many were content to "turn on" with the relatively mild marijuana; others sought the greater experiences and discoveries ostensibly awaiting them with doses of heroin, amphetamines such as methedrine, or psychedelic compounds like lysergic acid diethylamide, popularly known as "acid" or LSD. They pursued their new habits with much abandon, attracted much publicity, and acquainted a fascinated "straight" society with the definition, if not the experience, of turning on, freaking out, tripping, and the rest of the harsh argot of the drug world.

Drugs were only one avenue to the liberation these earnest young people sought. Some of them formed communes and pursued happiness through communal self-sufficiency and rural simplicity.[9] Many were fascinated by mysticism and magic, astrology, witchcraft, and religions (Oriental, Occidental, or primitive) with transcendental or supernatural emphases. In general, the counterculture exhibited a romantic, antirational, intuitive outlook that worried intellectuals (including many who otherwise sympathized with the movement) and a blatant style of dress and deportment that brought numbers of older Americans to the verge of apoplexy.[10]

Reaction actually ranged all the way from cautious emulation through amusement and shock to contempt and panic, but the prevailing response was one of hostility. Many were offended by the repudiation of conventional morality and the calculated fondness for four-letter words and unkempt appearance. The drug problem, now that it had climbed from the ghetto to the middle and upper-middle classes, alarmed nearly everyone—and probably, at the price of numerous domestic tragedies, set in motion a long overdue reevaluation of society's proper posture toward drug use and its treatment. As young people's hatred of a war that seemingly would not end escalated to include a savage indictment of government, business, and America generally, great numbers of citizens who still set store by such things grew deeply resentful.

[9]The communes, like the suburbs whence so many of these discontented young people had come, lent themselves too readily to hostile stereotypes. In actuality, they showed great variety—in size, degree of success and longevity, philosophic underpinning, and manners and customs. Some were consciously religious and enforced strict standards of behavior; some forbade drugs while others encouraged or permitted them; some were havens for sexual freedom and license and others were not. Beyond the fact that the communes represented efforts, however pathetic or half-baked, to escape conventional society and find a better mode of existence, few generalizations would seem to apply.

[10]Like most nonconformist movements, the counterculture developed customs of its own to which adherents slavishly conformed—none more so than in matters of dress. Although the combinations varied, the emphasis was upon faded levis, beads, Indian headbands, bangles, discarded military clothing, fringed buckskin shirts and vests, leather garb, long stringy hair, and (to the extent that sex, age, and natural endowments permitted) sideburns and beards.

Part of the hostility reflected perennial disagreements between youth and age. Another part reflected a certain class antagonism between blue-collar Americans and the more affluent, more fortunately situated middle-class individuals who formed the central element in the counterculture. But in essence, the gulf that yawned across American society in the late sixties was ideological—between a rebellious minority, mostly young and college-educated, who felt that the nation and its values were in dire need of overhaul; and a majority, rather less young and less (or less recently) educated, who felt that the biggest single thing wrong with the nation lay in what this minority had done to it.

This split added to the growing social malaise, but it was not all. The beleaguered majority saw trouble at every turn, and its morale plummeted. Resentment of youthful dissidents was superimposed across a rising fear of black militance, ghetto riots, crime, and the alleged permissiveness that had encouraged it all. Suspicion, alienation, and hostility throve in such an atmosphere. Appeals to "law and order" became a potent political weapon, and a corrosive fear for one's personal safety became an overriding fact of urban life.

Yet other pressures worked to prevent a cohesive, repressive majority from forming on the basis of such fears. Millions who were neither youthful nor rebellious were coming to share the young rebels' sense that environmental deterioration had reached a crisis stage, that credibility and responsiveness in high places were at a discount, and that the war in Vietnam was an abomination that had to end. In short, Americans had seemingly reached a collective state of mind that bordered on despair by 1970. Never before had larger numbers of people been so convinced that things had got out of control, that the problems confronting them had become too big and too complex to solve, and that the very political, economic, and social institutions from which answers ought to be forthcoming had become unresponsive, corrupt, or irrelevant. The solitary human being seemed dwarfed and isolated, his individuality crushed by huge impersonal forces, vast organizations, and a runaway technology. Worried intellectuals spoke in doom-laden tones about a "sick society," and enough people seemed to be agreeing with them as to make it a kind of self-fulfilling prophecy.

It was manifestly impossible, in the face of all that had happened, to answer Cassandra with Pollyanna. And yet the period offered grounds for hope as well as despair. These were also years of enormous vitality and experimentation; the challenges to tradition were not all destructive, extreme, or barren. New styles and variety were the order of the day, including much that was needed and some that was good.

In matters of dress, for example, young innovators did far more than popularize faded blue jeans and bare feet. They also revolutionized the fashion world for women and men in striking and positive ways. In design, color, pattern, fabric, and the ways in which these components were combined, fashions exhibited an unprecedented boldness and variety.[11] Hair styles, reinforced by a new vogue in wigs, displayed a similar range and diversity. Some of the innovations were abortive and some were grotesque, but the overall effect must be adjudged favorably. One of the most significant differences between these and earlier stylistic changes was that the major impetus came from below rather than above; fashion designers on the whole were responding rather than setting the pace, and their former stranglehold upon what was acceptable (and therefore available) was broken.

A comparable phenomenon was evident in the arts. The lines hitherto separating high culture from so-called pop or mass culture were becoming more and more blurred as eager amateurs kept experimenting, often with scant regard for professional canons or training. If the results were frequently deplorable, the uneven quality and debased standards were partly offset by diversity, vitality, and a joyous willingness to innovate. This was the age, as current slang had it, of doing one's own thing.

And it was precisely here that those who searched American society for signs of health and vigor could take heart. If something indefinable and a bit frightening was happening to culture and the arts, the best of it was rather good and a lot of it showed promise. American music, for example, was undeniably enriched by the ways in which rock, soul, country, folk, and rhythm and blues styles were arranged and blended by imaginative writers and performers. Popular singer-composers like Bob Dylan, Paul Simon, and the four young Englishmen who achieved world fame in the mid-sixties as the Beatles displayed real musical talent. Similarly, American art, architecture, and dance (all of which had flourished in the quiet fifties as well) were invigorated by the eclectic, intuitive, personal approach that characterized the times.

The assault on conventional standards made a shambles of the moral codes that had hitherto regulated what was permissible in literature, film, the theater, and places of entertainment. One unfortunate but predictable result was a flood of cheap pornographic books and movies specializing in nudity, sex, perversion, and obscene language. Yet at their best, writers and filmmakers used their new freedom tastefully and explored sensitive themes with realism and frankness. The emphasis upon experimentation resulted not only in blurred standards but also in a conscious, sometimes fruitful search for new techniques and styles. A healthy indirect result of

---

[11]The famous miniskirt was undoubtedly the period's most spectacular offering—but it should be noted that the relaxed standards that permitted such record-breaking public exposure of the female form did not demand public conformity to the new style; for more modest spirits and less youthful or comely forms there were attractive alternatives like the maxi and the pants suit.

Men's clothing styles, which had exhibited a drab sameness and glacial rate of change for decades, were similarly affected. Variety in color, cut, weave, and pattern, once confined to sportswear and other off-duty garb, was applied daringly across the entire range of male attire. Not since the eighteenth century had Western man been able to dress as colorfully or choose as widely.

the new moral freedom was that it enabled society to begin looking at complex subjects like abortion and homosexuality with vision less clouded by preconceptions and shibboleths.

The common denominator beneath all this ferment was a new search for meaning and identity. Many regarded it as both fitting and hopeful that black Americans should blaze the trail toward greater self-awareness and group pride, and that other groups—Indians, Chicanos, Puerto Ricans, ethnic minorities, women, young people—should follow their lead. For what was happening in art, film, music, dance, dress, and language was happening, essentially, as a result of immensely variegated human activity. And what these activists were doing, in the words of one observer, was seeking to "possess one's experience rather than be possessed by it, . . . to live one's own life rather than be lived by it, and [to] drive for a more various selfhood than men have known before."[12]

Many bewailed the seeming breakdown in moral and aesthetic standards and values that accompanied this ferment, often failing to realize that the process had been under way for over half a century and was, even in its excesses, as much an indication of vitality as of decadence. Fearfully or hopefully, but withal consciously, Americans stood on the threshold of a new era in the seventies. Like all new eras, this one would partake more of past traditions and values than either young rebels or frightened conservatives could readily imagine. Yet it seemed likely that the emphases and tone of the years ahead would be different from much that had gone before.

The legacy that this new era would inherit from the sixties was confused and uncertain, but it included some things of essential value. If that restless decade had found few answers, it had learned to ask some of the right questions. It had lost nearly all of its illusions, including many that had served as blinders. It had not merely recognized but put into practice the notion that cultural diversity, unorthodoxy, and the freedom to experiment might be the best keys to psychic survival in a highly industrialized society undergoing rapid change. And at the very center of its restless search was, after all, an abiding concern for individual dignity, freedom, and fulfillment.

3. American Fiction, Drama, and Poetry

The historian can pass no more than tentative judgment on the literary achievements of his own day, yet a few comments about the period after 1940 appear warranted. The quality of American fictional writing did not

[12]Benjamin DeMott, "The Sixties: A Cultural Revolution," *New York Times Magazine* (December 14, 1969), p. 124.

match that of the preceding generation. The Second World War marked the close of a great literary epoch. Young authors seemed less clear of purpose than their predecessors of the twenties and thirties; and the giants of that earlier day, with one or two exceptions, spoke with declining power after 1940.

The one outstanding exception was William Faulkner, whose reputation as America's foremost living novelist was firmly established by 1945 and endured until his death in 1962. In all of his major novels Faulkner probed the meaning of life through a many-sided portrayal of southern society, with its tensions between a meaningful but archaic past and a rapidly changing present, and between the established but often degenerate older families and the rapacious, materialistic instincts of the rising poor whites. Racial antagonism added malign tensions of its own. Readers could not be sure from his earlier novels whether Faulkner was affirming or denying the values of the past. But in the impressive array of later works—*The Hamlet* (1940), *Go Down, Moses* (1942), *Intruder in the Dust* (1948), *Requiem for a Nun* (1951), *A Fable* (1954), *The Town* (1957), and *The Mansion* (1960)—Faulkner's purpose emerged with greater clarity. It was, as he said in accepting the Nobel Prize for literature in 1955, to reaffirm the eternal worth of human beings and the dignity of the human spirit. For all his preoccupation with the bitter antagonisms and dark violence that he saw in southern life, Faulkner insisted that his ultimate message was one of hope. "I believe that man will not merely endure," he said. "He will prevail. He is immortal . . . because he has a soul, a spirit capable of compassion and sacrifice and endurance."

Ernest Hemingway's position as the other undisputed master of American fiction survived, but he did relatively little to sustain it after 1940. Between his triumph with *For Whom the Bell Tolls* in that year and his apparent suicide in 1961, Hemingway produced only two major works. One of these, *Across the River and Into the Trees* (1950), was a disappointment, full of unlikely dialogue, shallow philosophizing, and carping criticism that amounted almost to a parody of his earlier writing. The other was a successful short novel, *The Old Man and the Sea* (1952). In this tale of an aging fisherman adrift in the Gulf Stream, battling for his own survival while he stalked a great fish, the author's force and skill were once more in evidence. And the emphasis, as one critic observed, was again upon "the heroism of the solitary individual, set against a hostile universe, which Hemingway has always celebrated."

The other major voices of the Lost Generation spoke less effectively after 1940. F. Scott Fitzgerald died in that year, a tragic victim of his own disenchantment with American life. Sinclair Lewis survived until 1951, but his later writing never recaptured the quality of his great achievements of the twenties. In his last novels Lewis returned to old themes and took up a new one, racial prejudice; but withal he demonstrated "a continuous decline of powers and an irritable indecision concerning the meaning of what he is doing." John Steinbeck remained competently productive until shortly before his death in 1968, but none of his postwar novels duplicated the power and scope of *The Grapes of Wrath* (1939). John Dos Passos, who lived until 1970, allowed bitterness and an uncritically reactionary viewpoint to warp his work. Hypnotized by the belief that the greatest menace to the individual was no longer heartless capitalism but expanding world communism and its domestic counterpart, the welfare state, Dos Passos gradually lost the power to capture the mood and tempo of twentieth-century America. His second trilogy, *District of Columbia* (1939–1949), though a vivid account of the depression years, was weakened by its distorted treatment of the New Deal. His later novels were undistinguished.

The survivors of the Lost Generation could not lead a literary revival, and the best writing of the postwar years—though much of it was quite good—hardly constituted one. A gifted younger writer, Ross Lockridge, Jr., whose *Raintree County* gave promise of richer development, cut himself off by suicide. Established authors like Robert Penn Warren, J. P. Marquand, and John O'Hara continued to produce readable and often penetrating novels, but blazed no new trails in form, viewpoint, or subject matter. The same was true, essentially, for a talented group of southern writers who maintained the genteel tradition and high literary standards established earlier by Ellen Glasgow, Willa Cather, and Katherine Ann Porter. Among the best postwar writers in this tradition, presenting sensitive, realistic, finely drawn sketches of southern society, were Caroline Gordon, Joan Williams, Carson McCullers, Harper Lee, Eudora Welty, and Reynolds Price.

There was also an outburst of war fiction, including a few books of more than passing interest. Among the best in this category were three probing portrayals of military life in which war formed a backdrop for a study of human relationships among men in uniform: James Gould Cozzens's *Guard of Honor* (1948), James Jones's *From Here to Eternity* (1951), and William Styron's *The Long March* (1953). There were also the neo-Hemingways, to borrow a name—Alfred Hayes, John Horne Burns, Norman Mailer, and Irwin Shaw—who wrote powerfully of war's horrors and brutality. Other young writers, like John Hersey, Herman Wouk, and James Michener, found courage and nobility in the great tragedy. But few of them, whether despairing or hopeful, were able to transcend the quality of their war novels in the years that followed.

The fifties accorded a burst of critical acclaim to James Gould Cozzens and J. D. Salinger, yet neither had much to say thereafter. Cozzens, who began writing in the twenties, achieved recognition with *Guard of Honor* (1948) and fame with his most ambitious novel, *By Love Possessed* (1957). The latter was an elaborate fictional treatise on justification by faith and man's failure to achieve true virtue by ordinary morality. His only additional novel in a decade and a half—*Morning, Noon and Night* (1968)—was less successful. Cozzens, whose values and outlook were uncompromisingly those of conservative white, Anglo-Saxon Protestant America, was no spokesman for the iconoclastic sixties. Salinger, meanwhile, wrote of regaining the purity of childhood through mystical religious experience. He explored this theme, with a masterful rendition of the idiom and thought processes of intelligent but bewildered young people in search of meaning, in *The Catcher in the Rye* (1951) and *Franny and Zooey* (1961). Yet his further output was confined to a few more stories, all written in the fifties, about the same endlessly introspective characters. Salinger, some felt, had been injured by too much early success.

Much postwar writing was vigorous and forceful, but it reflected indecision and a failure to find intellectual or moral bearings. The overriding concern was a familiar one in twentieth-century American literature: the attempt to discover how the isolated individual might survive in an increasingly impersonal and complex society. Perhaps the outstanding difference between most younger novelists and their illustrious predecessors lay in the assumptions with which this problem was approached. The Lost Generation had not avoided—had indeed looked searchingly at—the grimmer and seamier aspects of modern life. It might be fair to observe that they had shed all their illusions save one—an underlying, usually implicit hope that humankind yet retained enough heroic potential not merely to endure, as Faulkner had put it, but to prevail.

It was precisely this hope that many novelists after midcentury seemed to have lost. Moreover, as one critic observed, "the traditional novel depended and still depends on a reliable cosmos, a future, a society with predictable norms of moral response." These assumptions, too, became increasingly harder to make in the postwar years; writers, prefiguring the conscious anxieties of their society by about a decade and a half, began groping uncertainly for new approaches right after the Second World War. The times may have pressed too hard upon this generation of writers, most of whom could neither escape a mounting social concern nor find a way of voicing it that seemed adequate to the enormity of what they felt was happening.

Some moved in the direction of subjectivism and a new way of expressing or identifying the Self; this, at least in part, characterized the efforts of such otherwise dissimilar novelists as John Updike and Norman Mailer. Both were talented writers, yet Updike's brilliant style and sharp wit could not remove the taint of dullness and joylessness that marked the lives of most of his fictional characters; and Mailer often seemed so busy seeking experience in the various roles he liked to play—tormented genius, brash social critic, male sex symbol—that his potential as a novelist was not fully realized.

Others gave vent to their anger or strove to awaken society by propelling their readers along bleak trails into sordid or violent realms. Nelson Algren, for example, wrote viscerally and impressionistically of the underdogs in American society: "the jail and the whorehouse . . . the cockroach, the drunkard, and the pimp." He wrote, Algren himself said, out of "a kind of *irritability* that these people on top should be contented, so absolutely unaware of these other people, and so sure that their values are the right ones." Hubert Selby depicted the hopelessness and horror of life in New York with brutal effectiveness in *Last Exit to Brooklyn* (1964). Flannery O'Connor's haunting stories of the South were peopled by as grotesquely evil and spiritually deformed a set of characters as modern fiction had to offer, while William Burroughs recounted his experiences as a drug addict in *The Naked Lunch* (1959) with a lurid hallucinatory frankness that some found repellent. William Styron, another restless talent, hurled bombastic protest at the accretion of violence in the twentieth century and the way in which continual war had deadened conscience and sensibility. "Contemporary man for Styron," wrote one critic, "is an infinitely corruptible Adam repeatedly violating the terms of his existence, falling farther and farther out of Paradise."

Few leading writers could escape the familiar themes of alienation and isolation. Significantly, in their portrayals of the individual trying to face the world and discover who he is, they tended to find their heroes among the outcasts and misfits of American society: Jews, blacks, Indians, addicts, perverts. Jewish protagonists conducted introspective searches in the novels of Philip Roth, Bernard Malamud, and Saul Bellow. And whether their difficulties stemmed from overprotection, as with the obsessively self-centered hero of Roth's *Portnoy's Complaint* (1969); or from persecution, as with the hero of Malamud's *The Fixer* (1966); or simply from a sense of incommunicable isolation, as in Bellow's *Henderson the Rain King* (1959) and *Herzog* (1964), the characters were usually restless, tormented individuals who could find neither peace nor place in a cruel or indifferent world. A gifted Indian writer, N. Scott Momaday, in *House Made of Dawn* (1966), explored a comparable situation wherein red men struggled vainly to adapt to white standards. Similar themes received attention in the works of black authors like John A. Williams and John Oliver Killens.

The most important and certainly the most revealing new emphasis in American fiction after midcentury—in plot, style, situation, character, and tone—was upon the grotesque and the bizarre, upon horror and insanity, satire, parody, and black comedy. Groping for an approach suitable to their view of the times, many writers developed their stories by supplementing (or replacing) narrative with myth and fable, stream of consciousness, random flashbacks, unfinished letters, hallucinations and epiphanies, a surrealistic mingling of dream and reality. Such novels, as one critic observed, were "essentially plotless—held together by heroes whose anxieties are inexplicable, ambiguous, bizarre and sometimes laced with zest and comic sensuality."

Worth noting among the authors specializing in this unstructured, diverse genre were Ken Kesey, whose characters in *One Flew Over the Cuckoo's Nest* (1962) were inmates of an oppressive and machine-like insane asylum; Joseph Heller, whose hilarious *Catch-22* (1961) parodied the inherent insanity of modern war and modern society; Thomas Pynchon, who skillfully blended reality, fantasy, and farce in a comment upon man's dehumanization and enslavement at the hands of his own contrivances in *V* (1963) and *The Crying of Lot 49* (1965); John Barth, who satirized and probed the human condition by making his hero the offspring of a woman and a computer in *Giles Goat-Boy* (1966); Kurt Vonnegut, Jr., whose *Slaughterhouse Five* (1969) portrayed the terrors of mass destruction with trenchant force and macabre humor; and Joyce Carol Oates and John Hawkes, both of whom displayed a remarkable ability to evoke horror and nightmare in their novels and stories.

If such writing was often too obscure, too confusing, too mordant, or too outspoken for many readers, it yet appeared that the liveliest frontier in postwar American fiction was that of surrealism, satire, burlesque, and comic absurdity. The recurrent theme of insanity served to pose the dilemma of how to determine who was truly sane in an insane world. The emphasis upon social outcasts seemed appropriate enough to those who felt that mankind had become helpless in the face of modern technology; in such a world, Bernard Malamud remarked, "all men are Jews." Or, as Saul Bellow's Herzog put it, "honor or respect formerly reserved for justice, courage, temperance, mercy, may now be earned in the negative by the grotesque." When Ralph Ellison, a gifted black writer, was criticized for the confusing dashes of surrealism in his sensitive novel, *The Invisible Man* (1952), he answered with a comment that may stand as the watchword for an entire generation. "I didn't select the surrealism, the distortion, the intensity, as an experimental technique," Ellison said, "but because reality is surreal."

American fiction seemed to be in a transitional phase as the final third of the century began, with much talent and promise on display but with no outstanding spokesmen or clear sense of direction yet in evidence. American drama showed even fewer indications of having found a voice that could speak convincingly to or for the postwar era. To be sure, the brooding genius of Eugene O'Neill survived into these years. His productivity was slowed by illness, but he completed four plays after 1940—*The Iceman Cometh* (1946), *A Moon for the Misbegotten* (1947), *Long Day's Journey Into Night* (1956), and *A Touch of the Poet* (1957). O'Neill continued his intensive probing of human character, still convinced "that the only subject worth writing about was the eternal tragedy of Man in his glorious, self-destructive struggle." There were many outstanding musicals and light comedies in the forties and fifties, but only three new playwrights of any consequence: William Inge, Arthur Miller, and Tennessee Williams.

William Inge, a master of realistic plot and dialogue, reported the ordinary tragedies and tensions of middle-class life with sympathetic insight. He achieved four notable successes on Broadway with *Come Back, Little Sheba* (1950), *Picnic* (1953), *Bus Stop* (1955), and *The Dark at the Top of the Stairs* (1957). Arthur Miller fully shared the pervasive moral uneasiness of the postwar world and laid bare a variety of social ills. His plays— which included *All My Sons* (1947), *Death of a Salesman* (1949), *The Crucible* (1953), and *A View From the Bridge* (1955)—were eloquent if somewhat strident protests against materialism, dehumanized efficiency, and conformity.

Tennessee Williams, whose skillfully constructed plays established him as one of the most expert dramatists of modern times, both captivated and shocked audiences by liberally infusing his plots with sex and violence. These items were always relevant to his theme, but he showed an increasing tendency to probe to the very depths of human depravity, psychic disorder, and abnormality; some critics came to feel that he had carried his sympathy for the degenerate and the perverted to a repellent extreme. Nevertheless, his plays included many theatrical landmarks: *The Glass Menagerie* (1944), *A Streetcar Named Desire* (1947), *Summer and Smoke* (1948), *The Rose Tattoo* (1950), *Camino Real* (1953), *Cat on a Hot Tin Roof* (1955).

None of these three gifted playwrights, however, was able to carry the quality of his earlier triumphs into the 1960s. Inge's three productions during the period 1959–1966 were a disappointment. Miller explored human failings and searching with great passion and anguish, but not always with convincing dramatic mastery, in *After the Fall* (1964), *Incident at Vichy* (1965), and *The Price* (1968). And Tennessee Williams, after writing four relatively undistinguished plays in the years 1957–1960, achieved one of his greatest triumphs with *Night of the Iguana* (1962)—and then entered a decade of tortured uncertainty and decline. His later plays generated force and power, as always, but so little else as to suggest that Williams's various morbidities and private torments had become a source of weakness rather than strength to his talent as a dramatist.

Indeed, the sixties and seventies were relatively barren years for American drama. A promising young black playwright, Lorraine Hansberry, whose *Raisin in the Sun* (1959) depicted the anguish and pride of a sensitive black family attempting to rise in a hostile white environment, was tragically removed by an early death in 1965. The most important dramatist of the decade, beyond doubt, was Edward Albee, who gripped audiences with an unforgettable, painful view of tortured characters drunkenly flaying each other in *Who's Afraid of Virginia Woolf?* (1962). A master of living dialogue, Albee portrayed man "destroyed by his own acts, still clinging to life, still groping for meaning." Yet some critics felt that his skill at dialogue covered virtually plotless plays and thinly fleshed characters. His later productions leaned harder and harder on obscurity and unconventionality but displayed few signs of growth, and one unsympathetic observer concluded that Albee's fame derived chiefly from the fact that "he was all there was to talk about" in the sixties.

As Off-Broadway productions tended to move closer to the standards and commercial orientation of Broadway plays, so-called Off-Off-Broadway became the center of avant-garde efforts. Consciously trying to turn informal surroundings and unconventionality to their advantage, earnest dramatists experimented in bizarre ways. They subjected viewers to heavy doses of unstructured plots, surreal situations, audience participation, shock, noise, and—increasingly—nudity, obscenity, sex, and perversion. There was no indication, in the seventies, that these wild experiments and deep sojourns into noisy unorthodoxy had yet evolved playwrights of the first rank or drama that would be remembered.

American poetical writing displayed more excitement and virtuosity than were apparent in either drama or fiction. The best poetry revealed great vitality and a sustained interest in experimental forms. The influence of Ezra Pound and T. S. Eliot, who had cast long shadows across the field since the First World War, continued to be felt. Boldly experimental and frequently obscure, after the fashion of Pound and Eliot, much recent verse demanded rereading and careful study. Yet the experimentation helped give American verse its dynamic quality, and the vogue of obscurity was well adapted to the Western world's growing sense of individual isolation, "the man so far away from society that he no longer cares to talk with his fellows." If the ordinary reader remained baffled by the remote allusions and cryptic imagery of the more radical experimentalists, he could find other talented writers who made fewer demands on him. At least five poets who became prominent after midcentury—Phyllis McGinley, William Meredith, Reed Whittemore, Louis O. Coxe, and Richard Wilbur—chose to communicate with more directness and clarity.

American poetry exhibited a new-found maturity and self-assurance. An English critic noted that American poets displayed less "aggressive nativeness" than heretofore, a deeper awareness of the cultural traditions of other lands, and a fresher and less stylized use of classical and biblical allusions than those employed in England. In the poems of Robert Penn Warren, John Malcolm Brinnin, and Robert Lowell could be seen a thoughtful quest, relatively new in America, for identity with one's ancestors. Readers learned to appreciate the wide-ranging themes and varied styles of poets such as Lowell, Karl Shapiro, and Randall Jarrell, who began to publish during the Second World War, or the well-knit form and inner logic in the poems of Stanley Kunitz and Theodore Roethke, whose careers had begun a few years earlier. Robert Frost, the venerable dean of American verse, continued to captivate readers with his unique New England magic, controlled but exuberant energy, and dry humor and sympathetic wisdom. Frost remained cheerful, but he had no cures to offer. "Every poem," he said, "is an epitome of the great predicament; a figure of the will braving alien entanglements."

In striking juxtaposition at midcentury stood another venerable writer, Wallace Stevens, whom many regarded as one of the greatest of modern poets. Stevens, like Frost, began writing verse before the First World War. Unlike the New Englander, he did not win recognition beyond a small circle until late in life. Intuitive rather than rational, Stevens could write with eloquent simplicity about nature and the seasons and "gusty emotions on wet roads on autumn nights . . . the bough of summer and the winter branch." He was also a constant experimentalist in the Eliot-Pound tradition, a believer in bizarre words and obscure allusions. Yet persevering readers discovered that his poems contained much beauty, force, and profundity. Three well-established poets of the preceding generation, also in the Eliot tradition—Marianne Moore, William Carlos Williams, and E. E. Cummings—continued to display their diverse talents in the postwar years.

American poetry entered a period of transition in the sixties. Several major figures abruptly passed from the scene: Stevens died in 1955, Cummings in 1962, Roethke, Williams, and Frost in 1963, Jarrell in 1965. Yet American verse lost little of its force, momentum, or vitality. In truth, no form of creative writing was better suited for this disjunctive, unconventional, individualistic, desperately questioning era. Poets had been experimenting in these directions for half a century and were far less dependent than novelists or dramatists upon traditional forms and structure. Reflecting the mood of the times, contemporary verse became increasingly personal in subject matter, increasingly informal in style.

With the passing of the older generation, positions in the vanguard were readily taken by the developing talents of Robert Lowell and John Berryman. Lowell's achievements in the late fifties and early sixties were outstanding. His *Life Studies* (1959) stamped him as a master of the growing emphasis upon personal, informal verse. His *For the Union Dead* (1964) displayed maturity, force, and "the imagination of a great historian, reliving the past while relating to the troubles of the present." Another critic felt that Lowell was uniquely qualified to bear "the role of the great poet, the man who on a very large scale sees more, feels more, and speaks more bravely about it than we ourselves can do."

Lowell was overshadowed in the late sixties by John Berryman, whom many were acclaiming as America's greatest living poet when he committed suicide in 1972. Berryman's *The Dream Songs* (1969) revealed an almost matchless appreciation for the diversity of the language and an inventive skill at using it. As critic and poet Karl Shapiro noted, Berryman's "sense of the American idiom is unsurpassed. Where some poets twang on a single string . . . Berryman swoops through the inchoate medium of ex-English and with a Chaucerian confidence gathers the new language into his arms and *conducts* it."

With Berryman gone and Lowell less active, an even younger generation of poets—those born in the late twenties and thirties—moved toward leadership. Perhaps the most impressive of this younger generation was James Wright, who wrote feelingly and powerfully of Americans' maltreatment of nature and their fellow man in striving for financial success. "Our age," one critic noted, "desperately needs his vision of brotherly love, his transcendental sense of nature, the clarity of his courageous voice." Certainly the age was fortunate in having a vigorous, ongoing poetical tradition that seemed able, unlike fiction and drama, to rise with rather than be swamped by the flood tide of change and uncertainty.

4. Crises and Changes in American Education

American education felt the impact of accelerating social and economic change after 1940 in so many ways that a balanced assessment is difficult to make. They were years of genuine achievement, unremitting stress, and challenges as complex as they were formidable. Not surprisingly, huge increases were registered between 1940 and 1970 in nearly every statistic that helped to measure size and scope. Total enrollment—in public and private elementary and secondary schools, colleges, and universities—rose from under 30 million to over 60 million; total expenditures increased from $3.2 billion, representing 3.5 percent of the GNP, to over $70 billion, or 7.7 percent. Public school enrollment rose from 25.4 million to 46.5 million; the number of pupils in private schools, from 2.6 million to 5.5 million. Expenditures for public education below the college level expanded from $2.4 billion to nearly $44 billion. Even more significantly, expenditure per pupil shot up nearly tenfold, from $88 in 1940 to $858 in 1970.

National concern over education, dulled somewhat by the stringencies of the Great Depression, assumed the proportions of a crusade in the late forties as a result of wartime difficulties. The war placed huge burdens on the public schools. Severe overcrowding in urban areas, combined with shortages of material and equipment, forced many schools to go on double shift and use abandoned buildings. Even worse, by 1945 some 350,000 teachers—nearly 40 percent of the total employed in 1941—had left the profession for better paying jobs in business and government. Desperate authorities issued emergency certificates to over 100,000 teachers, but the shortage persisted: "Schools were closed or were conducted for short terms; many subjects . . . had to be abandoned for lack of adequately prepared teachers."[13] If anything, the situation worsened in the immediate postwar years.

[13]I. L. Kandel, *The Impact of the War Upon American Education* (Chapel Hill, N.C., 1948), p. 7.

AMERICAN PUBLIC EDUCATION
1940 - 1970
ENROLLMENT, *IN THOUSANDS OF STUDENTS*

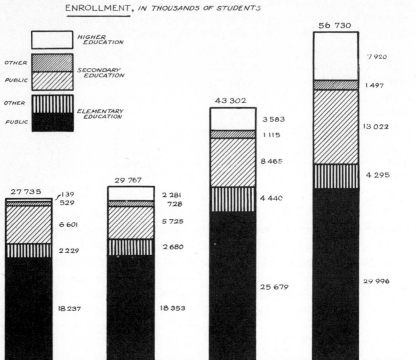

Public opinion was roused by disclosures of these problems. Influential groups like the National Association of Manufacturers, Chamber of Commerce, AFL, and CIO joined teachers' lobbies and citizens' committees to demand increased school appropriations and new buildings. Americans proved willing to spend large sums for education and sustain the effort for two decades, and many gains were recorded. While enrollments mounted and expenditures soared, parts of the educational plant underwent much-needed modernization. In hundreds of communities, grim old structures that had served generations of pupils were replaced by attractive, well-lighted, better-equipped modern buildings. Thousands of one-room country schoolhouses and inadequate small-town facilities gave way to new district-wide elementary schools[14] and county union high schools. Average daily attendance registered increases. Most important, the lot and status of the public school teacher began a slow but steady improvement that eventually restored the depleted ranks and outstripped demand.

[14]There were still 107,000 one-teacher elementary schools in the United States in 1940, representing over half of all elementary schools. This number had shrunk to 4,100 by 1968, representing less than 5 percent of the total.

The mid-fifties marked the turning of the tide. While public school enrollment rose by 50 percent between 1955 and 1970, the number of classrooms increased by 80 percent and the number of teachers doubled; the pupil-teacher ratio declined from about twenty-six to just over twenty-two. The percentage of teachers lacking full certification dropped from over 10 at midcentury to less than 5 in 1970. And teachers' salaries rose steadily from an average of $1,440 in 1940 to $3,000 in 1950, to almost $5,000 in 1960, to $9,300 in 1971.

The postwar crusade also strove to reassess current educational philosophy and improve the quality of what went on in the classroom. One manifestation of this was a sustained assault, by intellectuals, academicians, and other informed observers, upon that unsystematized and poorly understood body of principles known as progressive education. Despite its substantial contributions to a more enlightened public school system,[15] progressive education could not withstand this assault. It had lost much of its intellectual vitality and had become inbred, overprofessionalized, and torn by internal schisms. The end of its tenure as the reigning philosophy in American education was symbolized by the dissolution of the once powerful Progressive Education Association in 1955. As one authority put it, "a movement that had for half a century enlisted the enthusiasm, the loyalty, the imagination, and the energy of large segments of the American public and the teaching profession became, in the decade following World War II, anathema."[16]

The gist of the indictment was that modern progressivism had emasculated scholarship and subject matter in the interests of pedagogic technique and "life adjustment" and, consequently, had sapped much intellectual vitality, rigor, and discipline from the school system. Walter Lippmann sounded the tocsin as early as 1940, noting angrily that the modern school contained "no common faith, no common body of principle, no common body of knowledge, no common moral and intellectual discipline." Prominent educators like Albert Lynd, Robert M. Hutchins, and Arthur Bestor wrote penetrating elaborations upon this theme in the early fifties, and public dissatisfaction grew. Critics called for a shift in emphasis from "child-centered" to "subject-centered" education and

[15]The progressive impulse in education had had a profound if uneven influence upon American schools in the period 1915-1940. In a zealous attempt to apply the ideas of John Dewey and other pioneer reformers, progressive-minded educators had wrought a host of changes and improvements: a revamped and expanded curriculum, with increased attention to vocational, cultural, and extracurricular activities; greater variation and flexibility in the grouping of students, based on intelligence and achievement tests; a new mobility and informality in the classroom; fresher and more attractive textbooks and other materials; and improved facilities such as assembly rooms, gymnasiums, laboratories, shops, movable furniture and partitions, better lighting, and so on.

[16]Lawrence A. Cremin, *The Transformation of the School: Progressivism in American Education, 1876-1957* (New York, 1961), p. vii.

more rigorous training in basic academic disciplines like English, history, mathematics, science, and languages.

The drive for improved standards moved into high gear in the decade 1955-1965. College professors were enlisted to redesign public school courses, texts, and syllabi embodying recent scholarship and greater emphasis upon subject matter. A new approach to the teaching of mathematics won widespread adoption; however, it was generally pronounced a failure by the late seventies. Some schools experimented with team teaching; a few introduced programmed instruction, whereby a student could progress at his own speed by talking into a machine that corrected his mistakes as he went along. Greater attention to audiovisual devices included experiments with television as a means of enabling a single teacher to reach scattered classrooms and schools.

The Elementary and Secondary Education Act of 1965 (see p. 853) made large sums available to the public school system for library resources, textbooks, instructional materials, supplementary and mobile services, remedial programs, guidance counseling, field trips, and teacher aides. The act also underwrote cooperative research designed to stimulate innovation and broaden the intellectual and social base of the "educational establishment." Children from low-income areas received special attention, and preschool programs such as Head Start sought to assist youngsters from disadvantaged homes.

This impressive educational effort registered at least a few improvements in the finished product. The median number of school years completed, for all Americans aged twenty-five and over, rose from 8.6 in 1940 to 12.2 in 1970; in other words, a majority of adults had completed high school by the latter date, as opposed to less than 25 percent in 1940. For blacks aged twenty-five and over, the median number of school years completed rose from 5.8 in 1940 to almost 10 in 1970; the percentage of adult nonwhites who had completed high school rose from 7 to nearly 34. The high school dropout rate, contrary to general belief, declined markedly; the proportion of students finishing high school rose from 58 percent in 1955 to almost 74 percent in 1970. And although statistics were far from adequate, the results of a few comparable tests given over a period of years suggested that young minds were being better prepared by this expanding educational system. "Until better evidence is presented," the Department of Health, Education, and Welfare observed, "the tentative judgment must be that American children in the sixties are learning more than their older brothers and sisters learned in the fifties."

Despite real achievements, the great postwar campaign to improve the public schools was being adjudged a failure by informed observers as the seventies began. The system as a whole, they charged, had not really altered and was increasingly inadequate, even anachronistic. Few of the

FEDERAL OUTLAYS FOR EDUCATION
1955, 1965, and 1971

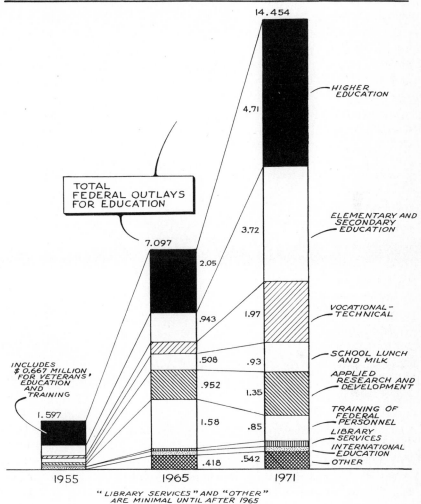

IN BILLIONS OF DOLLARS

14.454

HIGHER EDUCATION

4.71

TOTAL FEDERAL OUTLAYS FOR EDUCATION

7.097

ELEMENTARY AND SECONDARY EDUCATION

3.72

2.05

.943 1.97

VOCATIONAL – TECHNICAL

.508 .93

SCHOOL LUNCH AND MILK

INCLUDES $ 0.667 MILLION FOR VETERANS' EDUCATION AND TRAINING

.952 1.35

APPLIED RESEARCH AND DEVELOPMENT

1.597

1.58 .85

TRAINING OF FEDERAL PERSONNEL

LIBRARY SERVICES

INTERNATIONAL EDUCATION

.418 .542 OTHER

1955   1965   1971

" LIBRARY SERVICES " AND "OTHER" ARE MINIMAL UNTIL AFTER 1965

widely heralded innovations and reforms had lived up to expectation. Team teaching had often turned out to be "simply a new label for old-fashioned departmentalization." Neither television nor programmed instruction had had much impact. Courses, books, and teaching material designed by college professors, though often a distinct improvement in content over what they supplanted, turned out to be ill-designed for effective or imaginative teaching. "With the kind of casual arrogance only professors can manage," one dean remarked, the goal had been to make the new material communicate directly from scholar to pupil and in effect by-pass the classroom teacher altogether. The results had been disappointing.

Remarkably little seemed to have changed after years of strenuous effort; inertial resistance had tended to prevail. The Educational Testing Service concluded that the high school social studies curriculum in 1965-1966 did "not differ in any striking way from that which has been traditional in the United States for the past twenty-five years." Schools and classrooms remained, by and large, rigidly organized for administrative convenience: arbitrary units of time, fixed rows of desks facing the teacher, and an overemphasis upon facts, regimentation, discipline, and quiet. "It's easier to put man on the moon," one disillusioned educator observed in 1966, "than to reform the public schools." Another authority concluded that the dominant quality in the school system was one of mindlessness.

The indictment went deeper. It now appeared that the attack on progressive education had repeated one of progressivism's great errors by replacing an overemphasis on child-centered education with an equally unbalanced (and damaging) stress on subject matter. Curricular reform, critics insisted, would have little effect until basic methods of operating a school and teaching a class had undergone drastic change. The postwar crusade had merely sought to improve existing practice when what was needed was a complete reexamination and overhaul of the system's intellectual underpinning: educational philosophy, approaches to teaching and learning, social purpose and values, raison d'être.

While this kind of criticism gathered momentum in the late sixties, the school system also encountered a full share of the social turmoil that marked those years. Youthful rebelliousness spread downward from colleges to high schools and even junior high schools—as did increased drug use, disruption, vandalism, and violence. Racial and ethnic tensions became chronic in many urban schools, occasionally erupting into riotous outbreaks. Teenagers began demanding more academic and social freedom, a voice in curricular decisions, and an end to excessive regulation. Many pupils were caught in angry power struggles, often three-cornered, between local communities, central boards of education, and teachers' unions.[17] Disturbances and tension were by no means confined to inner cities and racial conflicts; a poll of high school principals revealed that 60

[17]Most spectacular of these conflicts was a bitter, prolonged battle between New York's Ocean Hill-Brownsville community, the central board of education, and the United Federation of Teachers, over the community's attempt to terminate the employment of thirteen teachers and six administrators it found unacceptable. Months of wrangling, replete with angry confrontations, sporadic violence, and furious reciprocal charges of racism and anti-Semitism, resulted in deadlock and a succession of teachers' strikes that kept most of New York City's public schools closed for thirty-six of the first forty-eight school days in the fall of 1968.

percent of them, including many schools in all-white rural and suburban areas, had experienced some form of unrest and disruption during 1968-1969. Schools also felt the pinch of inflation, and taxpayer resentment began to express itself in the form of slashed school budgets and a growing unwillingness to finance improvements or expansion.[18]

Though buffeted by searching criticism, social unrest, and financial pressures, the public school system continued to offer grounds for hope in the seventies. Charges of regimentation, sterility, and mindlessness were at least partly offset by the inventiveness, zeal, and talent displayed by countless thousands of dedicated classroom teachers. Promising experiments were taking place here and there in numerous directions: open and more flexible classrooms, informality in teaching and learning situations, individualized instruction, independent study, interdisciplinary and "problem" approaches to subject matter, new approaches to grading and teacher education, decentralized community control, and the use of neighborhood business, cultural, and scientific facilities to supplement and enrich conventional courses. Such experiments, sparked by imaginative teachers and principals, were recording successes in ghetto schools, crowded interracial urban areas, and poor rural districts as well as in wealthy suburbs. They suggested that high intellectual standards, structure, and "subject matter" were potentially compatible with greater freedom, informality, joy of learning, and child-centered emphases—and that in such necessary combinations a new approach to the whole complex matter of teaching, learning, individuality, and educational purpose might yet emerge.

These were years of phenomenal growth and achievement for American colleges and universities. Between 1940 and 1970, enrollment increased from 1.5 million to 8.3 million, expenditures from $606 million to nearly $25 billion. Whereas less than 16 percent of the eighteen-to-twenty-one age group attended college in 1940, nearly 43 percent did so in 1969. Only 11 percent of the adult population (aged twenty-five and over) and a bare 3 percent of nonwhite adults had had one or more years of college before the outbreak of the Second World War; by 1970 these figures stood at 21 and 10.4 percent. A college education, hitherto largely confined to those with money, social standing, or unusual talent and ambition, had come at least potentially within the range of nearly every American youth who so aspired.

The path that led to this outstanding accomplishment was strewn with pitfalls and problems. The Second World War made enrollments plummet and forced comparable cuts in the size of faculties and capital expenditures. Peace brought an inundation of students, as veterans enjoying liberal

[18]The nation's parochial schools encountered such serious financial stringency as to result in the closing of several hundred private schools, a leveling off (after two decades of steady growth) in private secondary school enrollment, and a 13 percent decrease—from 4.5 million to 3.9 million—in private elementary school enrollment, in the period 1966-1970. Some Roman Catholic officials predicted that their entire system of parochial schools might have to close down unless substantial public assistance could be obtained.

public support more than doubled enrollments between 1945 and 1948 and put almost unbearable strains on college housing, classroom, and library facilities. The Red scare of the late forties and fifties posed threats to academic freedom in the form of test oaths and campaigns aimed at driving nonconformist or liberal teachers from the classroom and unorthodoxy from the textbooks.[19] The result, for a few years at least, was to impugn the loyalty of thousands of professors and teachers, drive thousands of others into silence or extremes of orthodoxy, and cast a pall of fear and suspicion over many colleges and public schools.

And yet, despite such stresses, the period was one of remarkable academic progress, induced by continuing thoughtful inquiry into the philosophy, methods, and goals of higher education. First came a sweeping victory for the proponents of an integrated curriculum designed to afford a general education for American undergraduates. A revolt against the intellectual chaos of the free elective system, led in the thirties by President Robert M. Hutchins of the University of Chicago, came to a head with the publication of the Harvard Committee's *General Education in a Free Society* in 1945. A milestone in the development of educational philosophy in the United States, the Harvard report was an eloquent plea for greater emphasis upon general education that would acquaint students with the whole of human experience rather than with isolated fragments. Curricular changes embodying the substance of this concept were adopted in many colleges and universities in the years that followed.

The reexamination thus set in motion led to other changes and experiments. Recognition of the importance of Judaism and Christianity in the development of Western civilization led to the establishment of religion departments in many institutions that had once gladly abandoned such studies. Awareness of America's new responsibilities stimulated academic interest in international affairs and foreign areas, and especially in institutes to promote study about Russia, the Orient, and the Middle East. New or enlarged programs in American civilization and expanded offer-

---

[19]The number of actual Communists in American classrooms after the war was infinitesimally small. Yet great vigilance was in evidence everywhere. Important groups like the American Association of University Professors, National Education Association, and American Federation of Teachers all took stands against employing Communist teachers. Many states and cities imposed test oaths on teachers and established committees to scrutinize textbooks for subversive ideas. The University of Oklahoma virturally excluded any but native-born citizens from its staff; Kansas, Pennsylvania, and Massachusetts authorized schools to dismiss teachers for disloyalty; and Maryland, New York, and New Jersey forbade teachers to join certain proscribed organizations.

The dangers inherent in reckless assaults upon academic freedom were illustrated by a controversy that seriously hurt the University of California at midcentury. In order to protect the institution from attacks by certain demagogues in the legislature, the president and regents imposed a loyalty oath of their own in 1949. Forty-nine professors, among them the most distinguished scholars and teachers on the staff, were discharged when they refused to sign the oath on the ground that it impeached their loyalty and affronted their dignity. Other professors resigned in protest or refused to accept appointment in the ensuing battle, and the entire academic world watched in alarm. The regents rescinded the oath in 1951–1952 and reinstated the discharged professors who had not gone elsewhere.

ings in cultural anthropology, sociology, and psychology reflected new concerns, as did interdisciplinary courses and programs centered around urban problems, environmental studies, race relations, Afro-American history and culture, the American Indian, and others. Quantification and the computer greatly extended academic frontiers in the natural and social sciences, while tapes and other electronic equipment permitted new advances in the teaching of foreign languages.

Absorbed though they were with expansion and improvement, universities also participated actively, at times controversially, in the affairs of society. They associated closely with governmental, defense, and business institutions and with all of the professions, applying their talents and resources to matters that ranged from social medicine to chemical warfare and from ecosystems to the problems of the inner city.

Intellectual excellence, academic standards, and creative scholarship were not merely maintained but expanded during these years of proliferating effort and rapid growth; social involvement and quantity education were by no means achieved at the expense of quality.[20] The system had succeeded in combining "the traditional or 'elite' function of the university—the transmission of high culture and the creation of new knowledge—with its 'popular' functions, i.e., educating large numbers of students, particularly for professions and vocations, and providing other services to the society."[21] In sharp contrast to the situation in the twenties and thirties, American universities and the quality of their scholarship after midcentury compared favorably with any in the world.[22]

American higher education was at the flood tide of this expansive thrust when it ran athwart those powerful currents of social unrest that began overflowing their banks in the mid-sixties. The result was a sensational period of turbulence and a grave new threat to educational quality and progress.

Growing student activism became noticeable around 1960 as youthful idealism, kindled by the civil rights movement and John F. Kennedy's political candidacy, began to erode the passivity and conformity that had characterized most student bodies during the fifties. The concern boiled over into rebellion at the University of California at Berkeley in 1964, an

[20]A major reason for rising academic standards in the midst of swelling enrollments was a vast reservoir of youthful talent, hitherto untapped. In 1953, when the postwar (nonveteran) increase in college enrollment was just beginning, only 48 percent of high school seniors in the top quarter of their class were going on to college. By 1960 this portion had leaped to 80 percent and continued to climb, which meant that colleges and universities of every caliber could become more selective as they fished for freshmen in this larger pool. President Nathan Pusey of Harvard was hardly exaggerating when he told a group of alumni in the fifties that "unless your sons are a lot brighter than you they won't be able to get into Harvard."

[21]Charles E. Silberman, *Crisis in the Classroom: The Remaking of American Education* (New York, 1970), p. 14.

[22]Whereas in 1930 only 5 percent of the Nobel Prizes were held by Americans, by the late sixties the figure exceeded 40 percent.

episode that triggered a six-year period of collegiate unrest, agitation, and violent outbreaks. Campus revolt became worldwide in 1968, with major disturbances occurring at Columbia University, San Francisco State College, and several other American institutions and at universities in Egypt, Poland, Czechoslovakia, most of western Europe, and parts of Latin America and the Far East.

American colleges experienced a climactic and nationwide wave of uprisings in 1970. Students, already roused to new militance by a recent escalation of the war in Indochina (see pp. 929, 932), went wild upon hearing that five college youths had been killed and several others wounded by gunfire from national guardsmen during a violent outbreak at Kent State University in Ohio on May 4. Further inflamed by news of the killing of two black youths by police gunfire during a melee at Jackson State College in Mississippi ten days later, students proceeded to stage a virtual "general strike" of the nation's colleges and universities. Some 750 institutions, of every size and description from coast to coast, experienced upheaval in the tense weeks that followed, and at least 130 schools cancelled classes for the balance of the spring term.

Student tactics, usually formulated and initiated by a small radical minority—seldom more than 2 percent—and supported by a larger minority of aroused moderates, included protest meetings, demonstrations, nonattendance at classes, the occupation of buildings, the holding of faculty or administrators as hostages, sporadic vandalism and other destructive acts, and the purposeful disruption of all normal campus activity. The tragedies at Kent State and Jackson State were only the most dramatic of several illustrations that forcible attempts to suppress disorder by bringing in police or national guardsmen merely made matters worse. By the end of the decade it appeared that such disorders had brought American higher education to the verge of paralysis, if not outright chaos.

What were the causes and issues that fed this crescendo of collegiate unrest? Targets of student protest fell into two broad categories: internal institutional concerns and social and political questions of national or worldwide import. Among the former, which sparked the revolt at Berkeley in 1964 and remained a prominent part of many later uprisings, were a concern over the size and impersonality of the large university, the quality of undergraduate teaching, alleged neglect of individuality, and the oppressive or irrelevant nature of many rules and requirements. Students went from there to demands for a larger voice in curricular matters and in the hiring and retention of teachers, and greater freedom in a whole range of social questions: parietal hours, dormitory regulations, and the like.

These internal considerations were overshadowed after 1966 by mounting external resentments: against racial injustice, environmental deterioration, the alleged repressiveness of governmental policies and American society generally, and above all the war in Vietnam. Opposition to the war found several outlets. Along with general protests, sit-ins and teach-ins, letter-writing campaigns, and efforts in behalf of antiwar political candidates, students demanded that their institutions assert themselves against the war in a variety of ways: by official public pronouncements, by "decrediting" officer training courses and even removing ROTC programs altogether, by refusing to make the academic standing of students available to draft boards, by cutting off all research ties that furthered military technology, and by forbidding "tainted" institutions like the Central Intelligence Agency or the Dow Chemical Company (makers of napalm) to engage in job recruiting on campus.

The drive for racial equality featured demands for more black students, professors, and administrators, more courses and programs in Afro-American history and culture, and sometimes even for separate dining and social facilities for black students seeking to retain their identity at predominantly white schools. Urban institutions were urged to strive for better relations with blacks and other low-income minorities in nearby neighborhoods. Many students also became champions of the Women's Liberation movement and of campaigns to improve the status of Indian and Latin American minorities. They gave enthusiastic support to environmental action measures and to consumer advocates like Ralph Nader. Few social injustices escaped their attention. During the height of the unrest in 1968-1970 they periodically turned out by the thousands to march, demonstrate, agitate, picket, or simply work. (Campus turbulence subsided after the spring of 1970, and a period of calm ensued and continued through the 1970s.)

The internal effects of these rebellious years were so mixed as to defy easy analysis. On the one hand, many institutions were shaken out of a stifling complacency and took long overdue steps to bring students, faculty, and administration into better balance and closer contact in areas of curricular policy making and college governance. Minority representation on student bodies, faculties, and administrations improved noticeably. Many obsolete social regulations were discarded or eased, including the venerable notion of *in loco parentis*. Although greater social freedom was attended by a few excesses and missteps, the process was undoubtedly a necessary advance along the road to maturity. Many noncoeducational institutions, notably such symbolic bastions of male exclusiveness as Yale and Princeton, responded to the temper of the times and opened their doors to students of both sexes.

And yet the negative results were both depressing and disturbing. The vulnerability and fragility of academic institutions, so necessary to their proper functioning as agents of independent inquiry, had been dramatically underscored. Academic standards had deteriorated. Many schools, hoping to forestall or check disorder, bent so far over backward in acceding to student demands—for fewer requirements, pass-fail grading systems, longer reading periods, "relevant" course offerings of dubious academic worth, more independent study, and so on—that they seriously compromised their own intellectual convictions about higher education. So many curricula had so changed and loosened in response to the agitation that organic cohesion and purpose had well-nigh disappeared. Most important was a dramatic decline in reading and writing skills.

Moreover, response from outside was predictably hostile. Parents, alumni, state and federal lawmakers, and wealthy donors, whose combined support had underwritten the impressive expansion of college facilities since midcentury, were understandably alarmed or angered by all of this turmoil as well as by the shrill denunciation of country, government, economic system, and national values that accompanied it. Colleges seemed to have become havens for increased drug use, sexual license, and wildly uncritical subversive activity, all at the expense of legitimate educational purpose. Since campus unrest coincided with the inflationary recession of the late sixties, financial contributions to higher learning experienced a dual stringency that curtailed growth and development for the first time in twenty years and threatened some overextended institutions with actual bankruptcy. The emotional response from many older observers raised the specter of a new wave of repressive anti-intellectual attacks that would undo or jeopardize much of the real progress that American higher education had recorded. Colleges and universities faced the final quarter of the century in a mood of anxious uncertainty.

5. New Emphases in American Religion

Religious bodies grew remarkably in size and material resources during the war and postwar years. Church membership increased from 64.5 million in 1940, or almost 50 percent of the total population, to 114.5 million in 1960, or 63 percent. Nearly every religious group recorded substantial gains. Membership in the three Jewish bodies grew from an estimated 3 million in 1940 to over 5 million in 1960. All Protestant denominations grew faster than the general population, but the significant growth occurred among those that made an aggressive appeal to the lower middle and lower classes. The Baptists registered the biggest gains, increasing in numbers from 8.3 million in 1936 to 11.4 million in 1960. The various bodies on the social frontier of Protestantism—the Church of the Nazarene, the several Churches of God, the Pentecostal Assemblies, and the Foursquare Gospel movement—also grew rapidly and evolved from fringe sects into established denominations.

Although the United States remained a predominantly Protestant country, a striking feature of the fifties was the enormous gain in membership recorded by the Roman Catholic church. Total Protestant membership had increased by 66 percent between 1926 and 1950, from 31.5 million to 51.1 million, as compared with a Catholic increase of 55 percent, from 18.6 million to 27.6 million. But Catholicism far outstripped Protestantism in rate of growth between 1950 and 1960: Protestant membership expanded from 51.1 million to 63.5 million, or not quite 25 percent; Catholic membership from 28.6 million to 42.1 million, or nearly 50 percent.

Expanding church membership was only one evidence of a new interest in religion. The nation seemed to be undergoing a veritable "surge of piety" at midcentury, including much that was genuine and much that was superficial. A widespread yearning for relief from anxiety and insecurity produced a spate of sermons and religious books offering inner tranquillity, a new self-confidence, and heightened powers through prayer and "postive thinking." Leading figures in this so-called cult of reassurance included Rabbi Joshua Liebman, author of *Peace of Mind* (1946); Monsignor Fulton J. Sheen, author of *Peace of Soul* (1949); and above all the Reverend Norman Vincent Peale, whose parade of best-selling titles was indicative: *The Art of Living, A Guide to Confident Living, The Power of Positive Thinking, Stay Alive All Your Life.* Another manifestation of the postwar religious hunger was a new wave of revivalism. The unquestioned champion of the modern revivalists was the Reverend Billy Graham, who swayed huge crowds in all parts of the world with his impassioned oratory and persuaded thousands to come forward and declare for Christ. Elsewhere, dedicated laymen formed associations which enlisted the services of God and Christianity in behalf of freedom's crusade against communism, or more specifically in behalf of limited government and free enterprise.

It was difficult to escape reminders of the new religious impulse. A "Religion in American Life" campaign, pursuing its objective with the help of millions of dollars' worth of free advertising, used billboards and spot television and radio announcements to exhort Americans to "attend and support the church or synagogue of their individual choice." The phrase "under God" was added to the pledge of allegiance. A flood of religious and inspirational books enjoyed huge sales, and film extravaganzas like *The Ten Commandments* broke box office records. Campaign speeches seldom failed to pay tribute to church and religion. And the unremitting blare of the nation's juke boxes attested to the popularity of "hit" religious tunes like "The Man Upstairs" and "I Believe." Religion, as one authority put it, had "come into vogue."

The causes were complex and often obscure. The war had drawn millions of American families to church or synagogue to pray for the safe return of loved ones overseas. A basic underlying factor, certainly, was the change in popular attitudes toward man, society, and God that took place as the twentieth century wore on. Mass destruction in both world wars, revelations of Nazi barbarism and similar evidence of man's inhumanity, and fear of future annihilation weakened public faith in human progress and drove millions to seek understanding and guidance in religious worship.

Other factors had a more tenuous connection with meaningful religion. The pressures of conformity and social climbing—the advantages of "belonging" and the urge to advertise or confirm one's rising status by associating with a "respectable" denomination—undoubtedly played a role. As we have noted, part of the increase in church membership and in the activity of many local church organizations was related to the heightened quest for community on the part of the legions who moved to the suburbs after 1945.

Will Herberg, a professor at Drew Theological Seminary, advanced a related, if somewhat deeper, hypothesis. He explained the great increase in church membership in terms of a search for identity by many Americans—particularly third-generation immigrants. Sons and daughters of the original immigrants, growing up in the new country and usually more eager than their parents to be assimilated and "Americanized," had often abandoned the traditional family religion. But a third generation had come of age by the Second World War, and the pendulum swung back. This new generation, living in a mobile society that tended to blur ethnic, regional, and class differences, found that the religion of their ancestors offered the most convenient and satisfying path to social identity.

One of Herberg's conclusions genuinely disturbed orthodox believers from all three faiths. "By and large," he wrote, "the religion which actually prevails among Americans today has lost much of its authentic Christian (or Jewish) content. Even when they are thinking, feeling, or acting religiously, their thinking, feeling, and acting do not bear an unequivocal relation to the faiths they profess."[23] Other analysts made similar observations: modern religion was strongly secular; doctrinal differences were blurring or softening; and what one authority defined as "religion-in-general," a vague "national religion," was outstripping and eroding the three traditional faiths.

The prevailing emphasis was not only secular but humanistic—so much so that the essence of Christian doctrine was in danger of being lost. Scholars and ministers noted a tendency to stand biblical truth on its head by putting God to work in the service of man. Such, in effect, was the message of the "positive thinking" advocates, who made religious experience a kind of bargain-counter operation whereby God, in exchange for prayer, doled out peace of mind, worldly happiness, and success. Such also, more blatantly, was the message of those who identified God's will with the cause of democracy or free enterprise, in contravention of the scriptural reminders that the Almighty has purposes of His own. Even the

[23]Will Herberg, *Protestant, Catholic, Jew*, rev. ed. (Garden City, N.Y., 1960), p. 3.

revivalists, for all their emphasis upon salvation by conversion, implied that this vital process was the work of man rather than the unmerited gracious act of the Holy Spirit. True Christianity was giving way to a shallow, fuzzy, humanistic faith that dangerously oversimplified when it did not distort. The God of Abraham had become The Man Upstairs— friendly, manageable, eager to serve.

Critics did see a few grounds for hope. The surge of ignorant piety lost much of its fervor as the fifties ended. By no means all churches had surrendered to a watered-down religion; responsible elements in Judaism, Catholicism, and Protestantism steadfastly refused to conform. There was hope, too, in the nation's seminaries, most of which had turned from the liberal, humanistic doctrines of the prewar years toward Biblical theology and epistemology, building upon the neo-orthodox foundations laid by such outstanding Protestant theologians as Karl Barth, Paul Tillich, and Reinhold Niebuhr (see Vol. I, p. 277). Catholicism was similarly invigorated by the uncompromising theology of the French scholar Jacques Maritain, and Judaism found the basis for a sharper faith in the incisive theology of Martin Buber.

American religion, like every other aspect of life, felt the powerful impulses of the sixties in confusing and contradictory ways. On the one hand, the postwar trend toward secularity became so strong that organized religion sometimes seemed in danger of being engulfed by it. The growth rate in church membership, after two decades of spectacular gains, abruptly leveled off; the percentage of the total population that belonged to a church held remarkably steady at 63 percent between 1960 and 1970.[24] More and more people came to feel that religion was losing its importance: polls indicated that whereas only 17 percent of the respondents believed in 1957 that the influence of religion was declining, fully 70 percent believed this in 1969. A small but influential group of radical theologians proclaimed the "death of God" in the sixties, arguing (in brief) that "God . . . is the transcendent enemy of the fulness and the passion of man's life in the world, and only through God's death can humanity be liberated from that repression which is the real ruler of history."[25] Although the death of God movement attracted no more than a small following, it received much publicity and undoubtedly added to the general public sense of religion's declining importance.

---

[24] All the principal faiths experienced a sharp falling off in their growth rate after 1960. While the total population grew by a little over 13 percent from 1960 to 1970, Protestant membership expanded from over 63 million to around 70 million, or 11 percent (compared with a 25 percent increase in the fifties); Roman Catholic membership grew from 42 million to nearly 48 million, or 14 percent (compared with 50 percent in the fifties); Eastern Orthodox membership rose from 2.7 million to 3.7 million, or 37 percent (compared with nearly 70 percent in the fifties.) Jewish congregations showed the most modest increase, from an estimated 5.4 million to 5.8 million. Figures for religious membership are imprecise, but there could be no doubt that the rush to affiliate with "the church of one's choice" had all but ceased during the sixties.

[25] Thomas J. J. Altizer, *The Gospel of Christian Atheism* (London, 1967), p. 22.

And yet organized religion managed to confront the secular sixties with several constructive responses. The most influential of these, perhaps, was a kind of "neo-liberal" theology that sought to reapply God's teachings to current problems, after the fashion of the Social Gospel movement yet with less of the naive faith in human progress that had characterized the earlier impulse. Drawing upon the arguments of the German theologian Dietrich Bonhoeffer in the forties and those of Harvey Cox, a professor at Harvard Divinity School and author of *The Secular City* (1965), exponents of the new Social Gospel argued that modern man could only discover God and confront Him with faith and love by finding Him in the midst of life and meeting the world's problems head on, so to speak—and in His name.

"If we are to understand our present age," Cox wrote, "we must learn to live it in its unremitting secularity. We must learn . . . to speak of God in a secular fashion and find a nonreligious interpretation of Biblical concepts. It will do no good to cling to our religious and metaphysical versions of Christianity, in the idle hope that one day religion or metaphysics will again gain their centrality. They will become even more peripheral and that means we can let go and immerse ourselves in the new world of the secular city."[26]

While millions of believers were repelled or unaffected by this emphasis upon a secular God, the response from many seminaries and churches added up to one of the most vigorous reform impulses in modern religious history. Cautiously optimistic, by no means unmindful of neo-orthodoxy's strictures about man's limitations and essential depravity, much of organized religion threw itself into the battle for reform and human betterment. Protestant, Catholic, and Jewish leaders worked assiduously on behalf of the civil rights movement, taking prominent part in many activities—demonstrations, marches, boycotts, rent strikes, voter registration drives, testimony before Congress, and so on—designed to bring black Americans and other minorities closer to full and equal citizenship.

Finding targets everywhere, reform-minded church groups and leaders took forthright stands (in word, deed, and financial contribution) against poverty, discrimination, urban and environmental problems, the war in Vietnam, and other pressing issues. As Eugene Carson Blake, secretary general of the World Council of Churches, put it in 1966, "The Church must identify itself much more radically with the interests of the poor, the 'losers,' the outcasts, and the alienated."[27] This phenomenon, like most others in the sixties, was not limited to the United States or to Judaeo-Christian religious bodies. Seldom if ever had larger numbers of the world's churches, of all faiths, arrayed themselves so earnestly on the side of the downtrodden and the unfortunate.

[26]Harvey Cox, *The Secular City*, rev. ed. (New York, 1966), p. 3.

[27]Eugene Carson Blake, "The Church in the Next Decade," *Christianity and Crisis* (February 27, 1966), p. 17.

While one major impulse in modern religion spoke forthrightly to the secular problems of the age, another sought solace and fulfillment in various quests for a renewed or heightened spiritual experience. This became especially true toward the end of the decade, as social tensions and economic problems mounted and the optimism that had sparked recent reform activity faded. Oriental and primitive religions, with their meditative and transcendental overtones, appealed to increasing numbers, as did the range of cults, encounter and therapy groups, and other sects and experiments that flourished in parts of southern California. Experiments with peyote and LSD; popular rock operas like *Tommy* and *Jesus Christ Superstar*; and huge outdoor rock festivals like the one attended by hundreds of thousands of eager youths at Bethel, New York, in 1969, all included religious motivation of a genuine, if sometimes pathetically misguided, sort. Other young people, disillusioned or unimpressed by drugs, turned to more conventional religious experience and converted enthusiastically to Christ.

Revivalism, still led by Billy Graham, enjoyed another resurgence in the late sixties and early seventies. Graham's multimillion-dollar operation combined traditional revivalistic appeal, including the nostalgic vision of a simpler, older, purer America, with the latest communications technology and the methods of a modern big business. Graham reached millions through his films, books, radio programs, newspaper columns, and spectacular appearances at sports stadia and arenas. Though Graham spoke sincerely about the need for salvation through Christ, his insistence that true peace, brotherhood, and reform could only be achieved with the Second Coming and his tendency to link Christianity with American patriotism in a kind of civil religion worried progressives both within and without the religious sphere. Clearly, nostalgia and escape as well as social commitment were prominent features of religious life in the late twentieth century.

Of untold importance to the future of organized Christianity was the ecumenical movement. Gathering headway in the twenties and thirties, it moved by leaps and bounds after 1940 and accelerated even more sharply in the sixties. Protestantism took large strides toward unity both within and among its principal denominations. Two branches of the Society of Friends came together in 1955, two Presbyterian bodies in 1958. The Evangelical and Reformed church merged with the Congregational Christian churches in 1957 to form the United Church of Christ. Four major Lutheran bodies united between 1960 and 1963 to form the American Lutheran Church; four other Lutheran groups merged in 1962 to form the Lutheran Church in America. The Methodists and Evangelical United Brethren came together in 1968 to form the United Methodist Church, with over 10.6 million members.

Meanwhile, the Federal Council of Churches of Christ in America continued to speak for a growing majority of American Protestant churches.

The Federal Council combined with eight interdenominational agencies in 1941, and the entire structure was reorganized in 1950 and reintegrated into the National Council of the Churches of Christ, which included every important Protestant denomination except the southern Baptists and the Missouri Synod Lutherans. In an equally important move, the Consultation on Church Union was formed in the sixties to discuss a wide range of doctrinal matters. Though progress was slow and uneven, the group had brought most Methodist, Presbyterian, Episcopalian, and Congregational bodies, representing over one-third of American Protestants, measurably closer to union by the early seventies.

An even more heartening outgrowth of the ecumenical spirit was the World Council of Churches, organized in Amsterdam in 1948 after years of preparation. It combined practically all the non-Roman Catholic churches of the world, including the Russian Orthodox church by 1961, into a working fellowship. The Second Assembly of the World Council met in Evanston, Illinois, in 1954, the Third in New Delhi in 1961, the Fourth in Uppsala, Sweden, in 1968, and the Fifth in Addis Ababa, Ethiopia, in 1971. By the latter date the World Council represented over 250 Protestant, Orthodox, and non-Roman Catholic churches from ninety countries embracing over 400 million members. Its display of Christian unity and its fruitful attempts to formulate a basic, all-embracing Christian creed were impressive; and continuing association among churchmen of varying beliefs and traditions held great promise for the future.

For ecumenism, the most epochal development in the sixties was the marked, steady convergence of the Protestant and Roman Catholic faiths in many significant areas of doctrine and spirit. Despite occasional sharp clashes and undercurrents of bitterness between Protestants and Catholics over such traditionally touchy issues as federal aid to education and public support for parochial schools, the gulf of antagonism and prejudice that had yawned between the two Christian faiths for so many centuries had all but disappeared by 1970.

The Roman church contributed significantly to this new spirit. The Second Vatican Council, held from 1962 to 1965, and the brief but epochal tenure (1958-1963) of the most influential pontiff in recent Church history, John XXIII, featured a thorough reexamination and liberalization of Roman beliefs and doctrine and a comprehensive search for a new basis for Christian unity. As the Roman church began to reassess and at times soften its traditional views on birth control, divorce, intermarriage, liturgy, the celibate priesthood, and other doctrinal matters, the distinctions that had long set it apart from other Christian churches blurred and softened. Not since the Reformation had Roman Catholicism been so affected by internal criticism, questioning, and intellectual independence at all levels of its complex hierarchy. Catholic bishops participated more and more closely in meetings of the World Council and other interfaith bodies. Joint statements against war, poverty, and discrimination, and in favor of more vigorous efforts on behalf of underdeveloped nations, were issued with growing frequency.

Catholicism, Protestantism, and Eastern Orthodoxy were moving visibly closer in matters of doctrine; perhaps more importantly, all three Christian faiths were exhibiting a sense of mutual tolerance, understanding, and accommodation unprecedented since the beginning of the Christian era. It was not beyond the bounds of possibility that the most secular age in the history of the West might eventually witness—and indeed bring about—the reunification of Christendom.

25

Politics and Problems

of the Truman Era

Seldom had the American political scene seemed more confused than during the immediate postwar years. The Democratic party, torn by struggles over civil rights and labor policy, was further weakened by a growing conviction that the Truman administration was riddled with corruption and tainted with communism. The Republicans, out of power in Washington during most of this period, were equally beset with difficulties. Torn by divisions between internationalists and neo-isolationists and between progressives and reactionaries, weakened by a long absence from power, and plagued by reckless irresponsibility, they gave no brighter promise of uniting the country and providing constructive leadership than did the Democrats.

Yet never before had the problems confronting the American people been so great. What shall we say of the achievements of the postwar period? The following chapters will attempt to answer that question. It must suffice to say here that, in spite of seeming chaos and intense partisanship, Americans met the challenges of their time more courageously and with greater wisdom than their grandfathers had done during Reconstruction or their fathers during the decade following the armistice of 1918.

1. Harry S Truman and the Progressive Movement

A distraught man stood in the White House at 7:09 P.M. on April 12, 1945, and took the oath as president of the United States. Franklin D. Roosevelt had died a few hours before, and leadership was now entrusted to his vice-president, Harry S Truman. For Roosevelt, as for Lincoln, death was a merciful deliverer, sparing him a host of troubles at the moment of his greatest triumph. For Truman, Roosevelt's passing meant a new life of trial and yet such opportunity as rarely comes to any person.

"Who the hell is Harry Truman?" Admiral William D. Leahy had asked when Roosevelt told him of the vice-presidential nominee in the summer of 1944. That same question was repeated often if less profanely during the days of mourning that followed Roosevelt's death. Harry S Truman was born at Lamar, Missouri, on May 8, 1884, the grandson of pioneers from Kentucky, and grew up in the area around Kansas City. After graduation from high school in 1901, he worked as a bank clerk and farmer, then went to France with his National Guard artillery regiment and rose to the rank of major. He married his childhood sweetheart and entered the clothing business in Kansas City in 1919. Ruined by the postwar recession in 1922, Truman accepted nomination as county judge, or commissioner, of eastern Jackson County from the Kansas City Democratic machine. He was defeated for reelection in 1924, in part because of his opposition to the Ku Klux Klan, but he returned to the courthouse in Independence as presiding judge in 1927. During the next seven years he rebuilt the county's roads and courthouse, helped to plan a system of parkways for Kansas City, and earned a reputation as an able and incorruptible administrator.

Truman was nominated for the United States Senate in 1934 with the help of the Pendergast machine and won easily in the Democratic landslide that fall. In Washington he was known as the "Gentleman from Pendergast"; and his political career seemed at an end when his patron, Tom Pendergast, was sentenced to prison in 1939 for income tax evasion. Truman surprised friends as well as enemies when he won reelection to the Senate on his own in 1940 by attracting the votes of workers, farmers, and blacks in a campaign prophetic of his more famous battle eight years later.

His political stature, enhanced by this victory, increased still further when the defense crisis afforded an opportunity to render national service. Appalled by the waste in defense spending and the army's neglect of small business in awarding contracts, he obtained appointment in 1941 as chairman of a special Senate committee to investigate the defense effort. His committee worked assiduously to prevent waste and favoritism, and his fairness and insistence upon constructive criticism won him the admiration of President Roosevelt and the vice-presidential nomination in 1944.

Yet the country knew little of the character of Harry S Truman when he entered the White House. Because he was modest in demeanor, unpretentious in appearance, and obviously lacking in Roosevelt's histrionic abilities and patrician touch, many Americans assumed that Truman epitomized the average man. Never had a popular judgment been more mistaken; in most aspects the new president was extraordinary indeed.

He was extraordinary in his personal warmth and charm, breadth of learning that often astonished scholars, and ability to understand difficult situations. He was extraordinary in his personal honesty and integrity; although supported by a corrupt political organization, he never allowed the machine to use him, or misappropriated a single dollar of county funds. He was extraordinary in his devotion to duty and the general interest, and in his capacity for hard work. He was extraordinary in his feeling for the underdog, hatred of pretense, and broad sympathy that tolerated no racial or religious distinctions. Above all he was extraordinary in his courage— whether in defying the Ku Klux Klan in Jackson county, fighting a seemingly lost battle on the hustings, dismissing a renowned general, or leading his country in bold pursuit of peace and security.

A few traits, however, weakened Truman's force as a personal leader. Some weaknesses stemmed in the beginning from his undue modesty and feeling of inadequacy for the great tasks ahead. "I don't know whether you fellows ever had a load of hay or a bull fall on you," he told reporters on April 13, 1945. "But last night the moon, the stars and all the planets fell on me." He had inherited a cabinet and administration of strangers; and in his loneliness he turned at first to friends in the Senate and gathered around him a group of intimates known as the Missouri Gang. Some lowering of the tone of public service after the war was inevitable, for corruption permeated politics at all levels. And yet Truman in some measure contributed to the deterioration of public morality. Absolutely honest himself, he was so much a professional politician, who accepted the game as he found it, that he sometimes appeared unable to see dishonesty in others. He trusted too much and refused to move hard and fast against corruption in high places. He was president during a period of intense partisanship, and his own campaign oratory did little to elevate the tone of public discourse. Usually cautious in matters of state, he was often rash and impulsive in personal controversy and given to name-calling in public.

Even so, historians have been kinder to Truman than were many Americans in his own day. They have realized that his personal excesses were far outweighed by positive qualities: strength, courage, and an ability in large matters to put the national interest above personal and party advantage. They have remembered his many contributions, the difficulties of his tasks, and his great growth in leadership.

In spite of early indecision, Truman became not only leader of his party but also the true heir of Bryan, Wilson, and the two Roosevelts in perpetuating and developing the American progressive tradition. In the conviction that the president must be the one national spokesman and defender of the general interest, he preserved the executive branch against congressional assaults and even strengthened the office. He fought hard and successfully to prevent a normal postwar reaction from developing into a repudiation of progressive ideals and practices. Indeed, he actually succeeded in expanding them. This was a difficult task, for progressives were divided, confused, and uncertain at the end of the war. Some, including spokesmen of the CIO and non-Communist followers of Henry A. Wallace, wanted some form of full-fledged collectivism, with widespread nationalization and comprehensive planning and economic controls. Others, especially many southerners, demanded an end to further reform. Allying himself with neither extreme, Truman not only consolidated and enlarged the New Deal structure but also advanced the frontiers of progressivism in the important areas of civil rights, public health, and public power.

2. *Demobilization, Reconversion, and a New Federal Structure*

As we have seen, the immediate postwar years were characterized by inflation and labor unrest, but withal by tremendous economic expansion and prosperity (see pp. 566-569, 590-593). They were characterized also by growing international tension, which caused problems of foreign policy to intrude into all other calculations. The historian looking back over the tumult of these years is astonished by the constructive things that were done in spite of apparent chaos in Washington.

The first order of national business was demobilization of the armed forces and conversion of the economy from a war to a peace footing. It was apparent to the new president and his advisers even before Japan surrendered that the world was entering an uncertain period of potential conflict and realignment of power, and that national security demanded the retention of large armed forces. But the dimensions of future threats to peace were not clear in the autumn of 1945, while the popular demand for speedy and drastic demobilization was so overwhelming that probably no administration could have resisted it. As one writer has observed, "That rush to disarm in late 1945 was surely one of the most expensive economies—in terms of life and effort as well as of money—in which the United States ever indulged."[1] But it was inevitable.

[1] Walter Millis and E. S. Duffield, eds., *The Forrestal Diaries* (New York, 1951), p. 110.

The army began a limited demobilization in May 1945, and both armed services began discharging men as rapidly as possible once Japan had surrendered. When the army slowed its pace in January 1946, there were riots among enlisted men abroad and frenzied protests at home. The president and the army chief of staff, General Eisenhower, quieted the storm by appealing for patience and support. Nonetheless, demobilization had to proceed inexorably in response to public demand. "The program we were following," Truman later wrote, "was no longer demobilization—it was disintegration of our armed forces."[2] By its completion in midsummer of 1946 the great wartime army and navy had been reduced to 1.5 million and 700,000 men, respectively.

For the next four years the president and his military advisers pointed out time and again that American armed strength was barely sufficient to meet the country's minimum international responsibilities, much less provide for security in the event of new aggressions. Congress grudgingly extended a weak Selective Service from July 1946 to May 1947, and reinstituted the draft on a broader basis a year later. At the same time, the lawmakers refused to approve an administration plan for universal military training and insisted upon even further reductions in armed strength after 1946. There were momentary increases after the Communist coup in Czechoslovakia and the Berlin blockade heightened Soviet-American tension in 1948. But the president and his new secretary of defense, Louis Johnson, joined Congress in 1949 to effect new reductions that brought American armed strength to a postwar low point. By early 1950 they had imposed a $13 billion ceiling on defense expenditures and reduced the army to 600,000 men and ten active divisions.

Meanwhile, the country had confronted the tasks of reconversion. One major problem—assistance for veterans—was solved thoroughly and without partisanship. Everyone agreed that veterans should have generous help in finding jobs, adjusting to civilian life, and recovering lost educational opportunities. Congress in June 1944 had enacted the Servicemen's Readjustment Act, with good reason called the G. I. Bill of Rights,[3] and a grateful nation poured out its resources to help its former servicemen. Expenditures of the Veterans Administration rose from $723 million in 1944 to a peak of $9.3 billion in 1950, declining to about $6 billion in 1951 and 1952 and averaging $5 billion annually for the balance of the decade. The government during the peak period 1945–1952 gave $13.5 billion for education and training alone, and nearly $4 billion for unemployment benefits and self-employment help. In addition, the Veterans Administration guaranteed or insured nearly $16.5 billion in veterans' loans for

[2] Harry S Truman, *Memoirs by Harry S Truman*, 2 vols. (New York, 1955), I, 509.

[3] It provided large sums for new veterans' hospitals and vocational rehabilitation; guaranteed unemployment compensation of $20 weekly for a year to veterans who could not find work; provided substantial assistance in the purchase of homes, farms, and businesses; and offered free tuition, books, and subsistence for job training and four years of college or university education.

homes, farms, and businesses and operated a chain of some 150 hospitals that served over 100,000 patients a day in 1950.

Nor was there much controversy over the desirability of tax reductions and assistance to industry in its conversion to civilian production. Congress responded to public pressure by reducing taxes nearly $6 billion in November 1945, while the administration in 1945–1946 disposed of government-owned war plants representing a total investment of $15 billion and some 20 percent of the nation's industrial capacity.

The overshadowing domestic fear in 1944–1945 was dread of a catastrophic postwar depression that might end in national bankruptcy and world chaos. The government's success in marshaling industry and labor during the war stimulated bold ideas. For example, progressives like Henry A. Wallace and spokesmen of the CIO repudiated the assumption that the nation must inevitably career through alternating periods of "boom and bust." They proposed that the government assume responsibility for full employment through indirect stimulation of purchasing power and, if necessary, sufficient compensatory spending to prevent recession. The promise of "full employment" after the war, a major Democratic pledge during the campaign of 1944, was reaffirmed by Truman in September 1945 and set off the first full-fledged debate on postwar domestic policy.

The administration's plan was embodied in a full employment bill submitted by Democratic Senator James E. Murray of Montana. It stipulated that the president and his staff should prepare an annual budget estimate of the investment and production necessary to maintain full employment, and that a congressional committee should assume responsibility for "federal investment and expenditure as will be sufficient to bring the aggregate volume . . . up to the level required to assure a full employment volume of production." To conservatives, the Murray bill meant nothing less than a permanent program of deficit spending through partisan agencies. They countered by proposing a nonpartisan commission to advise the president and Congress on the state of the economy and measures necessary "to foster private enterprise . . . and promote a high and stable level of employment."

Although conservatives and progressives disagreed on means, the significant aspect of the debate over the Murray bill was that both groups agreed in placing chief responsibility for economic stabilization upon the federal government. The outcome was the Employment Act of February 1946, a compromise that affirmed national responsibility for prosperity without prescribing an inflexible method to achieve it. A three-man Council of Economic Advisers, presumably expert and nonpartisan, was created to study the economy for signs of weakness and advise the president and Congress on means of promoting national economic welfare; and a new congressional joint committee was to study and propose stabilization measures. The Employment Act was a milestone in American progressivism. It established machinery for mobilizing all public and private resources in order to sustain a high level of national production, employment, and income. Future experience would reveal that even "experts" on the council could disagree, and that ultimate decisions had to be made by political agencies. And it was not until the 1960s that the Council of Economic Advisers emerged as a really powerful force in Washington. Nonetheless, the Employment Act established the first machinery for systematic investigation and planning for national welfare.

Devising a postwar policy for development of atomic energy was, as events turned out, considerably more urgent. Most Republicans and Democrats agreed that national security demanded retention of a governmental monopoly on all aspects of research and production of fissionable materials, at least until effective international machinery had been established to prevent the manufacture of atomic bombs. On the issue of civilian or military control of the program, however, a heated controversy ensued when a special Senate committee headed by Brien MacMahon of Connecticut set to work on an atomic energy bill in late 1945. At Truman's urging, MacMahon drafted a measure establishing exclusive civilian control through an Atomic Energy Commission (AEC). It won the support of most progressives, scientists, and religious and educational leaders. On the other hand, Senator Arthur H. Vandenberg of Michigan won committee support for a proposal giving military and naval leaders a full voice, even a veto over civilian authorities, in determining atomic energy policies.

The dispute came to a head in early 1946, after the committee adopted Vandenberg's amendment to the MacMahon bill providing for military participation. So violent was Truman's opposition and the public reaction that Vandenberg agreed to a compromise amendment. It established a Military Liaison Committee to work with the AEC but placed exclusive control in civilian hands. Thus the Atomic Energy Act, approved in August 1946, preserved governmental monopoly on fissionable materials, vested control of research and production in the hands of a five-man AEC, and gave to the president alone the power to order the use of the atomic bomb in warfare. It also barred divulgence of information to foreign governments, even friendly ones, which drew a sharp protest from the British.

One problem—unification of the armed services—was entirely nonpartisan but gave rise to a bitter controversy. Almost everyone, including military and naval spokesmen, agreed that the Pearl Harbor disaster and wasteful interservice competition during the war had proved the need for common control and direction of the defense establishment. But disagreement arose on almost every practical suggestion. The army's friends in Congress favored unification, but the navy's champions feared that army domination of a unified defense structure would eliminate the Marine Corps and favor land-based air forces at the expense of sea power. Partisans of the two services maneuvered and skirmished from the end of 1945 until mid-1947. Secretary of the Navy James V. Forrestal, although opposed to complete integration, supported greater unity and held rebellious admirals in check, while the president mediated skillfully.

The result of the give and take was the National Security Act of July 1947, which created a single Defense Department, headed by a secretary with cabinet rank and supervision over secretaries of the army, navy, and air force. It formalized the institution of the Joint Chiefs of Staff representing the three services, to prepare defense plans and consider matters of strategy. Finally, it created the Central Intelligence Agency, supreme in that sphere, and two advisory bodies, the National Security Council and the National Security Resources Board. As Forrestal, the first secretary of defense, soon discovered, it was easier to erect the façade of a new defense structure than to compel genuine unification.[4] Even so, the National Security Act was a major accomplishment. If it had done nothing more than establish an independent air force and provide a framework for gradual unification, the measure would have justified all the labor that went into its writing and adoption.

There was little partisan bickering and considerable agreement on the need for a thorough overhaul of federal administrative structures. They had grown wildly, often without plan or overall purpose, during the New Deal and war periods. The most significant step came in 1947, when Truman appointed a commission on executive reorganization headed by for-

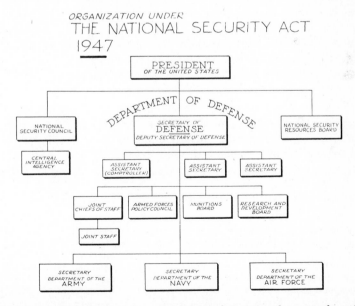

ORGANIZATION UNDER
THE NATIONAL SECURITY ACT
1947

---

[4]Forrestal, in fact, broke under the strain, resigned on March 2, 1949, and committed suicide soon afterward in a moment of depression.

mer President Herbert Hoover. It undertook a comprehensive study and issued reports in early 1949 recommending many consolidations.[5]

Largely at Truman's insistence, Congress approved another major governmental change, the Presidential Succession Act of 1947, which placed the speaker of the House and president pro tem of the Senate ahead of cabinet members in line of presidential succession after the vice-president. Another constitutional alteration was the Twenty-second Amendment, passed in 1947 and ratified by the thirty-sixth state in 1951. It forbade election to the presidency for more than two full terms, or the reelection of a president for more than one term if he had served over two years of an unfinished term. The amendment, which specifically exempted Truman from its interdiction, reflected a widespread conviction that the powers of the office were too great to justify the risk of unlimited reelections.

3. Truman's Struggles with Congress, 1945-1948

Republicans in Congress, often joined by conservative Democrats, also engaged in bitter controversies with the president over several aspects of economic and social policy. Truman, by gestures of friendship toward congressional leaders during the first months of his presidency, led conservatives to believe that he planned to preside over the liquidation of the progressive movement. This brief "honeymoon" came to an end on September 6, 1945, when the president sent his first important domestic message to the Capitol. "It was on that day and with this message," Truman later wrote, "that I first spelled out the details of the program of liberalism and progressivism which was to be the foundation of my administration."[6] He called for a full revival of progressive policies—extension of social security, increase in the minimum wage, national health insurance, renewal of the New Deal's war against slums, regional developments along lines of the Tennessee Valley Authority, a full employment bill, executive reorganization, and extension of wartime economic controls through the reconversion period.

[5]Among the most important recommendations were those for reducing the number of federal departments and agencies from sixty-five to twenty-three; establishing a Department of Welfare to consolidate activities in the fields of public health, education, and social welfare; and thoroughly reorganizing the Post Office Department. The Reorganization Act of June 1949 authorized the president to submit plans for reorganization, which would go into effect unless Congress specifically disapproved. Truman submitted thirty-six such plans in 1949-1950. All were allowed to go into effect except one establishing a Department of Welfare, defeated in 1950 by Republicans and southern Democrats who feared approval might imply acquiescence in the president's proposal for national health insurance. The plan for a Department of Health, Education, and Welfare was revived by President Eisenhower and approved by Congress early in 1953.

[6]Truman, Memoirs, I, 481-482.

Truman's manifesto of September 6 showed clearly enough that he knew what he wanted. But it was not always easy to find majority support in Congress. Despite his success on nonpartisan issues and some acceptable compromise solutions, a conservative coalition of Republicans and southern Democrats often controlled both houses. They blocked the president on advanced measures of welfare and civil rights and defeated him in hard battles over economic controls and revision of federal labor policies.

The president and Office of Price Administration announced soon after the Japanese surrender that they would undertake "continued stabilization of the national economy" by gradual relaxation of wartime controls over prices, wages, and scarce commodities. During late 1945 and early 1946 the OPA was able to end most rationing, continue priorities on scarce industrial materials, and hold wholesale prices and the general cost of living to increases of only 7 and 3 percent. Yet inflationary pressures were mounting powerfully to burst the bounds of price controls. Consumers were buying in black markets; organized labor was driving for higher wages; and manufacturers and farmers had combined with Republican leaders in Congress to demand an end to all controls.

A battle raged all through the spring of 1946 over extension of the OPA. The conservative coalition presented Truman with a price control bill in June that extended the agency for one year but severely weakened its power and commanded it to decontrol prices "as rapidly as possible." Instead of acquiescing, Truman vetoed the bill on June 29 and allowed price controls to end altogether on July 1. Prices rose wildly in the severest inflation since 1942. After much debate, Congress approved a second bill extending price and rent controls for one year on July 25, 1946, but the damage was already done. Moreover, the new measure was, if anything, even weaker and more confusing than the one Truman had vetoed. The president gave up the fight after the Republican victory in the congressional elections that fall. He ended all wage and price controls, except for those on rents, sugar, and rice, on November 9, and the OPA began to wind up its affairs a month later.

The wild inflation occurred just as GOP leaders were beginning their drive to capture Congress in the autumn elections. Republican speakers and advertisements all during the campaign played on the theme of confusion and failure of the price control program. One incident was particularly damaging to Democratic fortunes. The OPA restored price ceilings on meat in August, and farmers withheld beef from the market in anticipation of a change in policy. While housewives waited in line in vain for hamburger at any price, Republicans pressed their telling question, "Had enough?"

All signs pointed to an overwhelming Republican victory. Truman had alienated almost every major group. Labor was embittered by his bridling of John L. Lewis and his stern action in breaking the railroad strike that spring (see pp. 590-591). Conservatives were already disenchanted by his advocacy of welfare and civil rights legislation. New Dealers, on the other hand, were disgruntled by two incidents that threatened to disrupt the Democratic party. The first was the dramatic resignation of the "old cur-mudgeon," Harold L. Ickes, as secretary of the interior, following a dis-pute with Truman over a recent appointment. The second was Truman's dismissal of Secretary of Commerce Henry A. Wallace on September 30, soon after the former vice-president had publicly attacked the administra-tion's policy of stiffening resistance to Russian demands. The president, actually, had to choose between Wallace and Secretary of State James F. Byrnes, who had threatened to resign if Wallace remained in office. But the Democratic party's chief liability that fall was Truman himself. He had given millions of Americans an impression of total inability either to lead or govern.

Few observers were surprised, therefore, when the GOP won control of the House and Senate for the first time since 1928 and captured governor-ships in twenty-five of the thirty-two nonsouthern states on November 5, 1946. What was surprising were the dimension of the landslide and the sharp decrease in the urban Democratic vote. Party machines in many cities had been weakened by prosperity and the suburban migration, and the hitherto solidly Democratic labor bloc had disintegrated.

The significance of the Republican triumph became evident soon after the Eightieth Congress convened in January 1947. There were many new faces and new conservative leadership in both houses, but above them all stood Robert A. Taft of Ohio, chairman of the Republican policy commit-tee in the Senate, champion of business interests, and trenchant foe of advanced progressivism. This son of a former president would lead such a vigorous opposition during the next five years as to earn the title "Mr. Republican" and come within a few votes of winning the presidential nomination in 1952.

Republican leaders in Congress fought with the president and his sup-porters all during 1947 and 1948. The noise emanating from Washington might well have prompted a superficial observer to conclude that effective government was impossible in the melee. Actually, president and Con-gress cooperated to achieve an outstanding record in foreign policy. Even so, sharp differences over domestic policies provided abundant grist for the mill of partisanship. Truman, for example, fought hard against the Taft-Hartley bill (see p. 593), even though he had moved severely against arrogant labor leaders. Adoption of Taft-Hartley over the president's veto in June 1947 was the most important conservative triumph of the postwar era. A second controversy centered on ways of combating inflation. The president pleaded against further tax reduction, which he said would in-crease inflationary pressures. But the Republicans, their eyes on 1948, adopted a tax bill over Truman's veto in July 1947 that gave greatest relief to persons on low and middle incomes. When prices continued to rise during the summer and autumn, Truman called Congress into special session in November to consider an anti-inflation program. Republican leaders responded with a bill that carefully avoided giving the president effective power. Congress extended rent controls for another year in March 1948, but added to inflationary pressures by adopting, again over Truman's veto, another measure for tax reduction.

President and Congress also fought pre-campaign battles over housing and agricultural policies. Truman and moderate Republicans, led on this occasion by Senator Taft, supported a bill that would have inaugurated a broad program of public housing designed to benefit lower income groups. All that the Republican majority would permit, however, was a measure providing governmental credit for veterans' homes and cooperative housing projects. As for agriculture, Congress approved a measure in June 1948 continuing support of farm prices at 90 percent of parity through 1949, to be followed by a program of flexible supports ranging from 60 to 90 percent.

4. The Election of 1948

Not for two decades had the GOP been so confident as it was in early 1948. Among Republican hopefuls the most eager candidate for the presidential nomination was former Governor Harold E. Stassen of Minnesota, who won much popular backing by his frank support of progressive policies at home and American leadership in world affairs. After victories in the Wisconsin and Nebraska presidential primaries in April, Stassen seemed on his way, but party leaders looked elsewhere. They preferred Taft, whose conservatism had won enthusiastic support from the business community, particularly in the Middle West. Taft's chances, however, were weakened by his isolationist background and lukewarm support of postwar internationalism, and by a popular feeling that he was cold and a poor campaigner. Republican leaders were too eager for victory to run such risks. They approached General Eisenhower, who declined. Then they turned to their titular leader, Governor Thomas E. Dewey of New York, who had gained a reputation as a progressive and an internationalist. The Republican national convention, meeting in Philadelphia in June 1948, nominated Dewey on the third ballot and named Governor Earl Warren of California as his running mate. A brief platform approved the New Deal reform structure and postwar bipartisan foreign policy. It also promised further tax reductions, greater efficiency, and more civil rights, welfare, and housing legislation.

In the meantime, civil wars were apparently destroying the Democratic party. The chief rebel was Henry Wallace, who sought to rally Americans behind an advanced collectivistic program and against the administration's policy of resisting Soviet demands. He appealed especially to idealistic college students. When he announced in December 1947 that he would run for president on a third-party ticket, observers predicted that he would poll between five and eight million votes and blast Democratic chances.

While the Wallace rebellion took shape, Democratic progressives, now organized in Americans for Democratic Action (ADA), maneuvered desperately to avoid having to choose between Truman and Wallace. They tried to force Truman to retire and sought a winning candidate in Justice William O. Douglas or General Eisenhower. Powerful urban Democrats like Edward Flynn of New York and Jacob Arvey of Chicago also joined the movement to oust Truman and draft Eisenhower. As if to make a party rupture certain, southern Democrats were up in arms against the president's civil rights program and threatened to bolt if the convention adopted a strong civil rights plank.

It was, therefore, a gloomy and contentious Democratic convention that assembled in Philadelphia in July 1948. ADA progressives, led by Mayor Hubert Humphrey of Minneapolis and supported by city leaders, were determined to draft a program for the future even while they expected defeat in 1948. They put through a platform that strongly reaffirmed the progressive tradition. Then, after a bitter floor fight, the convention adopted a civil rights plank demanding a fair employment practices commission and federal antilynching and antipoll-tax legislation. Finally, a harassed convention early on July 15 named Truman for president because it had no other choice. As his running mate it chose Alben W. Barkley, president pro tem of the Senate, after Justice Douglas had declined to run.

What Democratic leaders most feared, a party rupture, occurred a few days later. The rebel left wing met in Philadelphia in late July, organized the Progressive party, and nominated Wallace for president and Senator Glen Taylor of Idaho for vice-president. Their platform demanded gradual nationalization of basic industries, an end to segregation, and reorientation of foreign policy toward friendship with Russia. This was, actually, the high point of Wallace's strength, for the convention revealed what many already suspected: the Progressive organization was controlled by Communists and fellow travelers, and Wallace had allowed himself to be used in a Communist attempt to disrupt progressive ranks. Few progressives or former New Deal leaders remained in the new party, and Wallace's support dwindled steadily.

Meanwhile, the smoldering southern rebellion had also erupted. So-called Dixiecrats met in Birmingham on July 17, waved Confederate flags, formed the States' Rights Democratic party, and nominated Governor J. Strom Thurmond of South Carolina and Governor Fielding L. Wright of Mississippi. Their opposition to the president's civil rights program had a powerful appeal to southern white sentiment and enabled them to control the Democratic party in four southern states. But they failed to achieve their main objective—an all-southern rebellion that would throw the election into the House of Representatives.

Republican confidence mounted as both wings of the Democracy pummeled Truman. Governor Dewey conducted a mild and dignified campaign. He repeated old strictures against alleged Democratic incompetence but made it clear that he approved the essentials of Democratic domestic and foreign policy. Dewey was so encouraged by the Gallup Poll, which showed him far in the lead, that he bestirred himself only to make plans for his inauguration. Most newspapers and magazines shared his confidence.

Indeed, Truman was one of the few men in the country who thought that he had a chance to win. He startled everyone by announcing that he would call Congress into special session and give the Republicans an opportunity to enact their platform into law. Congress met from July 26 to August 7 without, as he expected, adopting any important legislation. Then Truman went to the country in perhaps the most strenuous personal campaign in American history. Traveling more than thirty thousand miles, he made 351 speeches, many of them "whistle-stop" talks in railroad yards from the rear platform of his car, to an estimated 12 million people. "The technique I used," he later wrote, "was simple and straightforward. . . . I had simply told the people in my own language that they had better wake up to the fact that it was their fight."[7] Castigating the "do-nothing" Eightieth Congress, he urged a bold resumption of progressive policies: repeal of Taft-Hartley, strong civil rights protection for minorities, national health insurance, new antitrust legislation, federal aid to education, broadening of social security benefits, a minimum wage increase, and high parity support for farm prices. Moreover, he went into Harlem to become the first presidential candidate ever to appeal in person for black votes.

Americans admired the president's pluck and assumed that Dewey was bound to win. As one writer observed, they seemed willing to give Truman anything but the presidency. But he knew better than the pollsters and commentators, and he went to bed on election night, November 2, 1948, confident and serene. In the most surprising political upset in American history, Truman won 24,105,695 popular and 303 electoral votes, Dewey 21,969,170 popular and 189 electoral votes. Thurmond, with 1,169,021 popular and 39 electoral votes, and Wallace, with 1,156,103 popular votes, trailed far behind. The Democrats won control of the next Congress by majorities of ninety-three in the House and twelve in the Senate.

Republican critics like the Chicago *Tribune* charged that Dewey had no one but himself to blame for his debacle because he had offered no alternative to Democratic policies. But a careful survey later indicated that

[7]Truman, *Memoirs*, II, 211.

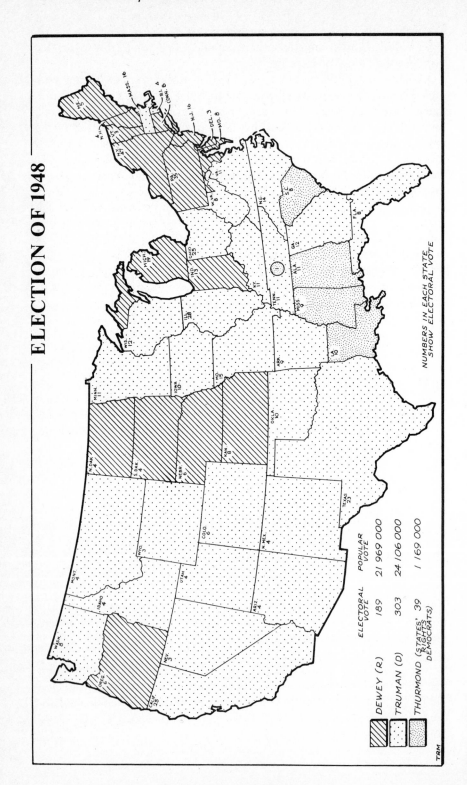

ELECTION OF 1948

NUMBERS IN EACH STATE SHOW ELECTORAL VOTE

	ELECTORAL VOTE	POPULAR VOTE
DEWEY (R)	189	21 969 000
TRUMAN (D)	303	24 106 000
THURMOND (STATES' RIGHTS DEMOCRATS)	39	1 169 000

TRM

Dewey had polled about the maximum normal Republican vote, and that Truman would have been the gainer by a larger turnout on election day. Truman and the Democrats retained control of the federal government for a number of reasons. The country was at peace, prosperous, and relatively united on foreign policy. The party recaptured labor support by its advocacy of repealing Taft-Hartley and gained an almost solid black allegiance by its firm support of new civil rights legislation. Ironically enough, the Wallace and Dixiecrat rebellions probably assured Democratic victory by removing the Communist issue from the campaign and making it clear to blacks and other minority groups that the southern wing did not dominate the party. Another decisive factor was the unexpected behavior of farmers in the Middle West and border states, all of which went for Truman except Indiana. Farmers had feared a depression since the war, and farm prices began a precipitate decline in 1948. Yet Republicans advocated "flexible" price supports that could mean disaster in the rural areas, while Truman promised to maintain a program that had brought prosperity. "I talked about voting for Dewey all summer," one Iowa farmer declared, "but when the time came I just couldn't do it. I remembered the depression and all the good things that had come to me under the Democrats."[8] Finally, the party ticket was strengthened in crucial areas by strong local candidates like Humphrey in Minnesota and Adlai E. Stevenson in Illinois, who ran far ahead of Truman and probably helped him to carry their states by small majorities.

5. The Fair Deal: Revival of Progressivism

Truman was a new political creature after the election of 1948—a president in his own right, sustained by the people's supreme gift. Progressives were happier than at any time since 1936. They had a host of new and vigorous leaders in Congress and a champion in the White House who was dedicated to the cause of further reform. Chastened Republican leaders, surveying the wreckage of their hopes, agreed with Dewey that the GOP's only hope lay in a less conservative posture. Progressivism, therefore, seemed once again ascendant when Harry S. Truman formally launched what he called the Fair Deal in his Annual Message in January 1949. In this and subsequent messages he consolidated past proposals into a comprehensive program. Let us now see how his efforts fared before a new international crisis set the nation upon the path of war and partial mobilization.

[8]Quoted in Samuel Lubell, *The Future of American Politics* (New York, 1952), p. 161.

To state the matter briefly, Truman won less than he asked for and a good deal more than cynics thought he could get from the Eighty-first Congress. For labor, he obtained an amendment to the Fair Labor Standards Act increasing the minimum wage from 40¢ to 75¢ an hour, plus amendments to the Social Security Act that brought 10 million new beneficiaries into the system and increased benefits for retired workers by an average of 77.5 percent. For the millions who lived in rented homes and apartments, he won extension of rent control to March 31, 1951. Another triumph, climaxing a bitter four-year struggle, was the Housing Act of 1949. It provided large sums for slum clearance and authorized construction of 810,000 units for low-income families during the next six years. Truman failed to win approval for the St. Lawrence Seaway, a Missouri Valley Authority, and other regional projects. But he obtained large increases for the Reclamation Bureau's ambitious hydroelectric, water-control, and irrigation program in the West. He won higher appropriations for the TVA, the Rural Electrification Administration, and the Farmers' Home Administration, which since the war had continued the work of the Farm Security Administration in extending loans to farmers for rehabilitation and farm ownership. Finally, he gained approval in June 1950 of a new Displaced Persons bill to admit some 400,000 European refugees.

However, in striving to achieve labor's most important goal—repeal of the Taft-Hartley Act—the president and the unions tried to gain too much and failed. Congress and the public were obviously unwilling to give up many features of the measure that unions condemned as a "slave labor" law. The Senate, with Taft's approval, did adopt a series of amendments that revised the measure substantially in labor's favor. But Truman and his labor allies, gambling on the future, ruined the opportunity by rejecting the compromise and demanding nothing less than complete repeal.

The president and his friends also pushed too hard too fast on other important Fair Deal objectives. The administration's program for agriculture, the Brannan Plan,[9] was probably the best solution of the farm problem. But it aroused charges of regimentation and socialism and provoked much opposition from large farmers. Although the Brannan Plan failed, the administration could claim that the Agricultural Act approved by Congress in October 1949 redeemed Democratic pledges and reaffirmed a progressive policy. It continued rigid price supports at 90 percent of parity through 1950 and provided for flexible supports ranging from 75 to 90 percent afterward.

[9]This plan, proposed by Secretary of Agriculture Charles Brannan in April 1949, was the first serious effort since 1938 to eliminate weaknesses in federal farm policy. It proposed to maintain a "farm income standard," or a dollar income as high as the average of the preceding ten years. To accomplish this goal, it would continue the program of price supports through loans and storage of nonperishable commodities. But for perishable items like meat, eggs, and dairy products it suggested a new method of distribution and maintenance of parity income—the immediate sale of all such commodities at the market price, followed by federal payments to the farmer to make up the difference between what he received and the official support price.

In other and more controversial projects, Truman encountered bitter opposition and defeat. His proposal for national health insurance was beaten by the American Medical Association's gigantic advertising and lobbying campaign. His plan for federal aid to education had substantial bipartisan support, but it met resistance from the Roman Catholic church because it did not include subsidies to parochial school children.

The president suffered his most discouraging defeat in the field of civil rights. He had appointed a Committee on Civil Rights in 1946, composed of distinguished southerners, blacks, educators, and churchmen, to investigate and recommend "more adequate and effective means and procedures for the protection of the civil rights of the people of the United States." The committee report, *To Secure These Rights*, issued in 1947, exposed the operation and consequences of the caste system and called for a systematic federal-state program to root out racial injustice—by strengthening the civil rights section of the Justice Department, using the FBI in cases involving violations of civil rights, enacting antilynching and antipolltax laws, establishing a permanent FEPC, and other measures.

Truman appealed to Congress year in and year out to implement these recommendations, but he could never overcome the threat of a southern filibuster in the Senate. However, he had other recourses; and through them he struck hard at the caste system. He strengthened the civil rights section of the Justice Department and began a practice of having the department assist private parties in civil rights cases. He invited blacks to the inaugural reception and ball in 1949. He appointed the first black governor of the Virgin Islands and the first black federal judge. Most important, he began abolition of segregation in governmental departments and the armed services in 1948.

Looking back over the first eighteen months of Truman's second term, the historian must wonder at how much, not how little, the Fair Deal accomplished during a period of prosperity and relative social contentment. One fact of supreme importance stood out at midcentury. Most Americans, regardless of party affiliation, were so fundamentally progressive that their differences involved only the degree and speed of further movement toward the welfare state.

6. The Second Red Scare

By that fateful day in June 1950 when North Korean Communists invaded South Korea, the American people were convulsed by fear of Communist infiltration of their government and institutions. This second Red scare, so reminiscent of the hysteria after the First World War, would grow even larger before it began to ebb and would leave a residue of personal and partisan bitterness unparalleled since Reconstruction. Its effects were tragically disruptive during a time when Americans needed unity of will and purpose. Unhappily, in contrast to the Red scare of 1919-1920, fear of Communist infiltration after 1945 was in some measure justified. Even more unhappily, millions of Americans turned receptive ears to demagogues who used the Communist issue to seek power and attack freedom in politics, the press, and education.

In an earlier chapter we noted the rise and decline of communism in the United States during the 1930s and the success of underground party members in infiltrating into key positions in the federal government (see Vol. I, pp. 428-432). That infiltration continued unabated after 1941. As one writer put it, "During the war years, Communists and fellow travelers had entered the government in droves. . . . During wartime, most government agencies had considered Communist affiliations to be unimportant. In the Office of Strategic Services, it was common knowledge that the employment of pro-Communists was approved at very high levels provided they were suited for specific jobs."[10]

The impetus for a full-scale drive to root Communists out of government came from two specific events in 1945 and 1946. The OSS discovered early in 1945 that certain of its most secret documents had fallen into the hands of Philip J. Jaffe, editor of *Amerasia*, a Communist-sponsored magazine established for the purpose of influencing American policy in the Far East. OSS officers raided the *Amerasia* offices on March 11, 1945, and found piles of diplomatic and military documents. The FBI then took jurisdiction and established an intimate connection between Jaffe and his associates and Soviet and Chinese Communist officials. Jaffe and an accomplice subsequently received light fines for conspiring to receive government property illegally. Even more jarring was the report issued in 1946 by a Canadian royal commission appointed to investigate charges of Communist espionage. The commission proved that the Communist party in Canada was an arm of the Soviet government and exposed the operation of several Soviet spy rings. More important, it revealed that at least twenty-three Canadians in "positions of trust," one of them a member of Parliament, another a leading atomic scientist, were agents of the Communist ring and had sent atomic secrets and samples of uranium to Moscow.

These revelations spurred the FBI and security officers of Washington departments into action. President Truman issued an executive order in March 1947 inaugurating a comprehensive investigation of all federal employees. Some features of the program evoked strong opposition from liberals, who charged that the government had introduced the principle of "guilt by association" and failed to provide adequate safeguards against

[10]Nathaniel Weyl, *The Battle Against Disloyalty* (New York, 1951), p. 180.

discharge on account of rumors and unknown accusers. On the whole, however, the administration moved with regard for justice and civil rights during its loyalty probe. The gigantic task was completed by early 1951. The Civil Service Commission had cleared more than 3 million federal employees. The FBI had made some fourteen thousand full-scale investigations of doubtful cases. Over two thousand employees had resigned, and 212 persons had been dismissed on the ground that their loyalty was in reasonable doubt. In addition, the president approved a bill in August 1950 authorizing heads of ten so-called sensitive departments and agencies to dismiss persons who, though not necessarily disloyal, were deemed bad security risks. Persons thus accused might demand a hearing by the security board of their own agency but were denied the right of appeal to a review board.

In spite of the thoroughness and severity of the administration's loyalty probe,[11] it was not enough to quiet popular alarm or prevent Republicans from exploiting the issue. This was true not only because demagogues went to work, but also because sensational exposures revealed the former extent of Communist infiltration and the devastating effectiveness of Soviet espionage in acquiring secrets vital to American security. It was true, most poignantly, because the president and several public leaders were drawn into a compromising position in one of the most celebrated cases in American history—the trial of Alger Hiss, ostensibly for perjury but actually for espionage.

Hiss, a member of an important Communist cell in Washington during the New Deal era, had risen rapidly through various departments to a position of considerable trust in the State Department. He had in a sense become the model of the able young civil servant. Among a host of friends he could count a justice of the Supreme Court and a future secretary of state. He resigned from the State Department in 1947 to accept the presidency of the Carnegie Endowment for International Peace.

Whittaker Chambers, a former Soviet agent, had denounced Hiss and other Communists to the State Department in 1939 but had failed to offer proof or even describe the espionage network to which Hiss belonged. Events subsequently convinced Chambers that democracy and communism were engaged in a death grapple, and he told his story to the public and the House Un-American Activities Committee in 1948. Hiss sued for libel, and Chambers produced microfilms of sixty-five State Department documents that he said Hiss had passed to him in early 1938. Called before a federal grand jury in New York, Hiss denied that he had ever delivered such documents to Chambers. He was then indicted for perjury and convicted on January 21, 1950, after a first trial had ended in a hung

[11] Perhaps the best testimony to the program's effectiveness was the failure of security officials or congressional committees to find any Communists in government after the Republicans came to power in 1953.

jury. Hiss's personal tragedy was awful enough. Even more tragic was his betrayal of the president, who had earlier denounced the House committee's investigation as a "red herring," and of a large body of distinguished public leaders who testified to his integrity. The Hiss trials, more than any other event, contributed to a growing public conviction that the Roosevelt and Truman administrations had been oblivious to the danger of Communist subversion.

Other shocks followed. While the rehabilitated House Un-American Activities Committee launched new investigations, a young employee in the Justice Department named Judith Coplon was arrested, tried, and convicted in 1948 for passing vital information on the FBI's counterespionage system to a Soviet agent. Virtual hysteria followed the revelation in 1950 that a group of Anglo-American agents had succeeded in delivering full information on the atomic bomb to the Soviet government from 1943 to 1947.[12]

These disclosures and their implications set the stage for the spectacular rise of Joseph R. McCarthy of Wisconsin and the peak of the second Red scare. Elected to the Senate in 1946, McCarthy had already acquired a reputation for moral callousness, doubtful integrity, and utter ruthlessness. He decided early in 1950 to use the issue of Communist infiltration to improve his ebbing political fortunes. By his indiscriminate and reckless attacks during the next four years he won clear title as the most unprincipled man in public life since Aaron Burr and the most successful demagogue since Huey Long. He also did more than any other living American to confuse and divide the people and discredit his country's good name abroad.

McCarthy opened his campaign on February 9, 1950, by announcing that he had the names of 205, or 57, Communists in the State Department. Unable to point out a single one, McCarthy countered by naming Owen Lattimore of The Johns Hopkins University, an expert on the Far East, as leader of "the espionage ring in the State Department." When J. Edgar Hoover, head of the FBI, affirmed that there was no evidence on which to substantiate this charge,[13] a special Senate committee headed by Millard Tydings of Maryland gave Lattimore a clean bill of health. Such failure

[12] All during the war Soviet agents made fantastic attempts to obtain information about the atomic energy program. Army intelligence and FBI agents frustrated most of these efforts but failed to discover the important atomic spy ring led by Dr. Klaus Fuchs, a German-born physicist and naturalized British subject. Sent to Los Alamos in 1944 to help make the atomic bomb, Fuchs succeeded in delivering apparently complete information on the bomb to Soviet agents. The American people learned the shocking news of his betrayal when Fuchs was arrested in February 1950 and confessed to British authorities. Soon afterward the FBI arrested his accomplices in the United States.

[13] The only serious charge against Lattimore was that he consciously sought to influence American Far Eastern policy in order to further Soviet interests. The Senate internal security committee, which reopened the Lattimore case in 1951, made this accusation and obtained an indictment (later dismissed by a federal court) charging Lattimore with perjury.

only stirred McCarthy to more brutal attacks. He turned next against Philip C. Jessup, American representative in the General Assembly of the United Nations, charging savagely that this distinguished public servant had Communist connections; against Senator Tydings, whom he helped defeat for reelection in the autumn of 1950; and finally against Generals George C. Marshall and Dwight D. Eisenhower, both of whom he accused in June 1951 of assisting the Russians in their drive for world domination.

McCarthy's smear campaign and use of the "big lie" tactic, so reminiscent of the methods of Adolf Hitler, filled many with loathing, but millions of Americans were so frightened by revelations of Communist espionage and infiltration that they turned receptive ears to his propaganda. Moreover, Republican leaders encouraged the Wisconsin demagogue and used him with telling effect in the congressional campaign of 1950. For a time it seemed that "McCarthyism" had won at least the approval, if not the open endorsement, of the great GOP.

7. Communism, the Courts, and Congress

McCarthyism was only the most violent manifestation of the anti-Communist hysteria that engulfed the United States from 1948 to 1953. In varying degree it affected the press, schools, churches, courts, the executive branch, and Congress. It created an atmosphere of fear and stimulated a belief that it was safer to conform than to disagree with the majority. While many bold voices pleaded for sanity and preservation of civil liberties, the government carried through and the courts approved an anti-Communist program that greatly diminished such liberties.

The Truman administration opened the drive in 1948 by obtaining the indictment of eleven Communist leaders for conspiring, in violation of the Smith Act of 1940, to *teach* the violent overthrow of the United States. The government had prepared its case thoroughly and could support its charges by the testimony of FBI agents and former Communists. The long trial culminated in conviction of all eleven defendants in 1949. After the court of appeals upheld the decision, the case—*Dennis et al.* v. *United States*—came before the Supreme Court for final review.

The court upheld the Smith Act and confirmed the convictions by a vote of six to two on June 4, 1951. The charge was not conspiracy to overthrow the government by force, but conspiracy to teach or advocate revolution. Chief Justice Vinson spoke for the majority in this important decision. He reconciled the conviction with the right of free speech by affirming that the government had proved the Communist threat sufficiently substantial to justify conviction under the doctrine of "clear and present danger." The Justice Department then obtained the conviction and imprisonment of some forty other Communist leaders for violating the Smith Act. Defenders of civil liberties were further shocked by two Supreme Court decisions in 1951 and 1952 that seemed to condone police censorship and state suppression of free speech on broad grounds.[14] Indeed, many wondered whether the court had not been sucked into the vortex of the reaction against communism.

Congress, too, reacted violently in 1950 by approving over the president's veto the McCarran internal security bill—easily the severest measure since the Sedition Act of 1918 and one of the most confused. It required Communist organizations to register with the attorney general and furnish membership lists and financial statements. But it specifically declared that membership or officeholding in a Communist organization was not, per se, a crime. In a second breath, the bill made it illegal knowingly to conspire to perform "any act" that would "substantially" contribute to the establishment of a totalitarian dictatorship in the United States. It also forbade granting passports to Communists or employing them in defense plants; authorized their internment in time of war; and established a bipartisan Subversive Activities Control Board to assist in exposing such organizations.

If, as the president charged in his veto message, the McCarran Act's internal provisions were mainly blundering and ineffective, then the ones relating to immigration, deportation, and naturalization actually damaged American security. By forbidding the entry into the United States of any person who had once been a member of a totalitarian organization, for example, the measure deprived the American government of its most effective means of inducing Russian and other Communist leaders to defect to the free world.

Anti-Communist sentiment flared again two years later when Congress passed over Truman's veto the McCarran-Walter immigration and nationality bill in June 1952. It rectified an old injustice by permitting naturalization of resident Asiatics and annual admission of two thousand Orientals on a quota basis. But the President and many liberals thought that its provisions for exclusion and deportation of aliens and control of American citizens abroad were unnecessarily harsh and subversive of fundamental rights.

---

[14]In *Feiner* v. *New York* and *Beauharnais* v. *Illinois*. Feiner had been arrested for disorderly conduct while making a soapbox speech in Syracuse during the campaign of 1948. The shocking aspect of the verdict, which upheld the conviction, was the implication that police were justified in arresting any person who *in their opinion* was provoking a riot. Beauharnais, head of the racist White Circle League of Chicago, was convicted of violating an Illinois statute forbidding the libeling of any person or group on account of race, color, creed, or religion. In upholding the conviction by a five-to-four majority, the Court specifically approved the new theory of "group libel" and thus further enlarged the state's control over speech and expression.

26

Vain Struggles for a Brave New World,

1945–1949

Americans thanked God in the summer of 1945 that the war was over and hoped that a new world order would banish fears and rivalries upon which wars bred. Events soon made a mockery of these hopes. The Allied victory had raised a new menace—the threat of Soviet expansion—which seemed at the time to be almost as great as the Nazi danger had been. The total defeat of Germany and Japan had removed counterbalances to Soviet power, and Americans now faced two unwelcome alternatives. They could either allow Russia to fill the European and Far Eastern power vacuums or they could build and support a new power structure to prevent it.

In due time Americans would learn that perils and hardships inevitably accompany world leadership. The grave danger after 1945 was that they were still so inexperienced and naive as to expect prompt and easy solutions, and that they would shirk responsibility when their hopes were frustrated as they had done in 1919-1920. Let us now see what triumphs and failures awaited them during this second postwar period, and how they groped toward effective participation in world affairs.

1. The Brave New World

President Roosevelt and Secretary Hull worked diligently after 1941 to achieve their primary postwar objective, creation of an international organization to prevent aggression and preserve peace. They found an almost unanimous response in the United States; abroad they found disagreement only upon details. Leaders of the three great powers resolved their differences at the Dumbarton Oaks and Yalta conferences in 1944 and early 1945 (see pp. 546–550). They also approved the structure of a United Nations and convoked an international conference to meet in San Francisco in April to draft a charter for the new organization.

Allied disagreement over Poland threatened to disrupt the conference before it could meet. But President Truman made it clear to Foreign Minister Molotov on April 22 that the United States intended to lead in forming an international organization whether or not Russia cooperated, and the Soviets abruptly changed their attitude. Thus the conference opened on schedule on April 25, and representatives of forty-six nations met to transform a wartime alliance into a permanent structure for world peace.

The San Francisco Conference was an inauspicious beginning for the reign of universal brotherhood. American and Russian delegates wrangled incessantly over questions large and small; and Truman saved the conference from disruption on one occasion only by appealing personally to Stalin. In the end, the Charter of the United Nations—signed on June 26, approved by the United States Senate on July 28, and promulgated on October 24, 1945—embodied a minimum of concessions to Soviet demands and every important objective for which the United States had contended. It was an American document in all its strengths and weaknesses—Wilson's League covenant embellished and revised.

The charter created a United Nations with a bicameral legislature. The Security Council, or "upper house," had initiative and authority in fundamental matters. It was composed of representatives of five powers with permanent seats[1] and six other members elected biennially by the other house. The vote of any seven members could settle procedural questions, but action on substantive questions required unanimous approval by the five permanent members. The General Assembly, or "lower house," in which each member nation had one vote,[2] was empowered to discuss any question and to recommend to the Security Council on any matter within the scope of the charter, except in the case of a dispute already on the council's agenda.

[1] The United States, Great Britain, Russia, France, and China.

[2] The exception was Russia, which in effect had three votes. In return for Soviet concessions on other matters, the Ukrainian and Byelorussian "soviet republics," though actually part of the USSR, were given seats in the assembly.

The charter also created a Secretariat, headed by a secretary-general, to perform administrative tasks, and an International Court of Justice endowed with such jurisdiction as member states chose to grant. There were dozens of subsidiary and allied agencies: an Economic and Social Council; a Trusteeship Council, established to supervise old League mandates and territories taken from Japan and Italy; an International Monetary Fund, with resources of nearly $9 billion for currency stabilization and trade expansion; an International Bank for Reconstruction and Development, with subscribed capital of $9.1 billion to facilitate investment in war-ravaged and undeveloped areas. There was, finally, the United Nations Relief and Rehabilitation Administration (UNRRA), eventually given nearly $4 billion to provide food and clothing for war-stricken peoples of Europe and Asia from 1945 to 1947.

It was an imposing structure, calculated to fit every need and to please all but the most extreme nationalists. But it was a structure for world confederation and cooperation, not for effective world government. On paper the charter inaugurated an era of universal peace, for members agreed to follow the path of arbitration rather than the road to war. And yet the United Nations lacked power sufficient to its task. Like the American union established by the Articles of Confederation, the UN was an association of sovereign states, with no authority except such as leading members condescended to let it use. Established primarily to prevent war, it could be blocked in performing this elementary function by the veto of any permanent member of the Security Council. Powerless to prevent aggression by its leading members, the UN in this respect was a weaker peace-keeping instrument than the League of Nations. Nor was there much hope of reform, for permanent members of the Security Council had the right to veto proposed amendments.

American leaders, notably Roosevelt and Hull, were largely responsible for these constitutional defects. Fearing isolationist sentiment at home and willing to make concessions to obtain Russian membership, they insisted upon an agency that would not impair national sovereignty and could function effectively only so long as all great powers agreed. Thus the veto was more an American than a Russian invention; the provision for "regional" defensive associations, creation of which later emphasized the UN's failure as a peace agency, was also included at American insistence.

These weaknesses were only dimly perceptible as people set about creating a new and better world in 1945. To the first and most urgent task, that of relief for war-ravaged areas, Americans responded generously. The United States contributed some $2.7 billion through UNRRA in food and supplies to the peoples of China and central and eastern Europe. The army assumed the burden of relief in Japan and the American zone of Germany, while the Red Cross, church groups, and private organizations

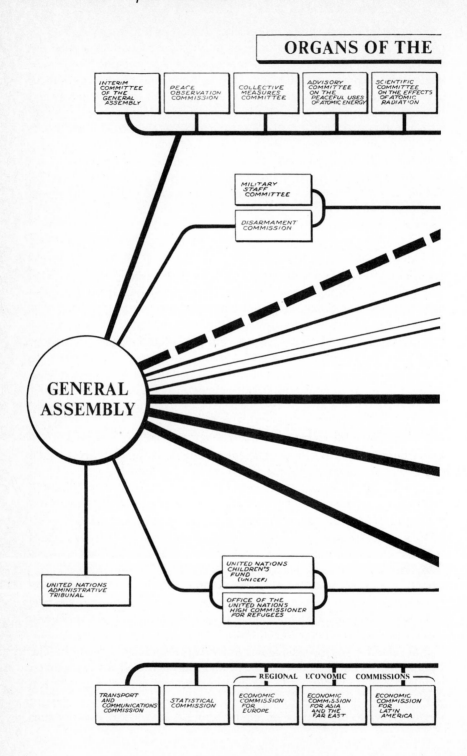

ORGANS OF THE

INTERIM COMMITTEE OF THE GENERAL ASSEMBLY

PEACE OBSERVATION COMMISSION

COLLECTIVE MEASURES COMMITTEE

ADVISORY COMMITTEE ON THE PEACEFUL USES OF ATOMIC ENERGY

SCIENTIFIC COMMITTEE ON THE EFFECTS OF ATOMIC RADIATION

MILITARY STAFF COMMITTEE

DISARMAMENT COMMISSION

GENERAL ASSEMBLY

UNITED NATIONS ADMINISTRATIVE TRIBUNAL

UNITED NATIONS CHILDREN'S FUND (UNICEF)

OFFICE OF THE UNITED NATIONS HIGH COMMISSIONER FOR REFUGEES

REGIONAL ECONOMIC COMMISSIONS

TRANSPORT AND COMMUNICATIONS COMMISSION

STATISTICAL COMMISSION

ECONOMIC COMMISSION FOR EUROPE

ECONOMIC COMMISSION FOR ASIA AND THE FAR EAST

ECONOMIC COMMISSION FOR LATIN AMERICA

UNITED NATIONS

UN RELIEF AND WORKS AGENCY FOR PALESTINE REFUGEES IN THE NEAR EAST

UNITED NATIONS KOREAN RECONSTRUCTION AGENCY

INTERNATIONAL LAW COMMISSION

COMMITTEE ON INFORMATION FROM NON-SELF-GOVERNING TERRITORIES

ADVISORY COMMITTEE ON ADMINISTRATIVE AND BUDGETARY QUESTIONS

COMMITTEE ON CONTRIBUTIONS

SECURITY COUNCIL

INTERNATIONAL ATOMIC ENERGY AGENCY

INTERNATIONAL COURT OF JUSTICE

TRUSTEESHIP COUNCIL

SECRETARIAT

ECONOMIC AND SOCIAL COUNCIL

ADMINISTRATIVE COMMITTEE ON CO-ORDINATION

TECHNICAL ASSISTANCE BOARD

S P E C I A L I Z E D   A G E N C I E S

INTERNATIONAL LABOR ORGANIZATION

WORLD HEALTH ORGANIZATION

FOOD AND AGRICULTURE ORGANIZATION OF THE UNITED NATIONS

UNIVERSAL POSTAL UNION

UNITED NATIONS EDUCATIONAL, SCIENTIFIC, AND CULTURAL ORGANIZATION

INTERNATIONAL TELECOMMUNICATION UNION

INTERNATIONAL CIVIL AVIATION ORGANIZATION

WORLD METEOROLOGICAL ORGANIZATION

INTERNATIONAL MONETARY FUND

INTER-GOVERNMENTAL MARITIME CONSULTATIVE ORGANIZATION

INTERNATIONAL BANK FOR RECONSTRUCTION AND DEVELOPMENT

INTERNATIONAL FINANCE CORPORATION (AFFILIATE OF INTERNATIONAL BANK)

INTERNATIONAL TRADE ORGANIZATION (INTERIM COMMISSION)

COMMISSION ON HUMAN RIGHTS

SOCIAL COMMISSION

COMMISSION ON THE STATUS OF WOMEN

POPULATION COMMISSION

COMMISSION ON NARCOTIC DRUGS

COMMISSION ON INTERNATIONAL COMMODITY TRADE

added several hundred million dollars' worth of clothing and food. Through the sale on credit of surplus property and extension of credits by the Export-Import Bank, Washington made some additional $4.7 billion available, chiefly to western Europe.

To the second task, restoration of foreign trade, the American government addressed itself with boldness and success. The fundamental problem was Europe's continued dependence upon the United States for food, supplies, and industrial equipment, and her inability to pay in full, either in dollars, goods, or services, because of war damage and the termination of Lend-Lease assistance in 1945. Accumulated foreign deficits—over $19 billion in 1946-1947—were so staggering that world trade would simply have collapsed without decisive American support. Washington solved the problem before 1948 by stopgap expedients: UNRRA and other aid, loans by the Export-Import Bank, a credit of $3.75 billion to Great Britain in 1946, and so on. The world economy was not much healthier in 1948 than it had been in 1945; but stopgap aid had prevented its collapse until a comprehensive reconstruction program could be launched.

The third and perhaps most difficult task was the reconstruction and reform of Germany and Japan and the punishment of individuals allegedly responsible for the war. Americans were unprepared for this undertaking, and in retrospect many of the occupation policies seem unwise, unnecessarily harsh, and utopian. Not even during the heyday of Wilsonian missionary interventionism had the United States embarked upon so stupendous an effort to reform other nations; never had an American government practiced such terrible vengeance upon former enemies. Policy makers blithely ignored the possibility that the vexatious problem of "war guilt" might someday return to haunt the American people.

American policy in Germany was shaped by a desire to visit condign punishment and then to make German society over in the American image. All four occupying powers were pledged to destroy nazism and help build new democratic institutions, but American authorities outshone all others in zeal. The United States cooperated with other powers in limiting German steel production, destroying armament plants and industries with war potential, and dismantling other plants and sending them to Russia, Poland, and elsewhere as reparations. The result was to limit the German contribution to European recovery and aggravate the huge burden of relief for refugees, displaced persons, the homeless, and the unemployed.

By 1949, when "denazification" was supposedly complete, military authorities and German courts had punished 1,635 major and some 600,000 minor Nazi offenders. Allied vengeance culminated in the trial of some twenty-two high Nazi officials by an International Military Tribunal at Nuremberg from November 21, 1945, to October 1, 1946. Three of the defendants were acquitted and nineteen were convicted, of whom twelve were sentenced to death.[3] The tribunal tried hard to avoid the appearance of a kangaroo court and observed some of the forms of justice. Even so, the trial violated nearly every tradition of Anglo-American jurisprudence. Conviction of political officials for planning and waging aggressive war, for example, violated the ancient prohibition against ex post facto laws. Execution of military commanders established the new and impossible doctrine that soldiers might be punished for obeying orders. Above all, the trial of defendants for war crimes and atrocities established the principle that, as Churchill put it, "the leaders of a nation defeated in war shall be put to death by the victors."

The United States exercised complete control over occupation and reconstruction policies in Japan, vesting all authority in General Douglas MacArthur as supreme commander for the Allied powers. Thousands of alleged militarists and supporters of aggression were purged, and hundreds of military leaders were tried and executed for war crimes. An International Military Tribunal for the Far East prosecuted twenty-eight high officials for waging aggressive war in violation of international law.[4] But MacArthur and his subordinates came to reform as well as to punish. They sought not only to destroy or modify institutions and customs that had served the Japanese people for hundreds of years, but also to create a new political, economic, and social order with roots deep in American utopian traditions. This new order included renunciation even of defensive war, demilitarization, land distribution, an antitrust campaign, and social democracy. A few "reactionaries" protested; a few "realists" suggested that destruction of Japanese power would only serve the interests of the Soviet Union. But most Americans hailed the building of this new democratic society in the far Pacific.

2. *The Breakup of the Grand Alliance, 1945-1947*

President Roosevelt worked hard until his death to remove Soviet suspicions and create an atmosphere of mutual trust in which genuine collaboration could develop. There were increasing evidences of Russian bad faith and expansionistic ambitions, and warnings from Moscow by Ambas-

[3]The death sentence was executed by hanging eight defendants. Another, Martin Bormann, was never apprehended and was presumed to be dead; another, Hermann Goering, cheated the hangman by committing suicide.

[4]This "trial" began in Tokyo in June 1946 and ended in April 1948. The tribunal found all defendants guilty on November 11, 1948, and sentenced seven of them, including two former premiers, to death by hanging.

sador W. Averell Harriman and his assistant, George F. Kennan, that such collaboration was impossible. Even so, President Truman and his new secretary of state, James F. Byrnes,[5] continued Roosevelt's quest.

Russian action in imposing a Communist government on Rumania, dissension over Poland, and Stalin's accusation that Roosevelt and Churchill conspired during the last weeks of the war to make a separate peace had raised grave doubts about the permanence of the Grand Alliance even before Germany surrendered. The rift widened at the San Francisco Conference, and Truman sent Harry Hopkins to Moscow in May 1945 to join Harriman in frank talks with Stalin. The dictator, in an angry mood, accused the American government of insulting the USSR at San Francisco and ending Lend-Lease aid abruptly after the German surrender in order to apply pressure on Russia. But Stalin mellowed in conversation and agreed to admit non-Communist Poles to the Polish government and to meet President Truman and Prime Minister Churchill for a full discussion of outstanding problems.

Truman, Stalin, Churchill, and Clement Attlee, soon to be Churchill's successor, assembled in Potsdam, outside shattered Berlin, on July 17, 1945, for the last meeting of the chiefs of state of the Grand Alliance. The conferees quickly agreed to demand the immediate surrender of Japan and establish a Council of Foreign Ministers to prepare peace treaties for Italy and the Balkan states. There was, however, almost interminable disagreement over the sensitive issues of reparations and implementing the Yalta Declaration on Liberated Countries. Under strong pressure from Truman and Churchill, the Russians finally agreed to permit Anglo-American observers in Rumania, Hungary, Bulgaria, and Finland to move about freely. In return, the American and British leaders approved Polish occupation and administration of German territory east of the Neisse River until a peace conference could settle German boundaries. As for reparations, Stalin accepted Byrnes's proposal that each power obtain reparations from its own zone, and that the Western Allies transfer 15 percent of the capital equipment in their zones to Russia in exchange for food, coal, and other raw materials. Other unsettled issues were deferred for future discussion.

Soviet-American relations were not helped by Washington's failure in the immediate postwar period even to acknowledge a Soviet request for a large loan from the United States. However, on the whole it must be said that Byrnes and his advisers struggled during the next seventeen months, in the face of mounting obstacles, to reach accord with the Russians on outstanding problems—a united policy for Germany, peace treaties for Italy and the central European and Balkan countries, and international agreement for disarmament and control of atomic energy. Byrnes, who shared Roosevelt's conviction that American cooperation with Russia was the indispensable cornerstone of postwar peace, sought to overcome Rus-

[5]Truman appointed Byrnes in June 1945 to succeed Edward R. Stettinius, Jr.

sian suspicion by concession and compromise. His failure prepared the way for a different policy of firm support of western Europe and stern resistance to feared Soviet aggressions.

Germany, that cockpit of Europe, was the source of greatest potential conflict. In order to destroy the German threat to European security and world peace, Roosevelt had envisaged and seemingly won Stalin's cordial support for united action in demilitarizing and neutralizing Germany for years to come. Byrnes urged the Russians at London in September 1945 and again at Moscow in December to join in a twenty-five-year alliance to prevent a resurgence of German militarism. When Truman, Stalin, and the British and French foreign ministers approved, Byrnes hopefully prepared a treaty, only to encounter insuperable Russian opposition in early 1946. Byrnes's successor, George C. Marshall, raised the proposal again in April 1947 and met the same response. By this time the Grand Alliance had become permanently disrupted and Russian policy was clear—to keep Germany divided so as to preserve Soviet control of the eastern zone.

Byrnes also worked hard to conclude peace treaties for Hitler's erstwhile junior partners. The Russians stubbornly refused to approve an Austrian treaty, as such action would have compelled them to withdraw from a vital outpost in central Europe and destroyed their excuse for retaining troops in Hungary and Rumania. On the other hand, Byrnes finally obtained treaties for Italy, Hungary, Rumania, and Bulgaria at Paris in February 1947. They confirmed Western supremacy in Italy and North Africa and Soviet predominance in Hungary and the Balkans. It was perhaps the only settlement possible, but it marked American recognition of Russian control of southeastern Europe, which, in the circumstances and in view of Russian security needs, was inevitable in any event.

On the other overshadowing issue of 1945-1946—international disarmament and control of atomic energy—American leaders formulated a bold plan to relieve world anxiety over atomic warfare and lay the foundations for future peace. With sole possession of atomic bombs from 1945 until the Russians detonated their first in mid-1949, Americans might have pursued "atomic imperialism," that is, policies of threat and coercion. Instead, they came forward with a truly revolutionary disarmament proposal. Submitted to the United Nations Atomic Energy Commission by Bernard M. Baruch in June 1946, the plan called for an international statute and Atomic Development Authority to own, control, and operate all uranium and thorium mines and production facilities and alone conduct research in atomic explosives. The authority might permit use of atomic energy for peaceful purposes, but it would have full power, unrestrained by any veto, of inspection and punishment of violators of the atomic energy statute.

This was a breathtaking proposal, but it was more than the Russians believed they could safely approve. They correctly perceived that the authority would be controlled by the Western nations. They therefore countered with a proposal simply to outlaw manufacture and use of atomic bombs and to vest enforcement in the Security Council, where

CENTRAL
AND EASTERN
EUROPE
———
TERRITORIAL CHANGES
1939–1947

300 MILES

NORTH CAPE

Petsamo

Murmansk

WHITE SEA

NORWAY

SWEDEN

FINLAND

GULF OF BOTHNIA

Oslo

PORKKALA-UDD
(LEASED TO
U.S.S.R.)

Helsinki

LAKE LADOGA

Stockholm

Tallinn

GULF OF FINLAND

Leningrad

DENMARK

BALTIC SEA

ESTONIA

S O V I E T

Riga

LATVIA

Copen-
hagen

FORMER GERMAN
TERRITORY
ADMINISTERED
BY U.S.S.R.
AND POLAND

LITHUANIA

Moscow

Gdansk
(DANZIG)

Kaunas

Vilna

ANNEXED BY THE
SOVIET UNION

E. PRUSSIA

Minsk

Szczecin
(STETTIN)

(ALLIED
OCC.)

WEST
GERMANY

Berlin

EAST
(U.S.S.R.
OCC.)

POLAND

Warsaw

EASTERN

POLAND

Bonn

Wrocław
(BRESLAU)

GERMANY AND
AUSTRIA DIVIDED
AND OCCUPIED

Prague

Cracow

Kiev

BERLIN AND
VIENNA JOINTLY
OCCUPIED

CZECHOSLOVAKIA

U N I O N

SWITZ.

AUSTRIA
(U.S.S.R.
OCC.)

Vienna

Bratislava
BRIDGE-
HEAD

Budapest

SUB-
CARPATHIAN
RUTHENIA

NORTHERN
BUKOVINA

BESSARABIA

Odessa

(ALLIED
OCC.)

HUNGARY

TRANSYLVANIA

Trieste

VENEZIA
GIULIA

RUMANIA

FREE
TERRITORY
OF TRIESTE

ANNEXED
BY
YUGOSLAVIA

Belgrade

Bucharest

DOBRUJA

*BLACK
SEA*

Zara
(CEDED
TO YUGO.)

YUGOSLAVIA

Rome

LAGOSTA
IS.

Sofia

BULGARIA

ANNEXED BY
BULGARIA

ITALY

ALBANIA

Tirana

Istanbul

(TURK.)

SASENO I.
(CEDED TO
ALBANIA)

TURKEY

GREECE

SICILY

Athens

TRM

they might veto action against violators. The Russians subsequently made important concessions by accepting unlimited international inspection, but they would never yield the power to veto punishment of violators. The American government, unwilling to accept any compromise that impaired the principle of effective international control, rejected the Soviet overtures and in effect ended all serious hopes for atomic disarmament.

Failure here merely underscored the larger failure of the United States and the Soviet Union to find a basis for common action on Germany, disarmament, and creation of armed forces for the UN. Perhaps Russia would have been more cooperative had the United States extended material aid for civilian reconstruction after the termination of Lend-Lease, shared the secrets of the atomic bomb (which Roosevelt had also refused to do), and more readily conceded what in retrospect seem to have been Russia's legitimate security needs in eastern and central Europe. Perhaps American leaders, by moving too boldly and quickly on disarmament, confirmed Russian suspicions that the United States sought world domination. On the other hand, it does seem fair to say that Russian leaders, out of ignorance, isolation, a distorted view of international politics, or desire to extend their own power, were primarily responsible for wrecking the world's hopes for a stable peace.

3. *The Chinese Tragedy*

The Chinese Communist victory of 1949 upset the world balance of power and destroyed American hopes for peace and stability in the Far East. It also had a supremely ironic quality. The American government had sought for half a century to maintain Chinese independence and give China what it regarded as the benefits of Western civilization, democracy, and Christianity. The United States, among all of the major Far Eastern powers, had been the least imperialistic, and had defended Chinese integrity even to the point of a long and bloody war with Japan. Yet, only five years after the Japanese surrender, the American people found themselves at war with a Chinese government that reviled them as China's most dangerous enemies.

The stage was set for Communist triumph during the war years. By the end of 1941 Chiang Kai-shek's Nationalist government at Chungking was exhausted and nearly fatally weakened after four years of seemingly hopeless resistance to Japan. It managed to survive after 1941 only because the Japanese concluded that its final destruction was not worth the effort. The American government did its best to keep China in the war—by extending a half-billion-dollar credit in 1942, airlifting supplies over the treacherous Himalayan Hump, and dispatching military advisers to Chungking. But these efforts were totally inadequate to the main task of strengthening and supplying Chinese armies. Allied forces in Burma finally broke the siege of China and opened a supply route from India to Kunming in early 1945—with the war nearly over and the Nationalist government weaker than ever.

Meanwhile, Roosevelt and his advisers had been maturing plans to strengthen China after the war and establish her as a great power even while lifeblood drained from the Chungking regime. The president won Churchill's and Stalin's seeming approval of the Cairo Declaration of December 1943, which promised the return of Manchuria and Formosa to China. At Yalta the president won a permanent seat on the Security Council for China and Stalin's pledge of support for the Nationalist government. These were great plans but dangerous ones, unless the Soviets honored their promises and the United States was prepared to support and strengthen the Nationalists. Yet even while the leaders talked at Yalta, China stood on the verge of civil war. Its outcome would make China a great power, to be sure, but one seemingly allied with the Soviet Union.

Chiang Kai-shek all through the war faced not only the outward Japanese menace but also the internal peril of Communist conquest. The Chinese Communists, driven out of southern China in 1934–1935, had fought their way to Yenan, in the Shensi Province in northwestern China. There they established a precarious government, harassed but never conquered by Nationalist forces. Growing stronger after the Japanese invasion in 1937, the Communists rejected Chiang's appeals to submit to the central government and join in common defense of the motherland. They were so strong by early 1944, in fact, that Chiang had diverted 400,000 of his best troops in order to contain them.

At this point the Allied need for manpower in Burma and the beginning of a new Japanese offensive in China led Washington to try to unify the Chinese forces. Stalin and Molotov reassured Roosevelt that Russia had no interest in controlling China and that, in any event, Chinese Communists were not good Communists. Vice-President Wallace went to Chungking in June 1944 and urged Chiang to come to terms with Yenan so that all Chinese troops could combine against the common enemy. A short time later Roosevelt sent General Patrick J. Hurley as his personal representative to Chiang. Hurley went by way of Moscow and learned that the Kremlin was not interested in or responsible for the Chinese comrades and would take no part in the civil war.

But the more American leaders urged Chiang to come to agreement, the more stubbornly did he insist that Chinese Communists were revolutionaries bent upon domination of China. And the more Chiang refused to approve unification upon any basis except Yenan's military submission, the stronger the American conviction grew that Chiang and his government were unreasonable, corrupt, incompetent, and unrepresentative. Chiang did allow American newspaper reporters and official observers to go to Yenan in the spring of 1944. These reporters sent back glowing accounts, while foreign service officers confirmed the newsmen's reports that the Communists were primarily agrarian reformers, extraordinarily efficient, and devoted to the cause of democracy. At the same time, these observers emphasized the obvious shortcomings of the Chungking regime so heavily that "The main effect of their reporting was . . . to weaken faith in the power of the Generalissimo [Chiang] and his group to govern China."[6]

A rational American policy would have been difficult at best as the showdown between Communists and Nationalists approached in 1945. It was, however, virtually impossible because of the irresponsible way that Washington was then doing business in China. Its two chief officials there—General Hurley, who became ambassador in December 1944, and General Albert C. Wedemeyer, who succeeded General Joseph W. Stilwell as Chiang's chief of staff and commander of American forces in China in October 1944—tried hard to work with Chiang. Foreign service experts, on the other hand, argued that the Nationalist government was hopelessly corrupt and tyrannical, and that the Communists would prevail because they were genuinely representative of the people. They appealed over Hurley's head to Washington, urging that the United States should either compel Chiang to come to terms with the Communists or else, if he refused, join hands with the Yenan regime.

When Roosevelt backed Hurley at a showdown meeting in Washington in March 1945, American policy became reasonably clear. The United States would continue to support Chiang but would also seek to arrest the civil war by bringing the Nationalists and Communists together in a coalition government. Hurley cordially supported this decision, convinced, like most Americans, that Russia would not intervene and that the Yenan leaders were neither genuine Communists nor Soviet allies.[7] He set more intensively to the task of mediation upon his return to Chungking in May 1945. In Moscow Harry Hopkins received Stalin's unequivocal pledge of support for the Nationalist government.

Then the war in the Pacific suddenly ended, and the United States had to redefine its policy. It quickly came to Chiang Kai-shek's assistance in the first task ahead—accepting the surrender of Japanese forces and occu-

[6]Herbert Feis, *The China Tangle* (Princeton, 1953), p. 259.

[7]Hurley's views were "confirmed" in Moscow by Stalin and Molotov in April 1945. It is only fair to add, however, that Ambassador Harriman and Kennan were not deceived by Stalin's assurances and warned against taking them seriously.

pying key Chinese ports and cities before the Communists could occupy them. Thus, American air power moved three Chinese armies from the interior to eastern and northern provinces during September and October 1945. The navy later transported an additional 400,000 Nationalist troops to Manchurian ports. American marines occupied strategic cities like Tsingtao, Tientsin, and Peking until Nationalist forces could take over. By the end of 1945, American and Chinese troops had accepted the surrender of Japanese forces everywhere in China but Manchuria, and Chiang controlled the important cities in Manchuria and the southern and eastern provinces.

Even so, the situation was fraught with danger. The Chinese Communists were powerfully entrenched in the north and in Manchuria, where Russian occupation forces were supplying them with Japanese arms. Nationalist armies were badly overextended, while Chiang's political agents were often inexperienced, inefficient, and corrupt. Before the Russians withdrew from Manchuria in February 1946, they stripped that province of some $2 billion worth of industrial and railroad equipment, thus leaving the area useless to assist in national rebuilding. Worst of all, it was obvious that China stood on the brink of full-scale war.

Clearly, this was a crucial moment of decision in Washington. Should the United States occupy China and Manchuria, at least with token forces, and give material assistance to the Nationalists? Should it seek to halt the civil war through mediation and threaten to withdraw support if Chiang refused to cooperate? Or should it withdraw from China altogether and let the two opposing forces fight it out?

The final decision was not adopted because of any lack of reliable information. General Wedemeyer warned in a series of messages that the task of unifying and pacifying China was too great for Chiang and his incompetent government to accomplish. Other military observers confirmed this analysis and agreed that abandoning Chiang meant abandoning China to the Communists. And yet there was no disposition in Washington or the country at large to give wholehearted support to Chiang's discredited regime in a war against what many thought was an honest, efficient, and democratic opponent. In fact, the administration's desire to stay out of the civil war enjoyed almost universal support in the United States.

Thus supported, the Washington leaders made their decision in late 1945. They sent General Marshall to China to press for a truce and conduct mediation looking toward a coalition government in which both the Kuomintang, or Nationalist, and Communist parties would compete peacefully for power. Marshall arrived in Chungking at the end of December and set to work at once. It seemed for several months that his efforts to achieve peace and unity might succeed, as the opposing groups approved a cease-fire and a plan for governmental reorganization. Actually,

Marshall merely delayed the inevitable war—inevitable because neither side would trust the other or yield on essential points—during a time when delay worked to Communist advantage. He abandoned his mission in January 1947 with a blast at Nationalist reactionaries and Communists alike, declaring that the hope of Chinese salvation lay with a liberal group who were without power and prestige in the Kuomintang.

Marshall returned to Washington to become secretary of state, and the war in China began in earnest. The Nationalists were well equipped[8] and greatly superior in numbers at the outset. But the Communists had the edge in training, discipline, and leadership, plus the advantage of interior lines, while Nationalist commanders were content to occupy isolated cities and seemed unable to wage aggressive campaigns. The tide was beginning to turn by mid-1947. Defeatism swept through the Nationalist armies, and Chiang's government at Nanking lost further popular support through its failure to curb inflation, suppress warlords and bandits, and govern competently.

Resumption of civil war forced Washington to face a new situation. Convinced that Nationalist armies were adequately equipped, American leaders felt that they could do nothing more without running heavy risks of full-scale participation. Hence they withdrew all military forces, except for a small contingent of marines at Tsingtao, and refused to extend any large new assistance to Chiang in 1947. President Truman did send General Wedemeyer back to China in July to investigate and recommend. The general reported on the dangers of the Chinese situation in September 1947. While admitting that "reactionary leadership, repression and corruption" had caused the people to lose faith in Chiang's government, he held out hope for genuine reform, provided that the United States gave effective moral and material support. Communist control of China, Wedemeyer warned, would imperil American interests and peace in the Far East because Chinese Communists were agents of Soviet expansion in that area. The situation, he went on, was far from hopeless. The United States should insist that the UN take control of Manchuria to prevent that province from falling into the Soviet orbit. It should also inaugurate a large program of "moral, advisory, and material" assistance to China "to protect United States strategic interests against militant forces which now threaten them."

Even such action would probably not have sufficed, given the incompetence of Chiang's regime and Chinese Communist determination to win and reconstruct their country. In this conviction, and knowing that the American people would not have tolerated a full-scale participation in the

---

[8]They had obtained the arms and equipment of some 1.2 million Japanese soldiers and received some $700 million worth of lend-lease supplies, in addition to large quantities of surplus American military equipment, in 1945-1946.

Chinese civil war, the administration not only refused to sanction Wede-meyer's report but kept it secret until Chiang had been driven from the mainland. As Secretary Marshall declared, there was nothing the United States could do to "make the present Chinese Government capable of reestablishing and then maintaining its control throughout all of China."

The Communists captured Mukden in October 1948 and then, assisted by the rapid disintegration of the Nationalist government and armies, swept on to victory with incredible speed. They crossed the Yangtze in April 1949 and quickly captured Hankow, Shanghai, Canton, and other southern ports and cities. Chiang retired to Chungking in October and fled by air with remnants of his government to Taiwan in December. Meanwhile, the Chinese Communist leaders, Mao Tse-tung and Chou En-lai, had established the People's Republic of China at Peking, declared their friendship for the USSR, and begun an intensive campaign to expel American officials, missionaries, and citizens.

4. *The Decline of the Good Neighbor Policy*

Evidence of the success of the Good Neighbor policy came within a few days after Pearl Harbor, as twelve Latin American governments either declared war upon the Axis or broke diplomatic relations. All the rest save Argentina and Chile followed suit after approving a United States resolution to that effect at a conference in Rio de Janeiro in January 1942.[9] The American republics joined hands in genuine collaboration as the war progressed. Brazil participated in the campaign against German U-boats, provided airfields for an "air ferry" to Africa, and sent a division to the Italian front. Most other Latin American countries cooperated by sending vital raw materials, offering air bases, and joining with American agents to root out Axis influences.

The one important and dangerous exception was Argentina. Her leaders not only refused to break with the Axis but also maintained intimate relations with Nazi agents and sympathized with the German cause. A group of army officers seized control of the Buenos Aires government in June 1943 and launched a campaign to destroy the democratic opposition. When a new president, General Edelmiro Farrell, consequently came to power in February 1944, Washington undertook to persuade the other American republics to withhold recognition and several months later froze Argentina's gold assets in the United States.

The State Department, to quiet Latin American fears that even stronger unilateral measures impended, called a special Pan-American conference

[9]Chile broke relations in January 1943; Argentina, in January 1944.

to meet in Mexico City in February 1945. The delegates first invited Argentina to return to the inter-American fold. Then they approved the Act of Chapultepec on March 3. It completed the mutualization of the Monroe Doctrine by declaring that any attack upon the territory or sovereignty of one American state would be met by the combined forces of all of them. The Argentine government soon afterward declared war on Germany and Japan and ratified the Act of Chapultepec, and the United States accorded diplomatic recognition.

For a brief time the breach appeared healed, especially when the American delegation at San Francisco joined Latin Americans in winning UN membership for Argentina. Actually, however, the United States was already hard at work on daring new strategems against the Farrell government, which had suppressed free speech, opposition parties, and the press. Not content to stand by in silent disapproval, Washington went so far as to attempt to destroy the militaristic regime. Chief American agent was Ambassador Spruille Braden, who worked secretly with opposition leaders and made speeches and public statements virtually calling upon *Argentinos* to change their government as the price for retaining American friendship.

The leader of the antidemocratic forces, Colonel Juan D. Perón, answered Braden's challenge by demanding a national election and by announcing in December 1945 that he would be a candidate for the presidency. Two weeks before the election, in February 1946, the State Department issued a so-called Argentine Blue Book. It accused the militaristic clique of "aid to the enemy, deliberate misrepresentation and deception in promises of hemispheric cooperation, subversive activity against neighboring republics, and [forming] a vicious partnership of Nazi and native totalitarian forces." American friendship could be restored, the document warned, only when the Argentine people were represented by a government that commanded "full faith and confidence at home and abroad."

This intervention in the political affairs of a sovereign, suspicious, and proud people was stern but ill-fated diplomacy. In what was probably a fair election, *Argentinos* gave a large majority to Perón and a clear answer to their northern neighbor. Washington had no alternative but to recall Braden and accept the verdict. However, it refused to cooperate with the movement then under way to construct a regional defense association, declaring that it would wait for evidences of the good faith of the new Perón government. Relations between the United States and Argentina remained tense enough during 1946 to imperil the entire structure of hemispheric unity. Most Latin governments disliked the Perón regime; but for obvious reasons they disliked American intervention in Argentine affairs even more. In the face of mounting criticism, Truman and Marshall agreed that the pointless feud must end. The president duly announced in

June 1947 that his government was ready to begin discussions looking toward a hemispheric defense pact.

In response, delegates from all twenty-one American republics met in Rio de Janeiro in August 1947 to consider enforcement machinery for the Act of Chapultepec. What emerged was the Inter-American Treaty of Reciprocal Assistance, signed on September 2. It obligated all signatories, when two-thirds of them so voted, to sever diplomatic and economic relations with any internal or external violator of the Act of Chapultepec, but no signatory would be required to use its armed forces without its consent. The treaty also specified a broad security zone around the North and South American continents, including Greenland and Alaska, and defined an attack anywhere within this zone as an attack against all American republics. A ninth Inter-American Conference assembled at Bogotá in early 1948 to improve the political machinery. Its charter for an Organization of American States gave full constitutional status to the hemispheric system.[10] Its Pact of Bogotá provided for the peaceful settlement of disputes. And its agreement on economic cooperation pledged all signatories to treat foreign capital fairly and not to expropriate foreign-owned property without just compensation.

The structures erected at Mexico City, Rio, and Bogotá were signs that the Good Neighbor policy had been thoroughly mutualized. Yet they provided more form than substance, for hemispheric cooperation actually declined in practice after 1945. For one thing, the postwar era was a time of severe economic dislocation in Latin America, caused mainly by the region's inability to sell as much to the United States as it wished to buy, and by failure of American investors to help remedy the resulting "dollar gap" that disrupted inter-American trade. Washington, burdened by huge financial commitments to Europe, gave scant attention to this problem.[11] For another, it was a time of great political unrest, as leaders of the downtrodden masses and representatives of the privileged classes, usually military cliques, contended for power. Perhaps the chief factor was that, in contrast to the 1930s, Latin America had ceased to be of prime importance to the United States. Large new responsibilities after 1945 inevitably shifted the direction of foreign policy and popular interest to Europe and Asia. Yet Latin American economic, political, and social institutions were so unstable that a Good Neighbor policy of superficial political and military cooperation would no longer suffice to preserve the peace of the hemisphere.

---

[10]The charter established three representative bodies—the Inter-American Conference, the Meeting of Consultation of Foreign Ministers, and the Council—and constituted the Pan American Union in Washington as its permanent secretariat.

[11]Huge American purchases of raw materials after the outbreak of the Korean War momentarily eased Latin America's economic problems. Small amounts of American Mutual Security Aid made possible some technical assistance, and the Export-Import and World banks furnished modest funds for internal development.

5. Beginnings of Containment: The Truman Doctrine

A change in American foreign policy occurred in the spring of 1947 that ranks in importance with the Monroe Doctrine and the decisions to enter both world wars. The Truman administration, after struggling for two years to find accommodation with Russia, undertook a bold program aimed at nothing less than halting further Soviet expansion in the Middle East and Europe. The idea did not stem merely from irritation and disappointment over Russian behavior. It was a radical new departure grounded upon certain harsh assumptions and devised to meet a specific threat of Soviet control of the eastern Mediterranean.

Many leaders in the United States and Great Britain had abandoned the assumptions of collaboration with Russia well before the containment policy went into effect. It is not possible to surmise from President Truman's memoirs precisely when he concluded that such collaboration was impossible. Certainly he never fully shared Roosevelt's illusions about the chances of successful cooperation; he was aware of the danger of Soviet expansion in the Middle East and Greece as early as January 1946. To thwart it, Admiral Leahy and Secretary Forrestal urged reestablishment of American naval power in the eastern Mediterranean. Winston Churchill warned of the peril of Soviet aggression in his celebrated "iron curtain" speech at Fulton, Missouri, in March 1946. Ambassador Harriman also admonished the State Department about Soviet plans and ambitions.

However, it was George F. Kennan, counselor of the American embassy in Moscow, who first fully elaborated the assumptions behind the policy of containment. Stalin declared in February 1946 that international peace was impossible "under the present capitalist development of world economy" and called upon the Russian people to prepare for "any eventuality." This prompted Kennan to draft an eight-thousand-word dispatch to clarify the character, tactics, motivation, and ambitions of the Soviet state and the international Communist movement. After exploring the historical background of Russian distrust of the West, Kennan pointed up the danger: "We have here a political force committed fanatically to the belief that with the U.S. there can be no permanent *modus vivendi*, that it is desirable and necessary that the internal harmony of our society be disrupted, our traditional way of life be destroyed, the international authority of our state be broken, if Soviet power is to be secure."[12]

If it was true, as Kennan and others asserted, that Soviet leaders and their adherents throughout the world believed in a death struggle between communism and democracy and were at work to promote the violent overthrow of non-Communist governments, then how could the United States most successfully meet the threat? Again it was Kennan who best

[12]Quoted in Walter Millis and E. S. Duffield, eds., *The Forrestal Diaries* (New York, 1951), pp. 138-139.

summarized what many other Americans were thinking. He elaborated the doctrine of containment in an anonymous article in the July 1947 issue of *Foreign Affairs*. The nation could live at peace with the Soviet Union only by building its own strength and by erecting effective counterweights in order to contain Communist power at least in Europe. "It is clear," he wrote, "that the main element of any United States policy toward the Soviet Union must be that of a long-term, patient but firm and vigilant containment of Russian expansive tendencies."

Truman and Secretary of State Marshall, appointed in January 1947, were suddenly impelled toward an open containment policy by Soviet threats in the Middle East. The Russians had attempted during the war to create a puppet regime in the Iranian province of Azerbaijan, withdrawing their troops early in 1946 only after sharp State Department protests and "a blunt message" from Truman to Stalin. But the threat to Iran persisted. Even more threatening was extraordinary Russian pressure on Turkey for cession of territory and the right to build naval bases in the Bosporus. The Soviet foreign ministry pressed these demands from 1945 to 1947, while Russian propaganda warned of dire consequences if Turkey refused to yield. In brief, Soviet leaders seemed determined to achieve a historic Russian objective—control of the Straits and the eastern Mediterranean. Another threat was the possibility that Communist forces would capture Greece, thus outflanking Turkey and imperiling the entire Middle East. The British had supported a rightist Greek government since late 1944 in a protracted and bloody effort to suppress a Communist-led faction known as the EAM. The British ambassador informed Washington in February 1947 that Great Britain could no longer bear the burden of resisting communism in the eastern Mediterranean and would soon have to withdraw entirely from Greece.

This declaration marked the end of historic British supremacy in one of the most strategic areas in the world, and Truman's response marked a fateful turning point in American foreign policy. He thought that he saw the implications clearly enough: "If Greece was lost, Turkey would become an untenable outpost in a sea of Communism. Similarly, if Turkey yielded to Soviet demands, the position of Greece would be extremely endangered."[13] After discussions with congressional leaders he went to Capitol Hill on March 12 to seek $400 million for military assistance to Greece and Turkey. Even more important was his bold enunciation of the so-called Truman Doctrine, which went far beyond Kennan's concept: "I believe that it must be the foreign policy of the United States to support free peoples who are resisting attempted subjugation by armed minorities or by outside pressures. . . . The free peoples of the world look to us for support in maintaining their freedoms. If we falter in our leadership, we may endanger the peace of the world—and we shall surely endanger the welfare of our own Nation."

[13]Harry S Truman, *Memoirs by Harry S Truman*, 2 vols. (New York, 1955), II, 100.

It was in fact the beginning of the cold war, that posture of semihostility between the United States and Russia that would threaten the peace of the world for nearly two decades to come. To be sure, mutual suspicion and bad feeling had existed since 1945. However, the two powers had reached at least tacit agreement to respect each other's spheres of influence. Whether the president overreacted in seeking aid to Greece and Turkey and enunciating the Truman Doctrine, it is impossible to say, since the documents essential to any understanding of Soviet plans and purposes are not open to scholarly purview. But one thing can be said with confidence. Truman *reacted*, quickly and decisively, to what he and his advisers considered dire threats to the security of the United States.

The meaning of Truman's pronouncement was clear and shocking to the American people, then inadequately prepared to assume such enormous new responsibilities. But the administration stood firm against charges that it was supporting British imperialism and needlessly provoking Russia. And with the crucial help of Arthur Vandenberg of Michigan, chairman of the Senate foreign relations committee, the president won congressional support for his Greek-Turkish aid bill in May 1947. "Congress took the plunge and, in taking it, confirmed a new departure in American foreign policy. The United States served notice that henceforward, to deny further strategic advantages to Russia, it would act to bolster up nations and governments resisting Soviet pressure and penetration."[14]

The United States did not falter in its effort to save Greece and strengthen the Turkish bastion. All told, Washington spent some $659 million under the Greek-Turkish aid program from 1947 to 1950. The task in Turkey was quickly and inexpensively accomplished, as the Turkish government was relatively honest and undisturbed by internal warfare. American aid helped the Turks achieve economic stability and modernize their sizable army without the slightest show of friction on either side.

The Greek problem, on the other hand, proved immensely difficult. The United States found itself in the embarrassing position of defending democracy in Greece by supporting a reactionary government that refused to do anything effective about basic economic and social evils that had stirred the masses to revolt. In any event, American supplies and a military mission enabled a reorganized Greek army to undertake a determined campaign to end the civil war. It cleared the Peloponnesus of guerrillas and then turned northward toward the EAM stronghold. Success was assured when Yugoslavia broke with the Soviet bloc in 1948 and abandoned support of the Greek Communists in mid-1949. The long civil war was over by October, and the Greek people could turn to urgent problems of domestic reconstruction.

Thus the Truman Doctrine accomplished its first major objectives. Aid to Greece saved that country from certain Communist conquest. Aid to

[14]John C. Campbell et al., *The United States in World Affairs, 1947–1948* (New York, 1948), p. 48.

Turkey won a powerful ally on Russia's southern flank and at least temporarily prevented Russian power from bursting into the eastern Mediterranean or threatening the Middle East.

6. To Save Western Europe: The Marshall Plan

As winter turned into spring in 1947 there were alarming signs that the Greco-Turkish situation merely reflected a graver crisis that threatened all of western Europe. In varying degree Britain, France, Italy, and other nations were staggering under nearly impossible burdens of reconstruction, careening from one economic crisis to another, and facing violent social upheaval if they failed to accomplish miracles of recovery. The United States had kept western Europe from starvation and economic collapse since 1945 by an outlay of some $11 billion in UNRRA aid, loans, credits, and other assistance. But this huge outpouring had mainly helped Europeans acquire dollars for food, clothing, and other elementary necessities, not to build a sound recovery. The situation grew worse as 1947 wore on; an outright Communist triumph in France and Italy became a distinct possibility.

Leaders in Washington appreciated the dimensions of the problem, and the State Department's policy planning staff, headed by Kennan, was hard at work upon a radical remedy. Its purport was indicated in a speech in May 1947 by Undersecretary of State Dean Acheson, who cited a need to strengthen governments that were "seeking to preserve their independence and democratic institutions and human freedoms against totalitarian pressures, either internal or external." Then Secretary Marshall, in an address at Harvard University in June, became more specific. European states should work out a comprehensive program and tell America how it might best help in achieving lasting recovery. "Any government willing to assist in the task of reconstruction," he promised, "will find full co-operation on the part of the United States."

Marshall envisaged nothing less than the rebuilding of western Europe's economy in order to provide a more stable social order. Indeed, he, Kennan, and others in the State Department thought that Russia might also be willing to cooperate in a gigantic European effort. Nothing but good, they believed, could come of such an enterprise. They also realized that Russian cooperation might wreck the plan in Congress, although this danger was remote. The Russians had been consolidating their control over eastern Europe since 1945 and were not likely to relinquish it. And they had revealed, only two months before Marshall's speech, their determination to prevent solution of Europe's most urgent problem, unification and rehabilitation of Germany. Issuing an invitation to all European nations to join in a common effort seemed safe enough.

In any event, the showdown came soon after Marshall made his memorable address, when the British, French, and Russian foreign ministers met in Paris in late June to consider a reply. The British and French ministers voiced the overwhelming enthusiasm and gratitude of western Europe, while Molotov expressed the sullen opposition of the Communist bloc and left the meeting when he could not disrupt it. Representatives from Britain, France, Italy, Turkey, and other non-Communist nations met in Paris on July 12 and appointed a Committee of European Economic Cooperation (CEEC). It submitted a master recovery plan two months later calling for $22.4 billion in American assistance and loans. By the autumn of 1947, therefore, the lines were drawn for "a struggle which was to be waged with weapons of politics and propaganda as well as with loans, grants and trade agreements."[15] That struggle was already acute in France and Italy. Communists, expelled from coalition cabinets early in the spring, were now working to destroy moderate governments.

Meanwhile, lines were also being drawn in the United States between champions of the European Recovery Program (ERP), as the Marshall Plan was called, and an incongruous company of opponents. Debate began in earnest when the president submitted an economic cooperation bill in December 1947 calling for $17 billion in aid during the next four years. Opponents of the measure, fatally handicapped by Communist opposition to it, were soon overwhelmed by a coalition that included farm organizations, the AFL and CIO, the National Association of Manufacturers, and other pressure groups. Any doubts that Congress would approve the bill were ended when a Communist minority in Czechoslovakia seized control in February 1948 and destroyed a democracy for which millions of Americans felt strong emotional attachment.

The main burden of leadership in Congress fell upon Senator Vandenberg, who mollified critics by eliminating authorization of the full commitment and slightly reducing the first appropriation. After the hearings had ended, Vandenberg opened debate on March 1, 1948, with an address that brought senators and spectators to their feet in applause. "The greatest nation on earth either justifies or surrenders its leadership," he declared. "We must choose. . . . The iron curtain must not come to the rims of the Atlantic either by aggression or by default."

The Senate approved the bill by a huge majority on March 13. Then, while the House dallied, Truman and Marshall began a public campaign to point up the dangers of Soviet expansion and the immediate menace of a Communist victory in Italy if the House did not act before the Italian elections on April 18. Popular pressure was almost irresistible; and the House voted approval on March 31. It was a momentous law that received President Truman's signature on April 3, 1948. The launching of the ERP meant that hereafter American destinies were inextricably intertwined

---

[15]Campbell et al., *The United States in World Affairs, 1947-1948*, p. 444.

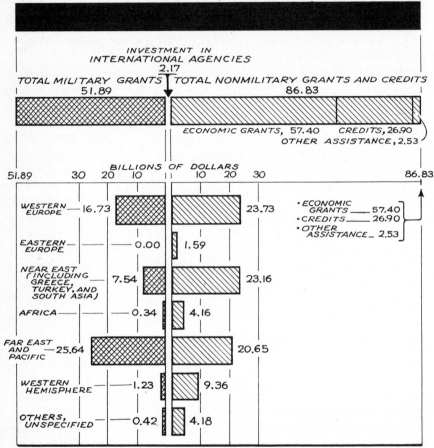

AMERICAN FOREIGN AID
1945 – 1971

IN BILLIONS OF DOLLARS

TOTAL *(NET)*
U.S. FOREIGN AID, 1945 – 1971
140.9

INVESTMENT IN
INTERNATIONAL AGENCIES
2.17

TOTAL MILITARY GRANTS | TOTAL NONMILITARY GRANTS AND CREDITS
51.89 | 86.83

ECONOMIC GRANTS, 57.40   CREDITS, 26.90
OTHER ASSISTANCE, 2.53

BILLIONS OF DOLLARS
51.89   30   20   10   10   20   30   86.83

WESTERN EUROPE — 16.73 | 23.73   • ECONOMIC GRANTS ___ 57.40
                                     • CREDITS ___ 26.90
                                     • OTHER ASSISTANCE __ 2.53

EASTERN EUROPE — 0.00 | 1.59

NEAR EAST (INCLUDING GREECE, TURKEY, AND SOUTH ASIA) — 7.54 | 23.16

AFRICA — 0.34 | 4.16

FAR EAST AND PACIFIC — 25.64 | 20.65

WESTERN HEMISPHERE — 1.23 | 9.36

OTHERS, UNSPECIFIED — 0.42 | 4.18

with the destinies of other peoples who stood on the dangerous frontier between a world dominated by Stalin and a world struggling for a new birth of freedom.

From April 1948 until it was supplanted by the Mutual Security Agency in December 1951, the Economic Cooperation Administration joined hands with the CEEC to carry forward one of the most ambitious and successful reconstruction programs in history. The United States gave some $12 billion in assistance through ECA during this period, but initiative and chief direction came from CEEC. Results were astonishing even by 1950, before American rearmament during the Korean War gave further economic stimulus to the Western world. From 1947 through 1950, gross national product in Marshall Plan countries as a whole increased 25 percent; industrial production, 64 percent; and agricultural output, 24 percent. In most categories recovery not only attained but exceeded prewar levels.

7. The Berlin Crisis and the North Atlantic Treaty

We have thus far viewed the European Recovery Program partially out of the context of other great events that were impelling Western nations toward closer unity and driving the Soviet Union into opposition and a desperate campaign to consolidate its control over eastern Europe. The crux of the problem lay in war-ravaged Germany. American, British, and French leaders continued to plead for German unification and neutralization until the end of 1947. But the Russians made it clear at Moscow and London meetings of the Council of Foreign Ministers in 1947 that they would approve no agreement on Germany that did not give them a large voice in the control of the Ruhr Valley, the industrial heart of Europe.

Western leaders now realized that agreement with Russia on their terms was impossible, and that one alternative was to agree upon their own plan for Germany. This undertaking, by arousing French fears, might drive France into the arms either of extreme nationalists or Communists. And yet the effort had to be made, for German recovery was the key to European recovery, and the defense of western Germany was the key to the defense of western Europe. British and American leaders moved fast. After consolidating their zones in February 1948 and creating a limited German government at Frankfurt, they won French approval for a West German Federal Republic with limited sovereignty. They also won French consent to currency reform in the three Western zones and measures to include West Germany as a full partner in the ERP. The Germans organized state governments in October 1948, adopted a federal constitution in May 1949, and elected a federal Diet that met at Bonn in September and established a full-fledged constitutional government.

Russian reaction to the Marshall Plan and to Western policy in Germany was immediate. Soviet leaders created the Cominform in October 1947 to unite eastern Europe in a campaign of complete "sovietization," that is, a final destruction of all anti-Communist elements. They launched a campaign of strikes and violence through Communist parties and Communist-controlled trade unions that impeded but did not prevent Italian and French recovery. They engineered the coup that overthrew a coalition

DIVIDED **GERMANY** AND **AUSTRIA**

BERLIN'S CHANNELS TO THE WEST

DIVIDED **GREATER BERLIN**

government in Prague in February 1948 and established a Communist regime in Czechoslovakia.[16]

The grand and perilous climax was the Berlin blockade. In April Soviet authorities began to restrict movement of people and freight from the Western zones into Berlin, then under four-power control but isolated in the Russian-held Eastern zone of Germany. This action provoked violent controversies in the Allied *Kommandatura*, the four-power control council for the German capital, eventuating in Soviet withdrawal from that body on July 1. Meanwhile, in retaliation against Allied introduction of the new West German currency, Russia halted all traffic to Berlin from the Western zones on June 23. Soviet propaganda made no effort to conceal the objectives of the Berlin blockade—either to force the Allies from their advanced position in East Germany or else to compel them to abandon their plans for West German unification. Yet withdrawal would signify surrender in the face of superior force, the end of Allied influence in Germany, and a Soviet diplomatic victory of catastrophic proportions. Free men everywhere turned to Washington for leadership in this first open test of strength between the West and the Soviet Union.

The thought of retreat apparently never troubled the mind of the stubborn Missourian in the White House. When army leaders raised the question of withdrawal on June 28, Truman "interrupted to say that there was no discussion on this point, we were going to stay." Rejecting the suggestion that the army send armed convoys and fight its way into Berlin if need be, the president approved a more ingenious and less risky plan—to supply West Berlin by air and thereby force the Russians to make the decision for peace or war. Soon afterward he sent two groups of B-29 bombers to English bases. At the same time he refused to give physical possession of atomic bombs to the military because, as he said, he did not propose "to have some dashing lieutenant colonel decide when would be the proper time to drop one."

While the siege of Berlin lasted, from June 1948 to May 1949, the British RAF and the United States Air Force accomplished a miracle. The airlift was soon carrying a daily average of 4,000 tons of supplies, including quantities of coal, to the Western sectors. All told, British and American planes made over 277,000 flights and carried nearly 2.5 million tons of supplies, enough to sustain the outpost.

The airlift succeeded, but it was no permanent solution. That would have to come through diplomacy. "Some voices," Truman later wrote, "were raised in America calling for a break with the Russians. These people did not understand that our choice was only between negotiations

---

[16]On the other hand, their efforts to control Marshal Tito's Communist government in Yugoslavia backfired in a violent break between Belgrade and Moscow and, subsequently, a partial alignment of Yugoslavia with the West.

and war. There was no third way."[17] Thus the American, British, and French governments opened negotiations in July 1948 that forced the Soviets to admit that they had instituted the blockade in retaliation against Allied policy in Germany. In a full-dress meeting with Stalin, Molotov, and the British and French ambassadors in Moscow on August 2, the American ambassador warned that the Western powers would not be bullied, and that the Soviet threat "could not be allowed to succeed." Stalin was seemingly conciliatory, but efforts at compromise foundered for months upon Russian insistence that the Allies abandon their plans for West German unification without Soviet participation, and Allied refusal to discuss this larger issue so long as the blockade was in effect.

Russia finally yielded and lifted the blockade on May 12, 1949, in return for Allied agreement to hold a prompt meeting of the Council of Foreign Ministers in Paris. It was a small price to pay for so large a victory. The Paris conference brought no important agreement on Germany, but it did reveal Soviet indecision and obvious unity among the Allied powers. As the new American secretary of state, Dean Acheson, observed upon his return to Washington, "the position of the West has grown greatly in strength, and . . . the position of the Soviet Union in regard to the struggle for the soul of Europe has changed from the offensive to the defensive."

It was a masterful understatement, for by the time Acheson spoke the western European nations and the United States were united in a military alliance for common defense. Let us review the background of this epochal event.

The first major thrust toward Atlantic unity was the Marshall Plan. This project reflected a dramatic reversal of economic nationalism and a determination by Western statesmen to create an integrated economic community. The second thrust came at the height of debate over the ERP. British Foreign Secretary Ernest Bevin, in a speech in the House of Commons in January 1948, announced his country's readiness to join a western European union. Britain, France, the Netherlands, Belgium, and Luxembourg signed a fifty-year treaty of economic cooperation and military alliance at Brussels in March and quickly established machinery to speed such collaboration. A council of Europe, created in January 1949, included not only the Brussels powers but Italy, Ireland, Denmark, Norway, Sweden, the Saar, and the German Federal Republic as well.[18]

Western European leaders now turned to Washington. The Vandenberg resolution, adopted by the Senate in June 1948, had implicitly promised

---

[17]Truman, *Memoirs*, II, 128.

[18]The first important outcome of this drive toward European union was the so-called Schuman Plan, originated by Jean Monnet of France and pressed by Robert Schuman, French foreign minister. The treaty implementing it was signed by France, Germany, Italy, the Netherlands, Belgium, and Luxembourg in March 1951. It established a High Authority to pool all coal and steel resources, production, and distribution in the signatory countries.

American cooperation. Negotiations looking toward an Atlantic alliance began in the American capital in July. A draft treaty was completed in December and signed in April 1949 by representatives of the United States, Britain, France, Italy, the Netherlands, Belgium, Canada, Iceland, Luxembourg, Denmark, Norway, and Portugal. This North Atlantic Treaty declared that an armed attack against any member in Europe, North America, or French Algeria would be considered an attack against all signatories; and it looked forward to the creation of joint military forces. Congress in September 1949 approved the Mutual Defense Assistance Act appropriating $1 billion for arms and equipment for the signatories and an additional $211 million for Greece and Turkey.

One meaning in these momentous events stood out above all others. In signing the North Atlantic Treaty, the United States revealed a determination to abandon its historic traditions against alliances and do what was necessary to protect western Europe. President Truman and Secretary Acheson had wisely drawn Republican as well as Democratic senators into the negotiations. Consequently, a solid bipartisan phalanx overwhelmed the opposition when debate opened in the Senate in July 1949. It approved the pact without reservation on July 21 by a vote of 82 to 13.

27

The Korean War
and the Election of
1952

The years between the signing of the North Atlantic Treaty and the inauguration of Dwight D. Eisenhower were a time of mounting international crises, domestic tension, and moral challenge. Catapulted into leadership of what was commonly called the free world, Americans now had to demonstrate whether they could lead courageously and wisely. American policy won a series of victories in western Europe. On the other hand, the Communist victory in China upset the precarious balance of power in the Far East and presaged a dire new threat to peace—the North Korean assault upon South Korea.

1. Prelude to the Korean Crisis

The American people were convulsed and confused at midcentury by a bitter debate over foreign policy in general and Far Eastern policy in particular. Despite the marked development of a neo-isolationism, especially in the Midwest, and of a conviction that the United States could not keep spending billions on foreign aid, the administration continued to enjoy large bipartisan support for its policy of assistance to western Europe. President Truman also mustered considerable Republican support in 1950 in obtaining $35 million to launch his "bold new program" of checking communism by rendering technical assistance to underdeveloped areas.

By this time, however, Republicans were eager to disrupt bipartisan unity and use foreign policy as a major issue in the midterm elections. The Republican leader on foreign policy in the Senate, Arthur Vandenberg, was so disturbed that he violated his doctor's orders after a severe lung operation and returned to Washington in January 1950 to head off the revolt. He succeeded momentarily; but his great services were ended by renewed illness that finally took his life on April 18, 1951. Long before he died, his Republican colleagues had raised a violent storm over China that was subdued for a time by war in Korea, then renewed on an even greater scale when the Chinese intervened.

The government had meanwhile been trying to formulate a policy to meet the new situation in the Orient. It would perhaps have followed Britain, India, and other powers in recognizing the Chinese People's Republic had Peking not launched a violent campaign in the autumn of 1949 to expel American diplomats, missionaries, and private interests. Reaction in the United States was bitter. Anti-Peking sentiment was further exacerbated by a so-called China lobby, and by a Republican campaign to discredit the administration and force it to extend military assistance to the Chinese Nationalists on Taiwan.

The State Department had washed its hands of responsibility for the Chinese debacle by releasing a white paper that blamed the Nationalists for their defeat. The president, in January 1950, reaffirmed his determination not to be drawn into the Chinese civil war, even if such a policy resulted in Communist capture of Taiwan. And a week later Secretary of State Dean Acheson, who had succeeded Marshall in January 1949, announced what was in effect a new American policy in the Far East. The United States, he declared, desired only to help the peoples of Asia to realize their democratic aspirations. It would protect a "defensive perimeter" that ran from the Aleutians to Japan, the Ryukyus, and the Philippines. But aggression against areas outside the perimeter—Korea, Taiwan, and Southeast Asia—would have to be met by the peoples involved and by the United Nations.

This speech gave new impetus to the Republican attack. It took an extreme turn as Senators McCarthy, Taft, Kenneth S. Wherry of Nebraska, and other GOP spokesmen opened a campaign to drive Acheson from office and prove that the State Department was riddled with Communists and fellow travelers who, as Taft put it, had "surrendered to every demand of Russia . . . and promoted at every opportunity the Communist cause in China." So violent was this assault that it wrecked the bipartisan policy, made formulation of a rational Far Eastern program impossible just when it was most needed, and raised grave doubts abroad about the quality of American leadership.

These were times of further soul-searching because thoughtful men began to wonder whether the world was heading for destruction. The president's revelation in September 1949 that Russia had detonated an atomic bomb upset all assumptions upon which American defensive stategy had been based since 1945. It also renewed a fierce debate in administration circles, particularly between scientists J. Robert Oppenheimer and Edward Teller, over the development of a hydrogen or tritium bomb, potentially a thousand times more powerful than the atomic bombs that destroyed Hiroshima and Nagasaki. When Truman announced in January 1950 that he had ordered the AEC to proceed with work on the hydrogen bomb, thoughtful Americans were stunned by the gloomy prospects even while agreeing that their government had no other recourse. The American people were entering, as Acheson put it, a new era of "total diplomacy," in which their fortitude and wisdom would be put to severe and numerous tests.

2. *The Korean Crisis*

Not many months after Acheson spoke, an invasion of South Korea threatened world peace and sorely taxed American courage and capacities. The background can be briefly told. Roosevelt and his advisers had decided that Korea should be freed from Japanese control, but they gave no thought to a postwar policy—even though Japan and Russia had fought a war for control of this strategic peninsula in 1904-1905, and Russian dominance there would gravely threaten Japanese security. Russian troops entered northern Korea in August 1945; American forces occupied southern Korea in September. The two powers agreed to divide their occupation zones at the thirty-eighth parallel, which runs north of the capital city, Seoul.

American leaders assumed that the Korean people would soon organize a government and occupation forces would thereupon be withdrawn. The Russians in fact approved a plan in December 1945 to create a Korean government guided by a joint American-Soviet commission. But Russian representatives on the commission blocked all efforts at unification, established a Communist "people's government" in North Korea, and trained and equipped an army of 150,000 men. The United States then appealed to the UN General Assembly, which established a Temporary Commission on Korea in November 1947. It visited Seoul in January 1948 and, after being denied entry into the Soviet zone, held elections in South Korea. A constituent assembly met in July 1948, adopted a constitution, and elected Syngman Rhee as president. The UN, the United States, and other non-Communist powers recognized Rhee's regime as the only lawful government of Korea. Washington, following advice of the Joint Chiefs of Staff and General MacArthur in Japan, withdrew its last troops from South Korea in June 1949. It also gave substantial assistance to Rhee's government.

This, in general, was the situation when North Korean forces crossed the thirty-eighth parallel in an all-out invasion of South Korea at 4 A.M., Korean time, on June 25, 1950. The Soviet government's precise role and objectives remain unclear. In all likelihood, the withdrawal of American troops and Acheson's statement that Korea lay outside the Far Eastern defense perimeter encouraged a belief that the United States would not fight to prevent Communist control of the entire Korean peninsula. Such a notion was obviously strengthened by general American military weakness and inability to fight a limited war.

News of the invasion reached Washington at 9:26 P.M., June 24, Washington time. Acheson held hurried conferences and called the president, who was then in Independence, at about midnight. Truman agreed that the secretary should bring the matter before the Security Council at once. By the following afternoon, when the council met in emergency session, it was evident that North Korea had launched not a border raid but a full-scale war. With the Russian representative absent,[1] the council by a vote of nine to zero adopted a resolution condemning the invasion as aggression and demanding withdrawal of Communist troops from South Korea.

The president hastened to Washington on June 25 and conferred immediately with civilian and military advisers. He decided to order the Seventh Fleet to neutralize Taiwan and to direct General MacArthur to furnish arms and limited air support to South Korea. Conferences with army and intelligence officials on June 26 revealed, incidentally, that intelligence agents knew next to nothing about the strength of the North Korean forces or the object of their assault. That evening Truman summoned his advisers. After hearing their views, he announced that American naval and air forces in the Far East would render full assistance to the South Koreans. "Everything I have done in the last five years," he declared, "has been to try to avoid making a decision such as I have had to make tonight."[2]

Events now moved swiftly to a climax. The president called congressional leaders to the White House on June 27 and told them of his decision to resist the invasion and his determination to rally the United Nations in a

---

[1]The Russians had boycotted the Security Council since January, because it had refused to seat a delegate from Communist China.

[2]Quoted in Beverly Smith, "Why We Went to War in Korea," *Saturday Evening Post*, 224 (November 10, 1951), 80.

bold collective effort to repel aggression. The Security Council that same day adopted an American-sponsored resolution calling upon member nations to render all necessary assistance to the Republic of Korea. And on June 29 and 30, after it had become evident that the Communists would quickly conquer the peninsula unless American forces stopped them, the president made the hardest decision of all—to send two divisions of ground troops from Japan to Korea and authorize a naval blockade of North Korea. This action was approved by the Joint Chiefs of Staff, the State Department, General MacArthur, and other advisers, all of whom assumed that limited American support would turn the tide, and that Russia and China would not intervene. In fact, it was the reception in Washington on June 29 of a Russian disclaimer of responsibility for the attack that paved the way for the decision to use American ground troops. Obviously, the full costs were not known in advance.

3. *The Korean War: First Phase*

"This is the Greece of the Far East," Truman said to one reporter. "If we are tough enough now, there won't be any next step." The president's decision was, as one writer put, "like a gust of wind blowing away a fog of uncertainty and gloom. . . . Here at last was the courage to tackle an aggressor."[3] Republican leaders like Governor Dewey and John Foster Dulles were effusive in praise. Members of the House of Representatives stood and cheered when they learned that the president had ordered air and naval forces to defend South Korea. Even Senator Taft declared that he would vote for a resolution authorizing use of American forces in Korea, though he opposed the president's acting without congressional consent. Elsewhere men and governments rallied. The Security Council established a UN command and requested the American government to name a commander in chief. Some nineteen nations soon made a military contribution; by the end of 1950, British, Turkish, Australian, and Philippine troops were fighting beside Americans and South Koreans with General MacArthur in command.

Meanwhile, however, North Korean troops almost overran the entire peninsula before American power could be brought to bear. They had pressed the defenders into the southeastern corner by September 12 and were threatening to drive them from Pusan, their remaining supply port. But Allied defenses stiffened and held firm, and MacArthur counterat-

---

[3]Albert L. Warner, "How the Korea Decision Was Made," *Harper's Magazine*, 202 (June 1951), 104.

tacked with large American reinforcements. Opening an offensive on September 15 with a daring landing on the North Korean flank at Inchon, he soon recaptured Seoul, reoccupied southern Korea, and destroyed or captured more than half the invaders. UN forces had reached the thirty-eighth parallel by October 1 and were preparing to launch an invasion of North Korea.

Although Americans watched breathlessly and went on a buying spree that caused sharp price increases and momentary scarcities, their most significant reaction was an awakening to the peril of new and more portentous Soviet aggressions, perhaps against the Middle East, perhaps against western Europe. And it was obvious that the peril was great precisely because the Western world lacked an effective counterforce. As one observer put it, "The vital question was whether time still remained to create the armed strength which alone might deter the Kremlin from undertaking further and even more dangerous adventures."[4]

Thus the chief issue was not *whether*, but *how*, the United States should prepare. Resisting demands for all-out mobilization, the government moved swiftly to set a limited, orderly mobilization under way. Congress approved the Defense Production Act in August. This measure, announcing a determination to "oppose acts of aggression and . . . to develop and maintain whatever military and economic strength is found to be necessary," empowered the president to institute allocations and priorities, authorize tax incentives to encourage defense production, build industrial plants, and impose limited price and sweeping credit controls. Congress also approved plans to double the armed forces from 1.5 million to 3 million men by mid-1951. It adopted a revenue bill designed to raise nearly $4.5 billion in additional income and corporate taxes, and appropriated another $12.6 billion for defense and over $5 billion for military assistance, chiefly to western Europe.

The president, assuming that the Korean War would soon end, did not establish special mobilization machinery or invoke price controls. He also assumed that the greatest danger was Soviet aggression in Europe. Hence the United States embarked upon a bold program to stimulate western European rearmament and create a unified North Atlantic Treaty Organization army. With the promise of new mutual defense assistance, Britain, France, and other NATO countries made plans to rearm. The North Atlantic Council met in Brussels in December 1950 and approved plans for unifying all NATO forces under the command of General Eisenhower.

This summer and autumn of fear and crisis witnessed one of the bitterest congressional campaigns in American history. Republicans did not openly repudiate the Korean intervention, but they charged that Truman and Acheson had blundered so badly as to make that war inevitable. They also warned of further inflation, socialization, and federal aggrandizement

[4]Richard P. Stebbins et al., *The United States in World Affairs, 1950* (New York, 1951), p. 244.

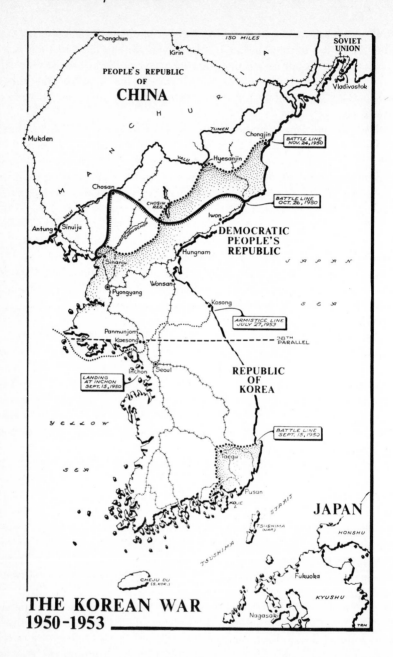

**THE KOREAN WAR
1950-1953**

if the Truman policies were not abandoned. But the main Republican
issue was communism—the alleged Democratic failure to recognize and
cope with Communist infiltration and influence in government. Not all
Republican leaders emulated the example of McCarthy, who used the
issue to defeat the veteran Democratic senator from Maryland, Millard

Tydings, or of Representative Richard M. Nixon, who exploited the popular fear in his successful campaign for a California Senate seat. Even so, Republican campaigners highlighted the issue almost everywhere with considerable success.

The Democrats retained narrow control of both houses in the election of 1950, but the results were a smashing reversal for the administration. Two Fair Deal stalwarts, Senators Frank P. Graham of North Carolina and Claude W. Pepper of Florida, had been defeated by anti-Truman conservatives in the primaries, and a whole host of the president's friends followed them into retirement after November 7. An all-out Democratic effort to unseat Senator Taft in Ohio failed so dramatically as to make Taft a leading contender for the Republican nomination in 1952. Even more important were underlying developments—the return of the agrarian Middle West to the Republican fold; the obvious success of the Communist issue; and the fact that Republicans polled a larger vote than Democrats in contests for House seats.

4. *The Korean Crisis Threatens a Third World War*

Having cleared South Korea, victorious allied forces halted at the thirty-eighth parallel until the General Assembly, on October 7, 1950, called upon MacArthur to take all necessary steps to establish UN control throughout Korea. The Chinese foreign minister had warned only a few days before that China would not "supinely tolerate seeing their neighbors being savagely invaded by imperialists." And he had told the Indian ambassador in Peking that "if the U.S. or U.N. forces crossed the Thirty-eighth Parallel, China would send troops to the Korean frontier to defend North Korea." But few leaders in the free world took the threat seriously. MacArthur assured the president at a conference on Wake Island on October 15 that there was little danger of Chinese intervention and promised a great slaughter if China's armies entered the fight. Washington shared his confidence. Indeed, Truman had approved military operations north of the thirty-eighth parallel as early as September 11. Western European leaders were equally enthusiastic.

MacArthur's forces drove triumphantly northward toward the Yalu River separating Korea from Manchuria. Just as it seemed that North Korean resistance had entirely collapsed, advanced American troops encountered large Chinese units fifty miles south of the Yalu in late October. Later reconnaissance revealed that China had massed armies of some 850,000 men in Manchuria and moved advanced units into northern Korea. While the Western world waited anxiously, Chinese soldiers skirmished defensively and the Security Council heard Peking's representatives demand prompt American withdrawal from Korea.

But MacArthur launched a final great offensive on November 24 to drive the Chinese beyond the Yalu and end the war before Christmas. In this action he violated the spirit if not the letter of his instructions. It was Washington's policy to send only South Korean troops into this area in order to avoid provoking the Chinese. MacArthur's decision was also a nearly fatal strategic blunder, for he drove his men into a huge trap. The Chinese counterattacked on November 26 and split the center of the UN line held by South Korean troops. The United States Eighth Army on the western flank withdrew in an orderly retreat toward the thirty-eighth parallel, but X Corps on the northeastern flank was isolated and cut off. It took them two weeks of desperate fighting to reach the port of Hungnam. From there they were evacuated and transferred to the main defensive line north of the thirty-eighth parallel, in one of modern warfare's most spectacular operations.

Washington, meanwhile, had gravely accepted the challenge and begun to prepare for a possible general war. "This new act of aggression," Acheson declared, "has created . . . a situation of unparalleled danger. . . . No one can guarantee that war will not come." During December, the president denounced the Chinese intervention, outlined a vast new defense program, declared a state of national emergency, and announced creation of an Office of Defense Mobilization and the beginning of production and stabilization controls.

On the whole, American mobilization proceeded smoothly and successfully during the next two years. Congress opposed the president on nearly every other score, but it granted his requests for unprecedented peacetime appropriations for defense and assistance to NATO countries.[5] The result was a considerable increase in the military strength of the Western allies. NATO had created forces probably capable of withstanding a Soviet invasion by the end of 1952.

5. The Second "Great Debate" and the MacArthur Affair

It would be pleasant for the historian to record that Americans met these new foreign threats calmly, wisely, and in firm conjunction with their European allies. The truth is, however, that the people nearly lost their heads, the administration nearly lost control of foreign policy, and the

[5]In all, Congress appropriated over $100 billion for national defense and some $14 billion for Mutual Security assistance from 1951 to 1953.

United States almost lost its allies as a result of the "great debate" and events that followed the Chinese intervention.

The debate began on November 10, 1950, when Senator Taft, reacting to the president's announcement that he would send additional divisions to Europe, proposed a reexamination of foreign and military policies and questioned whether defense of western Europe was essential to American security. Former President Hoover declared in December that the United States should defend the Atlantic and Britain, and the Pacific to Japan, but should withdraw troops and withhold further support until western Europe had organized and equipped sufficient forces to withstand a Russian assault. These were only two indications of the surging growth of Republican neo-isolationism, based partly upon fear of excessive governmental spending and the expansion of presidential power.

The debate exploded with exceptional bitterness in January 1951, when Senator Wherry offered a resolution declaring that "no ground forces of the United States should be assigned to duty in the European area for the purposes of the North Atlantic Treaty pending the adoption of a policy with respect thereto by Congress." Administration and military spokesmen replied that defense of western Europe was essential to defense of the United States. General Eisenhower returned from his command in Paris to report to Congress that western European nations could build a strong anti-Russian barrier if America did not desert them. Even so, debate raged and the issue was long in doubt, especially after a majority of House Republicans signed a manifesto in February endorsing Hoover's proposals. Resolution came in April when the Senate reaffirmed American commitments under the North Atlantic Treaty, approved sending four more divisions to Europe, but warned the president not to send additional troops without "further Congressional approval."

This furor was nothing as compared to the fury that erupted following the president's recall of General MacArthur from his command in Tokyo. Indeed, few episodes in American history have been so extraordinary or revealing. The MacArthur affair brought the Republican campaign against Truman and Acheson and the bitter controversy over American foreign policy to a head.

The conflict between Truman and MacArthur first centered around relations between the United States and Nationalist China. MacArthur made an ostentatious visit to Taiwan in July 1950. He then addressed a message to the annual convention of the Veterans of Foreign Wars in August calling for incorporation of Taiwan into the American security system and talking about "offensive strategy" in the Far East. Truman was shocked and considered relieving the general of his command. Instead, he met MacArthur on Wake Island in October, again explained that he had no intention of becoming involved in the Chinese civil war, and warned the general to make no more provocative statements.

MacArthur was silent for a time, but after the Chinese intervention he opened a campaign to force the administration to permit him to bomb Chinese bases in Manchuria. Truman replied on December 6, forbidding the release of any statement on foreign policy by civilian or military officials without prior approval by the State Department. During the following weeks, when the Chinese and North Koreans seemed about to drive UN forces from Korea, the president and Joint Chiefs of Staff deliberated possible responses to such a catastrophe. MacArthur suggested in late December that the United States blockade the Chinese coast, bombard China by air and sea, and support a Nationalist invasion from Taiwan. Otherwise, he intimated, it might be necessary to evacuate his forces. The Joint Chiefs replied that such retaliatory actions could not then be permitted; at the same time they began to prepare for similar desperate measures should the United Nations be driven out.

Events in Korea soon decided the issue. The American Eighth Army halted the enemy drive and began a limited offensive in January 1951. Since it was now evident that UN forces could remain in Korea, the president and Joint Chiefs quickly agreed upon a policy of conducting a limited war for the limited objective of maintaining the integrity of South Korea. This would avert the danger of a general war with China—"the wrong war, at the wrong place, at the wrong time, and with the wrong enemy," General Omar N. Bradley, chairman of the Joint Chiefs of Staff, later called it. A war with China might absorb all available manpower and resources and thus invite a Russian attack on western Europe. To be sure, limited and essentially defensive operations in Korea would not destroy the Peking regime. Yet such operations could inflict such punishment on Chinese and North Korean forces that they would have to abandon their aggression and thereby acknowledge a defeat that would vindicate the principle of collective security. NATO leaders fully shared these convictions.

MacArthur, however, was temperamentally incapable of accepting the concept of a limited war. He was prepared to abandon Europe to its inevitable doom, for he believed that destiny lay with the Orient. He also believed that blundering, if not treasonable, political leadership was depriving America of an opportunity to settle the Far Eastern question for generations to come. He therefore resorted to extreme measures. Informed on March 20, 1951, that the president was about to attempt to settle the Korean conflict by diplomacy, MacArthur issued a public statement aimed at preventing a peaceful settlement. Then, in reply to a letter from House minority leader Joseph W. Martin, Jr., of Massachusetts, the general called for a war to defeat communism in the Far East. "We must win," he concluded. "There is no substitute for victory."

Martin read this letter to the House of Representatives on April 5. The country was now convulsed by a frenetic Republican campaign to force the administration to adopt MacArthur's proposals for a victory offensive in Korea and possible war against China. Publication of MacArthur's letter was an open challenge to the president's foreign policy by a military commander who had joined hands with the opposition. Reluctantly but resolutely the man from Independence took the inevitable step. On April 10, 1951, he relieved MacArthur of his commands in Japan and Korea.[6] "I could do nothing else and still be President of the United States," he concluded. "Even the Chiefs of Staff came to the conclusion that civilian control of the military was at stake and I didn't let it stay at stake very long."[7] "If I allowed him to defy the civil authorities in this manner," Truman afterward wrote, "I myself would be violating my oath to uphold and defend the Constitution."[8]

The recall of a general who was the greatest living American in the eyes of millions required courage. And all the furies of hell seemed abroad in the country in consequence. Republicans, the China lobby, and many commentators poured out streams of invective and abuse. MacArthur, with a large entourage, returned to his native land for the first time in more than a decade. He made triumphal tours in San Francisco, Chicago, New York, and Washington, and basked in the warmth of popular applause. His climax was a melodramatic address before a joint session of Congress on April 19, calling for stern action against China.

While the nation reverberated from this din, congressional leaders agreed that the Senate Armed Services Committee should investigate MacArthur's recall and review American policy. The committee heard more than two million words of testimony from MacArthur, Bradley, Acheson, and dozens of others during May and June 1951. Chairman Richard B. Russell of Georgia would tolerate no nonsense, and the committee acted like neither partisans, prosecutors, nor circus performers, but rather like men in search of truth. Most Americans recovered their senses as the hearings ground on.

In retrospect, we can see that the MacArthur affair cleared the air of popular confusion over Far Eastern policy. As Marshall, Acheson, and Bradley emphasized, the United States would neither adopt MacArthur's program nor evacuate Korea. It would continue to "inflict the greatest number of casualties . . . in order to break down not only the morale but the trained fabric of the Chinese armies." Unification of Korea remained a political and diplomatic objective; but as it had never been a military objective, the UN could accept a compromise that provided for Communist withdrawal above the thirty-eighth parallel. In brief, the United States would fight a limited war for limited objectives in order to avert the risk of world conflict.

[6]Truman appointed General Matthew B. Ridgway, commander of the Eighth Army in Korea, as MacArthur's successor.

[7]Quoted in William Hillman, *Mr. President* (New York, 1952), p. 133.

[8]Harry S Truman, *Memoirs by Harry S Truman*, 2 vols. (New York, 1955), II, 444.

6. *Decision in Korea: Truce and Armistice*

Washington had meanwhile moved on several fronts to convince Peking that some kind of settlement would be advantageous. Secretary Acheson won United Nations approval in May 1951 of an embargo against the shipment of arms, munitions, and critical raw materials to China. He made it clear that the United States would strenuously oppose Peking's effort to join the UN and would prevent Communist seizure of Taiwan. In Korea, UN forces repulsed two great offensives in April and May with staggering losses to the attackers. It was obvious by midyear that American policy was succeeding. The Communists had suffered over a million casualties; the best Chinese armies had been decimated; and China was isolated diplomatically and economically from the free world and had no hope of forcing a military decision.

Moreover, Chinese hostility confirmed American determination to conclude a peace treaty with Japan that would both restore sovereignty to the island empire and make it the cornerstone of a new security system in the far Pacific. Negotiations directed by John Foster Dulles, Republican adviser to the State Department, proceeded smoothly during 1950 and 1951. To be sure, the Russians objected, but their opposition only strengthened Western unity and facilitated signing of a "peace of reconciliation" in San Francisco in September 1951. The treaty stripped Japan of its overseas empire but was extraordinarily generous in all other respects. It imposed no restrictions upon Japanese economic development, levied no reparations, and recognized Japan's right to rearm. By this time a new security system in the Pacific had taken shape. The United States concluded a Mutual Defense Treaty with the Philippines in August and a Tripartite Security Treaty with Australia and New Zealand in September. A Security Treaty with Japan that same month permitted the United States to maintain land, sea, and air bases in Japanese territory.

While America thus began to marshal Pacific countries, the Communists showed the first sign of retreat in the Far East. Jacob A. Malik, head of the Russian delegation in the UN, declared in June 1951 that the Korean conflict could be ended if the belligerents began discussions looking toward a "cease-fire and an armistice providing for the mutual withdrawal of forces from the 38th parallel." When Moscow endorsed the suggestion, General Ridgway opened truce negotiations with Chinese and North Korean officials on July 10. While the negotiators haggled at Kaesong and later at Panmunjom, UN forces conducted defensive operations to hold their line north of the thirty-eighth parallel. It seems fairly certain that their strengthened armies could have cleared the Communist forces from North Korea that summer, and that Russia proposed truce talks chiefly to avert this catastrophe. Whether the Washington leaders knew this at the time, we cannot say. In any event, they instructed Ridgway and his successor, General Mark W. Clark, to maintain an impregnable defensive position and prevent a Communist buildup through unrelenting air assaults upon North Korea.

Meanwhile, truce negotiations proceeded amid charges and countercharges. The first break came in November 1951, when the Communists yielded their demand for UN withdrawal southward to the thirty-eighth parallel and accepted the American demand for demarcation along the military line at the time an armistice was signed. Then the negotiators reached an impasse over the question of repatriating prisoners of war. The Communists demanded the forcible delivery of some 46,000 Chinese and North Koreans who did not wish to return. The Americans adamantly refused, and the Communists broke off discussions in October 1952.

The Eisenhower administration, inaugurated in 1953, was determined to end this impasse even if it involved resumption of hostilities. The Communists responded by agreeing to exchange wounded prisoners, and armistice talks resumed in earnest on April 26. The new secretary of state, John Foster Dulles, now used veiled threats to assure speedy conclusion. He intimated to Indian Prime Minister Jawaharlal Nehru in May that the United States meant to have peace by one means or another. The warning certainly went at once to Peking, and with prompt results. Communist negotiators conceded all essential United Nations demands. Trouble now arose from President Syngman Rhee of South Korea, who threatened to withdraw his troops from the UN command and resume hostilities if his allies approved an armistice that left Chinese troops in North Korea. Rhee later gave in and agreed to support the armistice even though he would not sign it. In return, the American government promised to train and equip a South Korean army of twenty divisions, extend $1 billion in economic aid, and conclude a mutual security pact to protect South Korea against further aggression. An elaborate armistice, signed at Panmunjom on July 27, 1953, vindicated every important objective for which Americans and their allies had been fighting.[9] Thus ended the Korean War. It had cost the United States 54,246 dead, 103,284 wounded, and billions of dollars.

---

[9]The agreement established a demilitarized zone along a boundary that coincided with the military lines and a joint UN-Communist Military Armistice Commission and a Neutral Nations Supervisory Commission to enforce a cease-fire and prevent violations. To supervise repatriation of prisoners of war and release of prisoners who refused to return to their homelands, the agreement established a Repatriation Commission, composed of representatives of Sweden, Switzerland, Poland, Czechoslovakia, and India. Finally, the signatories recommended a conference within three months "to settle through negotiation the question of the withdrawal of all foreign forces from Korea, the peaceful settlement of the Korean question, etc."

7. Challenges to Democratic Supremacy

There were abundant signs after 1950 of mounting popular discontent with administration policies at home and abroad. Indeed, probably a majority of Americans for one reason or another desired a change of government by early 1952. Practically the entire white South was on the verge of revolt against the president's civil rights program and in a state of tense fear lest the Supreme Court outlaw public school segregation. In addition, Democratic leaders and private interests in Texas, Oklahoma, Louisiana, and Florida were near rebellion because of presidential and northern Democratic opposition to their demands for state ownership of offshore oil lands and exclusive state regulation of the natural gas industry.

This was also the time when Senator McCarthy pressed his campaign to expose alleged Communist infiltration in high places. Other Republican leaders were less abusive, but they joined his attack by charging that Roosevelt had "sold out" to Stalin at Yalta and asserting that sympathizers in the State Deparment had facilitated Communist victory in China. These persistent attacks succeeded in planting in millions of minds the suspicion that the Democratic party was tainted with treason and communism.

Opposition to Democratic rule was also generated by revelations of widespread corruption in Washington. A Senate investigation of the Reconstruction Finance Corporation in 1951 revealed corrupt influences in the granting of loans and exposed a ring of so-called five percenters. Soon afterward, in a nationally televised investigation, a Senate committee headed by Estes Kefauver of Tennessee exposed embarrassing connections between Democratic city machines and crime syndicates. Americans also learned that the Bureau of Internal Revenue was riddled with corruption, and that the assistant attorney general in charge of tax evasion cases had accepted large gifts, including two mink coats for his wife, from "fixers" and persons accused of income tax fraud.

Such scandals were good grist for the Republican mill, even though they were much less significant than those of the Grant and Harding eras. Even more damaging to Democratic prestige was the president's failure to take dramatic leadership in ousting the corrupt elements. To be sure, he reorganized the RFC and Bureau of Internal Revenue; but he acted slowly and, it seemed, reluctantly. And when he finally launched a housecleaning early in 1952, the affair turned into a farce. Attorney General J. Howard McGrath would not permit the special investigator to question Justice Department employees about their incomes. Truman upheld McGrath, causing the investigator to resign, then dismissed his attorney general in April and appointed James P. McGranery—who quietly abandoned the project of a special investigation.

Economic developments also contributed to the general dissatisfaction. Wholesale prices rose 13 percent from June 1950 to January 1952, and this spurred new rounds of wage demands and a sharp increase in the number of work stoppages. Although income kept pace with higher taxes and prices,[10] certain groups—persons on fixed incomes, for example, or farmers, whose costs mounted faster than their receipts—suffered much hardship.

Ironically, the Korean War itself generated the greatest popular discontent. Almost everyone had cheered when the president intervened, but disillusionment and a kind of despair swept through large elements of the country following China's entry and the administration's refusal to make an all-out bid for victory. Few Americans actually wanted to risk a third world conflict, but millions of them could not comprehend the concept of limited war and longed for some quick and easy way out of the stalemate. Casualties mounted while the truce talks ground on to no seeming end or purpose, and a tide of peace sentiment threatened to engulf the party in power.

8. The Campaign and Election of 1952

Republican leaders thus had reason to be confident as they prepared for the 1952 elections. But basic disagreement between the two important wings of the GOP quickly erupted into a battle for party control. Since his smashing reelection in 1950 Senator Taft was more than ever the unchallenged Republican leader in Congress, spokesman for the nation's conservatives and neo-isolationists, and preeminent foe of Democratic foreign and domestic policies. He had the support of powerful business interests, conservative-isolationist newspapers like the Chicago *Tribune*, and party organizations in the South and Middle West. He seemed irresistible as he opened an all-out campaign to win the presidential nomination and wrest control from the eastern internationalist leaders who had guided the party since 1940.

The eastern wing moved to counter this challenge. Led by Governor Dewey of New York and party heads in New England, Pennsylvania, New Jersey, and Maryland, the easterners enjoyed a working alliance with West Coast GOP leaders. They were moderately progressive in domestic affairs and favored preserving the New Deal reform structure. In foreign policy they were firmly committed to support of the United Nations and the non-Communist world. Their task was to find a candidate who could defeat Taft and then go on to win the presidency in November.

[10]Per capita disposable personal income was, in constant 1953 dollars, $1,509 in 1950, $1,508 in 1951, and $1,517 in 1952.

At first it seemed an impossible undertaking. Former Governor Harold E. Stassen was eager but unacceptable. Their most prominent spokesman, Governor Dewey, was already a twice-beaten candidate. They turned, therefore, to General Eisenhower, supreme commander of NATO forces, and implored him to run. Eisenhower reluctantly agreed to do so—only, as he told intimate friends, in order to prevent Taft's nomination and the triumph of isolationism in the Republican party.

Eisenhower's manager, Senator Henry Cabot Lodge, Jr., of Massachusetts, entered the general's name in the New Hampshire primary in January 1952 while Taft's forces began a drive in the South and Middle West. Eisenhower won easily in New Hampshire, Pennsylvania, and New Jersey, but Taft won such impressive victories in Wisconsin, Nebraska, and elsewhere in the Midwest that Eisenhower resigned his NATO command, returned to the United States, and entered the campaign in person in early June. Not since the William H. Taft-Theodore Roosevelt contest in 1912 had Republicans waged such a close and bitter prenomination battle. Taft and Eisenhower each garnered about five hundred delegates. The prize would go to the man who won Minnesota and California, committed to favorite sons, and contested delegations with sixty-eight votes from Texas, Georgia, and Louisiana.

The Taft forces controlled the Republican National Committee when the convention opened in Chicago on July 7, 1952. But they were out-maneuvered by Dewey and Lodge in a struggle for the crucial contested delegates. The easterners won a savage floor fight and were thereby able to nominate Eisenhower on the first ballot on July 11. It was an impressive victory but a potentially fatal one, for Taft and his embittered supporters were threatening to bolt or stay at home. GOP chances would depend upon Eisenhower's success in closing this breach. Meanwhile, the convention had nominated Senator Richard M. Nixon of California for vice-president and adopted a platform broad enough to accommodate both factions.[11]

The Democrats also waged a long hard campaign to determine party control and a presidential ticket. There were a host of contenders—Vice-President Alben W. Barkley of Kentucky, Averell Harriman of New York, Senators Robert S. Kerr of Oklahoma, Richard B. Russell of Georgia, and Estes Kefauver of Tennessee. Kefauver made the most vigorous bid and scored the earliest successes by open opposition to the Truman administration. Yet power rested with leaders of the northern and midwestern organizations and in large measure with the president himself. Truman

---

[11]It promised reductions in federal expenditures and taxes, extension of social security, maintenance of high farm price supports, and exclusive state control of the tidelands. It condemned corruption in government; approved the Taft-Hartley Act but promised revision favorable to labor; approved in principle an FEPC but declared that states should have primary control of race relations; and denounced the president's alleged usurpation of the warmaking power by intervening in Korea without congressional consent. Finally, it announced a new policy of the "liberation" of peoples under Soviet domination, to replace the allegedly futile policy of containment.

played a cautious game at first. Then he announced on March 30 that he would not run again; and soon afterward he began a campaign to draft Governor Adlai E. Stevenson of Illinois. But Stevenson insisted that he was not a candidate and continued his protestation until right before the convention.

Truman and his allies thereupon promised to support Barkley, who left for Chicago "with the assurances of party leaders from President Truman down, that Adlai Stevenson would not take the presidential nomination and that . . . [he] would be the convention's choice."[12] But on the eve of the convention a group of "certain self-anointed political labor leaders," including Walter Reuther of the CIO and George M. Harrison of the AFL, told Barkley that he was too old to run and asked him to withdraw. They spoke without authority, but they gained their objective.

The Kefauver forces made a gallant effort when the Democrats assembled in Chicago on July 21. But Truman and his friends were in the driver's seat. They turned again to Stevenson, who consented this time and won the nomination on the third ballot. The convention named Senator John J. Sparkman of Alabama as his running mate and adopted a platform demanding repeal of the Taft-Hartley Act, enactment of a full civil rights program, including a compulsory FEPC, and maintenance of high price supports for farmers. The platform also promised continuation of administration policies in Asia and Europe.

Stevenson, once he accepted the nomination, acted like a man who wanted to win. In a series of addresses unparalleled for literary excellence since Wilson's day, he told the American people that there was no easy road to peace and security. On domestic issues he began as a moderate but was drawn inevitably into full espousal of Fair Deal progressivism. He won AFL and CIO endorsement by demanding repeal of Taft-Hartley. He won wide support among blacks by championing advanced civil rights legislation. He drew most intellectuals to his side by his high seriousness and obvious intellectual capacity. On the other hand, he was less successful in his bid for general support. Many farmers and suburbanites, tired of both the war and the administration, simply refused to listen to a Democratic candidate.

Stevenson's eloquence was not enough to withstand the Republican assault. Eisenhower took the lead, launching a "great crusade" for honest and efficient government at home and for "freedom in the world." Then he took up the theme of liberation of captive peoples, first developed by John Foster Dulles and included in the party platform. Condemning the administration's "appalling and disastrous mismanagement" of foreign affairs, Eisenhower promised a surer road to peace than the policy of containment, although he was never precise in pointing to the new way. On domestic issues he talked in generalities broad enough to please almost all classes and interests.

[12] Alben W. Barkley, *That Reminds Me—* (New York, 1954), p. 233.

In early weeks Eisenhower struck a posture of national leadership above the din of political strife. He soon persuaded himself, however, that national salvation lay as much in a sweeping party triumph as in his own election; and he shifted his ground accordingly. He invited Senator Taft to New York City to conciliate the right wing. At their conference on September 12, Eisenhower signed Taft's articles of surrender, won the Ohioan's promise of cooperation,[13] and soon afterward opened a strongly partisan attack upon the Truman administration and the president personally. He also clearly endorsed Taft's view that one objective of his administration would be to destroy such products of "creeping socialism" as the TVA and federal hydroelectric projects in the Northwest. Finally, he tried to cement party unity by supporting all Republican candidates, including his bitter enemies, Senator McCarthy and Senator William Jenner of Indiana.

Eisenhower's most important move was to take up the Korean issue in an effort to capitalize upon the overriding popular desire for peace. He did not specifically say that intervention had been unwise. But he did charge that Truman's blundering had helped to cause the conflict, and that the United States had walked into a Soviet trap by agreeing to a cease-fire in 1951. He struck the high note of his campaign at Detroit in October by promising "an early and honorable end" to the war. "That job," he said, "requires a personal trip to Korea. I shall make that trip. Only in that way could I learn how best to serve the American people in the cause of peace. I shall go to Korea."

Meanwhile, a united Republican party had waged one of the most powerful and best financed campaigns ever seen. Utilizing all the techniques of advertising through television, radio, and the press, GOP spokesmen mounted a devastating attack. Practically all Republican campaigners used the Communist issue; a few, like McCarthy, went so far as to charge that Stevenson was tainted with Communist associations. Even more effective was the attack on American participation in Korea. The Republican momentum was halted only once, when the Democrats published proof that Nixon had enjoyed access to a modest fund provided by friends in California. Eisenhower was so furious that he commissioned Dewey to ask Nixon to withdraw. But Nixon fought back in an emotional television broadcast on September 23 that won new support for his ticket. Eisenhower was convinced and rushed to a dramatic public reconciliation.

All signs pointed to a Republican victory on November 5, but the pollsters were unsure of themselves, and GOP campaigners fought hard to

[13]Taft had earlier made it clear that he regarded Eisenhower as another Dewey, a "me-too" candidate who would carry the GOP to defeat by agreeing with the Democrats on all important points. At this New York conference, Eisenhower agreed that the main issue of the campaign was "liberty against creeping socialization" and promised to defend the Taft-Hartley Act and treat Taft's followers fairly in dispensing patronage. The two men disagreed on foreign policy; but Taft added, "I think it is fair to say that our differences are differences of degree."

ELECTION OF 1952

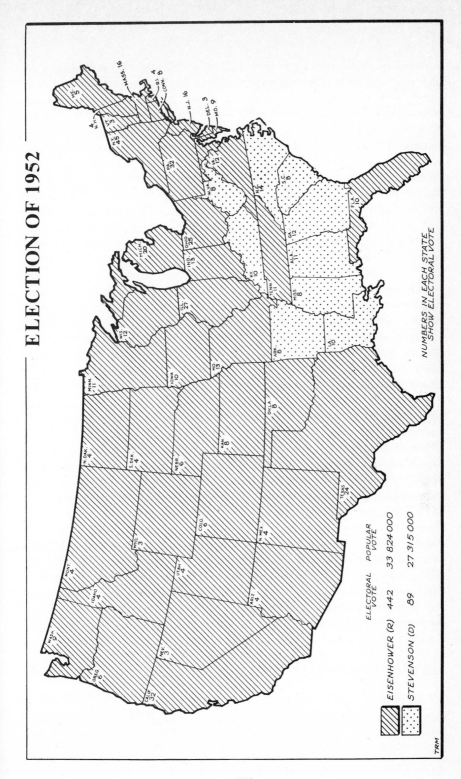

NUMBERS IN EACH STATE
SHOW ELECTORAL VOTE

	ELECTORAL VOTE	POPULAR VOTE
EISENHOWER (R)	442	33 824 000
STEVENSON (D)	89	27 315 000

ME. 5
MASS. 16
R.I. 4
CONN. 8
N.J. 16
DEL. 3
MD. 9
N.H. 4
VT. 3
N.Y. 45
PA. 32
W. VA. 8
VA. 12
N.C. 14
S.C. 8
MICH. 20
OHIO 25
IND. 13
KY. 10
TENN.
GA. 12
FLA. 10
ALA. 11
WIS. 12
ILL. 27
MISS. 8
ARK. 8
LA. 10
MINN. 11
IOWA 10
MO. 13
OKLA. 8
N. DAK. 4
S. DAK. 4
NEBR. 6
KAN. 8
TEXAS 24
WYO. 3
COLO. 6
N. MEX. 4
MONT. 4
IDAHO 4
UTAH 4
ARIZ. 4
WASH. 9
OREG. 6
NEV. 3
CALIF. 32

TRM

721

avert a a last-minute swing to Stevenson. It did not occur. Stevenson, with 27,314,987 popular votes, carried only West Virginia, Kentucky, the Carolinas, Georgia, Alabama, Mississippi, Louisiana, and Arkansas. Eisenhower won 33,824,351 popular votes and carried thirty-nine states with a landslide electoral total of 442 to Stevenson's 89.

This victory was, in part, the personal triumph of a much-loved and widely respected national hero. In addition, the Republicans won because they were the opposition at a time when discontent was great enough to destroy normal voting habits and break the Democratic coalition of farmers, workers, ethnic minorities, and southerners. Many southern Democrats voted as much against Truman's civil rights program and for state ownership of the tidelands as for Eisenhower. Many Democratic workers defected because as Catholics or persons of eastern European ancestry they were particularly susceptible to Republican denunciations of Communists and Yalta. Midwestern farmers voted Republican, in part, because Eisenhower simply outbid Stevenson for their support. Persons on fixed incomes were obsessed by fear of inflation.

But all observers agreed that the issue with the greatest impact was the Korean War. It crystallized all accumulated discontent. "In marking their ballots for Eisenhower," one analyst observed, "many persons, of course, hoped to bring their sons and husbands back home. Still, the election should not be interpreted as a vote for peace at any price. It was more a vote of impatience with the frustrating state of neither war nor peace."[14]

And yet we can easily exaggerate the results by emphasizing only Eisenhower's triumph and the divisive issues. The astonishing phenomenon was the Democratic party's continued strength. In spite of Eisenhower's personal popularity, widespread discontent, and an effective campaign against an increasingly unpopular administration, the Republicans only managed to elect a majority of eight in the House and, because of the defection of Wayne Morse of Oregon from the GOP, to break even in the Senate. As Eisenhower ran far ahead of most other Republican candidates, it was clear that he carried this slight congressional majority along with him into office. Nor could reactionaries or neo-isolationists claim that the election signified a repudiation of either progressivism or internationalism. Actually, differences between parties and candidates were slight compared to their substantial agreement on the necessity of preserving both the New Deal reform structure and the postwar alliance-assistance system.

[14]Samuel Lubell, "Who Elected Eisenhower?" *Saturday Evening Post*, 225 (January 10, 1953), 74.

28

Politics and Problems

of the

Eisenhower Era

The confusion and uncertainty that had permeated the American political scene since 1945 were in no way resolved by the inauguration of a Republican president in 1953. The GOP was back in power for the first time in twenty years, and Dwight D. Eisenhower had just received one of the most impressive personal mandates on record. But Americans who believed that new leadership would bring deliverance from postwar anxieties were doomed to disappointment. The pressures and crises of the cold war continued undiminished. Inflation and recession posed threats to prosperity. Racial, religious, and ideological tensions added their disruptions to the normal problems of a mobile society. Social and economic changes altered old voting patterns, and the period was one of flux and partial deadlock in politics. The emphasis had shifted somewhat, but doubt and uncertainty were as rife at the end of the Eisenhower era as they had been at the beginning.

Despite confusion and deadlock, there were positive gains during these eight years. Before the end of Eisenhower's first term the nation had largely recovered from the excesses of its Red scare. There was progress in the field of civil rights. The new administration prevented runaway inflation and presided over the most prosperous decade Americans had ever known. And the GOP's return to power resulted in a cautious expansion of the New Deal reform structure, rather than its dismantling. The anticipated break with the Democratic era did not occur.

But these were not years of vigorous leadership or bold action in domestic affairs. Thoughtful Americans came to deplore the government's refusal to move more forcefully against growing problems of technological unemployment, urban decay, education, transportation, and the farm surplus. This inactivity stemmed from the overriding urgency of foreign affairs, a general public mood of complacency, fear of inflation and excessive spending, and disagreement over specific means and goals. Perhaps no leadership could have made much headway in the face of such obstacles. But many felt that the president's failure to use his prestige and power more effectively in behalf of needed domestic reform was an abdication of responsibility.

1. The New Republican President

Dwight David Eisenhower brought to the White House, and retained, a degree of popularity accorded to few if any of his predecessors. Not since Hoover had a new presidential candidate been as widely known and respected at the time of his nomination. Not since Grant had the American people turned so hopefully to a military hero.

Eisenhower was born in Denison, Texas, on October 14, 1890, and grew up in Abilene, Kansas. Graduation from West Point in 1915 was followed by twenty-seven years of routine duty at regular army posts, attendance at various service schools, and a tour of duty as aide to General MacArthur in the Philippines from 1935 to 1940. Eisenhower was a lieutenant colonel with the temporary rank of brigadier general when the Japanese attacked Pearl Harbor. During the next three years, after brief service in the War Department, he commanded United States forces in the European theater, directed the North African campaign, led the Allied Expeditionary Force that landed on Norman beaches in June 1944, and achieved the five stars of a general of the army. He commanded American occupation forces in Germany following the Nazi surrender, succeeded George C. Marshall as chief of staff in late 1945, and resigned from active service in 1948 to become president of Columbia University. In 1950 he took leave of absence from Columbia to become supreme commander of the newly formed NATO forces.

How well had this long and distinguished military career prepared General Eisenhower for the nation's highest office? His lack of ordinary civilian experience was a liability. No previous president—with the possible exception of Zachary Taylor, whose example was not overly comforting—had had a briefer exposure to civilian life prior to his election. He entered the campaign of 1952 with no experience and almost no working knowledge of the political process. Indeed, his political views were so ill defined after the war that no one, including the general himself, was quite sure of his party preference, with the result that both parties besought his candidacy in 1948. This was in one sense an asset, since it freed him from the kind of intense partisanship that the nation had experienced all too frequently. But the long army career had insulated him from civilian concerns and taught him to rely too heavily upon the initiative and judgment of subordinates.

Military experience also provided a positive legacy. He had learned to direct gigantic operations, developed a talent for working harmoniously with others and reconciling divergent viewpoints, and become accustomed to the burdens of large responsibility. At a time when such questions were crucial, he brought to the presidency a high level of competence in the field of national defense. His overseas experiences had instilled a mature internationalist outlook, an invaluable familiarity with European leaders and problems, and a determination to maintain and strengthen the Western alliance system and the non-Communist world generally. This all gave a strength and a focus to his presidency that no specific errors or failures could undermine.

The new president was not an intellectual, nor was he given to serious reading in history, politics, or current affairs. "Eisenhower's mind is, like his personality, standard-American," one observer noted. "It is unschematic, distrustful of fine distinctions into the realm of matter and things, concerned with the effect of ideas rather than with their validity."[1] He sometimes expressed commonplace ideas in a rambling and labored syntax. Yet he spoke in terms and voiced sentiments that millions of Americans understood and shared.

Indeed, Eisenhower was "standard-American" almost to the point of caricature. He liked westerns, bourbon, bridge and poker, golf, fishing, gardening, and hunting. His admiration of the successful businessman reminded historians, rather uneasily, of U. S. Grant. In a generation that had experienced bewildering changes and looked nostalgically toward a vanished past, Eisenhower seemed to embody traditional American virtues: decency, self-reliance, thrift, individualism. The political views that began to emerge with his candidacy in 1952 smacked of orthodox Republicanism: devotion to free enterprise and a balanced budget, a preference for liberty over security, respect for state rights, distrust of "creeping socialism." Yet he agreed that the essentials of New Deal reform should be maintained. To critics, right and left, this seemed like inconsistency and fuzzy thinking. But it exemplified the middle-road position that Eisenhower consciously sought to occupy, and it was an excellent approximation of majority sentiment in the 1950s. Most Americans, in short, wanted freedom *and* security. Moderation was the keynote of both the man and his administration.

[1] Richard H. Rovere, *Affairs of State: The Eisenhower Years* (New York, 1956), p. 17.

It also characterized his methods of leadership. A gifted coordinator, Eisenhower detested controversy and constantly sought to reconcile opposing viewpoints. He employed approaches that were second nature to him: persuasion, discussion, tact, charm, patience, good will. Cooperative teamwork was the key to accomplishment. The leader's role was to harmonize the functioning of the team and ratify decisions and policies carefully prepared by subordinates.

Results, however, were often disappointing. The military staff system, with its chains of command and sweeping delegations of pyramided authority, lent itself only moderately well to the ill-assorted operations of the federal executive. The teamwork and coordination that had made Allied landings on D-Day so huge a success were poorly designed to absorb the frictions and pressures of the political process. Conciliation and compromise had a way of deferring or diluting decision, and moderation began to look like drift. Eisenhower seemed to lack the will to make the executive branch operate efficiently. He avoided, when possible, systematic exposure to the details, close political contacts, and daily burdens of the office. Beneath his seemingly open and uncomplicated manner, it turned out, lay an impressive fund of political skill and shrewdness. But he refused to grasp the immense possibilities that his skills, prestige, and the powers of his office had placed at his disposal.

And yet it can be said that an Eisenhower was both inevitable and necessary for this troubled era. His outlook, temperament, and style fitted the public mood like a tailored uniform. Americans wanted just such a president—a respected figure above the political battle, a cautious moderate, an embodiment of the "American way." Twenty years of one-party dominance had weakened the vitality and responsibility of Republicans and Democrats alike. New Deal reform needed the kind of bipartisan ratification that only a well-disposed Republican administration could provide. Republicans needed to learn, as only the burdens of leadership could teach them, that neither the New Deal nor the postwar world could be wished into oblivion.

2. The Second Red Scare: Peak and Decline

National alarm over alleged Communists in government, so great an issue during the Truman era, persisted well into Eisenhower's first term. It exhibited a bizarre cast of characters; but the central figure during this heyday of the second Red scare, the man who did most to shape its course and stamp it with his own personality and character, was Senator Joseph R. McCarthy of Wisconsin.

It was widely assumed as the Eisenhower administration took office that McCarthy's days of power and influence were about to end. He had made his reputation as a savage and reckless critic of the party in power. Now that the Democrats were gone, taking with them their softness toward communism, conspiracies, and twenty years of treason, there seemed to be no need for further assaults. "It is this newspaper's hope and belief that McCarthyism would disappear overnight if Eisenhower were elected," the Washington *Post* had said in 1952. This confidence persisted for a few weeks after the election. Senator Taft, who disapproved of McCarthy while condoning his scurrilous attacks for the past three years, believed that GOP strategists could now contain the Wisconsin demagogue. Even McCarthy saw a new role ahead for himself. "The picture has so infinitely changed," he told newspapermen. "Now it will be unnecessary for me to conduct a one-man campaign to expose Communists in government. We have a new President who doesn't want party-line thinkers or fellow travelers. He will conduct the fight."[2]

Taft planned to render McCarthy impotent by assigning the chairmanship of the Internal Security Committee, which would handle loyalty investigations, to the devoutly anti-Communist but colorless William Jenner of Indiana. McCarthy would be safely pigeonholed as chairman of the innocuous Committee on Government Operations. "We've got McCarthy where he can't do any harm," Taft concluded happily—as mistaken a judgment as the astute Ohioan ever made. Part of McCarthy's new committee was a permanent subcommittee on investigations. Although *investigations* applied ostensibly to governmental contracts, McCarthy saw the word as a convenient turret that could be aimed in any direction. Making himself chairman of the subcommittee, he quickly resumed his flamboyant crusade against Communists in government.

For the next year and a half McCarthy was rarely out of the headlines. He piled accusations, wild charges, sensational "disclosures," and widely publicized investigations one upon another. His shadow seemed to grow ominously longer, and only the president of the United States wielded comparable influence. Few men in public life were willing to challenge him when opinion polls reported in early 1954 that 50 percent of the people approved of McCarthy and another 21 percent "did not know." The Senate was reluctant to oppose him, for McCarthy had demonstrated more than once what he could do against a senator in an election campaign.[3] Except for a small band of conservatives, senators despised him—and feared him even more.

The president also stayed aloof as long as he could. This was not due to fear, but rather to his desire for party harmony and inveterate dislike of personal controversy—especially of the sort McCarthy relished. "I will

[2] Quoted in Richard H. Rovere, *Senator Joe McCarthy* (New York, 1959), p. 187.

[3] Millard Tydings of Maryland, William Benton of Connecticut, Scott Lucas of Illinois, and Ernest MacFarland of Arizona were among those defeated senators who counted themselves McCarthy's victims.

not get in the gutter with that guy," Eisenhower reportedly snapped.[4] He also wished to avoid a break with the Republican right wing and apparently hoped that forbearance and time would solve the problem with the least friction and damage.

The president's forbearance was sorely tested during his first eighteen months in office. McCarthy conducted a tirade against the appointment of Charles E. Bohlen as ambassador to Russia in 1953. Taft finally intervened to secure Bohlen's confirmation, but at the price of a virtual agreement by the administration to make no further appointments that McCarthy disapproved. The State Department meekly chose what everyone regarded as a "McCarthy man" for its security officer, thereby giving the senator from Wisconsin a virtual veto over the secretary of state in departmental personnel policy. McCarthy announced in March 1953 that he had "negotiated" an agreement with Greek shipowners to stop trading at Soviet and other Communist ports. When this drew from Harold Stassen, director of mutual security, the indignant charge that McCarthy was usurping executive functions and undermining American foreign policy, the administration made peace by issuing a mild rebuke to McCarthy and forcing Stassen to tone down his statement.

McCarthy charged ahead on many fronts. His subcommittee probed for alleged Communists in the Voice of America program, finding none but managing to destroy that agency's efficiency and morale. He performed a similar operation in 1953 upon the State Department's overseas information program. In the process, two irresponsible young members of his staff conducted a farcical "investigation" abroad and brought shame and despair to every American embassy in Europe. The State Department dutifully removed from its overseas libraries, and in some instances actually burned, books by authors whom the McCarthy subcommittee regarded as subversive.[5] Another member of his staff wrote a magazine article charging that the American Protestant clergy was riddled with subversion. The administration did manage to take a stand against burning books and attacking clergymen, but not in such fashion as to deter the freewheeling senator. Millions of Americans were too impressed by the range and variety of his charges to notice that in four years of strenuous activity he had not unearthed a single Communist in government or anywhere else.

Meanwhile, the Justice Department and other federal agencies conducted loyalty probes of their own. The government had become so

---

[4]Quoted in Robert J. Donovan, *Eisenhower: The Inside Story* (New York, 1956), p. 249.

[5]These "subversive" authors included Bert Andrews, chief of the Washington bureau of the New York *Herald Tribune*; Richard Lauterbach, former European correspondent of *Time* magazine; Clarence Streit, internationalist author; Walter White, distinguished Negro leader; and Foster Rhea Dulles, professor of history at Ohio State University and a cousin of the secretary of state.

hedged about with suspicion and security regulations that its very functioning was adversely affected, especially in the vital fields of scientific research, national defense, and foreign policy. Attacks on the State Department shattered morale among loyal public servants and caused a sharp decline in the number of young men entering the diplomatic corps. Equally damaging and deplorable was the sustained attack upon J. Robert Oppenheimer, former director of the Los Alamos laboratory and a scientist of international renown. The Atomic Energy Commission, on the initiative of its new chairman, Lewis L. Strauss, barred Oppenheimer from access to classified materials in July 1953 on the ground that he was a poor security risk. A special board affirmed Oppenheimer's loyalty in May 1954 but agreed that security regulations required that he be denied access to classified data. Perhaps the most revealing aspect of these proceedings was that not a single prominent political figure raised his voice against them, even after their shameful character had been laid bare.[6]

The climax came with McCarthy's attack upon the army in early 1954. He discovered that a reserve corps dentist at Fort Monmouth had been promoted and honorably discharged despite his refusal to sign a loyalty certificate. From this insignificant episode, which the army admitted having mishandled, came wild charges about subversion in the armed forces and a new round of hearings. When McCarthy bullied and humiliated Brigadier General Ralph Zwicker, the dentist's commanding officer, Secretary of the Army Robert Stevens rushed indignantly to the general's defense. He denounced the subcommittee, ordered Zwicker and other officers not to testify before it, and prepared a strong statement which he planned to read before it himself. McCarthy, calling Stevens an "awful dupe," conferred with the secretary and obtained his signature to articles of surrender permitting Zwicker to testify after all. The army struck back with the charge that McCarthy had attempted by various improper means to obtain preferential treatment for Private G. David Schine, former "consultant" to the subcommittee.

This embroilment led to televised hearings that captivated millions for six weeks during the spring of 1954. McCarthy dominated these proceedings as he had dominated all such affairs—interrupting, raising "points of order," evading questions, bullying witnesses, glowering, sneering, obstructing. Many Americans saw McCarthy in action for the first time. They saw uncouth arrogance, frank brutality, and a callous disregard for established rules, law, the rights of others, and human decency. They saw the face of evil and recognized it.

Equally important, McCarthy's performance goaded both the Senate and the president into open defiance. Democratic members of the subcommittee could hardly acquiesce or look away before a national television audience, and bluntly opposed their chairman for the first time. President Eisenhower delivered a sharp rebuke. During the hearing, McCarthy had produced a letter containing secret material from the FBI files and announced that federal employees were "duty bound" to give him information "even though some bureaucrat may have stamped it secret." This was open aggression, and the White House responded with the flat statement that executive responsibility could not "be usurped by any individual who may seek to set himself above the laws of our land or to override orders of the President of the United States."[7]

McCarthy's star was on the wane when the hearings closed in June 1954. They ended in victory for neither side, but McCarthy was the real loser. His investigation of Fort Monmouth had collapsed; he had lost his dictatorial control over the subcommittee; and both the Senate and the president were now in open opposition. In August, following debate over a censure resolution introduced by Ralph Flanders of Vermont, the Senate voted to appoint a committee to investigate McCarthy's conduct. After prolonged hearings, in which McCarthy for once appeared as defendant rather than prosecutor, the committee recommended censure on two counts. By a vote of sixty-seven to twenty-two, the Senate adopted a resolution in December 1954 "condemning" certain of McCarthy's actions.

There followed a downhill trail to obscurity and death. The Democratic victory in the election of 1954 cost McCarthy his committee chairmanships. The Senate thereafter ignored him. Physical ailments drained his vitality. His will to resume the struggle seemed to have been sapped, and he never again captured the headlines or strode dramatically into the limelight. A hard core of devoted followers remained loyal to the end— and afterward—but most Americans simply forgot about him. When McCarthy died on May 2, 1957, of complications induced by neuritis, hepatitis, and inflammation of the liver, the era to which he had given his name was already dead.[8]

---

[7]In reply, McCarthy referred again to the "evidence of treason that has been growing over the past twenty—twenty-*one* years."

[8]McCarthy's decline was as much symptom as cause. Except for a determined minority on the far right, Americans began to realize that there were more important problems than the search for Communists in government. Common sense was reasserting itself, especially after the loyalty probes received a deadly blow in early 1955. Harvey Matusow, a voluble ex-Communist and prize witness in the government's case against certain individuals, suddenly went back on his testimony, confessed to perjury, and admitted having lied about the individuals in question. A few other ex-Communists, some of whom had been retained by the Justice Department as consultants in preparing cases against alleged subversives, also repudiated earlier testimony. The country could not help but laugh at the spectacle of committees actually trying to persuade these gentlemen that they were lying now about having lied earlier; the whole process of anti-Communist investigation was thrown into confusion and disrepute, and it never fully recovered.

3. The Anomaly of American Politics, 1953–1960

Although the new president was instrumental in restoring a measure of unity and confidence to a nation torn by fear of communism at home and abroad, the most striking feature of American politics during the 1950s was its confused and unstable condition. Eisenhower's huge majority in 1952 signaled the breakup of the Roosevelt coalition of laborers, farmers, urban minorities, and southerners, but no new majority coalition took its place. The result was stalemate, and positive leadership proved difficult to assert.

Not only did cleavages within and between the two parties limit constructive action on domestic affairs. Consistency and pattern seemed to vanish from the political scene. Traditional party allegiance declined in almost every group, class, and section. A huge "swing vote" appeared, varying in size and composition with each election. Millions of Americans adopted the practice of voting a split ticket, supporting a man or an issue rather than a party, and shifting sides in response to circumstances. For the decade as a whole, the two parties were more nearly equal in voting strength than at any time since the early 1890s. An unstable and unpredictable equilibrium had become the political norm.

The reasons were many. Fear of communism and resentment over the Korean War, as we have seen, swung many traditionally Democratic votes into the Republican column in 1952. Extreme charges of Democratic disloyalty—"twenty years of treason," the "sellout" at Yalta, and so on—had their most telling impact upon Americans of German descent, and upon Catholics. Genuinely fearful of communism, these elements reacted more strongly to the loyalty issue perhaps because their own Americanism had been suspect in times past. Many clung to their suspicions and resentments long after the Red scare had subsided.

Prosperity also eroded older voting habits. Among farmers, for example, the dire economic plight that had produced Democratic majorities in most rural areas in the 1930s was largely gone. The farmer continued to rely upon governmental price supports and other New Deal benefits, but since 1941 he had exchanged problems of poverty for those of relative affluence. By midcentury most farmers had escaped tenancy by moving to the cities, and many farm owners had paid off the mortgage and put cash in the bank. Debtor psychology had vanished. Steadily rising costs accompanying the purchase and upkeep of farm machinery made inflation a matter of concern. Thus the farmer now disapproved of governmental spending—except, of course, for agricultural price supports—and tended to regard Democratic fiscal and welfare policies as inflationary. Moreover, rural voters shared a widespread public feeling that labor unions had grown too strong and exercised undue influence in the Democratic party.

Comparable pressures were at work in cities, where regular Democratic majorities of 60 and 70 percent had been the rule in the 1930s and 1940s. The urban masses were joining the middle class. As millions of families moved from city tenements to suburban homes after 1945, a new property-owning, taxpaying outlook often outweighed older class prejudices and party loyalties. A Republican majority in the suburbs began to offset the Democratic big-city vote. Moreover, urban political machines lost much of their cohesion and power as the federal government assumed most of the welfare burden, and as once-submerged ethnic groups climbed the social ladder and challenged the dominance of former leaders. Among urban groups, only blacks retained the staunch Democratic loyalty fostered during New Deal days.

Unions, for comparable reasons, had also ceased to be a reliable bulwark of Democratic power. The goals that had united labor politically during the thirties had been won, and Democratic allegiance was undermined by fear of inflation, dislike of taxes, resentment against the Korean War, and dissatisfaction with certain trade and tariff policies. Attempts by AFL-CIO leaders to influence Democratic policy and marshal labor support for Democratic candidates alienated many nonunion Democrats and frequently, as in the abortive campaign to unseat Senator Taft in 1950, backfired even among union members.

Conditions changed even more in the South. Backward one-crop agriculture, tenancy, rural poverty, and wool-hatted rustics were giving way to growing cities and plush modern suburbs, booming industries, a large urban middle class, prosperous farms, and an economy more nearly in tune with that of the nation than ever before. At the same time, the southern tradition of white supremacy faced a challenge unparalleled since Reconstruction. The nature and impact of this challenge will be discussed later. It had, among other things, a profoundly unsettling effect on southern politics. Economic transformation and the assault upon segregation produced two insurgent political factions. One, drawing its main strength from old "black belt" counties and low-income urban wards, was frankly dedicated to preservation of white supremacy. The other consisted of rising business and professional elements in southern cities who increasingly resented their impotence in a one-party system.

An odd paradox resulted. These factions had only one thing in common—opposition to the national Democratic party. Segregationists were arrayed against its stand on civil rights; southern businessmen resented its dominance by the northern urban-labor wing and its economic progressivism. Both factions began voting for Republican presidential candidates in order to deprive the Democracy of federal power, yet they were at odds beyond that point. Many rural and labor voters who favored segregation were progressive on economic and welfare issues. The urban business element was not willing to jeopardize southern economic and moral progress by all-out resistance to desegregation. As a result, the two factions could not cooperate effectively in state and local politics. But in presidential elections the Solid South had vanished. The GOP carried four southern states in 1952, five in 1956, and three in 1960. Whereas it won a paltry 22 percent of the southern major-party vote in 1940 and 28 percent in 1944, it polled 49 percent in 1952, almost 51 percent in 1956, and 48 percent in 1960.

Notwithstanding all these changes, Republicans were unable to construct a stable national majority of their own. The Roosevelt coalition had been broken because conditions that gave it birth were largely gone, but the Democrats still retained a majority of several million registered voters throughout the 1950s. It was no longer a reliable majority, but the country remained "normally" Democratic, and neither prosperity, Eisenhower's popularity, nor the frustrations and resentments of the cold war could make permanent Republicans out of the millions of Democrats who backed Eisenhower in 1952.

America had in effect become a nation of moderates who withheld blind allegiance from either party. Voters were keeping their freedom and security in delicate balance. If prosperity had engendered a new sensitivity to inflation and opposition to governmental spending, depression memories prevented any return to Republican "normalcy" of the 1920s and produced a Democratic reaction in times of recession. "I voted for Eisenhower to turn the tide of too much reliance on government," an Illinois farmer explained in 1954. "Now I'm voting Democratic again to see that things don't go too far the other way."[9]

4. National Elections in the 1950s

Election results reflected this political ferment. The GOP could do no better in 1952 than break even in the Senate and win a majority of eight in the House. The balance of the decade, with one major exception, witnessed a resurgence of Democratic strength. A mild recession in 1954 caused a rise in unemployment and touched off fears of depression. These alarms, when added to rural discontent over administration farm policy, contributed to a Republican reversal in the midterm elections. Although

[9]Quoted in Samuel Lubell, *Revolt of the Moderates* (New York, 1956), p. 118.

the president stumped for Republican candidates, the Democrats won a precarious majority in the Senate and regained control of the House by a margin of 232 to 203. Yet the turnover had been below average for a midterm election, and fear of depression had not revived the huge Democratic majorities of New Deal days.

Even more indicative were results in 1956. The only serious question for Republicans was the president's health. He had suffered a major heart attack in the autumn of 1955 and had undergone an operation for ileitis in the spring of 1956. His recovery in both cases had been so remarkable as to remove most doubts about his ability to serve a second term, and Republican leaders well knew that defeat impended if he did not run again. They were also determined to renominate the more controversial Nixon for vice-president. Nixon had outraged Democrats and offended liberal Republicans by his vigorous use of the Communist issue in 1952 and 1954, but GOP strategists regarded him as an indispensable link between the moderate and conservative wings. No real opposition appeared, and a jubilant Republican convention met in San Francisco on August 20, 1956, and quickly renominated Eisenhower and Nixon. The platform promised flexible price supports, federal aid to schools, revision of Taft-Hartley, and tax reductions if possible. It approved the Supreme Court's desegregation decision of 1954 but opposed the use of force to implement it.

Meanwhile, the Democrats had met in Chicago on August 12 and renominated Adlai Stevenson, who had retained most of his prestige and following within the party and had been its major spokesman since 1952. But he did not win the second nomination without a struggle. Senator Kefauver, a southern liberal whose national reputation was based largely upon his investigations of crime, announced in early 1956 that he would enter certain primaries and seek the nomination. A long, exhausting, and uninspiring primary battle between Stevenson and Kefauver ensued. The Tennessean scored early successes in New Hampshire and Minnesota by dint of prodigious energy, then lost to Stevenson in Florida, California, and Oregon. When Democrats in state after state named pro-Stevenson or favorite-son delegates to the national convention, Kefauver withdrew. Stevenson encountered a second challenge when former President Truman came to Chicago to work for the candidacy of Governor Averell Harriman of New York. But the Stevenson forces were able to beat down this threat, and the Illinoisan won the nomination on the first ballot.

The only surprise occurred in the selection of a running mate. Stevenson announced after his nomination that he would leave the convention free to choose a vice-presidential candidate. A feverish battle immediately broke out, with several younger aspirants—notably Senators Hubert Humphrey of Minnesota, Albert Gore of Tennessee, and John F. Kennedy of Massachusetts—competing for delegate support. Kefauver also entered the contest, which soon became a Kefauver-Kennedy duel. Kefauver finally won, but the most noteworthy aspect was the South's willingness to support Kennedy, a Roman Catholic.

The Democratic platform promised more generous price supports, a higher minimum wage, and repeal of Taft-Hartley. It advocated a balanced budget, federal atomic energy plants, better conservation of natural resources, and tax reduction for lower-income groups. The civil rights plank cautiously endorsed the recent Supreme Court decision and called for continued efforts to wipe out discrimination, but it contained no pledge to implement desegregation and was weaker than its Republican counterpart. The platform also attacked the Eisenhower foreign and domestic policies, charging that they had weakened the defense establishment, damaged America's standing with her allies, increased the risk of war, and ignored the needs of farmers, small businessmen, low-income groups, and elderly citizens.

The second Eisenhower-Stevenson campaign was a dull affair. The Democrats, to be sure, labored under huge disadvantages. The president was at the peak of his popularity and almost invulnerable to criticism, and Stevenson groped vainly for an issue. Charges that Eisenhower's uncertain health would impair his leadership made no impact. Nothing in the Democratic arsenal could possibly match the Republican appeal of "peace and prosperity." Neither farm discontent nor unemployment was acute enough to cause a major upheaval. No matter how they treated it, the civil rights question was more liability than asset to the Democrats. They did their best to make an issue out of Nixon, but with little success. When Stevenson tried to discuss the perils of radioactive fallout and the need to stop nuclear testing, the country seemed satisfied that Eisenhower knew best about such matters. As in 1952, the press was overwhelmingly Republican. To make matters worse for the Democrats, Stevenson seemed unsure of himself and ran less effectively this time.

In retrospect, it is doubtful that anything Stevenson might have said or done would have affected the outcome. The sudden eruption of the Hungarian and Suez crises right before the election (see pp. 787, 804–806) raised questions about the wisdom of recent American diplomacy; but the Democrats could not profit from it. Most Americans apparently believed that the soldier-statesman's experienced leadership was more necessary than ever now that war seemed possible.

The result on November 6 was an Eisenhower landslide of almost staggering proportions. The Republican candidate received a record number of 35,582,236 popular votes and carried forty-one states with 457 electoral votes. Stevenson, with 26,028,887 popular votes, won only the 73 electoral votes of Missouri, Arkansas, Alabama, Mississippi, Georgia, and the Carolinas. Only in Missouri, California, and a few farm states did Eisenhower fail to run more strongly than in 1952.

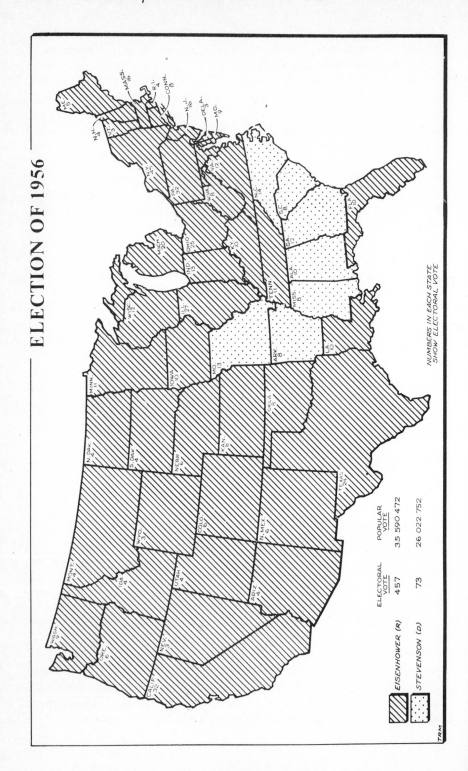

ELECTION OF 1956

NUMBERS IN EACH STATE
SHOW ELECTORAL VOTE

	ELECTORAL VOTE	POPULAR VOTE
EISENHOWER (R)	457	35 590 472
STEVENSON (D)	73	26 022 752

Given the magnitude of this victory, the results in Congress were striking and without precedent. The Democrats carried both houses, retaining their narrow majority in the Senate and slightly enlarging their House margin to 234-201. Never before had a party won both branches of Congress while losing the presidency.[10] In part, of course, the outcome was a personal tribute to Eisenhower. It also indicated that a normal Democratic majority survived but had lost cohesion at the national level.

Two years later the Republicans suffered one of the worst midterm defeats in American history. The country was shaken from its complacency by a series of events that weakened public confidence in the administration; for the first time, even the president's own popularity declined. A recession beginning in late 1957 brought a sharp rise in unemployment and reawakened fears of depression. Launching of the Russian *Sputnik* satellites caused dissatisfaction over the state of American education, science, and defense. The need to enforce desegregation with federal troops in Little Rock, Arkansas, drew criticism from several quarters. International crises in the Middle and Far East in 1958 increased the threat of war. Finally, labor opposition solidified in response to GOP attempts to enact "right to work" laws and other antiunion measures in several states.

Beset by these liabilities,[11] the Republicans received a stunning rebuke at the polls in 1958. The Democrats enlarged their congressional majorities to veritable New Deal proportions: 64-34 in the Senate and 283-153 in the House. There was a resurgence of Democratic strength among white-collar workers, young voters, and suburbanites. There was also a revival of progressivism. Dozens of able young liberals in both parties swept into office, while a host of diehard conservatives, notably Republican Senators William Jenner of Indiana, William F. Knowland of California, and John Bricker of Ohio, retired or went down to defeat.

However, neither the huge Democratic majorities nor the new progressive impulse pulled the nation from its middle course. The country emerged from recession in 1959, and the president, warning against inflation, used the veto to block what he regarded as overly ambitious or costly legislation. On most domestic matters the Democratic majority was less

[10]The Republicans in 1860 and the Whigs in 1848 won the presidency without carrying either chamber, but in both instances third-party blocs prevented any party from claiming a majority in the House.

[11]To complete Republican discomfiture, the public learned in early 1958 that Sherman Adams, influential assistant to the president, had accepted gifts and favors from a New England industrialist under compromising circumstances. Though hardly a flagrant example of official misconduct, the episode was highly embarrassing to the administration—first, because the GOP had made clean government a major talking-point in every campaign, with Adams hailed as a leading watchdog against corruptionists and influence-peddlers; and, second, because Eisenhower insisted upon retaining Adams in his post for months after the disclosure, despite a mounting chorus of criticism. When he finally resigned in September the political damage had already been done.

impressive than it looked. A coalition of southern Democrats and conservative Republicans often modified or blocked progressive measures. Moreover, the skillful Texas politicians who led the Democrats in Congress—Senate Majority Leader Lyndon B. Johnson and veteran Speaker Sam Rayburn—followed a deliberate strategy of compromise and cooperation in their dealings with the White House. Moderates and political realists, they preferred to keep party ranks intact and work for victory in 1960 rather than risk internal disruption by sponsoring an overly progressive program.

Moderation thus remained the keynote in American politics as the decade ended. Progressivism had stirred noticeably in 1958, and increasing numbers of Americans seemed in a mood for more positive leadership. But complacency, fear of inflation, and uncertain political allegiance remained forces to reckon with. Few experts felt overly confident in their predictions about the 1960 campaign.

5. *Dynamic Conservatism: The Cabinet, Fiscal Policy, and Public Power*

A rightward swing in domestic policy was generally expected as the Eisenhower administration took office in 1953. Actually, it proved far less conservative than many progressives feared and many Republicans hoped. Emphasis would be, as the president expressed it, upon "dynamic conservatism"—caution in financial and economic matters, but careful attention to problems of human welfare.

To be sure, the early months were more conservative than dynamic. The new cabinet seemed a citadel of orthodox Republicanism. For secretary of state, the president chose John Foster Dulles, experienced diplomat and wealthy corporation lawyer. Two prominent business executives, George Humphrey of the M. A. Hanna Steel Company and Charles E. Wilson of General Motors, headed the Treasury and Defense departments. The new attorney general was Herbert Brownell, Jr., of New York, legal aide and political ally of Thomas E. Dewey. Automobile distributor Arthur E. Summerfield became postmaster general. Governor Douglas McKay of Oregon went to the Interior Department. Ezra Taft Benson, conservative farm marketing specialist, became secretary of agriculture, while the Commerce Department went to Sinclair Weeks, a New England industrialist. For the secretaryship of labor, Eisenhower turned to Martin P. Durkin, president of the Plumbers and Steamfitters Union.

So studded with wealth and business connections was this group that the *New Republic's* irreverent description—"eight millionaires and a plumber"—enjoyed wide circulation.[12] Early appearances could not help but alarm progressive observers. Secretary Humphrey, firm advocate of a balanced budget, tighter credit, reducing spending, and lower taxes, made news when he restored a portrait of Andrew W. Mellon, high priest of economic normalcy in the 1920s, to the wall of his office. Secretary Benson, an outspoken believer in free enterprise and rugged individualism, wanted to reduce if not eliminate federal aid to farmers. Secretary Wilson delivered the first of several memorable utterances while his appointment was being confirmed. Denying any potential conflict of interest between his position in the Defense Department and his large holdings of GM stock, Wilson bluntly affirmed that "what was good for the country was good for General Motors, and vice versa." Progressives exchanged more grim nods when Secretary of Labor Durkin resigned in mid-1953, charging that the administration had not kept its promise to revise the Taft-Hartley Act.[13]

By and large, the cabinet was much less conservative than it sounded. For all their orthodox talk, men like Humphrey and Wilson were hard-headed pragmatists in action. They had gained their business experience in the age of Roosevelt, and were accustomed to operating within the New Deal-Fair Deal framework. Adaptable and flexible, serving a president whose approach was as untheoretical as their own, they had no intention of trying to turn the clock back to 1921.

Even so, Republicans were determined to make it tick more slowly in certain areas. The new administration promptly eliminated wartime price, wage, rent, and other controls, sold twenty-eight federally owned synthetic rubber plants to private companies, and allowed the Reconstruction Finance Corporation, created by Hoover during the depression, to go out of business in 1953. Even more indicative was the new fiscal policy, which reflected the views of Secretary Humphrey and Senator Taft. Tax reductions for individuals and corporations went into effect in January 1954, and a vigorous attempt was made to balance the budget. The attempt failed, but the Republicans did succeed in slashing federal expenditures in 1954 by fully $6.5 billion, or almost 10 percent. At the same time, Secretary Humphrey, in cooperation with the Federal Reserve Board, moved to avert inflation by raising interest rates and tightening credit.

[12] A ninth "millionaire" was added in April when the president appointed Oveta Culp Hobby, wartime commander of the WAC and wife of a wealthy Texas publisher, to head the new Department of Health, Education, and Welfare.

[13] Durkin was succeeded by a department store vice-president and labor relations specialist, James P. Mitchell.

Despite this initial application of doctrinaire conservatism, the Eisenhower administration's basic realism was nowhere more evident than in the realm of fiscal policy. Humphrey believed in a balanced budget and tighter credit, yet he quickly learned that a too rigorous application of deflationary policies was both dangerous and impossible. Raising interest rates on new government bond issues hurt the market price of older bonds and stirred complaint from bankers. Tightened credit induced a slump in economic indices that contributed to a recession in 1954. As investment, employment, production, and profits declined, tax revenues fell off, and balancing the budget became correspondingly harder. Furthermore, federal expenditures could not be slashed indefinitely; the government cut military appropriations by another $6 billion in 1955, but could not hold the line elsewhere. Upon investigation, Humphrey awoke to international reality and agreed to a 30 percent increase in foreign aid for 1955. "Before coming in here," he admitted frankly, "I had no idea of the extent to which our own security was involved in whatever happens in the world." The demand for larger appropriations for veterans' benefits, welfare, agriculture, and housing was also impossible to ignore, and the second budget ended with a larger deficit than the first.

The administration thereafter followed a flexible policy. Though still on guard against inflation, the Treasury Department and Federal Reserve Board were quick to ease credit and apply other "countercyclical" measures whenever the economy lagged. Insistence on a balanced budget was frankly abandoned. The government accepted another deficit in 1958 and a much larger one in 1959—the largest in thirteen years—as higher appropriations for defense and welfare were approved in the face of decreased revenues. Balance was achieved again in 1960, only to disappear before a $4 billion deficit in 1961. Financial reality also triumphed in the matter of tax reduction. Excise taxes were lowered slightly in 1954, and revision of the internal revenue code relieved individuals and certain businesses of some $1.4 billion in income taxes during 1955. But thereafter, despite pressure for further reductions, the government maintained taxes at existing rates.

The most "conservative" of the Eisenhower policies involved the role of government in developing electrical power and natural resources. Eisenhower believed that too much federal activity in these areas resulted in waste and "creeping socialism," both of which he deplored. In regard to conservation, he felt that governmental ownership of natural resources often infringed upon state rights and should be circumscribed. On the power issue, he advocated a kind of partnership between government and industry that would both serve the public interest and strengthen so-called free enterprise. The two subjects were dramatized by three specific controversies: the tidelands oil deposits, the Hell's Canyon Dam project, and the Dixon-Yates contract with the Atomic Energy Commission.

The tidelands oil controversy went back to the 1930s, when discovery of huge oil deposits off the California and Gulf coasts provoked a dispute between state and federal governments over ownership of the submerged lands. President Truman vetoed bills in 1946 and 1952 granting title to the states, and Supreme Court decisions in 1947 and 1950 affirmed the federal government's "paramount rights" to the offshore lands. President Eisenhower, however, felt differently. Sworn to oppose what he termed "federal encroachment upon the rights and affairs of the states," Eisenhower signed a Submerged Lands Act in May 1953 after it had passed both houses by large majorities. The act gave title to submerged coastal lands within their "historic boundaries"[14] to the states but recognized federal jurisdiction over the continental shelf extending beyond these boundaries. Opponents denounced the new law as a gigantic "giveaway" and agreed with its defenders that the principle of state rights had won a notable victory.

Meanwhile, the historic power controversy flared anew during the 1950s. Public-power advocates wanted the government to build and operate a huge dam and hydroelectric plant in Hell's Canyon on the Snake River in Idaho. Adverse to such expansion of federal activity, the president opposed Democratic bills for the Hell's Canyon project and threw his support behind the counterproposal of a private firm, the Idaho Power Company, to develop power in the region by building three smaller dams. After a bitter two-year battle, the Idaho company obtained a license from the FPC for its project in 1955. Democratic attempts to pass a Hell's Canyon bill in the next two sessions of Congress ended in failure. An insurmountable veto would have awaited it in any case, the president having fought and condemned the proposal as wasteful.

The Dixon-Yates controversy began in 1953 over the means of providing increased electrical power to the AEC's atomic energy plant at Paducah, Kentucky. Congress rejected a $100 million request by the Tennessee Valley Authority to erect a new steam plant for this purpose, and the president supported a proposal already under consideration by the AEC to obtain its power from private sources. A newly formed group headed by utilities executives Edgar H. Dixon and Eugene A. Yates had offered to construct a generating plant at West Memphis, Arkansas, and sell power to the TVA, which could then divert more of its own electricity to the AEC.

This proposal immediately became the focus of a slashing battle between friends and opponents of public power. After five months of disagreement, the AEC fell in line with a White House directive and voted approval of the Dixon-Yates contract in November 1954. But the Joint

[14]Three miles in the case of Louisiana, Alabama, and Mississippi, ten and a half in the case of Texas and Florida. Supreme Court decisions in 1960 upheld these differences on the grounds that only the two latter states had produced evidence that their historic boundaries extended beyond the normal three-mile limit.

Congressional Committee on Atomic Energy, whose approval was also necessary, had found that there had been no competitive bidding, that an allegedly better offer had been rejected, and that the TVA, which bitterly opposed the plan, had not been adequately consulted. Democrats attacked the Dixon-Yates project in force, claiming that the administration sought to scuttle the TVA. Although the joint committee also endorsed the contract by a strict party vote after obtaining a few revisions, new disclosures and heightened Democratic opposition finally brought the project to defeat. Senator Kefauver, staunch defender of the TVA and a member of the subcommittee that conducted hearings on the contract, bluntly asserted that the Dixon-Yates power company would be a "risk-free, government-granted, and government-guaranteed monopoly." Republicans indignantly denied this, but the new company's financial arrangements, expected profits, and ultimate effect on the TVA raised serious questions. Then in early 1955 it was revealed that the special consultant who had advised the government to accept the contract was a vice-president of the investment firm that had been engaged to market Dixon-Yates securities.

The whole affair had taken on an unsavory look, and Eisenhower was quick to seize an alternative. When the city of Memphis announced that it was ready to build a municipal power plant with ample capacity to supply the needed electricity, the president ordered cancellation of the Dixon-Yates contract in July 1955. Later that year, the AEC formally ruled the contract invalid because of a possible conflict of interest in its negotiation. Progressives were relieved at this defeat of an alleged threat to the TVA, while the president could take comfort from the fact that a municipal rather than a new federal power plant was being constructed.

Another phase of the power controversy centered around the president's program for the development of atomic energy. In a celebrated "Atoms-for-Peace" address before the United Nations in December 1953, Eisenhower proposed the international pooling of atomic information and materials and the use of this common fund in peaceful pursuits. The plan was favorably received at home and abroad, and Congress embodied it in the Atomic Energy Act of 1954.[15] But the domestic side of this program rekindled the power controversy. Eisenhower's idea of sharing atomic information blended with his distrust of too much government to prompt

[15]The result was the International Atomic Energy Agency, approved by the Senate in June 1957 and joined by seventy-nine other nations. The agency was to report annually to the UN, cooperate in peaceful atomic research, disseminate information, and establish safeguards to prevent military misuse. The United States agreed to pay one-third of the agency's administrative expense.

The government concluded an agreement in 1958 with the new European Atomic Energy Community (Euratom)—France, West Germany, Italy, and the Benelux countries—to promote production of nuclear power in Europe. The United States pledged a loan of $135 million and enough uranium to operate several reactors for twenty years. These reactors, under a $100 million research program financed jointly by the United States and Euratom, were to be used to seek ways of cutting the cost of atomic power. Congress also amended the Atomic Energy Act in 1958 to permit greater exchange of information and materials between the United States and its allies.

the suggestion that American atomic development be opened under proper safeguards to private industry rather than remain a governmental monopoly. Battle lines formed immediately in Congress, and private-power clauses in the Atomic Energy Act did not pass without a long struggle that included a thirteen-day filibuster by Democratic opponents of the bill. As finally adopted, the act made atomic material and production facilities available to private companies under AEC safeguards. It also authorized the AEC to license private construction of nuclear reactors and pay a fair price for their output. All in all, though somewhat modified by Democratic revisions,[16] the act was a victory for the president.

6. The Middle Road: Maintenance of the New Deal

Eisenhower tried throughout his tenure to implement a moderate expansion of New Deal economic and social policies. He was constantly hampered by conservatives who wanted no expansion at all, by progressives who wanted more than he was willing to approve, and by representatives of special interests. Sectional, religious, and racial antagonisms often led Congress to defeat or weaken important bills. The president's desire for an adequate welfare program was also circumscribed by his own dislike of spending and big government. Yet he succeeded, despite setbacks in some areas and small results in others, in preserving and enlarging the complex body of welfare legislation initiated by Franklin Roosevelt and Harry Truman.

It was not easy going during Eisenhower's first two years in office, for Old Guard Republicans were in the saddle in Congress. They refused to permit revision of Taft-Hartley, notwithstanding the platform pledge in 1952. They rejected Eisenhower's proposals for federally supported health insurance, larger highway appropriations, and aid to education. They nearly approved a constitutional amendment offered by Senator John W. Bricker of Ohio to limit the president's treaty-making power.[17] The tragic death of Senator Taft due to cancer in 1953 only exacerbated this rift

---

[16]The most important of these was a "patent-licensing" provision calling for compulsory sharing of commercial atomic patents for five years, to prevent the formation of patent monopolies.

[17]The Bricker amendment reflected both isolationist and state rights sentiment. It invalidated all treaties dealing with matters constitutionally reserved to the states, unless individual state legislation gave specific approval of such treaties, and empowered Congress to regulate and pass upon all executive agreements with foreign nations and international organizations. Designed to give Congress a dominant role in foreign policy, the amendment was the subject of hearings and acrid controversy for months. The Senate finally rejected it in February 1954 by a vote of fifty to forty-two.

between moderate and reactionary elements within the Republican party, for Taft had supported the administration in its first months and used his great prestige and influence to win a measure of cooperation from the right wing.

On the whole, Eisenhower's programs fared better in the narrowly Democratic Eighty-fourth and Eighty-fifth Congresses (1955–1958) than in the Republican Eighty-third (1953–1954). The large Democratic majorities in the Eighty-sixth Congress (1959–1960) tended to be more progressive than the president, but the record was generally one of cooperation. Except for the power controversy, differences between Eisenhower and the Democrats on matters of domestic reform and welfare were differences of detail and degree.

The most difficult policy to maintain rationally was that of support for farm prices to assure parity income to agriculture. The nation's farmers were more efficient than ever before, but they were caught in an inexorable vise of rising costs of equipment, labor, and distribution. As a result, net income per farm declined by 29 percent from 1947 to 1957. The farmer's share of the retail cost of his product dropped from 51 percent in 1947 to 39 percent in 1960; the parity ratio, from 115 to 79. Large commercial farms were often prosperous, but all farmers felt the price squeeze in one way or another.

Overproduction was the major problem, as increasing use of machinery, fertilizer, and better scientific methods swelled the yield per acre in startling fashion.[18] Farm prices sagged hopelessly beneath a gigantic surplus that overburdened granaries and warehouses every year.[19] The government remained committed, as it had been since 1933, to the basic principle of farm price supports, but there was little agreement over the formula that would best achieve reduced production and fair prices. Whether supports were raised or lowered, whether acreage allotments were increased or reduced, the farmer's natural tendency was to expand his yield in order to achieve maximum profits. Hence total farm production mounted steadily.

Most farm spokesmen favored the highest supports obtainable and opposed any reduction in the 90 percent parity payments established by the Agricultural Act of 1949. The Eisenhower administration, however, followed the lead of Secretary Benson and advocated lower supports on a flexible sliding scale. Benson's theory was that high and rigid price supports only stimulated overproduction and thereby insured falling prices for the farmer and a costlier and less manageable surplus for the government. Congress, mindful of the farm vote, was cool to the Benson pro-

---

[18]The yield per acre for corn was 41 percent higher in 1958 than the 1946–1950 average. The wheat yield increased 44 percent; cotton, 70 percent; potatoes, 38 percent; tobacco, 32 percent.

[19]In 1960, for example, the government owned 1.1 billion bushels of wheat and 1.5 billion bushels of corn.

gram, but the administration succeeded in making it the basis for the Agricultural Act of 1954. It established a flexible scale of supports on basic commodities ranging from 82.5 to 90 percent of parity for the 1955 crop, and from 70 to 90 percent in succeeding years. Rural dissatisfaction with Benson and his program contributed no little to Republican losses in the midterm elections of 1954.

Nevertheless, the administration continued to work for lower and more flexible price supports. The principle was retained in the Agricultural Act of 1956, which Eisenhower signed after vetoing a Democratic bill that reestablished 90 percent supports. The main feature of the act of 1956 was the "soil-bank" plan, which set up acreage and conservation reserve programs in an effort to reduce the farm surplus. Farmers who agreed to reduce their acreage below their normal allotments, or to devote a portion of their land to soil-conserving rather than commercial use, were eligible to receive governmental payments as compensation for the smaller crop. Although farmers set aside several million acres each year under the soil-bank program, higher yields per acre produced a succession of record-breaking bumper crops from 1956 through 1960, and the formidable surpluses remained as large as ever.

The last major farm legislation during the Eisenhower era was the Agricultural Act of 1958, signed in August after another hard battle between proponents of rigid and flexible price supports. The act was a compromise, achieved with the aid of Democratic votes after Eisenhower had vetoed a bill in March freezing price supports at their existing level. Under the new law, supports were to be lowered gradually to a minimum of 65 percent on most basic crops in 1961–1962. Critics claimed that a progressive lowering of price supports was self-defeating because it merely encouraged farmers to produce more and thus create larger surpluses. Defenders responded that high supports had the same effect at greater cost to the taxpayer. The farm problem, surely one of the most intricate dilemmas confronting the American people, had clearly not been solved by 1960.

The basic principle of federal support had, however, become permanently established, and the government maintained and expanded other forms of aid. Agricultural research programs continued their valuable work. The Rural Electrification Administration celebrated its twenty-fifth birthday in 1960 with the proud announcement that 97 percent of all American farms now had electricity, as compared with 11 percent in 1935. The Farmers Home Administration made and insured farm loans at a rate of over $300 million a year during the late 1950s. And a Rural Development Program, designed to provide opportunities for farmers and rural dwellers in low-income areas, was operating in 262 counties in thirty-one states by 1960, with more than two thousand local improvement projects under way.

Meanwhile, those huge farm surpluses were being put to good use. The Agricultural Trade Development and Assistance Act of 1954, renewed and expanded by nearly every succeeding Congress, empowered the government to finance the sale and export of surplus farm products to other nations in exchange for foreign currencies, to make outright gifts of surplus food to needy nations, to provide milk for American school children, and, by an amendment in 1959, to make up to $1 billion in surplus food available to needy families by issuing free stamps redeemable at grocery stores.

Promotion of American commerce, a major goal of the Eisenhower adminstration, led to increased governmental activity in two areas—expansion of liberal trade policies begun during the New Deal,[20] and creation of the St. Lawrence Seaway Development Corporation. The project of improving navigation on the St. Lawrence River by means of locks and dredging, in order to open the Great Lakes to large ocean-going vessels, had been advocated without success by Presidents Hoover, Roosevelt, and Truman. Eisenhower finally overcame the opposition and persuaded Congress to authorize American participation in 1954. Jointly constructed by the Canadian and United States governments, the St. Lawrence Seaway was opened in 1959. Tonnage passing between Montreal and Lake Ontario during the first season was 75 percent greater than in 1958, and several foreign shipping lines took steps to inaugurate or enlarge direct trade between European and Great Lakes ports. The president justly regarded the Seaway as one of the most valuable achievements of his administration.[21]

Support of the Seaway was one of several indications that Eisenhower was more sympathetic to public works projects than progressives maintained. To be sure, he disapproved of pork-barrel legislation and shared Secretary Humphrey's opposition to federal spending as an antidote to recession. He continued to favor federal partnership with state, local, and private enterprise whenever possible. He insisted that public works pro-

---

[20]Stimulation of America's foreign commerce was a major purpose of the Agricultural Trade Development and Assistance Act of 1954. It empowered the president to use foreign currencies accruing from the sale of farm surplus to build new markets abroad. An amendment in 1957 permitted up to 25 percent of such currencies to be lent to American or foreign companies to promote expanded markets for American products. The act was further liberalized in 1958 to permit the use of these currencies to finance American participation in international trade fairs.

The Trade Agreements Act of 1934, which authorized the president to enter reciprocal agreements with other nations lowering specific duties up to 50 percent without requiring approval of Congress, was regularly extended during the 1950s.

[21]The Seaway had long been opposed by eastern business and railroad interests fearful of adverse effects. Eisenhower overcame the objections by pointing, first, to Canada's announced determination to construct the Seaway without American help; and, second, to the growing need of midwestern steel producers for Laurentian ore as the great Mesabi deposits neared exhaustion. Seven new locks (five constructed by Canada, two by the United States) formed the nucleus of the Seaway and permitted the passage of ships up to 750 feet in length with drafts up to 27 feet. Power development, an important adjunct, was turned over to the state of New York in a compromise between public and private power advocates.

FOREIGN TRADE
1940 – 1970

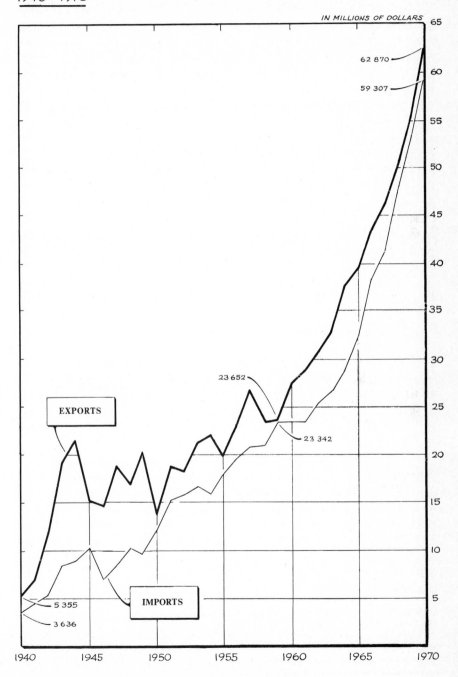

IN MILLIONS OF DOLLARS

65

62 870

60

59 307

55

50

45

40

35

30

23 652

25

EXPORTS

23 342

20

15

10

IMPORTS

5 355

5

3 636

1940   1945   1950   1955   1960   1965   1970

grams meet tests of legitimate need and fiscal responsibility. And, as we have seen, he wanted to restrict governmental activity in the realm of power development. Yet within these limits Eisenhower supported a variety of public works measures. These included increased funds for flood control and other projects in the Columbia River Valley in 1953; a $1 billion appropriation for river, harbor, and flood control projects in 1954; a gigantic Colorado River Storage Project, including reservoirs, power plants, and irrigation facilities, in 1956; and an agreement to participate with Mexico in building a huge dam and power plant on the Rio Grande in 1960.

The president and Congress generally saw eye to eye on the scope of public works programs until late in his second term. In 1959, however, the big Democratic majorities in the Eighty-sixth Congress ignored his plea for fiscal caution and adopted, over his veto, a large public works bill that included sixty-seven new flood control and reclamation projects. "The lure of the pork barrel was a little too much for Congress," the president commented wryly. But Eisenhower himself had done much to keep the public works program alive.

This was also true of housing and highway construction, although Congress again tended toward more liberal programs than the president thought advisable. New low-income housing units were authorized at an annual rate of some 35,000. Progressives denounced this figure as inadequate for American needs, and Congress occasionally enlarged the appropriation. But most housing legislation during the 1950s merely liberalized FHA terms for purchasers of low-income housing. Eisenhower's plan for a massive federal-state highway project failed in 1955, but a compromise measure became law in 1956. The Federal Aid Highway Act projected a 42,500-mile network of superhighways linking all major urban areas, with the government paying 90 percent and the states 10 percent of the estimated cost of $27.5 billion.[22]

Eisenhower also moved to expand New Deal welfare legislation. Amendments to the Social Security Act in 1954 and 1956 extended coverage and benefits to millions not previously covered—salaried and self-employed professionals; religious, domestic, and clerical workers; farm operators and workers, and members of the armed forces. A 7 percent increase in social security benefits, though opposed by the administration, received bipartisan support in Congress and became law in January 1959. Social Security legislation covered some 58 million individuals by 1960.

---

[22] Money was to be raised by increased "user" taxes on gasoline, tires, diesel fuel, trucks, buses, and trailers. An additional $5 billion for primary and secondary roads was included in the act, the cost to be shared equally by federal and state governments. Administration insistence on "pay-as-you-go" financing, whereby construction would not start until user taxes were actually in the highway trust fund, was suspended by Congress in 1958 for two years in order to speed the work.

In a related measure, the Transportation Act of 1958 authorized the ICC to use up to $500 million to guarantee loans to railroads for equipment and maintenance, attempted to tighten ICC control over discriminatory rates, and made all interstate motor traffic subject to ICC regulation.

Moreover, Congress amended the Fair Labor Standards Act in 1955 to increase the minimum wage from 75¢ to $1 an hour. Though Congress twice refused to act on the president's request for federal participation in a national health insurance program, the level of federal spending on public health, medical research, hospital construction, and similar items increased steadily during the Eisenhower years—from $290 million in 1954 to almost $1 billion in 1961.

7. *Expansion of the New Deal: Education and Civil Rights*

In response to popular demand, the Eisenhower administration also worked to expand New Deal reform in two important and hitherto slighted areas—education and civil rights. Progress was blocked or limited during the 1950s, sometimes by disagreement over method or detail, more often by conservative coalitions in Congress. Yet the president could justly claim that significant beginnings had been made by 1960.

Mounting pressure on the nation's public school system, in consequence of the new high birth rate and a growing shortage of classrooms and qualified teachers, was an inescapable fact of the postwar era (see pp. 631–633). State and local budgets were already strained to the utmost, and many authorities believed that only federal aid could prevent massive deterioration in educational standards.

Several controversies raged over the school question. Many persons opposed federal aid on principle, alleging that it would result in federal control, infringe upon state and local rights, and cost too much money. Spokesmen for the nation's private schools, many of which were Catholic, feared that federal spending for public education would damage if not destroy the private schools unless they received a share of the funds. Conversely, the stoutest champions of federal aid were often irrevocably opposed to any measure that granted public funds to private education. Southerners tended to oppose federal aid because it offered a means of enforcing desegregation, while many black leaders insisted that schools refusing to desegregate should receive no aid. All these groups were represented in Congress. It is not surprising, therefore, that complex political maneuvering, setbacks, and slow progress marked the development of a school-aid program.

Eisenhower's first education bill, in 1956, proposed aid on a basis of per capita income and relative state expenditures on schools. The Democrats substituted a bill making population the basis for apportionment of aid. In a maneuver that was to be repeated, the House first adopted an amendment offered by Adam Clayton Powell of New York, making compliance with the Supreme Court's desegregation decision a requisite for receiving school aid. Then a bipartisan conservative majority defeated the measure altogether. A similar fate befell the administration's school-aid bill in 1957.

Eisenhower's lone accomplishment in this field came a year later, in the shocked aftermath of *Sputnik*. The National Defense Education Act of September 1958 provided funds for long-term, low-interest loans to college students, with half the loan to be canceled if the student taught in elementary or secondary school for at least five years after graduation. It offered matching grants to public schools for laboratories, textbooks, and other facilities in the sciences, mathematics, and foreign languages, as well as funds for 5,500 fellowships for graduate students interested in college or university teaching. Finally, it provided grants to state agencies for counseling, vocational education, and other purposes.

The act's major defect was that it sidestepped the crucial issue of federal aid for new classrooms and teachers' salaries. Bills containing such provisions were debated by Congress in 1959 and 1960. A compromise measure providing funds for classrooms but not salaries seemed within reach in the latter year; but the House rules committee, controlled by its four Republican and three southern Democratic members, stubbornly refused to authorize the official House-Senate conference that was prepared to adjust differences and devise an acceptable bill.

The record of achievement was better in the more controversial field of civil rights, and the adoption of a Civil Rights Act in September 1957 was a landmark—the first federal legislation in this area in eighty-two years. It was attended, of course, by months of bickering and southern obstruction. But southern senators abandoned their filibuster after winning minor concessions, and the bill became law. It established a bipartisan commission with power to subpoena witnesses and investigate denial of voting rights and equal protection of the laws on account of color, race, religion, or national origin. It also provided for a new assistant attorney general who might initiate injunctive proceedings in federal district courts when voting rights were interfered with.[23] Appointed in November 1957, the Civil Rights Commission set to work at once.

Congress extended the commission for two more years in 1959 as black movements for equality met increasing violence (see pp. 760–764). But more legislation was clearly needed, and Congress finally responded, after

---

[23] To secure compliance with its orders, the courts could issue injunctions and begin *civil* contempt proceedings without jury trial, thus bypassing the problem of selecting an unbiased jury. If the courts began *criminal* contempt proceedings, as punishment for actual violation of court orders, defendants could demand a jury trial if the judge imposed a fine of more than $300 or a jail term longer than forty-five days.

In *United States* v. *Raines*, 1960, the Supreme Court upheld the provision of the Civil Rights Act that permitted the attorney general to enjoin state officials from discriminating against voting rights on grounds of race or color. The *Raines* decision also upheld the provision of the act that permitted the Civil Rights Commission to conduct hearings without permitting persons accused of denying voting rights to be apprised of specific charges against them or the identity of their accusers. The court reasoned that this violated neither the Fifth Amendment (because the Civil Rights Commission was an investigative and fact-finding agency), nor the Sixth Amendment (because the proceedings were not in the category of "criminal prosecutions").

long debate, with another Civil Rights Act in 1960. In order to afford added protection, this law empowered federal courts to appoint referees to consider state voting-qualification laws whenever a petitioner had been deprived of the right to register or vote because of race or color.[24] It also imposed heavy penalties against illegal acts by private citizens. With what seemed to civil rights advocates like agonizing slowness, but nonetheless surely, the power of the federal government was finally being extended in behalf of fair and equal treatment for all Americans.

8. The Warren Court: Civil Rights and Civil Liberties

Less than nine months after taking the oath of office, President Eisenhower named Governor Earl Warren of California to succeed the late Fred M. Vinson as chief justice of the United States. Future historians may well decide that the new chief justice and his eight associates did far more to shape the course of American history after midcentury than Eisenhower, Congress, or the political parties.

Civil rights and civil liberties had been the Supreme Court's major concern since the late 1930s. It had begun to undermine the barriers of racial discrimination in the forties and early fifties, especially with regard to denial of voting rights to southern blacks. In *Smith* v. *Allwright*, 1944, the court reversed a previous decision and declared that because Negroes were an integral part of the electoral process they could not be denied the right to participate in party primaries. When South Carolina tried a subterfuge by removing all regulations for party primaries from its statute books, District Judge J. Waites Waring of Charleston refused to approve and ordered Democratic registrars to enroll qualified black voters in 1948. The Supreme Court upheld Waring by refusing to review the case. And in *Terry* v. *Adams*, 1953, the court outlawed a Texas organization known as the Jaybird Association, which limited its membership to whites and chose nominees for the local Democratic primary. Noting that Jaybird candidates almost invariably won both primary and election, the Court identified this as another illegal method of circumventing the *Allwright* decision and excluding blacks from voting. Such decisions brought southern blacks measurably closer to political citizenship.[25]

[24]The act also permitted suits to be brought against states for violations, and required federal election officials to preserve all election records for a least twenty-two months.

[25]As compared with a negligible number of black voters in the South before 1944, an estimated 1.3 million Negroes in eleven southern states (25 percent of their adult Negro population) had registered by 1959, chiefly in cities. The figure was far from adequate, and older patterns of discrimination against Negro voting persisted in rural areas, but the advance in fifteen years had been significant.

It was on the educational front that the court found cause to strike down the historic "separate but equal" concept, the legalism upon which southern states had built their elaborate system of Jim Crow legislation. Chief Justice Hughes had opened the assault in the *Gaines* decision in 1938 (see Vol. I, pp. 424-425). In *Sweatt* v. *Painter*, 1950, the court decreed that separate law school facilities could never be really equal and ordered the University of Texas to admit a black student who had refused to attend the state law school for Negroes in Houston. One effect was to compel many southern state universities to admit blacks to law, medical, and graduate schools. More important was the clear implication of the *Sweatt* case: segregated public education on any level was unequal education. Thus encouraged, the National Association for the Advancement of Colored People stepped up its campaign to end segregation in public schools. Southern states, mindful of the court's growing hostility to Jim Crow, spent large sums improving black schools in an effort to achieve equality *within* the separate system and thus stave off the ruling that they feared.

Thus the stage was set for the epochal decision in 1954. A number of cases challenging public school segregation had come before the Vinson court in 1952. Unable to reach a decision, the justices ordered reargument of these cases in 1953 and requested counsel to answer certain key questions regarding the intent and meaning of the Fourteenth Amendment. With Warren on the bench during the reargument, the justices handed down their decision on a representative case—*Brown* v. *Board of Education of Topeka*—on May 17, 1954. A unanimous court held that public school segregation was unconstitutional under the Fourteenth Amendment, thus completely reversing the "separate but equal" doctrine enunciated in *Plessy* v. *Ferguson* in 1896. Impressed by the trenchant logic of Thurgood Marshall, counsel for the NAACP, the justices emphasized sociological and psychological factors in their decision. "In the field of public education," Warren declared, "the doctrine of 'separate but equal' has no place. Separate educational facilities are inherently unequal."

The court outlined implementation procedures a year later. It instructed federal district courts to order school desegregation in their respective areas and to require "good faith," "a prompt and reasonable start," and "all deliberate speed" from local authorities. Though demanding compliance with the principle, these instructions recognized that the timing and mode of desegregation would vary according to conditions, and they permitted district judges to use discretion in setting specific deadlines and other details. Nevertheless, the broad import of the *Brown* decision was momentous and unmistakable. Affecting the school systems of twenty-one states and the District of Columbia,[26] it promised to alter the pattern

---

[26]The *Brown* decision affected seventeen states where segregation was required by law, and four that permitted it by local option. Segregation in the nation's capital was invalidated by a companion decision, *Bolling* v. *Sharpe*, which the court pronounced immediately after *Brown* v. *Board of Education*. The due process clause of the Fifth Amendment, rather than the Fourteenth, was held to forbid segregation in the District of Columbia.

of education for over 8 million white and 2.5 million black children, representing nearly 40 percent of American public school enrollment. The Warren court had erected a historic landmark in American constitutional law.

And legalized Jim Crow was systematically obliterated. Having destroyed the "separate but equal" doctrine in public school education, the court quickly rendered it inapplicable elsewhere.[27] It steadily ruled in favor of blacks seeking admission to southern colleges, universities, and graduate schools. As a result, out of 195 formerly all-white public institutions of higher learning in fourteen southern states, fully 124 had admitted Negro students by 1960. In a series of other rulings, federal courts also invalidated segregation in parks, public housing, municipal golf courses, public beaches and bathhouses, intrastate buses, and bus, railway, and air terminals serving interstate passengers. On the basis of the *Brown* decision the ICC in 1955 ordered railroads to end all rules and practices maintaining segregation. Like emancipation a century earlier, the long-overdue extension of equal justice under law to black Americans was a beginning, not an end. It was, nevertheless, a forward step of lasting importance.

On the race question the court had moved with boldness, unanimity, and devotion to principle. On the related issue of civil liberties, involving reconciliation of individual freedoms with demands of national security, the justices proceeded somewhat cautiously. The difference was understandable. The former question, though complex, was essentially a contest between elementary justice and entrenched prejudice; the latter found legitimate needs and rights at stake on both sides. Rather than attempt to enunciate a fundamental principle that would guide and control future action, as in the *Brown* case, the court dealt with civil liberties on a pragmatic, ad hoc basis. It questioned procedure and wording, sought to curb excesses, and invited state and federal bodies to tighten and improve their loyalty programs. Often divided on details, the justices groped for a middle ground that would preserve the substance of individual liberties without crippling the government's right to protect itself from disloyalty and subversion.

We have noted the general timidity of the Vinson court, which sat during the worst years of the second Red scare (see pp. 671–672). As McCarthyism declined after 1954 and the influence of the new chief justice began to be felt, the federal judiciary moved toward a bolder stand. Two lower court decisions in 1956, for example, narrowed the investigative authority of the Senate Committee on Government Operations by

---

[27]As with education, the Vinson court had paved the way. In 1946 it invalidated a Virginia statute requiring segregated seating in interstate buses by decreeing that such segregation was an undue burden on interstate commerce. It struck a blow at residential segregation in 1948 by ruling that convenants forbidding the sale of real estate to persons on account of race or color were not enforceable in the courts. All-white hotels, restaurants, and theaters in the District of Columbia were opened to Negroes in 1953.

applying the standard of pertinency.[28] The Supreme Court in 1955 strongly upheld the controversial right of witnesses to avoid incrimination by invoking the Fifth Amendment before congressional committees. It added, moreover, that a "veiled claim" of the privilege was permissible in view of the opprobrium often attached to its use. Congress attempted to circumvent the Fifth Amendment by passing the Immunity Act of 1954, under which witnesses could be granted immunity from criminal prosecution and then be *compelled* to testify in national security cases. Not unmindful of the government's need, the court upheld the Immunity Act in *Ullman* v. *United States*, 1956. It warned, however, that protection afforded by the Fifth Amendment must not be downgraded or diminished.

The court upset several actions of the executive branch in disloyalty proceedings. Though all of these cases raised constitutional issues, the justices avoided them by settling each on narrow procedural grounds.[29] However, the effect of one decision—*Greene* v. *McElroy*, 1959—was to invalidate the government's security program for private defense plants; the effect of another—*Cole* v. *Young*, 1956—was to render some 80 percent of all federal employees immune from the security program by ruling that it applied only to "sensitive" positions and agencies.

The court did not take a bold stand on the rights of aliens. In 1954 it broadly upheld the provision of the Internal Security Act of 1950 that required deportation of any alien who had been a member of the Communist party when he entered the United States or at any time thereafter. The effect of later decisions in 1956-1957 was to limit and reform governmental procedures in deportation and denaturalization cases. But in *Jay* v. *Boyd*, 1956, the court, in a five-to-four decision, upheld the Department of Justice in a case involving deportation on the basis of confidential information not disclosed to the alien. The four dissenters included Warren and the veteran New Deal appointees—Felix Frankfurter, Hugo Black, and William O. Douglas. They variously objected to certain features of the case: undisclosed information, faceless informers, dubious delegation of authority, and the shifting of deportation trials from courts to temporary removable appointees.

[28]In *United States* v. *Kamin*, a district judge held that a study of subversion in private defense plants was not within the committee's authority. In *United States* v. *Lamont*, a federal circuit court found a similar lack of pertinency in the committee's inquiry into how long someone had spent on a trip to Russia. Both cases had arisen out of contempt prosecutions initiated by the committee while McCarthy was its chairman.

[29]Specifically, in *Communist Party* v. *Subversive Activities Control Board*, 1956, the court simply returned a subversive listing to the board with the request that it base its findings on "untainted evidence." *Peters* v. *Hobey*, 1955, involved the problem of whether a federal employee might be discharged when findings against him reflected statements of secret informers. The court sidestepped this issue and upset the dismissal on technical grounds. In *Service* v. *Dulles*, 1957, the court condemned the discharge of John Stewart Service on the ground that the State Department had violated its own regulations in dismissing him. And in *Kent* v. *Dulles*, 1958, the justices held that Congress had not authorized the secretary of state to withhold a passport because of an applicant's political beliefs and associations.

An early high-water mark in the court's defense of civil liberties came in 1957, with a spate of decisions that left legal experts breathless and conservatives enraged. In *Jencks* v. *United States*, the court held that in certain circumstances a defendant was entitled to inspect FBI reports used in his trial, and ordered the government to dismiss criminal action if it chose to withhold such reports. In *Yates* v. *United States*, the justices narrowed the meaning of the Smith Act by ruling that an individual might advocate the "abstract principle" of overthrowing the government so long as he did not advocate specific action to that end. And in *Watkins* v. *United States*, the court invalidated a contempt conviction by the House Un-American Activities Committee because its legislative mandate was "loosely worded" and "excessively broad," and because it had failed to show the pertinency of its questions to the inquiry at hand. Detecting a threat to First Amendment freedoms, the court took occasion in the *Watkins* ruling to remind Congress that it was not a law enforcement agency, and that an inquiry was not an end in itself but must be directly related to some legitimate congressional task.

The justices also reviewed and set aside certain state actions against subversives. The most important of these rulings was *Pennsylvania* v. *Nelson*, 1956, in which the court invalidated a conviction under a state sedition law on the ground that Congress had in effect preempted the field of sedition, which was a national question, and had thus "superseded" state laws on this subject. The effect was to set aside, at least temporarily, anti-Communist laws in forty-two states. In *Slochower* v. *Board of Higher Education of New York*, 1956, the court ruled that a state could not discharge a teacher for using the privilege against self-incrimination in a congressional investigation, on the ground that the state had construed the mere claim of the privilege as "conclusive presumption of guilt." And in *Sweezy* v. *New Hampshire*, 1957, the justices invalidated a state legislative inquiry into subversive activities.[30]

Although progressives hailed these decisions as a clarion reaffirmation of individual liberties, the loudest reaction came from voices of dissent. Conservatives tended to feel that the Warren court had protected Communists, done great if not irreparable harm to the national security program, and encroached upon the rightful powers of coordinate branches and state governments alike. "Well, Comrades," one newspaper fumed in 1957, "you've finally got what you wanted. The Supreme Court has handed it to

[30]The Warren court limited state and local authority in other fields as well. In 1955 and 1956 it held that federal labor legislation (1) preempted the right of a state supreme court to bar certain strikes by injunction, and (2) prevailed over a state "right to work" provision that had been used to bar a union-shop contract.

In the realm of censorship, the court in 1957 struck down a Chicago ordinance against "immoral and obscene" movies as unconstitutionally vague, and invalidated a similar New York statute in 1959 on the ground that it prevented the advocacy of an idea—in this case, that under certain conditions adultery may not be improper or immoral behavior. However, in 1957 the court upheld both a federal and a California antiobscenity statute by excluding obscenity from the protections afforded by the First and Fourteenth Amendments.

you on a platter."[31] J. Edgar Hoover, director of the FBI, lamented "the mounting success of criminal and subversive elements in employing loopholes, technicalities, and delays in the law to defeat the interests of justice."[32] A conference of governors in 1956, an assemblage of state chief justices in 1958, and the American Bar Association in 1959 all voiced criticism of recent decisions and asked for more judicial restraint. Extremists on the far right denounced the nine justices with a virulence unrivaled since the aftermath of the *Dred Scott* decision a century earlier.

Efforts to persuade Congress to bridle the court ended in failure. Southern congressmen repeatedly introduced bills to nullify the desegregation decision of 1954. Among the more extreme and far-fetched proposals, backed by an angry coalition of segregationists and reactionaries, were constitutional amendments aimed at destroying the power of judicial review, limiting the Supreme Court's appellate jurisdiction, and choosing justices by popular election or by vote of state supreme court judges. Such schemes got nowhere. Measures to strengthen the government's security program likewise failed. Bills protecting state antisubversion laws and broadening the "violent overthrow" provision of the Smith Act passed the House in 1959 but died in the Senate. The one enactment that emerged from the debate was a law adopted in 1957 that protected the security of FBI files against undue exposure, but did not overturn the basic principle affirmed in the *Jencks* decision.

Congress failed to move more decisively, in part because of a general reluctance to tamper with the judiciary, and in part because anti-Communist hysteria ebbed steadily after 1955. Moreover, later decisions did much to mollify conservative fears and provide additional leeway for antisubversion measures. The court clarified and qualified its ruling in the *Slochower* decision by twice declaring, in 1958, that state and city employees, including teachers, might be dismissed upon reasonable determination of "unfitness," even though alleged disloyalty was the root cause for dismissal. In *Uphaus* v. *New Hampshire*, 1959, the court narrowed the implications of the *Nelson* and *Sweezy* decisions by sanctioning a state attorney general's efforts to obtain information about subversive activities. States, it appeared, were not powerless in the battle against communism after all. And in *Barenblatt* v. *United States*, 1959, the court ruled that a congressional committee *could* compel a witness to answer its questions about his Communist affiliations, thus modifying the *Watkins* decision of 1957. "The balance between the individual and the government interests here at stake," the court noted in the *Barenblatt* case, "must here be struck in favor of the latter."

---

[31] Quoted in Alpheus T. Mason, *The Supreme Court from Taft to Warren* (Baton Rouge, La., 1958), p. 4.

[32] Quoted in Leon I. Salomon, ed., *The Supreme Court* (New York, 1961), p. 114.

Though doubt and confusion were sometimes created by the effect of various decisions, the policy of avoiding broad constitutional pronouncements and requiring greater procedural care from state and federal authorities was undoubtedly a wise approach. Individual rights had been greatly strengthened, yet not at the price of undermining legitimate governmental powers.

9. Blacks in the 1950s

For American blacks, the postwar era was one of unparalleled striving, ferment, and progress. It was also, inevitably, a time of heightened tension, as new onslaughts against racial discrimination challenged traditional attitudes, altered the status quo, and met the resistance born of prejudice, ignorance, and fear. The most significant feature in this changing pattern of race relations was neither black progress nor the tension that accompanied it, but rather that various developments at home and abroad had finally forced the nation, after generations of evasion and indifference, to begin facing its biggest social problem.

Such a confrontation could no longer be deferred. A few Americans had long been aware that the status of the Negro represented American democracy's most glaring failure. The New Deal, with its concern for the plight of all underprivileged citizens, emphasized the extent to which poverty and lack of opportunity were a way of life for the great majority of blacks. At the same time, as the nation recoiled from the theory and practice of Nazi racist doctrines, the injustice of systematic racial discrimination at home became more apparent. The unswerving loyalty with which blacks supported the democratic cause during the Second World War, and the implications of America's position as leader of the so-called free world after 1945, made the anachronism of second-class citizenship more insupportable than ever. The United States could manifestly never win the respect or cooperation of emergent peoples in Asia and Africa while it degraded its own darker-skinned minority. By midcentury, therefore, increasing numbers of white Americans were prepared to extend the benefits of democracy to all citizens regardless of race or color.

Even more important, black Americans had reached a point where they were both able and determined to advance their own cause. The New Deal had provided the first relative economic security that millions of them had ever known. They had shared largely, if somewhat belatedly, in wartime job opportunities and high wages, and they further expanded their economic strength in the prosperous postwar years. Their growing concentration in northern urban centers conferred a political power which both parties had to recognize. The federal courts, as we have seen, were becoming a potent ally. Though still far below the national average, the percentage of blacks with comfortable incomes, white-collar jobs, high-school diplomas, college degrees, and professional skills increased markedly after 1945.

Moreover, blacks were now ready psychologically to launch a campaign for first-class citizenship. Economic, political, and educational advances not only provided new strength but spurred ambition for further gains. The Negro was keenly aware of the relevance, for him, of democracy's struggle against fascist and communist totalitarianism. His confidence was further stimulated by the efforts of President Truman and other national leaders in behalf of civil rights. The greatest emotional turning-point was undoubtedly the desegregation decision of 1954. As a noted black psychologist, Kenneth Clark, put it: "For the first time every Negro felt that he was a man in his own right and that his government would help him prove it."[33]

There were other grounds for optimism. Negroes were encouraged by the collapse of the color line in major league baseball in the late 1940s, and exulted in the achievements of Jackie Robinson, Roy Campanella, Willie Mays, and other black stars. They took pride, too, in the national distinction accorded increasing numbers of their race in other sports, and in music, literature, scholarship, and entertainment. They were also stirred by momentous international developments after 1945—the breakup of European colonial empires, the growing power and influence of nonwhite nations like China, and above all the steady emergence of black Africa from colonial subservience to independence.

Hope for the future was matched by increasing dissatisfaction with the status quo. The retreat of white supremacy in most other parts of the world had become a rout; how long would it continue to be tolerated in the United States? Patience began to wear thin. Blacks bore surprisingly little malice and emphasized loyal and peaceful methods in their drive for equal treatment. But a pressure for change had built up and would continue to mount.

Numerous public and private organizations supported the Negro's campaign. The federal government, as we have seen, instituted desegregation in both the civil service and the armed forces, promoted equal job opportunities, and eventually legislated in behalf of black voting rights. Most northern states passed or strengthened antidiscrimination laws aimed at removing inequities in employment, housing, and public accommoda-

---

[33]Quoted in Harry S. Ashmore, *The Other Side of Jordan* (New York, 1960), p. 121.

tions.[34] National labor organizations strove to end segregation and other discriminatory practices in union membership, although many local unions remained strongholds of prejudice. Corporations evinced a growing willingness to hire qualified Negroes for positions formerly closed to them. Youth organizations and urban welfare agencies were active in promoting racial harmony.

Religious bodies, including nearly all of the great Protestant denominations, took a far more liberal and enlightened stand on the race question than in previous times. Ministers and religious leaders reminded worshipers that prejudice and discrimination were a gross violation of the Christian law of love. Many churches attempted to practice what they preached by establishing interracial congregations.[35] According to one historian, "every major church body in the South has made some pronouncement in agreement with the Supreme Court decision regarding segregation."[36] Unquestionably, the moral weight of official religious statements in behalf of tolerance, brotherhood, and equality did much to erode racist attitudes.

Interracial organizations occupied the vanguard in the civil rights campaign. The Southern Regional Council, with headquarters in Atlanta, worked quietly but effectively to promote equal opportunity and friendly contact between the races. The National Urban League, founded early in the twentieth century, was operating in forty-one states by 1960. Moderate in approach, dependent largely upon local resources and contributions, the Urban League maintained a variety of services but concentrated primarily upon advancing black employment opportunities. A more recent organization, the Congress of Racial Equality (CORE), supported a wide range of antidiscrimination campaigns with emphasis upon direct though nonviolent action.

---

[34]New York State, with its large and politically powerful Negro population, was a leader in this movement. Its Fair Employment Act of 1945, the first of such statutes, was amended in 1952 to cover discrimination in public accommodations and in 1955-1956 to include public housing. Its Commission Against Discrimination investigated and attacked discriminatory practices. Massachusetts, Connecticut, Washington, Colorado, and Oregon led the way in combating discrimination in private housing.

[35]According to one authority, an estimated 10 percent of all Protestant churches were interracial by 1957—a fivefold increase in ten years. Many large churches in downtown areas, crippled by the mass migration of white parishioners to the suburbs, refused to close or relocate, choosing instead to welcome blacks and other minorities and rebuild their congregations on an interracial basis. The once aristocratic Episcopal church had noteworthy success with this policy in several urban parishes.

[36]Thomas D. Clark, *The Emerging South* (New York, 1961), p. 260. Roman Catholic bishops in the South also took steps to begin the integration of parochial schools in the wake of the *Brown* decision. When white Roman Catholics in New Orleans, where the problem of integrated parochial schools was largest, attempted to defy the order, Archbishop Joseph F. Rummel did not hesitate to employ the weapon of excommunication to secure compliance.

The most influential of these groups was undoubtedly the National Association for the Advancement of Colored People. Supported by 350,000 members, white and black, the NAACP conducted an intensive and highly successful legal campaign to destroy segregation. Victorious in all but four of forty-six appeals to the Supreme Court, the NAACP was instrumental in the epochal decisions that advanced voting rights, invalidated restrictive housing covenants, and upset the "separate but equal" doctrine in transportation, public facilities, and education.

Progress often seemed slow, but it was remarkable by comparison with any previous period. Even more gratifying, the northern white community did not respond with large-scale acts of violence. To be sure, racial tension mounted in many areas and found expression in sporadic outbreaks of vandalism, terrorism, and mob action, especially in urban neighborhoods undergoing racial transition and all-white suburban communities resisting the "invasion" of a black family. Such incidents were numerous, and it would be fatuous to claim that harmony prevailed over old prejudices.

Yet the record was surprisingly good. Comparable black migrations during and after the First World War had touched off some of the bloodiest race riots in the nation's history; and as late as 1943, a wartime influx of black and white job-seekers had sparked a major riot in Detroit. But law-enforcement agencies and citizens' groups managed to keep most racial incidents from getting out of hand in the postwar years, despite continued black migration into and within metropolitan areas. In some transitional neighborhoods, public officials and residents cooperated to reduce friction, prevent "panic selling," and establish relatively harmonious biracial communities. Here and there, white employees grew accustomed to working with blacks in skilled, professional, and white-collar positions; restaurants, theaters, and other social facilities increasingly accepted black patrons without incident. If success was partial and uneven, it was substantial enough to indicate that racial bias was gradually diminishing, and that blacks were measurably closer to acceptance as equal citizens.

Inevitably, progress was slower in the South. Not only were notions of white supremacy more deeply entrenched, but the full weight of state and local authority as well as custom bore down upon blacks who attempted to cross the color line. Even here, however, a softening of traditional attitudes took place—*before* the *Brown* decision. White southerners were by no means prepared to grant social equality, but many had come to admit that blacks were entitled to greater economic and educational opportunities. The old rural South's devout bigotry was being leavened by a more enlightened outlook in the new urban-industrial South; and a sizable body of moderate white opinion, typified by religious and professional leaders who worked on the Southern Regional Council, now fairly offset the old viewpoint. The *Brown* decision was greeted with alarm and shock in some quarters, but also with a rather widespread, if reluctant, willingness to comply with the law of the land.

Unfortunately, southern extremism triumphed over southern moderation within twelve months of the *Brown* ruling. Some observers blamed
the federal government, and more particularly the president, for failing to
exert positive leadership and moral influence in the crucial first months.
Others concluded that powerful adverse opinion simply overawed moderate sentiment.

In any case, while moderates spoke in muted tones or not at all, southern politicians assumed postures of defiance, and segregationists mobilized
to meet the challenge. Most important among their numerous local organizations were the White Citizens Councils, modeled after a prototype that
sprang up in Indianola, Mississippi, in 1954. The idea spread rapidly, especially in the black-belt regions of the lower South, until a network of
Citizens Councils had appeared in several southern states. In contrast to
the Ku Klux Klan—which never attained a fraction of the following or
influence it had enjoyed in the 1920s—the Citizens Councils officially renounced violence, terrorism, and hooked night raids.[37] Instead, they employed the weapons of propaganda, pressure, persuasion, and agitation to
solidify white opinion. They relied heavily upon state rights arguments and
denounced the *Brown* decision as unconstitutional. Familiar white-su-
premacy shibboleths, including many that were hoary in John C. Cal-
houn's time, were circulated in a flood of pamphlets, books, speeches,
letters, radio programs, and lectures. So effective a pressure group did the
councils become in most southern states that opposition was silenced;
even rational discussion of the problem soon became impossible. Southern
legislatures passed a barrage of resolutions, laws, and constitutional
amendments designed to circumvent the *Brown* ruling, including measures
that would permit or require state officials to close public schools rather
than allow integration. Every legal device, maneuver, and gambit that
imaginative southern attorneys could conjure up was mobilized to delay or
thwart the desegregation process.

The white South, of course, was not monolithic on this or any other
question, and the speed and degree of compliance with the *Brown* decision varied greatly. On the whole, school integration was accomplished
rapidly and without undue difficulty in the District of Columbia and the
border states. "Token integration" was achieved in North Carolina, Tennessee, Arkansas, and Texas by 1957. Despite resistance from state authorities and the pressure of local opinion, most federal district judges
went resolutely about the task of implementing the *Brown* decision. Appellate courts were quick to sustain their integration orders or reverse
their rulings and demand more vigorous action when they countenanced
undue evasion or delay.

---

[37]Some councils, however, used economic coercion, anonymous telephone calls, and other forms
of intimidation against both black and white citizens. Moreover, the councils' language and tactics
were sufficiently inflammatory to encourage acts of violence on the part of others and generally
foster a spirit of defiance of law and order.

The first major clash between federal and state authority occurred in Arkansas. Governor Orval E. Faubus posted state national guardsmen outside Central High School in Little Rock to bar the entry of nine black students in the fall of 1957. President Eisenhower immediately federalized the national guard and sent federal troops to Little Rock to preserve order and enforce integration. Openly encouraged by state policy, aroused white citizens prepared to bar the reentry of the black students in 1958. So threatening had the situation become that a federal district judge granted the local school board a two-and-a-half-year delay in integration in order to avoid violence. This order was quickly appealed, and the Supreme Court, in *Cooper* v. *Aaron*, September 1958, unanimously set it aside. "Law and order," the Supreme Court announced, "are not here to be preserved by depriving the Negro children of their constitutional rights." The state of Arkansas thereupon closed the four Little Rock high schools but reopened them again in 1960 with limited integration.

Schools facing integration were also closed in 1958-1959 in Virginia, another bastion of "massive resistance." But both state and federal courts in 1959 held Virginia's school-closing law unconstitutional, and local opinion soon concluded that a little integration was better than no schools at all. State authorities yielded, and token integration was peacefully accomplished in several Virginia schools in 1959 and 1960. Even in the deep South the wall was finally breached: a few blacks began attending formerly all-white schools in Florida in 1959 and, despite an angry boycott by white parents, in Louisiana in 1960. When Georgia yielded to the extent of permitting local school boards to comply with federal court orders if they chose, Atlanta drew up an integration plan, and nine black students entered a white school there in 1961. By the latter date, only South Carolina, Alabama, and Mississippi had failed to make at least a token compliance with the *Brown* decision.

And yet the "tokens" were small. White citizens soon realized that they could better preserve the substance of segregation in practice by accepting a small measure of integration in principle. Devices to limit integration by "pupil placement" laws, permitting assignment on some basis other than race—psychological factors, mental aptitude, availability of classrooms and teachers, and so on—appeared less apt to be struck down if carefully drawn. The Supreme Court held in 1958, for example, that an Alabama school-placement law was not unconstitutional on its face. As of 1960, six years after the *Brown* decision, only about 181,000, or 6 percent, of some 3 million black students in the South were attending public schools with white students, and all but a fraction of these were in the border states and the District of Columbia. As we will see, however, this was by no means the end of this story.

Meanwhile, blacks were striking more directly and dramatically at other parts of Jim Crow. A Negro Baptist minister, Martin Luther King, Jr., of Montgomery, Alabama, founded an association in 1955 to protest against segregated seating on local buses. Supported eventually by nearly all of Montgomery's 50,000 blacks, the group organized car pools and conducted a massive boycott against the bus line. Though exposed to harassment and indignities from local authorities and white citizens, King and his followers maintained the boycott for over a year and nearly drove the company into bankruptcy. A court decision in 1956 struck down segregated seating in local transportation, and Montgomery Negroes triumphantly returned to the buses to sit where they chose. Many other southern cities soon instituted desegregation in local transit.

The basis of King's philosophy was the doctrine of nonviolent or passive resistance that Mohandas Gandhi had made famous in India. Following King's example, black college students proceeded to challenge Jim Crow by deliberately breaking local segregation ordinances in peaceful and orderly fashion. Seeking to dramatize the injustice of such laws, the demonstrators offered no resistance to violence and actually courted arrest. Major targets of this movement were southern department stores, which uniformly maintained segregated lunch counters while welcoming Negro trade in other sections of the store. The first "sit-in" demonstration occurred in Greensboro, North Carolina, in 1960, when four black students sat at a Woolworth lunch counter, requested service, and continued to wait patiently after being refused.

The technique caught on immediately. Dozens of similar demonstrations took place in other southern cities in ensuing weeks. Many sit-ins were spontaneous and locally organized, while others were sponsored by CORE and similar groups. The idea particularly captured the imagination of college students, black and white. Demonstrators were often heckled, spat upon, chased, and beaten; scores were arrested for violating local ordinances, trespassing, or disturbing the peace. Nevertheless, the movement continued and soon bore results. Chain stores in dozens of southern communities desegregated their lunch counters during 1960 and 1961.

Notwithstanding the bitterness, fear, racial tension, and sporadic violence that attended the Negro's bid for equal treatment in the South, there were grounds for cautious optimism. To begin with, the amount of actual violence was relatively small—either by comparison with the record of past decades, or when measured against the depth and variety of the postwar challenge to old customs and attitudes.[38] A powerful pressure,

---

[38]There were, to be sure, a number of tragic episodes. Six Negroes were lynched during the decade of the 1950s (as compared, however, with the dismal record of 1,100 Negroes lynched in the years 1900–1917, and 70 in 1919 alone). In addition to the brutality often meted out to sit-in demonstrators, vicious mob outbreaks occurred in Nashville and Clinton, Tennessee, over school integration. Unruly white students forced a black girl off the campus of the University of Alabama in 1956 when she attempted to enroll there. Several churches and synagogues were bombed during the bus boycott and sit-in campaigns. Economic coercion was frequently applied; there was much intimidation.

Yet the record was far less stained than it might have been—or would have been, fifty or even twenty years earlier.

hitherto insignificant in the South, was acting not only to restrain lawlessness and violence but to weaken the caste system. This pressure, of course,
was industrialization—impatient of Jim Crow and any other impediment
to the orderly transaction of business. Still dependent upon northern capital and eager to attract more industry, southern business leaders deplored
and often worked to prevent mob outbreaks that hurt trade and discouraged investment. Moreover, industrial development had drawn blacks to
southern as well as northern cities; over half the Negroes *in the South*
were urban dwellers before 1960. Their purchasing power was far greater
than ever before, and white merchants were loath to offend so large a bloc
of customers.

Not all enlightened voices had been stilled by segregationist pressure. A
few courageous ministers, writers, and editors continued to speak forthrightly in favor of common sense, tolerance, obedience to law, and adjustment to reality. Many southerners, though opposed to desegregation, were
aware of the bad name their section had acquired at home and abroad and
realized that some modification of the old order was necessary. Finally,
even segregationists were not of one mind about actually closing public
schools to avoid integrating them; the experiences in Arkansas and Virginia
had been sobering. Several southern communities, notably Atlanta in
1961, showed that careful planning could avert trouble and insure peaceful integration.

One further aspect of black protest remains to be noted. Blacks as a
whole, and especially young people, were becoming impatient with the
legal gradualism advocated by older leaders and favored direct action to
achieve more immediate results. A harmonious biracial society of equal
citizens remained their goal, but one restless element had set its sights in a
far different direction. The phenomenon known as black nationalism, first
observable in Marcus Garvey's "Back to Africa" campaign in the 1920s
(see Vol. I, p. 237), enjoyed a resurgence during the 1950s. It was most
powerfully represented by the so-called Black Muslims, a quasi-religious
organization professing allegiance to its own version of Mohammedanism.
There were other black nationalist groups, but the Muslims alone
achieved a significant following. Founded in Detroit in the early 1930s, the
group soon passed under the leadership of a Georgia Negro, Elijah Poole,
who adopted the name of Elijah Muhammad and achieved absolute authority over the movement. Under Muhammad's aggressive guidance, the
Black Muslims became a well-knit, dedicated body of over 100,000 adherents by 1960. Muhammad enforced a stern morality upon members, organized a cadre of highly disciplined young blacks, levied contributions from
the faithful, acquired real estate and various business enterprises for the
organization, and established over fifty temples in urban centers from
coast to coast, South as well as North.

The core of early Muslim doctrine was black supremacy—an explicit, uncompromising racism. Locally, Muhammad spoke of the day when blacks would have an entire culture and economy of their own in the United States, totally separate from the white. Ultimately, he predicted the downfall of white civilization and world dominance by the colored races. He was deliberately vague as to just when and how all of this would take place, being careful to avoid openly seditious utterances or invitations to violence. Though he preached a race hatred as bitter as that of the most ardent Ku Klux Klansman, he insisted that Black Muslims should avoid aggressive or hostile acts against whites. The most significant feature of the Muslim movement was that a message based firmly upon outspoken racism and hatred of the white man could attract so large a following— especially among young and lower-class blacks. And the Muslims were a mere precursor of the militancy that would accompany black demands in the sixties.

29

⧉

The United States
in a Turbulent World,
1953–1960

A mericans had become well acquainted with crisis and tension in international affairs by the time that Eisenhower came to the presidency. But the winds of change were blowing everywhere with stronger force. The Soviet Union worked to undermine Western unity and bid for the loyalty of impoverished but aspiring millions in Asia, Africa, and Latin America. The United States and its allies worked earnestly if not always harmoniously to preserve their security and contain the spread of communism. East-West rivalry and the cold war came to have limitless scope—featuring a costly arms race that increased the dangers and destructive potential of nuclear war at every step and impelled both sides toward involvement in border quarrels, political upheavals, and social revolutions in every corner of the globe.

1. "New Look" in American Foreign and Defense Policies

The Republican landslide in 1952, as we have seen, in large measure reflected widespread public dissatisfaction with Democratic foreign policy. Some Americans believed McCarthy's charges of treason and betrayal. Many more, while rejecting such fantasies, believed that Roosevelt and Truman had made a series of disastrous blunders: conceding too much at Yalta, letting Russia solidify its control in eastern Europe and develop the atomic bomb, permitting Communist triumph in China, bogging down in indecisive war in Korea. To these distraught Americans the Democratic policy of containment now seemed defensive, almost defeatist—a far cry from the splendid old American objectives of total victory and unconditional surrender. Republican spokesmen in 1952 therefore stressed the need for a "new look" in foreign policy and promised to recapture the initiative that Democrats had allegedly lost. Eisenhower's pledge to go to Korea, if elected, and work for a satisfactory conclusion to that stalemate was undoubtedly the most effective statement of the entire campaign.

Chief spokesman for the new look was John Foster Dulles, who served as secretary of state from 1953 until a fatal illness forced his retirement in 1959. An experienced diplomat and international lawyer, grandson of one secretary of state and nephew of another, Dulles was eminently qualified for his important post.[1] His most recent and significant work had been as major architect of the Japanese Peace Treaty and security pacts with Japan and other Pacific countries in 1950-1951 (see p. 714).

In office, Dulles proved to be a patient, canny statesman whose efforts on behalf of European unity and collective security showed vision and courage. He also had superabundant energy, profound self-assurance, and a domineering personality. He was seldom plagued by doubt, and it was often difficult to distinguish between his moral certitude and self-righteousness. He traveled nearly half a million miles during his tenure, visited some forty-six countries, and dominated the State Department so completely that subordinates, including ambassadors and members of the Policy Planning Staff, declined in importance; Dulles, people said, carried foreign policy under his hat. He enjoyed the complete confidence of President Eisenhower. All in all, he was one of the most forceful, influential, and controversial secretaries of state in American history.

Much of the controversy stemmed from Dulles's penchant for making phrases. A general expectation that the new administration would completely reshape American foreign policy owed much to his rhetoric. In the GOP platform of 1952, which he drafted, Dulles condemned Yalta by promising to repudiate all "secret understandings," indicted the Democrats for "neglect of the Far East," and promised that Republicans would find a "dynamic" substitute for the "negative, futile and immoral" policy of containment. Later he spoke confidently, if somewhat vaguely, of a "rollback" of Soviet power in eastern Europe and "liberation" of coun-

---

[1] He had served his apprenticeship as observer at the second Hague Conference in 1907 and as legal adviser on reparations at Paris in 1919 and Berlin in 1933. He had been a delegate at the San Francisco Conference that created the United Nations in 1945, a delegate to the General Assembly in the late 1940s, and an adviser at four foreign ministers' conferences from 1945 to 1949.

tries under Communist domination. He also helped to popularize the notion that Chiang Kai-shek and his Nationalist forces on Taiwan would be "unleashed" to recapture China.

The urge to make phrases continued after Dulles became secretary of state. He warned in December 1953 that France's failure to approve German rearmament in a European army would force the United States to make an "agonizing reappraisal" of its commitments—a thinly veiled threat to withdraw American troops from Europe. Next came "massive retaliation," enunciated in January 1954, implying that the United States would hereafter rely upon nuclear weapons instead of ground forces in responding to Communist aggression. Finally, there was his remark in 1956 that he had taken the United States to "the brink of war" on three occasions since 1953 in order to preserve the peace. Democrats derisively referred to this as "brinkmanship."

Actually, the new look consisted largely of old policies obscured by new language. Bold rhetoric notwithstanding, the Eisenhower administration did not have a workable alternative to containment. In fact, the basic principles of Truman-Acheson diplomacy—regional alliances, collective security, foreign aid, and support of the UN—were not only maintained but extended after 1953. It could hardly have been otherwise. Both Eisenhower and Dulles had helped to formulate American policy during and after the Second World War. Both were firmly committed to the postwar system of alliances and mutual obligations. The extreme revisions advocated by neo-isolationists—whose agenda included elimination of foreign aid, abandonment of the UN, retreat to a highly armed "fortress America," instant nuclear response to Communist aggression, attacks on China, and even preventive war—were totally unacceptable to the new president and secretary of state. Any changes they undertook would be made within the framework of internationalism and collective security.

Furthermore, world realities simply precluded most of the actions that Dulles forecast in announcing the new look. Repudiation of "secret understandings" like Yalta would invite Russia to make further repudiations of her own. Attempts to end alleged "neglect of the Far East" could not prevent further changes in that area. Despite rebellious outbreaks in Russian satellite countries during the 1950s, the United States could manifestly do nothing to "roll back" Soviet power or "liberate" so-called captive nations without courting a third world war, and Dulles was careful not to go to the brink when vital Soviet interests were at stake. As for "unleashing" Chiang Kai-shek, administration leaders knew that he could not invade the mainland without massive American support, which they never seriously contemplated providing.

Reality likewise reduced the import of "massive retaliation"—which was never intended to mean that the United States would rely solely upon nuclear weapons. Republican defense policy aimed at achieving the power to deter most attacks and the flexibility to counter all. The United States hoped to be able, as Dulles put it, "to retaliate, instantly, by means and at places of our choosing. That permits a selection of military means instead of a multiplication of means." It would thus permit economy—a prime goal of the new administration—by obviating the need to maintain extensive ground forces deployed against potential attacks. Instead, "highly mobile naval, air, and amphibious units" would be poised in combat readiness, equipped where feasible with tactical atomic weapons and backed by the growing "massive deterrent" fleet of medium- and long-range bombers in the Strategic Air Command. As Admiral Arthur W. Radford, chairman of the Joint Chiefs of Staff, put it: "We must be ready for tremendous, vast retaliatory and counter-offensive blows in event of a global war, and we must also be ready for lesser military actions short of all-out war."

Advancing technology and emphasis on air power enabled the administration to effect substantial reductions in defense spending and conventional armed forces from 1953 to 1956.[2] The army dwindled from a postwar peak of 1.5 million men in 1953 to less than 900,000 by 1960; navy personnel (including marines), from over 1 million to less than 800,000. Army expenditures dropped from $17 billion in 1953 to an annual average of under $10 billion in 1955–1960. Naval expenditures were reduced from almost $12 billion in 1953 to $9.7 billion in 1955 and 1956, then began to rise. Air force expenditures, in contrast, mounted steadily from $15 billion in 1953 to over $19 billion in 1959 and after. Effective use of radio, radar, and electronic computers brought phenomenal progress in air defense. The Defense Early Warning (DEW) Line, a string of radar stations above the Arctic Circle, was completed in 1958 and later extended to Greenland and reinforced by the even more sensitive Ballistic Missile Early Warning System (BMEWS).

The navy undertook many improvements, adding several big carriers, guided-missile surface craft, and nuclear-powered vessels, notably the gigantic 86,000-ton carrier *Enterprise* in 1961. Most importantly, the navy in 1955 introduced the nuclear submarine, capable of almost indefinite submersion, and equipped it with intermediate-range Polaris missiles by 1960. The fleet of Polaris nuclear submarines authorized or building by the latter date promised to provide a powerful, mobile, and seemingly invulnerable deterrent force.

The army, too, modernized equipment and techniques. Most spectacular among a bewildering array of new hardware were various tactical atomic weapons—rockets, atomic cannon, surface-to-surface and surface-to-air missiles—that began appearing in more potent and sophisticated versions each year after 1955. Reorganization into lighter, mobile "pento-

[2]The defense budget for fiscal 1954 was reduced some $3.5 billion from the 1953 figure, and $6 billion more was slashed in 1955, bringing total defense expenditures down to about $40 billion. They remained at that level in 1956 and then began an inexorable upward climb as mounting costs defied attempts at further reductions.

mic" divisions took place in 1957, with emphasis upon a Strategic Army Corps maintained in combat readiness in the United States and capable of quick dispatch anywhere to reinforce overseas units or provide initial resistance in case of war.

President Eisenhower also overhauled the entire defense establishment, seeking to achieve greater efficiency and reduce waste. Defense reorganization acts in 1953 and 1958 centralized power and responsibility in the hands of the secretary of defense and increased the authority of the Joint Chiefs of Staff. The government faced the challenges of the space age by creating the National Aeronautics and Space Administration (NASA) out of an older advisory body.

Air power, of course, figured most prominently in a defense system based on massive retaliation.[3] Concentration on the air arm was doubly attractive to policy makers: it offered savings in reduced manpower and equipment for ground and naval forces, and it seemed to provide a way of meeting aggression without heavy commitment of troops and attendant casualties. But technological change was nowhere more dynamic than in the field of aviation, and maintaining an up-to-date air force belied hopes for economy. No sooner had jet planes replaced propeller-driven aircraft than supersonic fighters and bombers—each new model faster, more powerful, and costlier than the one it supplanted—began going from design into production. Jet fighters achieved "Mach 2" (twice the speed of sound, or about 1450 miles per hour) by 1957. Greater range, maneuverability, and firepower likewise added to rapid turnover and mounting costs of combat planes—as did other advances like aerial refueling, all-weather navigational and bombing systems, and air-to-air and air-to-surface rockets.

All these improvements were eclipsed in the late 1950s by progress in missile development. Pioneer "anti-missile missiles" offered hope for an effective defense against enemy nuclear rockets, while intercontinental (ICBM) and intermediate-range (IRBM) ballistic missiles promised to supplement, and perhaps eventually replace, the manned bombers of the Strategic Air Command as America's ultimate offensive weapon.[4]

---

[3] Recognizing that the air force had become a coordinate military arm, the administration implemented plans long in the making and established the Air Force Academy in 1954, opening its new plant and campus near Colorado Springs in 1958.

[4] The armed services had registered several triumphs in the field of strategic offensive missiles by 1960. The navy's Polaris was matched by Jupiter and Thor, IRBMs with a range of 1,500-2,000 miles, which completed their tests and went into production in 1958. Thor missile squadrons were deployed two years later at RAF bases in Great Britain, Jupiter squadrons at NATO bases in Italy and Turkey.

America's first ICBM was the Atlas, test-fired at a range of 6,325 miles in 1958 and deployed in its first squadron by 1960. Maximum range was increased to 9,000 miles by reducing its weight and expanding the thrust of its liquid-fueled rocket engine. Titan, with comparable range, became war-ready in 1961, while construction proceeded on base sites in various parts of the country. The air force also developed the Minuteman, a simpler and less costly ICBM that could be launched from underground silos and movable railroad cars.

Despite these achievements, the administration's defense policy became caught in a sustained cross fire of criticism. To many foreign observers, America's seeming reliance on massive retaliation increased the danger of total war and endangered all humankind. NATO allies suspected that the United States planned to withdraw its troops and "protect" Europe solely with nuclear weapons—a form of protection which they regarded as militarily useless, diplomatically unreliable, and morally repulsive. At home, the policy drew fire from a host of critics, including Adlai Stevenson, former Secretary of State Dean Acheson, and Henry A. Kissinger, of Harvard University's Center for International Affairs. General Ridgway resigned as army chief of staff in 1955 out of disagreement with the policy, and his successor, General Maxwell D. Taylor, became no less critical.

The essence of the indictment was that dependence upon massive retaliation placed American policy in a dangerous strait jacket. By reducing the nation's capacity to fight limited wars, it positively encouraged the Communists to "nibble" at peripheral and remote areas. Since it was unlikely that the United States would bomb Moscow whenever such local aggression occurred, the policy was no more than a patent bluff. Except for direct Soviet attacks upon the United States or western Europe, critics argued, the policy was doubly harmful: it was useless as a deterrent because it lacked credibility, and emphasis upon it deprived the country, when faced with lesser thrusts, of any alternative save yielding.

Worse still, it could easily lead to war by miscalculation—the very contingency Secretary Dulles sought to avoid. He hoped to prevent it by making clear in advance how the nation would respond. Yet talk of massive retaliation made for ambiguity rather than clarity, and the ambiguity increased each time the deterrent was not employed. If Communist leaders ever concluded that the American threat was pure bluff, they would sooner or later act on this assumption once too often—in which case, as Kissinger remarked, " 'massive retaliation' may bring about the total war it seeks to prevent."

Criticism grew apace as a result of unwelcome shifts in the military balance of power. When Russia developed the hydrogen bomb in 1953, only nine months after the United States had done so, "nuclear deterrence" became a two-way street. The Soviets continued to make formidable progress in military technology. Already boasting the world's most powerful army, they built a navy second only to America's after midcentury and a submarine fleet second to none. They acquired, by 1956, enough long-range bombers and a sufficient nuclear stockpile to devastate the largest American cities. Their progress in tactical atomic weapons and short-range rockets equaled that of the United States. The disturbing climax came in 1957, first with the Russian claim that they had successfully test-fired an ICBM in August, a year before America's pioneer Atlas proved its merit, and then with the launching of *Sputnik* space satellites in October and November.

Americans took alarm. Their vaunted technological genius had not only been matched but apparently surpassed. To be sure, the United States launched an impressive number of its own space satellites beginning in January 1958, with technical equipment superior to the Russian ventures. But in one crucial matter—development of a thrust sufficiently powerful to orbit large vehicles with heavy payloads—the Soviet Union was clearly ahead of the United States. Even substantial American progress in long-range missile development after 1958 did not quiet the fear that a danger-ous "missile gap" was tipping the balance of nuclear power in Russia's favor.

Unfortunately, furor over this alleged missile gap broke out just as the administration discovered sharply rising costs in its defense budget. De-spite efforts at economy, expensive new weapons and research programs more than offset money saved by reductions in manpower and conven-tional equipment. With Secretary Humphrey warning of a "depression that will curl your hair" unless budget and taxes were reduced, the admin-istration slashed its military program drastically in 1958. It made further troop reductions, shelved defense contracts, abandoned or postponed re-search projects on missiles and other weapons, retired nearly one hundred warships, and eliminated five tactical wings from the air force. Four army divisions, two proposed missile commands, and several antiaircraft battal-ions were also pared from the rolls. All this coincided with *Sputnik* and Russia's first ICBM.

Angry critics now accused the government of mutiple failure. It had first weakened conventional forces and limited-war capability in the inter-ests of economy and nuclear air power, then fallen behind Russia in missile development while failing to keep costs down. Foremost critic of the missile gap was Senator Stuart Symington of Missouri, secretary of the air force under Truman and now chairman of the Senate armed forces sub-committee. Symington added to the disquietude in 1959 by charging that the administration, "far from planning to close the current ICBM gap . . . is actually allowing it to widen." Defense expenditures rose in response, reaching record peacetime highs of over $45 billion annually from 1959 through 1961. But public confidence, despite official reassurances, was badly shaken.

Actually, the state of American defenses was sounder than critics claimed. Progress in some aspects of missile development lagged behind Russia's, but American strength was clearly sufficient, at any time during the Eisenhower era, to deter an all-out Russian attack or retaliate with crushing effectiveness. It is probably true that less concern for economy would have advanced the missile and space programs and reassured the nation's allies about its ability to fight limited wars by nonnuclear means. But the overshadowing fact of the decade was that both Russia and the United States were acquiring and enlarging nuclear arsenals capable of destroying each other, and possibly the rest of the world as well.

2. America and the Soviet Union: Summit Diplomacy and Cold War

The inauguration of President Eisenhower virtually coincided with the death, on March 5, 1953, of Joseph Stalin. The vacuum thus created at the top of the Soviet hierarchy, after twenty-five years of dictatorial rule, led to a long struggle for power. The new premier, Georgi M. Malenkov, shared authority with such high-ranking Communist party officials as Vyacheslav M. Molotov, who again headed the foreign office; Lavrenti P. Beria, minister of internal affairs; Nikolai A. Bulganin, minister of defense; and Nikita S. Khrushchev, first secretary of the Communist party's Central Committee.

Control shifted with bewildering frequency for several years. Beria was shot in 1953. Malenkov gave way as premier to Bulganin in early 1955. Molotov resigned from the foreign office in 1956 and was ousted from the Central Committee. Malenkov followed him in humiliation a year later. Many other figures rose and fell during this turbulent period. Although Defense Minister Rodion Malinovsky, Foreign Minister Andrei Gromyko, and First Deputy Premier Anastas I. Mikoyan were among the principal leaders after 1957, the man who solidified his power with each shake-up and maneuvered his way to the top of the hazardous Russian pyramid was Khrushchev. He exercised virtual control during Bulganin's premiership and formally succeeded Bulganin in March 1958. This volatile, stockily built Russian, with his histrionic speeches and expressive countenance, became a familiar figure to Americans after 1955.

The power struggle that followed Stalin's death had barely begun before the Soviets inaugurated a tactical change in foreign policy. Underlying objectives remained the same, but the Kremlin concluded that a less provocative diplomacy would best serve Russian interests. They talked of relaxing tensions, evinced a seeming readiness to negotiate deadlocked questions, and hinted at concessions. They also began to speak of the "peaceful coexistence" of socialist and capitalist nations.

Eisenhower responded cautiously, displaying a willingness to explore possibilities but indicating that words were not enough. "We welcome every honest act of peace," he said on April 16. "We care nothing for mere rhetoric. We are only for sincerity of peaceful purpose attested by deeds." The Soviets did in fact make conciliatory gestures during 1953, notably an endorsement of the Chinese and North Korean proposal to resume the armistice negotiations at Panmunjom. These actions lent some weight to Premier Malenkov's assertion that "there is not one dispute or undecided question that cannot be decided by peaceful means on the basis of mutual understanding of interested countries. This is our attitude toward all states, among them the U.S.A." Prime Minister Churchill, meanwhile, continued to urge a four-power meeting of heads of government, or summit conference, a step he had been advocating for three years. But Eisenhower was loath, as Truman had been, to go to the summit until some assurance of progress and cooperation could be had in advance.

Gradually, the two sides maneuvered toward a summit meeting. The first break occurred at a foreign ministers' conference in Vienna in May 1955. Russia finally agreed, after a decade of haggling, to conclude a treaty restoring Austria's freedom and ending the four-power occupation. Never before had the Soviets consented to pull completely out of an area where their troops had established a foothold. It did much to persuade the West that the new Russian leaders genuinely desired better relations. Plans for a summit meeting were quickly drawn, and President Eisenhower, Premier Bulganin, Prime Minister Anthony Eden of Great Britain, and Premier Edgar Faure of France met at Geneva in July 1955 to define and review the issues dividing East and West. It was the first time that an American and Soviet chief of state had talked directly since Truman's meeting with Stalin at Potsdam ten years before.

The Geneva meeting raised high hopes. Its relaxed atmosphere, stimulated by an abundance of vodka, martinis, and mutual cordiality, seemed to suggest that a major turn for the better in world affairs was taking place at last. The Russian leaders, smiling and seemingly well disposed, made a favorable impression; they were obviously impressed in their turn by Eisenhower's manifest good will and desire for peace. These feelings of harmony, often invoked as the "spirit of Geneva," remained in evidence for over a year and kept hopes for an East-West détente alive.

Actually, the summit conference amounted to little more than an earnest gesture. It had been decided in advance that the heads of state would try to formulate rather than solve the pressing issues, and agree, if possible, only upon methods to be followed. The four leaders defined the paramount problems as German reunification, European security, disarmament, and greater East-West contacts. They recommended free elections in Germany, a general treaty renouncing force or aid to aggressors, pursuit of disarmament by the UN, and elimination of barriers to the flow of people and ideas between East and West. But these were truisms, and nothing tangible came of them. A follow-up conference of foreign ministers in Geneva in late 1955 was totally unable to realize summit directives. Neither side would make vital concessions, and harmony was preserved at the price of avoiding all public discussion of such explosive issues as freedom in eastern Europe and admission of Communist China to the United Nations.

Peace hopes and the spirit of Geneva crumbled in October 1956 when Soviet tanks crushed a rebellion in Hungary just as English, French, and Israeli forces launched an invasion of Egypt (see pp. 787, 804–806). Worldwide instability brought a new freeze to the cold war, and chances of East-West accord faded. When Switzerland proposed another summit meeting to halt the threat of war, Eisenhower coldly replied that the UN should handle the crisis. There seemed little point in further top-level discussions with Moscow.

Yet the Russians, while attempting to turn every new trouble spot to their advantage and hammering at Western unity, tried repeatedly to bring about a second summit meeting. They began this agitation late in 1957 and finally induced a reluctant assent from Eisenhower and Dulles in March 1958. England and France also accepted, but the three Western powers insisted that conversations at the ambassadorial and foreign minister levels precede such a meeting.

Khrushchev replaced Bulganin as premier just as the Western leaders agreed to return to the summit, and the Russian attitude underwent several reversals. Khrushchev's public criticisms of Eisenhower in early 1958 seemed to destroy the chances of a meeting. But Russia's sudden challenge to Western rights in Berlin in November (see pp. 789–790) provided new impetus. The Berlin crisis led directly to a foreign ministers' conference at Geneva, and tension momentarily subsided. Khrushchev, following a visit to the United States in September 1959, dropped the time limit for a Berlin settlement; and Eisenhower, who had refused to go to the summit under the seeming duress of a Berlin deadline, forthwith consented. Khrushchev's American tour ended in such a friendly mood, induced especially by cordial private talks between premier and president at the latter's mountain retreat west of Washington, that observers soon began speaking hopefully of the "spirit of Camp David."

This spirit proved even more illusory and short-lived than that of Geneva. Well in advance of the summit meeting, scheduled to open in Paris in May 1960, it became evident that little would be achieved there. The powers had made slight progress toward agreement on a nuclear test ban but none whatever on German reunification, Berlin, or arms control. Khrushchev's general posture for some weeks before the conference did not augur well for its success.

Two weeks before it opened, a high-altitude American U-2 reconnaissance plane was shot down on May 1 far over the interior of Russia. Washington first claimed that a routine weather flight from an overseas base near the Soviet border had gone astray. Then Khrushchev revealed that the pilot had been captured and had freely confessed that aerial espionage was the real purpose of the flight. The American government not only admitted this but added, in a display of frankness that amazed foreign diplomats, that such photo-reconnaissance flights had been taking place over Soviet territory since 1956.

Khrushchev came to Paris in a dangerous temper. He voiced all manner of threats, not only against the United States but against nations that permitted "spy flights" to take off or land on their soil. (The U-2 aircraft in question had been flying across Russia from Pakistan to Norway.) He demanded that the president apologize for these violations of Soviet air space and promise their immediate discontinuance. He added that whatever the United States did about the U-2 flights, it would be necessary to cancel Eisenhower's scheduled visit to Russia in June because the Soviet people were too upset by the recent episode to greet the American president with proper "cordiality."

Eisenhower ordered suspension of the flights, but refused to apologize. His own temper mounted wrathfully as Khrushchev's diatribes continued, and efforts of Prime Minister Harold Macmillan of Great Britain and President Charles de Gaulle of France to restore harmony and save the meeting were futile. It broke up in mutual frustration and anger before it actually convened.

Many observers felt that Khrushchev had used the U-2 incident as a pretext for disrupting a conference he no longer saw advantage in attending. Certainly the propaganda value of the affair was of greater benefit to him than the inevitable deadlock would have been. Despite his anger, the Soviet premier spoke in favor of a summit conference at some future date—adding, however, that it could not take place while Eisenhower was president. Eisenhower left office, therefore, with Soviet-American relations at a low ebb and the record of summit diplomacy a distinct failure.

3. America and the Soviet Union: Nuclear Stalemate and the Quest for Disarmament

A grim dilemma confronted American policy makers after 1945. The appalling destructive force of new thermonuclear weapons made their control and, if possible, their elimination a matter of increasing urgency. Tragically, the deep mutual distrust that underlay the world rivalry between East and West placed a huge obstacle in the path of effective arms control. Given this distrust, the demands of national security impelled the United States and the Soviet Union, as we have seen, into the vicious ascending spiral of a nuclear arms race. Pressures to enlarge and contract the dread arsenals thus mounted simultaneously; quests for a disarmament formula and more devastating weapons proceeded hand in hand. It was sadly true, however, that modern science made the latter quest all too successful, while cold-war diplomacy compiled for the former a record of little save frustration and deadlock.

That record was already seven years old when President Eisenhower and Secretary Dulles renewed a long-standing American quest for a workable arms control agreement in 1953. Various UN commissions had tried since 1946 to produce such agreements, but progress had been stymied by unyielding attitudes on both sides. Though both ostensibly favored disarmament, a fundamental difference separated their views. The Western allies, not trusting Russia, had insisted that disarmament could neither begin nor proceed save under an effective system of international inspection and control. The Russians had flatly rejected this approach and hammered away on a sweeping formula of their own: immediate abolition of atomic weapons, a one-third across-the-board reduction in conventional forces by all countries, and abandonment by every nation of all military bases on foreign territory. This was in effect asking the United States to abolish the Strategic Air Command and emasculate NATO while the Red Army retained its decisive numerical superiority; not surprisingly, the West found it unacceptable.

Shifts, new proposals, and partial concessions on both sides marked negotiations from 1953 to 1960, but no real change in basic positions and no substantive progress took place. The United Nations Disarmament Commission, having failed to accomplish anything since its creation in 1952, delegated its task in 1954 to a five-power subcommittee representing the United States, the Soviet Union, Great Britain, France, and Canada. The subcommittee held private meetings in London for three years and probed every facet of the subject. They concentrated on an inspection system for controlling nuclear weapons, a method of preventing surprise attacks, and a ban on nuclear testing. At times they seemed on the verge of accord. Invariably, however, some item that one side considered indispensable was felt by the other to place it at a disadvantage, and no agreement was reached.

None of the various allied proposals for "phased" and controlled disarmament or international inspection was acceptable to the Russians, whose deep-seated dislike of opening their country to foreign observation stemmed in part from fear of espionage. For this reason they also opposed Western suggestions for preventing surprise attacks, including Eisenhower's "open skies" plan put forth at Geneva in 1955. The president proposed that the United States and Russia exchange complete information about military installations, equipment, and organization, and allow monitored but unrestricted aerial reconnaissance over each other's territory. The Soviets endorsed this in principle, but later discussions resulted in the customary failure to agree on detail. Although some Russian proposals for controlled and inspected reductions were quite similar to earlier Western formulas, one or more of the allies inevitably boggled over some point on which Russia refused to retreat; and the stalemate persisted.

The powers came closest to accord on the issue of a nuclear test ban. World opinion justly regarded this as the least difficult and most imperative aspect of the disarmament controversy, especially as repeated tests by the United States, the Soviet Union, and Great Britain (which developed the hydrogen bomb in 1957) demonstrated the weapon's terrifying potential. Agitation for discontinuance of nuclear testing mounted steadily everywhere.[5]

The Russians soon made a test ban one of the principal items in their disarmament proposals. They used the issue effectively in appealing to worried neutral countries, particularly when Eisenhower gave the impression of rejecting the test ban by insisting that it be tied to a larger settlement and contain adequate safeguards. Though the president's reaction was understandable, given American distrust of Soviet intentions, it seemed obstructive in other quarters and compared unfavorably with the Russian proposal that a moratorium on testing precede rather than follow an inspection system or other agreement.

Gradually the two sides moved toward a more constructive approach. The Soviet demand for a test ban culminated in a dramatic announcement in March 1958 that the USSR would suspend nuclear tests, although it reserved the right to resume them if other powers did not join the moratorium. Washington countered with a plea for joint technical studies to examine methods of detecting violations of a test-ban agreement. Russia agreed unenthusiastically. A panel of scientific experts from four Communist states (the USSR, Poland, Czechoslovakia, Rumania) and four Western nations (the United States, Britain, France, Canada) held closed meetings in Geneva in mid-1958. Conducting their deliberations in a cooperative spirit and with remarkable objectivity, the scientists submitted a constructive and encouraging report. It was technically feasible, they agreed, to establish a workable control system that would detect violations of a test ban. The system would require land-based control posts on every continent, including both Russian and American territory, plus naval and air patrols and mobile inspection groups, all to be operated by an international agency.

The American and British governments now seized the initiative by announcing their willingness to negotiate a three-power treaty that would establish an international control system and provide for permanent cessation of nuclear tests. Moreover, they agreed to suspend their own tests for one year if Russia accepted the principle of a controlled test ban and agreed to negotiate to that end. Both allies made it clear that they would conclude their present test series before invoking the proposed one-year

---

[5]There was a growing fear that the tests were highly dangerous in themselves because of the increased amount of radioactive fallout with which they poisoned the atmosphere. This was dramatized in 1954 when several crew members of a Japanese fishing boat that had strayed near American nuclear tests in the Pacific suffered burns. Horrifying predictions of the genetic damage that a higher rate of fallout could wreak upon future generations strengthened the conviction that nuclear tests posed their own threat to civilization.

suspension and would resume testing if Russia did so; otherwise, however, the suspensions would be subject to one-year extensions if the negotiations made satisfactory progress.

The Russians could hardly refuse this invitation to negotiate after years of urging a test ban. They accepted in August, and a three-power Conference on the Discontinuance of Nuclear Weapons Tests duly assembled in Geneva in October 1958. Prospects of success seemed bright for a time, then dimmed in 1960. As in almost all previous negotiations, the issue of controls proved an unbridgeable gap. Despite agreement on principle, America consistently held out for a more extensive system and a larger number of on-site inspections than Russia was willing to grant.

The conferees continued the sessions in good spirit until the end of 1960, gradually narrowing their differences, then recessed to await the inauguration of President Kennedy. Even though many American experts now doubted that an effective control system was possible and favored a resumption of testing, hope for a test-ban treaty remained alive. As the decade ended, the unilateral suspensions that all three nuclear powers had proclaimed in 1958 were still in force. The atmosphere had been untainted by new fallout for over two years.

Meanwhile, the powers had resumed their search for agreement on broader issues. In the brief aura of good feeling that emerged during Khrushchev's visit to the United States in 1959, the Soviet leader had offered a sweeping four-year plan for "universal and complete" disarmament. The Big Four foreign ministers agreed upon a ten-nation disarmament conference which met in Geneva in March 1960 to explore "avenues of possible progress" toward reducing armaments "under effective international control." Notwithstanding a generally cooperative tone, deliberations ran aground on the same unyielding reefs. Compromise proposals could not alter the fact that, in sum, the West insisted upon adequate controls before disarmament could take place, while the Communists insisted that disarmament could begin at once and a control system devised later. Gradually, as the irreconcilable nature of this impasse took shape, the Geneva talks degenerated into a propaganda battle.

The conference recessed in April in hopes that the forthcoming Paris summit meeting would provide an improved basis for further discussion. But Paris was a fiasco, as we have seen, and the outlook was dim when talks resumed in June. The Soviets first juggled their disarmament formula. Then, after the American delegate returned from Washington with a revised counteroffer, the Communist delegations walked out without listening to it, charging that the West had not negotiated in good faith. The ten-nation conference, like the summit meeting, thus ended in shambles. Khrushchev announced on June 27 that further meetings were useless, and the decade ended with no agreements reached and few in sight on the crucial question of disarmament.

4. Europe and the United States in the 1950s

Europe remained the central battleground in the cold war. The strength and solidarity of the North Atlantic alliance continued to be America's primary concern; the weakening or disruption of that alliance retained a high priority among Soviet goals. There was no doubt in either Washington or Moscow that the renascent countries of western Europe, with their booming economies, vast industrial and human resources, and quickening sense of unity, were the pivot in the world balance of power. Conversely, maintenance of its adjoining satellite empire in eastern Europe was of crucial importance to the Kremlin. Overarching all these problems was the future status of divided Germany and Berlin.

NATO allies had concluded by midcentury that they could not rely solely upon American strategic air power to deter a Soviet attack on western Europe. Conventional ground forces would also be necessary, although numerical parity with Russia was never contemplated. It was hoped, rather, to raise and equip a sufficient number of divisions (the so-called defensive shield) to prevent Europe from being overrun before American retaliatory bombing—NATO's "striking sword"—could take effect. The alliance promptly took steps to formulate a defensive strategy, integrate its command system, and rearm, backed by a flood of American supplies. By 1953 NATO could deploy five thousand tactical aircraft and had large stockpiles of weapons and equipment. Troop strength was another matter. Main reliance was on a handful of well-equipped divisions, mainly American, British, and French, backed by a larger number of undermanned reserve units. The entire NATO army was less than half the size of the forces immediately available to the Soviet bloc. Nevertheless, the new defensive shield had become strong enough by 1953 to provide at least a measure of military security.

Graver problems lay just ahead. Three concurrent challenges beset NATO: shifts in Soviet policy after Stalin, a lengthening thermonuclear shadow, and a violent cresting of the nationalist wave in Asia, Africa, and the Middle East. These challenges magnified normal divisive tendencies, and the outstanding fact was not that NATO encountered difficulties after 1953 but that it survived at all.

Germany held one important key to success. The Atlantic allies, faced with a persistent Soviet refusal to permit German reunification on terms they could accept, had adopted the alternative in 1948-1949 of uniting the three Western zones in the West German Federal Republic (see p. 697). NATO's campaign for rearmament and military integration in 1950 included a "forward strategy" that placed West Germany within the allied defense perimeter and anticipated meeting a Soviet thrust at or near the Communist border. Even more important, the United States put forth specific proposals in September 1950 for a West German army. This question threatened to disrupt NATO for years. No European country could view the prospect of Germans in uniform without misgiving so soon after Hitler's Reich; the strongest opposition came, understandably, from France. Yet Europeans agreed reluctantly with the American view that German manpower was indispensable, and the first major design for re-arming West Germany came from French Premier René Pleven in 1950. He called for an integrated European Defense Community, linked to NATO, with German units submerged in a supranational army under joint control of the member nations. A treaty creating the EDC was signed in Paris in May 1952 by France, Belgium, the Netherlands, Luxembourg, Italy, and West Germany. But the French National Assembly rejected it in August 1954, after over two years of debate. Neither firmer British pledges, nor assurances from President Eisenhower, nor Secretary Dulles's threats of "agonizing reappraisal" were sufficient to muster a French majority in favor of the treaty. Dulles, who had labored mightily to make this blueprint for European unity a reality, termed defeat of EDC a "shattering blow" to the North Atlantic treaty system.

Fortunately, Prime Minister Eden of Great Britain came forward with an acceptable alternative. The British proposal was hammered into final form in London in September 1954, signed in Paris in October, ratified by the nations concerned, and put into force in May 1955. In brief, the Paris agreement ended the joint occupation, restored full sovereignty to the West German government, and admitted West Germany to NATO. It also provided for a maximum of twelve German divisions and expanded NATO's authority over the armed forces of all member nations.

This agreement contained two revolutionary features: a positive commitment by Great Britain, far more binding than its earlier pledges to EDC, to maintain substantial armed forces on the continent; and acceptance by the major European powers, including France, Britain, and Italy as well as West Germany, of limitations and controls upon their armed forces.[6] The United States, pleased with this workable substitute for EDC, repeated its assurances that American troops would remain in Europe.

But admission of West Germany alleviated none of NATO's difficulties. Its military posture, which German adherence was designed to improve, had begun to slip well before the agreement of 1954 made possible the raising of German contingents. An ambitious three-year program to in-

---

[6]The Paris agreement embodied these unprecedented features in a complex series of arrangements. First, it enlarged and revised the Brussels Pact of 1948, under which France, Britain, and the Benelux countries had formed the Western European Union (WEU), which in turn became a subdepartment of NATO. The Brussels Pact was amended by deleting references to German aggression, and its purpose was redefined as that of promoting the unity and "progressive integration" of Europe. The WEU Council was reconstituted and empowered to fix the maximum size of the armed forces that each country could contribute to NATO. In addition, West Germany specifically agreed not to manufacture atomic, biological, or chemical weapons, and to refrain from producing certain other weapons save upon request of NATO.

COLLECTIVE DEFENS

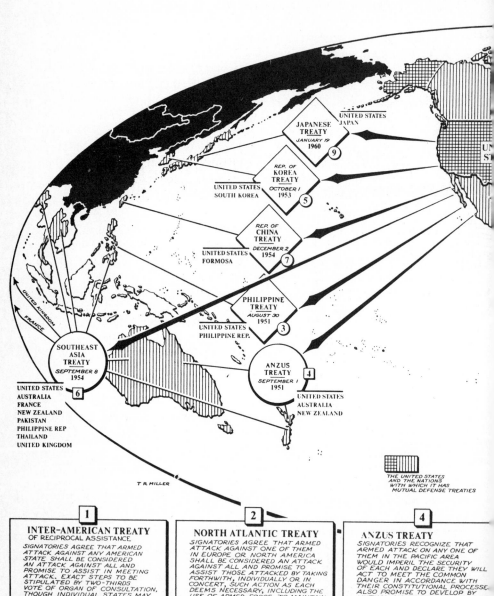

UNITED STATES
JAPAN

JAPANESE
TREATY
JANUARY 19
1960
9

REP. OF
KOREA
TREATY
OCTOBER 1
1953
5

UNITED STATES
SOUTH KOREA

REP. OF
CHINA
TREATY
DECEMBER 2
1954
7

UNITED STATES
FORMOSA

PHILIPPINE
TREATY
AUGUST 30
1951
3

UNITED STATES
PHILIPPINE REP.

SOUTHEAST
ASIA
TREATY
SEPTEMBER 8
1954
6

UNITED STATES
AUSTRALIA
FRANCE
NEW ZEALAND
PAKISTAN
PHILIPPINE REP
THAILAND
UNITED KINGDOM

ANZUS
TREATY
SEPTEMBER 1
1951
4

UNITED STATES
AUSTRALIA
NEW ZEALAND

UNITED KINGDOM

FRANCE

U
S

T R MILLER

THE UNITED STATES
AND THE NATIONS
WITH WHICH IT HAS
MUTUAL DEFENSE TREATIES

1
INTER-AMERICAN TREATY
OF RECIPROCAL ASSISTANCE.

SIGNATORIES AGREE THAT ARMED ATTACK AGAINST ANY AMERICAN STATE SHALL BE CONSIDERED AN ATTACK AGAINST ALL AND PROMISE TO ASSIST IN MEETING ATTACK. EXACT STEPS TO BE STIPULATED BY TWO-THIRDS VOTE OF ORGAN OF CONSULTATION, THOUGH INDIVIDUAL STATES MAY ACT PRIOR TO THAT VOTE. NO STATE SHALL BE REQUIRED TO USE ARMED FORCE WITHOUT ITS CONSENT.

2
NORTH ATLANTIC TREATY

SIGNATORIES AGREE THAT ARMED ATTACK AGAINST ONE OF THEM IN EUROPE OR NORTH AMERICA SHALL BE CONSIDERED AN ATTACK AGAINST ALL AND PROMISE TO ASSIST THOSE ATTACKED BY TAKING FORTHWITH, INDIVIDUALLY OR IN CONCERT, SUCH ACTION AS EACH DEEMS NECESSARY, INCLUDING THE USE OF ARMED FORCE, TO MAINTAIN THE SECURITY OF THE NORTH ATLANTIC AREA. ALSO PROMISE TO DEVELOP BY MUTUAL AID THEIR INDIVIDUAL AND COLLECTIVE CAPACITY TO RESIST ARMED ATTACK.

4
ANZUS TREATY

SIGNATORIES RECOGNIZE THAT ARMED ATTACK ON ANY ONE OF THEM IN THE PACIFIC AREA WOULD IMPERIL THE SECURITY OF EACH AND DECLARE THEY WILL ACT TO MEET THE COMMON DANGER IN ACCORDANCE WITH THEIR CONSTITUTIONAL PROCESSES. ALSO PROMISE TO DEVELOP BY MUTUAL AID THEIR INDIVIDUAL AND COLLECTIVE CAPACITY TO RESIST ARMED ATTACK.

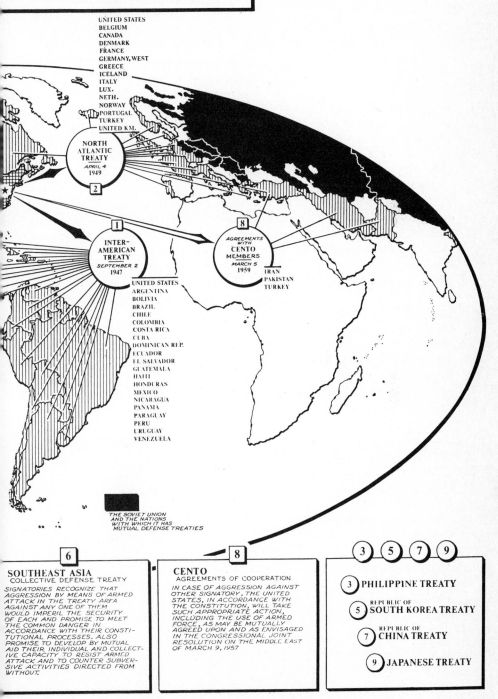

RANGEMENTS, 1961

UNITED STATES
BELGIUM
CANADA
DENMARK
FRANCE
GERMANY, WEST
GREECE
ICELAND
ITALY
LUX.
NETH.
NORWAY
PORTUGAL
TURKEY
UNITED KM.

NORTH ATLANTIC TREATY
APRIL 4
1949

2

1 **INTER-AMERICAN TREATY**
SEPTEMBER 2
1947

8 AGREEMENTS WITH **CENTO MEMBERS**
MARCH 5
1959
IRAN
PAKISTAN
TURKEY

UNITED STATES
ARGENTINA
BOLIVIA
BRAZIL
CHILE
COLOMBIA
COSTA RICA
CUBA
DOMINICAN REP.
ECUADOR
EL SALVADOR
GUATEMALA
HAITI
HONDURAS
MEXICO
NICARAGUA
PANAMA
PARAGUAY
PERU
URUGUAY
VENEZUELA

THE SOVIET UNION AND THE NATIONS WITH WHICH IT HAS MUTUAL DEFENSE TREATIES

6
SOUTHEAST ASIA
COLLECTIVE DEFENSE TREATY
SIGNATORIES RECOGNIZE THAT AGGRESSION BY MEANS OF ARMED ATTACK IN THE TREATY AREA AGAINST ANY ONE OF THEM WOULD IMPERIL THE SECURITY OF EACH AND PROMISE TO MEET THE COMMON DANGER IN ACCORDANCE WITH THEIR CONSTITUTIONAL PROCESSES. ALSO PROMISE TO DEVELOP BY MUTUAL AID THEIR INDIVIDUAL AND COLLECTIVE CAPACITY TO RESIST ARMED ATTACK AND TO COUNTER SUBVERSIVE ACTIVITIES DIRECTED FROM WITHOUT.

8
CENTO
AGREEMENTS OF COOPERATION
IN CASE OF AGGRESSION AGAINST OTHER SIGNATORY, THE UNITED STATES, IN ACCORDANCE WITH THE CONSTITUTION, WILL TAKE SUCH APPROPRIATE ACTION, INCLUDING THE USE OF ARMED FORCE, AS MAY BE MUTUALLY AGREED UPON AND AS ENVISAGED IN THE CONGRESSIONAL JOINT RESOLUTION ON THE MIDDLE EAST OF MARCH 9, 1957

3 5 7 9

3 **PHILIPPINE TREATY**

5 REPUBLIC OF **SOUTH KOREA TREATY**

7 REPUBLIC OF **CHINA TREATY**

9 **JAPANESE TREATY**

crease the size and strength of defensive-shield forces had been adopted in February 1952, only to prove unworkable within a few months and slide steadily further out of reach.

A primary reason was economic. Both western Europe and the United States were prospering, and the peoples involved had little taste for high taxes, austerity, and sacrifice in peacetime. The Eisenhower administration's economy drive in military spending had its counterpart in every NATO capital. As the threat of general war receded after the Korean armistice, each ally scaled down its rearmament program in response to popular demand. While drainage of this sort became chronic, the expected transfusions from Germany were slow to arrive; rearmament was no more popular there than elsewhere. As late as 1959 only seven of the projected twelve divisions were ready, and NATO never achieved the thirty-division strength described by its commanders in 1958 as a necessary minimum.

Diplomatic solidarity, in the face of changing circumstances and a new international climate, likewise weakened steadily after 1955. Economic recovery instilled new confidence in European leaders and lessened European dependence upon the United States. Prosperity alleviated popular discontent and stabilized national politics to the point where local Communist parties, though still a potent force in states like Italy and France, no longer threatened any European government with paralysis, civil war, or takeover. And changes in Russian foreign policy after Stalin's death dissipated the fear of war. Responsible European statesmen did not necessarily accept Soviet talk of peaceful coexistence and disarmament at face value, but they felt that Western policy needed overhauling in order to respond effectively. Unfortunately, they could agree upon the need for a new departure but not upon a specific policy. Western unity eroded as Russian leaders, redoubling their efforts, warned that Europe would suffer most in a future war, stressed disarmament formulas that would eliminate American bases on the continent, and proposed a new all-European security pact led by Russia and excluding the United States.

European dissatisfaction with American policies and leadership became more outspoken. The United States seemed too rigid in its approach to Russia, unreasonable in its refusal to recognize Peking, obsessed with internal security and military preparedness, and intolerant of its allies' needs and problems. Liberal opinion disapproved of America's close military ties with the Fascist regime of Generalissimo Francisco Franco in Spain.[7] Americans in turn sometimes felt that Europeans were "soft" on communism (or at least not sufficiently alarmed by it), prone to appease the Soviets, and unwilling to assume a fairer share of the Western defense effort. European trade with China vexed the United States.

[7]The United States and Spain concluded agreements in 1953 whereby the former provided economic and military aid to the Franco government in return for the right to build and maintain air and naval bases in Spain.

Other quarrels also took their toll. Distrust of a resurgent Germany remained strong even after the Federal Republic joined NATO in 1955. Sporadic manifestations of neo-Nazi sentiment, West Germany's growing military and economic power, the chance that it would embrace neutralism or seek accord with Moscow in order to reunite with East Germany, and its desire to adopt tactical atomic weapons all added to European apprehensions.

The Soviet government naturally tried to exploit these fears. When its attempt to prevent German rearmament failed, it created a regional grouping of its own—the Warsaw Pact of May 1955, binding Albania, Bulgaria, Czechoslovakia, East Germany, Hungary, Poland, and Rumania to the USSR in close military alliance. Still hopeful of driving a wedge between America and western Europe, the Soviets later renewed their proposal to form a Continental security system by excluding the United States from a merger of the NATO and Warsaw Pact countries.

They also sought to woo the Federal Republic. Reunification was the Soviet trump card, and all Western efforts to reach agreements with Moscow on this important issue ended in failure. From the very beginning, the Eisenhower administration had sought to rearm the Federal Republic within NATO and unify the two Germanys through free elections. These were not easily reconcilable goals, and achievement of the former made the latter more remote than ever. The Western allies had urged reunification upon Russia at the Berlin conference in 1954 without success. They tried again at Geneva in 1955 and did obtain Bulganin's agreement that free elections should be the basis for future settlement. But Soviet intransigence had not abated. Russia first insisted that the two Germanys negotiate directly, in order to guarantee East Germany a voice in any united government thus formed. Next came a plan suggested by Polish Foreign Minister Adam Rapacki in October 1957. It called for the military disengagement of central Europe by banning nuclear weapons in both Germanys, Poland, and Czechoslovakia. Another Soviet proposal, in 1959, demanded withdrawal of all foreign troops from German soil, restricted German armaments, and forbade a reunited Germany to join any alliance that did not include the Western Big Three and the USSR.

Another serious challenge to Western unity was colonialism, shattering beneath the hammer blows of nationalist and independence movements in Asia and Africa. Whether by war and revolution or patient negotiation— or both—most of the colonies and protectorates in the once extensive empires of Great Britain, France, and the Netherlands either won independence or advanced to its threshold between 1945 and 1962. By the latter date only Portugal, oldest of the imperial powers, still clung tenaciously to most of its overseas possessions. All in all, some thirty-five new countries, with a total population of over 600 million, emerged from colonial status during the postwar years.

It was a difficult transition. For European powers, the economic and psychological readjustments were enormous. Public opinion elsewhere opposed even the vestiges of colonialism. Newly freed nations clamored incessantly, while the Communist bloc quickly took up the anti-imperialist cry and posed as champions of self-determination. NATO suffered both because it included all the major imperial powers and because Americans were highly critical of colonialism. The United States, seeking to combat the rising anti-Western sentiment that European imperialism had fostered, was not always patient in urging decolonization upon its allies—who often felt that Washington failed to appreciate the complexity of their problems and was oversensitive to the frequently unreasonable demands of the anti-colonial nations. This tension laid foundations for a rupture that almost destroyed NATO in late 1956.

Meanwhile, the solidarity of the eastern European bloc was also crumbling. The first break had occurred in 1948, when the Yugoslav leader, Marshal Tito, defied Stalin and embarked upon independent foreign and domestic policies. He adhered to a policy of noncommitment, although intense Russian hostility during Stalin's final years nearly drove Yugoslavia into the Western camp. Encouraged, the American government provided economic and military aid during the 1950s and pursued a policy of restrained friendship toward this unaligned Communist state. After Stalin's death, Soviet leaders abandoned all hostility toward Yugoslavia and attempted to effect a reconciliation. Tito welcomed better relations with Moscow but hewed steadfastly to his policies of neutrality and independence.

Soviet control in eastern Europe eased somewhat after 1953. The satellite nations, emboldened by this new leeway and encouraged by Tito's example, stirred restlessly. Their peoples dreamed variously of greater independence, improved economic conditions, and possibly even freedom from communism. The Kremlin's partial repudiation of Stalinism in early 1956 raised such hopes; Tito's visit to Russia in June, where he won Soviet approval of a joint declaration that every country should be permitted to choose its own road to socialism without interference, raised them even more.

Pent-up economic and political discontent burst forth that summer and fall. Unorganized riots by workers demanding "bread and freedom" broke out in the Polish industrial city of Poznań in late June, and demands for an end to Soviet control over Polish affairs reached revolutionary proportions by October. With strong public support, a major element within the Polish Communist party moved to end Soviet domination by elevating Wladyslaw Gomulka, who had once been jailed in a Stalinist purge, to the important post of first secretary. Soviet leaders hastened to Warsaw to face down this challenge, backed by Soviet troops moving into Poland from Russia and East Germany. Minor clashes between Polish and Russian military units seemed to presage an imminent full-scale war. But tense discussions resulted in a victory for Polish nationalism. The Soviets backed down on October 20, withdrawing their troops and acquiescing in Gomulka's installation as first secretary and head of state. He won enough concessions from Moscow to launch Poland on a "national Communist" policy along Titoist lines.

Nationalist dissent immediately erupted in Hungary, beginning with a revolt in Budapest on October 23–24. It led to bloodshed and intervention by Soviet military forces, then proceeded to get out of hand. The Hungarians lacked a leader of Gomulka's stature and ability, and what had begun as another Titoist bid for national Communist autonomy soon broadened into a sweeping, ill-organized movement to overthrow Communist rule altogether. The Hungarian regime replaced unpopular leaders with moderates who made concession after concession to the rebels—now backed by an almost nationwide general strike—and virtually dismantled the Communist edifice. In what sounded like a major retreat, Moscow announced on October 30 that it would withdraw all Soviet troops at Hungary's request and reexamine its policy of military and economic influence in the affairs of fellow-Communist states.

President Eisenhower hailed these developments as "the dawning of a new day" in eastern Europe. But the situation quickly passed from bright hope to darkest tragedy. The Hungarians sealed their own fate by asking for more than Russia could possibly grant. While anti-Soviet strikes and demonstrations continued, Budapest informed the Soviet ambassador on November 1 that Hungary was about to renounce the Warsaw Pact, declare its neutrality, and appeal to the United Nations for support. This bold attempt to withdraw entirely from the Communist bloc was met by the prompt dispatch of Soviet divisions to Budapest and bloody suppression. In less than a week the movement had been crushed and a new puppet government installed. The West was horrified, but it could not intervene without risking a third world war. Appeals and condemnation from the UN and expressions of sympathy and relief appropriations from the United States were no more effective than the poorly armed Hungarian rebels in fending off Russian tanks.

Tragedy in Hungary coincided with an Anglo-French-Israeli invasion of Egypt in early November 1956 (see pp. 804–806). Events leading to the Suez crisis revealed a basic Western disagreement on the colonial question, and the crisis itself transformed this disparity into a split that almost wrecked the Atlantic alliance. The United States not only refused to back its allies in their assault on Egypt but joined the Soviet Union and most other countries in condemning it. Although suspicion and animosity within the Western camp lingered for months, Soviet bellicosity had effectively dramatized the need for unity, and allied statesmen worked patiently to heal the breach.

They had no sooner restored reasonably harmonious relations when the dawning of the missile age in 1957 provided a new basis for discord. The

United States proposed to strengthen Western defenses by equipping its NATO contingents with tactical atomic weapons and installing IRBM bases on the territory of its European allies. Control over nuclear warheads for these weapons would remain in American hands. This policy, together with the appearance of Soviet ICBMs and threats of instant retaliation against any country that permitted the launching of nuclear missiles from its soil, raised twin fears in the minds of European statesmen. Could they rely upon an American nuclear response to a Soviet invasion of Europe now that Russian rockets threatened American cities? And did they dare permit deployment of American atomic arms and missile bases on the continent without some voice in the decision to use them?

Europeans grew increasingly restive under America's nuclear preponderance. Seeking to escape it, the British developed their own nuclear capability.[8] France, determined to follow suit, conducted successful atomic explosions in the Sahara desert in 1960, despite objections from allied and neutral countries. Yet neither Britain nor France, much less other Western allies, could develop an adequate nuclear arsenal in the near future unless the United States shared closely guarded scientific information and fissionable materials. If these were not forthcoming, European countries wanted at least a measure of control over any decision to use American nuclear weapons on their territories.

For a time, Americans wanted to retain their nuclear monopoly almost as badly as Europeans wanted to break it. But the need to mend fences after Suez demanded concessions. The United States agreed in 1957 to a larger measure of collaboration with Great Britain in missile and atomic research and began providing its allies with more nuclear information after Congress amended the Atomic Energy Act in 1958. European NATO contingents received training in the use of American tactical atomic weapons and rockets, and the United States built large stockpiles of nuclear warheads in Europe, to be available to the shield forces in the event of war.[9] In return, Great Britain agreed in 1958 to permit establishment of Thor IRBM squadrons on British soil.[10] Italy and Turkey concluded missile-base agreements with the United States a year later.

But real accord on this touchy question had not been achieved. No other NATO ally was willing to allow American missile bases on its soil, and the United States retained full control over nuclear warheads for the

[8] With the perfection of a hydrogen bomb in 1957, Britain followed America's example and overhauled her defensive strategy with emphasis upon nuclear striking power and reductions in conventional armament.

[9] Even the new German forces, despite objections from the allies and Soviets alike, demanded and began to receive instruction in the use of tactical weapons. The United States retained control over the decision actually to provide the Federal Republic and other nations with full use of these weapons.

[10] The British also agreed in 1960 to let Polaris submarines operate from a base in Scotland.

missiles and tactical weapons it deployed in Europe. French President Charles de Gaulle, who came to power in 1958, voiced dissatisfaction with NATO and proposed creation of a three-power *directoire* (France, Britain, and the United States) to direct alliance policy. When this plan was rebuffed, de Gaulle refused to place French units at the complete disposal of the supreme commander and became generally uncooperative. NATO's strategic adjustment to the nuclear age and cohesiveness as an effective supranational force were far from complete by 1960.

Meanwhile, the city of Berlin had once again sparked a crisis that threatened to lead to war. Still under four-power control, the city was divided in two by a line running irregularly north and south along city streets. On one side was East Berlin, Soviet sector since 1945 and capital of East Germany since 1949. Its 1.2 million inhabitants lived drably amid a few well-lit modern avenues and vast dismal neighborhoods that still carried the scars of war. Across the street lay West Berlin, embracing the three Western sectors, a prosperous beehive of 2.2 million energetic inhabitants.

West Berlin was both affront and menace to the Communist system. It afforded an escape route for the thousands of East Germans who deserted the unpopular puppet state each year, and its very existence kept discontent alive among those who remained. It contributed substantially to East Germany's economic problems, and the Soviets viewed this situation with understandable nervousness. They had had to quell one East German uprising in 1953. Since then they had experienced major difficulties in Poland and Hungary. Chronic unrest in the German Democratic Republic remained strong.

One further development set the stage for crisis. In 1955 the Russians transferred to East Germany the power to supervise civilian traffic and freight on the surface arteries that linked West Berlin to the Federal Republic. Russian troops continued to inspect military traffic supplying the allied garrisons, but after 1955 East Germany possessed the ability to harass, delay, or block the flow of civilian goods upon which West Berlin's prosperity depended. The Western powers, which had never recognized the East German regime, warned that they would continue to hold Russia accountable for any disruption of the Berlin traffic or any infringement of their right of access.

Three years passed without major incident. Then Khrushchev announced in November 1958 that four-power occupation of Berlin was out of date and should be terminated. Russia, he said, would shortly hand over its functions in the city to the East German government. If they did not follow suit, the Western allies would henceforth have to deal directly with East Germany. Russia would meet forcible resistance to this new arrangement with force. The allies promptly reiterated their right to remain until a peace treaty with a reunited Germany had been concluded. They also renewed their promise to protect West Berlin. Khrushchev replied on

November 27 that Russia no longer recognized any Western right of access or presence. Continued occupation, he said, was a threat to the security of East Germany, the Soviet Union, and the entire Communist bloc. As an alternative to absorbing all of Berlin into East Germany, he offered to make West Berlin a disarmed and neutralized "free city." But a satisfactory adjustment was imperative, and Russia would sign a separate peace treaty with East Germany in six months if no such adjustment were made. The treaty would transfer to the East German government all controls then exercised by the Red Army in and about Berlin. Thereafter a showdown over access or occupation rights would confront the allies with the unpalatable choices of abandoning West Berlin, recognizing East Germany, or war.

The West met this challenge firmly. The British, French, and American governments made it clear that they did not recognize Russia's right to act unilaterally in altering the four-power occupation, that they would not abandon West Berlin, and that negotiation was possible only in connection with the entire German question and in the absence of an ultimatum. Tension eased in 1959 after visits by Deputy Premier Mikoyan to the United States and Prime Minister Macmillan to Moscow, and Khrushchev's six-month deadline expired without incident.

No progress, however, could be made toward a settlement. Negotiations at the Geneva conference of foreign ministers in mid-1959 ended in the usual impasse. Package offers that included minor concessions never reconciled Russian insistence upon allied withdrawal and allied determination to stay until the entire German problem was settled. Khrushchev wanted to discuss Berlin at the summit. He also wanted to visit the United States and talk informally with President Eisenhower, and Russian demands were toned down somewhat. In his talks with the president at Camp David in September the Soviet premier agreed that no new time limit should be imposed upon a solution to the Berlin problem, thus removing the ultimatum that had barred a path to the summit. Yet neither side altered its position before the ill-fated Paris summit meeting of May 1960.

The Soviet premier, having despaired of winning concessions from Eisenhower, laid the groundwork for pressure upon his successor by announcing that Russia would not sign a separate peace treaty with East Germany until after the American presidential election. As this event drew nearer, Khrushchev set April 1961 as a new deadline for settlement of the Berlin question. Since Russia would accept no settlement that did not include withdrawal of allied troops, it was clear that another test of Western firmness had been prepared. The fear grew stronger that both sides, while not wanting war over Berlin, had assumed irreconcilable positions from which neither dared to retreat.

If hardening attitudes on Berlin gave cause for concern, the early success of the Common Market cast a bright ray of hope across the European scene. Ever since the inception of the six-nation Coal and Steel Community in 1951 (see p. 700, n. 18), statesmen had been laying plans to broaden the area of economic unity. New impetus stemmed from European resentment against both superpowers in the aftermath of Suez and Hungary. As French Premier Guy Mollet put it: "Between an America which is now too impulsive and now too slow to understand perils and a Soviet Union which is disquieting and sometimes still menacing, how often have we wished for a united Europe acting as a world force, not neutral, but independent."[11]

Plans for economic integration went quickly forward, and the six nations in the Coal and Steel Community signed a treaty in Rome in March 1957 creating the European Economic Community. It called for free movement of labor and capital and gradual abolition of all internal tariff barriers and trade restrictions within the six-nation area; eventual adoption of a uniform external tariff; and direction by a network of supranational executive, legislative, judicial, and advisory bodies. The agreement was purposely designed to provide a framework for eventual political union. A companion treaty formed the European Atomic Community, or Euratom, to conduct joint development of atomic power for economic purposes. Both treaties went into force in January 1958.

The first 10 percent reduction in internal tariffs and quota restrictions took place in January 1959, the second a year later. More important, the ability of the supranational governing bodies to prepare long-range programs, resolve complex technical questions, and harmonize conflicting policies gave evidence that this experiment in unity had the power to survive and grow. Economies of member nations flourished spectacularly under the integrated system. A powerful new aggregation with human and industrial resources on a par with those of the United States and the Soviet Union was emerging in Europe.

The new arrangement inevitably posed problems for the West as a whole. Plans to link the Common Market with a broader trade area were temporarily stalled when Great Britain, Sweden, Norway, Denmark, Switzerland, Austria, and Portugal formed the European Free Trade Association in 1959—the so-called Outer Seven, as distinguished from the Common Market's Inner Six—in a somewhat looser agreement. Differences in policy between the two groups threatened to become a trade war in 1960, as the Common Market effected its second internal tariff reduction and the Outer Seven their first. American concern that its exports to Europe would be adversely affected led the administration to warn against exclusive policies that might damage world trade and place other nations at an unfair disadvantage.

[11]Quoted in Richard P. Stebbins et al., *The United States in World Affairs, 1957* (New York, 1958), p. 104.

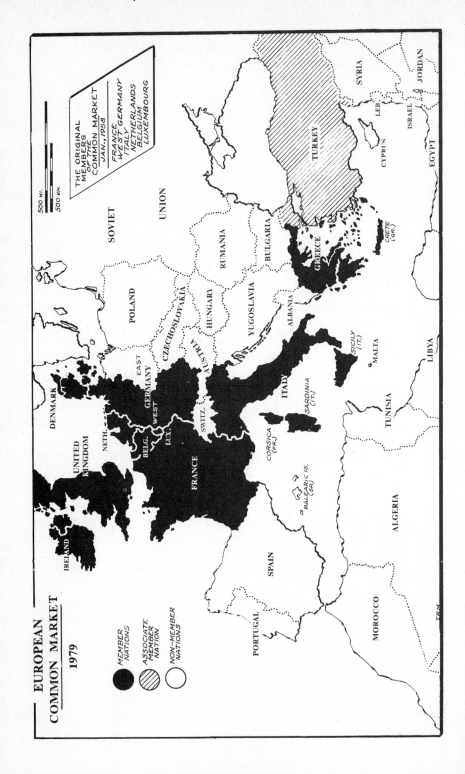

EUROPEAN
COMMON MARKET
1979

MEMBER
NATIONS

ASSOCIATE
MEMBER
NATION

NON-MEMBER
NATIONS

THE ORIGINAL
MEMBERS
OF THE
COMMON MARKET
JAN., 1958

FRANCE
WEST GERMANY
ITALY
NETHERLANDS
BELGIUM
LUXEMBOURG

500 MI.
500 KM.

SOVIET

UNION

TURKEY

SYRIA

JORDAN

LEB.

CYPRUS

ISRAEL

EGYPT

RUMANIA

BULGARIA

GREECE

CRETE
(GR.)

POLAND

CZECHOSLOVAKIA

HUNGARY

YUGOSLAVIA

ALBANIA

AUSTRIA

DENMARK

EAST
GERMANY

WEST
GERMANY

NETH.

BELG.

LUX.

SWITZ.

FRANCE

ITALY

SICILY
(IT.)

MALTA

SARDINIA
(IT.)

CORSICA
(FR.)

BALEARIC IS.
(SP.)

UNITED
KINGDOM

IRELAND

SPAIN

PORTUGAL

MOROCCO

ALGERIA

TUNISIA

LIBYA

T.R.M.

The Common Market's economic success and political promise soon showed signs of overcoming most of these troubles. The British government, which had been loath to associate with the Inner Six for fear of endangering its important ties with the Commonwealth nations, reversed a historic policy and made a bid for membership in 1961. In the United States, respect for the Common Market led to adoption in 1962 of one of the most liberal and far-reaching trade bills in American history (see p. 827). And the Soviets, in a not unfamiliar pattern, revealed their respect for this capitalist device by first denouncing it and then copying it. The Soviet bloc's Council for Mutual Economic Assistance, or Comecon, began duplicating Common Market institutions and procedures in wholesale fashion in 1962. This was the sincerest form of flattery, confirming a general conviction that the European Economic Community marked a historic turning point.

5. *Recurrent Troubles in the Far East*

Termination of the Korean War in 1953 brought neither peace nor stability to the troubled Orient. Antagonism between China and the United States grew apace. Because China's emergence as a great power under Communist auspices was an ironic perversion of long-standing American hopes, and because the United States felt responsible for what had happened there, Americans tended to view all matters pertaining to China after 1949 with frustration and resentment. The government of Mao Tse-tung, in turn, demonstrated hostility toward the West from the very outset. It intervened in Korea and assisted Indochinese rebels in their struggle against France. It defied the United Nations, mistreated prisoners of war, and showed a cynical disregard for international law and human rights. It confiscated American property, imprisoned American citizens, conducted a barrage of virulent anti-American propaganda, and accused the United States of aggression and use of germ warfare. It proclaimed its intention to "liberate" Taiwan and the smaller offshore islands held by Chiang Kai-shek's Nationalist government. And after July 1953 it repeatedly violated the terms of the Korean armistice.

For these reasons, both the Truman and Eisenhower administrations pursued a policy of rigid opposition to the Chinese People's Republic. Although this course did not lack critics at home or abroad, the prevailing mood in America and the hostility emanating from Peking left little alternative. The United States continued to withhold recognition and used all its influence to block admission of the People's Republic to the United Nations. Save for Secretary Dulles's grudging confrontation with Premier Chou En-lai at Geneva in 1954, Washington kept its diplomatic contacts with Peking on an indirect and subordinate level.[12] It refused to trade with China and tried to persuade its allies to maintain the broad embargo on strategic materials recommended by the UN in May 1951.

Washington adhered to this policy even though many allies abandoned it. Great Britain and most other Western states sooner or later accorded recognition and accepted Peking's sovereignty as an accomplished fact. The majority mustered by the United States against admitting China to the UN dwindled each year in the General Assembly. Britain acted unilaterally to ease the embargo on strategic materials in 1957. A year later Japan and most NATO countries agreed upon a reduction in the number of strategic items that could not be sold to the Communist bloc.

The Eisenhower administration also gave firm support to the Chiang Kai-shek Nationalist government. Though Chiang had been confined since 1949 to Taiwan and smaller islands off the Chinese coast, the United States continued to recognize his regime as the legitimate government of all of China and upheld Chiang's envoy in the UN as the proper occupant of China's permanent seat on the Security Council. American arms and equipment bolstered Nationalist military strength.

This much was a continuation of Truman's policy, but the Republicans, mindful of their promise to end alleged neglect of the Far East, attempted to do more. First, they encouraged the belief that a Nationalist reconquest of the mainland was imminent. President Eisenhower announced in February 1953 that the United States Seventh Fleet would no longer be used to "shield" China from a possible Nationalist offensive. Second, Secretary Dulles moved to bring Taiwan more formally within the Western defensive perimeter by negotiating a mutual defense pact with the Nationalist government in December 1954.

By this time, however, the administration had ceased to look for an alternative to containment in the Far East. Abandoning even the pretense of a possible Nationalist invasion of mainland China, Washington took pains to insure—by official correspondence and by senatorial reservations to the mutual security treaty—that Chiang would undertake no major offensive operations against Peking without American consent. In the treaty, Taiwan and the adjacent Pescadores were specifically named as the Nationalist territory that would be jointly defended against armed attack. Other Nationalist-held islands—notably Quemoy and Matsu, within actual sight and artillery range of the Chinese coast—were not mentioned.

The importance of a strengthened containment policy in the Orient was brought home by the final stages of the Indochinese war in 1954. France, reluctant to grant full independence to the new Indochinese states of Laos, Vietnam, and Cambodia, had been struggling vainly since 1947 to put down local nationalist movements in her Asiatic colony. The strongest of these movements, the Vietminh, was centered in the coastal state of

---

[12]During attempts to negotiate a cease-fire in Formosa Strait in 1958, for example, the United States talked with China in Warsaw through the two ambassadors to Poland.

Vietnam. Increasingly dominated by a well-disciplined Communist element, assisted by arms and equipment from Peking, the Vietminh employed effective guerrilla tactics and successfully resisted a growing French military effort to crush the uprising.

The Truman administration, seeing a connection between the struggles in Korea and Indochina, had provided increasing military aid to the French forces. Eisenhower continued this policy, and by 1953 the United States was bearing nearly half the cost of France's Indochinese campaign. Fearful that a truce in Korea would enable China to divert troops to aid the Vietminh, Dulles warned in September that Chinese aggression in Southeast Asia would have "grave consequences which might not be confined to Indochina." But Mao Tse-tung did not need to intervene directly. Despite American aid and the commitment of some of France's best troops, an all-out French drive to suppress the rebellion made no progress, and the war dragged on. It became obvious that France could not win without full-scale American participation.

Public opinion in the United States was highly averse to such a step, which promised to mire American soldiers in an even more remote and costly Korea, but the Eisenhower administration moved to the brink of military action in Indochina. Prospect of French defeat loomed in early 1954 when the Vietminh surrounded and besieged some of France's finest troops in the fortress of Dienbienphu in northern Vietnam. Washington learned on March 20 that only a heavy air attack against Vietminh supply lines and siege forces could avert a French surrender. Dulles and Admiral Radford sought a congressional resolution authorizing an American carrier-based air strike to aid Dienbienphu.

In this venture the government lacked support at home or abroad. A bipartisan group of congressmen, upon learning that the other Joint Chiefs opposed Radford's views and that the British had not been consulted, advised strongly against sending such a request to Congress. Consultations between Dulles and British Prime Minister Eden failed to produce agreement on Dulles's proposal to form an immediate military coalition in Southeast Asia along NATO lines. Mutual distrust between the two allies grew when Dulles then tried to go ahead with this project against Eden's express wishes. It grew still further when Dulles suddenly proposed dispatch of a token Anglo-American military force to Indochina. The British government wanted no part of an operation that seemed to risk a third world war.

The possibility of American intervention ended when the Dienbienphu garrison surrendered in May 1954, and the foreign ministers' conference then sitting in Geneva soon managed to end the Indochinese war. Eisenhower had warned that Communist victory there might topple other Asian governments like a row of dominoes, but the growing supremacy of the Vietminh in most of Vietnam and French determination to come to terms after Dienbienphu precluded any chance of continuing the struggle.

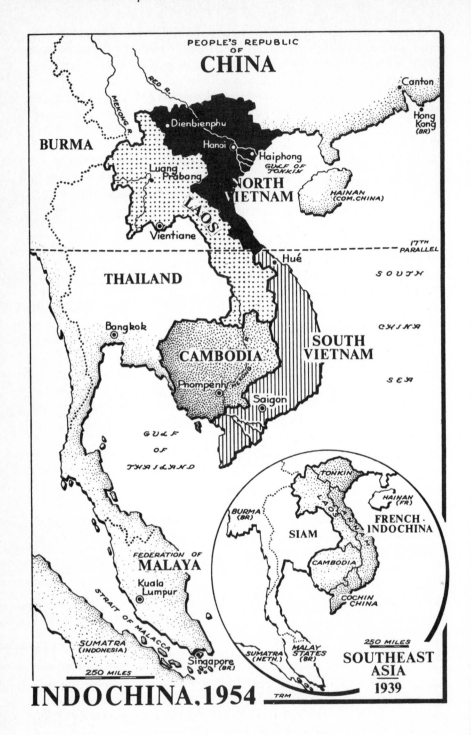

INDOCHINA, 1954

The armistice of July 1954 duly recognized Communist military successes in Indochina. Vietnam was divided at the seventeenth parallel between Vietminh Communists led by President Ho Chi Minh, in control of the northern Democratic Republic, and the Western-backed regime of President Ngo Dinh Diem in South Vietnam.[13] An international truce commission directed cease-fire arrangements. All the Indochinese states became fully independent. Laos and Cambodia were in effect neutralized by agreeing not to join regional alliances or allow foreign bases on their soil. Parties to the Geneva agreement, which included China but not the United States, promised to respect the independence and territorial integrity of the Indochinese states. The settlement was generally unsatisfactory to the American government. Dulles acquiesced in it because he had no choice, but he avoided endorsing it and announced that the United States would resist future Communist attempts to overrun Southeast Asia.

Anxious to forestall this possibility, Dulles strove to erect a regional defense system. The result was a treaty, signed in Manila in September 1954 and soon transformed into the Southeast Asia Treaty Organization, or SEATO. It included the United States, Great Britain, France, Australia, New Zealand, the Philippines, Thailand, and Pakistan. Each signatory agreed that its own safety would be endangered by an armed attack upon any other member within the carefully defined treaty area, or upon any additional state or territory in that area which the members, acting unanimously, might later designate. The signatories promised to consult in the event of threatened subversion and act together in accordance with their respective constitutional processes. The pact also called for economic cooperation and strengthening of free institutions and military defenses. A declaration endorsing equal rights and self-determination, designed to remove any colonialist taint, was signed in conjunction with the treaty. A SEATO Council with headquarters at Bangkok was charged with the tasks of promoting social and economic welfare and preventing invasion and subversion.

Dulles hailed this as the capstone of an already elaborate Pacific defense system. SEATO, however, was full of weaknesses. It possessed no military forces of its own and no centralized command system. More than half of its members were far removed from the actual treaty area, and no two of those within it were geographically contiguous. Strategically, the region posed enormous defensive problems, especially for the United States, upon whom the main burden of defense would fall. The alliance was crippled by the absence of India, Burma, and Indonesia, whose governments believed neutralism a safer course than military alignment with the West.

[13]The armistice called for internationally supervised elections in 1956 to determine the reunification of Vietnam. When the time came, however, the United States supported President Diem of South Vietnam in refusing to join in the procedure despite prodding from North Vietnam. It was too apparent, both to Diem and the American government, that the Communists would win nationwide elections. Thus Vietnam, like Germany and Korea, remained divided with few prospects of peaceful reunification.

The Indochinese armistice had scarcely been concluded before a new threat to peace loomed in Formosa Strait. Peking talked menacingly of an early liberation of Taiwan, and President Eisenhower countered with the blunt statement that an invasion from the mainland "would have to run over the Seventh Fleet." Peking tested American intentions in September 1954 by opening a bombardment of Quemoy and Matsu. Washington postponed decision to defend these islands until the extent of the assault could be determined. The bilateral security treaty with Nationalist China in December committed the United States to the defense of Taiwan but deliberately omitted specific mention of the offshore islands. Probing still further, Communist forces in January 1955 captured one of the Tachen Islands, northernmost group of the offshore chain. The president, concluding that defense of Taiwan did not depend upon the Tachens, ordered the Seventh Fleet to cover the evacuation of the Nationalist troops stationed there. At the same time, he warned Peking that attacks on the other offshore islands might encounter American resistance. To make the country's position clear, he asked Congress for a resolution authorizing him to use armed force to defend not only Taiwan and the nearby Pescadores, already covered by treaty, but also certain unidentified "closely related localities." Congress granted this discretionary authority on January 28 by huge majorities, stipulating that the resolution would remain in effect until the president deemed it no longer necessary.

Intermittent bombardment of Quemoy and Matsu continued for another three months, but Peking did not expand its military action, and Washington carefully dissociated itself from Chiang's warlike flourishes. The crisis tapered off, then subsided completely in April when Chou En-lai offered to negotiate for a relaxation of tensions. The bombardment ceased, and Americans temporarily forgot about Quemoy and Matsu.

More than three years of relative calm followed. But no solution of underlying problems in the Far East had been reached, and, with a few exceptions, the Western position continued to deteriorate. Communist troop build-ups and subversive activity remained constant along uneasy armistice lines in Korea and Vietnam. China's economic strength, industrial progress, prestige, and diplomatic influence increased steadily.[14] As the shadow of the Chinese giant grew longer, neutralist sentiment increased in most other Asian countries; Washington tended to aggravate this problem by reacting to neutralism with ill-disguised impatience.

There were a few bright spots. Though its neutralist posture frequently annoyed Western diplomats, the Indian government under Prime Minister Nehru strove to make progress under a form of guided democracy, and

[14]This was shown in the prominent role played by Premier Chou En-lai at the Bandung Conference in April 1955, when representatives of twenty-nine Asian and African states assembled in the Indonesian city to issue an anticolonialist manifesto and demand freedom for all remaining colonies. Chou En-lai successfully cast the People's Republic in the role of anticolonial leader and champion of emergent nations.

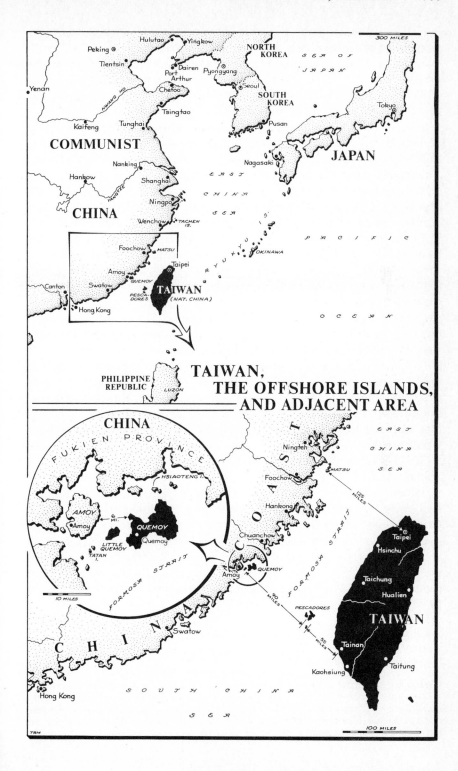

TAIWAN,
THE OFFSHORE ISLANDS,
AND ADJACENT AREA

lost all illusions about the peaceful intent of its huge neighbor when Peking laid claims to Indian territory in the Himalayas in 1959. Border clashes and tension resulting from these claims, together with China's repressive policy in Tibet, drew India closer to the West and contributed to a rift between China and the Soviet Union. Peking's sweeping attempt to communize Chinese agriculture proved a failure in the early 1960s, adversely affecting industrialization and forcing a lowering of economic and diplomatic sights. President Ramon Magsaysay of the Philippines managed to preserve representative institutions while stamping out an internal Communist movement. Communism also suffered a setback in Malaya, where the British were able to eradicate a large subversive element and lead this former colony to independence in 1957 under a stable native regime. Highly industrialized Japan, the West's vital bastion in the Orient, recorded economic gains and mounting prosperity. Despite Communist threats and cajolery, Japanese leaders kept the nation firmly within the Western orbit.[15]

Crisis returned to the Far East when China abruptly resumed bombardment of the offshore islands in August 1958. The American government responded firmly. It would be unwise to assume, Dulles warned, that an invasion of the islands could be a "limited operation." He added on September 4 that the congressional resolution of January 1955 might apply to Quemoy and Matsu. A huge naval and air striking force assembled in Formosa Strait, and American warships escorted Nationalist supply convoys from Taiwan to Quemoy. Tension mounted when Khrushchev promised Russian support to the People's Republic in any clash with the United States and called for an end to American intervention in what he said were China's internal affairs.

The possibility of war over Quemoy and Matsu set off an adverse public reaction in the United States and expressions of alarm from western Europe, and both sides showed signs of retreat. Dulles announced on September 30 that the American government had no commitment to defend Quemoy and Matsu. He spoke in favor of reducing Nationalist forces on the islands and added that a dependable cease-fire would make this possi-

---

[15]Japanese neutralist sentiment increased during the decade, claiming the allegiance of perhaps a third of the electorate by 1960, but communism made little headway. The USSR tried to exploit neutralist sentiment by a policy of friendship and cooperation, supporting Japan's bid to join the UN (which took place in 1956), and pointing out the disadvantages and dangers in Japan's alliance with the United States.

Washington soon agreed to revise the 1951 security treaty in Japan's favor. The new treaty, signed in January 1960, placed the Japanese on a more equal footing. Most important, it gave them a voice in the placing of American military units, including missile bases and reconnaissance planes, on Japanese soil. Premier Kishi, a leader of the pro-Western Liberal Democratic party, succeeded in the face of stiff neutralist opposition and domestic turmoil in obtaining approval of the new treaty by the Japanese Diet. Antitreaty demonstrations were so riotous that a projected visit by President Eisenhower in 1960 had to be cancelled. Order was soon restored, and elections that fall kept the Liberal Democrats in power under Kishi's successor, Hayato Ikeda, but the strong Socialist party continued to oppose the treaty and the Western alliance.

ble. At the same time, the Chinese seemed almost to welcome the chance to call off what had become a profitless venture. Peking first suspended the bombardment for three weeks in October, then proclaimed the bizarre policy of not shelling Quemoy on even-numbered days while reserving the right to do so on odd ones. It kept up an intermittent and desultory shelling for some months and then abandoned the effort.

Southeast Asia, meanwhile, returned to the spotlight. Domestic political conflict in the landlocked kingdom of Laos became an issue in the cold war, and the ordinary tranquility of life in this remote land was shattered by the cumbersome maneuvering of the great powers and their agents. Forbidden by the Geneva armistice to join regional alliances or solicit military aid from East or West, Laos was largely occupied in pacifying the Pathet Lao, its pro-Communist political faction, which received aid from North Vietnam. After years of effort, Prince Souvanna Phouma, neutralist premier, managed to bring Pathet Lao leaders into a unified national government in July 1958. Souvanna Phouma then resigned in favor of another middle-road premier, Phoui Sananikone, and the political situation in Laos worsened steadily. Neither the Communist bloc nor the United States had approved Souvanna Phouma's neutralist policy. With his departure both sides, in unabashed contravention of the Geneva armistice, maneuvered for advantage in the tiny kingdom. Communist pressure mounted during the Quemoy crisis. The United States countered with an expanding program of military and economic assistance. Thus strengthened, the new premier first excluded all Communist elements from his cabinet, then tried in early 1959 to subdue the Pathet Lao altogether. Fighting spread as guerrillas crossed into Laos from North Vietnam, and the royal government announced in July that the reinforced Pathet Lao was endangering the kingdom.

This internal struggle, temporarily quieted by a UN investigation in late 1959, gradually took on dimensions of an international crisis in 1960. A pro-Western general, Phoumi Nosavan, ousted Premier Sananikone in January and supported a new government which made certain that subsequent elections went against the Pathet Lao. Then an enterprising neutralist captain, Kong Le, engineered a coup in August which returned Souvanna Phouma to power. Souvanna argued that only a government of all factions—pro-American, neutralist, pro-Communist—could restore peace. The Eisenhower administration disagreed, and when neither diplomacy nor clumsy economic pressure dissuaded Souvanna Phouma from this coalition policy, Washington supported a counterrevolution recently launched by General Nosavan. Nosavan's army, after defeating Kong Le's forces in a battle near the capital, installed a pro-Western government under Prince Boun Oum in December 1960. Souvanna Phouma went into exile in Cambodia, while Kong Le and his followers joined the Pathet Lao.

The tide quickly turned against the new government. Laotian Communists controlled large segments of the kingdom by early 1961 and threatened the capital itself; they defeated Boun Oum's forces decisively whenever they met. With Boun Oum's collapse imminent, the Eisenhower administration sought the neutralist compromise it had earlier helped to defeat. But Souvanna Phouma, still in exile, blamed the impending disaster on Washington and refused to cooperate, while the resurgent Pathet Lao scented total victory and rejected all compromise proposals. Ngo Dinh Diem's government in neighboring South Vietnam was menaced by guerrilla bands. The row of dominoes to which Eisenhower had likened the fragile governments of Southeast Asia six years before seemed about to topple.

6. The Middle East and Africa

The spread of the cold war to the Middle East and sub-Saharan Africa during the 1950s raised new threats to world peace and drew the United States into areas it had hitherto relegated to secondary importance. Responsibility for protecting Western interests in the Middle East had largely been borne by Great Britain and France until midcentury, when postwar economic and political realities forced these nations to abandon or reduce imperial commitments. This disengagement soon encouraged Soviet penetration and prompted American activity in response.

The Middle East was made to order for Communist exploitation. It contained the world's richest known oil deposits, historic land and sea routes connecting three continents, and underdeveloped countries ruled by inexperienced, unstable, or reactionary regimes. It fairly seethed with resentments born of poverty, anticolonial bitterness, extremist agitation, clashing nationalist ambitions, and religious strife.

Specific ingredients in the incipient Middle Eastern crisis were Arab-Israeli antagonism, American attempts to erect a regional defensive system, inept Western diplomacy, and the ambitions of the new Egyptian strong man, Gamal Abdel Nasser. The mortal conflict between Arab and Jew, bitterest of postwar quarrels, stemmed from the irreconcilable determination of Israel to protect her hard-won independence and of Arab neighbors to destroy her. Boundaries between Israel and the encircling ring of hostile Arab nations had been set by an armistice that ended the Arab-Israeli war of 1948-1949, and the armistice lines were supervised by a UN truce team and upheld by an Anglo-American-French pledge of 1950. But neither armistice nor pledge brought peace to the troubled region. Israel became a virtual garrison state whose well-trained, well-equipped forces were an object of envy, alarm, and attempted duplication in Arab countries. Constant raids and terrorism by both sides flashed across the armistice lines. These episodes kept mutual hatred and suspicion at fever pitch, defied outside efforts to harmonize or soothe the quarrel, and continually threatened to touch off a second Arab-Israeli war.

Western diplomacy faced a well-nigh impossible task. It wanted to preserve peace and remain neutral in the Arab-Israeli impasse while courting Arab favor in erecting a Middle Eastern defensive system. Its efforts were hampered by touchy nationalist and anticolonial feelings in the area, directed primarily at Britain and France, and by Arab resentment over Western sponsorship of Israel in the late 1940s, directed primarily against the United States.

Secretary Acheson had hoped to forestall Soviet penetration by creating a Middle East Command along NATO lines, but his successor did not consider this project immediately realizable. Instead, Dulles sought Arab friendship by promoting settlement of an Anglo-Egyptian dispute over Britain's huge base at Suez. His efforts were crowned by a treaty in October 1954, whereby England gave up rights to the base and agreed to evacuate all armed forces from the canal zone within twenty months. Egypt agreed in return to keep the base in combat readiness and permit reentry of British forces in the event of attack by an outside power against Turkey or any Arab state. Abandonment of Suez weakened Western defenses, but Dulles and Eden hoped that Egypt under Nasser's new regime would cooperate in reducing Arab-Israeli tensions and building a collective defense system. American offers of economic and military aid to Egypt followed immediately upon conclusion of the Anglo-Egyptian treaty of 1954.

Nasser was loath to align himself with the West. He wanted arms, but mainly for use against Israel and not at the price of pledges demanded in return for American aid. He professed to see in this program a potential new form of Western imperialism, and he did not share American alarm about the menace of communism. Moreover, Nasser aspired to establish Egyptian primacy in the Arab world. He resented the rival aspirations of pro-Western Iraq and suspected that Iraq's interest in stronger Western ties was designed to bolster her bid for Arab leadership.

Events in 1955 embarked Nasser on the international high road to adventure and trouble. A major raid by Israeli armed units on the Egyptian territory of Gaza in February revealed the relative weakness of Nasser's military forces and whetted his desire for preparedness. At the same time, Dulles's efforts to create a regional defense system culminated in a defensive alliance—the Baghdad Pact—between Turkey and Iraq, soon expanded to include Great Britain, Pakistan, and Iran. This new alliance, which the United States encouraged and aided but did not join, seemed to close the ring of containment around the Communist perimeter.[16] But it also infuriated Nasser, worried the other Arab states, and evoked warnings from Russia.

[16]The Baghdad Pact was linked to NATO through Turkey and to SEATO through Pakistan, while Great Britain belonged to all three.

Nasser took advantage of Soviet resentment and concluded a big arms agreement with the Communist bloc in September 1955, exchanging Egyptian rice and cotton for Czechoslovakian tanks, planes, artillery, and other equipment. Arab nationalists in every country now turned to Nasser for leadership against Israel. Egypt concluded defensive alliances and military arrangements with Syria and Saudi Arabia in October. Israel, alarmed by this prospective enhancement of Arab military strength, began laying plans to strike while the advantage still lay in her favor. Armed clashes and raids across the tense armistice lines during 1955 were bloodier than any since 1949.

Nasser moved more boldly into the center of East-West rivalries in 1956 by seeking foreign loans for a high dam across the Nile at Aswan, eight hundred miles south of Cairo. It was an ambitious project, designed to increase Egypt's supply of arable land and stimulate industrial expansion. The British and American governments had already made a trial offer of some $200 million to underwrite initial construction, and the World Bank would advance another $200 million when preliminary work was completed. Nasser rejected the Anglo-American offer in January 1956, claiming that it threatened Egyptian independence, and hinted that better terms were available in Moscow.

By this time Nasser was also conducting an intensive anti-Western propaganda campaign, plotting against pro-Western governments in Iraq and Jordan, aiding Algerian rebels in their war against France, proclaiming the doom of Israel, and praising the USSR. Soviet and East German technicians abounded in Cairo. Communists exercised a strong and potentially decisive voice in the government of Syria. Though Nasser continued to proclaim his neutralism in the cold war, he had all but mortgaged Egypt's economy to the Communist bloc in exchange for arms, and Egypt seemed on the verge of becoming a new Soviet satellite.

When Dulles heard rumors in June 1956 of a $1 billion Russian loan to finance the Aswan Dam, he informed the Egyptian ambassador that the United States had decided not to participate in the project. Events quickly led to the most serious international crisis since Korea. Stung by Dulles's public rebuff, Nasser cast about for a new way to finance his cherished dam. He found it by nationalizing the Suez Canal Company in July. Its net annual profits of $30 million would provide money for the dam. Assuming adequate compensation to shareholders, which the Egyptian government readily promised, there was nothing illegal in Nasser's action. The canal lay in Egyptian territory, and the company that operated it held an Egyptian charter and was subject to Egyptian law. The company's concession, in any case, was due to expire and revert to Egypt in 1968.

What alarmed western Europe about Nasser's abrupt maneuver was the economic and strategic importance of the Suez Canal. It carried over 100 million tons of cargo a year, three-fifths of which was Middle Eastern oil bound for western Europe, and its traffic had become a mainstay of European prosperity, NATO security, and world trade. Nasser took pains to announce that in operating the canal Egypt would abide by the Constantinople Convention of 1888, which guaranteed all nations free navigation in peace and war.

Great Britain and France took no comfort from these assurances. Convention and UN protests notwithstanding, Nasser had barred Israeli shipping from the Suez for years. The British doubted that Egypt would operate the canal efficiently. The French had long resented Nasser's open support of the Algerian rebels. Both governments regarded this act as a blow to their prestige and a threat to their security, and they decided to tolerate neither. Prime Minister Eden cabled Eisenhower on July 27, 1956, that Britain was prepared to use force as a last resort if Egypt did not relinquish the canal.

More than two months of intricate, futile negotiations followed. Nasser refused to accept any scheme of outright international control of the canal, and Britain and France refused to accept any system that left unfettered control in Nasser's hands. Partial concessions from both sides seemed at last to place agreement within sight, but a compromise resolution containing guarantees acceptable to the European allies was killed by a Russian veto in the Security Council on October 13.

The Atlantic allies proved unable to coordinate their policy or, in the end, even to communicate. Dulles had initially conceded that Nasser must be made to "disgorge" the canal and had not ruled out force if other measures failed. But his view soon changed. Washington did not share the Anglo-French sense of urgency or deem vital principles at stake, and it insisted upon settlement by negotiation. Eisenhower declared his unwillingness to be a party to aggression, and Dulles insisted that the United States would not "try to shoot its way through the Canal." Britain and France went ahead with their plans in full knowledge that they would lack American support. Indeed, after October 13, when actual preparation for an attack on Egypt began, London and Paris concealed news of the operation from Washington.

Israeli forces launched a sudden invasion of Egypt on October 29, 1956, and their rapid advance across the Sinai peninsula toward the canal gave Great Britain and France a pretext for their own assault. Justifying intervention as a means of insulating the canal from Israeli-Egyptian hostilities, the European allies sent an ultimatum to Cairo and Tel Aviv on October 30. They demanded an end to the fighting, a ten-mile withdrawal of all military forces from the canal, and a temporary right to occupy positions along the route in order to safeguard free transit. England and France vetoed American and Soviet resolutions in the Security Council requesting all members to refrain from use of force, and opened an aerial bombardment of Cairo and the canal area on October 31 when Egypt ignored the ultimatum. The attack coincided almost exactly with the ill-fated Hungarian revolt.

American leaders, caught completely off guard, were nettled because they had not been consulted or even notified in advance, and embarrassed by this attack at the climax of a presidential campaign. They recognized that Great Britain, France, and Israel were acting under provocation, but they could not condone an action that betrayed so many commitments. It violated the charters of both the United Nations and the North Atlantic alliance. It flouted an Anglo-American-French pledge of 1950 to oppose any breach in the Arab-Israeli armistice lines and an American promise of 1956 to "support and assist" any country under attack in that region. It went against American policies of keeping the Arab-Israeli and canal controversies separate and excluding Russia from the area. Washington took its stand against the allied assault regretfully but firmly. "There can be no peace without law," Eisenhower declared on October 31. "There can be no law if we work to invoke one code of international conduct for those who oppose us and another for our friends."

Events followed swiftly. Israeli forces occupied most of the Sinai peninsula within a few days. The Anglo-French invasion moved so slowly, however, that Egypt had time to block the canal with sunken ships before allied troops could occupy the route. Meanwhile, an emergency session of the General Assembly passed an American-sponsored cease-fire resolution by a huge majority on November 2, then created an international emergency force to "secure and supervise the cessation of hostilities." Belligerent threats from Moscow added to the growing tension. The United States rejected Bulganin's proposal for joint Soviet-American military action to end the fighting, but the Kremlin avowed its readiness to "crush the aggressors and restore peace in the East through the use of force" and spoke of recruiting "volunteers" to aid the Egyptians. Such threats led Eisenhower to order a global alert of American armed forces on November 6.

The British decided on that day to accept a cease-fire. Israel, having gained most of its military objectives, did the same, and France had no choice but to follow suit. Although arrival of the United Nations Emergency Force (UNEF) enabled the European invaders to withdraw without complete humiliation,[17] their operation had been a fiasco. They had failed to destroy Nasser, whose prestige in Egypt and the Arab world was higher than ever. Their offensive had been mounted too slowly to prevent obstruction of the canal and called off too soon to guarantee their possession at the time of the cease-fire. The Suez Canal not only remained in Egypt's hands but was closed to traffic until obstructions could be removed, forcing Europe in the interim to rely upon American oil and the long route around Africa.

---

[17] Anglo-French withdrawal took place in December when the UNEF arrived, but Israel would not relinquish the Egyptian territory it had occupied until March 1957. By this time the Israelis were convinced of UNEF's effectiveness and had established their shipping rights in the Gulf of Aqaba.

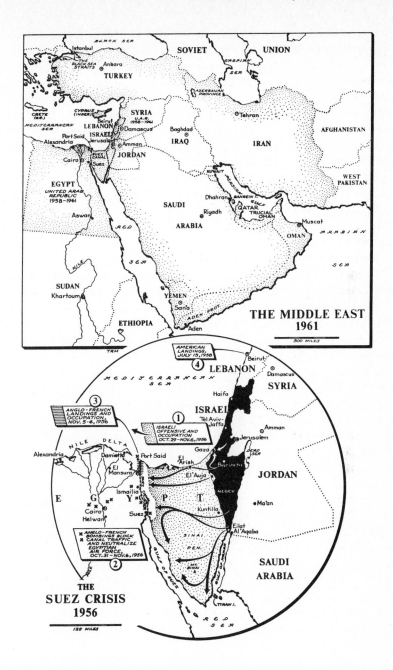

THE MIDDLE EAST
1961

THE
SUEZ CRISIS
1956

Anglo-French prestige was at an all-time low, and anticolonial sentiment had been fanned to new heat. The United States had won approval
in neutral quarters for its resolute opposition to the assault, but the Western position had been badly weakened, and the Atlantic alliance was a

shambles. Russia had reaped huge advantages by standing as defender of Arab nationalism against imperialist aggression. Afro-Asian opinion could overlook Soviet brutality in Hungary in its greater sensitivity to this seeming resurgence of European colonialism.

The Middle East remained a storm center in international politics. The UNEF managed to maintain relative peace and stability in and about Suez and the armistice area, and a UN salvage team removed all obstructions and reopened the canal by April 1957. Contrary to European fears, Egypt thereafter proved cooperative in not interfering with canal traffic (save Israel's) and efficient in operating the busy waterway. But political ferment was on the rise. Communist and Nasserite nationalist elements enlarged their influence in every Arab state. They dominated the Syrian government and endangered shaky pro-Western regimes in Iraq, Jordan, and Lebanon.

America's first response, in the dazed and tense aftermath of Suez, was the so-called Eisenhower Doctrine. A joint congressional resolution of March 1957 authorized the president to use up to $200 million for economic and military assistance to Middle Eastern nations that desired it, asserted America's vital interest in preserving the independence and integrity of all countries in the region, and offered American armed assistance upon the request of any such nation facing "armed aggression from any country controlled by international communism."

As an attempt to deter aggression and clarify American policy in the Middle East, the Eisenhower Doctrine contained certain ambiguities and omissions. It deliberately left the Suez and Arab-Israeli disputes to the United Nations. It did not precisely define the area covered and could not be applied until a nation requested it. It did not mention subversion, which many regarded as a far greater danger than outside aggression. The new doctrine was denounced by the Soviet bloc, described as an imperialist plot by Egypt, hailed by Iraq, Iran, and Turkey, and cautiously approved in Jordan, Lebanon, and Saudi Arabia.

Alarm signals flashed again and again during 1957. Young King Hussein of Jordan, who had recently cut traditional ties with Britain under pressure from anti-Western elements, abruptly ousted his pro-Nasser cabinet in April and appealed to loyal Bedouin tribes to protect his throne. Eisenhower moved to forestall Soviet exploitation and possible Nasserite intervention by pronouncing Jordan's independence "vital" and ordering the Sixth Fleet to the eastern Mediterranean. This action momentarily stabilized Hussein's throne, but charges of American plotting in Syria culminated in October with a blast from Moscow and a new war scare. Russia accused the United States of inciting a Turkish attack upon Syria and threatened Turkey with rocket attacks. Syria requested a UN investigation while American and Soviet delegates exchanged accusations, and Egypt sent troops to reinforce Syrian concentrations along the Turkish border.

King Saud of Saudi Arabia stepped forward to mediate the Turko-Syrian dispute before UN action was necessary.

American intervention, threats of war, and new Western setbacks followed in 1958. Syria and Egypt merged to form the United Arab Republic in February and stepped up subversive activities against pro-Western Arab regimes. A Nasserite revolt broke out in Lebanon in May. The Lebanese government accused Egypt and Syria of border violations and interference in its internal affairs and requested an investigation, but a UN observation group proved unable to seal the frontier, stop the fighting, or substantiate Lebanese charges. When appeals to the Arab League also failed, Lebanon asked for American assistance. The president hesitated, loath to risk a clash between Americans and Arabs and fearful of Russian intervention. Then a nationalist group led by General Abdel Karim al-Kassim overthrew the pro-Western regime in Baghdad in July and signed a mutual defense pact with Nasser. Iraq's apparent withdrawal from the western into the Egyptian orbit threatened to produce like results in Lebanon, Jordan, and Saudi Arabia. Alarmed, both Lebanon and Jordan sent out desperate calls for Western help.

President Eisenhower, after hurried conferences with advisers and congressmen, ordered the Sixth Fleet to deploy off Lebanon for an amphibious landing. Some eight thousand American troops went ashore unopposed in mid-July "to encourage the Lebanese government in defense of Lebanese sovereignty and integrity," while Great Britain sent three thousand men to Jordan in response to Hussein's appeal. The operations were executed brilliantly, but diplomatic reactions were ominous. Nasser flew to Moscow, and Russia responded with warnings and charges of aggression. Khrushchev, saying that the world was on the "brink of disaster," demanded an immediate conference with Eisenhower, Macmillan, de Gaulle, Nehru, and Secretary-General Dag Hammarskjold. "I am not aware," Eisenhower replied drily on July 22, "of any factual basis for your extravagantly expressed fear." In the Security Council, attempts to stabilize the situation met Soviet vetoes. The United States thereupon asked for an emergency session of the General Assembly.

The outlook had brightened somewhat when this session convened on August 8. Khrushchev had been quoted as saying that Russia had no intention of sending "volunteers" or regular troops to the area. There had been no bloodshed in Lebanon, and a new president acceptable to all factions had been found. The United States had quieted Arab fears of intervention in Iraq by recognizing Kassim. While the General Assembly argued over Soviet demands for Anglo-American withdrawal and American proposals for a condemnation of indirect aggression, the Arab states presented a resolution on August 21 that passed unanimously. It accepted assurances that none of those states would take "any action calculated to change established systems of government," asked members of the United Nations to refrain from interfering in the internal affairs of other states, and requested the secretary-general to "make . . . such practical arrangements as would adequately help in upholding the purposes and principles of the Charter in relation to Lebanon and Jordan." Hammarskjold arranged matters so effectively that all American and British units withdrew from Lebanon and Jordan by November 1958.

Temporary calm then descended upon the strife-torn Middle East. The United States and the Soviet Union continued to maneuver for advantage, but no large-scale violence or war scares occurred. Fewer bloody incursions disturbed the Arab-Israeli impasse. Ships continued to pass undisturbed through the Suez Canal.

Actually, genuine neutrality gained ground at the expense of both East and West. Iraq withdrew from the Baghdad Pact in 1959, and the alliance was transformed five months later into the Central Treaty Organization (CENTO), with headquarters in Ankara. Supported but not formally joined by the United States, CENTO lacked a unified command or armed forces of its own, and was more a symbol than a bastion of Western power in the Middle East. Nasser remained strong in Egypt and influential in the Arab world, but he concentrated more on internal affairs after the Lebanese crisis. Although he accepted a $100 million loan from Russia in 1958 and began work on the Aswan Dam with help from Russian engineers, his neutralism grew less belligerent and less aligned with Moscow. Indeed, he clamped down ruthlessly on Communist activity in Egypt. Despite grave economic troubles, Iraq managed to maintain itself without sliding under control of either Egypt or Russia. Lebanon became neutral, and Hussein still occupied an uncertain throne in Jordan, but both countries preserved more independence than had seemed possible in 1958.

Meanwhile, the world spotlight had turned toward Africa, where the movement for independence reached flood tide. As late as 1955 there were only five independent nations in Africa; twenty-eight more had joined their number by 1962. Only a scattered handful of small dependencies and the two large Portuguese colonies of Angola and Mozambique remained under European rule by this date. American diplomatic interest had been limited, by and large, to expressions of good will and friendship toward the emergent African peoples.

Only in North Africa, close enough to the main theaters of the cold war to possess strategic value, did the United States show active interest before 1958. The former Italian colony of Libya achieved independence in 1953, French Morocco and Tunisia in 1956. In Tunisia the pro-Western orientation of President Habib Bourguiba, an influential figure in the Arab world, was an important counterweight to Nasser. Libya's continued friendship became vital in 1954 when that country leased the huge Wheelus Air Force base near Tripoli to the United States. Morocco figured even more prominently in American planning because of the airfields and naval base that the United States had built there in 1950–1951. Libya remained well-disposed, but Morocco demanded cancellation of American bases on its soil. This demand became so insistent that Washington promised in 1959 to relinquish them by 1963—an agreement made possible by completion of the new network of bases in Spain.

Between Tunisia and Morocco lay the French colony of Algeria, oldest and richest possession in France's diminishing empire. American concern here stemmed from the diplomatic and military ramifications of France's prolonged efforts to put down the rebellion of non-French Algerians that broke out in 1954. This war became one of the West's biggest liabilities. It crippled NATO's military strength by draining off nearly all French contingents, strained French relations with her allies, embarrassed Western standing with neutral and ex-colonial nations, and transformed Bourguiba from pro-Western champion to neutralist. Washington was torn between loyalty to an ally, on the one hand, and sympathy for the Algerian rebels and concern for anticolonial opinion, on the other. Its attempts to offend neither side ended by displeasing both, and it was no more able than Bourguiba, the UN, or any third party to effect a settlement. France ultimately found a leader, General de Gaulle, who terminated the bitter struggle in 1962 by granting independence to Algeria.

Meanwhile, the cold war had sucked sub-Saharan Africa into its vortex. Soviet attacks on Western imperialism and white supremacy in this region began in 1958, as new nations began to emerge from colonial status. Ghana, for example, maintained a policy of nonalignment but espoused a pan-African nationalism that frequently arrayed her against the West. Guinea went much further toward direct alignment with Moscow. The Soviets, unencumbered by liabilities of imperialism in Africa or traditions of white supremacy, enjoyed advantage over the Western powers in bidding for the friendship of new African nations. The United States again found itself caught between sympathy for African aspirations and the demands of its NATO partners with colonies in the area.

The first real test came when Belgium granted freedom to the Congo in June 1960. Congolese leaders had barely taken the reins of government before mutiny in the native army and looting and violence broke out. Belgium, alarmed for the safety of its nationals still on the scene, reinforced the handful of white troops remaining in the Congo and thereby touched off new violence. Congolese Premier Patrice Lumumba asked the United Nations on July 10 for assistance against "external aggression" and hinted that he would seek help elsewhere if the UN did not provide it.

Chaos quickly engulfed the unhappy Congo. The province of Katanga, from whose rich mineral resources and prosperous mining companies the new republic planned to derive much of its revenue, seceded in July under the leadership of Moise Tshombe. Lumumba, seeking a unified state under a strong central government, tried to put down this secessionist movement and soon won the support of Ghana, Guinea, and the Soviets, who sent technicians and military equipment. Joseph Kasavubu, the Congolese president, grew alarmed at Lumumba's Communist leanings and dismissed him in September. Parliament restored him to power, but the army disbanded parliament, arrested Lumumba, ousted the Soviet and Czechoslovakian missions, and endeavored to come to terms with Katanga. The internal struggle became three-cornered when the followers of Lumumba, still recognized by the Soviets as premier, organized a new separatist movement. Virtual anarchy prevailed in much of the country.

The United Nations did what it could. The Security Council asked Belgium to withdraw its troops, authorized Hammarskjold to create a multinational peace force, and recommended that all states refrain from interfering. While the Soviets accused NATO of plotting to restore colonialism in the Congo and affirmed their readiness to combat this move, Moscow and Washington exchanged warnings about keeping troops out of the new republic. In assembling the peace force Hammarskjold was careful to draw largely upon African and Asian contingents and sought no aid from the major powers. Tshombe's recalcitrance added to the difficulty. He defied the central government, refused to permit UN forces to enter Katanga, and drew threats from Ghana and Russia to force his adherence to a unified Congo. This produced another Security Council resolution on August 7, proclaiming that the UN command would have to enter Katanga but must not be employed, as Lumumba and the Soviets wished, to assist any party in the Congo's internal dispute.

This last proved an impossible directive. The United Nations force, eventually totaling twenty thousand men, could not restore peace to the Congo without inadvertently aiding one faction or another. Khrushchev was convinced that the UN had connived against Lumumba in favor of Kasavubu, especially after the General Assembly voted in November to seat Kasavubu's delegates instead of Lumumba's. When Congolese factionalism became more sharply three-cornered after Lumumba's arrest in December 1960, the Soviets supported his cause against both the central government and Katanga and wanted the UN command to do the same. The West backed Kasuvubu, and UN troops tried to avoid partisanship in coping with an impossible situation. Involvement led to tragic death for Hammarskjold when his airplane crashed in Northern Rhodesia on September 18, 1961, on a flight to Katanga.

A moderate new premier, Cyrille Adoula, won support from both Western and African governments and achieved a measure of stability for his beleaguered country. He brought Tshombe to terms with the help of UN troops, while Lumumba's Communist-oriented movement gradually faded into impotence after the former premier was kidnaped and murdered in Katanga in 1961 under mysterious circumstances. Even so, the situation remained confused and volatile. The Congo had vividly illustrated both the disruptive effects of East-West rivalry upon local conditions and the internal difficulties that threatened stability and progress in emergent Africa.

7. The Western Hemisphere

The New World, oldest and until recently the paramount sphere of American diplomatic activity, was overshadowed after 1945 by the greater urgency of new commitments elsewhere. But conditions in Latin America offered a tempting target for Communist exploitation. Poverty, overpopulation, social discontent, reactionary or unstable governments, sensitive nationalism, and hatred of imperialism were facts of life in most countries south of the Rio Grande. The status quo was under massive assault. The United States did not awaken to the full implications until communism established a beachhead in the very center of the hemisphere in 1960.

The United States was partly negligent and partly a victim of circumstances. It could not change the fact that its wealth was a source of envy, its power a source of alarm, its diplomacy in earlier years a source of resentment, and its footholds in Panama and Guantánamo, Cuba, a source of irritation south of the border. There were no easy solutions to Latin America's economic problems: a rate of population increase that nullified gains in productivity; and overdependence upon foreign trade, the United States market, and a single-export commodity subject to fluctuating world prices.[18] A wave of revolutions in Latin America during the 1950s swept away traditional military dictatorships in favor of more or less democratic governments, but the United States lost rather than gained by these upheavals. In the interests of hemispheric solidarity, it cultivated friendly relations with despotic regimes and thereby antagonized democratic leaders who came to power later. Careful adherence to the doctrine of nonintervention, upon which Latin America insisted, meant that triumphs over dictatorship were achieved without help from Washington. Though it often had no real alternative, the United States was widely criticized for alleged lack of sympathy with democratic movements.

Washington occasionally contributed more actively to this Latin American image of a reactionary and neo-imperialist "colossus of the North." It was sometimes unduly lavish in its praise of Latin tyrants. It often seemed to prefer an orderly dictatorship, however unpopular and repressive, to an unstable or radical democracy. It did not always act promptly in suspend-

---

[18]A few figures suggest the dilemma. Economic growth rate for Latin America was high—approximately 5.5 percent each year in the decade 1946–1956, as opposed to 5 percent in western Europe and 4 percent in the United States; total GNP increased from $32.2 billion to $47.2 billion. But these gains were largely canceled by inequitable distribution, inflation, and population increases that kept per capita income low. Whereas the United States normally exported about 10 percent of its total production, many Latin American countries exported as much as 80 percent. The United States took about 80 percent of Latin America's copper; 70 percent of its coffee, lead, and zinc; and similar percentages of other basic items. And nearly every Latin American country depended largely upon a single product, such as coffee, sugar, copper, or tin, in its export trade. Washington was cool to Latin American requests that it grant preferential treatment and stabilize prices of these commodities, since any such action would mean higher consumer prices in the United States.

ing arms shipments when such weapons were used to suppress domestic opposition to authoritarian regimes. And it persisted in stressing the importance of private investment rather than its own aid as the best means of promoting Latin American economies. Although the large volume of United States private investment south of the border conferred undeniable benefits, Latin Americans were far from satisfied with the overall results.[19]

Communism made its first New World incursion in the republic of Guatemala, where a long overdue social revolution in 1944 had overthrown a reactionary regime. Guatemala, eager for reform, moved farther to the left after the election of Jacobo Arbenz in 1950, and a small Communist party won control of the government by 1953. It immediately sought to expropriate foreign assets in Guatemala and launched subversive movements in neighboring countries.

Dulles wanted the Organization of American States to consider some form of joint action or strong protest, but Latin American respect for nonintervention limited the possibilities. All he could obtain was a resolution, passed at an Inter-American Conference in Caracas in March 1954, defining "domination or control of the political institutions of any American State by the international communist movement" as a threat to the "sovereignty and political independence of the American States, endangering the peace of America." Unabashed, Guatemalan leaders obtained Czechoslovakian military equipment and fomented strikes in neighboring Honduras. Washington denounced these actions, accused Guatemala of planning aggression, and furnished weapons to Honduras and Nicaragua. Arbenz invoked martial law in Guatemala on June 8, claiming that a foreign plot to overthrow him was under way. A few days later a small force of exiles crossed into the country from Honduras and united with dissident army units to challenge his regime. Guatemala requested an emergency meeting of the Security Council and charged Honduras and Nicaragua with aggression "at the instigation of certain foreign monopolies."

---

[19]Compared to expenditures in Europe and Asia, aid to Latin America under the Mutual Security Act was minuscule—only 3 percent, for example, of the $2.76 billion appropriation for 1955. The United States also provided technical assistance, short-run aid in the form of stabilization programs and emergency credits, and indirect aid through the Export-Import Bank, International Monetary Fund, and World Bank. But public assistance was far from able to meet the region's basic capital or welfare needs.

On the positive side, the $6.5 billion of private United States investments in Latin America in 1955 (the figure reached $9 billion by 1957) underwrote goods and services with an annual market value of $5 billion. In 1955, United States companies produced 30 percent of Latin America's exports and 20 percent of its industrial output, paid over $1 billion in taxes to Latin American governments, and employed over 600,000 Latin American citizens.

However, critics argued that this investment was unevenly applied (45 percent confined to Venezuela and Brazil, and 30 percent in the petroleum industry alone). To many reformers it smacked of imperialism and economic thralldom to the United States. It certainly did not provide the kind of balanced, comprehensive, long-range assistance that most Latin American countries needed.

A heated debate followed, with Russia demanding instant action and vetoing an American resolution to refer the problem to the OAS. While the Soviet delegate charged that the OAS was controlled in Washington, the American delegate angrily warned the Russians to "stay out of this hemisphere." The council finally passed a French resolution calling for immediate cessation of hostilities. A few days later Guatemala and Russia charged that the resolution had not been complied with, and the council met again. It decided, over Soviet protests, to defer action until an investigation by the Inter-American Peace Committee (a mediatory adjunct of the OAS) had been completed. Before this happened, Arbenz had fled and Guatemala had come under control of an authoritarian anti-Communist government approved by the United States. The Eisenhower administration denied complicity in the movement to overthrow Arbenz, but it had in fact been engineered by the CIA.

Meanwhile, Communist agitation in other parts of Latin America continued, backed by the strategy of cultural and economic penetration that Russia and China were pursuing in other areas. The United States awoke to the danger when Communist-inspired mobs assaulted Vice-President Nixon in Peru and Venezuela in 1958. Elsewhere, Washington had revised its treaty with Panama in 1955 in response to Panamanian demand[20] and was endeavoring within limits to promote progress and better relations south of the border. But its unwillingness to provide large-scale aid or modify certain trade and tariff policies remained a continual source of irritation. Economic and social discontent in many countries had clearly passed the point where assurances, palliatives, or stopgap aid would serve. Nixon warned upon his return that there were many non-Communists in the crowds that menaced him in Lima and Caracas. The United States reexamined its economic policies, promoted regional free trade agreements, and supported an international program to stabilize the price of coffee. Most important, it agreed in 1959 to participate (by subscribing 25 percent and guaranteeing another 20 percent) in an Inter-American Development Bank with a capital of $1 billion, for loans to Latin American countries.

But time was running out. Communism found its next opportunity with the overthrow of Fulgencio Batista's harsh dictatorship in Cuba on January 1, 1959. The successful revolutionary movement was led by Fidel Castro, whose new regime veered with unexpected rapidity down the path of extremism and Communist alignment. Castro had announced a sweeping land reform program that worried foreign investors, and he had never concealed his antipathy toward the United States for its tolerance of

[20]The revised treaty increased the American annuity to Panama from $430,000 to $1.9 million, enabled Panama to tax its citizens who worked in the Canal Zone, transferred certain lands back to Panama, and altered American economic privileges in and about the Zone in Panama's favor.

Batista and other dictators. The administration was therefore expecting some difficulty even after extending prompt recognition and friendly gestures to the new Cuban government. But Washington was not in any way prepared for the intensity of Castro's anti-American policy or the violence of his assault upon the status quo in the Western Hemisphere.

While Castro leaned more and more toward views held by Communist supporters and became increasingly virulent in his denunciations of the United States, Cuba became a headquarters for intrigue and subversive planning. Communists and radical exiles from other Caribbean republics converged on the island to plot and prepare invasions, accumulate weapons, and conduct training exercises. Reports of imminent armed expeditions led to an inter-American foreign ministers' meeting in August 1959, but Washington's hopes for joint action were reduced to a pair of resolutions condemning totalitarianism and reaffirming democratic principles. Meanwhile, Castro accused the United States of harboring and equipping his enemies, inciting sabotage and counterrevolutionary activity, and permitting air attacks on Cuba. His domestic reform program moved markedly leftward, and Cuban seizures of American property totaled $1 billion by 1960. Relations between the two countries worsened steadily.

American exasperation grew, but a policy of restraint toward Castro remained in force. The United States was in a dilemma. Military retaliation was unthinkable, and economic retaliation would provoke cries of dollar diplomacy and imperialism throughout Latin America. Yet continued passivity in the face of Castro's sweeping confiscations might encourage other Latin demagogues to follow suit. American forbearance weakened when Castro abandoned the hemispheric bloc in the General Assembly and proclaimed a neutralism that echoed the Soviet position; signed an extensive five-year trading agreement with Russia in February 1960; and hinted at a military alliance with the USSR. Eisenhower's patience snapped when Castro, in response to an American memorandum to the Inter-American Peace Committee accusing Cuba of "systematic and provocative" slander, seized a $25 million Texaco refinery in June 1960 for refusing to process Russian crude oil. The president retaliated by cutting American imports of Cuban sugar.

The shadow of the cold war was lengthening across the Western Hemisphere. While Cuba complained of American action before the Security Council, Khrushchev entered the controversy on July 9 by declaring that "Soviet artillerymen can support Cuba with rocket fire" in event of an American attack on the island. He struck at the very cornerstone of America's New World policy a few days later by proclaiming that the Monroe Doctrine was obsolete, had "died a natural death," and should not be permitted to "poison the air by its decay." The State Department replied with the flat statement that the doctrine was as valid in 1960 as it had ever been, and that attempts to extend the Russian system to the New World would be considered dangerous to the peace and safety of the United

States. The Security Council, after hearing the Soviet delegate call the doctrine a cloak for American territorial greed, voted to refer the dispute with Cuba to the Organization of American States.

The OAS was badly torn by the turmoil that seemed about to engulf Latin America. Unstable democratic governments were being threatened from both left and right, as Castro's subversive activities were matched by similar plots emanating from Rafael S. Trujillo's dictatorship in the Dominican Republic. An attempt by the latter to overthrow the democratic regime of Romulo Betancourt in Venezuela was sharply condemned in August 1960 by the inter-American foreign ministers, who voted unanimously to break off diplomatic relations and impose sanctions on the Dominican Republic.

But the OAS would not take similar action against Castro. It condemned Sino-Soviet meddling and criticized Cuba indirectly for allowing Russia to exploit its internal situation, but the resolutions contained neither overt condemnation nor sanctions. Although other Latin nations disapproved Castro's military flirtation with the Soviet Union, many of them sympathized with the broad social objectives of his revolution. Some admired his successful defiance of the "colossus of the North." Those who might otherwise have condemned him were frankly fearful of the effects of such a move upon restive elements in their homelands.

Castro was unintimidated by the tepid OAS resolution. He recognized Communist China, expropriated what remained of American business in Cuba, threatened to seize the naval base at Guantánamo, and drilled his militia in preparation for an alleged American invasion. The United States, deprived of any hope of joint inter-American action, did all it could unilaterally short of military intervention. It imposed an embargo in October 1960 on all exports to Cuba save food, medicine, and medical supplies; set up a naval patrol in the Caribbean in November to prevent rumored Cuban invasions of Nicaragua and Guatemala; and formally severed relations in January 1961. The American public did not yet know that the CIA had begun to train and equip Cuban exiles in Florida for a military assault. As the decade ended, the United States faced a choice between tolerating a Communist outpost on its very doorstep or courting obloquy and world war by trying to destroy it.

30

New Frontiers
at Home and Abroad

The 1960s saw the return of the Democratic party to power in Washington. From the very outset, the young and vigorous president, John F. Kennedy, faced grave challenges to his relatively untried leadership. A succession of international crises led the United States to the brink of nuclear war with Russia in 1962. Although relations between the two superpowers later improved, troubles aggravated by the cold war continued to plague American diplomacy on four continents. At home, Kennedy defined programs to deal with the increasing complexities of American society and asked for renewed dedication and sacrifice from the people. But Congress responded grudgingly, and the president's major tasks lay unfinished at the time of his tragic death.

1. The Election of 1960

Americans went about the task of choosing a new president in 1960 in an atmosphere of uncertainty, induced largely by vague fears that the nation's position in world affairs had somehow deteriorated. The Democrats, freed by the Twenty-second Amendment from the prospect of running against Eisenhower again, engaged in one of their customary uninhibited contests for the nomination. Four Democratic candidates formally entered the race: Senators Hubert H. Humphrey of Minnesota, John F. Kennedy of Massachusetts, Lyndon B. Johnson of Texas, and Stuart Symington of Missouri. There was also considerable support for Adlai Stevenson, the nominee in 1952 and 1956. Stevenson never became a formal candidate in 1960 but was amenable to a draft.

The forty-two-year-old Kennedy, the first Roman Catholic to contend seriously for the presidency since 1928, emerged as Democratic front runner. His triumph over Humphrey in the Wisconsin primary by a six-to-four margin in April was inconclusive, since most of the Kennedy support had come from Catholic districts. But five weeks later, in heavily Protestant West Virginia, Kennedy's efficient and well-financed campaign ended with a decisive triumph over the Minnesotan. Humphrey thereupon withdrew, and Kennedy went on to record impressive primary victories in Nebraska, Maryland, and Oregon. These, together with earlier successes in New Hampshire and Indiana, caused Democratic leaders in the East and Midwest to climb on his bandwagon. Working hard for support in other areas, Kennedy's well-disciplined organization came to the convention in Los Angeles on July 11 confident of at least 600 of the 761 votes necessary for the nomination.

Democrats converged on Los Angeles in a perplexed and sober mood, shaken by recent international events. The party platform proclaimed that an enduring peace could be obtained only by restoring American "military, economic and moral" strength. Charging the Eisenhower administraton with having lost America's "position of pre-eminence," it promised to "recast" national military capacity along more effective lines. Other pledges included better planning for disarmament, reshaping of foreign aid with more emphasis upon economic assistance and international cooperation, promotion of economic growth without inflation, and an end to the Republican "high-interest, tight-money policy" that had allegedly stifled expansion in recent years. The platform also contained the strongest civil rights plank in American history.[1]

The convention then proceeded, after intricate and strenuous maneuvering, to nominate John F. Kennedy on the first ballot. Symington's chances had faded with Kennedy's victory in West Virginia; Johnson's, with his failure to gain substantial western backing. Efforts by Stevenson strategists to win support from favorite-son candidates in a few key states and their attempts to break the tenuous allegiance of certain Kennedy

---

[1] It pledged full use of federal power and leadership to assure equal rights and opportunities in housing, employment, schools, and public facilities; promised to move toward elimination of literacy tests and poll taxes as voting requirements; called upon every state affected by the *Brown* decision to submit desegregation plans by 1963; and openly endorsed sit-in demonstrations and similar peaceful protests.

delegates proved unsuccessful. In a move that surprised nearly everyone, Kennedy then requested and obtained Johnson's nomination for the vice-presidency.

"The world is changing," Kennedy proclaimed in his acceptance speech on July 15. "We stand today on the edge of a New Frontier . . . a frontier of unknown opportunities and perils—a frontier of unfulfilled hopes and threats. . . . But the New Frontier of which I speak is not a set of promises—it is a set of challenges. It sums up, not what I intend to offer the American people, but what I intend to ask of them."

No such struggle for the nomination took place within the GOP. It had been clear for months that Vice-President Nixon enjoyed overwhelming support from party regulars in all sections of the country. His only serious contender was Governor Nelson A. Rockefeller of New York, a progressive Republican who had won national prominence with an impressive victory over incumbent Averell Harriman in 1958. Rockefeller formed an organization and sought support during 1959. He was popular among independents and party liberals, but he withdrew his candidacy in December upon discovering that Republican regulars and important financial backers were firmly committed to Nixon.

Rockefeller could not win the nomination, but he was nevertheless able to exert decisive influence on the party platform. Disturbed by recent developments and convinced that the administration had permitted America's military and economic strength to deteriorate, Rockefeller submitted a sweeping program for reform in these and other areas, including civil rights. It amounted to frank repudiation of many Eisenhower policies. The governor let it be known that he would accept a draft and threatened an open fight for his program on the convention floor if the platform did not incorporate his views.

Nixon privately agreed with much of Rockefeller's indictment and dreaded a rupture with the governor's wing of the party. Yet he hardly dared endorse so open a repudiation of Eisenhower. Rockefeller flatly rejected a compromise draft platform offered by the Nixon forces. Then the vice-president met the governor secretly at the latter's New York apartment three days before the GOP convention opened in Chicago on July 25 and accepted nearly all of Rockefeller's demands. The "Compact of Fifth Avenue," published in the press on July 23, called for a more imaginative foreign policy, an accelerated defense program, reorganization of the executive branch "to cope effectively with modern problems and challenges," stimulation of the economy, strong federal action in behalf of civil rights, a program of medical care for the aged, and aid to education.

News of the compact touched off explosions within the GOP. Senator Barry M. Goldwater of Arizona, leading spokesman of the right wing, denounced it as the "Munich of the Republican Party." From President Eisenhower, then on vacation in Rhode Island, came angry retorts. The platform committee, made up entirely of conservatives, felt betrayed and rebelled openly. The Nixon forces had to use every ounce of political leverage they possessed to placate these dissidents and win partial acceptance of the compact.

The GOP platform was unquestionably more progressive as a result. It praised the Eisenhower record in foreign affairs and national defense but pledged thorough modernization and acceleration of military programs and promised not to let budgetary concerns put a "price ceiling on America's security." The economic plank, while praising the prosperity of the past eight years, admitted the need for a higher growth rate. Warning against "massive new federal spending," the document promised to stimulate economic expansion through tax reform, a stable dollar, an end to featherbedding, and other stimulants to private initiative and investment. The civil rights plank, representing a complete victory for Rockefeller, was almost as strong as that of the Democrats. The convention proceeded to nominate Nixon by acclamation on the first ballot. With equal celerity it nominated Nixon's choice for the vice-presidency: Henry Cabot Lodge, Jr., of Massachusetts, ambassador to the UN.

Personalities and emotions played a more important role than issues in the campaign. The two candidates were in basic agreement on most major questions. Both were internationalists and moderate progressives; their programs differed in detail and emphasis but hardly in kind. Kennedy's central theme was the need for positive leadership, public sacrifice, and bold national effort to "get America moving again." Nixon, while denying that the military and economic situation was as grave as his opponent claimed, also affirmed that the United States could not afford to stand still or rest upon past laurels.

The early advantage lay with Nixon, who was free to launch his campaign while Kennedy was tied down in Washington by the barren postconvention session of Congress. Nixon was far better known in the country at large because of his active role in the Eisenhower administration. He emphasized this point over and over, abandoned the narrow partisanship and hard-hitting tactics of his early career, and made use of the argument that he and Lodge were more qualified for the task of national leadership than the youthful, inexperienced Kennedy. Nixon enjoyed a substantial lead in late-summer opinion polls.

The picture changed drastically, however, on account of an innovation that may have been the most decisive single feature of the campaign: four nationally televised debates between Nixon and Kennedy from September 26 to October 21. Although the candidates were unable to explore issues thoughtfully and few clear distinctions in their positions emerged, Kennedy profited greatly from these encounters. October polls showed him in the lead, and reporters were impressed by the growing size and enthusiasm of his crowds. Democratic confidence and Republican gloom waxed steadily as election time neared. But effective stump speeches by President Eisenhower and a massive Republican television effort during the final week produced a resurgence of Nixon strength and reduced Kennedy's margin to the vanishing point.

Early returns from the East and South on election night, November 8, indicated a Kennedy landslide. But his lead dwindled steadily as returns from the western states came in. The decision remained in doubt until the next morning. Then returns from Illinois, Texas, and Minnesota gave the presidency to Kennedy by a narrow margin. He received 34,227,000 popular and 303 electoral votes; Nixon, 34,108,000 popular and 219 electoral votes.[2] Kennedy's popular majority of 120,000 votes was less than one-fifth of 1 percent of the total cast! The large Democratic majorities in Congress were reduced slightly, by a loss of 2 seats in the Senate and 22 in the House, to 64–36 and 263–174.

The election provided much material for analysis. Voting patterns displayed, superficially at least, a sectional hue. The historic Democratic coalition of East and South gave Kennedy the bulk of his electoral support. He swept the populous Northeast, losing only Maine, New Hampshire, and Vermont. In the South, with the help of Lyndon Johnson, Texas and Louisiana renewed their Democratic allegiance and five other states returned Democratic majorities, although Nixon duplicated Eisenhower's triumphs in Virginia, Florida, and Tennessee. In the border region, Kennedy lost Kentucky but won handily in West Virginia and narrowly in Missouri. Michigan, Illinois, and Minnesota were his only triumphs in the Middle West. And beyond the hundredth meridian Nixon carried every state except Nevada, New Mexico, and Hawaii.

But sectionalism was an inadequate key to American sentiment in this complex campaign. Closer examination revealed that changes in popular voting habits observable during the 1950s—ticket splitting, independent voting, erosion of traditional party loyalties—were more pronounced than ever. Both candidates ran ahead of their tickets in some areas and behind in others. The returns indicated that the disappearance of the Solid South in presidential elections was no temporary phenomenon; the anti-Democratic coalition that had emerged there after midcentury gave Nixon nearly half of the southern popular vote—almost as large a share as Eisenhower had received in 1952 and 1956. Conversely, Kennedy ran quite well in such traditionally Republican areas as northern New England, parts of the Middle West, and the suburbs. He also received heavy support from blacks and other minorities, and demonstrated that a Roman Catholic was no longer automatically barred from winning the nation's highest office.

[2] Six of Alabama's eleven Democratic electors and all eight of Mississippi's were unpledged. These, together with a defecting Republican elector in Oklahoma, cast their votes for Senator Harry F. Byrd of Virginia.

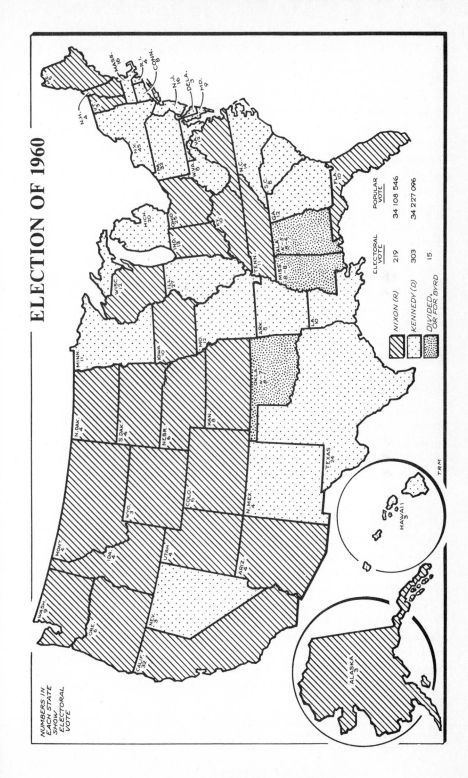

ELECTION OF 1960

NUMBERS IN
EACH STATE
SHOW
ELECTORAL
VOTE

	ELECTORAL VOTE	POPULAR VOTE
NIXON (R)	219	34 108 546
KENNEDY (D)	303	34 227 096
DIVIDED, OR FOR BYRD	15	

T.R.M.

2. *The New Frontiersmen*

Kennedy's inaugural address was a clarion call for renewed dedication in behalf of traditional American ideals. "Let the word go forth from this time and place, to friend and foe alike," he proclaimed, "that the torch has been passed to a new generation of Americans—born in this century, tempered by war, disciplined by a hard and bitter peace, proud of our ancient heritage." Pledging loyalty to America's allies, support to the United Nations, and aid to underdeveloped countries, he called for a "grand and global alliance" against "the common enemies of man: tyranny, poverty, disease and war itself." As for the cold war, he suggested that "both sides begin anew the quest for peace." He concluded with an eloquent appeal: "In the long history of the world, only a few generations have been granted the role of defending freedom in its hour of maximum danger. . . . The energy, the faith, the devotion which we bring to this endeavor will light our country and all who serve it—and the glow from that fire can truly light the world. And so, my fellow Americans: ask not what your country can do for you—ask what you can do for your country."

As presidential backgrounds go, John Fitzgerald Kennedy's was both unusual and instructive. He was born in Brookline, Massachusetts, on May 29, 1917, the second of nine children. Both his grandfathers were second-generation Irish Catholic immigrants who rose to prominence in Boston's Democratic politics. His father, Joseph P. Kennedy, made a large fortune in banking, stocks, and real estate, later supported Franklin Roosevelt, and served as ambassador to Great Britain during the late 1930s.

Graduating *cum laude* from Harvard in 1940, Kennedy became a junior naval officer during the Second World War. He won the Navy and Marine Corps Medal for rescuing the surviving crew members of his PT boat after a Japanese destroyer had sunk it off the Solomon Islands in 1943. After the war he entered Democratic politics in Massachusetts and was elected in 1946 to the House of Representatives from the Boston area. After three terms in the lower house he ran for the Senate against the Republican incumbent, Henry Cabot Lodge, Jr., in 1952. It was a formidable undertaking. Eisenhower was headed for a landslide presidential victory; and Lodge, who was serving as the general's campaign manager, had a distinguished name and record. The young Democrat stumped Massachusetts with tireless energy and defeated Lodge by 70,000 votes, while Eisenhower carried the state by over 200,000.

Kennedy's congressional career was marked by moderate progressivism, ambition, and remarkable vote-getting ability. He was reelected to the Senate in 1958 by 875,000 votes, the largest majority in Massachusetts history. Almost from the moment of his defeat for the vice-presidential nomination in 1956, Kennedy launched an unrelenting campaign for the presidency that led him to his convention victory at Los Angeles and culminated in his narrow triumph over Nixon in November 1960.

Kennedy, the youngest man ever elected to the presidency, displayed an impressive, if frequently baffling, combination of personal qualities. He had an abundance of poise, charm, self-assurance, and energy, together with a keen sensitivity to the American political process and a leader's fascination for political power. He was well informed, incisive, and articulate, and he respected these qualities in others. Eager to accept responsibility, he inspired fierce devotion and loyalty among his followers. Critics detected a streak of ruthlessness and sometimes worried about his ambition and love of power. Coolly level-headed, he was able at all times to view situations, associates, enemies, and himself with remarkable detachment. This was a practical asset, but some believed that it might also reflect a basic limitation. He was a realist, a believer in the art of the possible; his wife called him "an idealist without illusions." Kennedy's progressivism and interest in human welfare were undoubtedly genuine, but they seemed to represent more of an intellectual than an emotional commitment.

Kennedy's cabinet included a few surprises. Chief among these was the appointment of Dean Rusk, then president of the Rockefeller Foundation, as secretary of state. Rusk was an experienced diplomat, but his name had not been among those mentioned. Adlai Stevenson, mentioned frequently and favored by liberal Democrats for that important office, was named instead as ambassador to the UN. Another surprise, aimed at reassuring "sound money" conservatives, was the appointment of New York banker C. Douglas Dillon, Eisenhower's undersecretary of state, as secretary of the treasury. Another Republican, Robert S. McNamara, left the presidency of the Ford Motor Company to become secretary of defense.

Most of the other posts went to experienced Democratic politicians. They included the president's brother, Robert F. Kennedy, as attorney general; J. Edward Day of California, postmaster general; former Representative Stewart L. Udall of Arizona, secretary of the interior; former Governor Orville L. Freeman of Minnesota, secretary of agriculture; former Governor Luther H. Hodges of North Carolina, secretary of commerce; and former Governor Abraham Ribicoff of Connecticut, secretary of health, education, and welfare. Arthur J. Goldberg, a prominent labor lawyer, became secretary of labor.

The emphasis in many cabinet appointments, and in most high-level advisory and assistant positions in the executive branch, was upon people with the kind of qualities Kennedy himself possessed and admired. He wanted to be surrounded by vigorous, activist intellectuals who prided themselves upon their pragmatism and their hard-headed, modern approach to the solution of problems. Confident in their ability to control events, these youthful appointees buzzed energetically about the White House and Capitol Hill during the Kennedy years.

3. *Kennedy and Congress*

As Kennedy had hoped, public imagination was stirred by the new administration's vigor, spirit, and industry. Polls taken shortly after the inauguration indicated that fully 75 percent of the people "approved" of their new president. But this popularity, he soon discovered, could not be easily translated into congressional support for his legislative program. A major obstacle was the coalition of conservative Republicans and southern Democrats that had been blocking or diluting welfare legislation since 1938. Kennedy usually had a reliable working majority in the Senate. But the 263 Democrats in the lower house included some 100 southerners, at least half of whom voted consistently with the Republicans against progressive measures.

The only parts of Kennedy's program that came through this gauntlet relatively unscathed were those pertaining to defense and foreign policy. Fear of Communist aggression enabled the president to command strong legislative support for nearly all his proposals to strengthen the free world. Congress readily appropriated $47 billion for defense in 1961 and over $48 billion in 1962, on both occasions actually exceeding the amount Kennedy had asked for. Congress also approved requests for authority to call reservists into the armed forces for twelve-month periods in 1961-1962 and for a space program designed to put a man on the moon before 1970.

The president encountered more resistance to his far-reaching aid and trade programs, but he obtained much of what he wanted. Congress cut his $5 billion foreign-aid requests in 1961 and 1962 by about 20 percent. They refused to grant long-term borrowing authority, which would have enabled him to avoid the annual battle for new appropriations and develop foreign-aid projects on a long-range basis. But these defeats were more than offset by a number of triumphs. Congress responded to his proposal for a five-year program of aid to underdeveloped countries by creating the Development Loan Fund in 1961 with an appropriation of $1.2 billion in its first year and $1.5 billion annually for the next four years. Kennedy also won approval of his comprehensive program for Latin American aid: the Alliance for Progress. Formally launched at an Inter-American Conference in Uruguay in August 1961 and signed by all the American republics except Cuba, the alliance envisaged a massive ten-year program for economic and social development. It promised at least $20 billion in aid, over half to be provided by the United States and the balance by international agencies, European countries, and private capital.

There were other victories. The Senate ratified a treaty in March 1961 making the United States a member of the newly created Organization for Economic Cooperation and Development. Also including Canada and eighteen western European nations in its membership, the OECD was designed to improve world trade, promote closer economic ties among members, and evolve a program allocating their future aid contributions to underdeveloped countries. The most dramatic of Kennedy's aid proposals was the Peace Corps, created by executive order in March 1961 to train volunteers for educational and technical service abroad. Thousands of Americans volunteered, and Congress established the Peace Corps on a permanent basis in September.

Kennedy's biggest legislative achievement was passage of the Trade Expansion Act in September 1962. Designed to establish closer ties with the European Common Market through reciprocal concessions, the act permitted him to reduce tariffs by 50 percent, and by as much as 100 percent on articles in which the United States and Common Market countries together accounted for four-fifths of world trade. Another major feature was a system of "trade adjustment assistance" to aid American firms and workers adversely affected by lower tariffs.

In fiscal matters the new administration proceeded cautiously. Kennedy's economic views were moderate; his plans to stimulate the economy did not envisage massive federal spending or a marked increase in the role of government. Moreover, he was caught in a financial dilemma that jeopardized almost any course of action. On the one hand, the recession that had begun in 1960 was growing worse; business investment and construction had declined and unemployment was rising. On the other hand, the country faced a near crisis in its international balance of payments. During the last three years of the Eisenhower administration, money spent abroad (for imports, economic and military aid, private investment) had exceeded income *from* abroad (from exports, interest, and services) by a total of $11 billion. The result was an outflow of gold that was increased after the election by the action of European speculators who feared that the new administration would devalue the dollar. Recognizing that this crisis would become more acute if he attacked the recession through large-scale pump-priming measures, Kennedy moved swiftly but circumspectly to ease both problems.

Instead of asking for large appropriations, he countered the recession through a variety of executive actions that did not weaken confidence in the dollar.[3] At the same time, he took action to restore the balance of payments without resorting to the remedies of raising tariffs or reducing foreign aid. Announcement of these measures, together with his financial restraint in domestic policy and his appointment of the conservative Dillon as secretary of the treasury, restored European confidence and ended

[3]For example, he reduced the interest rate on FHA loans to stimulate housing construction, released $274 million in highway improvement funds, ordered early payment of $258 million in veterans' insurance dividends, and accelerated governmental procurement and construction programs in depressed areas. The Defense Department released $690 million of ready funds for this latter purpose, and the Federal Home Loan Bank Board liberalized its lending rules for savings and loan associations and thus released over $1 billion in credit to stimulate residential building.

speculation in gold. The balance of payments deficit began to decrease as these policies took effect, and American exports rose sharply. The country began climbing from the recession in 1961.

With the economy expanding again, the president took pains to reassure suspicious businessmen that he was not an irresponsible spender. Eager to avoid inflationary action that would nullify returning prosperity, he found it ironic and galling that the first real assault upon a relatively stable price level came from an important segment of the business community. Negotiations between the steel companies and the United Steelworkers over a new wage contract broke down in March 1962. Kennedy and Secretary Goldberg were instrumental in persuading the two sides to renew negotiations, and they were heartened when a noninflationary two-year wage contract was signed on March 31. Kennedy, with assurances from steel executives that the agreement obviated the need for a price rise, praised both labor and management for their "industrial statesmanship" in holding the line against inflation. Ten days later, however, Roger M. Blough, chairman of the board of United States Steel, informed the president that his company was raising its prices by six dollars a ton. Five other major steel companies announced an identical increase on the following day.

Feeling betrayed, Kennedy scathingly denounced the companies in a press conference on April 11. Quoting figures, he denied any justification for the rise. He was shocked, he said, that "a tiny handful of steel executives, whose pursuit of private power and profit exceeds their sense of public responsibility, can show such utter contempt for the interest of 185,000,000 Americans." The president did more than denounce, and the nation looked on in awe as he mobilized the massive power of the federal government. The FTC launched an inquiry into the possibility of collusive price-fixing. The Treasury Department spoke of a tax investigation. The Department of Justice announced that it would see whether antitrust laws had been violated. The Defense Department hinted that its steel purchases would be made from companies that had not raised their prices.

The offending companies quickly surrendered. Bethlehem Steel announced on April 13 that it was rescinding its price rise, and the others followed suit a day later. Kennedy's attempts to cultivate better relations with the business community suffered heavily, but the public on the whole was impressed by the president's firmness under pressure.

None of this, however, had changed the situation in Congress, where Kennedy's New Frontier program—designed to bring the country out of recession, stimulate growth, and assist needy groups by economic and social welfare measures—encountered strong opposition from the conservative coalition. Administration Democrats, led by venerable Speaker Sam Rayburn, moved to render the coalition less effective by striking at one of its strongest bastions, the House Rules Committee. This committee included eight Democrats and four Republicans. Its chairman and one other Democrat were southern conservatives who consistently voted with the Republicans to deadlock the committee and bottle up progressive bills. Rayburn, after a bitter contest, won House acceptance in January 1961 of a resolution enlarging the Rules Committee from twelve members to fifteen. He appointed two pro-administration Democrats and one Republican to the new seats, thereby making possible an eight-to-seven Kennedy majority.

Administration forces then waged a succession of hard-fought battles over each item in the Kennedy program, usually winning or losing by a handful of votes. Honors were about evenly divided during the two sessions of the Eighty-seventh Congress. Conservatives scored a major triumph in the first session by defeating an ambitious school-aid bill. It called for a three-year federal grant of $2.3 billion to the states for school construction and teachers' salaries and the allocation of another $3.3 billion over five years for colleges and federal scholarships. The bill passed the Senate easily in May 1961, but Roman Catholic bishops then demanded that parochial schools receive aid on an equal basis with public schools. Kennedy refused to accept this amendment, and the search for a compromise proved futile. Two Catholic Democrats on the Rules Committee joined with conservatives to bury Kennedy's bill, and the House later defeated a weak substitute measure.

The New Frontier recorded a few victories during 1961. One was a new Housing Act authorizing nearly $5 billion for local urban renewal projects over a four-year period. Strenuous administration efforts also mustered a majority in favor of a higher minimum wage bill. The new law, which went into effect in September, raised the hourly minimum in two stages over a two-year period from $1 to $1.25 for the 24 million workers already covered, and extended the same coverage to some 3.6 million new workers, primarily in retail and service industries. A third triumph, the Area Redevelopment Act of May 1961, provided nearly $400 million in federal loans and grants for assistance to "distressed areas" of economic stagnation and high unemployment. Kennedy also obtained liberalization of social security benefits and new funds for the Federal Water Pollution Control Act, which permitted construction of sewage treatment plants.

The record was different in 1962. Speaker Rayburn, stricken by a fatal cancer, died on November 6, 1961. His successor was less able to enforce House discipline in the administration's behalf, and the unrepentant southern chairman of the Rules Committee once again kept several bills from coming to a vote. Aside from the Trade Expansion Act, the New Frontier's successes were few and unimportant, far outweighed by the defeat or crippling of key measures.

Three such measures finally passed, but without the provisions that Kennedy wanted most. One, the Revenue Act of 1962, granted business $1 billion a year in special tax credits to encourage new outlays for machinery and equipment. But it omitted Kennedy's proposals for withholding income taxes on dividends and interest and curtailing expense account deductions. The second, a farm bill designed to impose strict production controls on wheat and feed grains, was beaten in the House in June; a weak substitute measure merely extended the existing voluntary control program for another year. In a third compromise, Congress authorized the president to channel $900 million in public-works projects into areas with high unemployment but denied his request for stand-by authority to initiate a $2 billion antirecession public-works program.

Conservatives defeated several important measures outright during 1962. Chief among these was a bill to provide health insurance for the aged through the Social Security system. This so-called Medicare program, advocated by Kennedy since 1960, was killed in the Senate in July by a vote of fifty-two to forty-eight. Another major loss was a proposed new Cabinet Department of Urban Affairs. The House Rules Committee stifled bills that sought to aid unemployed youth, migrant workers, commuter transit, and medical schools. All in all, the legislative record of Kennedy's first two years fell considerably short of fulfilling the New Frontier program.

Nor did the midterm elections figure to improve his prospects. If the past was any guide, the Democrats could expect to lose at least forty seats in the House and six in the Senate. None of these losses was likely to occur in the South. Kennedy wanted to fight for a more amenable Congress, even though (as Franklin Roosevelt and Dwight Eisenhower could testify) presidential intervention frequently backfired. But Kennedy, bent on defeating Republicans because of their opposition to domestic reform, ignored the warnings of his advisers and launched an energetic nationwide campaign on behalf of Democratic candidates. The effects of this bold move will never be fully known, for Kennedy abruptly ended his tour in mid-October in order to deal with the Cuban missile crisis (see pp. 837-838). Although the Democrats went on to score an impressive midterm victory, gaining four seats in the Senate and losing only two in the House, the results could neither be attributed to Kennedy's electioneering nor interpreted as a mandate for his domestic program. More likely, the victory reflected public approval of his firm stand against the Soviet missile threat.

A time of peace and prosperity appeared at hand as the president faced the new Congress in January 1963. Russian-American relations had improved; Berlin was quiet; Southeast Asia appeared relatively tranquil. The economy was humming. Yet in his Annual Message Kennedy warned against any temptation to relax and insisted that complacency was unwarranted. Deeply rooted social problems persisted. Material prosperity was only one side of the coin. "The quality of American life," he emphasized, "must keep pace with the quantity of American goods." The United States had to be strengthened by investing in its youth, by safeguarding the health of its citizens, by protecting the basic rights of *all* the people, and by prudent use of its resources. Furthermore, the rate of economic growth had to be sustained and unemployment reduced.

The administration's program, however, fared no better in the first session of the Eighty-eighth Congress than it had in the Eighty-seventh. The lawmakers slashed Kennedy's $4.5 billion foreign aid request by fully 33 percent and pared more than 10 percent from NASA's $5.7 billion space program. The fight for a reduction in federal income taxes, which Kennedy had called the "essential" step toward accomplishment of his goals, was symptomatic. The president was determined to sustain an economic growth rate of at least 5 percent. The economy, advisers argued, could be stimulated through either large-scale governmental spending or a tax reduction that would increase consumer purchasing power. Choosing the latter course, Kennedy submitted a detailed proposal cutting federal tax revenues by $11 billion from individuals and $2.6 billion from corporations. Tightening present schedules would raise an additional $3.4 billion, thus making a net tax reduction of $10.2 billion. The plan immediately came under fire from all sides. Labor demanded further cuts favoring lower-income groups; business claimed discrimination against middle-income groups; and Congress complained that federal revenues could not be cut in the face of a projected $8.3 billion budget deficit. Despite a White House request for prompt action, Congress moved slowly. The Ways and Means Committee did not order the bill reported until September. The House finally passed it, substantially in the form Kennedy had requested, in September 1963, but the Senate adjourned without taking action.

Kennedy's program for improving the quality of American life scored a few successes. Congress approved $150 million in grants to states for construction of nonprofit community health centers for the mentally ill. It also authorized construction grants and student loans for medical and dental schools, an expanded campaign against air pollution, and a one-year extension of the National Defense Education Act. Yet 1963, in terms of congressional response to administration requests, was the least productive of Kennedy's three years in office. Frankly viewing these years as educative and preparative, the president confidently anticipated further legislative triumphs during the 1964 session and the fruition of his program during his second term.

4. The Black Revolt

Meanwhile, discontent among black Americans had grown by leaps and bounds; the 1950s, it now appeared, had been mere preamble. The new president's first reminder came with the "freedom rides" that began in the spring of 1961. Sponsored by several interracial organizations, black and white citizens attacked segregation in interstate travel by chartering buses and riding through the deep South, deliberately entering segregated restaurants and terminals en route. White resentment quickly boiled over. In Anniston, Alabama, one group of riders was attacked and beaten; a second freedom bus was halted, bombed, set afire, and destroyed by a mob. When the riders tried to proceed from Anniston to Montgomery, the situation deteriorated still further. The governor of Alabama denounced them as "rabble rousers" and made no attempt to curb resentful white citizens. Thus encouraged, they mobbed the riders so ferociously that Washington, in the absence of effective action by state or local authorities, had to intervene. Only after Attorney General Robert Kennedy sent several hundred federal marshals to Montgomery to prevent further violence did the governor act, proclaiming martial law and employing state national guardsmen and police to restore order.

The freedom rides continued. Bruised but unintimidated, most of the original group left Montgomery for Jackson, Mississippi, in a bus under heavy police escort. Many of them were arrested in Jackson for violating a segregation ordinance, but officials were scrupulously careful to prevent further acts of violence. Thereafter, in fact, the riders met with little more than epithets, angry stares, and occasional mass arrests. State authorities, aware of the unfavorable publicity that Anniston and Montgomery had received in the North and abroad, took steps to avert similar outbreaks.

Results came in late 1961 when the ICC ordered all bus companies to desegregate interstate routes, post signs to that effect on every bus, and cease stopping at restaurants and terminals that maintained segregated facilities. The bus lines complied, and an increasing number of local terminals took down "white" and "colored" signs and grudgingly admitted blacks who sought to enter the white section. The freedom rides resulted in partial rather than total victory, but another area of Jim Crow practice had been broken.

Yet growing numbers of blacks were less impressed by victories won than by dismal evidence of what remained to be done. They were far from free, a century after Emancipation. In the South, they still encountered discrimination at nearly every turn. They could not eat in most white restaurants or register at white hotels. Few of their children, despite the *Brown* decision, attended schools with whites. In many southern counties they still lacked the power to vote and thus seek redress through political action. In the North, millions of blacks were mired in urban slums where high unemployment, inadequate opportunities, inferior schools and housing, and disproportionate crime and disease rates were facts of life.

Kennedy's commitment to civil rights was genuine, but his initial performance was, as Martin Luther King, Jr., observed, "essentially cautious and defensive." The president named a few blacks to positions of high responsibility, including Robert C. Weaver for the sensitive post of federal housing administrator. A new Committee on Equal Employment Opportunity, headed by Vice-President Johnson, persuaded more than fifty of the nation's largest defense contractors to sign "plans for progress" embodying agreements to provide equal opportunity. Firms holding governmental contracts in excess of $10,000 were required to file periodic reports proving compliance with federal antidiscrimination policy. An executive order in November 1962 prohibited racial and religious discrimination in housing built or purchased with federal aid.

Presidential action grew progressively stronger and more forceful in response to events in the deep South. First came the case of James H. Meredith, a black Mississippian who had instituted a suit charging racial bias after the state university had rejected his two applications to enroll. A variety of legal means to secure his admission all failed in the face of Governor Ross Barnett's defiance of judicial authority. Finally, after Meredith's fourth attempt to register was rebuffed by two hundred state police on September 27, 1962, the United States Circuit Court in New Orleans announced that its powers were exhausted and that further action was up to the executive branch. President Kennedy moved decisively to insure compliance with the court's orders. On September 30 he ordered several hundred federal marshals to accompany Meredith to the university campus at Oxford; sent federal troops to a base at nearby Memphis, Tennessee; and federalized the Mississippi National Guard. That evening a mob of students and bystanders attacked the marshals with rocks and occasional rifle fire, and a fierce riot ensued until dawn of the following day. State police withdrew, and only the prompt arrival of federal troops saved the lightly armed and outnumbered marshals. Two civilians were killed and seventy wounded before order was restored. State resistance thereupon melted away as federal bayonets kept order. Meredith was registered on October 1 and began attending classes under heavy armed guard.

Impressed by a need for stronger action, President Kennedy requested new civil rights legislation in February 1963. He sought to secure greater protection for voting rights, assist areas in process of desegregating their schools, and extend the Civil Rights Commission. Black leaders demanding "Freedom Now" were less than satisfied with this moderate program, but the southern catalyst was still at work. Dr. King began a campaign in April 1963 to end discrimination in shops, restaurants, and employment in Birmingham, a center of deep southern resistance. The protest, small at first, began with lunch counter sit-ins, picketing, and demonstrations. The mood grew uglier as King met the full force of Birmingham law enforcement authorities, led by Police Commissioner Eugene "Bull" Connor. The climax came on May 3, when Connor used fire hoses and police dogs to break up a protest march. Television forced these events upon the nation's attention and helped rouse white middle-class consciences. Civil rights protests spread rapidly; over 750 demonstrations occurred across the nation in the spring and early summer, bringing nearly 14,000 arrests in eleven southern states alone.

Kennedy addressed the nation on June 11 with a call for action. "We face," he declared, "a moral crisis as a country and as a people." Black aspirations could no longer be denied. The United States could not preach freedom abroad and practice discrimination at home. "This is one country," the president emphasized. "It has become one country because all of us and all the people who came here had an equal chance to develop their talents." But this had not been true for blacks, and prompt governmental action was imperative. He then submitted a new civil rights bill containing all the features of his February proposal, plus many new ones in the areas of desegregation, equal employment, and equal access to public accommodations. Demonstrations, continuing while Congress considered this proposal, were climaxed by a march on Washington on August 28. Although many feared that the remonstrance would alienate congressmen and might lead to violence, the 250,000 participants conducted themselves with remarkable decorum and dignity. The House of Representatives passed a strengthened version of Kennedy's bill. But the Senate Judiciary Committee, headed by James O. Eastland of Mississippi, held the bill so long that little action in the upper house was possible before adjournment. Although a hard fight loomed and a Senate filibuster appeared certain, Kennedy was reasonably confident that Congress would enact civil rights legislation during the next session.

5. *The Cold War Continues*

These domestic strivings were largely overshadowed by foreign difficulties. The most nettlesome, beyond doubt, concerned Cuba. Kennedy's long-range plans for Latin America, exemplified in the Alliance for Progress, seemed threatened by Fidel Castro's foreign and domestic policies. The Cuban dictator hoped to export his radical social and economic revolution throughout the Western Hemisphere, and few Latin American governments were sufficiently stable, popular, and progressive to feel immune. The trend in Castro's domestic program, and the network of economic, military, and technical agreements he had recently concluded with the Soviet bloc, suggested that Cuba was about to become a full-fledged Communist state. Many feared that his subversive activities and radical doctrines, if unchecked, would lead to Communist gains all over Latin America.

The United States government had concluded that the only feasible prospect of overthrowing the Castro regime lay in supporting the thousands of anti-Castro Cubans who had fled from their homeland after 1959. The Eisenhower administration therefore decided, as early as March 1960, to equip and train Cuban refugees under CIA auspices in camps in Central

America and the southern United States. The CIA was convinced that a well-timed assault by these refugees would set off a massive general uprising of disaffected Cubans and topple Castro. Blueprints for such an invasion, prepared before Eisenhower left office, awaited only Kennedy's approval before being put into action.

Kennedy, despite some misgivings, ordered the assault to take place. He did so against the advice of several White House staff members and Senator J. William Fulbright, chairman of the Foreign Relations Committee. Kennedy thus became responsible for one of the most ill-conceived, dismally planned, carelessly managed, and ineptly executed episodes in American history. Cuban airfields were attacked on the morning of April 15, 1961, by B-26 fighter bombers, which the United States claimed were flown by defecting Cuban air force pilots, but which were later revealed to have taken off from a refugee base in Central America. The actual landing took place before dawn on April 17 in the *Bahía de Cochinos*—the Bay of Pigs—on the southern coast of Cuba. An estimated fifteen hundred Cuban refugees took part in the landing, which in the absence of air or naval artillery cover was pinned down and overwhelmed within three days by Castro's armed forces. Contact with the underground was not made, and the anticipated anti-Castro uprising did not occur.

The fiasco had disastrous repercussions. The United States suffered widespread condemnation and loss of prestige. Khrushchev combined threats of possible Soviet intervention in defense of Cuba with pious lectures to Kennedy on good conduct and the importance of observing international law. Other Latin American governments, disturbed by this apparent recrudescence of Yankee imperialism, refused to cooperate with Washington's attempts to induce inter-American action against Cuba. Castro, strengthened rather than weakened by the episode, proceeded to make Cuba an even greater storm center in hemispheric affairs. He reaffirmed his ties with Russia, claimed that only Soviet offers of armed assistance had deterred further American assaults, formally proclaimed Cuba a socialist country, and quickened the pace of socialization. The one benefit accruing to the United States from the Bay of Pigs disaster was its effect upon the president. Shaken but not demoralized, he publicly accepted full responsibility for the failure and obviously learned much from it.[4]

Cuba was only the first of sobering international experiences in store for President Kennedy. The second was his conference with Premier Khrushchev in Vienna on June 3-4, 1961. It was not a summit meeting but a private encounter, permitting the two leaders to exchange views and take each other's measure. Khrushchev, perhaps hoping to overawe the youn-

---

[4]The overconfidence with which Kennedy and his youthful advisers had approached foreign affairs gave way to caution. Determined never again to be so dependent upon a single source of information, Kennedy ordered a reexamination of the intelligence-gathering and policy-making functions of the CIA and appointed General Maxwell D. Taylor to the White House staff as special military adviser.

ger man, adopted a truculent and at times bellicose posture. He handed Kennedy a memorandum defining the Soviet position on Berlin. Without setting a deadline, it renewed demands for an "immediate" peace treaty with Germany and an end to the present four-power occupation of Berlin. Khrushchev made it plain that he would sign such a treaty with East Germany whether the Western allies participated or not, thus forcing them to negotiate their rights in Berlin directly with a government they refused to recognize.

Berlin had once again become the focus of a crisis that could lead to war. Months of tension followed the Vienna meeting. The Western allies, though uncertain and divided as to how much, if anything, was negotiable in this tangled controversy, were united in their determination not to back down. Their responses flatly rejected any solution to the Berlin problem that did not guarantee Western presence, Western access, and unhampered freedom for the citizens of West Berlin. President Kennedy drew the line most sharply in a national broadcast on July 25, 1961. "We do not want to fight, but we have fought before," he said. "We cannot and will not permit the Communists to drive us out of Berlin, either gradually or by force."

The situation grew steadily more ominous. Both the United States and the USSR announced increases in their armed forces and military budgets. East Germany, determined to block the flow of refugees to the West, closed the boundary between the Eastern and Western sectors in August while Soviet troops surrounded the city. Transit to and within the city by West Berliners, West Germans, and allied personnel was theoretically unaffected by the maneuver, which sought to control the movement of East Germans and thus shut their escape hatch to the West. Yet all but twelve—soon all but seven—of the eighty crossing points between the sectors were completely closed, and other restrictions further encroached upon Western rights of movement in East Berlin. While the Soviets ignored allied notes protesting the illegality of this action, East German authorities physically sealed off the entire Berlin border by a wall of concrete blocks and barbed wire running across the city. To many, the Berlin wall was a perfect symbol of the barrier that divided East and West, a monument to communism's failure in the battle for the mind of man.

The wall and the city it bisected were scenes of violent and dangerous incidents for months. To reassure the anxious West Berliners, who feared that allied acquiescence in the building of the wall heralded their abandonment of Berlin, President Kennedy provided three tokens of Western determination to remain. He sent Vice-President Johnson on a visit to the city to renew American pledges of support. He appointed General Lucius D. Clay, symbol of Western firmness during the airlift crisis of 1948–1949, as his personal representative there. And, in a dramatic move, Kennedy reinforced the American garrison by dispatching a battle group of fifteen hundred troops down the hundred-mile *Autobahn* from West Germany to Berlin.

Although diplomatic exchanges failed to break the impasse, tension eased when Premier Khrushchev announced in October that he would no longer insist upon a settlement before the end of the year. Soviet harassment of Allied air corridors was halted in March 1962. General Clay, expressing the belief that Berlin was no longer in immediate peril, returned to the United States in May.

While these tensions relaxed, the Cuban situation grew worse. By early 1962 the island had virtually become a Soviet satellite and military base, capable of supporting guerrilla operations and subversion all over Latin America. The other Latin American republics became sufficiently worried to vote Cuba's exclusion from the inter-American system in January. The United States tightened its trade embargo against the Castro regime. Large numbers of Soviet technicians began to arrive in Cuba during the summer. Many Americans favored stronger action, and Republicans began to criticize the administration for failing to prevent the Cuban arms build-up or cause Castro's fall. Kennedy replied in August that he was opposed to an armed invasion, adding that the United States would take no stronger action so long as arms shipments to Cuba remained "defensive" in nature. He received explicit assurances from Soviet Foreign Minister Andrei Gromyko in a White House meeting on October 18 that such arms were in fact defensive. But four days earlier, the president had learned from aerial reconnaissance that medium-range ballistic missiles were already present in Cuba, and that the construction of launching pads was nearing completion.

Reporters detected unusual activity and an air of incipient crisis in Washington during the week of Gromyko's visit. Then the White House announced on Monday afternoon, October 22, that the president would address the nation at seven o'clock that evening in a message of "national urgency." He began this address by announcing that the crisis concerned Cuba. He then proceeded to stun the world with a series of uncompromising statements. "Within the past week," he said, "unmistakable evidence has established the fact that a series of offensive missile sites is now in preparation" on Cuban soil. Announcing establishment of a "strict quarantine of all offensive military equipment under shipment to Cuba," the president asserted that the United States would demand "prompt dismantling and withdrawal" of all offensive bases at an emergency meeting of the Security Council and would maintain the quarantine—actually a selective blockade—until the bases had been removed.

Kennedy put the issue squarely in one of the most chilling statements of intent ever uttered by an American president: "It shall be the policy of this nation to regard any nuclear missile launched from Cuba against any nation in the Western Hemisphere as an attack by the Soviet Union on the United States requiring a full retaliatory response on the Soviet Union." He also made it clear that he was not thinking solely of the Caribbean: "Any hostile move anywhere in the world against the safety and freedom of peoples to whom we are committed, including in particular the brave people of West Berlin, will be met with whatever action is needed."

It was the most direct and ominous confrontation in the history of Soviet-American relations, and the world hovered on the brink of war for a few tense days. The Soviets, caught off balance, replied hesitantly and with restraint. Secretary-General U Thant called upon Khrushchev and Kennedy to suspend both the missile build-up and the blockade and negotiate the dispute peacefully. Kennedy's reply did not close the door to negotiations but insisted that suspension of the blockade depended upon the removal of offensive bases and international inspection to insure compliance. American warships and planes in the Atlantic and Caribbean began the quarantine patrol and prepared to intercept all vessels bearing offensive equipment to Cuba.

The American people, their Western allies, and the OAS rallied overwhelmingly behind President Kennedy, and Russia backed away from the challenge. American planes reported on October 24 that Soviet vessels carrying jet aircraft and other "contraband" had altered course away from Cuba. Two Cuban-bound Soviet ships bearing no offensive equipment submitted to American inspection and were permitted to proceed. Khrushchev first offered to remove Russian bases in Cuba in exchange for American evacuation of its obsolete bases in Turkey. When Kennedy refused, the Russian premier agreed to the substance of the president's demands on October 28. The USSR would remove all offensive weapons and submit to international inspection if the United States would pledge not to invade Cuba. Kennedy agreed to these terms and suspended the blockade, while U Thant went to Havana to arrange details for the inspection. Dismantling and removal of the bases took place promptly.

Khrushchev, having grossly underestimated American resolve, shifted back to an emphasis upon peaceful coexistence, and Soviet-American relations improved markedly. Control of nuclear testing provided the key to a détente. Russia, at the height of the Berlin crisis in 1961, had announced the resumption of atmospheric nuclear testing on an unprecedented scale. The first detonation in the new series occurred in September, and nearly two dozen others, including one massive superbomb in the 50 megaton range (equivalent to 50 million tons of TNT), took place in Siberia and the Arctic during the next two months. The United States responded in March 1962 by announcing plans for its own tests but stipulated that it would cancel them if Russia agreed to a test ban treaty. When Moscow refused, America conducted extensive atmospheric and underwater tests in the Pacific during the spring of 1962. Meanwhile, the tripartite test ban conference, responding to UN appeals, had resumed its sessions in Geneva in November 1961. The talks proceeded intermittently until the following September but the two sides could not reach agreement on the crucial question of inspection.

Following its Cuban misadventure, the Soviet Union evinced a willingness to reopen negotiations. Private talks began in January 1963. The United States, with improved methods of detection, had lowered its previous demand for twenty on-site inspections per year to seven. Russia, heretofore unwilling to accept any inspections, now conceded that two or three might be allowed. But the two nations could not bridge this narrow gap. On the other hand, minor progress at the Geneva test ban talks—an agreement to install a "hot line" for direct communication between Moscow and Washington—kept hopes for a détente alive.

President Kennedy took the initiative in a speech at American University on June 10, 1963. Calling for a reexamination of American attitudes toward the Soviet Union and the cold war, he emphasized that negotiation of a test ban treaty was the first step along the road to peace. He dispatched Undersecretary of State Averell Harriman, one of the nation's ablest and most experienced negotiators, to Moscow in July. Harriman found the Russians both willing and eager to conclude a treaty. The question of underground testing, which would require on-site inspections, was put aside in favor of an agreement banning atmospheric explosions. The treaty, initialed on July 25, provided that there should be no atmospheric or underwater testing and banned other tests that would spread radioactive debris outside the territorial limits of the testing state. Both nations pledged to refrain from "causing, encouraging, or in any way participating in" tests anywhere else. Either party could withdraw from the agreement upon three months' notice if its supreme interests were in jeopardy. Eventually, more than one hundred nations signed the treaty, but the two powers closest to a nuclear capacity, France and China, refused.

The test ban treaty was favorably received in the United States, notwithstanding claims that the agreement endangered American security. The Senate ratified it by a vote of eighty to nineteen on September 24, 1963. Other signs of lessening tensions followed. President Kennedy proposed a joint Soviet-American expedition to the moon and authorized the sale, through private channels, of American wheat to the Soviet Union. Indeed, as the year ended, Russian-American relations were more cordial than at any time since the Second World War.

6. Trouble in Southeast Asia

Even as East-West relations began to show positive signs of transcending the cold war at last, the mentality that it had fostered was propelling the United States toward unalloyed disaster in Indochina. Among the earliest dilemmas confronting President Kennedy upon taking office in 1961 were those centered in this region. Native Communist movements, aided and encouraged by Ho Chi Minh's energetic government in North Vietnam, threatened pro-Western regimes in Laos and South Vietnam (see pp. 801–802).

Three rival "governments" contended for primacy in Laos. The right wing faction of Prince Boun Oum, despite diplomatic and material support from the United States, was suffering defeat after defeat at the hands of Prince Souphanouvong's Pathet Lao forces and seemed about to collapse. Other Laotians supported the neutralist regime of the exiled premier, Prince Souvanna Phouma—whom Russia, while airlifting equipment to the Pathet Lao, still recognized as the rightful ruler.

Only large-scale American intervention could save Boun Oum, and Kennedy chose to avoid this course. Instead, he affirmed the goal of a "neutral and independent Laos" and pressed for a diplomatic solution along that line. The Soviets agreed in April 1961 to discuss the problem at an international conference and join other powers in requesting a cease-fire. All three Laotian princes and representatives of thirteen nations—the Western Big Three, Russia, China, Canada, Poland, India, Burma, Thailand, Cambodia, and North and South Vietnam—assembled in Geneva on May 16. In session almost continuously for fourteen months, the conferees hammered out terms for an international agreement safeguarding Laotian neutrality and independence. But their attempt to persuade the three princes to form a coalition government proved more difficult to achieve than East-West accord. The princes, especially Boun Oum, were refractory and suspicious, and the Pathet Lao repeatedly violated the cease-fire in order to improve their strategic position. Communist subversive activity from Laos became so menacing that Kennedy sent naval units and five thousand marines to Thailand in May 1962 to prevent border violations.

The United States suspended aid to the uncooperative Boun Oum in March and virtually forced him to come to agreement. Souphanouvong, Souvanna Phouma, and General Phoumi Nosavan, who had replaced Boun Oum, signed a compact on June 12 establishing a "troika" coalition with Souvanna Phouma as premier. The new government approved a cease-fire on June 24. The Geneva conference thereupon approved two neutrality pacts, signed by all fourteen nations on July 23. The first was a joint declaration pledging respect for Laotian neutrality, territorial integrity, and independence. The second was a joint protocol specifying procedures for the withdrawal of foreign troops and the future safeguarding of Laotian neutrality.[5] The United States began withdrawing its troops from Thailand on July 1.

Meanwhile, the situation in South Vietnam had deteriorated steadily. Despite American aid, the pro-Western government of Ngo Dinh Diem

[5]This agreement prohibited reentry of foreign troops, forbade Laos to join or accept protection from SEATO or any other regional alliance, and reestablished the International Commission (composed of Indian, Polish, and Canadian truce teams) that had overseen Laotian neutrality after the Geneva armistice of 1954.

was unable to cope with the mounting subversive activities of Vietcong nationalist guerrilla forces. A veritable Greek tragedy was taking shape for the United States—and for millions of Vietnamese as well—in this unfortunate land.

The tragedy had its origins in France's long, vain struggle to retain her Indochinese colony from 1946 to 1954. Its prologue and theme could be read in America's response to the cold war, which froze an entire generation of leaders into a position of unyielding anticommunism. Reality, for makers of American foreign policy, stopped short of questioning the basic assumption of the cold war: the notion of a monolithic world Communist movement whose agents were at work in every corner of the globe as part of a vast, coordinated campaign to destroy the "free world." In this view, anyone who proclaimed himself an enemy of communism—including not a few petty tyrants and reactionary feudal princes—became an ally to be wooed, aided, and sustained in the great death struggle. Such a leader was Ngo Dinh Diem, supported by Secretary Dulles after the Geneva armistice of 1954 as a bastion against further Communist incursion in Southeast Asia (see pp. 795–797). Diem, a relic of a dying order whose regime grew more repressive and narrowly based each year, had become as out of tune with political and social reality in Southeast Asia as Chiang Kai-shek had in China a few years before.

Nowhere in the United States did the cold war's constricting world-view press more heavily than upon the Democratic party. Vulnerable since midcentury to McCarthyite charges ("soft on communism," "twenty years of treason"), the party's normally progressive-minded leaders were, by and large, committed "cold warriors" whose hard-line anticommunism was built upon both a deep conviction and a sense that as Democrats they had no choice.

John F. Kennedy, for all his cool-headed pragmatism and awareness of complexity, never quite transcended the cold war mentality. He knew that world communism was no monolith and that new policies, especially with regard to China, would have to be evolved. But he did not feel that his administration, with its hairline margin of victory and its legacy from the McCarthy era, dared even hint at a revision of America's devout anti-China posture during his first term. Meanwhile, in a world full of problems demanding prompt attention, the pragmatic approach put a dangerous premium on quick makeshift solutions and the short-run view. Kennedy, anxious to satisfy suspicious conservatives at home and convince watchful enemies abroad, felt a need to prove the nation's firmness and resolve in the wake of the Bay of Pigs fiasco and Khrushchev's militant challenge at Vienna.

Vietnam, a peripheral and relatively remote area of American concern, appeared to offer such a test of firmness. An ineffectual regime, crumbling under the pressure of a determined nationalist movement, therefore became a focus for American attention in the battle to keep another country from falling to communism. "It was the irony of the Kennedy Administration that John Kennedy, rationalist, pledged above all to rationality, should continue the most irrational of all major American foreign policies, that policy toward China and the rest of Asia. . . . Because he did not look back on America's China policy, it was easier for him, in 1961, to move forward in Vietnam."[6]

Washington had few illusions about Diem; but, as Vice-President Johnson observed after a visit to Saigon in May 1961, "he's the only boy we got out there." The United States accordingly embarked upon ambitious programs of expanded economic assistance and military training. The latter program was enlarged again in the fall, and by early 1962 over four thousand American military personnel were on the scene, instructing and at times assisting South Vietnamese troops in more efficient supply and combat operations. American military forces in Vietnam gradually swelled to over sixteen thousand during the next eighteen months; sixty American soldiers were killed in action in 1963. The costs of supporting Diem's regime skyrocketed.

To make matters worse, the United States government stumbled into a systematic process of self-deception. The tragedy unfolded in piecemeal fashion, but inexorably: an American military assistance mission that reported only favorable news about the progress of the war (ignoring what its own field officers said was happening); an ambassador who spoke only with Diem's small clique and unquestioningly passed on the regime's dreamlike version of reality; a pledge of support by Vice-President Johnson; a request by Diem for American combat troops, eagerly seconded by American military men whose formula for success, then and thereafter, was invariably *more*—more men, more weapons, a wider war.[7] Thus by slow degrees, imperceptible save in retrospect, did the United States become more firmly attached to what one reporter aptly called "the tar baby of Saigon."

The administration, knowing from independent news sources that the situation in South Vietnam was neither good nor promising, proceeded to employ every device of press agentry to make their venture *look* viable because they believed it *had* to be. The commitment grew with the rhetoric, step by fateful step—until the rhetoric came to be believed by the very people who had papered over the truth in order to justify what they were doing. And the commitment tended to become absolute, even in the

---

[6]David Halberstam, *The Best and the Brightest* (New York, 1972), pp. 102, 104.

[7]President Kennedy opposed the sending of combat troops, despite pressure from both Diem and American military advisers. But he agreed, by way of compromise, to a progressive enlargement of the military advisory and support mission. The voice of the military thus grew louder, and their demand for a wider American role became harder to ignore. In opposing pressure for escalation and trying to resist it, Kennedy learned that bureaucracies and programs generate a momentum of their own that can sometimes be slowed but rarely stopped altogether.

face of continued political and military deterioration in South Vietnam. Diem's well-equipped but poorly led and unenthusiastic army was no match for the purposeful, well-trained Vietcong forces. At the same time, non-Communist opposition to his regime grew steadily. Buddhist leadership rose in protest in June 1963, and when Diem crushed this uprising, Buddhists turned to the tactic of suicide by immolation in hopes of mobilizing public opinion. Diem, who had never responded to American pleas that he initiate needed reforms and broaden the base of his government, declared martial law and attacked the Buddhist pagodas. Washington finally gave up on him, virtually conceding the bankruptcy of its previous policy. In November a military coup that had the tacit support of the Kennedy administration finally overthrew the regime and assassinated Diem. The year ended with the Vietnamese situation in turmoil and future prospects bleak.

7. Tragedy at Dallas

In the autumn of 1963, President Kennedy's thoughts turned to next year's election. His first term had been a time of preparation. He confidently expected reelection, a clear mandate, and the fulfillment of his legislative program. He journeyed to Texas in late November, in the company of the vice-president, for the purpose of mending political fences. Texas was badly split between the liberal Democratic forces of Senator Ralph W. Yarborough and a conservative faction led by Governor John B. Connally. Kennedy sought unity for the coming election. He arrived in Dallas, a center of extremist right wing activities, on the morning of November 22. Ambassador Stevenson, attending the celebration of United Nations Day in the city a few weeks earlier, had been spat upon and hit by a picket sign. But there was no sign of hostility as the president's motorcade proceeded into downtown Dallas. Friendly, cheering people lined the streets, and Kennedy twice halted the motorcade to greet them.

At 12:30 P.M., CST, just as the motorcade turned on to Elm Street and went past the Texas Book Depository Building, shots rang out. The first hit Kennedy in the back of the neck, exiting through his throat. He stiffened, then lurched slightly forward in his seat. Governor Connally, sitting in front of the president, was also hit. Then Kennedy received a bullet in the back of the head and fell into his wife's lap. The president was sped to Parkland Memorial Hospital, four miles away, but it was too late. He was pronounced dead at 1:00 P.M.

The apparent assassin, soon captured by police, was a twenty-four-year-old malcontent named Lee Harvey Oswald, with a record of emotional disturbance and grievances against society. Another killer murdered Oswald two days later. A special commission headed by Chief Justice Warren later concluded that Oswald's guilt was certain beyond any reasonable doubt and that he had acted as an individual rather than as "part of any conspiracy, domestic or foreign, to assassinate President Kennedy."

No single event in American history had ever caused such trauma. The president's body, taken to the White House, remained there until Sunday, when it was placed in the rotunda of the Capitol on the same catafalque that had held the body of Abraham Lincoln nearly one hundred years before. More than 250,000 people passed by to pay their last respects. Monday, November 25, was clear and cold, and a million people lined the streets of Washington to view the funeral, while millions more watched on television. Eight heads of state, ten prime ministers, and most of the world's remaining royalty added to the pomp and pageantry of the somber occasion. The cortege moved from the Capitol to St. Matthew's Cathedral, where the late president's life-long friend Richard Cardinal Cushing, Archbishop of Boston, said a funeral mass. The procession then moved down Connecticut Avenue to Constitution Avenue, past the Lincoln Memorial, and over Memorial Bridge to Arlington National Cemetery. There, on a hill overlooking the city of Washington, John F. Kennedy was laid to his final rest.

31

The Great Society
and the Vietnamese War

President Kennedy's successor, Lyndon B. Johnson, guided the nation during a turbulent and eventful period. Despite recurrent troubles in Europe, Latin America, and the Middle East, the United States and the Soviet Union moved closer to détente than they had been since the Grand Alliance of 1941–1945. In domestic affairs, while the aspirations of black Americans assumed revolutionary proportions and other minorities stirred restlessly, the new Democratic president was able to secure the enactment of a comprehensive program of social and economic welfare legislation. Yet Johnson's domestic reforms, comparable in scope to those of the New Deal, were soon overshadowed and weakened by deepening American involvement in Southeast Asia. Unable to extricate itself from this tragic struggle, rocked also by angry criticism and social turmoil at home, the Johnson administration drew to a close in 1968 with American society in a condition of violence, dissension, and disarray unequaled since the 1860s.

1. Johnson Takes the Helm

With Kennedy's death the eyes of the world turned to the new leader of the American people, Lyndon Baines Johnson. Born near Stonewall, Texas, on August 27, 1908, Johnson knew adversity as a youth. He completed his education at Southwest State Teachers College and taught school for a year. Politics, however, strongly attracted the young man. Both his father and grandfather had served in the Texas legislature, and he soon developed his own political ambitions. Johnson first came to Washington in 1932 as secretary to Representative Richard M. Kleberg. Four years later, at age twenty-seven, he was appointed national youth administrator for the state of Texas. This office proved a springboard for his election to the House of Representatives in 1937. Johnson, a staunch supporter of the New Deal, received President Roosevelt's attention and patronage in return. The rising politician won the Texas senatorial primary, tantamount to election, in 1948, defeating his opponent by eighty-seven votes. The Senate soon recognized his political talents, electing him minority leader in 1953—a rare tribute to a freshman senator. From 1955 to 1960 he compiled a distinguished record as majority leader.

Johnson's bid for the presidential nomination in 1960 was swept aside by the Kennedy bandwagon, as we have seen. Kennedy, aware of the strength Johnson would bring to the Democratic ticket, offered him the vice-presidential nomination. Few, including Kennedy, believed that Johnson would abandon his powerful position in the Senate, but he ignored the advice of close friends and accepted, eager to become a national instead of a sectional figure. He proved a loyal lieutenant to his young chief, and Kennedy, in turn, treated him with respect and kept him fully informed. While it is undoubtedly true, as Kennedy once said, that there is no adequate preparation for the presidency, no man ever came to the office with greater knowledge and mastery of the national political process than Lyndon Johnson.

But what of the man? Johnson, one astute commentator observed, was "the first uninhibited product of the American frontier to take over since Andrew Jackson."[1] The new president was direct and earthy, and his speeches frequently sounded like the homilies of a rural preacher. Vain and sensitive, he desired constant praise and approval and what he termed a national consensus. He was a hard-driving, quick-tempered man, harshly intolerant and abusive of associates who displeased him or critics who opposed him. His most striking personal characteristics were immense energy, drive, and determination—all of which, lacking outside interests, he channeled into politics. Though unideological in political philosophy,

[1] Michael Davie, *LBJ: A Foreign Observer's Viewpoint* (New York, 1966), p. 5.

he had a deep and passionate concern for the poor, the elderly, and the downtrodden. Government, he believed, existed to serve people and do for them what they were unable to do for themselves. Johnson, far more than Kennedy, was thus a direct inheritor of the New Deal tradition and its commitment to social and economic justice.

The new president promptly announced that his first task was to complete the Kennedy program. Knowing that economy had been the main congressional excuse for rejecting it, Johnson ordered a review of all federal programs and warned that expenditures had to be pared wherever possible. His final budget figure of $97.9 billion for 1965 envisioned a deficit of only $4.9 billion, less than half the estimated deficit for 1964. The president called this "an important first step toward a balanced budget."

Johnson's strategy enabled Kennedy's program to sweep through Congress. It passed his tax reduction bill (see p. 831) in February 1964, enacted a variety of conservation measures, and voted $375 million to aid in developing urban transit systems. When Johnson submitted a "bare bones" foreign-aid program calling for the expenditure of $3.5 billion— $1.1 billion less than the previous year's request—Congress reduced it by only $250 million, the lowest percentage cut in the seventeen-year history of the program.

President Johnson also continued the fight for civil rights legislation with unrelenting determination. "No memorial oration or eulogy," he stated in his first address to Congress, "could more eloquently honor President Kennedy's memory than the earliest possible passage of the civil rights bill for which he fought so long." The bill passed the House easily enough in February 1964, but a southern filibuster delayed matters in the Senate. However, only nineteen southerners participated; many were old men, and the ablest of them, Richard B. Russell of Georgia, did not seem to have his heart in the struggle. The bill's managers, Majority Whip Hubert Humphrey of Minnesota and Minority Whip Thomas H. Kuchel of California, maintained unrelenting pressure. They kept two senators on the floor at all times and enough supporters on hand to answer quorum calls. Finally, on June 10, fifty-seven days after formal consideration began, the Senate voted cloture on a civil rights debate for the first time in its history. The bill passed handily a week later by a vote of seventy-six to eighteen.

The Civil Rights Act of 1964, the most far-reaching law of its kind since Reconstruction, was quite similar to the bill President Kennedy had proposed a year earlier, together with strengthening features added by the House of Representatives in October 1963. At its heart was a section guaranteeing equal access to public accommodations. It also strengthened existing machinery for preventing employment discrimination by governmental contractors, established a Community Relations Service to help localities resolve racial disputes, and empowered the government to file school desegregation suits and cut off funds wherever discrimination was practiced in the application of federal programs. The Justice Department was authorized to enter civil rights suits pending in federal courts and to initiate suits to desegregate public facilities.

President Johnson could also point to a major legislative triumph of his own. In his first State of the Union message in January 1964 he had declared "unconditional war on poverty in America." One-fifth of the nation was impoverished in an affluent society, and legislation was urgently needed to combat illiteracy, unemployment, and the lack of public services. Congress responded with the Economic Opportunity Act of 1964, authorizing $947.5 million in 1965 to begin a three-year program. It provided, among other things, for a Job Corps to train youths in conservation camps and urban areas; a community action program aimed at job training and improved health and housing; and a domestic peace corps to cooperate with state and local authorities in combating poverty. The act established the Office of Economic Opportunity to supervise the program. R. Sargent Shriver, Jr., director of the Peace Corps, became head of the new agency in October.

2. *The Election of 1964*

While Johnson enhanced his strength, Republicans searched for a candidate to oppose him in 1964. Volunteers for the GOP nomination did not abound. The early favorites, Senator Barry M. Goldwater of Arizona and Governor Rockefeller of New York, had their first confrontation in the New Hampshire primary in March. To everyone's surprise, the voters rejected both men, writing in the name of Henry Cabot Lodge, Jr., ambassador to South Vietnam. Goldwater, who had advocated voluntary participation in Social Security and suggested giving NATO commanders the right to order the use of nuclear weapons, had acquired a reputation for irresponsibility. Rockefeller, on the other hand, had been hurt by a recent divorce and remarriage.

Lodge was the front runner as the Republican aspirants faced Oregon's voters in May, but Rockefeller came out on top after a vigorous campaign. With the Lodge boom deflated, Rockefeller and Goldwater again faced each other, and the California primary became the crucial test. Goldwater, who already controlled a large number of delegates to the national convention, had to prove his popularity with the voters before he could capitalize on this advantage. A victory for Rockefeller in California might not guarantee him the nomination, but it would assuredly give him a decisive voice in naming the candidate and writing the platform. California was thus a major showdown, bitter and intense. On June 2 California Republicans chose Goldwater by a narrow margin.

Although the Arizonan's nomination was now virtually assured, the liberal elements of the party, headed by Governor William W. Scranton of Pennsylvania, rallied in a last-minute "Stop Goldwater" movement. It was too late. The GOP convention, meeting in San Francisco on July 13, was a Goldwater affair all the way. This first became apparent when the platform committee, drafting the most conservative major party platform in modern times, pledged "limited, frugal and efficient" government at home and "a dynamic strategy aimed at victory" abroad. Party liberals, rebuffed in committee, carried the fight to the convention floor. They offered amendments to strengthen the civil rights provision, condemn by name extremist groups of the left and right, and reaffirm the president's exclusive control over nuclear weapons. A partisan convention booed, heckled, and raucously shouted them down, then nominated Goldwater on the first ballot on July 15. Showing no inclination to heal wounds, Goldwater chose Representative William E. Miller of New York, a former GOP national chairman known for his conservative views, as his running mate. Goldwater's acceptance speech further exacerbated the division between the two wings of his party. "Any who join us in all sincerity," he said, "we welcome. Those who do not care for our cause we do not expect to enter our ranks in any case." Finally, in a statement that became notorious, he declared: "I would remind you that extremism in the defense of liberty is no vice. And let me remind you also that moderation in the pursuit of justice is no virtue."

Goldwater had sounded the battle cry, saying that he had embarked upon a crusade, not a campaign. The conservative wing of the GOP, after years of frustration, had finally nominated one of their own. His political views left little role for the federal government in coping with the problems of modern society. Big government was unnecessary and usually corrupt. Americans should stand on their own feet and meet problems with the same self-reliance exhibited by their forefathers on the frontier. In foreign relations, the United States had to stand firm against world communism. There would be no more "capitulation" through fear of nuclear catastrophe. Freedom could not be compromised.

The Democratic convention, held in Atlantic City in August, was an anticlimax to the spectacle at San Francisco. Johnson, who managed the affair from beginning to end, was duly nominated. Some Democrats wanted Robert Kennedy for vice-president, but Johnson turned instead to Hubert Humphrey, an old friend and staunch liberal. The convention ratified the president's choice on August 26. To no one's surprise, the Democratic platform endorsed the Great Society.

The presidential campaign proved a dull affair. From the beginning, the polls indicated an overwhelming triumph for the Democrats. Even so, Goldwater's supporters talked bravely of a silent conservative majority that might carry their candidate to victory. They also hoped to capitalize on the white reaction against the black revolution. Governor George C.

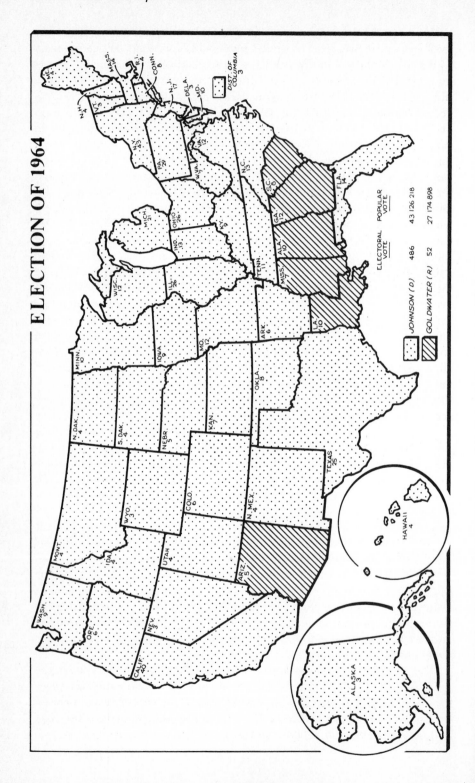

ELECTION OF 1964

	ELECTORAL VOTE	POPULAR VOTE
JOHNSON (D)	486	43 126 218
GOLDWATER (R)	52	27 174 898

Wallace of Alabama had demonstrated that such a backlash did exist. In the Democratic primaries Wallace, a strident segregationist, had captured 34 percent of the vote in Wisconsin, 30 percent in Indiana, and 43 percent in Maryland. Republican hopes of profiting from the backlash rose when riots erupted in black areas of northern cities during the summer. The first occurred in Harlem on July 18–23, leaving 1 dead and 140 injured. Others broke out in Rochester, Jersey City, Philadelphia, and suburban Chicago. But Goldwater, ignoring the wishes of many supporters, refused to exploit this touchy situation, and civil rights leaders worked effectively to quiet the restive black population as the campaign got under way. Johnson, shrewdly reading the signs, conducted a limited and restrained campaign. Dramatic events abroad diverted the nation's attention in mid-October when Premier Khrushchev was ousted from power in the Kremlin and China exploded its first nuclear device. National uneasiness redounded in Johnson's favor, and only the size of his majority now remained in doubt.

On November 3, 1964, the American people accorded Lyndon Johnson the largest popular vote, 43 million, that any presidential candidate had ever received to that time. His electoral majority was a thumping 486 to 52. Goldwater, trailing far behind with 27 million popular votes, carried only Alabama, Georgia, South Carolina, Louisiana, Mississippi, and Arizona. The sweeping Democratic triumph cut deeply into GOP strength at all levels. The Democrats gained 38 House seats, giving them a 295 to 140 margin in the next Congress, and picked up 2 seats in the Senate, making their majority 68 to 32. The GOP lost over 500 seats in state legislatures across the country. Republican inroads in the South brought more concern than satisfaction to party leaders in other sections, for these gains had been achieved largely by appealing to segregationists and other reactionary elements. Most Republican spokesmen frankly acknowledged the real significance of the election returns—that the American people had overwhelmingly affirmed their allegiance to the progressive tradition.

3. The Great Society

President Johnson, buoyed by his popular mandate, set forth the goals of the Great Society in his message of January 1965. Such a society, he observed, rested on abundance and liberty for all. Opportunities enjoyed by most Americans had to be opened to everyone, and the quality of life had to be improved. This could be accomplished by stimulating the economy, continuing the antipoverty programs, and developing imaginative solutions for the complex problems of modern urban society. It was imperative to control water and air pollution and preserve the country's natural beauty. A new and expanded program of aid to education was needed. In the following months Johnson submitted a flood of specific proposals to implement the Great Society.

Congress responded with an alacrity rarely seen on Capitol Hill. Its first major enactment was the Appalachian Regional Development Act, signed in March. Appalachia, extending from Pennsylvania to northern Alabama and encompassing 182,000 square miles and 17 million people, was a region of poverty, with a per capita income 40 percent lower than the national average and an unemployment rate 50 percent higher. Emphasizing economic development rather than welfare support, the act provided $1.1 billion in subsidies for highway construction, health centers, and development of resources. A joint federal-state agency, the Appalachian Regional Commission, would implement the program; the states would design projects to fit their needs and execute them following commission approval.

The administration also strove to alleviate one of the nation's most pressing problems, that of urban decay. The Housing and Urban Development Act of 1965, the most comprehensive legislation of its kind since 1949, extended the major programs of the Housing and Home Finance Agency, provided assistance for the construction of some 240,000 additional units of low-rent public housing, and authorized $2.9 billion in federal grants for urban renewal over a four-year period. Controversy over payment of direct federal rent supplements to low-income families temporarily stalled this provision, but funds for the purpose were obtained in 1966. Congress, at the president's request, also created a cabinet-level Department of Housing and Urban Development to administer the act and related programs. Robert C. Weaver, the first black ever named to the cabinet, became head of the new department in January 1966.

A further milestone was reached in 1965 with passage of the most significant piece of welfare legislation since the New Deal. President Truman had proposed a comprehensive plan for medical care for the aged, to be financed through Social Security, in 1945. During the next twenty years the proposal had faced the vehement and successful opposition of the American Medical Association. But Johnson, having made the program a major issue in his campaign, now had both a mandate and the necessary votes. Congress approved the Medicare bill by large majorities, and President Johnson signed it on July 30 in Independence, Missouri, with Truman at his side.[2]

Education, the president repeatedly emphasized, was the key to the

---

[2]The act, covering most persons sixty-five and older, included a basic health plan that provided up to ninety days of hospital care, one hundred days of nursing-home care, and one hundred home health-care visits. A supplementary plan, available to those who elected to pay a $3 monthly premium, covered 80 percent of the costs of a variety of health services, including doctors' fees, after a standard deduction of $50. General revenues and an increased Social Security tax, rising progressively to 11.3 percent in 1987, would fund the program.

Great Society. Although school and college enrollment approached 54 million and the nation spent a record $39 billion on education during the 1964-1965 school year, many Americans remained unable to provide their children with full educational opportunities. The Elementary and Secondary Education Act of 1965, passed in April, was a historic breakthrough, settling a twenty-year controversy over the use of large-scale federal funds to support primary and secondary education. The $1.3 billion program was designed primarily to aid schools with large numbers of children from low-income families. The act contained a formula for handling the thorny issue of federal aid to parochial schools: aid would be supplied to children attending both private and public schools, but public agencies would control expenditures. The president also won approval of the Higher Education Act of 1965 to expand federal aid on another level. It made scholarships available to more than 140,000 capable but needy college students and authorized a National Teachers Corps to provide qualified personnel for schools in poverty-stricken areas.

Although the scope and quantity of reform legislation fell off somewhat after 1965 in the face of mounting war costs, inflation, and a less cooperative Congress,[3] President Johnson added considerably to the Great Society's legislative foundations during his final three years in office. New welfare enactments included a series of provisions for expanded federal activity in the field of public health in 1966.[4] An amendment to the Social Security Act in 1967 raised pensions and enlarged the coverage for some 24 million persons. The minimum wage was raised in 1966 to $1.60 an hour, effective in 1968, for some 30 million workers already covered; in addition, over 8 million service employees, farm workers, and workers in retail stores, hotels, and restaurants were brought under the provision of the law for the first time. The president won firm congressional support— in excess of the amount he requested—for further massive infusions of federal aid to education at all levels in 1966, including $3.9 billion over a three-year period for colleges and universities and $6.1 billion for public schools in a two-year extension of the Elementary and Secondary Education Act.

Continued concern for the quality of urban life was reflected in the Demonstration Cities and Metropolitan Area Redevelopment Act of 1966—America's most ambitious effort on behalf of its hard-pressed

[3] The 1966 elections, in a fairly normal midterm reaction against the party in power, cost the Democrats 48 House seats and 4 Senate seats. In the Ninetieth Congress, which was more conservatively inclined than its predecessor, the Democratic majorities were 247 to 187 and 64 to 36.

[4] For example, amendments to existing statutes changed the pattern of federal assistance to state public health programs and made federal grants available for the establishment of regional medical centers for heart disease, stroke, and cancer. Other new or amended laws made federal funds available for constructing facilities in nursing schools, setting up scholarships for students in schools of nursing and public health, making grants to universities to improve their facilities in these areas, building community facilities for the mentally ill, and modernizing obsolete hospitals.

cities.[5] A housing act in August 1968 called for the construction or rehabilitation of 1.7 million units of low- and middle-income housing by 1970
and 6 million units by 1978. New concern for consumer protection was
reflected in so-called Truth-in-Packaging and Truth-in-Lending acts in
1966 and 1968. The former required sellers to provide accurate labeling of
the contents and quantity of packaged household goods; the latter required lenders and retailers to provide information about the exact interest charges on loans and credit purchases.

The government addressed itself to the nation's multifaceted transportation problem in a variety of ways. It granted funds for urban mass transit
and the development of fast trains on the metropolitan corridor between
Boston and New York and Washington. It created a new cabinet-level
Department of Transportation in 1966, embracing and coordinating many
federal agencies dealing with air, highway, and rail transport. And, as we
have seen, it passed a series of highway and traffic safety and automobile
emission control laws in 1966–1967.[6]

Since President Johnson's vision of the Great Society centered on an
interest in the quality of American life, it is not surprising that environmental issues took on increasing importance. Federal activity in the areas
of water and air pollution first became significant under President Kennedy and expanded markedly during the Johnson administration. Each
year brought new legislation and increased appropriations, the cumulative
effect being to widen the scope of federal responsibility and attack the
problem through formation of regional control agencies and planning commissions.[7] Other laws, notably the Highway Beautification Act of 1965,
which the president's wife, Lady Bird Johnson, was instrumental in obtaining, began attacking the man-made blight that lined America's roadways.
Concern for an industrial society's steady encroachments upon natural

[5]In brief, the act sought to encourage slum clearance and rehabilitation in some sixty to seventy
cities by covering up to 80 percent of the costs of planning and construction, to finance metropolitan area planning, and to underwrite the building of new model communities by providing land-
development mortgage insurance. The law attempted to improve the "total environment" of the
slumdweller by concentrating on better schools, hospitals, and job opportunities, as well as housing units, in the area being rehabilitated.

Another portion of the act sought to stimulate and coordinate comprehensive metropolitan
planning and construction by making supplementary grants to localities and other public bodies
seeking improved transportation facilities, water and sewer systems, hospital and medical facilities, recreational and open-space areas, and other needs.

[6]Moreover, the administration began to take greater account of human concerns in its highway
policy, as evidenced by innovations in the Federal Aid Highway Act of 1968 providing for more
equitable relocation payments to persons and businesses displaced by new highway construction.
The act also ordered equal employment opportunity on all highway projects receiving federal aid.

[7]Research, planning, coordination, establishment of mandatory standards and enforcement procedures, and construction of sewage and waste treatment plants were among the assorted goals of
such enactments as the Water Quality Act of 1965, the Solid Waste Disposal Act of 1965, the
Water Resources acts of 1964 and 1966, the Rural Water Supply Act of 1965, the Water Resources Planning Act of 1965, the Clean Water Restoration Act of 1966, the Air Quality Act of
1967, and several others.

surroundings led to a host of important legislation, beginning with the Land and Water Conservation Act and the National Wilderness Preservation Act in 1964. These were followed by statutes setting aside land for parks and recreational use, protecting various endangered species, and safeguarding such threatened national treasures as the Indiana dunes along Lake Michigan, California's giant redwoods, and several wild and scenic rivers.

As we shall soon note, the president won landmark victories in 1965 and 1968 in the field of civil rights. Although he lost a few minor battles and occasionally had to be content with partial or limited victories—as in his efforts to obtain home rule for the District of Columbia, which Congress grudgingly permitted on a rudimentary basis in 1967—his only conspicuous legislative defeat was a failure, in 1965-1966, to secure repeal of the "right-to-work" provision of the Taft-Hartley Act.

What brief general assessment of the Great Society legislation—and of its architect—is possible? A few judgments, certainly, appear warranted. Aided though he was for two or three years by generally favorable circumstances (uninterrupted prosperity, large congressional majorities, a sympathetic court, the groundwork and inspiration bequeathed by his predecessor), Lyndon Johnson earned full credit and the gratitude of posterity for achieving the most ambitious and many-sided program of welfare reform in American history. That some of the steps were tentative or long overdue—Medicare, urban renewal, concern for the disadvantaged and the elderly, environmental reform, fair housing—should not detract from the magnitude of the achievement. They were worthy beginnings that promised to light the way ahead.

And yet the program was no more than a beginning, and its momentum had largely disappeared even before Johnson left the White House. Changed circumstances rather than inherent defects were partly responsible for this. Congress, reflecting voter anxiety about crime, disorder, and inflation, became less favorably disposed toward large welfare expenditures after 1966. The blighting shadow of the war in Vietnam, which fell across the entire American landscape during the late sixties, soon diverted funds and attention from the Great Society. Johnson's approach, which grew out of a reluctance to raise taxes and a hope that the nation could afford both war and continued reform—guns *and* butter—added greatly to inflationary pressures and eventually proved a failure. Reform programs and appropriations were steadily reduced after 1965 as the war absorbed more and more of the mounting federal budget, until one reform-minded Democrat could announce in 1967 that "the Great Society is now, except for token gestures, dead. The fight for equal opportunity for the Negro, the struggle to save our cities, the improvement of our schools—all must be starved for the sake of Vietnam."[8]

---

[8] Arthur M. Schlesinger, Jr., *The Bitter Heritage: Vietnam and American Democracy* (Boston, 1967), p. 50.

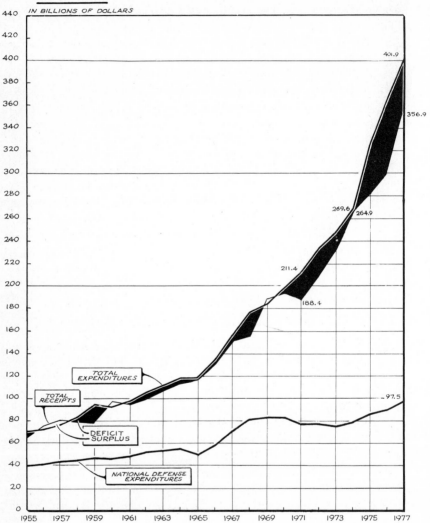

THE FEDERAL BUDGET
1955 - 1977

IN BILLIONS OF DOLLARS

TOTAL
EXPENDITURES

TOTAL
RECEIPTS

DEFICIT
SURPLUS

NATIONAL DEFENSE
EXPENDITURES

401.9

356.9

269.6 264.9

211.4

188.4

97.5

But the problem went deeper than this. Johnson's reforms, even at meridian, were all too often eclipsed by the complexity and magnitude of the problems they attempted to solve. The president's desire for consensus, his politician's sense of the art of the possible, often steered him away from the kind of all-out effort that most of these problems demanded. The new Department of Transportation, for example, was denied jurisdiction over the regulatory and rate-making functions performed by independent agencies like the ICC. And as one city planner bitterly noted, the authorization in 1966 of $2.3 billion for urban renewal projects over a six-year period would "scarcely meet the needs of a large slum area for a single year." The so-called War on Poverty was in reality little more than a pilot project; a truly successful campaign in this area, many felt, demanded not merely increased appropriations but a substantial redistribution of the nation's wealth—which the president, eager to retain business support, never really considered.

Indeed, American prosperity in the sixties was marred by a basic imbalance which Johnson's efforts, well intentioned though they were, barely touched. "The performance of the economic system," John Kenneth Galbraith observed in 1970, "is highly uneven. . . . For those who belong, there is no poverty. In consequence, our supply of automobiles, gasoline, highways, household appliances, detergents, gargles, space vehicles, and weapons is excellent. Outside of the world of the large corporation, the performance is far less reliable or satisfactory. This is especially true of that part of the economy which makes urban life agreeable or even tolerable. . . . And the reforms required to make it work uniformly and for individuals, not the corporations, are far more fundamental than anything contemplated by the cheap and easygoing liberalism of these last years."[9]

4. The Black Revolt Becomes Revolution

Black Americans vastly increased the scope and force of their drive for equal treatment and improved conditions during Lyndon Johnson's presidency. The progress of this revolutionary movement, though uneven and marred by violence and controversy, was dramatic; not since the 1860s had blacks taken comparable strides toward full citizenship. If at the end of Johnson's tenure the distance yet to be traveled along this lonesome road remained long, the distance already covered—in terms of psychological, social, economic, and political gains—was many times greater still.

To nearly everyone's surprise, the movement made its most striking

[9]John Kenneth Galbraith, "Who Needs the Democrats?" *Harpers Magazine*, 241 (July 1970), 47.

progress in the South—though not, of course, without a bitter struggle. Unabashed by recurrent white hostility, which had resulted in the murder of three civil rights workers in Mississippi in 1964, Martin Luther King launched a voter registration campaign centered in Selma, Alabama, in January 1965. When two months of intense effort managed to add only fifty names to the voting list, King decided to publicize the plight of the Negro in the deep South by staging a protest march from Selma to the state capitol in Montgomery, fifty miles away. It began on March 7 and was quickly broken up by state and local police using billy clubs and cattle prods. Federal Judge Frank M. Johnson, Jr., ordered Governor Wallace to permit the march and protect the marchers. When Wallace claimed that the state was unable to implement this order, President Johnson called the Alabama National Guard into federal service. The march took place without incident on March 21–25, culminating in a rally of twenty-five thousand persons in front of the first capitol of the Confederacy. White violence flared savagely in response.[10]

These events spurred new federal action. The president, appearing before a joint session of Congress on March 15, insisted that there be "no delay, or no hesitation or no compromise," and he used the language of the black revolution in an impassioned plea for justice. "Their cause must be our cause too," he said. "Because it is not just Negroes, but really it is all of us who must overcome the crippling legacy of bigotry and injustice. And we shall overcome."

Duly impressed, Congress responded with the Civil Rights Act of 1965. It suspended literacy and other voter tests and authorized federal supervision of registration in states and counties where such tests or devices had been employed prior to November 1964 and where less than half the adult residents had been registered or had voted in the presidential election of 1964. Federal examiners were empowered to register qualified applicants if state officials refused.

Thus during the Johnson years, and in no small part because of his leadership, did the executive, legislative, and judicial branches show what could be accomplished when they coordinated their efforts in behalf of Negro rights. As federal registrars and other officials proceeded to implement the provisions of the Civil Rights acts of 1964 and 1965, the walls of

---

[10]James J. Reeb, a Unitarian minister from Boston, died on March 11, 1965, after being beaten on the streets of Selma. Mrs. Viola Liuzzo, a civil rights worker from Detroit, was shot and killed on March 25 while driving her car on an Alabama highway after the march to Montgomery.

And yet even these tragic episodes were not without their ultimate ray of hope. Although state courts acquitted certain suspects in both the Reeb and Liuzzo killings, in December 1965 an all-white federal jury in Montgomery found three Klansmen guilty, under an old Reconstruction statute, of conspiring to deprive Mrs. Liuzzo of her civil rights; the three received the maximum prison sentence (ten years) permitted by the 1870 law. Another all-white jury in Anniston, Alabama, found a white man guilty of the slaying of Willie Brewster, a black, in July 1965. And in October 1967 an all-white jury in Mississippi convicted seven of eighteen white defendants, under the same Reconstruction statute, of conspiring against the rights of the three workers murdered in that state in 1964.

segregation crumbled. Encouraged and protected, southern blacks registered and voted in numbers unprecedented since Reconstruction.[11]

In consequence, the political climate in the deep South underwent a marked shift toward moderation, following a pattern that had begun a few years earlier in southern border states. Ardent segregationists like Wallace of Alabama and Governor Lester Maddox of Georgia still spoke the traditional language of angry defiance. But this sort of leadership declined visibly as the new black voting strength manifested itself. White politicians generally, even in such bastions of white supremacy as Mississippi and South Carolina, showed an increasing willingness to abandon racist postures and even, in many instances, to win support from both white and black voters for enlightened policies based on fair treatment for all. Moreover, black leaders began to win election victories now and then. There were about one hundred elected black officials, state and local, in the southern states in 1966. By 1972 this number exceeded one thousand and was still growing. It included over twenty state legislators; a few mayors, notably Charles Evers (brother of martyred civil rights leader Medgar Evers, murdered in 1963) of Fayette, Mississippi; and dozens of sheriffs and other law enforcement officials, state and local officers, school board members, and the like.

In this changing atmosphere the courts, aided also by executive support and new federal laws, quickened the pace of school desegregation from a crawl to a trot. White southerners, in the face of such efforts, demonstrated that obedience to law and acceptance of change could prevail over traditional racist responses. These persisted, of course; sporadic violence and ugly episodes continued to plague southern life. But such occurrences were far overshadowed by the degree of peaceful compliance. Whereas a bare 4 percent of black students in southern states attended public schools with whites in 1957 and no more than 9.2 percent did so in 1964, the figure leaped to 25.8 percent in December 1966 and reached 40 percent in 1968. Two years later, over 3.2 million black students, representing 84.3 percent of southern black enrollment, were attending desegregated schools. Subterfuges and evasions continued, to be sure, and the amount of actual classroom integration was frequently much less than the enumeration of "desegregated districts" might indicate. Hundreds of thousands of white children were sent to private schools of dubious quality by parents who would not tolerate integration. And yet the degree of acceptance, whether sullen or cheerful, was truly astounding. The black revolution had been accompanied, in the South as a whole, by something no less revolutionary in the realm of white attitudes.

[11]In 1960, 29.1 percent of voting-age blacks in eleven southern states (compared with 61.1 percent of that region's voting-age whites) were registered voters. By 1970 fully 62 percent of voting-age blacks (compared with 69.2 percent of whites) were registered in those eleven states. Black registration had gone up from 13.7 to 66 percent in Alabama, from 29.3 to 57.2 percent in Georgia, from 13.7 to 56.1 percent in South Carolina, and from 5.2 to 71 percent in Mississippi.

If the South was still far from having achieved a biracial millennium as the seventies began, it had so altered its traditional posture as to begin attracting a small but noticeable number of *northern* blacks to migrate *southward* in search of better opportunities and a more hospitable environment! "The tide of reverse migration of middle-class Negroes to the South from all parts of the country is setting in," columnist Roscoe Drummond reported in 1971. "It is visible and it is rising."[12] Even *Ebony*, a skeptical black periodical, observed that southern white attitudes had changed.

The situation in northern cities, where nearly half of the nation's blacks now resided, was less encouraging. Mass exodus to the suburbs by white families (and much retail trade and light industry) had narrowed the inner-city tax base, contributing to a steady deterioration in the quality of transit, sanitation, and other public facilities. This exodus also created a high degree of residential segregation in metropolitan areas. De facto school segregation was one result; another was a pattern of real estate values that acted to deprive many middle-class blacks of housing opportunities commensurate with their income. Many lower-middle-class blacks, similarly, were forced to remain in or near overcrowded slums. At the bottom of this uneasy urban pyramid were the ghetto poor, trapped in a vicious circle of inadequate education and training, inadequate job opportunities, inadequate wages, inadequate housing, and all of the debilitating problems of crime and squalor that festered around them. Rising expectations, resentment, and a collective impatience at the disparity between white liberal rhetoric and white actions had combined to induce a militance of revolutionary proportions among northern blacks.

One manifestation was a series of ghetto riots that rattled through metropolitan America like a chain of lethal firecrackers during the mid-sixties. An outbreak in Harlem in 1964 pointed the way, but the nation's attention first became riveted upon the unrest in its inner cities when riots convulsed the Watts section of Los Angeles during the week of August 11–16, 1965, killing 34 persons, injuring over 1,000, and doing an estimated $40 million in damage. Few cities with a substantial black population—North, West, or South; large, medium-sized, or small—escaped some sort of racial disorder in the years that followed. Hundreds of communities experienced major riots, the worst of which took place in Newark and Detroit in July 1967. The statistics were dismal and frightening: 26 dead, 1,000 injured, 1,400 arrested, and whole neighborhoods gutted in Newark; over 40 deaths, 350 injuries, 3,800 arrests, 5,000 burned out of their homes, and some 3,000 business establishments sacked and looted in Detroit. Firebombs and rooftop sniping tore the latter city, which required some 4,700

[12]Roscoe Drummond, "South Lures Blacks to 'Promised Land,' " *Chicago Today*, August 16, 1971.

federal troops to restore order and reminded a few awed observers of war-shattered Berlin in 1945.

Nearly all of these riots were triggered by minor episodes—an arrest, a routine police raid, a shooting, a thrown rock, a street corner argument. By and large, they were not "race riots" between black and white citizens of the sort that many American cities had experienced decades earlier. Most of the action took place within or on the fringes of slum areas; most of the destruction was wreaked upon ghetto homes, stores, and businesses (largely white-owned and operated); and most of the violence occurred between black rioters and police or national guardsmen. Studies indicated that the real trouble was rooted in chronic slum conditions aggravated by resentment of police tactics.

While such outbreaks dramatized the discontent among slumdwellers, a comparable militancy began to surface in the rhetoric and tactics of black leaders. As the sixties began, the dominant pattern of black leadership resided in veteran interracial groups like the NAACP, the Urban League, and the Southern Regional Council. The emphasis was upon working peaceably within the system to destroy discrimination, promote opportunity, and bring about the goal of a racially integrated society. Such leaders were increasingly challenged after 1960 by younger, angrier blacks who had come to feel that traditional goals and methods were no longer sufficient.

These new voices spoke in harsh and uncompromising tones. There was Malcolm X, for example, a forceful Black Muslim who broke with Elijah Muhammad to found his own Muslim group, the Organization of Afro-American Unity, in 1964. He won wide praise from blacks both within and beyond the Muslim movement for his clarion utterances in behalf of black dignity, full equality at once, and no compromise with white men. There was Stokely Carmichael of Trinidad and New York, educated at Howard University, who became chairman of the recently formed Student Non-Violent Coordinating Committee in 1966 and proceeded to shock the nation by enunciating a doctrine of "black power" that carried unmistakable overtones of violence. Texas-born Bobby Seale helped found the Black Panther Party for Self Defense in Oakland in 1966 to organize and instill self-respect among ghetto youths and induce better treatment from police by a series of aggressive confrontations and pressure tactics. The Black Panthers soon dropped "Self Defense" from their title and spoke the language of military preparedness and revolutionary socialism. There was Eldridge Cleaver, later the Panthers' "minister of information," who wrote *Soul on Ice*, a searing, inflammatory look at the race problem, while serving a prison term in California for narcotics possession. H. Rap Brown, an outspoken advocate of black power, urged guerrilla warfare against the white establishment. Playwright and poet LeRoi Jones and essayist and novelist James Baldwin contributed with bitter eloquence to the black protest movement during this period. So, a little later, did Angela Davis, a gifted young assistant professor of philosophy at the University of California at Los Angeles and an avowed believer in communism and revolutionary action. The League of Revolutionary Black Workers, organized in the late sixties by black union members in Detroit, battled racist practices in industry, labor unions, and local communities.[13]

Although the specific programs advocated by this new wave of leadership varied widely, certain common emphases stood out: a tendency to disavow integration in favor of some form of black separatism, a more or less radical economic agenda, a determination to instill greater dignity and race pride among blacks, a willingness to consider and employ violence and revolutionary tactics, and a profound distrust of the white man and all his works. Whatever the dangers and drawbacks in such an approach, there could be no denying that its advocates did much to give millions of black Americans a new sense of pride and potential.

There was considerable disagreement among observers (of all shades of political opinion and skin color) as to whether the northern racial picture was improving or worsening as the black revolution accelerated. Pessimists could certainly cite evidence to support their view. Fractured leadership hurt the civil rights movement as suspicion and animosity between black militants, black moderates, and white liberals flourished. Racial tensions undoubtedly increased in the face of mounting black demands. White suburbanites met open-housing demonstrations by Dr. King and CORE with stones, epithets, and mob violence, and they vehemently resisted the building of low-income housing projects. Congress, responding to this backlash, moved to crack down on rioters and checked or weakened various federal attempts to achieve better racial balance through housing laws or by busing students. A bill to prohibit discrimination in the sale or rental of private housing, put forth by President Johnson in 1966, was emasculated in the House and rejected altogether by the Senate when two attempts to halt a southern filibuster by voting cloture failed. Police and FBI activity against the Black Panthers included so much harassment and so many controversially violent raids that some saw it as a war of extermination. Far from crumbling, the walls of white resistance appeared to be rising higher than ever to contain the tide of black aspirations.

---

[13]Violence, in deed as well as word, flowed both to and from many of these new black leaders. Malcolm X was assassinated (allegedly by embittered followers of Muhammad) in New York in 1965. Eldridge Cleaver went into exile in Algeria to escape charges of assault and attempted murder after a gunfight with Oakland police in 1968. Seale served a prison term for carrying guns to a session of the California legislature. H. Rap Brown, indicted in Cambridge, Maryland, in 1967 for arson and inciting racial violence, disappeared before the indictment was handed down, and was missing for years; he resurfaced in time to be involved in (and eventually found guilty of) armed robbery and assault with a deadly weapon in New York in October 1971. Angela Davis was sought, held, tried, and ultimately acquitted on controversial charges of having aided and conspired in an attemped courtroom escape by Black Panther defendants in California in August 1970.

This somber picture was confirmed in March 1968 when the National Advisory Commission on Civil Disorders, recently appointed by the president to investigate the causes of the riots, issued its report. The commission, headed by former Governor Otto Kerner of Illinois, set forth the appalling conditions in America's inner-city slums and uncompromisingly placed primary blame for these conditions upon a deep-seated, pervasive pattern of white racism. An all-out effort to provide slumdwellers with adequate housing, jobs, training, education, and welfare was imperative. Otherwise, the commission concluded starkly, America would continue irrevocably along the path it was now following: toward "two societies, one black, one white—separate and unequal."

A startled president and Congress had barely begun to respond when a sniper's bullet placed a tragic exclamation point upon the Kerner commission report. Martin Luther King, visiting Memphis to aid the city's striking sanitation workers, was assassinated on April 4, 1968, on the balcony of the Lorraine Motel.[14] A new wave of riots erupted in many cities, although police restraint and determined efforts by black leaders and municipal authorities helped contain these outbreaks.

Further indication that the civil rights movement had reached a dead end came with the failure of the Poor People's Campaign that Dr. King had been about to launch in Washington, D.C., following his visit to Memphis. Led by the Reverend Ralph Abernathy, King's long-time associate and successor as president of the SCLC, some fifty thousand persons came to Washington in June and lined the Mall with the tents of "Resurrection City" in an effort to dramatize the plight of the nation's poor. But the campaign floundered from start to finish—plagued by divided and uncertain leadership, bad weather, and an unsympathetic response from local authorities, Congress, the president, and the public.

The historian who attempts to estimate the future prospects of anything as complex as American race relations is hazarding a dangerous guess indeed—especially if he chooses to fly in the face of such evidence. And yet there were grounds for believing that the nation had not really turned its back on the vision of a harmonious biracial society, and that progress was still taking place, North as well as South, in a variety of ways.

To begin with, there were the spectacular achievements of numerous blacks at the top—a more important and relevant factor than disillusioned militants, their eyes on the beleaguered urban poor, might admit. National recognition and acclaim were being won by blacks in unprecedented numbers. Memorable "firsts" included Robert C. Weaver's appointment to the cabinet; Edward Brooke's election to the United States Senate from Massachusetts in 1966 (the first black to sit in the upper chamber since Reconstruction, the first ever from a northern state or by popular vote); and

[14]The self-confessed killer, apprehended and extradited after a flight to Canada and England and eventually sentenced to ninety-nine years in prison, was James Earl Ray, a rootless ex-convict of checkered background and shadowy ties with white racist groups.

Thurgood Marshall's appointment to the Supreme Court in 1967. Black candidates won mayoral elections in Cleveland, Gary, Newark, Atlanta, New Orleans, and several smaller cities. Charles Evers ran a strong though unsuccessful race for the governorship of *Mississippi* in 1971; Shirley Chisholm, a black congresswoman from New York, contended seriously for the Democratic presidential nomination in 1972. Psychologist Kenneth Clark and historian John Hope Franklin reached the top of their professions, as did editor LeRone Bennett, reporter Carl Rowan, and writers like Ralph Ellison and James Baldwin. There was also a great galaxy of black superstars in the sports and entertainment worlds, including (to name a few of the very best) slugger Henry Aaron and pitcher Bob Gibson, opera singer Leontyne Price and rock singer Diana Ross, basketball players Wilt Chamberlain and Kareem Abdul-Jabbar, actor Sidney Poitier, running backs Jim Brown and Gale Sayers, comedians Bill Cosby and Flip Wilson. The impact of this outstanding array of achievement was considerable. Whites were visibly impressed. Blacks of merely adequate as well as stellar talent found that opportunities and conditions in the field of their choice had improved. And most important, the hopes, aspirations, and pride of a whole people were reinforced and enhanced.

The battle for full citizenship was also being waged on dozens of less spectacular fronts. Participants in these campaigns, which attracted fewer headlines than riots or mobs, included thousands of men and women of both races and all walks of life. Hundreds of riot-torn communities were shaken out of decades of neglect, complacency, or unawareness into constructive action. Many states and cities adopted or strengthened fair employment and open-housing ordinances. Many unions, churches, municipalities, business groups, foundations, and community-action groups launched remedial campaigns: to recruit and hire qualified blacks in white-collar and other skilled positions, to create new job opportunities and training programs for ghetto unemployed, to aid and underwrite black businesses and self-help efforts, to improve community recreational facilities, to hire more black policemen and teachers, and so on.

Congress, in the shocked aftermath of Dr. King's death, roused itself to overcome a Senate filibuster and pass the open-housing legislation that it had rejected in 1966 and 1967. The Civil Rights Act of 1968, prohibiting discrimination in the sale or rental of most public and private housing, applied to some 80 percent of the nation's dwelling units. The act also protected civil rights workers and provided severe penalties for interfering with the exercise of certain specified rights, such as attending school or working.

Moreover, sensational clashes tended to obscure the fact that hundreds of interracial communities and neighborhoods, urban and suburban, were quietly proving that whites and blacks could coexist in orderly and peaceful fashion. Noisy resistance in some areas to busing students into integrated schools was offset by the successful use of this technique in other communities. Many dedicated lawyers, doctors, teachers, and other professionals were devoting part or all of their skills and time on behalf of disadvantaged groups.

What it added up to, notwithstanding tension, the persistence of a hard core of prejudice, and a formidable economic problem, was a heightened *awareness* on the part of both blacks and whites—of themselves, and of one another. This was the beginning of wisdom, upon whose foundation much could be built. It offered hope that mutual understanding and respect would someday prevail, and that the words of Dr. King's favorite spiritual—"Free at Last, Free at Last, Thank God Almighty I'm Free at Last!"—would yet come to describe the relations between black and white in the United States.

5. *The Supreme Court in the 1960s*

The Supreme Court continued, under Presidents Kennedy and Johnson, to affirm and expand its new role as protector of individual rights. Historians will probably agree that in the sixties, as in the fifties, no legislative or executive actions—not even the most ambitious of the Great Society enactments—could match the significance of certain landmark decisions on civil rights, on due process in criminal cases, and, most notably, on the nature of the electoral process.

Problems raised by the black revolution occupied much of the court's time. Many cases coming before it involved the review of convictions obtained by state and local authorities on trespass or criminal mischief statutes against civil rights workers for sit-ins, protest marches, and demonstrations. The court, in *Burton* v. *Wilmington Parking Authority*, 1961, expanded the coverage of the Fourteenth Amendment by ruling against the exclusion of blacks by private owners of restaurants located on state property. *Peterson* v. *City of Greenville*, 1963, extended this principle, under certain conditions, to privately owned facilities. *Cox* v. *Louisiana*, 1964, reversed the conviction of a civil rights leader under a Louisiana statute prohibiting disturbance of the peace. Such laws, aimed at protests against discrimination and segregation, were an infringement of the rights of free speech and assembly. But this decision, the court pointed out, should not be interpreted as approving riotous conduct, or even peaceful demonstrations, which conflicted with honest efforts to promote law and order, regulate traffic, and protect property.

Federal civil rights legislation fared well in the courts. The validity of the public accommodations section of the Civil Rights Act of 1964 was sustained in *Heart of Atlanta Motel* v. *United States*, 1964. Prohibitions against racial discrimination by hotels providing lodging to transient guests, the court ruled, constituted a legitimate exercise of federal power over interstate commerce. The same principle was applied to restaurants in *Katzenbach* v. *McClung*, 1964. The court unanimously dismissed *South Carolina* v. *Katzenbach* in March 1966, thereby upholding the validity of the Civil Rights Act of 1965. In a related matter, the court struck down the Virginia poll tax in state and local elections,[15] holding, in *Harper* v. *Virginia State Board of Education*, 1966, that such a tax violated the Fourteenth Amendment's equal protection clause.

The Civil Rights Act of 1968 was actually upheld even before it went into effect. In 1967 the justices affirmed a decision of the California Supreme Court invalidating a recent amendment to the state constitution which sought to protect a property owner's right to sell or lease to whomever he pleased. The effect of this decision was to reinstate a California law of 1963 forbidding discrimination in the sale or lease of houses containing more than four dwelling units. And in *Jones* v. *A. H. Mayer Co.*, 1968, the Supreme Court went the whole distance and swept aside discrimination in the sale or lease of all public and private housing by finding applicability in a century-old civil rights statute. "Racial discrimination which herds men into ghettos and makes their ability to buy property turn on the color of their skin," the court proclaimed flatly, "is a relic of slavery."

Striking at the very core of white supremacy dogma, the court, in *Loving* v. *Virginia*, 1967, swept aside state laws prohibiting interracial marriage. Chief Justice Warren, calling marriage a "basic civil right," declared that a denial of this freedom "on so unsupportable a basis as the racial classification so directly subversive to the principle of equality at the heart of the Fourteenth Amendment, is surely to deprive all the state's citizens of liberty without due process of law." A public interracial marriage took place in Mississippi without incident in 1970.

Indigent defendants in criminal cases often found it difficult to make full use of the judicial process to protect their legal rights. The court moved to rectify this situation in a number of historic decisions. In *Gideon* v. *Wainwright*, 1963, it held that a state was obliged to supply defense counsel to indigent defendants even in noncapital prosecutions. The *Gideon* decision applied retroactively to all convicts who had been tried and found guilty of noncapital offenses without benefit of counsel. *Fay* v. *Noia*, 1963, expanded the right of prisoners to obtain judicial review of questionable court procedures used in their trial. The court also continued to expand the coverage of the Fourteenth and Fifth Amendments in protecting individuals against the harsh administration of criminal law. *Escobedo* v. *Illinois*, 1964, decreed that a conviction was invalid when the police had either refused to permit a suspect to have counsel during interrogation or had failed to inform him of his right to remain silent. A series of decisions

---

[15]The Twenty-fourth Amendment, passed in 1964, had banned poll taxes in federal elections.

on June 13, 1966—notably *Miranda* v. *Arizona*—established firm guide-lines for the treatment of arrested persons. Such persons had to be advised of their right to remain silent or have a lawyer present during interroga-tion, and counsel had to be provided, even at state expense, if requested by the suspect.

This last decision, applying the privileges of the Fifth Amendment to the police station, provoked vigorous dissent from several justices. John M. Harlan termed it a dangerous experiment in view of the increasing crime rate. "Nothing in the letter or spirit of the Constitution or in the prec-edents," he maintained, "squares with the heavy-handed and one-sided action that is so precipitously taken by the court in the name of fulfilling its constitutional responsibilities." Chief Justice Warren, speaking for the ma-jority, countered that the right against self-incrimination was enshrined in the Constitution and "cannot be abridged."

The court continued to scrutinize and occasionally demand revision of state criminal process. One of its most significant assumptions was that the applicability of the Bill of Rights to federal power and procedure was fully extendable to the states under the terms of the Fourteenth Amendment. For example, in *Duncan* v. *Louisiana*, 1968, the court held that a misde-meanor case entitled the defendant to a trial by jury under the Fourteenth Amendment's due process clause because the Sixth Amendment would accord him this right in a federal court. Earlier, in a related application of the Bill of Rights, the court (in *Engel* v. *Vitale*, 1962, and *School District of Abington Township* v. *Schempp*, 1963) outlawed local or state laws requir-ing Bible reading and prayers in public schools on the ground that such practices constituted an establishment of religion contrary to the First Amendment. These decisions set off much public furor, but a movement to reverse them by constitutional amendment ran aground on a national conviction, expressed officially by several major Protestant denominations, that the court was right.

Decisions affecting civil rights and criminal due process were overshad-owed by the court's application of the "one man, one vote" principle. *Baker* v. *Carr*, 1962, made legislative apportionment by the states subject to the scrutiny of the federal courts. The case involved representation in the legislature of Tennessee. The make-up of that body, as in most states, reflected the rural-urban balance of forty or even sixty years earlier. Not wishing to lose their power, rural lawmakers had blocked reapportion-ment decade after decade, while their districts lost population and metro-politan areas mushroomed. Urban voters had grown restive under this form of inequality, and when *Baker* v. *Carr* opened the question to judicial review, suits demanding reapportionment were immediately brought in over two dozen states.

The first significant case to be decided involved the legality of Georgia's county unit system, used in primary elections for state offices and United States Senate seats. *Gray* v. *Sanders*, 1963, struck down this system as a violation of the Fourteenth Amendment's equal protection clause in that undue weight had been accorded rural votes. The high-water mark came with *Reynolds* v. *Sims,* 1964, and a series of related cases. The court now held that representation in *both* houses of a state legislature had to be based upon districts having roughly equal population. The court was widely criticized for exceeding its prerogative and usurping functions assigned to the legislative branch, but Chief Justice Warren disagreed. "Legislators," he wrote, in *Reynolds* v. *Sims,* "represent people, not trees or acres. Legislators are elected by voters, not farms or cities or economic interests. As long as ours is a representative form of government, and our legislators are those instruments of government elected directly by and directly representative of the people, the right to elect legislators in a free and unimpaired fashion is a bedrock of our political system."

Casting a wider net, the court declared in *Wesberry* v. *Sanders,* 1964, that the "one man, one vote" mandate was inherent in Article I of the Constitution as applied to seats in the national House of Representatives. States were instructed to draw the boundaries of their districts so that members of Congress would represent areas of roughly equal population. "One man, one vote" became the ruling principle across the entire spectrum of American politics when the court extended it, in *Avery* v. *Midland County,* 1968, and several related cases, to most *local* governmental units.

6. Continued Perplexities in a Changing World

The Johnson administration faced mounting problems abroad in meeting the responsibilities of American power. The Atlantic community seemed on the verge of breakup, while unrest in Latin America and a brief but portentous war in the Middle East posed threats to world peace. At the same time, internal stresses within the Communist bloc were accompanied by further slow improvement in Soviet-American relations.

The Common Market and NATO's unified command structure represented important steps toward a united Europe in close partnership with the United States, but centrifugal pressures were increasing in the sixties. One of the strongest of these was a prolonged controversy over the control of nuclear weapons. Washington's proposal to resolve this difficulty by creating a multilateral nuclear force—a fleet manned by mixed crews and equipped with atomic weapons—encountered opposition from both Great Britain and France.

British obstacles to Atlantic unity dated from the late fifties. One was a reluctance to enter the Common Market and thus loosen ties with Commonwealth partners; the second was a dislike of surrendering their independent nuclear capability. American sympathy for this attitude led

President Eisenhower to promise in 1960 that Britain could share in the Skybolt missile system then being developed by the United States. Skybolt, a bomber-launched rocket with a thousand-mile range, seemed to offer Britain and her obsolete V-bombers a relatively low-cost independent deterrent. But Skybolt proved so slow and costly a project, in comparison with the growing effectiveness of America's Minuteman and Polaris missiles, that President Kennedy decided to cancel it. The British, having abandoned their own medium-range missile project in anticipation of Skybolt, were understandably upset. Kennedy sought to restore Anglo-American harmony in December 1962 by offering Britain some Polaris missiles if the British agreed to assign their Polaris-equipped forces to NATO's projected multilateral nuclear force. Prime Minister Macmillan finally agreed, with the proviso that Britain could withdraw these missiles if its national security seemed in jeopardy.

The United States also offered to supply Polaris missiles to France under comparable conditions. But President de Gaulle, who both reflected and fanned a resurgent French nationalism, flatly rejected this proposal and added that France would continue to develop her own nuclear weapons. De Gaulle also blocked Great Britain's belated bid to join the Common Market, implying that a unified western Europe should be led by France rather than what he termed the "Anglo-Saxon nations." The French president remained unalterably opposed to Washington's plan for a multilateral nuclear force, and Franco-American relations worsened markedly both before and after Kennedy's death. Paris announced in March 1966 that it was withdrawing all French troops from NATO, though France would remain a member of the organization. De Gaulle then requested the removal of NATO headquarters and all American military personnel and installations from French soil, setting April 1967 as a deadline for this withdrawal. NATO duly transferred its headquarters to Brussels and American forces were relocated, although President Johnson reaffirmed America's determination to maintain NATO with or without France. "We shall not," he said, "abandon an institution which has proved itself in the hour of peril."

But the North Atlantic alliance had come upon lean days. Plans for the multilateral nuclear force got nowhere. A small group of senators led by Mike Mansfield of Montana began urging a substantial reduction of American forces in Europe. A quarrel between Greece and Turkey over the relative political status of their respective nationals on the island of Cyprus strained the alliance and threatened to result in war. The irrepressible de Gaulle infuriated most English-speaking Canadians by ostentatiously proclaiming his sympathy for the French-speaking separatist movement in Quebec. Members of the Common Market further integrated their economies and various supranational administrative structures in 1967, but followed French lead in refusing bids by Great Britain and most of her partners in the European Free Trade Association for membership in the Market.[16]

Actually, NATO's difficulties reflected the accomplishments of the alliance. The United States, determined to reconstruct Europe after 1945, had poured its treasure into the continent; the resultant prosperity testified to the effectiveness of those efforts. Yet as a strong and vital community emerged, it became less dependent upon American support. Disunity seemed the price of success.

Latin American unrest presented more immediate problems, with Panama affording the first serious crisis. Relations between Panamanians and American residents of the Canal Zone, long strained, broke out in violence in January 1964 when Panamanian students demanded that their national flag be flown alongside the American flag at Balboa High School in the Canal Zone. Twenty-one Panamanians and three American soldiers were killed in the riots that followed, and Panama broke off diplomatic relations. When tempers cooled the two nations agreed to let the OAS mediate the dispute. These efforts, reinforced by secret talks between Panama and the United States, resulted in a joint declaration in April 1964 calling for renewed diplomatic intercourse and "the prompt elimination of the cause of the conflict." Negotiations produced draft treaties in 1967 providing for Panamanian participation in the canal's management and profits and an end to exclusive United States sovereignty in the Canal Zone. But obstacles to ratification arose in both countries. Internal upheavals in Panama, which brought a military junta to power in 1968, further impeded negotiations. Meanwhile, considerations induced by the size of many new warships and supertankers led the United States to begin looking to the possibility of a new sea-level canal across Central America.

More serious trouble erupted in the Dominican Republic. The United States had become involved there following the overthrow of the dictatorial Trujillo regime in 1961. The Kennedy administration, seeking to make the country a showpiece of the Alliance for Progress, supplied economic aid and encouraged the election of Juan Bosch, a distinguished novelist and political liberal, in December 1962. Bosch proved unable to alleviate his country's chronic social and economic problems, however, and military leaders ousted him in September 1963. Kennedy, disappointed at this turn of events, withheld recognition from the new regime and suspended American economic aid. President Johnson restored diplomatic relations

---

[16]Despite political discord, economic relations in the Atlantic community had never been closer. Within the Common Market, intracommunity tariffs on industrial goods were lowered another 5 percent in 1967, reaching a point 15 percent of their level ten years earlier; another reduction in 1968 removed such internal tariffs altogether, along with quotas. In December 1966, three years ahead of schedule, the seven members of the European Free Trade Association removed the last tariffs on industrial goods traded within the group, thus establishing a single home market of 100 million persons. And completion of the so-called Kennedy round of tariff reductions in May 1967 among members of the OECD—a move made possible by the Trade Expansion Act of 1962— acted to stimulate an already thriving trade among all members of the North Atlantic community.

in December but maintained an attitude of cautious reserve. Donald Reid Cabral, head of the civilian junta that came to power after Bosch's fall, was equally unsuccessful. Sabotage, strikes, and undergound resistance kept the country in turmoil. Any hope of solving its economic difficulties vanished when the price of sugar, the island's major product, dropped sharply in 1964. Cabral's efforts to restore stability by reducing wages and military spending only served to fuse most elements of the population in opposition to his regime. Antigovernment forces, led by the army, rebelled on April 24, 1965, toppling Cabral. But pro-Bosch elements of the coalition, distrusting the army's promise to hold free elections, demanded that the constitution of 1963 be restored and that Bosch resume the presidency. Violence broke out in the city of Santo Domingo when the army refused to meet these demands; the army attacked the city, while the defiant rebels elected a provisional president.

These events caused consternation in Washington. The administration knew that Communist elements had infiltrated the rebel forces and feared, not knowing the extent of their influence, that they might be able to seize power and turn the island into another Cuba. Determined to prevent such an outcome, President Johnson landed a contingent of marines on April 28, 1965. Over twenty thousand American troops soon followed. The United States tried to generate support for the intervention by requesting the creation of an Inter-American Peace Force, which the OAS, with some reluctance, approved on May 6. Units from Paraguay, Nicaragua, Honduras, and Brazil later joined American forces in the Dominican Republic.

On September 3 the United States installed a provisional president, Héctor García-Godoy, to serve until elections could be held. The rebels, reduced to their last stronghold, had no choice but to submit. The army capitulated after the United States threatened to cut off its funds. Unrest continued to simmer, occasionally erupting in violence, but the situation remained under control. García-Godoy, backed by American troops, cleared the way for free elections by assigning most military and rebel leaders to diplomatic posts abroad. The elections in June 1966 resulted in a surprising victory by Joaquin Balaguer, a moderate, over the favored Juan Bosch, who had returned from exile. A measure of peace and stability returned to the Dominican Republic, and Johnson withdrew American troops in September.

The Middle East, meanwhile, posed a continual threat to world peace. The tensions that had made the area a storm center since midcentury were in no way abated during the sixties. Poverty, political instability, and unrest plagued most of the Arab states. Egyptian President Nasser's aggressive efforts to foster pan-Arab unity under his hegemony by harnessing and abetting the forces of revolutionary nationalism merely added to the antagonisms that underlay Middle Eastern politics. His ambitions, fanned by Soviet technological, economic, and military aid, were resisted by conservative rulers like Feisal of Saudi Arabia and pro-Western leaders like Tunisia's Habib Bourguiba. Soviet interest and influence in the region waxed steadily. Further complications stemmed from the tangled network of economic and political interests bound up with oil, pipelines, and strategic trade routes.

Arab-Israeli antagonism, of course, remained the most serious and explosive of these interrelated problems. A UN Emergency Force, created after the war of 1956 as a peace-keeping measure, patrolled the Israeli-Egyptian border, but the danger of another war remained constant. The sparks that continually threatened to ignite this tinderbox included periodic shelling and raids into Israeli territory by Palestinian Arab guerrillas and terrorists, launched from neighboring Arab states with or without the knowledge (and at times with the connivance) of the government involved. Such episodes invariably provoked drastic reprisals from Israel and kept the region in turmoil.

The predictable eruption took place in the spring of 1967. Terrorist raids from Syria's Golan Heights, just across the Israeli border near the Sea of Galilee, touched off a retaliatory air attack on April 7 that destroyed several Syrian planes and penetrated within sight of Damascus. Renewed raids prompted a severe warning from Tel Aviv in early May. Syria, claiming an Israeli military build-up along its borders, invoked the defense pact it had concluded in November 1966 with Egypt, and both Arab countries began to mobilize. Nasser now moved recklessly to the fore. During the week of May 18–22 he requested the UN to withdraw its forces from the Israeli-Egyptian border, sent his own troops into the buffer region thus vacated (including strategic Sharm El Sheikh, commanding entry to the Gulf of Aqaba), and proclaimed a blockade of Israel's Red Sea port of Elath.

Israel could only regard this as a blow at its vital interest—virtually an act of war.[17] When two weeks of futile international diplomacy failed to persuade Egypt to lift her blockade, Israel prepared to take matters into her own hands. Nasser, whose posture became more bellicose each day, concluded an agreement with King Hussein of Jordan on May 30 placing Jordanian armed forces under "united" Arab command. This action further convinced Tel Aviv that an all-out Arab attack was imminent.

Accordingly, Israeli forces launched a sudden offensive on the morning of June 5. Flying low to avoid radar detection, Israeli aircraft attacked enemy air bases and destroyed Egypt's air force. Armored columns, enjoying complete air protection, fanned out swiftly across the Sinai peninsula, routed the Egyptian army, and captured or destroyed hundreds of Egypt's

---

[17]It was partly to break such a blockade—Elath being a vital pipeline inlet and commercial link to Asia and East Africa—that Israel had launched its attack upon Egypt in 1956. Israeli forces had invaded the Sinai peninsula, captured Sharm El Sheikh, and lifted the blockade, relinquishing their hold upon this strategic spot in 1957 only after guarantees—by the United States, among others—that the UNEF would remain there and keep the Gulf of Aqaba open to Israeli shipping.

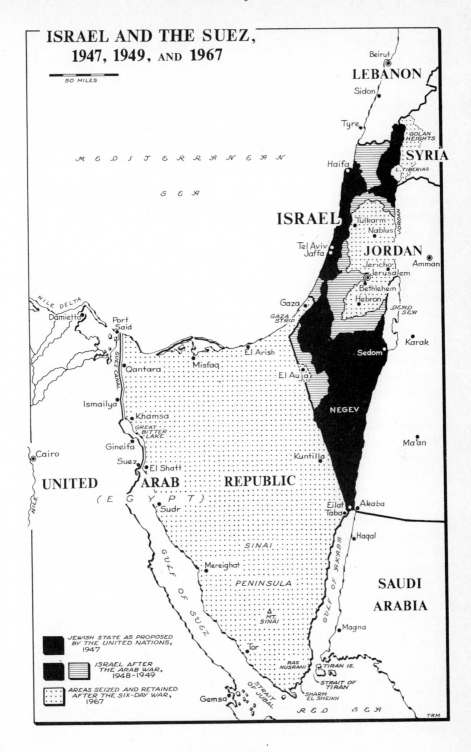

ISRAEL AND THE SUEZ, 1947, 1949, AND 1967

50 MILES

JEWISH STATE AS PROPOSED BY THE UNITED NATIONS, 1947

ISRAEL AFTER THE ARAB WAR, 1948-1949

AREAS SEIZED AND RETAINED AFTER THE SIX-DAY WAR, 1967

Soviet-made tanks and other armored vehicles. When Jordan loyally entered the war, Israel struck similarly devastating blows at this enemy. Other units kept Syria at bay.

By the time both sides agreed to a UN cease-fire on June 10—six days after the offensive began—Israel had achieved one of the most brilliant and stunning military successes in modern history. Her forces occupied the entire Sinai peninsula and camped along the east bank of the Suez Canal. They held all Jordanian territory west of the Jordan River and were entrenched inside Syria on the Golan Heights. Nasser's military capacity had been wiped out, his prestige shattered.

The Six-Day War had convincingly demonstrated Israel's prowess and resolve, but little seemed to have changed. Israel ignored Soviet and Arab protests and retained possession of the captured territories—determined to use them to protect her security, either as buffer zones or bargaining counters in return for Arab recognition and related guarantees. Military success had reopened the Gulf of Aqaba and blocked the Suez Canal, thus depriving Egypt of a major source of revenue. But Nasser proved amazingly resilient. Egyptians supported him despite the debacle, and new infusions of Soviet aid brought Egypt's military strength back to its prewar level within a few months. UN diplomacy made no progress in bringing the irreconcilable Arab-Israeli dispute appreciably closer to solution. President Johnson and Soviet Premier Kosygin conferred briefly in Glassboro, New Jersey, in late June to try to find a settlement of the Middle Eastern question, but no significant progress resulted from this meeting. Terrorist activities and violations of the cease-fire persisted.[18]

Russia intensified its involvement in the area—refurbishing Egypt's armed forces, supporting Arab demands that a return of all captured territory precede negotiations with Israel, and enlarging its naval forces in the Mediterranean until they rivaled the strength of the United States Sixth Fleet. It seemed apparent that Russia would not permit another Arab humiliation at Israel's hands; and it was equally apparent that the United States would not let the Zionist state suffer defeat and destruction. Neither power seemed able to contribute to a diplomatic resolution of the quarrel. As the sixties ended, the danger of a renewed Arab-Israeli war remained strong, with the attendant possibility that such a conflict would involve the great powers.

Notwithstanding the persistence of such trouble spots on the world scene, Soviet-American relations continued the gradual improvement that had begun during President Kennedy's final year in office. The two powers followed the nuclear test-ban treaty of September 1963 with several other steps toward détente and a lessening of tensions. Progress was not disrupted by Nikita Khrushchev's fall from power in October 1964. His suc-

---

[18] Egyptian missiles sank an Israeli destroyer in the eastern Mediterranean in November 1967, and Israel retaliated with a bombing raid that wiped out some 80 percent of Egypt's oil refining capacity.

cessors—Aleksei N. Kosygin, who became premier, and Leonid I. Brezhnev, who replaced Khrushchev as party chairman—were sober, cautious leaders who seemed desirous of maintaining satisfactory relations with the United States and avoiding risky or flamboyant diplomacy. There were several symbolic gestures of accord: cultural exchange agreements, a treaty establishing consulates in both countries, the inauguration of direct air service between New York and Moscow.

Of more substantive importance was a treaty banning the use or deployment of nuclear weapons in outer space, agreed to by both countries in 1967. A five-year attempt to reach accord in the matter of preventing the spread of nuclear weapons culminated in a nonproliferation treaty, initialed by the United States, the USSR, Great Britain, and fifty-eight nonnuclear countries in July 1968. Even the invasion and occupation of Czechoslovakia by Russian troops a month later, ruthlessly crushing a liberalization policy being pursued by Czech party leader Alexander Dubcek, did not seriously impair Soviet-American relations. Sympathy for Czechoslovakia and condemnation of the Russian move were voiced in all quarters—not only in the United States and other Western nations but in most Communist countries and even among Russian intellectuals. And yet the United States Senate, after delaying consideration of the nuclear nonproliferation treaty for a number of months, voted to ratify it in March 1969. Before President Johnson left office the two countries had also agreed to hold talks on the crucial subject of limiting the arms race.

Meanwhile, the so-called Communist monolith, however real it might have been at midcentury, was clearly and irrevocably sundered. Suspicion and antagonism between the Soviet Union and China expanded into outright hostility during the late sixties. Relations between the two countries deteriorated to the breaking point, featuring a stream of shrill recriminations between Moscow and Peking, troop build-ups and armed clashes along the Sino-Soviet border, and a fierce rivalry that divided or confused Communist party organizations in other countries. Smaller Communist countries deviated or dissented from the overlordship of either Russia or China with increasing frequency and boldness. All of these developments encouraged a belief in the United States and elsewhere that the era of the cold war was essentially over.

7. War in Vietnam

It was therefore all the more ironic that America's involvement in Southeast Asia, which had been a product of cold war assumptions from start to finish, should deepen and widen into full-scale military conflict even as the cold war receded. Conditions in South Vietnam grew considerably worse during 1964. While more and more North Vietnamese troops infiltrated across the border to reinforce their Vietcong allies, the political situation in Saigon became chaotic. No fewer than nine governments came and went within sixteen months after Diem's overthrow in November 1963. A Communist victory appeared inevitable.

Hoping to forestall it, the Johnson administration reviewed its policy and undertook a variety of measures short of total military involvement. General Maxwell Taylor, former chairman of the Joint Chiefs of Staff and special military adviser to President Kennedy, replaced Henry Cabot Lodge as ambassador to South Vietnam in June 1964, while General William C. Westmoreland took command of the American military mission in Saigon. Deciding on an expansion of the war effort, Washington strengthened American forces in Southeast Asia and launched a program of covert military operations against North Vietnam: U-2 observation flights, South Vietnamese commando raids and American naval intelligence operations along the North Vietnamese coastline, selected bombing of "targets of opportunity" by American airmen over Laos. Contingency plans for full-scale American bombing of North Vietnam were also prepared, and administration officials spoke in early 1964 of seeking a congressional endorsement for "wider U.S. actions" in Indochina.

Although intelligence reports and estimates to the contrary were not lacking, Washington had now become convinced, first, that Hanoi was in fact directing and controlling (rather then merely aiding) the Vietcong insurgency, and, second, that a combination of threats and actual military damage above the seventeenth parallel would eventually succeed in persuading the North Vietnamese to withdraw. (Beneath these convictions lay a third, upon which the whole superstructure of American policy was being erected: that a Communist victory in South Vietnam would bring about the collapse of all of Southeast Asia and the domination of that region by Red China.) As events would reveal, the gravest American misapprehension, which can only be defined as total, concerned the expectation that North Vietnamese resolve would crumble if sufficient American power were applied.

It was not surprising that a policy based upon such assumptions led to an expansion of the war. The first test came in August 1964, when American destroyers conducting intelligence operations in the Gulf of Tonkin were attacked by North Vietnamese patrol boats—apparently in the mistaken belief that the American craft had taken part in recent commando raids. Planes from *U.S.S. Ticonderoga* promptly took off on a retaliatory strike that destroyed some two dozen North Vietnamese patrol boats and support facilities. A deployment of American planes and bases looking toward the projected full-scale bombing campaign was ordered at about this time.

Anxious to obtain congressional approval both of what it had done and of what it might feel compelled to do, the administration backed a joint resolution pledging full support for American action in Vietnam "to promote the maintenance of international peace and security in Southeast Asia." The House approved the Gulf of Tonkin Resolution by a vote of 416 to 0 on August 7. In the Senate, where Wayne Morse of Oregon spoke in opposition, J. William Fulbright of Arkansas, chairman of the Foreign Relations Committee and later an outspoken critic of administration policy, responded by claiming that North Vietnam was guilty of aggression. The United States, Fulbright added, had no choice but to fight back and make it clear to the Communists "that their aggressive and expansionist ambitions, wherever advanced, will meet precisely that degree of American opposition which is necessary to frustrate them." The Senate speedily approved the resolution by a vote of 88 to 2.

Though now armed with the authority to escalate American activity, President Johnson resisted pressures to begin bombing the North during the fall of 1964, even after a Vietcong mortar attack on an American base at Bien Hoa, near Saigon, in November. Within a month, however, Johnson approved a plan for retaliatory air strikes followed by graduated air warfare against North Vietnam, together with "possible" deployment of ground combat forces. Part of this plan—Operation Rolling Thunder, a sustained bombing offensive against the North—was put into action in February 1965 following Vietcong attacks on American installations and billets at Pleiku and Quinhon in which some thirty Americans lost their lives. A contingent of 3,500 marines went ashore to protect the huge Da Nang air base in March, bringing the total of United States forces to 27,000. Johnson took the decisive step in April when he ordered a "change of mission" for these marines "to permit their more active use"—in short, from defensive to offensive operations. Troop build-ups began in earnest. U.S. forces in Vietnam reached 74,000 by June and 190,000 by the end of 1965.

A dismal pattern, differing only in detail, began to repeat itself in the long months that followed. Taking the offensive against their elusive foe, American forces undertook a series of "sweep" or "search and destroy" operations. These would be accompanied by enthusiastic or guardedly hopeful communiqués: detailed "body counts" showing that enemy forces were sustaining casualties ten and fifteen times those of the United States and South Vietnam; predictions that the enemy's prospects of winning had now been seriously crippled or destroyed, later that an American victory was only a matter of time; reports that the "pacification" and "Vietnamization" of rural areas once dominated or strongly infiltrated by the Vietcong were proceeding satisfactorily.

And such announcements were usually issued along with requests for more men and material—to consolidate recent gains and achieve the strength that would make a final victory possible. American troop strength approached 250,000 in April 1966. At this time B-52 bombers began large-scale raids on North Vietnam, extending their strikes to include oil installations in the Hanoi-Haiphong area in June. A steady stream of reinforcements brought U.S. strength in South Vietnam to nearly 400,000 by the end of 1966. The figure reached half a million a year later and continued to grow. Costs and casualties mounted in their turn, yet a kind of deadlock rather than victory appeared to be all that this massive effort was able to achieve.

The deadlock, in turn, took on an air of permanence. The American effort undoubtedly prevented a total Communist triumph in Vietnam, but neither incessant bombing attacks nor heavy casualties among their ground forces appeared to diminish Hanoi's capacity or will to continue the struggle. The South Vietnamese government achieved a measure of stability after June 1965 under a military regime headed by Air Vice-Marshal Nguyen Cao Ky as premier and Nguyen Van Thieu as chief of state. This government later acquired a certain legitimacy when relatively peaceful elections in September 1967 led to the choice of Thieu as president and Ky as vice-president. But Vietcong terrorism, internal power struggles, and continued dissent on the part of Buddhists and other non-Communist elements inclined the Saigon government toward repressive policies. Its capacity to endure was not accompanied by much achievement or effort in the important areas of social and economic reform, and its progress in winning the allegiance of substantial numbers of Vietnamese peasants was unconvincing. Corruption, favoritism, and low morale continued to be debilitating features of most South Vietnamese military and political units.

Washington strove earnestly, within the confines of its assumptions about the struggle, to achieve a peaceful settlement. While constantly reaffirming America's determination to halt aggression, President Johnson made numerous efforts to end the war. These included several partial or complete bombing halts, a number of peace feelers, repeated offers to negotiate, and offers to assist in the economic restoration and development of Southeast Asia. North Vietnam was invited to participate in a huge Mekong Valley development project along TVA lines.[19] The obvious sincerity of these attempts, and of Johnson's desire to bring peace and progress to all of Indochina, was negated by the fact that American conditions

---

[19]There were several notable examples of efforts to promote Asian development along non-Communist lines during the late sixties. An Asian Development Bank, created under UN auspices in 1965, became operational in December 1966 with headquarters at Manila and an authorized capital of $1.1 billion, the United States and Japan being the largest investors. A Mekong Development Committee consisting of Cambodian, Laotian, South Vietnamese, and Thai representatives began promoting plans for water-resources projects in the Mekong basin. Malaysia, the Philippines, and Thailand revived the Association for Southeast Asia in 1966 looking toward the formation of a common market. A nine-nation Asian and Pacific Council (Japan, Taiwan, Australia, Thailand, New Zealand, South Vietnam, South Korea, Malaysia, the Philippines) was set up to discuss economic, technical, and social matters. An attempted Communist coup in Indonesia was defeated in October 1965, resulting in a takeover by the Indonesian army and a violent anti-Communist and anti-Chinese reaction that cost President Sukarno most of his power and led to the killing of hundreds of thousands of Indonesians. Indonesia broke completely with Peking and rejoined the United Nations.

VIETNAM, 1966

for a negotiated peace—an independent non-Communist South Vietnam—remained irreconcilable with those of Hanoi and the Vietcong. Each side, unalterably convinced that the other was the aggressor, fought on. Attempts by third parties—Secretary-General U Thant, British Prime Minister Harold Wilson, and others—to bring the opposing forces to the negotiating table made no progress whatever.

American public opinion became increasingly divided and restive as the war ground inconclusively on. President Johnson strove to steer a middle course, continuing to send reinforcements and strike at North Vietnam while resisting demands of so-called hawks that he step up the bombing, mine Haiphong harbor, use atomic weapons, and generally keep applying more power till the enemy gave up. He also resisted pressure from the growing ranks of doves, who variously advocated an end to the bombing, an unconditional cease-fire and immediate negotiations, and even a unilateral withdrawal of American forces.

A decisive break in the psychological, if not the military, deadlock occurred in early 1968 when the Communists launched their so-called Tet (lunar New Year) offensive. Catching both American and South Vietnamese authorities completely off guard, North Vietnamese and Vietcong units attacked all of the major South Vietnamese towns and cities, including Saigon. Some of the bitterest fighting of the war took place before the onslaught was contained. The Tet offensive inflicted great material damage, hurt the rural pacification program by forcing Saigon to divert funds and manpower to the shattered cities, shook the Saigon government, and proved that Communist forces could strike almost at will in the very heart of southern urban centers. Yet from the military and political point of view the offensive fell short of its major objectives. Communist efforts to topple the Saigon government, retain control of the areas under attack, improve their strategic position, or touch off an uprising of disaffected southerners all ended in failure. They suffered heavy casualties, which weakened the impact of follow-up offensives in May and August.

Nevertheless, Tet was an unquestioned psychological victory for the North Vietnamese. Its greatest impact and most decisive influence was upon the American people, who were misled by the news media into believing that the Tet offensive had been a great victory for the Vietcong. It seemed that recent optimistic reports—General Westmoreland had proclaimed as recently as November 1967 that he had "never been more encouraged in my four years in Vietnam"—had been wide of the mark. No part of South Vietnam was secure; Saigon could not defend itself adequately; search and destroy campaigns had not weakened the enemy's capacity to strike hard blows. By mid-1968 there were some 530,000 American military personnel on the scene. It had become the longest war in American history and one of the bloodiest: over 35,000 Americans had died in combat, another 75,000 had been injured, and hundreds more were confined in North Vietnamese prison camps. The financial cost approached $100 billion. Nearly 5,000 planes and helicopters with a value exceeding $5 billion had been destroyed by enemy action. The cost to the people of Vietnam—in deaths, injuries, suffering, dislocation, devastation of homes, villages, towns, and the very land itself—had been staggering and incalculable.

The conviction that victory in Southeast Asia was neither attainable nor worth such a cost quickly rose to dominance in the United States. Antiwar sentiment, which had been gathering force for three years, swelled to the bursting point on college campuses and among intellectuals. It grew much stronger in Congress, where Senators Fulbright (long regretful of his support for the Tonkin resolution), Mansfield of Montana, Eugene McCarthy of Minnesota, and George McGovern of South Dakota had been outspoken critics for some time. Antiwar demonstrations became more vociferous and angry, and attracted more support from the general public. Disillusionment, bitterness, and distrust of the credibility and motives of the United States government reached ominous proportions. No more divisive or agonizing issue had ever confronted the American people, and the Johnson administration moved into its final months with the nation's collective morale at an all-time low.

32

The Nixon Years, I:
The First Term

The triumph of Richard M. Nixon in the presidential election of 1968 marked the beginning of another period of Republican rule in Washington and, more importantly, of a new era in American politics and diplomacy. In foreign affairs, he brought the nation's longest war to its conclusion. He presided over the liquidation of the postwar system of international exchange based upon American financial hegemony. His diplomacy recorded progress in disarmament, the status of Berlin, and improved relations not only with the Soviet Union but with the Chinese People's Republic, ending nearly a quarter century of unbroken hostility between Washington and Peking. At home the most important development was in the emergence of a tentative new GOP coalition—an anxious "silent majority" of disaffected blue-collar workers, southern whites, middle- and lower-middle-class urban dwellers, and traditional Republican voters in the Middle and Far West. This political realignment was accompanied by a gradual shift from the underlying progressivism of the Truman, Eisenhower, Kennedy, and Johnson administrations to a conservatism unequaled since the 1920s. Yet Nixon's conservatism was far from doctrinaire. He first applied an un-Republican dose of Keynsian deficit financing in an effort to bolster the economy, then resorted to an equally un-Republican experiment with partial wage and price controls in an effort to stem inflation.

The Nixon years displayed a jumble of contradictory developments, defying easy analysis. Achievement and progress went hand in hand with the ugliest and meanest of disclosures. Americans inspired all mankind when the Apollo astronauts walked the moon's surface in 1969; a few months later the nation began to hear shocking rumors, which were later confirmed, about atrocities committed by American military personnel in Vietnam. Assassins' bullets played a role in both of Nixon's presidential campaigns, taking the life of one candidate in 1968 and permanently crippling another in 1972. Hopes for peace, dramatized by the signing of arms agreements and the sight of President Nixon speaking cordially with Premier Chou En-lai in Peking, were offset by the spectacle of young American students dying of gunfire on strife-torn college campuses. The incidence of urban rioting declined after 1969, but unrest and antagonism continued to smolder in America's cities; the problems that beset them were no closer to solution.

If the future meaning of these disparate events remained unclear, it was not inappropriate that they should be presided over by Richard Milhous Nixon. This was indeed the Nixon era. The man and the hour had truly met: a controversial and enigmatic figure elevated to leadership during the most controversial and enigmatic of periods; a leader who stressed traditional American values in a society that longed for such reaffirmation, yet a man whose interest in success, which reflected his country's outlook to its very marrow, had a way of giving pious affirmations of honor, justice, and fair play a hollow sound; a professed conservative leading a people who were fearful of change, and yet a bold and unpredictable policymaker who often refused to be bound by conventional wisdom; a versatile man whose very inconsistencies and ambiguities were a mirror for his generation.

This elusive rapport with the hopes and fears of millions of Americans, together with four years of genuine achievement, led to Nixon's reelection in 1972 by a stunning popular and electoral landslide. Yet even in his hour of greatest triumph, faint rumblings of trouble could be heard; the crazy-quilt pattern of events that led to his ultimate rendezvous with disaster was already unfolding.

1. The Election of 1968

The Communist Tet offensive in Vietnam, exploding upon the American consciousness in late January, did much to set the tone and direction of the 1968 campaign. In the previous November Senator Eugene McCarthy of

Minnesota, long critical of administration policy in Vietnam, had announced that he would enter several state primaries in an effort to block
President Johnson's renomination and provide a rallying point for antiwar
sentiment. For some time neither supporters nor critics of the administration took McCarthy's candidacy seriously because they were convinced
that Johnson's hold upon the Democratic party was unshakable. But Mc-
Carthy's quiet eloquence and conviction attracted a host of eager volunteers, and reaction to Tet badly weakened public confidence in the
administration.[1] McCarthy and his hard-working staff scored a surprising
upset victory over Johnson in the New Hampshire primary in March,
polling over 42 percent of the vote and capturing twenty of the state's
twenty-four convention delegates.

The campaign promptly picked up speed and interest. Senator Robert
Kennedy of New York, brother of the slain president and most sought
after among possible Democratic contenders, announced his candidacy on
March 16. Kennedy had wavered for some time on the question of when
and whether to declare his candidacy, holding back in the interest of party
unity and in hopes that the president would appoint a commission to
restudy American policy in Vietnam. Johnson's refusal to move in this
direction finally persuaded Kennedy to break with the administration and
actively pursue the nomination.

While the two antiwar candidates bickered and marshaled their forces,
President Johnson placed the entire campaign upon a different footing
with a dramatic address to the nation on March 31. He first proclaimed an
indefinite suspension in the bombing of North Vietnam in the interest of
bringing the opposing forces to the negotiating table. Then he announced
that he would not be a candidate for reelection but would devote the
remaining months of his tenure to an effort to bring the war to a satisfactory conclusion. Hanoi soon agreed to begin negotiations, and formal
peace talks between the United States and North Vietnam began in Paris
in May.

The race now became a three-cornered scramble among McCarthy,
Kennedy, and Vice-President Hubert Humphrey, who declared his candidacy on April 27 with the tacit support of President Johnson and most
organization Democrats. Humphrey filed too late to enter the primaries,
most of which became battlegrounds between McCarthy and Kennedy.
McCarthy's victory over Johnson in Wisconsin on April 2 was inconclusive, since the president had withdrawn from the race two days earlier.

---

[1] Public dissatisfaction rose even higher after North Korean naval forces captured *U.S.S. Pueblo*,
an electronic surveillance vessel operating off the Korean coast, on January 23, 1968. Johnson
handled the ensuing tense diplomacy with restraint and skill, but most segments of public opinion
found something to deplore in the *Pueblo* incident. Hawkish critics denounced the administration
for not retaliating or forcibly obtaining the release of the captured crew members (whom North
Korea finally set free in November, after an unnecessarily harsh confinement); others felt that the
whole affair reflected badly on the effectiveness and alertness of American intelligence operations; still others, remembering the U-2 incident of 1960, questioned the wisdom or utility of such
operations in the face of the obvious risks involved.

Kennedy, his own campaign now fully launched, proceeded to score decisive triumphs over McCarthy in Indiana and Nebraska in May, only to lose an upset contest to his tenacious rival in Oregon on May 28. McCarthy refused to respond to Kennedy's overtures that the two men join forces in an effort to stop Humphrey at the convention. Kennedy, whose ability to strike enthusiastic sparks from crowds and capture public imagination was fully on a par with his late brother's, now poured all of his famed energies into the California primary in early June, knowing that a decisive victory in this crucial state would constitute a major step toward the Democratic nomination.

Democrats approached this climactic event against a backdrop of almost unrelieved anguish and violence. The assassination of Martin Luther King in April (see p. 863) and the wave of riots in its aftermath, including a long night of fire and destruction in the nation's capital, served as savage reminders that urban America was one vast cauldron of discontent and unresolved problems. Then, on the evening following Kennedy's narrow victory over McCarthy in the California primary on June 4, a confused Arab alien named Sirhan Bishara Sirhan—another of those haunted marginal malcontents who made history alter course during the sixties—fatally wounded the New York senator in his hotel in Los Angeles just before a victory celebration. Shot through the head, Kennedy never regained consciousness and died several hours later on the morning of June 6. Almost numb with shock, the nation sorrowfully paid its last respects to the second of the slain brothers and watched, on television and at graveside, as he was laid to rest beside the first in Arlington National Cemetery.

From this point on the Democratic campaign was little better than a shambles. McCarthy was unable to pick up more than scattered support from the dazed and bitter Kennedy followers, many of whom wavered toward the last-minute candidacy of Senator George McGovern of South Dakota. Nor could McCarthy make much headway in state convention battles against organization Democrats favoring Humphrey, who came to the convention in Chicago on August 26 with most of the regular party delegations pledged to his support. As expected, the convention nominated Humphrey on the first ballot, giving him 1,761¾ votes to 601 for McCarthy and 146½ for McGovern. A bitter platform battle between proponents of "peace" and "proadministration" Vietnam planks resulted in adoption of the latter, which praised the president's efforts to end the war, approved the negotiations, and proposed an end to the bombing of North Vietnam when such action would not endanger American troops.[2] The rest of the platform was a mildly progressive document calling for

[2]Johnson had suspended some but not all of the bombing with his proclamation of March 31. In ensuing months, however, he had gradually stepped up the tempo of the raids in the vain hope that victory (or an end to North Vietnamese intransigence, which had helped to stall progress at the peace talks) might yet be forthcoming. In the late summer and early fall of 1968 the bombs were falling at a rate little reduced from that of March, although targets in the Hanoi-Haiphong areas were still being spared.

improvements in consumer protection, expansion of farm markets and income, new labor laws to assure collective bargaining, continued "reliance on progressive taxes," flexible policies to stabilize prices, and "an attack on the root causes of crime and disorder" as a means of achieving equal justice under law. Accepting Humphrey's recommendation, the convention nominated Senator Edmund S. Muskie of Maine as his running mate.

The Democrats had a candidate and a platform, but they were riddled with dissension over both and in a virtual trauma over their convention experience, which had been a prolonged orgy of recrimination within and violence without. The thousands of youthful antiwar demonstrators who had converged on Chicago in hopes of pressuring the convention into coming out firmly for peace were savagely set upon by Chicago police in a series of brutal clashes. Verbal provocation had not been lacking, but the police response—which had been virtually insured by the deployment and tactics prescribed for them by Mayor Richard J. Daley—amounted to outright aggression.

The violence in Chicago had underscored both a party problem and a national mood. Millions of liberal Democrats (without whose support the party could not win in November) were appalled at the repressive savagery of Democratic Mayor Daley's police. Millions of other Democrats, in white-collar suburbs and blue-collar wards the country over (and without whose support the party could not win in November), were either delightedly or reluctantly in full support of Mayor Daley's police, seeing in the youthful activists and their heralded life-style a threat to cherished values, among which were order, stability, and middle-class aspirations generally.

The Republicans, as usual, went about the task of selecting a candidate in more orderly, if duller, fashion. Although several aspirants were more or less in contention, the front runner from first to last was Richard Nixon. Engaged in a successful law practice in New York, Nixon had kept all of his political fences in good repair since his defeat for the California governorship in 1962. Running largely unopposed in the Republican primaries, he won impressive vote totals, accumulated a mass of delegates, and attracted favorable notice for his calm, knowledgeable manner and grasp of local and national issues.

Liberal Republicans who hoped to find an alternative to Nixon were first attracted to Governor George Romney of Michigan, but he soon revealed a degree of gullibility and ineptitude that deflated his stature. Governor Rockefeller of New York, quadrennial aspirant, had spent so much time backing coyly away from a formal candidacy that when he finally entered the race, at the end of April, he could not generate real momentum or support outside his home state. The GOP right wing was attracted to conservative, tough-talking Governor Ronald Reagan of California, but their behind-the-scenes efforts to build support for him came to little.

The Republican convention, which opened in Miami on August 5, proceeded to give Nixon an easy first-ballot victory with 692 votes to 277 for Rockefeller, 182 for Reagan, and 182 scattered elsewhere. The convention also ratified Nixon's rather unexpected choice of Governor Spiro T. Agnew of Maryland as his running mate. The GOP platform, like its Democratic counterpart, was a moderately progressive document with generalities designed to please all and offend none. The Vietnam plank favored peace, but "neither peace at any price nor camouflaged surrender." The party promised a "comprehensive program to restore the preeminence of U.S. military strength" and advocated "more selective use of our economic strength" and multilateral cooperation in foreign affairs. The platform called for federal "encouragement" of job opportunity, fair farm prices, education, health, social security, and control of violence. Metropolitan and rural blight were to be attacked by enlisting "new energies by the private sector and by government at all levels."

Behind this bland platform and the choice of a relatively unknown border-state governor for the vice-presidency was a firm understanding between Nixon and the southern wing of the party. Key figure in this "southern strategy" was the militantly reactionary Senator Strom Thurmond of South Carolina. Nixon's decision to cultivate this element rather than the liberal northeastern wing was highly significant, both as a key to the candidate's own priorities and as an indication of how much the political climate had changed since Goldwater followed such a strategy to disaster in 1964.

In private conversations before and during the convention Nixon took pains to clarify his position on issues of particular concern to southern Republicans. He would not, Nixon said, accede to demands that he choose a liberal running mate. He told the hawkish Thurmond that the way to get the Vietnamese Communists to the negotiating table was to make it clear that "unless you negotiate, this and that is going to happen." He spoke in favor of an expanded missile program, a project dear to Thurmond's heart. Moreover, Nixon stressed his disapproval of the recent open-housing law and the busing of school children to achieve desegregation. He came down hard in favor of law and order, affirming that "the first civil right of every American is to be free from domestic violence" and promising to find an attorney general "who is going to observe the law" and a chief justice who would "interpret the law . . . not make it." This kind of talk clinched the southern delegations for Nixon at Miami; that it did not clinch as many southern electoral votes for him in November was due to special circumstances.

These circumstances centered about the person and appeal of Governor George Wallace of Alabama, who became the most popular third-party candidate since Robert M. La Follette headed the Progressive ticket in 1924. Wallace, a nominee of the loosely organized, newly formed American Independent Party, declared his candidacy in February 1968 and launched an aggressive campaign that alarmed both major parties. Though avowedly southern, the Alabamian was by no means a sectional candidate. During the Democratic primaries in 1964 he had learned the extent of his appeal in many northern and midwestern states, and he was now determined to repeat that venture on a larger scale, and on his own. Well financed by wealthy conservatives and many small grass-roots donations, Wallace was able to get his name on the ballot in all fifty states.

His message was one of fear and demagoguery. The bogeys from whom he stridently promised deliverance included blacks, radicals, spenders, planners, bureaucrats, peace demonstrators, hippies, integrationists, do-gooders, big government, high taxes, and "pointy headed professors" whose fuzzy dogmas were responsible for the country's woes. He favored free enterprise, state rights, property rights, local control over school policy, a hawkish stance in Vietnam, and, above all, law and order, including the use of troops if necessary. He was appealing to all the fears, prejudices, and frustrations that a half-century of accelerating social and economic change had engendered; the dark hysterical current of response that carried his candidacy forward seemed on its way to becoming a flood. It was not generally believed that Wallace could win, but experts were predicting that he would poll from 15 to 20 million votes and might well carry enough states to throw the election into the House of Representatives.

Nixon, however, was heavily favored until late in the campaign. He spoke effectively, with a quiet confidence. His message, though tending toward generalities, was one of peace and healing—in contrast to the demagogic Wallace and the divided Democrats, whose failings in both foreign and domestic affairs Nixon promised to repair. While avoiding Wallace's overt appeals to prejudice, Nixon was actually, subtly, casting his net in a similar direction. His acceptance speech had sounded a principal theme of his campaign: a promise to heed the "quiet voice" of "the great majority of Americans, the forgotten Americans . . . the non-shooters, the non-demonstrators" who worked, saved, and paid their taxes. Republican campaigners invoked "law and order" less stridently but no less frequently than did Wallace; Governor Agnew, Nixon's running mate, specialized in hardhitting attacks on rioters and antiwar demonstrators.

The Democrats, meanwhile, floundered badly. The McCarthy people were ostentatiously refusing to support the Humphrey ticket; some were even talking of a vote for Wallace or Nixon as a way of punishing their party. Kennedy people were still dazed. And Humphrey, for all his enthusiasm, was badly handicapped by his close association with the unpopular Johnson and his unpopular war. Humphrey tried to take an independent line without actually repudiating the president, and it was an almost impossible assignment.

And yet, toward the end, Humphrey began to gather momentum and make a real race out it. His assets—vigor, sincerity, compassionate progressivism—began to come through. Many disaffected liberals drifted back into the ranks as they took clearer stock of the alternatives. Wallace's campaign, though he ran well and attracted enthusiastic crowds, entered a visible decline in the final weeks. Many disgruntled union workers and suburbanites whose frustrations first inclined them toward Wallace now began to remember old party loyalties. Labor unions redoubled their efforts in Humphrey's behalf, and Senator Muskie proved a distinct asset to the ticket. Humphrey's candidacy received last-minute boosts when McCarthy officially endorsed him on October 29 and when President Johnson, hoping to get the stalled peace talks moving and help his party, proclaimed a total bombing halt on November 1. Polls showed Nixon's early lead dwindling steadily as election time neared, and on the eve of the election canvass experts were terming it "too close to call."

A record number of 73 million voters went to the polls on November 5 and, in one of the closest elections in modern times, chose Richard Nixon as their next president. Nixon received 31,785,000 popular votes (43.4 percent of the total) as against 31,275,000 (42.7 percent) for Humphrey and 9,900,000 (13.5 percent) for Wallace.[3] Nixon carried thirty-two states with a total of 301 electoral votes, the smallest number by a winning candidate since Wilson's narrow triumph over Hughes in 1916. Humphrey won thirteen states and the District of Columbia, with a total of 191 electoral votes, while Wallace's 46 votes were based on winning margins in Alabama, Arkansas, Georgia, Louisiana, and Mississippi.[4] The Democrats retained control of Congress by slightly reduced margins: 58 to 42 in the Senate, a net loss of 5 seats, and 243 to 192 in the House, a net loss of 4.

The electorate had spoken in a babel, accurately reflecting the confusion and uncertainty of the times. Wallace's strength had been more confined to the South than many observers had predicted. Concern for law and order, of which white racism was one but by no means the only component, and disapproval of administration policy in Vietnam undoubtedly cost the Democrats heavily. Labor and so-called ethnic voting was widely split among the three candidates. Humphrey retained more support among this element than seemed likely at convention time, but the old New Deal coalition had clearly vanished. Only black voters supported the Democrats with any consistency. Humphrey's successes were mainly in the Northeast, where he carried four of the New England states plus New York, Pennsylvania, Maryland, the District of Columbia, and West Virginia. His lone southern triumph was a hairline victory in Texas; his

[3] These figures were mildly noteworthy. Wallace's percentage had not been exceeded by a third-party candidate since La Follette's 17 percent in 1924. Save for Kennedy's 0.2 percent popular margin in 1960, Nixon's 0.7 percent edge over Humphrey in 1968 was the smallest since the 1880s. And except for the four-way race in 1824, which had to be settled in the House, only two victorious candidates ever received a lower percentage of the popular vote than Nixon's 43.4— but they were illustrious company indeed: Wilson in 1912, with 41.9 percent, and Lincoln in 1860, with 40 percent.

[4] Wallace's total also included one vote from a defecting Nixon elector in North Carolina.

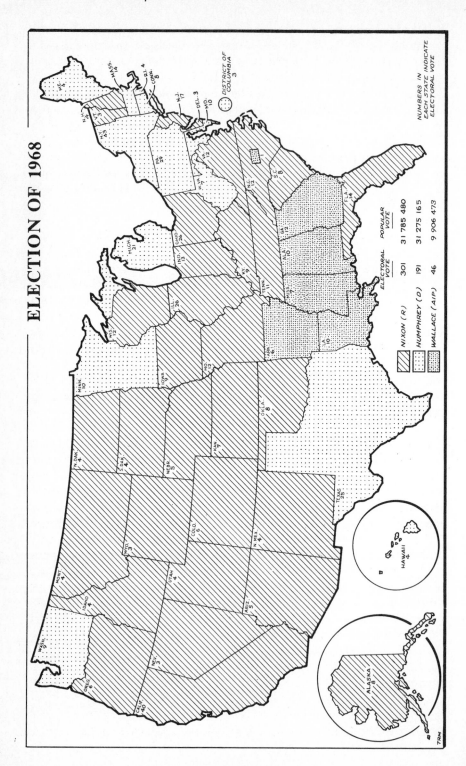

ELECTION OF 1968

NUMBERS IN
EACH STATE INDICATE
ELECTORAL VOTE

	ELECTORAL VOTE	POPULAR VOTE
NIXON (R)	301	31 785 480
HUMPHREY (D)	191	31 275 165
WALLACE (AIP)	46	9 906 473

DISTRICT OF
COLUMBIA
3

only midwestern achievements were in Michigan, where labor finally rallied to his support, and in his home state of Minnesota. In the vast region west of Texas and Minnesota he won only Hawaii and Washington.

Nixon could hardly claim a mandate on the basis of so narrow a margin, but Republicans had reason to be confident about the future. They had cut heavily into Democratic strength in all areas. Nixon's popular vote in the eleven former Confederate states exceeded both Wallace's and Humphrey's. Favorable response to Nixon's moderate but persistent emphasis upon "forgotten Americans," law and order, and retrenchment and re-examination of domestic welfare programs suggested that the bulk of Wallace's support could be attracted to the GOP in a normal two-party contest.

2. The New Republican President

The thirty-seventh president offers a perplexing and elusive target for historical analysis. The principal facts in his remarkable political career were identifiable enough, as were most of the motivating beliefs and character traits that make portrayal and explanation possible. But attempts to evaluate Richard Milhous Nixon can do little more than tumble the enigmatic components about in the hope that the kaleidoscope may prove to contain patterns after all.

Born on a farm in Yorba Linda, California, on January 9, 1913, Nixon grew up in nearby Whittier, where he worked long hours in his parents' grocery store and was raised in his parents' Quaker faith. Successively graduated from Whittier College and Duke University Law School in the 1930s, the young man practiced law in the Whittier area until the Second World War drew him to Washington in quest of government employment, and finally into military service as a naval supply officer. His political career began in 1946 when he ran for Congress on the Republican ticket in California's twelfth district and defeated Democratic incumbent Jerry Voorhis. Reelected easily in 1948, Nixon then sought and won a seat in the United States Senate in 1950. His reputation as an able, hard-line anti-Communist, in this ascendant period of the postwar Red scare, persuaded GOP strategists that he would be a good running mate for General Eisenhower in 1952. Eight active years in the vice-presidency were followed by the narrow loss to John Kennedy in the presidential election of 1960, and apparent oblivion with his decisive defeat by Democratic incumbent Edmund G. (Pat) Brown in the California gubernatorial election of 1962. But the tireless Nixon transferred his base to New York and rebuilt his political standing to the point where he could seek and capture the GOP nomination in 1968. His ensuing victory over Humphrey marked one of the most spectacular political comebacks on record.

The individual who had compiled this unusual success story was easy to describe but difficult to fathom. His entire life, from boyhood through college, law school, the navy, and on every rung of the political ladder, had been characterized by unremitting hard work, application, and intensive study, fired by a restless ambition that drove him relentlessly. These capacities, thus driven, enabled him to master whatever he set out to learn, and he became an acknowledged master of the art of politics. He had a politician's interest in power, a strong man's reliance on it, an ambitious man's craving for it.

The hard-scrabble rise from humble origins into an Establishment that snubbed and rebuffed as casually as it breathed had left its mark. Nixon was a secretive, private, and lonely man, aloof and remote from all save a small inner circle of family and close associates. Easily hurt, prone to lash back in anger and reveal too much of himself, he had practiced the discipline of self-control until it became a mask that sometimes quivered but rarely slipped; wariness and defensiveness seemed to inform every public gesture, every smile, every glance. No previous president had guarded or shielded himself so closely.

What values and attitudes prompted this intense political figure? Nixon was a devout patriot who believed passionately in the classic nineteenth-century version of the American Way: hard work, thrift, individual enterprise, self-reliance, the self-made man. His political hero was Woodrow Wilson, who had also believed in these things. Nixon proclaimed traditional American virtues with earnest sincerity, but there was a contradictory element that worried many observers. From his first entry into politics he had resorted to a deliberate technique of keeping his opponents on the defensive, using a mixture of smear and innuendo to identify them with some unpopular cause or issue. He had used communism in this way in his race against Voorhis in 1946 and against Helen Gahagan Douglas in 1950, and much of his campaigning during the fifties was conducted in a similar vein. He had adopted a more restrained and statesmanlike posture in 1960 and afterward, but memories and suspicions of the earlier Nixon lingered.

Perhaps the contradiction lay less in the man than in the very values of the system he so sincerely admired. Richard Nixon was not a hypocrite; his platitudinous invocations of freedom and the American Way came from the heart. Yet the American Way contained the same ambiguity that many detected in Nixon himself—a hard pragmatism that bordered on expediency, an ambition that did not stop at ruthlessness, a concern for success at any price. This was not contradiction but essence. America had made a moral virtue of success; it was the proof of the system. And winning, despite homilies to the contrary, could easily become more important than how one played the game. Expediency in the pursuit of success (like Goldwater's extremism in the defense of liberty) therefore derived not from a lack of moral scruple but from the all-out moral commitment of the zealot. Such a commitment could justify any action in furtherance of a holy cause—like freedom, or victory, or national security. Perhaps it was this quality that underlay his capacity to inspire fierce loyalty among followers and subordinates and equally fierce dislike among political opponents.

Nixon's compassion for the poor and the downtrodden tended, owing to his other convictions, to narrow down to a sympathy for the forgotten American, hero of his campaign oratory, with whom he clearly identified: the taxpaying, diligent, aspiring, law-abiding citizen. It was this sense of mutual identity rather than charisma or eloquence, which he conspicuously lacked, that underlay Nixon's growing rapport with many voters during and after his election. He not merely voiced but actually embodied the aspirations of an older America, and of millions who, cherishing it, desperately wanted to believe that their strivings and values still mattered.

Success had also circumscribed Nixon's compassion in another way. A highly sensitive man, he could exhibit a strange insensitivity in many of his utterances and dealings; there were subtle wavelengths on which his otherwise keenly attuned political antennae seemed numb. This insensitivity included a streak of ruthlessness and more than a touch of arrogance: the self-made man's contempt for those who had not made it, the winner's contempt for also-rans, the aloof zealot's inner conviction that he knew what was better for people than they did. Nixon's baffling combination of qualities unquestionably included consummate skill, courage, and dedication. At bottom, though, the combination also contained fatal flaws—hubris, insensate ambition, and susceptibility to the corruption of power.

3. President and Congress, 1969-1972

An air of calm confidence and quiet competence marked the accession of the Nixon administration in 1969. Nixon's cabinet included both moderates and conservatives, with an accent upon experienced men from a variety of business, academic, legal, and public service backgrounds. For secretary of state Nixon chose his long-time adviser William P. Rogers, a skilled negotiator trained in government and international law. The new secretary of defense was veteran GOP congressman Melvin R. Laird of Wisconsin. David M. Kennedy, prominent Chicago banker and believer in monetary restraint, was named secretary of the treasury. The president's erstwhile law partner, John N. Mitchell, a conservative who had specialized in bond financing, became attorney general. The Post Office Department, soon to become a public corporation, was assigned to Winton N.

Blount, an Alabama contractor and former president of the United States Chamber of Commerce. The new secretary of the interior was former Governor Walter J. Hickel of Alaska. Secretary of Agriculture Clifford M. Hardin, concerned with rural poverty and the marginal farmer, had been professor of agricultural economics and one-time chancellor of the University of Nebraska. The Commerce Department was headed by Maurice H. Stans, member of a large Chicago accounting firm and a former director of the Bureau of the Budget. George P. Shultz, former college professor and dean of the University of Chicago graduate school of business, became secretary of labor. A liberal lawyer from California with an interest in better opportunities for slumdwellers, Robert H. Finch, who had managed Nixon's campaign in 1960, became secretary of HEW. Governor Romney of Michigan was named to the Department of Housing and Urban Development, while the Department of Transportation was assigned to construction executive and former Governor John A. Volpe of Massachusetts.

Daniel P. Moynihan, labor expert and former Democrat, was named as the president's urban affairs adviser with cabinet rank. The major executive appointments included three key members of the White House staff who were destined to outrank cabinet members in importance and influence. Henry A. Kissinger, professor of government at Harvard and former consultant to Eisenhower, Kennedy, and Johnson, became Nixon's special adviser on foreign policy; John Ehrlichman was named special adviser on domestic affairs; and H. R. Haldeman became the White House chief of staff.

It is not surprising, given the president's greater concern with foreign affairs, the control of Congress by the opposition party, and the various problems besetting the economy, that domestic legislative accomplishments were relatively modest during Nixon's first term. Aside from marked activity in economic and environmental matters, which we shall discuss later, the record was one of moderate extensions of social-welfare legislation. Social security benefits were increased and liberalized by enactments in 1969, 1971, and 1972. Production of federally subsidized housing for low- and middle-income families proceeded at a brisk pace. An ambitious bill known as the Education Amendments, signed in June 1972, expanded the student assistance program.[5] Federal grants for education at all levels totaled $7.8 billion in 1969, $8.6 billion in 1970, and $5.1 billion 1971. The Tax Reform Act of 1969, though falling short of progres-

[5]The act made Basic Educational Opportunity grants (up to $1,400) available on a basis of need to every college student in good standing. Secondly, it created a government-sponsored corporation that would buy existing student loans from banks and other lending institutions so as to provide such lenders with more capital for the guaranteed student loan program. The amendments also created a National Institute of Education to conduct educational research, established interlocking support programs for community colleges, and authorized $2 billion in federal assistance to local school districts to meet needs incidental to desegregation and help minority children overcome disadvantages.

sive goals, was the most ambitious such measure in the history of American tax legislation.[6]

Two of President Nixon's most interesting and innovative reform measures—the so-called family assistance plan and a revenue-sharing program that would distribute a portion of federal monies to state and local governments—became embroiled in both partisan and ideological disputes that persisted throughout his first term. The proposals, first introduced in 1969, were key items in the president's general blueprint for reforming the welfare structure and creating what he called a "new federalism" that would decentralize (and theoretically democratize) many reform activities presently administered from Washington.

The family assistance plan was designed to provide a minimum income for all families with dependent children ($1,600 for a family of four). It contained a scale of reduced governmental payments supplementing existing wages so that all families earning less than $3,920 a year would be eligible for at least some aid. Many states and cities hailed the prospect of transferring their burdensome welfare expenditures to the federal government. But the idea became caught in a crossfire. Conservatives objected to the proposed increase in total welfare costs, and progressives maintained that the minimum income figures were unrealistically low. Conservatives were pleased and progressives further alienated by a "workfare" addition to the plan which would require all family assistance recipients who were deemed capable of holding a job to find work or enter a job training program.

The House of Representatives finally passed a family assistance bill in 1970, but the Senate blocked it. A new and more ambitious version, providing a minimum income of $2,400 for a family of four, passed the House in June 1971. The Senate remained unenthusiastic, and the whole project had to be postponed in the face of budgetary restrictions imposed by the president's new economic policy (see p. 914). Just before adjournment in December 1971, however, Congress suddenly passed the workfare provision, whereby all welfare recipients under the Aid to Families with Dependent Children program, save for a few exempt categories, would have to register for work or training beginning in July 1972.[7] It was indicative of

[6]The new tax law increased personal exemptions and standard deductions, cut some nine million low-income persons from the tax rolls, reduced the controversial oil depletion allowance from 27½ to 22 percent, and created a "minimum tax" designed to prevent individuals and corporations from amassing large tax-free incomes.

Tax-exempt state and municipal bonds were not affected by the law, and several loopholes remained unplugged, so that, much to the indignation of tax reformers, it remained possible for several individuals with extremely high incomes to end by paying low taxes or avoiding payment altogether.

[7]The law provided that the federal government would finance 100 percent of public service jobs for employable adults in the first year, 75 percent in the second, and 50 percent in the third. The government was also to pay 90 percent of the cost of day-care or babysitting services for children of working mothers.

a growing public hostility toward welfare that this single harsh feature of the family assistance plan was the only part of it to become law. Congress again rejected family assistance in 1972.

Revenue sharing, keystone of the new federalism, became similarly mired in disagreement. The president's repeated advocacy culminated in an outspoken call for action in his message to Congress in January 1971. Maintaining that "we have made the federal government so strong that it grows muscle bound and the states and localities so weak they approach impotence," he said that revenue sharing would open the way for "a new American revolution" in which power would be "turned back to the people." The plan called for distribution to states on a combined basis of population and taxable resources; a formula for subdividing this amount between a state and its localities was to be devised and agreed upon, if possible, by the governments concerned. The only federal restrictions would involve procedural safeguards against fraud and civil rights discrimination.

Although municipal and state governments were thrilled at the prospect of relieving their own financial difficulties by receiving an annual share of federal revenues, the objections to the plan were formidable. Some big-city leaders were fearful that its ultimate workings would not be to their advantage, and spokesmen for the poor were highly skeptical. Civil rights advocates doubted the effectiveness of the provisions against racial discrimination. There was considerable lack of confidence in the ability of state and local governments to make the best use of this money; it was the pervasive inadequacy of such units that had necessitated the transfer of power to Washington in the first place.

The revenue-sharing measure that finally became law was the State and Local Fiscal Assistance Act of October 1972. It provided for the sharing of $30.2 billion in federal revenue over a five-year period, with $5.3 billion to be distributed in 1972 on a basis of two-thirds to local governments and one-third to the states.[8] Although the plan was widely hailed, mostly by conservatives, as "reversing the flow of power" and inaugurating a new era of "refreshed and renewed" government at all levels, mayors and other spokesmen for urban areas and inner cities were soon complaining that the new system, coinciding as it did with drastic cutbacks or freezes in various federal programs (see p. 946), threatened to leave them worse off than before.

Reflecting the economic and social uncertainties of the day, both Congress and the president oscillated near the center of the political spectrum

---

[8] A complicated basis involving population, income, and tax effort would help to determine specific allocations. Localities had to spend their share within the broad categories of public safety, environmental protection, public transportation, social services, health, recreation, libraries, and financial administration. The grants were largely uninstructed, except that local governments were prohibited from spending shared revenues for education or from using them to match other federal grant programs.

in other areas of domestic policy. The tendency was toward a moderate and generally flexible conservatism, with the president inclining a bit more strongly in this direction than Congress. His inclination was most apparent in the field of civil rights. The administration did move boldly in the area of job opportunity by experimenting with the so-called Philadelphia Plan, which was designed to increase the ratio of blacks and other minorities in the building trades by assigning quotas to firms engaged in federally financed construction projects.[9] But the record was generally characterized by caution, lack of vigor, and a marked slowdown in implementing desegregation policies.

Nixon's southern strategy was much in evidence—in his nominations to the Supreme Court, in several administrative requests that school desegregation in the deep South be delayed, and above all in his stand against the busing of school children to achieve integration. While the courts, as we shall see, continued to move boldly in these areas, neither Congress nor the president was inclined to challenge conservative white opinion. In January 1971 Nixon announced his firm opposition to federal efforts to "force integration of the suburbs," calling such measures "counterproductive, and not in the interest of race relations."[10] In a special message to Congress in March 1972 he demanded a temporary halt to further court-ordered busing until mid-1973 and asked for legislation to control and limit the practice and establish "reasonable national standards." All Congress could agree upon was a measure prohibiting, until the end of 1973, the implementation of court busing orders until all appeals had been exhausted. Nixon signed this bill reluctantly in June 1972, saying that he did not believe its restrictions went far enough.

Civil rights advocates were variously depressed and enraged at the

[9]The plan was highly controversial, since the quota system appeared to go against the spirit if not the letter of existing civil rights legislation and practice. It was fiercely resisted by many of the predominantly white building-trades unions and criticized by the AFL-CIO. But its legality was upheld by the United States Court of Appeals in 1971, and the plan was extended directly or indirectly to several other major cities after the initial application in Philadelphia. A few cities came up with their own plans for increasing minority-group representation in the construction industry, and the participating firms in the original Philadelphia experiment managed to exceed the plan's goals ahead of schedule. It was pointed out, however, that quotas were sometimes being met simply by transferring minority workers from nonfederal to federal construction projects rather than by hiring appreciable numbers of new workers. Black labor leaders were not bowled over by the results of the plan, and progress in altering the lily-white complexion of most building-trades unions was minimal. Congress passed a law in 1972 empowering the Equal Employment Opportunity Commission to institute suits in the enforcement of federal laws against job discrimination. But President Nixon came out against the quota system in 1972.

[10]The administration's record on civil rights was mixed. Some government departments, notably HEW and HUD, proceeded more vigorously than others, but the momentum acquired during the Johnson years was visibly slowed. The Justice Department did bring suits now and then against racial discrimination by developers, apartment owners, and real estate dealers. But civil rights advocates accused the Justice Department of undue slowness and reluctance in many of these suits, citing a five-month delay in acceding to HUD's request that suit be brought against an all-white Missouri town for having deliberately incorporated with zoning ordinances expressly drawn to block construction of a federal low-income housing project.

president's stand on busing. School officials, North and South, who had devised and implemented busing plans in accordance with court orders, felt undercut to the point of betrayal. Although white resistance generated much protest and resulted in occasional ugly incidents, it remained true that large-scale busing was being employed successfully and peacefully in many northern and southern communities. Most liberals felt that the president had unnecessarily exacerbated the issue and encouraged white resistance at a time when forthright executive leadership in support of the policy might have induced general public acceptance.

Congress and the president also tended toward a conservative position on law and order issues, in keeping with much campaign rhetoric and widespread public concern. Ambitious laws aimed at organized crime and the drug traffic were passed in 1970, as was a stringent District of Columbia Criminal Justice Act, which President Nixon reportedly regarded as a model for all fifty states to copy. The administration stepped up the pace of wiretapping and other electronic surveillance of organized crime, and obtained increased funds for the Law Enforcement Assistance Administration. Attorney General Mitchell became an especially prominent advocate and implementor of a hard policy with regard to criminals, rioters, demonstrators, and other lawbreakers.

The Republicans overreached themselves slightly on the law and order issue in 1970 by trying to associate the Democrats, and especially Democratic liberals in the Senate, with the kind of softheaded and permissive policies that had supposedly encouraged lawlessness and social disorder. Not only organized crime but black militants, peace demonstrators, and campus radicals were the targets of this assault, which at times—notably in some of the outspoken remarks of Vice-President Agnew—broadened into an indictment of any and all who disagreed with administration policy. During the midterm elections Agnew campaigned extensively, and with the president's blessing, on the themes of biased news media, rioting, spoiled college youth, pornography, radicals, crime, drugs, Democrats, and various other social evils. "Will Americans be led by a president elected by a majority of the American people?" Agnew thundered in September. "Or will we be intimidated and blackmailed into following the path dictated by a disruptive radical and militant minority—the pampered prodigies of the radical liberals of the United States Senate?" Nixon, in one of his rare campaign appearances, responded to heckling by praising the administration record in stronger law enforcement and asking the silent majority to support Republican candidates at the polls.

It was a telling appeal in many quarters, but the irresistible flood of silent majority votes never quite manifested itself. Impatience and disillusionment with administration policy in Vietnam (see pp. 931–933) and objections to the intemperate nature of the Agnew assaults were offsetting factors, and the election of 1970 was a virtual standoff. The GOP made a net gain of 2 seats in the Senate, reducing the Democratic margin to

55-45, but the Democrats enlarged their House majority to 255-180, a net gain of 9 seats. At the state level the Democrats scored even more impressively, capturing 13 contested governorships from the GOP while losing only 2 and making substantial gains in many legislatures. The election was hardly a conservative mandate.

Although no great ideological gulf separated them, Nixon's relations with Congress were marked by recurrent deadlock, partisan wrangling (especially after the midterm elections, which brought Democrats back to Washington in a resentful mood), and small but growing signs of friction that pointed to an eventual power struggle between the executive and legislative branches. Congressional opinion was not monolithic, of course, but a sense that their power as a body was subject to erosion—even usurpation—gradually took shape in the early seventies. Democrats and progressive Republicans had been angered by the president's posture during prolonged battles over confirmation of two of his nominees to the Supreme Court in 1969-1970; they were further annoyed in 1970 when he vetoed a Democratic measure to impose limits on political campaign spending. Still smarting from Agnewesque attacks on pampered prodigies and radical liberals, progressive congressmen grew even more resentful when the president threatened to veto an administration-sponsored tax bill in 1971 if a campaign-reform amendment establishing federal financing of the 1972 presidential election were not deleted from the measure. The provision was duly stricken and the bill passed, but Nixon's reluctance to press for meaningful campaign reform would be remembered. His rightward swing was manifested in two major vetoes in 1971: he struck down a $5.7 billion public works and regional development bill and a $2.1 billion program for comprehensive child care for preschool children of lower- and middle-income families. The president termed both measures inflationary and called the latter a threat to the family structure.

Other sources of irritation slowly accumulated on Capitol Hill. There was widespread sentiment among senators of both parties, growing out of the Vietnam experience, that the president's authority as commander-in-chief should be so redefined and hedged as to prevent future involvements in war without congressional consent. There was marked recalcitrance, for the first time since the 1930s, over approving swollen defense budgets. Presidential claims of executive privilege, periodically invoked as a means of absolving members of the executive branch from testifying before congressional committees, became a source of friction. This was accompanied by a steadily growing resentment of the president's inaccessibility and remoteness and the studied arrogance and uncooperative posture of many of his chief advisers on the White House staff.

Congress also began to realize that its control over the federal budget, and specifically over the way in which authorized sums were actually allocated and spent, was fast disappearing. On a few occasions the president calmly proceeded to impound funds already appropriated by Congress when he disagreed with the purposes for which they had been authorized. This question of budgetary control, which promised to be a major issue between president and Congress during Nixon's second term, became a full-fledged quarrel in the fall of 1972. Congress angrily rejected an administration proposal that would have set a $250 billion ceiling on federal spending in fiscal 1973 and, more importantly, would have empowered the president to eliminate appropriations for any program, as he saw fit, in order to stay within that limit. Nixon, angered in turn, retaliated by vetoing a $24.7 billion, three-year program designed to clean America's polluted waterways. When the incensed lawmakers sweepingly overrode this veto, the president struck back in the name of fiscal responsibility by pocket vetoing eleven public works and social-welfare bills that exceeded the amounts he had requested. The political sky over Washington was piled high with thunderheads as 1972 drew to a close.

4. *The Supreme Court: Controversy and Change*

The changing political climate was also evident in the United States Supreme Court. Under Chief Justice Earl Warren, as we have seen, the court had greatly advanced the frontiers of American progressivism in such key areas as civil rights, criminal due process, and political reapportionment. The end of this historic epoch of judicial trailblazing had been twice signaled during 1968, first by Warren's announcement of his intention to retire at the end of the 1967–1968 term, and secondly by candidate Nixon's repeated assertions that he intended to fill vacancies with more conservative appointments.

Warren's announcement had been made early enough in 1968 to have enabled President Johnson, under normal circumstances, to appoint a successor. But Johnson's nomination of Justice Abe Fortas, an old friend and brilliant attorney whom the president had appointed to the Supreme Court in 1965, ran into senatorial opposition that proved too strong to overcome. The doctrine of separation of powers had been violated, many felt, by Fortas's continued service as close presidential adviser even after he took his seat on the court. Conservative Republicans and southern Democrats, highly critical of Fortas's trenchant liberalism, were able to mount a successful filibuster against his appointment. Warren, who had made his resignation effective at the president's pleasure, then agreed to remain for the time being. A little later he acceded to President-elect Nixon's request that he stay until the end of the 1968–1969 term.

Nixon's choice to succeed Earl Warren was Warren E. Burger, a Minnesotan who had served as assistant attorney general under Eisenhower and later as judge of the Court of Appeals for the District of Columbia. Burger, widely respected in legal circles though not a prominent public figure, was known as a strict constructionist who would interpret the Constitution with the kind of rigor and caution the new president had been advocating. Readily confirmed by the Senate in January 1969, the new chief justice began to preside at the opening of the 1969–1970 term.

Meanwhile, further difficulties had embroiled and finally engulfed the unhappy Fortas. It was learned in 1969 that he had agreed to accept an annual fee of $20,000 for services to a private foundation headed by a financier of dubious reputation who was then under prosecution in a federal court. Public pressure and charges of unethical conduct finally led Fortas to resign from the court in May, while Congress tried to frame a law that would define judicial ethics more explicitly.[11]

Nixon's search for a successor to Fortas touched off a revealing and bitter controversy. Conservatives, overjoyed to see Warren depart, exultant at the disclosure that had compelled Fortas to resign, and hopeful that similar charges would soon force the resignation of a third liberal, Justice Douglas, welcomed Nixon's nomination of Clement Haynsworth, a federal circuit court judge from South Carolina, to succeed Fortas. Strenuous liberal objections to Haynsworth's conservative opinions in certain labor and civil rights decisions would probably not have been sufficient, by themselves, to block Senate confirmation of this appointment. But matters took a different turn when the judiciary committee learned that Haynsworth, an active stock investor, had been insensitive to possible conflicts of interest growing out of his financial ties with litigants in cases where he had sat as judge. Though Haynsworth's integrity was not at issue, the dubious propriety of his extrajudicial connections bore sufficient resemblance to the Fortas imbroglio to embarrass conservatives and swing several moderate senators into opposition. Notwithstanding administration pressure, a bipartisan liberal majority finally rejected the Haynsworth nomination in November 1969 by a vote of 55 to 45.

Even more controversy raged over the president's second attempt to fill the Fortas vacancy. In a defiant gesture that infuriated liberals and dismayed moderates, Nixon turned to another southern circuit court judge, G. Harrold Carswell of Florida. Not only was Carswell tainted ineradicably with a segregationist, even a racist, background; he was a man of such modest judicial and intellectual caliber that many prominent members of the legal profession considered him unfit for a seat on the high court. Charges of mediocrity were so persistent and so convincing that a reluctant Senate majority was finally led to deny Carswell's nomination in April 1970 by a vote of 51 to 45. No other president in the twentieth century had been twice rebuffed on Supreme Court appointments. Nixon then

---

[11]The venerable New Deal justice, William O. Douglas, came under conservative attack on similar grounds and was forced to sever his salaried connection with an educational foundation whose chief assets were Las Vegas gambling houses. A judicial conference headed by Warren adopted resolutions in June 1969 requiring federal judges to decline all such extrajudicial fees, but Chief Justice Burger amended this in November to a request that judges merely report such income to a national council of their peers.

chose another strict constructionist from Minnesota, Circuit Court Judge Harry A. Blackmun, whom the Senate confirmed unanimously in May.

The retirement, in September 1971, of veteran justices Hugo Black and John M. Harlan enabled President Nixon to make two additional appointments to the Supreme Court. His choices—Lewis F. Powell, Jr., of Virginia, a respected corporation lawyer and former president of the American Bar Association, and Assistant Attorney General William H. Rehnquist—were readily confirmed by the Senate in December. Powell and Rehnquist joined Blackmun and Burger as moderate conservatives, and the Nixon court was thus visibly inclined away from the judicial activism of the Warren era. A delicate balance had been struck, with the four Nixon appointees offset by liberal justices Douglas, William Brennan, and Thurgood Marshall, while moderates Potter Stewart and Byron White were regarded as swing men.

The changed composition of the Supreme Court was reflected in many decisions, although in general its posture was marked by continuity and mild deceleration rather than dramatic reversal or pronounced rightward swing. In the field of civil rights, the justices continued to guard and advance the rights of minorities and reinforce most efforts to bring about school integration. In 1969, with Chief Justice Burger presiding, the court handed down one of the most significant school decisions since the *Brown* ruling. In *Alexander* v. *Holmes County Board of Education*, a unanimous opinion ordered an end to all school segregation "at once." Explicitly rejecting the previous standard of "all deliberate speed" as "no longer constitutionally permissible," the *Alexander* decision held that "the obligation of every school district is to terminate dual school systems at once and to operate now and hereafter only unitary schools." This opinion directly contravened a recent administration request to delay desegregation orders in Mississippi, Louisiana, and Oklahoma.

The court faced the problems of busing and neighborhood schools squarely, and again contradicted administration policy, in *Swann* v. *Charlotte-Mecklenburg Board of Education* and four related cases in April 1971. Finding a "presumption against schools that are substantially disproportionate in their racial composition," the *Swann* decision announced that the neighborhood school was not immune from desegregation, and that integration had to be achieved even if it necessitated "administratively awkward, inconvenient, and even bizarre" arrangements. Busing, the court added specifically, was an acceptable means of achieving desegregation. HEW officials promptly began working with southern school boards to draw up desegregation plans involving the use of buses. Many southern districts complied, and the schools in North Carolina directly affected by the *Swann* ruling were able to bus over 43,000 pupils daily without incident during the 1971-1972 session. In answer to southern charges that the nation was applying a double standard to the question of desegregation, district courts and federal and state officials began attacking the de facto segregation that prevailed in most northern and western urban centers. San Francisco, Philadelphia, Pittsburgh, Detroit, Los Angeles, Denver, and Boston were among the cities facing various desegregation orders in 1971 and after.

The Burger court had thus far displayed boldness of Warren-like dimensions, but in two crucial new areas of civil rights action it assumed a more cautious and conservative stance. The lower courts, in studying patterns of urban segregation, were beginning to conclude that in many instances school districts would have to be merged or ignored if desegregation were to be achieved. In two pioneer cases, District Court Judge Robert R. Merhige, Jr., of Richmond, ordered a merger in January 1972 of the predominantly black Richmond school district with the adjacent, largely white districts of Henrico and Chesterfield counties; and in June District Judge Stephen J. Roth ordered Detroit and fifty-two surrounding suburban districts to implement a cross-district busing plan, affecting nearly 800,000 pupils, to eliminate de facto segregation in the Detroit metropolitan area.

The Richmond case reached the Supreme Court first. Judge Merhige's order was ruled unconstitutional by the Fourth Circuit Court of Appeals in June 1972 on grounds that he had interpreted the Fourteenth Amendment in an "excessive" manner and slighted the Tenth Amendment's principle of federalism. In May 1973, by a four-to-four vote with Justice Powell (a former member of the Richmond and Virginia state boards of education) abstaining, the Supreme Court upheld the appellate court ruling, thus blocking the proposed merger of the Richmond school districts. But the court's action in this case, *School Board of Richmond* v. *State Board of Education*, was such that no legal precedent had been set. There remained the possibility, with the Detroit case still under review in the lower courts, that later merger orders might be upheld.

In an equally important issue, the court revealed its growing conservatism more decisively in *Rodriguez* v. *San Antonio Independent School District*, 1973. The four Nixon appointees were joined by Justice Stewart in holding that it was constitutional for states to finance their schools through local property taxes—as nearly every school system did—even if this resulted in disparities. The question involved a Texas school financing law based on local property taxes. Low-income residents of San Antonio had challenged this law on grounds that the result led to disparities, in school expenditures per pupil, of greater than ten to one between the richest and poorest districts. A federal district court had invalidated the law on grounds that it created unequal educational opportunities, but the five justices overturned that decision. "Education," wrote Justice Powell for the majority, "is not among the rights afforded explicit protection under our federal constitution. Nor do we find any basis for saying it is implicitly so provided. . . . At least where wealth is involved, the equal protection clause does not require absolute equality of precisely equal advantages."

Justice Marshall dissented strongly. "The Court decides," he wrote sadly, "that a state may constitutionally vary the quality of education it offers to its children in accordance with the amount of taxable wealth. . . . The majority's holding can only be seen as a retreat from our historic commitment to equality of educational opportunity and as insupportable acquiesence in a system which deprives children in their earliest years of the chance to realize their full potential as citizens."

American women, no less than American blacks, were finding the road to full citizenship studded with stoplights and detour signs. The court began to take more cognizance of women's rights in the early seventies. As with most complex legal issues, it was often a matter of chipping away at the problem. The justices ruled unanimously, in *Phillips* v. *Martin Marietta*, 1971, that women could not be denied a job merely because they had small children unless males were also denied employment on those grounds. *Reed* v. *Reed*, 1971, invalidated an Idaho law that gave preference to men as administrators of estates. *Drewrys Ltd.* v. *Bartmess*, 1972, forbade employers to set the compulsory retirement age for women lower than that for men.

In one of the most important and controversial areas connected with the Women's Liberation movement, the Supreme Court declared in *Roe* v. *Wade*, 1973, by a vote of seven to two, that a state could not prevent a woman from having an abortion (save for reasons connected with her health) during the first six months of pregnancy. The decision directly overturned abortion laws in Texas and Georgia and threatened existing statutes in forty-four other states. Although President Nixon had frequently voiced his opposition to liberalized abortion, three of his appointees—Burger, Blackmun, and Powell—were part of the majority in *Roe* v. *Wade*.[12]

Central to the concern of women's rights advocates was the unconstitutionality of any and all sex discrimination. The trend, beginning slowly in the sixties and gathering force very year, was in the direction of abolishing such discrimination wherever possible.[13] The Supreme Court resisted an

---

[12]Few issues of greater moral or philosophical complexity confronted this restless epoch. Most states, reflecting patterns of morality that were much under fire in the sixties and seventies, had laws forbidding abortion except under certain well-defined conditions, usually centering about the health and well-being of the mother (sometimes extending to pregnancies resulting from rape) or the likelihood of defects in the unborn child. Many religious and lay groups were vigorously opposed to legalized abortion; while champions of women's rights, the poor, and advocates of controlled population growth—to mention a few—were equally vociferous supporters of liberalization.

[13]The Equal Pay Act of 1963, which had required the same pay for men and women doing "substantially equal work," was extended in 1972 to some 15 million administrative, executive, professional, and outside sales employees. In the same year, Congress brought cases of sex discrimination within the jurisdiction of the Civil Rights Commission; and federal contractors (except in construction) with at least fifty employees and $50,000 contracts were required to file action programs covering the hiring and promotion of women as well as minorities.

opportunity to pronounce on this question in January 1973. After ruling, eight to one, that female members of the armed forces were entitled to the same dependency benefits for their husbands as men were for their wives, the justices stopped short, four to four, of deciding whether sex discrimination was basically unconstitutional. Justice Powell observed that the states should logically decide such a question, and as he spoke the states appeared well on their way to doing so.

An equal rights amendment to the federal Constitution had first been introduced in the early twenties. Half a century later it seemed to be an idea whose hour had arrived. Such an amendment, providing that "equality of rights under the law shall not be denied or abridged by the United States or by any state on account of sex," passed the House of Representatives in 1970 but failed in the Senate. The House repassed it unanimously in October 1971, and in the following March the Senate defeated crippling modifications and endorsed the measure by a vote of 84 to 8. Many legislatures were primed to receive it, and the equal rights amendment was approved by twenty-one states between March and September 1972. Then the pace slowed, and two years later it had virtually halted. There was uncertainty, as the decade ended, that the required number of thirty-eight endorsements could be achieved in the near future.

The Supreme Court's shift from activism to restraint was most evident in the complex field of criminal law. In his last year as presiding justice, Earl Warren made further contributions to the rights of defendants before giving way to his more conservative successor. The process of applying the Bill of Rights to state as well as federal activity (see p. 867) was further extended in *Benton* v. *Maryland*, 1969, in which the court ruled that the double jeopardy clause of the Fifth Amendment applied, under the Fourteenth Amendment's due process clause, to the states. *Chimel* v. *California*, 1969, further tightened the rule against unreasonable search and seizure. And in *Alderman* v. *United States*, 1969, the court struck a blow at unauthorized governmental eavesdropping by permitting defendants, even in national security cases, to examine all such material in order to see whether their rights had been violated. Altogether, during Warren's final term, the court decided against the prosecution in eighteen out of twenty-six appeals involving criminal law and procedure.

By contrast, during Chief Justice Burger's first term (1969–1970) the prosecution was successful in eighteen out of twenty-nine criminal law decisions. One such case, *Illinois* v. *Allen*, 1970, concerned a defendant who had disrupted his trial by disorderly action in the courtroom. The court held unanimously that such disruption, after due warning by the judge, warranted removing the defendant from the courtroom (or as a last resort, Justice Black added, binding and gagging him) without violating the constitutional right to be present at one's trial.[14] The Burger court made several decisions that eased the tasks of prosecution and conviction. It ruled in *Williams* v. *Florida*, 1970, that a six-person rather than a twelve-person jury would meet the requirements of the Sixth Amendment in noncapital cases. In *Johnson* v. *Louisiana*, 1972, a five-to-four majority upheld state laws that abandoned the requirement of a unanimous jury vote in criminal convictions. *Milton* v. *Wainwright*, 1972, another five-to-four decision, held that a confession obtained by unconstitutional means would not invalidate a conviction if there was enough legitimate evidence of guilt to render the error harmless. And in *Lego* v. *Twomey*, 1972, the court ruled that prosecutors could establish the admissibility of contested confessions by showing that they were voluntary "by a preponderance of the evidence" rather than, as the defense had argued, "beyond a reasonable doubt."

However, the court continued to be on guard against undue infringement of the rights of defendants.[15] In *Furman* v. *Georgia* and two companion decisions in 1972, the court ruled, five to four, that the death penalty as presently prescribed—capriciously rather than consistently imposed, with a tendency to fall more frequently upon minorities, the poor, and the powerless—was a violation of the Eighth Amendment's prohibition against cruel and unusual punishment. Most of the majority opinions, however, made it clear that an equitably administered death penalty would not be held unconstitutional.

Directly invalidating a prerogative claimed in 1970 by Attorney General Mitchell, the justices ruled, in *United States* v. *U.S. District Court, Eastern Michigan*, 1972, that wiretapping of alleged subversives and domestic radicals was not an inherent executive power that could be exercised without a court order.[16] Justice Powell, a Nixon appointee, read the administration a sharp lecture in his majority opinion. "The price of lawful

---

[14]The most notorious example of such courtroom disruption had occurred in 1969 during the conspiracy trial of seven youthful activists arrested in Chicago during the Democratic convention in 1968 under a federal antiriot statute. Two of the defendants were acquitted in February 1970 of all charges; the other five, convicted on the single count of crossing a state boundary with intent to incite a riot, were given maximum fines and five-year prison sentences. But in November 1972 a federal court of appeals overturned this verdict because of trial judge Julius Hoffman's "deprecating and antagonistic" behavior and certain remarks made by the government prosecutor.

[15]For example, *Baldwin* v. *New York*, 1970, required a jury trial if the offense was punishable by more than six months imprisonment; *Williams* v. *Illinois*, 1970, forbade holding defendants, who had been both fined and imprisoned, in jail beyond the maximum term because they were unable to pay the fine. *Coleman* v. *Alabama*, 1970, extended the right to counsel, under certain circumstances, to preliminary hearings. Provisions regarding an indigent defendant's right to counsel, laid down in *Gideon* v. *Wainwright*, 1963, were extended, in *Argersinger* v. *Hamlin*, 1972, to include misdemeanors as well as felonies if any term of imprisonment was involved.

[16]The Omnibus Crime Control and Safe Streets Act of 1968 had authorized wiretapping, without a court order, of suspected *foreign* agents in national security matters. The government had claimed the power to extend such surveillance to alleged *domestic* radicals.

public dissent," he noted, "must not be a dread of subjection to an un-checked surveillance power. . . . Unreviewed executive discretion may yield too readily to pressure to obtain incriminating evidence and overlook potential invasions of privacy. . . . We cannot accept the government's argument that internal security matters are too subtle and complex for judicial evaluation." This decision was handed down on June 19, 1972, in what had just become, as we shall see, a truly momentous week for "un-checked surveillance power" and "unreviewed executive discretion."

One or two other areas of judicial activity should be briefly noted. A few decisions in 1969 and 1970 further extended and amplified the "one man, one vote" principle.[17] The exact nature of the freedoms and obliga-tions of the news media, as they related to national security, crime, and the public's right to know, came under close but less than definitive scrutiny during the Nixon years. One issue arose out of the celebrated case of the Pentagon Papers, a multivolume, highly classified government study of American decision-making in Vietnam during the Eisenhower, Kennedy, and Johnson administrations. Daniel Ellsberg, a Defense Department ana-lyst, purloined and photocopied these papers and began making them available to the press in June 1971. The government, as soon as excerpts from these documents began to appear in the *New York Times* and the *Washington Post*, applied for injunctions to halt the publication in the interest of national security. After a flurry of contradictory rulings from district courts in New York and Washington, the lower courts ended by denying the government's request for injunctions, and the case was rushed to the Supreme Court for a final ruling.

In *New York Times* v. *United States*, June 1971, with each of the six majority justices filing a separate opinion, the court upheld the denial of the injunction and affirmed that publication of the Pentagon Papers could not be suppressed. The government, it was held, had not met the "heavy burden" of showing sufficient justification to warrant restraining the press in this instance. Exact guidelines governing the conflicting needs of na-tional security and a free press had not been set by the *Times* decision, however. The government, rebuffed in its attempts to halt publication of the Pentagon Papers, brought suit against Ellsberg for theft, conspiracy, and espionage.

[17]For example, a New York law limiting the right to vote in school board elections to property owners, lessees, and parents or guardians was invalidated in *Kramer* v. *Union Free School District No. 15*, 1969. Several other cases in that year laid down rigorous standards of equality between voting districts in ruling upon apportionment plans; in later years, however, the court showed a tendency to widen the limits of permissible disparity between the population of such districts. *Hadley* v. *Junior College District*, 1970, applied "one man, one vote" to any state or local election in which the official would perform governmental functions. And in *Phoenix* v. *Kolodziejski*, 1970, the court invoked the equal protection clause in forbidding municipalities to restrict voting rights to property owners in certain bond-approval elections. *Williams* v. *Rhodes*, 1969, made it easier for third parties to get on the ballot in many states by ruling that unreasonable restrictions on the right of political association violated the equal protection clause.

5. *Eagle Has Landed: Man Reaches the Moon*

"I believe," President Kennedy had told Congress in May 1961, "that this nation should commit itself to achieving the goal, before this decade is out, of landing a man on the moon and returning him safely to earth." This signaled the formal beginning of an effort that culminated eight years later in the landing of the Apollo 11 spacecraft upon the moon's surface. Upon the safe return of the three astronauts, much of mankind joined the American people in celebrating their accomplishment. In a decade that contained all too many episodes most people would have preferred to forget, the successful moon flight afforded a brief but welcome contrast; few of the hundreds of millions who watched or followed the progress of Apollo 11 failed to thrill at the magnitude of what was happening or share astronaut Neil Armstrong's sentiment that it constituted "one giant leap for mankind."

The major impetus behind the American moon program, beyond doubt, was the cold war. Getting to the moon per se, at least during the formative years of the project, was less important than getting there before the Russians did. Competition with the Soviet Union in outer space had begun in earnest in late 1957 when the Russians successfully launched their *Sputnik* space satellite some weeks ahead of the first American venture. The United States responded in 1958 by creating the National Aeronautics and Space Administration and inaugurating Project Mercury, a program designed to orbit a manned spacecraft. The first American in space was astronaut Alan B. Shepard, Jr., who made a brief fifteen-minute flight on May 5, 1961, three weeks before President Kennedy proposed to shoot the moon. The Russians were still "ahead" at this point; cosmonaut Yuri Gagarin had already completed a successful orbit of the earth. By the time American astronaut John H. Glenn, Jr., had surpassed this feat with a three-orbit venture in 1962, the Soviets were celebrating a much longer multiorbit flight of Gherman S. Titov. Taken all in all, honors between the two great powers during this competitive phase of the space race appear to have been divided fairly evenly.

Certain essential capacities of man, spacecraft, and rocketry having been established with the successful termination of Project Gemini in November 1966, NASA then proceeded to begin Project Apollo, the actual moon flight program. The Apollo spacecraft orbited the earth in satisfactory fashion in October 1968. Two months later Apollo 8 took three astronauts in a successful orbit of the moon. Apollo 9 featured performance and rendezvous tests of the various components of the spacecraft in earth orbit in March 1969. The major dress rehearsal came in May with Apollo

10, a ten-day lunar orbital trip during which the lunar module detached itself from the command module, descended to within ten miles of the moon's surface, and then rejoined the parent craft for the return trip to earth.

The stage was now set for Apollo 11, the flight that would culminate in an actual landing. Nearly a million spectators were on hand at Cape Kennedy, and tens of millions of others were glued to their television sets the world over. With astronauts Neil Armstrong, Edwin Aldrin, and Michael Collins aboard, the spacecraft was propelled from its launching pad by a huge Saturn 5 rocket on the morning of July 16, 1969. It entered a temporary "parking orbit" some 115 miles above the earth, and after its guidance system made the necessary computations, the men ignited the S-4B stage of the Saturn rocket, which shot them onto their translunar path at a speed of over 24,000 miles per hour. A bit later the command and service module was released, turned about in mid-space, and joined to the lunar module, at which point the Saturn launching rocket was left behind. On July 19, as they neared the moon, the astronauts reduced their craft's velocity and went into lunar orbit some seventy miles above the surface. They checked all systems and prepared for the descent. Armstrong and Aldrin climbed into *Eagle*, the lunar module; Collins remained in the command module *Columbia*, which was to continue orbiting the moon while *Eagle* made the actual landing.

Tension at the Houston space center and for millions of listeners became almost unbearable as Armstrong and Aldrin detached the lunar module from *Columbia*, fired the descent engines, and approached the surface under automatic control. They began manual control at an altitude of some 450 feet, surveyed the terrain until they found the agreed-upon landing site, and guided their craft slowly downward. Finally, at 4:17 P.M. eastern standard time on July 20, the world heard Neil Armstrong's quiet voice announce: "Tranquility Base here. The *Eagle* has landed."

Unbroken success continued to mark the remaining phases of this remarkable flight. Armstrong and Aldrin left their module, set up a television camera so that the world could get its first close-up view of the lunar landscape, and walked about in their bulky white space suits for some hours making observations and collecting rock and soil samples. They left a plaque in the Sea of Tranquility, proclaiming that "Here Men From the Planet Earth First Set Foot Upon the Moon, July 1969 A.D. We Came in Peace for All Mankind."

Excitement began to mount again as the two astronauts prepared to lift off and rejoin Michael Collins in *Columbia*. Collins had been orbiting the moon for nearly twenty-four hours in what one observer called a degree of human solitude unmatched since Adam's time. *Eagle* rose from the surface at 1:55 P.M. on July 21 and docked successfully with *Columbia*, whereupon the two moon walkers crawled back to rejoin Collins. *Eagle* was duly jettisoned, and the three men guided their craft through a sixty-hour return trip to a successful splashdown in the Pacific southwest of Hawaii on July 24, only two miles from their intended target point and about thirteen miles from *U.S.S. Hornet*, the recovery ship.

Apollo 11 was followed by five other successful manned flights to the moon, beginning with Apollo 12 in November 1969 and concluding with Apollo 17 in December 1972. Each voyage featured more complex and sophisticated experiments than its predecessor. The advances in scientific knowledge were considerable. The Apollo program was terminated at the end of 1972. Space appropriations had been subject to repeated cuts for some time in the face of high costs and charges that there were urgent things on earth that needed doing first. Some had grown impatient or bored with the space program, unmoved by later moon shots or by unmanned interplanetary satellites that both Russia and the United States were sending to Mars, Venus, and Jupiter. There was only mild public interest in the orbital sky-lab space station that the United States sought to establish in 1973. Some critics were loud in their demands that many domestic needs deserved priority over the shooting of costly hardware millions of miles into the void.

And yet the psychic significance of the Apollo program should not be underestimated. It had afforded a new and altogether priceless vision. At about the time of the first lunar orbit in late 1968, the childish competitive notion of a space race with Russia had begun to give way to a new and more mature perspective—induced primarily by a dramatic photograph, taken from Apollo 8 in lunar orbit, of the planet earth rising over the rim of the moon's horizon. Poet Archibald MacLeish had summed it up: "To see the earth as it is, small and beautiful in that silence where it floats, is to see ourselves as riders on earth together, brothers who know now they are truly brothers." Moreover, the Apollo program and its talented participants had convincingly demonstrated, in an age that stood in sore need of such reminders, that man's reach was magnificent indeed when he put his whole mind to it.

6. *The Environment and the Consumer*

Heightened concern over environmental issues and a growing self-awareness and assertiveness on the part of the American consumer had become significant political facts by the late sixties. They were related and frequently intertwined movements, since a concern for the quality of life and for the things that the American economic system seemed to be doing to it underlay both.[18] The two outstanding pioneers in provoking national awareness were Ralph Nader, whose career as the gadfly of assorted business practices and other vulnerable targets began with his book on automotive safety in 1965, and Rachel Carson, whose *Silent Spring* (1962), an eloquent study of the effect of pesticides upon bird life and the balance of nature, was probably one of the two or three most influential books of the age.

A great variety of private and public organizations had come into existence, in many cases quite recently, to deal with areas of consumer concern. At the federal level, a Consumer Advisory Council established by President Kennedy in 1962 was enlarged by President Johnson in 1964 to become part of a Committee on Consumer Interest, which included representatives of various federal agencies having consumer responsibilities. President Nixon also appointed such a committee, together with a special assistant to the president for consumer affairs. Pressure for the establishment of a stronger, more centralized body finally resulted in passage of the Consumer Product Safety Act in 1972. It created a new independent regulatory agency with authority to test, regulate, and set standards for product safety (incorporating certain safety functions of the Food and Drug Administration and the FTC), and to initiate court action against violators.

The consumer was also being aided by newly established public interest law firms, which for the first time enabled him to make effective use of the law in redressing his grievances. Interest in coordinating and centralizing the efforts of private bodies led in 1967 to the formation of the Consumer Federation of America, consisting of fifty-six organizations—state consumer associations, labor unions, local power cooperatives, and the like. Expanded to include 179 accredited groups by 1970, the CFA had become the consumer's chief lobbying agency in Washington. There was also a growing band of energetic young professionals and reformers associated with Ralph Nader. Known as Nader's Raiders, they followed their tireless consumer champion into a proliferating array of activities—pipeline and coal mine safety, land use, pension fund reform, mercury poisoning, insecticides, banking, meat adulteration, and the private-interest influence in federal regulatory agencies. All in all, the American consumer was armed as never before with ways of seeking redress for poor service, unhonored warranties, unreliable and unsafe products, deceptive advertising, frauds, high credit costs, and other examples of corporate irresponsibility.

Environmentalists also scored several victories. The Water Quality Improvement Act of 1970 sought to tighten existing safeguards against threats to water quality posed by acid mine drainage, thermal pollution from nuclear power plants, dredgings by the Corps of Engineers, sewage from

[18]Increased concern for consumer protection and environmental quality was observable in every industrial nation in the world by the late sixties, and international cooperation on such issues as air and water pollution, product safety, endangered species, and the like was significantly on the rise.

watercraft, public works projects, and oil pollution.[19] The National Air Quality Standards Act of 1970 contained several important provisions. It required car manufacturers to effect a 90 percent reduction in major pollutants from motor vehicles by 1975, required the government to set air quality standards for several contaminants, and gave the states three years in which to implement plans for meeting these standards. The act also authorized private citizens to file suit to enforce them, and imposed heavy penalties against violators. The Resource Recovery Act of 1970 took an important step toward satisfactory disposal of solid wastes by providing $453 million in demonstration grants for resource recovery systems, recycling, and planning waste disposal systems. President Nixon and Prime Minister Pierre Trudeau of Canada signed a Great Lakes Water Quality Agreement in April 1972, inaugurating a joint effort to clean up those badly polluted waterways.

An executive order of July 1971 combined several existing federal agencies that were concerned with such problems as pesticides, radiation, solid waste, auto exhaust emission, and water quality into a single department, the Environmental Protection Agency. Under the vigorous leadership of its first administrator, former Assistant Attorney General William Ruckelshaus of Indiana, the EPA immediately put its powers and mandate to work. Undeterred by backlash criticism from industry, several members of Congress, and other federal agencies with which he had collided, Ruckelshaus initiated action on several fronts. The EPA set emission control standards for the auto makers and brought dozens of suits against cities and corporations that appeared to be violating water quality standards or polluting navigable waterways.

In January 1971 public pressure finally forced the president to order a halt in the construction of a cross-Florida barge canal, designed to link the Atlantic with the Gulf of Mexico, after environmentalists had detailed the ecological and natural damages that would result. Similar disclosures persuaded the Senate in December 1970 to vote against further appropriations for a supersonic transport plane then under construction by the Boeing Company in Seattle. Despite pressure from private industry, the administration, and other advocates for a resumption of the project, the Senate was sufficiently convinced of the environmental hazards (and prohibitive costs) posed by the SST to vote in March 1971 to cancel it altogether. A $24.7 billion authorization to clean up American lakes and

---

[19]The threat to marine and wild life, public beaches, and ecological balance posed by oil spills was unforgettably dramatized by various accidents to oil tankers and leakages from offshore oil wells. The public first learned of this danger with the sinking of the tanker *Torrey Canyon* in the English Channel in 1967, damaging miles of beach in both France and England. An offshore drilling accident in the Santa Barbara Channel in 1969 had a similar effect on the California coast. The Chevron Oil Company was fined $1 million after a spill from its offshore platform near the Louisiana coast released some 20,000 barrels of oil into the Gulf. And the wreck of the tanker *Arrow* off Nova Scotia in 1970 polluted some 200 miles of shoreline with nearly 4 million gallons of fuel oil.

rivers was repassed over Nixon's veto in October 1972, as we have seen. Concern for the environment, which cut across party and liberal-conservative lines, was equally manifest on the state level.[20] The popularity of "earth day" programs and similar clean-up campaigns, the vogue of environmental studies programs in colleges, and an unprecedented boom in the sale of bicycles were among other evidences of the new public concern.

Such concern had done much to make Congress, corporations, and government at all levels more responsive, although neither the environment nor the consumer had thus far registered more than partial and occasional triumphs. But the level of public awareness and the determination with which many of the trouble spots were being attacked, by both public and private sources at home and abroad, gave grounds for the hope that an era of tragic abuse of the earth and the fulness thereof—an era dating back to the beginnings of the industrial revolution—might be on the verge of ending.

7. Economic Stress

The American economy behaved oddly during the Nixon years. Variously beset by inflation, unemployment, recession, surging expansion, a volatile stock market, imbalances in international trade and payments, and dangerous pressure on the dollar in foreign money markets, the situation was so contradictory and unstable as to defy most efforts at analysis or correction. The economy vaguely resembled a patient with several conflicting maladies and conditions; prescriptions designed to ease or rectify one aspect of the problem frequently exaggerated or endangered another.

In coping with this difficult situation the Nixon administration resorted to a variety of policies; the president's willingness to apply flexible and undoctrinaire approaches was never more in evidence. When he took office the most pressing issue was inflation, which had been rising sharply since the mid-sixties. The 7.7 percent growth in the GNP in 1969 was accounted for entirely by price increases rather than gains in real output, and the average worker's real spendable earnings declined by about a dollar during the year. The administration at first sought to ease the problem through conventional means, including reduced spending and re-

[20]Two or three examples of state action deserve brief mention. Michigan passed a law in 1970 authorizing every citizen of the state, whether directly affected or not, to go to court against public agencies and private companies thought to be damaging the environment. New Jersey, in an action later contested by New York and Pennsylvania, forbade the dumping of sewage sludge or industrial wastes within one hundred miles of its seacoast. A Delaware statute in 1971 banned all heavy industry along its shoreline, prohibited tanker-loading operations in Delaware Bay, and placed severe shoreline restrictions on other new industries. In signing this law, Republican Governor Russell Peterson knowingly turned down an estimated $750 million worth of proposed new industrial developments.

straints designed to curb the money supply and slow the pace of economic activity. With capital markets thus restricted in the face of increased demand for funds, interest rates shot up to the highest point in a century, affecting housing construction and the ability of state and local governments to raise money for needed social services. In further anti-inflationary moves in 1969 and 1970, the government raised certain taxes and effected large cutbacks in defense spending and missile and space projects.

The country soon found itself in a disastrous economic bind, scarcely foreseeable because it seemed to contradict all logic. Inflation continued unchecked during 1970 and much of 1971 at a rate of 4 to 5 percent a year. But the tight money policies, defense cutbacks, and high interest rates helped induce a falling off in construction, steel and auto output, and business expenditures for new plant and equipment. The corollary was a sharp, alarming rise in unemployment from 3.5 percent in December 1969 to 6.2 percent a year later, the highest level in nearly a decade. The United States thus faced a simultaneous onset of severe recession and continued inflation as the seventies began.

Moving to combat the recession, President Nixon startled orthodox Republicans by pronouncing himself a Keynsian and deliberately applying a dose of Keynsian economic policy: he would, he said, permit an unbalanced federal budget in the hope of stimulating economic recovery. Budget deficits were duly forthcoming—some $23 billion in fiscal 1971 and again in 1972, and an estimated $25 billion in fiscal 1973—but the expected recovery did not materialize. Both 5 percent inflation and 6 percent unemployment persisted through the spring and summer of 1971. Although all-time records in housing construction and the grain harvest were on their way to being set, business as a whole was stagnant. The stock market entered a dismal downward plunge from late April through mid-August. To make matters worse, a crisis was threatening the value of the American dollar in the international money market. In the face of such difficulties, the president addressed the nation on August 15, 1971, to announce a bold new economic stabilization policy.

The domestic side of this new policy began with the imposition of a three-month freeze on prices, wages, rents, and dividends. Phase Two, initiated in November 1971, imposed a system of controls to be administered by a price commission and a pay board. A cost of living council made up of government officials headed by the secretary of the treasury would oversee these two boards. The plan set maximum guidelines of 5.5 percent for most wage increases and 2.5 percent for price and rent increases. Raw foodstuffs and financial securities were among the items exempt from controls. Costs, productivity, and before-tax profits were among the factors to be weighed in approving specific increases. Advance permission was required for price increases by firms with $100 million or more in sales or wage increases involving five thousand or more workers. Firms in the $50-to-$100 million sales category and those employing between one thousand and five thousand workers were to report promptly after taking price or wage action. Smaller firms would simply be subject to periodic spot checks of their price and wage levels.

Nixon terminated Phase Two in January 1973, after fourteen months of operation. The results, while not earthshaking, represented a distinct improvement. Chiefly because of the sharp rise in the price of food, which farmers could sell free from controls, the overall cost of living rose about 3.5 percent in 1972. This was more than had been hoped for but markedly less than the rate that had prevailed for some years previously. Unemployment declined from over 6 percent to an average rate of 5.5 percent, which labor leaders denounced as far too high. But the economy came out of recession with alacrity. Industrial output, including steel and automobiles, registered sharp increases. Corporate profits soared. Rises in consumer spending, expenditures for plant and equipment, and other key indices also reflected the return of general prosperity during 1972. Public confidence had unquestionably been restored by the government's willingness to take strong action. Convinced that the worst was over, the president initiated Phase Three. Mandatory wage and price controls, except for "problem areas" like food, health care, and construction, were terminated in favor of a system of voluntary compliance whereby business and labor were to administer the controls themselves. Rent controls were abandoned and the pay board and price commission were abolished, although the cost of living council was retained and given a new labor-management advisory committee.

Meanwhile, the nation's economic policymakers had also been wrestling with an international monetary crisis. Nixon's announcement of August 1971 had proclaimed, in addition to the wage-price freeze, that the United States would no longer convert dollars into gold. He accompanied this startling announcement with the imposition of a 10 percent surcharge on imports in a further move to restore the nation's financial equilibrium.

The era that Nixon's statement brought to a close had been launched by an international monetary agreement signed by the United States and its allies at Bretton Woods, New Hampshire, in 1944. In a bold effort to provide stability and a reliable medium of exchange for future trading patterns in a war-shattered world, the United States had agreed at Bretton Woods to make the American dollar, then the world's only strong currency, convertible (by foreign governments or their central banks) into gold at a fixed rate of $35 an ounce. The postwar system of international exchange was thus based upon the dollar, with other currencies measuring their value in relation to it. Dollars were at a premium everywhere and remained so during the long slow months of postwar economic recovery. This recovery, fueled by American aid, touched off an unprecedented twenty-five-year boom in international trade.

The very world prosperity that American aid had underwritten began eroding the strength of the once almighty dollar. The United States had enjoyed an annual trade surplus uninterruptedly since 1893, and this surplus continued through the fifties and sixties as American goods remained in high demand. But other items in America's balance sheet with the rest of the world assumed increasing importance after 1945. Despite the annual trade surplus, the total annual outflow of dollars (for imports, foreign aid, military expenditures abroad, services paid to foreign shipping, tourist spending, private overseas investments, earnings on foreign investments in the United States) often matched and sometimes exceeded the total annual income (from exports, American shipping charges, foreign travelers and investments in this country, returns on American investments abroad, and so on). Deficits in this overall balance of payments had occasionally produced a momentary loss of confidence in the American dollar, with a resultant drain of gold from the country's reserve holdings. United States gold supplies shrank from a postwar high of $25 billion to a low of $10.5 billion in 1971.

The growing prosperity and productivity in those nations that constituted America's major trading partners—Western Europe, Japan, Canada, Great Britain—eventually altered the trade balance that constituted the dollar's last source of strength. As productive efficiency in these nations grew, American goods became subject to increasing competitive pressure in the world market. At first the pinch could be felt in items of low unit cost where labor differentials were a major factor, such as shoes, clothing, and textiles. Then foreign goods began elbowing American goods off the shelf, in both the international and domestic markets, where it hurt badly—in steel, photographic equipment, television and other electronics items, aircraft, automobiles. The American product, frequently matched or surpassed in quality by the foreign output, was placed at a further disadvantage by the effects of inflation. America's historic annual trade surplus began to shrink.

The turning point was reached and passed in early 1971, when monthly balances showed a trade deficit for the first time in nearly eighty years. Deficits continued, month after month, with a tendency to grow larger. By slow degrees, but with the kind of avalanche effect out of which panics are made, people overseas who held or dealt in American dollars—traders, investors, bankers, speculators, American individuals and corporations with overseas investments or funds to protect—began seeking to convert those dollars into foreign currencies. The rush to unload dollars grew in the summer of 1971 until it became a stampede that threatened to destroy the American currency as a medium of international exchange. Japanese, French, British, Belgian, and German central banks were inundated with dollars that nobody wanted, and for which not a fraction of enough American gold existed.

President Nixon responded with his announcement of August 15 ending convertibility into gold and imposing a 10 percent import surcharge. Leaders and financial experts from all the major commercial nations held meetings during the fall of 1971, and in December they produced a new interim agreement at the Smithsonian Institution in Washington. Its principal feature was a devaluation of the dollar by some 8 percent (in terms of gold, from $35 to $38 per ounce) and a corresponding upward revaluation of various foreign currencies to coincide more accurately with their relative strengths in the international money market. The dollar, under the Smithsonian agreement, would remain unconvertible into gold. The agreement also prescribed limits within which currencies would be allowed to fluctuate, in terms of one another, by the central banks and other financial institutions through which clearances were made. The United States dropped the 10 percent import surcharge, which foreign countries had criticized as conducive to future trade wars. By refusing to resume convertibility, the nation was in effect insisting that the dollar had become just another currency, to be exchanged with others at rates that would fluctuate according to commercial and financial realities. Its role as the western world's standard medium of exchange had ended.

The Smithsonian agreement represented a kind of holding action that would allow international monetary experts to ponder the situation and work out the basis for a more permanent system. During the first year of operation with a devalued dollar, American trade and payments balances showed a persistent, nagging deficit.[21] Pressure on the dollar continued accordingly; there was no return to the panic conditions of mid-1971, but the international money market still lacked confidence in the dollar's position. The result, in February 1973, was a second devaluation. It amounted to about 10 percent, with the value in relation to an ounce of gold officially adjusted from $38 to $42.22. The dollar remained unconvertible, as before. Although a completely successful international monetary system to replace the vanished Bretton Woods agreement had yet to be evolved, some financial experts believed that the system of flexible exchange rates was proving workable and ought to form a part of any future agreement.

---

[21] One major purpose of devaluing the dollar was to restore America's trade balance by stimulating American exports (since a given amount of marks or yen could now be converted into a greater number of dollars than before, more American goods could be bought) and reducing American imports (since, conversely, American dollars could be converted into fewer marks or yen). American exports did register increases, from a low of $2.7 billion in October 1971 to a high of $4.2 billion in January 1972, after which they fluctuated at an average monthly rate of about $4 billion through August. But the *short-run* effect of devaluation upon imports was to raise prices, as expected, *without* decreasing the volume of purchases. The sharp recovery of the American economy in 1972 vastly stimulated the demand for imports despite the increase in prices. As a result, imports rose from a low of about $3.4 billion in November 1971 to a high of over $4.5 billion in January 1972 and fluctuated slowly upward from that figure for the next eight months. The trade deficit, which had first appeared in early 1971, continued throughout 1972 at rates ranging from $200–500 million a month. The balance of payments also showed continuous deficits during 1972.

8. The Quest for Arms Control and Détente

President Nixon's record of bold initiative and positive achievement in the area of foreign policy contained elements of both logic and paradox. The logic stemmed from his career-long interest and experience in foreign affairs; this was where his priorities were known to lie, and prior to his election he had frequently spoken of the constructive diplomatic steps he hoped to take. Paradox lay in the fact that the major thrust of his foreign policy—a retreat from America's self-appointed role as world policeman and a determined search for accord with both Russia and China—represented a complete reversal of the hard-line anticommunism that had been the outstanding feature of his career before 1968. Nixon was a tough-minded realist in foreign affairs. He knew that the world of the cold war, in which his earlier views had been formed, bore little resemblance to the world of the 1970s. Yet his sense of realism cut both ways. A total repudiation of cold-war assumptions would have been, in his view, as unrealistic as a blind adherence to them.

The double-edged nature of Nixon's realism was most evident in the matter of disarmament and preparedness, prominent topics of debate in Washington during 1969-1970. The president's desire to seek accord with Russia and thus slow the nuclear arms race to a crawl, if not to a halt, led to several important steps. He hailed the Senate's approval of the Nuclear Nonproliferation Treaty in March 1969 (see p. 875). He won Russia's consent to a draft treaty covering the seabed, whereby the two powers agreed not to deploy nuclear, chemical, or biological weapons (save for missile submarines and defensive purposes in coastal waters) on the ocean floor. In November 1969, he proclaimed America's unilateral and unconditional renunciation of the use of biological warfare, and of chemical weapons save in defense; and he ordered the Defense Department to begin a phased destruction of the nation's stockpile of such weapons. His most notable achievement during 1969 came in December, when the Soviets agreed to begin the long-deferred strategic arms limitation (SALT) talks in April 1970 with an eye to reaching eventual agreement on arms control. But these forward steps on the road to disarmament were accompanied by an equal determination to maintain and even improve America's nuclear capacity. The president believed in negotiating from strength, frankly disagreeing with those critics who maintained that such a policy made the task of achieving meaningful arms control more difficult.

The specific dispute in 1969-1970 centered around new offensive and defensive weapons that well illustrated the grim dictates of nuclear technology and the inherent instability in the so-called balance of terror. Both the United States and the Soviet Union possessed enormous and approximately equal nuclear arsenals at the outset of Nixon's presidency. American military spokesmen, fearful that Russia's new SS-9 ICBM could destroy America's Minuteman missiles in their silos in a possible first strike, wanted the United States to deploy a new antiballistic missile (ABM) system, known as Safeguard, to defend against an SS-9 attack. The Russians, it was pointed out, were already deploying an ABM system around Moscow; as they expanded it they would become less vulnerable to, and therefore less apt to be deterred by, an American retaliatory attack. Nixon was a firm advocate of ABM; it was one of the items, as we have seen, that endeared him to Senator Thurmond before the 1968 election.

At the same time, the military was testing a new offensive weapon known, in the weird acronymic lingo of missile technology, as MIRV, or multiple independently-targeted reentry vehicle. In plainer words it could be described as a multiple warhead that could be fired from the parent missile in mid-flight at several targets in a kind of controlled buckshot effect. Interception of the MIRV by defensive missiles promised to be far more difficult than in the case of conventional single-warhead ICBMs. Hence, defense spokesmen argued, attaching MIRV warheads to some Minuteman and submarine missiles would restore the nation's deterrent credibility by reducing the effectiveness of the Soviet ABM system.

The Senate contained a growing number of opponents to this expanded missile strategy. Fulbright, Majority Leader Mansfield, McGovern of South Dakota, Edward Kennedy of Massachusetts, and John Sherman Cooper of Kentucky led a battle against the ABM that consumed most of the summer of 1969. Arguments about the high cost—an estimated $2.1 billion to emplace ABMs at two Minuteman silos—and the dubious effectiveness of the weapon were combined with basic questions about the logic behind such buildups. Russia, they pointed out, was also testing MIRVs. The adoption of an American ABM system would surely induce the Soviets to counter by equipping its SS-9s with MIRVs, the result being an escalation of the arms race at great cost to both countries and no advantage to either. After prolonged debate the Safeguard ABM system scraped through the Senate by a single vote in August 1969. It promptly passed the House, and preliminary work near Minuteman bases in North Dakota and Montana was begun. Congress authorized ABM emplacement around two more missile sites in 1970, and the Defense Department began equipping a few ICBMs and submarine missiles with MIRV warheads.

Whereas critics insisted that adoption of ABMs and MIRVs would damage prospects at the SALT talks, Secretary of Defense Laird and other proponents maintained that such action would deter the Soviets from adding to their own buildup and convince them of the need to negotiate. The SALT talks proceeded cordially but inconclusively during 1970, first at Vienna from April to August and then at Helsinki in November and December. The two sides were far apart in their proposals but agreed to keep talking. Missile buildups in both countries continued, especially on the part of the Russians, who were determined to achieve parity with the

United States in long-range weapons. But both powers slowed or halted work on ABM and MIRV projects, marking time while the talks proceeded.

For the American defense structure as a whole, President Nixon pursued a policy of moderate but steady reductions in conventional strength, including cancellation or cutbacks in a variety of installations and projects. He was reinforced in this posture by changing attitudes in Congress, and particularly in the Senate, where growing numbers of lawmakers were no longer willing to rubber-stamp all proposals from the Pentagon for new appropriations and hardware. They were shaken by discoveries of several appalling examples of waste, inefficiency, padded figures, and gigantic "cost overruns" in defense contracts. Nagged by a growing belief that blind acquiescence in military advice was at least partly responsible for American mistakes in Vietnam and elsewhere, Congress was moving toward growing assertiveness and intransigence on matters of defense and foreign policy.

Military retrenchment went hand in hand with a frank downward revision of America's global commitments. At Guam in mid-1969 the president proclaimed a new policy, sometimes known as the Nixon Doctrine, in which the nation's role was redefined in more modest terms as that of helpful partner rather than military protector. Looking first at Asia, the president gave assurances that the United States would continue to honor its treaty and mutual defense obligations. But its goal, he added, would henceforth be to help Asian countries, through economic and technological aid, to assume a larger share of the responsibility for their own development and security. American equipment and training might be available for any ally faced with internal subversion or external aggression, but American ground troops would not be employed in such cases—in sum, no more Vietnams. Nixon later extended these concepts of American partnership and greater self-reliance on the part of other nations to Latin America in a redefinition of the Alliance for Progress. He also made it plain to European leaders that he regarded the era of American hegemony as over, and he talked about applying the new partnership principle to NATO. Not since the late forties had an American president undertaken so large a reappraisal of the nation's role in world affairs.

Meanwhile, the SALT talks finally began to make progress. Three rounds of negotiations during 1971 produced an agreement that the two powers would seek to reduce the risks of nuclear war by concentrating upon limiting the number of ABMs and strategic offensive weapons.[22]

[22] Efforts to agree on the relative size and composition of the two arsenals were complicated by an awareness, in both Moscow and Washington, of signs of growing nuclear cooperation between France and Great Britain and of China's determined pursuit of a nuclear capacity. Peking had tested a medium-range missile (MRBM) in 1969 and launched a satellite in 1970; it was predicted that the Chinese would be able to deploy ICBMs by 1975. Both the United States and the Soviet Union were also aware that the facts of geography would enable Chinese ICBMs to threaten all of Russia and only a small portion of America.

They also agreed to modernize and strengthen the hot-line communications link between Moscow and Washington. The negotiators' persistence and dedication paid off in 1972 with the formulation and approval of the most significant arms accords of the atomic age. There were two documents, signed by President Nixon and party chairman Leonid Brezhnev in Moscow on May 26 and ratified by the legislative bodies of both countries in October 1972.

The first, a full-fledged treaty, limited the number of ABM sites in either country to two, one near its national capital and the other at least eight hundred miles distant. No ABM site could contain more than one hundred launchers and interceptor missiles, and both countries pledged not to develop, test, or deploy further ABM systems on land, sea, or in space. Rather than providing for international or on-site inspections, long a stumbling block in disarmament negotiations between the United States and the Soviet Union, the ABM treaty permitted each side to monitor the other by "nonintrusive" means, which meant photo-reconnaissance satellites. The treaty represented a recognition by both countries that a policy of mutual deterrence afforded the surest key to peace under present circumstances, and that only by prohibiting either side from working toward an effective nationwide ABM system could such mutuality be preserved.

The second accord was not a treaty but an Interim Agreement that put a five-year freeze on the number of strategic offensive missiles in both arsenals, including ICBMs, submarine-launched missiles (SLBMs), and modern ballistic missile submarines. Modernization of launchers and submarines on a one-to-one replacement basis was permitted, and no limits were placed on the number of nuclear warheads or upon programs such as America's current MIRV development. As with the ABM treaty, the Interim Agreement relied upon mutual monitoring via satellites rather than on-site inspections. The agreement gave the Soviet Union a distinct edge in the number of missiles and submarines but recognized a present American lead of 2.5 to 1 in the number of warheads.[23] The United States Senate ratified the ABM treaty promptly by a vote of 88 to 2 but expressed concern over the Soviet missile lead contained in the Interim Agreement (which, not being a treaty, did not require formal Senate ratification). The president asked Congress for a joint resolution endorsing the agreement, so as to strengthen his hand in negotiating a full-fledged treaty after the next round of SALT talks. In expressing its approval, Congress attached an amendment sponsored by Senator Henry Jackson of Washington urging that in future negotiations the United States should insist upon missile equality with the Soviet Union.

[23]Specifically, the Interim Agreement froze strategic long-range arsenals at their current levels. The Russian lead over the United States was thus set at 1,618 to 1,054 in ICBMs; 740 to 656 in SLBMs; and 62 to 44 in modern nuclear submarines. The American preponderance in nuclear warheads stemmed from both its strategic bomber fleet and its superior technology, as of 1972, in MIRV development.

The ABM treaty and Interim Agreement were clearly no more than first steps. Certain expansive features of the arms race—production of nuclear warheads, improvement of guidance systems, qualitative advances—were not only permissible but likely to continue, since each side would feel a competitive pressure to improve its strategic bargaining position in future talks. But the SALT accords of 1972 represented a genuine breakthrough in the long and generally unproductive record of East-West disarmament negotiations. The freeze on strategic weapons did not guarantee that there would be no war, as President Nixon said when signing the Interim Agreement on September 30, but he called it "the beginning of a process that is enormously important, that will limit now, and we hope, later reduce the burden of arms."

In fact, 1972 was a banner year for arms agreements. The Seabed Treaty, initiated and drafted by the United States and the Soviet Union in 1969 and submitted to the Geneva Disarmament Conference for multilateral approval, had been opened for signatures in February 1971. It went into effect in May 1972 when Great Britain, the Soviet Union, and the United States formally endorsed it, bringing the total number of signatures to eighty-six. Another outgrowth of a presidential initiative in 1969 came to fulfillment in April 1972 when a convention prohibiting the production and stockpiling of bacteriological weapons, negotiated by the Geneva Disarmament Conference during 1971, received the signatures of Great Britain, the United States, and the Soviet Union. Later signed by eighty-six other nations, the biological weapons convention was the first accord of the postwar era to provide for the actual destruction of existing weapons.[24] Conferences between NATO and Warsaw Pact nations regarding mutual reductions in armed forces were scheduled to take place in 1973. With such agreements in effect or pending and a new phase of SALT negotiations under way at Geneva, President Nixon could justly point with pride to his record in the field of arms control.

There were parallel accomplishments in other important areas of Soviet-American relations. The Big Four foreign ministers were able, after thirty-three sessions over a seventeen-month period in 1970-1971, to reach formal accord on the thorny subject of Berlin, periodic flash-point in East-West relations since 1945. In brief, the Quadripartite Berlin Agreement of 1971 pledged that "there shall be no use of force in the area and that disputes shall be settled by peaceful means." It also provided for "simplified and unhindered" access to and from West Germany; reaffirmed four-power responsibility for such access; and carefully defined the city's political status, the four-power presence, and regulations for visits

---

[24]Nixon had also, in November 1969, unilaterally renounced the use of chemical weapons, save for defensive purposes and with the exception of tear gas and defoliants. But attempts to include chemical with bacteriological weapons in the multilateral convention being negotiated at Geneva proved impossible because of an unbreakable deadlock between the United States and the Soviet Union on the issue of verifying compliance.

between East and West Berlin. The Berlin accord was followed by a series of agreements between East and West Germany. After signing pacts that provided for improving the flow of traffic to and from Berlin, easing travel and visit restrictions, and granting amnesty to many political prisoners, the two German states initialed a major treaty in November 1972. The document defined and established relations between the two countries to the satisfaction of both, including pledges of peaceful coexistence and mutual recognition of sovereignty and independence. This long-awaited normalization of German relations was followed in turn by the ratification of treaties of friendship and nonaggression between West Germany and Poland and between West Germany and the Soviet Union.

Relations between the United States and the Soviet Union reached a record high in 1972 with President Nixon's visit to Moscow in May and the conclusion of several agreements. Cordial talks between the president and the Russian leaders, which included signing of the two SALT accords, culminated in a cluster of pacts covering a variety of issues.[25] Most importantly, the presidential visit paved the way for a comprehensive Soviet-American trade agreement, signed in October. The agreement provided, among other things, for reciprocal credits, reduction of tariff levels on a most-favored-nation basis, availability of Soviet business facilities to American businessmen, and establishment of an American commercial office in Moscow and a Russian trade representative in Washington. It was estimated that the pact would result in a tripling of current trade levels between the two countries, from $500 million in 1969–1971 to $1.5 billion in 1973–1975. These figures, moreover, did not include a $1 billion contract for Soviet purchases of American grain over a three-year period, authorized by an agreement in July 1972. The two countries also signed a maritime treaty in October and agreed upon terms for liquidating an old Lend-Lease debt that dated back to the Second World War.[26] The Russians made several contracts for the purchase of industrial goods from American firms. Symbolic of the changed relations between the world's great centers of capitalism and communism was an announcement in the spring of 1973 that the Chase Manhattan Bank planned to open a branch in Moscow.

---

[25] In addition to a cultural exchange agreement, the two powers signed five-year pacts calling for extensive cooperation in several areas: medicine and public health, environmental protection, science and technology, and the exploration and use of outer space. They also signed a three-year agreement designed to prevent air and naval incidents.

[26] The maritime treaty opened forty ports in each country to the other country's ships, set rates on the shipments of American grain to Russia, and provided that one-third of Soviet-American marine trade would be in American and one-third in Russian vessels.

The total amount due the United States under the Lend-Lease debt, after portions had been written off in the immediate postwar years, was $2.6 billion. The United States later offered to settle for $1.3 billion, then for $800 million, but Russia had persistently refused to pay. The agreement in 1972 called for a Soviet payment of $722 million over thirty years in settlement of all claims, including interest.

It was quite true, notwithstanding these gratifying developments, that the two great powers remained in basic opposition on a number of matters involving both strategic self-interest and ideology. Yet the new Soviet-American détente represented genuine progress. The diplomacy of the Nixon years had advanced the possibility that the two countries could henceforth deal with one another on a basis of mutual awareness and understanding as to how their respective interests related. Peaceful coexistence between the United States and the Soviet Union had been a propaganda slogan and a mockery during the fifties; twenty years later it had become a reality.

Although the world offered a full quota of strife, political unrest, and upheaval during the Nixon years, relative calm rather than undue turbulence generally prevailed. In Europe, the retirement of Charles de Gaulle in 1969 helped pave the way for Great Britain to join the European Economic Community. Basic agreement was reached in June 1971, and formal admission of Great Britain, Ireland, and Denmark to the EEC took place in January 1973. Elsewhere, a few political changes resulted in minor setbacks for the United States.[27]

The most dangerous trouble spot continued to be the Middle East, where the immutable Arab-Israeli conflict smoldered and occasionally blazed across the new frontier lines that had come into existence after Israel's triumph in the Six-Day War of 1967. Little change in the status quo occurred during the next six years. The threat of war remained constant. American initiative and several months of negotiation with Israel, Jordan, and Egypt finally brought acceptance of a genuine cease-fire in August 1970, but it was little better than an uneasy armed truce. Nasser's death in September 1970 brought few changes; Anwar el-Sadat, who succeeded him, was no more able than his dynamic predecessor had been to face Israel down or promote Arab unity. The fear that Soviet artillerists and pilots stationed in Egypt might become dangerously involved in the periodic gun duels and air raids across the Suez Canal was eased when President Sadat, in a surprise move, ordered the expulsion of all Soviet technicians and military personnel from Egypt in July 1972. Terrorist ac-

---

[27] A reform-minded group of army officers led by Colonel Muammar al-Qaddafi seized power in Libya in 1969 and required both Great Britain and the United States to remove their armed forces and abandon their military installations on Libyan soil, including the big Wheelus air force base. An avowed Marxist, Salvador Allende, became president of Chile at the head of a coalition government in 1970 and secured a constitutional amendment expropriating the holdings of American firms in Chilean copper mines.

Civil war in Pakistan between the country's geographically and socially divided eastern and western sections in 1971 brought obloquy, war with India, crushing defeat, and dismemberment to the Pakistani regime led by General Agha Muhammad Yahya Khan. The Bengali rebels, after India intervened in their behalf, won their independence from Pakistan and entered the world family of nations as Bangladesh in early 1972. The Soviets, who had supported India, emerged with enhanced prestige in South Asia; while the United States, outspoken in its support of Pakistan, suffered accordingly.

tivities by Palestinian Arab guerrillas remained a chronic problem that showed signs of easing in the early seventies.[28]

The most startling development on the international scene during this period was the turnabout in relations between the United States and China. As Nixon took office the Chinese People's Republic was just beginning to emerge from several years of prolonged political and social upheaval. A self-induced Cultural Revolution had gotten out of hand, pitting party factions and students and troops against one another, ravaging parts of the countryside, retarding economic development, curtailing diplomatic activity almost to zero, and virtually destroying the country's political structure. As stability and cohesion returned in 1970, China sought to end its diplomatic isolation, cultivate friendships abroad, and strengthen its international position. Seeking to offset its badly strained relations with the Soviet Union, Peking made friendly gestures to Communist, Western, and third-world nations alike, and the atmosphere began to improve. Several countries, led by Canada and Italy in late 1970, responded to Chinese overtures by recognizing Peking as the sole legal government of China and establishing diplomatic relations. For the first time, the United Nations General Assembly in November 1970 cast a majority vote, though short of the necessary two-thirds, in favor of admitting China to the United Nations.

Nixon spoke several times, before and after his election, of an interest in opening a direct dialogue with Peking and seeking to review and improve the relationship between the two countries. China's only response to these overtures was an agreement to resume the Warsaw talks that it had broken off in 1968; intermittent conversations between the Chinese and American ambassadors to Poland had constituted the sole channel of direct communication between the two powers. The Warsaw talks duly reopened in February 1970, but American efforts to focus on relatively safe subjects like an exchange of visitors and expanded trade were met by a Chinese desire to discuss political problems, and particularly Taiwan. This issue, along with Indochina and Korea, was at the bedrock of Sino-American differences. Peking had never ceased to claim Taiwan as an integral part of China and hoped someday to "liberate" and absorb the island, thereby destroying the Nationalist regime to which the United States remained tied by mutual security obligations and a strong sense of commitment. The Warsaw talks consequently got nowhere, and Peking

---

[28]The Jordanian army, determined to halt this activity, finally managed to destroy Palestinian guerrilla bases in Jordan. Lebanon, too, tried to clamp down on guerrilla operations, leading to a series of clashes that almost toppled the Lebanese government in 1973. Terrorist exploits became more and more violent—the hijacking and destruction of airliners, the bloody random massacre of twenty-seven people by hired Japanese assassins in the Tel Aviv airport in May 1972, the brutal murder of eleven Israeli athletes at the Olympic games in Munich in September 1972. But the effectiveness and influence of the guerrilla organizations appeared to be on the wane.

discontinued them in May in protest against American military action in Cambodia.

Hence the basic disputes and the basic enmity remained. Yet potential mutual interests did exist. There was the problem of Russia; improved relations between Peking and Washington might induce a more cooperative spirit in Moscow toward both countries. And there was the problem of Japan. Japan's phenomenal economic growth since midcentury was one of the wonders of the modern world. She had become an industrial giant, with a GNP second only to those of the United States and the Soviet Union and a growth rate that promised to surpass both within a generation. The island nation fairly crackled with expansive energy. Japanese commercial, industrial, technical, and financial representatives were everywhere. In the Orient, they were making the Greater East Asia Co-Prosperity Sphere more of a reality in 1970 than militarist-imperialist Japan had ever been able to make of it in the thirties and forties.

Japan's surging expansion was accompanied by renascent nationalism, including an awareness that so powerful an economic aggregation had every reason to play a more forceful and independent role in world affairs. Relations with the United States were marked by friction in economic matters—Japan's strength was a major factor in the weakness of the dollar—and by growing Japanese demands for a redefinition of its diplomatic and military ties with the United States. In response to these pressures, Washington reduced its military forces in Japan, agreed to the transfer of certain military installations, and, after years of intricate negotiations, signed an agreement in June 1971 for the reversion of Okinawa to Japan in 1972. Japan's power and assertiveness were duly noticed in China and the United States.

In any event, Washington made a series of overtures to Peking in early 1971, chiefly in the form of relaxed trade and travel restrictions. The response emerged in calm, polite Oriental fashion during the spring and summer. It began with an indirect, good-natured gesture: an invitation in April for an American table tennis team to visit China and play a match with a Chinese team.[29] It emerged more tangibly from a series of private interviews between Premier Chou En-lai and a succession of American visitors, including James Reston of the *New York Times*. Chou reaffirmed China's Taiwan policy but called attention to the Japanese question, deftly outlining a possible agenda for more official conversations.

The breakthrough came with a secret visit to Peking by Henry Kissinger in early July. The world first learned of Kissinger's trip when Nixon addressed the nation on July 15 to announce that his adviser had conferred with the Chinese leaders and arranged for a presidential visit to China in early 1972. There would be no preconditions, Nixon added; the purpose

---

[29]The American team was cordially received and had a wonderful time during their one-week stay. The Chinese team won the match, 5–3 and 5–4.

was to seek "normalization" of relations between the two countries. Kissinger returned to China in October to arrange the details for Nixon's forthcoming visit.

The trip took place as planned during the last week in February 1972: the first meeting between an American and Chinese head of state since Roosevelt conferred with Chiang Kai-shek in Cairo in 1943, and the first time any American president had set foot in China or engaged in top-level negotiations with a country the United States did not officially recognize. Nixon had a frank and friendly interview with Mao Tse-tung on February 21, the day of his arrival in Peking. The entire American party were guests at a huge banquet that evening, at which American and Chinese officials, including the president and Premier Chou En-lai, mingled and drank to one another's health.

After a series of conferences, Nixon and Chou issued a joint communiqué on February 27 that summed up divergent but not irreconcilable views in certain key areas. Peking called itself the sole government of China and defined Taiwan's "liberation" as an internal Chinese concern; the United States agreed that Taiwan was part of China, affirmed its desire for a peaceful settlement, and spoke of reducing its forces "as the tension in the area diminishes." The Chinese placed priority upon unification in Korea; the United States again called for relaxing tensions there. China expressed concern over the revival of "Japanese militarism," while the United States emphasized the value it placed upon friendly relations with Tokyo. Peking's expression of sympathy for the peoples of Indochina was countered by an American stress upon self-determination for each country and an eventual withdrawal of American forces. Having expressed itself on the issues where differences were most acute, the communiqué went on to discuss areas of agreement and proposed wider contacts in the fields of science, culture, sports, technology, journalism, and trade development. The presidential party began its homeward trip on February 28.

The spirit of the joint communiqué was soon given practical form. A delegation of Chinese doctors visited the United States in October, and arrangements were made for several American editors to visit China. The Chinese bought ten Boeing 707 transports from the United States in September and followed this with the purchase of $50 million worth of American grain. In early 1973 the two countries agreed to exchange diplomatic missions. Both Nixon and Chou, as befitted veteran negotiators, were well aware that their meeting and the events flowing from it represented a mere beginning in what would perforce be a long search for full accord and normal relations. Yet the cordiality and good will in evidence on both sides during the presidential visit were obviously genuine, and few doubted that a historic turning point had been reached and passed.

These months of dramatic improvement in Sino-American relations also witnessed a veritable spate of diplomatic action elsewhere, as other nations tacked and yawed in trying to adjust their courses to the changing direction of the wind. The Soviet readiness to negotiate treaties with the United States and West Germany in 1971-1972 was not unrelated to this change. In the United Nations, where the United States had finally made known its willingness to support China's entry after years of blocking such a move, the enthusiastic delegates went far beyond the American goal of letting Peking join while Taiwan remained. In an emotional session in October 1971 the General Assembly rejected American resolutions looking toward "two China" membership. Instead, by a vote of 76 to 35, it exuberantly admitted Peking and ousted Taiwan altogether. The Nationalist seat on the Security Council as well as its membership in the United Nations was thus taken over by the mainland regime, twenty-two years after the displacement in China itself. Great Britain established full diplomatic relations with Peking in March 1972, acknowledging that Taiwan was a part of China and withdrawing its consular offices from Taiwan. Japanese elections in 1972 ended the long premiership of Eisaku Sato, who had rigorously upheld Japan's friendship with Taiwan despite mounting criticism. His successor, Kakuei Tanaka, visited Peking in September and arranged for an important accord between the two countries: Japan officially recognized Peking (and its claims to Taiwan), while China, in return, dropped its demand for indemnities stemming from Japanese damages during the Second World War.

9. Winding Down the War

The most important single challenge confronting President Nixon was that of bringing the war in Vietnam to some sort of satisfactory conclusion. He succeeded in doing so, at least tentatively. It took him four years, and a few of the tensions and leftover cold war assumptions that lurked within his special brand of diplomatic realism were on display as the effort unfolded. Credit for the achievement must be qualified, at best; he obtained nothing after four years of additional fighting that was not obtainable when he took office.

The war during the Nixon years had three concurrent, interrelated aspects: a military front, centered in Vietnam but spilling over into Laos and Cambodia; a diplomatic front, centered at Paris but rippling into other capitals as negotiators and emissaries hastened here and there; and a political-psychological front that throbbed irregularly across the length and breadth of the United States. The military phase was simply an extended version of what had gone on during the Johnson years, with one major difference: under Nixon the level of American troop strength was on the wane rather than on the rise. The American effort had two principal components. One was the process, called Vietnamization, of assigning larger shares of the action to the South Vietnamese as their units were deemed ready and as United States ground forces were withdrawn. The other was the massive use of American air power, tactical and strategic, in direct support of ground operations and in attacks upon North Vietnamese supply routes, bases, depots, and production centers. The war continued to be characterized by American search and destroy missions, North Vietnamese raids and mortar attacks, and other limited offensive operations by both sides.

The routine nature of the struggle was broken on three occasions during the Nixon years. In April 1970, a few weeks after Prince Norodom Sihanouk of Cambodia had been overthrown in a coup led by General Lon Nol, President Nixon ordered an invasion of this hitherto neutralist country in order, as he put it, to protect the lives of American servicemen and to continue the process of Vietnamization. The joint United States–South Vietnamese offensive was designed to locate and destroy North Vietnamese headquarters, sanctuaries, and supply caches in Cambodian territory, which the enemy had been using to support offensive operations around Saigon. Some supplies were located and destroyed, but the enemy command headquarters proved elusive. The president, terming the operation a success, withdrew the American forces at the end of June as planned, but Cambodia was thereafter an active supplementary theater of the Indochinese war. South Vietnamese troops remained there in force and conducted occasional operations, backed by American bombing sorties, against Communist units.

A familiar pattern proceeded to repeat itself in Cambodia. While American aid poured in to help sustain the Lon Nol regime and bolster its army and American planes roared overhead, a small indigenous Communist movement, the Khmer Rouge, proceeded to grow larger and stronger under North Vietnamese tutelage until a genuine Cambodian civil war raged alongside the struggle between North and South Vietnamese units. Khmer Rouge strength increased from an ineffective force of 3,000 in March 1970 to over 30,000 seasoned guerrillas in late 1972—by which time they and their North Vietnamese allies (reduced from 50,000 to about 12,000 during the same period) controlled some two-thirds of the country. South Vietnamese units and American bombing raids supported the 150,000-man government army, which two years of instruction and $340 million in United States aid had failed to make into an effective fighting force. American bombers also subjected Laos to heavy and repeated attacks during these years, both to disrupt North Vietnamese supply lines and to aid the Laotian government in its chronic campaigns against the indigenous Pathet Lao Communists.

In the major theater, meanwhile, Vietnamization had proceeded far enough by early 1971 to convince Washington and Saigon that a major offensive by South Vietnamese army units was feasible. After massing troops in its northernmost provinces, South Vietnam launched a heavy attack into Laos in February in an effort to cut the jungle trails by which Hanoi supplied its forces in the south. The operation was in part a costly setback, with some South Vietnamese units breaking in panic and others suffering heavy casualties in the face of determined North Vietnamese counterattacks. It was also partly successful, in that the military situation directly below the seventeenth parallel became more secure, and the withdrawal of American forces was facilitated.

The last major military operation began in March 1972 when Hanoi launched its heaviest offensive since the Tet onslaughts of four years earlier. Striking simultaneously in several areas, the Communists inflicted and sustained serious losses, captured considerable territory, and routed several South Vietnamese units. But southern resistance later stiffened and regained some of the lost territory. The United States, whose military role by this time was confined to air and support operations, retaliated in April by stepping up the bombing raids—hitherto in process of deescalation— on North Vietnamese installations, supply centers, and rail links to China. In an even bolder move, the president ordered the mining of Haiphong and other northern harbors in May in an effort to cut off the flow of Soviet military supplies and equipment that fueled the northern war effort. By autumn the situation had reverted to its customary stalemate. On the eve of an expected cease-fire in October, the Communists launched a series of minor attacks and raids in an attempt to improve their strategic position.

None of these operations had interfered with Nixon's sustained program of reducing the scope of the American military commitment while trying to negotiate a satisfactory peace. The withdrawal of American ground forces proceeded steadily, from a peak of 541,000 in March 1969 to 430,000 a year later, and on down to 280,000 in the spring of 1971. The president continued to announce withdrawals, reducing the total to 139,000 by November 1971 and to 70,000 by May 1972. The American ground combat role terminated that summer, with a residue of fewer than 60,000 advisers, technicians, and helicopter pilots remaining. These support forces had been reduced to 27,000 by December. The last GI in Vietnam stepped smilingly abroad a homeward bound airplane in March 1973, completing the cycle that had begun nineteen years and three presidents before when an American colonel heading a team of CIA agents arrived in Saigon to engage in "paramilitary operations" and "political-psychological warfare" against North Vietnam.

Progress at the bargaining table proved as tortuous and inconclusive as it was on the battlefield. The two sides had begun formal peace talks in Paris in May 1968, but for over a year the discussions were confined to bickering over the shape of the conference table and the related question of whether two, three, or four separate delegations—American, North Vietnamese, South Vietnamese, and National Liberation Front (Vietcong)—should be present and recognized. Indeed, a principal reason for the prevailing deadlock that beset the Paris negotiations from 1968 to

1972 was the intractable antagonism between the Thieu government in Saigon and the NLF, neither of whom, for a time, could even admit the other's claims to valid existence. The Thieu regime was determined to remain the controlling element in any postwar government, while the NLF demanded, at the very least, a coalition in which they would be powerful if not dominant. The United States, although trying from time to time to persuade Saigon to soften its position, opposed any settlement that might lead to Communist takeover, and it was unwilling to sacrifice the Thieu government—which American policymakers tended to identify with the South Vietnamese right of self-determination. That right, however it might ultimately be defined, was regarded by the United States as an essential item in the peace settlement.

A second issue that contributed to the deadlock had to do with the exact timing and relationship between a cease-fire, troop withdrawals by both sides, an end to American bombing, and a complete peace agreement. The North Vietnamese tended to insist that meaningful terms could only be reached after the last American troops and planes had left, while the United States insisted upon certain conditions—including the release by Hanoi of several hundred American prisoners of war—before removing its capacity to apply military pressure. Proposals and counterproposals involving different withdrawal timetables, peace terms, and postwar coalitions bounced unsuccessfully back and forth across the peace table and between the capitals. The talks dragged on, frequently stalled and occasionally broken off as recalcitrance, propaganda, and recrimination kept clouding the agenda. Perhaps only four years of diplomatic haggling and military stalemate could have brought so bitter and tangled a set of opposing viewpoints into accord. By this time it was impossible to tell what kind of government the battered Vietnamese peasantry, brutally handled as they had been by all four parties at the Paris peace table, would select if a true chance were ever given them.

In any case, the logjam finally broke. Washington and Hanoi had supplemented and at times replaced the formal Paris negotiations with secret talks between Kissinger and the principal North Vietnamese diplomats, Xuan Thuy and Le Duc Tho. These secret meetings became more frequent during 1972, and from them the basis for an acceptable agreement slowly emerged. Rumors of an impending settlement flew faster during early autumn, heightened by a Hanoi radio announcement in October claiming that the United States had agreed to sign a nine-point settlement by the end of the month. Kissinger, at a press conference, denied the deadline but told reporters that an agreement was indeed imminent. It could be reached, he thought, after one more round of private talks lasting three or four days. "Peace," the presidential adviser solemnly concluded, "is at hand."

The interminable struggle to bring the war to a close had been, for most Americans, a nightmare maze of anguished discoveries, thwarted hopes, and disillusionment. By the time Richard Nixon took the oath of office in January 1969, an overwhelming majority of his countrymen wanted out of Vietnam. For some, this meant unconditionally and immediately; for a greater number, it meant as soon as this could be done without sacrificing the South Vietnamese, or American interests, or whatever was rather vaguely felt to be still at issue. Antiwar sentiment found a few things to approve during the next four years: the Nixon doctrine disavowing further commitment of American troops in foreign countries, the earnest efforts to persuade Hanoi and Saigon to find a basis for agreement, and above all the steady, gratifying reduction of United States ground forces in Southeast Asia. But on the whole, the war did not get wound down as fast as American war weariness grew.

There was a disposition to be patient during the president's first year in office; he had claimed to have, without ever defining it, a plan to end the war, and most people agreed that he deserved a little time to put it into effect. Nevertheless, expressions of antiwar sentiment in Congress cropped up with growing frequency. The Senate came within a single vote of defeating the ABM project, as we have seen. It also passed a resolution setting forth the principle that overseas commitments required affirmative action by the legislative as well as the executive branch. A nationwide moratorium on behalf of peace received mass observances in hundreds of cities and campuses during the autumn of 1969 and drew over 250,000 quiet antiwar demonstrators to Washington in mid-November.

Then the shocks and revelations began, and the antiwar mood grew louder and uglier. News of the invasion of Cambodia in the spring of 1970 touched off a wave of protest in many quarters and a virtual scream of anguish from the nation's colleges and universities (see p. 640). This was the springtime of strikes, arson, disruption, shutdown, and violence on American campuses. A few scattered instances of bombing and arson—a bank here, a business office there—took place off-campus as well. (These student outbreaks and destructive incidents would seem to have been largely responsible, along with concurrent activities of the Black Panthers, for igniting some sort of mental process in Washington that the country would not really begin to learn about for another three years.)

Antiwar sentiment flared more strongly on Capitol Hill. The Senate, having gone on record in December 1969 against military involvement in Laos or Cambodia, responded sharply to the invasion of the latter country. It repealed the Gulf of Tonkin resolution of 1964, which had given President Johnson blank-check support for any action he might take to counter aggression in Southeast Asia. It passed an amendment to a military sales bill, sponsored by Democrat Frank Church of Idaho and Republican John Sherman Cooper of Kentucky, that sought to deny funds for American military action in Cambodia; the House later defeated this measure. Senators Mark Hatfield of Oregon and George McGovern of South Dakota put forth an amendment, which their colleagues finally rejected in September by a vote of 55 to 39, requiring withdrawal of all American troops from Vietnam by December 1971. The Senate again discussed and rejected this amendment in June 1971 by a vote of 55 to 42, but bipartisan opposition to administration policy was spreading.

The invasion of Cambodia was only one of the shocks that convulsed American public opinion during this period. In late 1969 the nation had begun to hear vague but shocking rumors about alleged massacres of Vietnamese civilians, including women and children, by American servicemen. And in the military trial of Lt. William L. Calley, Jr., that began in November 1970 at Fort Benning, Georgia, people learned that some of these appalling stories were true. Investigation confirmed that Calley and his platoon had been responsible for the killing of over one hundred men, women, and children in the hamlet of My Lai in 1968. On March 29, 1971, having examined all the evidence, a court composed of six army officers, all combat veterans, found Lieutenant Calley guilty, personally, of the premeditated murder of at least twenty-two unarmed civilians, and sentenced him to life imprisonment.

Public reaction verged on hysteria. Shocked and horrified by the atrocities, Americans disagreed sharply over the results of the trial and the extent of Calley's guilt. The verdict and sentence were criticized both by unreconstructed hawks who felt that no American soldier should be punished for work done in the line of duty, and by liberals and doves who felt that Calley had been made a scapegoat and that his superiors—all the way up through the Pentagon to the commander-in-chief—were the truly guilty ones. It was pointed out that the United States had insisted at the Nuremberg trials after the Second World War (see pp. 678-679) that guilt for war crimes extended to the highest levels of a command system. There was a distinct feeling in many quarters that the entire nation somehow stood convicted with Lieutenant Calley.

While this outcry raged, President Nixon intervened in an extraordinary and controversial move. Ordering Calley returned from the stockade and confined to his quarters until his legal appeals were exhausted, the president announced that he would review the case personally.[30] Some hailed and others denounced this action. Capt. Aubrey M. Daniel III, the prosecutor at the Calley court-martial, frankly accused the president of undermining public confidence in the military courts and the legal system generally. For a few agonized days in the spring of 1971 Americans of every political persuasion engaged in an orgy of lamentation and condemnation, bitterly attacking or defending Calley, the army, the president, the war, America, war protesters, and one another.

The furor passed, but the memory lingered. There was cold comfort in

[30]Calley's sentence was later reduced to twenty years, with further appeals pending. A later court-martial acquitted Calley's company commander, Captain Ernest Medina, of complicity in the tragic incident. But several Vietnam veterans admitted that they had seen, heard of, or even participated in similar actions; it appeared that My Lai was by no means an isolated occurrence.

the knowledge that both the Vietcong and the Saigon government had massacred tens of thousands of helpless civilians. Seared into the national conscience was the discovery, at My Lai, that what Kurt Schumacher, writing of the Nazi era, had called a hidden beast in every man—*der innere Schweinehund*—crouched balefully within Americans as well.

The next disturbing revelation came in June 1971 as the newspapers published excerpts from the Pentagon Papers that Daniel Ellsberg had purloined and photocopied for release to the press. Although a few were highly critical of Ellsberg and agreed with the government's claim that such actions threatened the national security, a greater number were depressed and angered by the purport and import of the documents. The Pentagon Papers suggested, at the very least, that the Kennedy and Johnson administrations had done far more than simply respond to Communist aggression in Indochina, that a fairly steady effort to widen America's role in the war had been made by various American civilian and military officials, and that the government's lack of candor in explaining certain details of this policy to the public included misleading statements amounting at times to outright deception. Faith in the credibility of government, visibly declining for some time, had been further undermined.

Peace advocates, their ranks swelled and their convictions strengthened by My Lai and the Pentagon Papers, were also profoundly disturbed by certain aspects of the president's policy and posture concerning Vietnam. They could not accept his assurances that he was bringing peace closer by periodic enlargements of the war—the Cambodian invasion, stepped-up bombing of North Vietnam and Laos, the mining of Haiphong harbor. Instead, they saw such actions as calculated to prolong and widen the conflict and imperil peace negotiations and other pending accords.[31] Moreover, they saw a dangerously trigger-happy aggressiveness in these actions, an urge to retaliate with violence when challenged or thwarted. And they were equally appalled, in view of all that was now known about the conflict, by the president's rhetoric—by his repeated insistence upon fighting until he obtained "peace with honor" and upon the need to maintain America's credibility "as a peacekeeper." They could only shudder at his occasional assertion that he did "not want to be the first American president who ever lost a war." They found this combination of words and deeds downright frightening, and they frequently despaired of ending the war behind such a leader.

There were, to be sure, many who retained their confidence in Nixon's Vietnam policy and tended to place the blame for delays and setbacks in peace negotiations upon enemy intransigence and bad faith. But war

[31] In a diplomatic sense, at least, the president was proved correct in his belief that the mining of Haiphong harbor in 1972 would not jeopardize America's pending détente with the Soviet Union or the improved relations with Peking. Both Communist powers protested the American action, but their objections were almost perfunctory. The president's visit to Moscow went smoothly and cordially, as though the mining had not taken place.

weariness had become truly nationwide months and even years before the end. In view of all that Americans had learned about their government, their war effort, and themselves, there could be little rejoicing at Kissinger's dramatic announcement in October 1972 that peace was at hand. At most they could feel a dull sense of relief.

Lacerated emotions were due for one final torment. It was altogether typical of this incorrigibly perverse war that an eleventh-hour impasse should suddenly arise to summon forth yet another round of violence before agreement was actually reached. Kissinger returned to Paris in November for that last brief round of talks with Le Duc Tho. Resolution of certain details stayed out of reach, and Saigon's chronic intransigence flared anew. Kissinger accused North Vietnam of procrastination and said that the talks were failing to produce a "just and fair" agreement; military buildups on both sides were reported in Vietnam. President Nixon announced that the United States would sign no agreement until these unresolved details were settled. Deep-seated differences between Saigon, Hanoi, and Washington over the number of supervisors, the control of territory, and the disposition of North Vietnamese troops below the seventeenth parallel threatened to disrupt the whole settlement.

Then the president, either convinced of Hanoi's bad faith or determined to display American resolve, ordered a renewal of massive B-52 bombing and mining attacks on North Vietnam in mid-December. Washington announced that these round-the-clock raids "will continue until such time as a settlement is arrived at." At the end of the month, after admitting losses of fifteen B-52s and ninety-three airmen killed or captured, the administration halted the bombing above the twentieth parallel. Kissinger and Tho went back to work in January, conferring in Paris for thirty-five hours over a six-day period. Reports of progress led the president to order an end to all bombing and mining of North Vietnam. Agreement was announced on January 23, 1973, and the accord was formally signed in Paris on January 27. A cease-fire went into effect in Vietnam on the same day.

In brief, the Paris accord called for the removal and deactivation by the United States of the mines it had sown along the Vietnamese coast, a withdrawal of all remaining American troops within sixty days, and the dismantling of its military bases in Indochina. All foreign troops, including Vietnamese Communist forces, were to be withdrawn from Laos and Cambodia. American prisoners of war, together with other military and civilian prisoners on both sides, were to be released at phased intervals over the next sixty days, with the Vietcong and Saigon to negotiate the status of various Vietnamese "political prisoners." Two truce teams—an international group composed of Canadian, Hungarian, Polish, and Indonesian observers and another representing each of the four participant factions (United States, North Vietnam, South Vietnam, NLF)—would supervise the cease-fire. An international conference that included Russia and China was to be convened to "guarantee peace in Indochina." And finally, a council composed of representatives of the Saigon government, the NLF, and South Vietnamese neutralist factions was to organize and conduct a national election for a new South Vietnamese government, with the present Saigon regime remaining in power until this was done.

And so the longest and by all odds the most unpopular war in United States history came to an official conclusion—eight years after American ground forces became actively engaged on a large scale, nearly fourteen years after the first Americans were killed by military action in Vietnam. All in all, the struggle had taken the lives of over 56,000 Americans. Other losses included some 300,000 wounded, nearly $100 billion in expenditures since 1965, and a psychic scar of undetermined proportions that touched nearly every citizen in one way or another. Hundreds of thousands of American servicemen, whose courage and fortitude under singularly bad conditions invited comparison with the best in a two-century-old tradition, came home to no hero's welcome, but only to a society that could not help but be embarrassed by their presence, half ashamed of what it had sent them to do, half fearful of what their future attitudes might be. Dry statistics that people might not otherwise have grasped— perhaps 650,000 South Vietnamese deaths, nearly 1 million North Vietnamese and Vietcong deaths, some 10 million refugees for Indochina as a whole, an American bomb tonnage many times greater than that of all the explosives dropped in all theaters during the Second World War—had come unforgettably alive day after day in photographs and on television: live action shots of napalmed children, grieving mothers, wounded soldiers, piled corpses, smoking rubble, wrinkled old refugees straggling down shell-pocked roads; these, too, were part of the price people paid.

10. The Election of 1972

The awareness, as 1972 began, that President Nixon would be difficult to beat in his bid for reelection that fall did not deter Democrats from engaging in one of their customary mad scrambles for the right to run against him. The party was in turmoil and disarray, ridden with factional quarrels, still scarred by the experiences of 1968, its various blocs and interests deeply divided over issues like busing, law and order, welfare, and related items. Reflecting these conditions, a veritable gaggle of candidates contended for the presidential nomination. The odds-on favorite at the start was Senator Edmund Muskie of Maine, a soft-spoken progressive who had made a favorable impression upon voters in 1968 and 1970. Muskie had put together an impressive-looking organization based upon the support of many party leaders at the state level. The other leading contender in early 1972 was Hubert Humphrey, the 1968 standard-bearer, who still commanded wide support among party regulars, organized labor, and blacks. In active pursuit of these front runners were Senator Henry F. Jackson of Washington, a firm advocate of a stronger defense program, and Senator George McGovern of South Dakota, chiefly known for his long record of outspoken opposition to the war. Two candidates from New York City also entered the campaign: Mayor John Lindsay, who had switched parties the year before because neither his urban progressivism nor his presidential ambitions had much future in the GOP, and black Congresswoman Shirley Chisholm.

Standing rather darkly in the wings on either side of these avowed contenders were two figures whose future decisions promised to have a bearing on the race: Eugene McCarthy of Minnesota and George Wallace of Alabama. At the beginning of the year McCarthy was still undecided whether to run at all, and if so whether to run inside or outside the party. Wallace, still nominally a Democrat, was bent on running again but had not yet decided whether he could exert more influence this time as a third-party candidate or within the Democratic ranks.

Looming even more hazily over the party scene was the figure of Senator Edward Kennedy of Massachusetts, last and youngest brother in the famous political family. Kennedy's stature had been reduced for a time by his questionable conduct following a tragic auto accident on Martha's Vineyard in 1969. But these memories had dimmed. Kennedy was able and attractive, and the magic of the Kennedy name was still potent among millions of voters, including many who agreed on nothing else. Although the young senator repeatedly insisted that he would not be a candidate, hopes persisted that the party situation would later pressure him into accepting a draft.

Recent organizational and procedural reforms affected the Democratic campaign in several ways. Party and convention machinery had been taken from the exclusive grasp of veteran professionals who represented the Democrats' overlapping power blocs—union leaders, southern senators, key governors and big-city mayors, black and ethnic-group spokesmen—and thrown open to grass-roots participation. The methods for selecting convention delegates had been democratized. Delegates had to be chosen during the election year rather than months or years earlier. Open voting, open competition for seats, and open procedures were to remove the control or undue influence that insiders, party bosses, and entrenched local organizations had long exercised in filling a slate. The party had also ruled that the composition of each delegation must "reasonably" reflect that state's relative proportion of minorities, women, and young people. There were contradictions, pitfalls, and unresolved problems in these new regulations, but the party's attempts to abide by them resulted in one of the liveliest preconvention campaigns in modern times.

It was a campaign full of surprises. Muskie, the favorite, faltered early and lost momentum badly. He made a poor impression with an emotional display during the New Hampshire primary in March,[32] and his vote total of 46 percent in a state deemed overwhelmingly in favor of him constituted a serious setback. After other unimpressive showings, Muskie announced in April that he would remain a candidate but would not continue in the primaries; his only hope now, it was felt, lay in a deadlocked national convention. But prospects of a deadlock began to fade as George McGovern, who had ranked well down the list of aspirants, steadily accumulated delegates from both state conventions and primary victories until he surged unexpectedly into the lead.

The other chief contenders, as Muskie faded from view and McGovern advanced, were Humphrey and Wallace, the Alabamian having decided to run as a Democrat. Wallace, campaigning as a conservative with emphasis upon opposition to busing and welfare spending, spoke with more restraint and less demagoguery than in his previous efforts. He showed considerable strength, beating Humphrey decisively in the Florida primary in March and winning handily in Tennessee and North Carolina in May, although Humphrey defeated him in West Virginia. The whole shape of the campaign altered on May 15 when Wallace was shot and critically injured while addressing a political rally in Laurel, Maryland.[33] Paralyzed from the waist down, Wallace was forced to withdraw as an active candidate; though he would attend and speak at the convention, the influence he had hoped to exercise upon the Democratic convention was much reduced by the tragedy. On the day after the shooting, Wallace defeated McGovern, Humphrey, and Muskie by a majority in Michigan and by a plurality in Maryland.

From that point on, McGovern advanced rapidly toward dominance in the Democratic race. He capped impressive primary victories in Oregon, Rhode Island, New Mexico, and New York with an important triumph in California in early June. His 44 percent plurality (Humphrey trailed close behind with 39 percent) enabled him to pick up all of the state's 271 delegates under California's unit rule. The senator from South Dakota came to the convention, which opened in Miami Beach on July 10, with enough delegates to win on the first ballot unless some of his strength could be pried loose. But it was basically a McGovern convention; chosen under new party rules, it contained unprecedently high ratios of women (40 percent), blacks (25 percent), people under thirty (21 percent), and relatively inexperienced grass-roots enthusiasts. While baffled Old Guard

[32]The nation learned a year later, in connection with the endless series of sordid disclosures coming out of the Watergate affair, that the Committee for the Re-election of the President, as part of their "dirty tricks" operation, had been responsible for the incident that triggered Muskie's emotional outburst.

[33]The would-be assassin was twenty-one-year-old Arthur Bremer, an emotionally unbalanced drifter with obsessions about his own importance and no consistent political orientation. His diary revealed that he had previously thought of assassinating Nixon. He wounded three other persons in the fusillade that felled Wallace, and was tried, convicted, and sentenced to a combined term of sixty-three years.

Democrats, feeling out of place and alienated in this energetic new breed of a gathering, sought vainly for ways to regain their ascendancy, McGovern's forces beat off an attempt to rule that 151 of California's delegates should be distributed among the other contenders. Then they held their ranks intact and nominated their man on the first ballot with 1,715 votes, comfortably more than the minimum required total of 1,509.

McGovern's triumph represented a stunning political upset that had analysts and professionals blinking in amazement. His earnest sincerity had made a favorable impression in the primaries. But he was neither charismatic nor a spellbinder, and experts had to look elsewhere for an explanation. It did not lie in his political philosophy, which made enemies as well as friends among Democrats. As Wallace had frankly aimed his appeal at the Democratic right and Humphrey at its moderately progressive center, so McGovern had stood on the party's left: he had called for advancing the rights of minorities, expanded social welfare legislation, tax reform aimed at high-income loopholes, and, of course, immediate withdrawal from Vietnam.

McGovern's success was chiefly a matter of technique. A long-time friend and associate of the Kennedys, he had some seasoned professionals working in his behalf along with legions of dedicated young people. He combined these elements into a superb organization that proved more adept than any rival group at turning the new party rules to its advantage and capturing delegates at the local and state level. Muskie and Humphrey had been well organized at the top, with Old Guard party leaders— but this was not the year of the Old Guard. Energy, dedication, teamwork, and shrewdness enabled the McGovern forces to find grass-roots support, organize it, get out the vote, and capture delegates right from under the noses of startled veterans.

For his running mate, after being politely refused in turn by Kennedy, Senator Abraham Ribicoff of Connecticut, and Governor Reubin Askew of Florida, McGovern chose Senator Thomas Eagleton of Missouri, a dynamic young liberal. The Democratic platform was a progressive document, reflecting the prevailing outlook among the delegates. It pledged a reduction in military spending, a restoration of "a meaningful role in decision on peace and war" to Congress and the people, and "immediate total withdrawal of all Americans from Southeast Asia." Full employment, tax reform, firm law enforcement, and social reform were among the domestic planks. The platform took a forthright stand on the controversial school issue, saying that quality education required both desegregation and "equalization in spending among school districts" and supporting busing as "another tool to accomplish desegregation." During the platform debate Wallace made a dramatic appearance in his wheel chair to plead for the inclusion of some of his views, but the convention firmly repudiated planks against busing and others advocating voluntary school prayers, a stronger defense structure, and continued American presence in Vietnam until all prisoners of war were returned.

In his acceptance speech McGovern made an eloquent appeal for America to "come home"—to heal its wounds, subordinate its differences, restore its confidence and its faith, and advance further toward the fulfillment of its democratic promise. It was a moving effort, well done enough to instill a momentary sense of unity and enthusiasm among the tired delegates. For the South Dakotan and his dedicated followers this was to be the high spot of the entire campaign.

No such struggles and expenditures of energy marked the selection of a GOP candidate. Richard Nixon had achieved an impregnable political position by the spring of 1972, and his renomination was a foregone conclusion. Meeting in Miami Beach on August 21, the GOP delegates enthusiastically chose Nixon and Agnew on the first ballot. The party also had no trouble in staking out its position for the coming campaign. This convention displayed a more traditional appearance and tone; it was far less "young, beautiful, and black" than its Democratic counterpart. Although the percentage of GOP women delegates had risen to 30 percent (from 17 percent in 1968), only 8 percent of the delegates were under thirty and only 4 percent were black. The GOP was looking elsewhere for its majority, as both the acceptance speech and the party platform made abundantly clear. On opening day Governor Reagan of California had declared that McGovern's nomination "disenfranchised millions of Democrats." Pursuing the same theme, Nixon called for "a new American majority bound together by our common ideals" and claimed that the differing philosophies of the opposing candidates constituted "one of the clearest choices of the campaign." The platform spelled it out: the choice, it said, was "between moderate goals . . . and far-out goals of the far left." The Democratic party, it added, "has been seized by a radical clique which scorns our nation's past and would blight our future." This "New Democratic Left" would weaken America's defenses and "retreat into virtual isolation."

The platform supported arms limitation, a volunteer army, full employment, and equitable tax reform. It favored a medical insurance program jointly financed by employers, employees, and government, but opposed a "nationalized compulsory" program. On the school issue, the GOP document supported equitable financing and an end to de jure segregation but opposed busing. Other planks touched all the bases: law enforcement with equal justice, fair prices for farmers, drug controls, urban development, low-income housing, preservation of natural resources, equal rights for women, and better opportunities for children, senior citizens, minorities, and veterans. In foreign policy the platform spoke of "a full generation of peace" based upon "a strategy of national strength" combined with "a new sense of international partnership." It called for a Vietnamese settlement that would guarantee self-determination for the peoples of Southeast

Asia and insisted that United States forces would not be completely with-drawn until all American prisoners were returned.

This campaign was subject to the shaping influence of two recent enact-ments. One, the Federal Election Campaign Act of 1972, was a long over-due attempt to tighten the rules governing political fund raising and spending. It replaced an ineffectual and widely evaded corrupt practices statute dating back to 1927, which one observer had called "more loop-hole than law." The new measure required detailed disclosure of cam-paign contributions and expenditures made after April 7, the date it went into effect. In an earlier move that gave every politician in the country something new to think about, Congress had passed the Twenty-sixth Amendment in March 1971 lowering the voting age in all federal, state, and local elections to eighteen.[34] State legislators bowed promptly to the inevitable: within ten weeks, an all-time speed record for constitutional change, the required number of states had ratified the new amendment. It thereby created some 14 million potential new voters, about half of whom were attending college. None of the predictions as to how this youthful infusion might affect the election sounded overly confident.[35]

The campaign was a one-sided affair that offered little excitement, less suspense, and no inspiration whatever. Nixon's reelection appeared to be a certainty, and public interest flagged. The Democrats labored under insu-perable disadvantages. The gulf between the Wallace and McGovern wings was absolutely impassable. Internal discords abounded. Veteran party leaders, including Chicago's Mayor Daley, were still smarting from treatment they had received at the hands of the McGovern organization before and during the convention; they had been outmaneuvered, dis-placed, rebuffed, and pushed around, and they were resentful. Organized labor was dissatisfied with McGovern at two levels: members of the high command were upset by his indifferent labor record and certain aspects of his program, and many among the rank and file regarded him as too radical.

Indeed, the taint of radicalism was McGovern's greatest liability. That George McGovern should acquire the image of a wild-eyed radical told more about his times than about him. He made a most improbable radi-cal—a minister's son and erstwhile history teacher with a distinguished combat record in the Second World War and signs of his middle-class South Dakota upbringing written all over him; a mild mannered, orthodox

[34] The Supreme Court, in December 1970, had ruled that eighteen-year-olds had to be given the vote in federal elections, though not necessarily in state and local elections. To avoid the admin-istrative problems that this ruling posed for the forty-seven states where twenty-one years was still the legal voting limit, Congress rushed the Twenty-sixth Amendment through in record time, with no committee hearings and only an hour of debate.

[35] The historian cannot resist an idle backward glance at the other two occasions when large new groups had been enfranchised by constitutional amendment. In 1868 and 1872, with blacks voting in large numbers for the first time, the nation elected Ulysses S. Grant. In 1920, just after passage of the woman suffrage amendment, the nation elected Warren G. Harding.

progressive straight out of the New Deal-Fair Deal tradition. The prevailing national mood had become so conservative on questions of busing, low-income housing, and public welfare that McGovern's mere advocacy of such measures made him seem radical. His early proposals for a guaranteed income, some of which were admittedly hasty, stamped him as an irresponsible spender; his later attempts to clarify and modify his stand did not undo this damage, but merely convinced opponents that he was confused or hedging.

What hurt him most was his alleged position on three emotion-packed issues. His desire to grant amnesty to those youths whose dislike of the war had led them to desert, flee the country, or go to jail was too advanced a view for many traditionalists. These folk were even more outraged because he had occasionally suggested that a liberalization of existing laws on abortion and marijuana might be in order. This was exaggerated into the charge that he stood for legalizing both. Such a position on abortion and marijuana, together with his willingness to forgive draft evaders ("ass, grass, and amnesty," as one cynical GOP opponent put it) marked him, in the eyes of many voters, as an ally and defender of hippies, traitors, promiscuity, and related evils, and the damage was irreparable. The Republicans made his ostensible radicalism an issue from the very start, and they used it effectively; it clung to him at every step.

To make matters worse for the Democratic candidate, ill fortune struck him a blow, early on, from which his campaign never recovered. His best hope, as he left Miami Beach in July to prepare for the race against Nixon, lay in extending the political momentum that had carried him so triumphantly up to and through the convention. He had shown signs of catching fire and capturing the public imagination, with his low-key prairie eloquence and his earnest, evangelical invocation of the best in the American dream. But this momentum collapsed with startling suddenness and was never to be regained. Shortly after the convention it was learned that his running mate, Senator Eagleton, had been hospitalized on three occasions during the sixties for "nervous exhaustion and fatigue" and had undergone brief psychiatric treatment for "depression." The McGovern staff had not discovered these facts when inquiring about Eagleton before the nomination, and he had neglected to tell them. Thrown off balance by the discovery, McGovern wavered—first declaring that he was "one thousand percent" behind his running mate and then abruptly deciding to drop him. He replaced the unfortunate Missourian with R. Sargent Shriver, former director of the Peace Corps and the OEO, who proved a good campaigner and an asset to the ticket.

But the damage had been done. McGovern was caught in a crossfire of criticism: for carelessness and poor staff work, in not having learned of Eagleton's background before selecting him; for indecisiveness, in having first backed and then dropped his running mate; for unfairness and disloyalty, in having abandoned Eagleton summarily rather than sticking by him. Eagleton had many sympathizers who felt that his background was neither unusual nor a discredit and that he should have been retained. Such a decision, however, would obviously have drawn heavy fire from other quarters. It was, in short, one of those dilemmas for which no right solution existed. The affair cost the McGovern headquarters a month, which they had planned to spend getting their campaign organized, and his hard-working forces never recaptured the drive or confidence that had swept them to victory in Miami Beach.

It probably would not have mattered. Nixon had, as they say, too much going for him. He had all the prestige and powers of his office, embellished by a range of achievements in foreign affairs and general approval of his vigorous policy to curb inflation and protect the dollar. The war appeared to be ending, and nearly all of the troops were back home. The economy was booming again. He was helped, too, by a general public disposition to worry far less about the hints of corruption and influence that clustered around his administration than about certain emotional issues upon which, everyone knew, the president stood four-square. Millions of voters were going to vote against radicalism, by which they did not mean a program or an ideology so much as an attitude. Radicalism had come to stand for permissive policies toward long-haired youth, nonconformity, drugs, sexual license, crime, draft resisters, welfare chiselers, busing—in a word, Sin. The Democratic candidate was somehow identified with these things, and the president was known to oppose them.[36]

McGovern was swimming against a powerful tide, and he made almost no headway. Among the minority who agreed with him he did well, speaking with earnest conviction and raising ample funds in hundreds of thousands of small contributions. He had found one potentially vulnerable spot in his opponent's formidable armor, and he pressed it hard. Charging the Nixon administration with being the "most corrupt in history," he cited several examples. There were indications that a $400,000 offer by the International Telephone & Telegraph Company to defray GOP convention costs in San Diego was connected with a favorable antitrust decision by the Justice Department in 1971 approving ITT's acquisition of the Hartford Fire Insurance Company. (The government denied any connec-

---

[36]Rough but interesting parallels with the election of 1896 come to mind. A prairie state agrarian indelibly stamped as a radical was matched against an able political veteran who stood for progress and profits and the American Way. Not least among William McKinley's assets in 1896 had been his shrewd millionaire campaign manager, Mark Hanna, who mustered voting support and campaign funds from workers and businessmen fearful of Bryan—Mark Hanna busily, in Vachel Lindsay's words, "rallying the bucket shops, rallying the roller tops." Three-quarters of a century later Richard Nixon had, as a kind of hydra-headed Mark Hanna to raise money and devise campaign strategy, something called the Committee for the Re-election of the President. It was raising millions of dollars for him, and it was engaged in carving itself a unique and enduring niche in the history of American politics.

tion but decided to move the convention site from San Diego to Miami Beach.) The Consumers Union charged in August 1972 that two officials in the Department of Agriculture had helped negotiate the recent grain purchases by the Soviet Union and then left the government to work for grain exporting firms involved in the shipments; huge illegal excess profits at the expense of grain farmers were alleged to have been made. There was also the matter of a sudden administration decision in 1971 to approve higher milk price supports and a $417,000 contribution by the dairy interests to the Republican party.

McGovern's most telling example, because there was no way on earth of denying that it had happened, concerned the break-in at the headquarters of the Democratic National Committee in Washington on June 17, 1972, in the huge hotel-office complex known as the Watergate. Seven men, including two former White House aides and a member of the Committee for the Re-election of the President, were apprehended and indicted—and later tried, convicted, and sentenced—on charges of conspiring to obtain information illegally, breaking and entering, planting wiretaps and electronic bugging devices, and stealing and photographing documents. It appeared that individuals connected with the Republican campaign and perhaps with the White House had been engaged in acts of espionage and sabotage against the Democratic party.

Administration officials tended to slough off the Watergate affair, dismissing it as a "caper" and a "third-rate burglary attempt" of no significance. This was the attitude of the president's campaign manager, former Attorney General John Mitchell. Continued expressions of concern and curiosity finally elicited a statement from the president himself. "I can say categorically," he announced on August 29, "that . . . investigations indicate that no one in the White House staff, no one in this Administration, presently employed, was involved in this very bizarre incident." There, for the time being, the matter rested. Try as he might, McGovern could not generate a groundswell of concern over corruption in Washington. The majority of voters, more impressed by returning prosperity, imminent peace, and other issues, were content to dismiss Watergate as a species of typical political infighting.

The president himself campaigned very little, content with a few personal and television appearances and the strength of his record. All indications pointed to a Nixon landslide, and the electorate responded according to prediction. On November 7, 1972, Nixon and Agnew received over 47 million votes (61 percent of the total) and carried forty-nine states with an electoral total of 520. McGovern and Shriver polled about 29.2 million popular votes and won only the 17 electoral votes of Massachusetts and the District of Columbia. Nixon's margin ranked with the victories of Johnson in 1964, Roosevelt in 1936, and Harding in 1920 as the greatest on record.

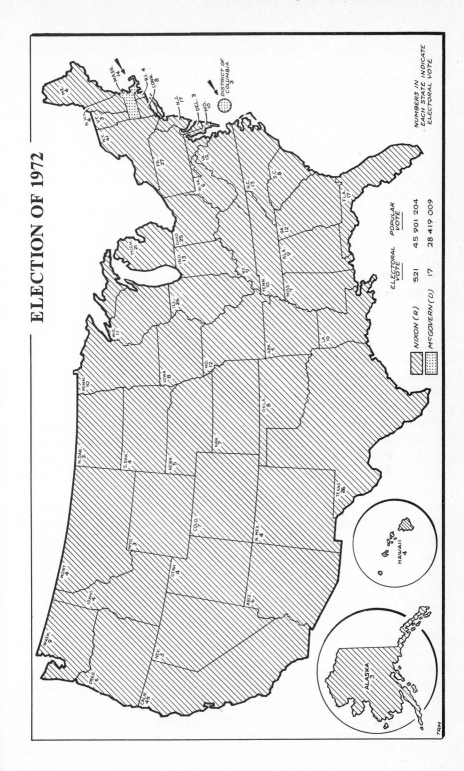

ELECTION OF 1972

NUMBERS IN EACH STATE INDICATE ELECTORAL VOTE

	ELECTORAL VOTE	POPULAR VOTE
NIXON (R)	521	45 901 204
McGOVERN (D)	17	28 419 009

TRM

As proof of the oft-repeated assertion that the voters had been choosing between the men rather than the parties, the Nixon landslide did not alter the situation in Congress. The Democrats easily retained control of both houses, picking up 2 seats in the Senate to make their new margin 57–43, and losing 12 in the House to reduce their majority to 242–192. Republicans gained 8 new southern congressmen, including 4 from the Deep South—and yet the South also sent 2 black members to Congress (both Democrats, from Texas and Georgia) for the first time in the twentieth century. The new House of Representatives would include record totals of 16 blacks and 14 women. The Democrats also won 11 of 18 gubernatorial races, increasing their total number of governorships from 30 to 31.

The presidential vote offered few surprises. It was obvious that nearly all of the Wallace supporters had cast their ballots for Nixon. Among minorities, only blacks, citizens of Latin American descent, and, by much reduced margins, Jewish voters appeared to have supported the Democratic ticket. The youth vote had had no impact; a majority of college students had voted for McGovern, but equal numbers of young voters did not attend college and tended to be more conservative. Something very like the silent majority that everyone had been talking about, and whom the president had cultivated for four years—middle- and lower-middle-class white voters, blue-collar workers, ethnic minorities, southerners, midwesterners—apparently existed, and it had voted for Nixon by the millions.

Thus bolstered, the confident president made no secret of the conservative tack on which he proposed to steer the nation in domestic matters. In October, as we have seen, he pocket vetoed several public works and welfare bills that contained larger appropriations than he had requested, saying that he would not go back on a promise to avoid raising taxes. His budget message in early 1973 announced the reduction or complete elimination of over one hundred federal programs, largely in the fields of public welfare, antipoverty, and education. Among the programs to be phased out were the Economic Development Act, a Great Society measure designed to stimulate growth in depressed rural and urban areas; and the Office of Economic Opportunity, coordinating agency in the network of antipoverty programs. A recent moratorium on new public housing and housing subsidy programs was extended. Manpower training, school and public library construction, regional medical programs, aid to state education departments, and a planned extension of the Head Start program were a few of the other items marked for cutbacks or elimination.

Although fiscal responsibility and the danger of higher taxes and more inflation were among the guiding factors in this new retrenchment policy, Nixon made it clear that the reasoning was, at bottom, ideological. His budget proposals, he said, would create "a leaner federal bureaucracy, increased reliance on state and local governments to carry on what are primarily state and local responsibilities, and greater freedom for the American people to make for themselves fundamental choices about what is best for them." Not since the early thirties had the nation's basic political orientation altered course more sharply. Was a great era of American progressivism drawing to a close? As though to symbolize its passing, the two living Americans who had contributed most substantially to the modern progressive tradition died less than four weeks apart as Nixon's second term began: Harry S Truman, on December 26, 1972, and Lyndon Johnson, on January 22, 1973.

33

▚▚▚▚▞▙▌▌▌▟▟▟

The Nixon Years, II:

Watergate

I f the 1960s, as a decade of violence, tragedy, and national anguish, really "began" with the assassination of John F. Kennedy in 1963, then the 1970s began with the Watergate disclosures that culminated in Richard M. Nixon's resignation as president of the United States in August 1974. Americans watched in growing dismay as the sordid affair unfolded. Nixon's resignation had been preceded a few months earlier by that of Vice-President Agnew, who also left office in disgrace. Never before had the American constitutional system been so abused and threatened. And not in many decades had the American people rallied so forcefully in its defense.

1. The Second Term Begins

Exhilarated by his sweeping victory at the polls in 1972, President Nixon entered upon his second term with confidence, displaying enough signs of pride and a haughty spirit to remind unsympathetic observers of the familiar injunction in the Book of Proverbs. He proclaimed Phase Three of the wage-price policy in January 1973 by announcing that the economy was behaving well enough to allow for voluntary compliance. He ignored the outcry against his welfare cutbacks and brusquely dismissed the claim that he lacked the power to eliminate such programs unilaterally or to impound funds specifically authorized by Congress. He reaffirmed his unshakable opposition to the granting of amnesty to draft evaders. In response to reports of violations of the cease-fire in Vietnam, he warned Hanoi not to expect that the United States would refrain from retaliation. He ordered a continuation of American bombing raids on Cambodia after the cease-fire (which did not cover the civil wars in that state or in Laos), partly as a means of pressuring North Vietnam and partly in support of the Phnom Penh regime. He began to implement a grandiose plan to reorganize and streamline the federal government and make the bureaucracy more responsive, efficient, and subject to presidential control.[1] His utterances in these and other matters were marked by a lofty self-assurance; he had received a gigantic vote of confidence from the people, and all seemed to be going well.

Then everything began to come apart. The peace settlement in Vietnam was not working; both Hanoi and Saigon were maneuvering troops and engaging in hostilities in repeated contravention of the accord. The bombing of Cambodia went on and on. It produced no discernible change in the conflict there, but it upset the American public and touched off a near-revolt in Congress. Each house moved more determinedly than ever before to curtail the president's unilateral freedom to engage in acts of war. In May 1973 the House voted, 219–188, to deny the administration permission to transfer defense funds to pay for the Cambodian bombing. When the secretary of defense claimed that the money could be found elsewhere in the budget, the Senate responded with an amendment banning the use of *any* funds for bombing or any other military action in either Cambodia or Laos.[2] Elsewhere, several federal courts ruled that

[1] Implementation had not extended beyond the stage of scrutinizing, reshuffling, and occasionally dismissing upper-level appointees when the administration became embroiled in Watergate and had to abandon its larger objectives. But the master blueprint—with its six-person executive council or "super cabinet" and its direct White House pipeline to key appointees in each department and bureau—affords some interesting insights. As Theodore White has observed, there was real need for a rationalized and more responsive bureaucracy, and some of Nixon's proposed restructuring made sense. But as White also observed, the plan bore no small resemblance to the system by which the Soviet government is controlled and directed by the Politburo. And far too many of the top positions in the proposed new structure would have been staffed by the men who were responsible for Watergate. One senior official later described the federal bureaucracy as "really, truly, at the point of breakdown. The trouble is that Richard Nixon thought he could solve it by putting sons-of-bitches in command." Quoted in Theodore White, *Breach of Faith: The Downfall of Richard Nixon* (New York, 1975), p. 227.

[2] This challenge to presidential authority ended in a compromise, although it would probably have proceeded further had the greater challenge of Watergate not intervened. Since both the House and Senate actions of May 1973 were in the form of amendments to an appropriations bill, a joint conference was necessary in order to reconcile the milder House measure with the more sweeping Senate version. Congress reached agreement and passed an amendment on June 26, requiring an end to the bombing by June 30. Nixon vetoed this, and the lower house was unable to muster enough votes to override. Congress proceeded to tack fund-ban amendments onto other appropriations bills, and Nixon finally won their consent to stop doing this in return for a pledge to cease bombing Cambodia by August 15.

Nixon had exceeded his powers by impounding certain funds and eliminating federal programs.[3] Inflation made a shambles of Phase Three as prices took off in the sharpest rise since the Korean War. A growing fuel shortage threatened to interfere with the harvest and led to angry charges against the major oil companies. Public criticism of the administration grew louder.

2. *Background to Disaster, 1969–1972:*
Sabotage and Spying

The smoldering Watergate affair burst into flames against this background in the spring of 1973. The burglary that administration officials had so airily dismissed the previous summer was transformed by a rash of new disclosures and confessions into the gravest political scandal in American history. The Watergate revelations, which did not cease until the president himself was driven from office, fell into two basic categories: those that pertained to actions *preceding* the actual break-in of June 17, 1972, and those involving actions that occurred afterward.

The break-in itself was revealed to be part of an extensive campaign, conceived and directed by leading members of the Committee for the Re-election of the President (CREEP) and others connected with the White House, to sabotage the Democratic campaign of 1972. Chief target of the break-in was the chairman of the Democratic National Committee, Lawrence F. O'Brien, whose political skills and connections were supposed to make his telephone conversations and office files worth tapping. (The Watergate burglars had broken in and tapped telephones in O'Brien's office a few weeks before the June 17 affair. They avoided detection on their first effort but failed to learn anything useful. The second break-in was designed to install more and better taps. The same crew had also tried, unsuccessfully, to break into Senator McGovern's campaign headquarters on several occasions during May 1972.) In addition, CREEP had been conducting a "dirty tricks" campaign since the summer of 1971—hiring people to write and distribute slanderous letters impugning Democratic candidates, concoct false telegrams and newspaper advertisements that would create an impression of popular support for the president, and disrupt and discredit opposition gatherings.

The scandal involved the misuse of millions of dollars of GOP campaign funds, much of which had been raised in violation of the Federal Election

---

[3] Specifically, District Court Judge Oliver Gasch of New York ruled in May 1973 that the president had no right to withhold $5 billion from an antipollution program authorized in the Clean Water Act of 1972. In April the district court in Washington invalidated the president's attempt to dismantle the OEO, and an appeals court in Missouri ruled that he had acted illegally in withholding $2.5 billion in federal funds for highway construction.

Campaign Act of 1972. Large donations, including $250,000 to finance the actual break-in, had been "laundered" through Mexican banks in an effort to make them untraceable, and then placed in unaudited funds that were used to support these sabotage and espionage activities.[4]

The Watergate disclosures extended remorselessly backward in time, upward in implication, and outward in scope. A committee working for Nixon during his California gubernatorial campaign in 1962, headed by H. R. Haldeman, had utilized "dirty tricks," and many of these were used against George Wallace in 1970. From 1969 on, the White House had employed a small group of investigators, paid out of private campaign funds, to gather information about the personal habits and finances of political opponents.[5] From 1969 to 1971, in the name of "national security," the White House had ordered the placing of taps on the telephones of several reporters and government employees suspected of leaking information or, as often as not, simply of being "anti-Nixon."[6] The president's aides compiled an "enemies list" and sought to harass them by instructing the Internal Revenue Service to investigate their tax returns; the threat of FCC action was similarly used on occasion to intimidate "unfriendly" newspapers, notably the *Washington Post*.[7]

There seemed no end to what came to be called the "White House horrors." In 1970 the president himself had approved an intelligence-gathering plan that called for the massive use of illegal mail surveillance,

---

[4]One of the most embarrassing disclosures involving campaign funds was a $200,000 contribution (in a black attaché case full of $100 bills) from financier Robert L. Vesco, who at the time was being sued by the Securities and Exchange Commission in a fraud case. Vesco had sought and obtained, through Attorney General Mitchell, interviews with SEC officials in an unsuccessful attempt to get the suit dropped. This episode led to a grand-jury indictment of Vesco, Mitchell, and former Secretary of Commerce Maurice Stans, CREEP finance chairman, for conspiring to defraud the government and obstruct the SEC investigation. Mitchell and Stans were tried and acquitted of these charges in April 1974, although both men were later found guilty of other illegal acts connected with the Watergate scandal.

[5]These investigators were urged to be especially zealous in their operations against Edward M. Kennedy, the political opponent Nixon feared above all others. They nosed about for scandalous or spicy episodes in the senator's private life, and particularly for details of his behavior during the driving accident on Martha's Vineyard in 1969 (see p. 937).

More seriously, one White House employee (later apprehended at Watergate) sought to embarrass Kennedy by discovering and disclosing that his brother, the late president, had directly conspired in the coup that overthrew and assassinated South Vietnam's Ngo Dinh Diem in October 1963 (see p. 843). When the State Department cables and CIA files failed to establish any such complicity, the investigator devised a pair of fake cables designed to expose President Kennedy's involvement.

[6]The existing wiretap law was flouted or stretched in some of these instances, and many of the taps were maintained long after the individuals in question had ceased to occupy positions even remotely involving "national security."

[7]John W. Dean III, counsel to the president from 1970 on and later a key figure in the Watergate cover-up, put the White House intentions beautifully in an office memorandum that translated bureaucratic language into enduring prose: "This memorandum addresses the matter of how we can maximize the fact of our incumbency in dealing with persons known to be active in their opposition to our Administration. Stated a bit more bluntly—how we can use the available federal machinery to screw our political enemies."

wiretapping, and burglary in order to acquire information about people and groups deemed to pose a threat to internal security. Although he later withdrew his approval of the scheme, reluctantly, in the face of adamant opposition by FBI director J. Edgar Hoover, the plan was not forgotten.

The techniques were frequently employed, for example, when the FBI, CIA, and Secret Service—often in violation of the law—were ordered to spy and collect dossiers on American citizens suspected of being "political dissidents." The same techniques were used by a special investigating group known as the "plumbers," which the White House formed in 1971 in order to find and plug security leaks like that of Ellsberg and his Pentagon Papers (see pp. 907, 934). In September 1971 a group of "plumbers"—much the same crew that would later attempt Watergate—broke into the office of Daniel Ellsberg's psychiatrist in Beverly Hills, California, in an attempt to find evidence that could be used against the defendant in his trial for theft and espionage.

No assignment was too far-fetched for these White House operatives. In May 1972, the group already recruited for the Watergate break-in was employed to heckle and rough up demonstrators at an antiwar rally at the Capitol. A few months earlier, the *Washington Post* had published an ITT memorandum indicating that the corporation's recent offer to contribute $400,000 toward GOP convention costs (see pp. 943–944) had indeed been connected with ITT's attempts to win governmental approval of its merger plans. Fearful that this would damage Nixon's reelection chances, the White House ordered one ubiquitous agent—already responsible for the Ellsberg break-in, later to help direct Watergate—to fly to Denver and talk to the alleged author of the memorandum, an ITT lobbyist named Dita Beard. The agent, using a false name and CIA credentials (improperly acquired) and disguised in a crude red wig, visited Mrs. Beard in her hospital room, spoke mysteriously of "high Washington level" connections, and urged her to deny her authorship of the memorandum and denounce it as a hoax, which she subsequently did.

All of these activities, which came to light piecemeal as the Watergate story unfolded in the spring of 1973, were either downright illegal or highly unethical or both; moreover, all had been connived at, approved by, and in most instances directly ordered by the president's principal lieutenants. To be sure, many of these practices had been employed by earlier administrations, as Nixon's defenders took pains to point out. But the scope of the Nixon administration's operations across the lines of legality and ethical conduct were markedly greater than anything that had occurred before.[8]

[8]The difference was neatly summarized in an exchange in May 1973 between H. R. Haldeman and a long-time Democratic opponent who was known to have used "dirty tricks" against the Nixon campaign in California in 1960.

"You s.o.b., you started this," Haldeman said.

"Yeah, Bob," the man replied, "but you guys ran it into the ground." Quoted in J. Anthony Lucas, *Nightmare: The Underside of the Nixon Years* (New York, 1976), p. 146.

3. *Highway to Disaster, 1972–1973: Cover-up*

Disturbing though they were, the "White House horrors" that culminated in the Watergate burglary were only the beginning. The burglars themselves had been caught red-handed. The administration that had dispatched them—or, more specifically, the network of officials in the White House and CREEP who were in various ways responsible—now faced a choice. A prompt admission of complicity, together with a few middle-level resignations, would, of course, have reflected badly upon the White House and the Republican presidential campaign and would have cost Nixon some votes in November, but hardly the election.

But the White House chose instead to avoid admitting anything, and the fatal damage to the Nixon presidency began at that point. Far from admitting complicity, the persons responsible for the Watergate break-in immediately launched an attempt at concealment.[9] This, the so-called cover-up, lasted through and beyond the election and indeed for as long as the surviving participants could manage it. And the cover-up led step by step through a deepening morass of illegality that threatened the constitutional system itself.

For the first few months the cover-up seemed to be working perfectly. Throughout their trial the seven Watergate defendants maintained a stoic silence about their connections with the White House and CREEP and denied that anyone else had been involved in the burglary. Nixon duly won his enormous victory in November. As the new year began, the cover-up strategists on the White House staff could congratulate one another. They had seemingly contained the incident and avoided contamination.

However, too many people had been involved; too many questions remained unanswered. Once any one person began to talk, it was only a question of time before larger and larger chunks of the story would come to light. This process began in March 1973 when one of the defendants—seeking to avoid a long prison sentence—started to tell everything he knew. The federal prosecutors, sensing that things were about to break, reconvened the grand jury and began a new round of interrogations. The newspapers, which with one or two exceptions had virtually abandoned Watergate as a live issue after the fall election, returned eagerly to the hunt. Suspicion on Capitol Hill that there was more to be learned had already led the Senate, by a vote of 77–0 on February 7, to establish a Select Committee on Presidential Campaign Activities, soon to become famous as the Watergate committee, with veteran North Carolina Democrat Sam J. Ervin, Jr., a respected constitutional lawyer, as chairman. The

[9]Alternative courses of action were apparently never seriously considered. "The cover-up began [immediately]," one Watergate conspirator later testified. "I do not think there was ever any discussion that there would not be a cover-up."

seven-man body[10] moved quickly to appoint a legal staff and prepare for hearings.

The cover-up dam was almost at once swept away by a flood of new disclosures. A self-perpetuating process had been set in motion. As more and more implicated parties engaged lawyers and raced to tell the prosecutors what they knew in hopes of obtaining immunity, various items would be leaked to the press. This provided sensational news stories, which in turn led to further investigations and a new round of leaks. The new testimony revealed, among other things, the break-in at the office of Ellsberg's psychiatrist. This and related disclosures led District Judge William Matthew Byrne, Jr., to dismiss the case against Ellsberg in May 1973 on grounds of gross misconduct on the part of the government.[11] April witnessed a flurry of resignations: Herbert Kalmbach, Nixon's private attorney and veteran fund raiser; John W. Dean III, counsel to the president; Attorney General Richard G. Kleindienst; the directors of the SEC and the FBI; several present and former White House aides; and the men closest to the president—John D. Ehrlichman, his adviser on domestic affairs, and H. R. Haldeman, the White House chief of staff.

Nixon, publicly affirming his determination to get at the whole truth, appointed Secretary of Defense Elliot Richardson, a Boston patrician of unassailable integrity, as the new attorney general. Events followed swiftly. In May, the Senate demanded, and Richardson was instructed to appoint, a special Watergate prosecutor with broad powers of investigation and subpoena. Richardson selected Archibald Cox, professor of law at Harvard and a blueblooded Yankee like himself. While Cox assembled a staff and started to gather evidence, the nationally televised public hearings of the Senate Watergate committee, which began on May 17, brought more and more testimony into open view.

And thus, throughout the spring and summer of 1973, a bewildered public learned about Watergate's sordid background and connections. They also learned about the cover-up and about the lengths to which its perpetrators had been willing to go in an effort to conceal the truth. These lengths, it developed, were considerable. They included promises of clem-

---

[10]It consisted of four Democrats—Ervin, Daniel K. Inouye of Hawaii, Joseph M. Montoya of New Mexico, and Herman E. Talmadge of Georgia—and three Republicans—Howard H. Baker, Jr., of Tennessee, Edward J. Gurney of Florida, and Lowell P. Weicker, Jr., of Connecticut.

[11]White House actions just before this news became public were suggestive. The president had learned (from his counsel and "cover-up director," John Dean) about the Ellsberg break-in, and about Ehrlichman's responsibility for it, as far back as mid-March 1973. Rather than inform either his attorney general or Judge Byrne of this patently illegal act, which, when disclosed, would inevitably destroy the government's case against Ellsberg, the president remained silent. And in the interim before it became known in mid-April—the Justice Department learned of it, ironically, from Dean himself, who was now telling all to the prosecutors—the president actually approached Byrne on three occasions, with the Ellsberg trial still in process, to see if the judge was interested in being appointed the next director of the FBI!

ency and future aid and the payment of hundreds of thousands of dollars in hush money, at times amounting to outright blackmail, in an attempt to keep the Watergate defendants quiet. They included perjured testimony, a parade of misleading statements and denials, constant evasions and distortions of the truth, and a good deal of unadorned lying. They included deceit, manipulation, subversion, and misuse of the Justice Department, the FBI, and the CIA.[12] These actions, moreover, had not been resorted to on rare or isolated occasions, or under sudden pressure. They had been performed repeatedly, calculatedly, and systematically. They amounted, in short, to criminal wrongdoing of massive proportions unparalleled in the history of the presidency.

4. The White House Tapes

As new revelations continued to expose the scandal, the main question now was whether Nixon himself had been involved. Senator Baker posed it to witness after witness while the Watergate hearings riveted a shocked audience to their television sets in the summer of 1973.[13] "What did the president know," Baker kept asking, "and when did he know it?"

The president's various public statements about Watergate did little to

[12]Examples of this subversion of government and law are worth noting. The administration had been making political use of the IRS, the intelligence agencies, and, at least by implication, the FCC for some time, as we have seen (p. 951). In its frantic attempt to conceal the truth after Watergate, the White House began by ordering the CIA to block FBI investigation of certain leads on the blatantly false grounds that some covert "national security" CIA operations were involved. At the same time, the acting director of the FBI (L. Patrick Gray III, who was appointed to succeed J. Edgar Hoover upon the latter's death in May 1972) was persuaded to destroy large amounts of incriminating material from the White House safe of one of the Watergate burglars.

From then on, the White House did everything it could to obstruct the government's attempt to pursue the course of justice. It concealed all the incriminating knowledge that it had from those officially responsible for investigating the case. It commandeered and used FBI files and confidential grand jury information to find out what was officially known, so as to assist implicated parties in concealing their guilt. It arranged to have its own staff members present during certain interrogations, which enabled them to find out more information, assist some witnesses, and intimidate others. It frankly and repeatedly ordered Henry Petersen, the assistant attorney general in charge of the Watergate prosecution, to stay away from "political" matters and anything that might lead to the White House.

The high-ranking officials of the bureaus and departments thus subverted were generally obedient to these orders, though increasingly troubled by them. Their obedience stemmed from an understandable reluctance to believe that the president of the United States, and ranking members of his staff who spoke authoritatively in his name, could have had anything but honorable motives in issuing such orders. It never occurred to them that they were being deceived and manipulated in furtherance of a criminal conspiracy.

[13]A Herblock cartoon captured the prevailing mood perfectly as the unsavory truths kept emerging. He pictured a man and a woman staring in unhappy disbelief at a TV screen labeled "Watergate" which had just flashed the message: "Do not try to adjust your sets; these things are really happening in America."

ease the growing doubts. The most damaging public testimony against him—and for a time the only direct charge that he had knowingly conspired in the cover-up—came from his former counsel, John W. Dean. But it was Dean's word against that of the president of the United States; and if Dean's testimony was often persuasive, it was not accompanied by proof. Moreover, by frankly admitting his own deep complicity, Dean was himself vulnerable; and the White House worked hard to discredit him and identify him as the "mastermind" of the cover-up. Despite such efforts, the doubts continued to grow. Nixon's approval rating in one public-opinion poll slipped from a high of 68 percent in February to 40 percent in July. Still, the case against him continued to rest entirely upon suspicious circumstances and unsubstantiated testimony.

Then, on July 16, the Watergate committee questioned Alexander Butterfield, a former presidential aide. He testified that in early 1971 the president had ordered a taping system installed in his White House offices for the purpose of recording conversations and telephone calls. Many of the high-level private conversations which Dean and others had tried to recall from memory or notes were presumably on those tapes.[14]

From then on the Watergate drama, which had yet another year to run, centered ever more closely upon the White House tapes and the prosecution's long running battle to find out exactly what they contained. The battle, intricate and sternly contested, involved all three branches of government and reached to the very heart of the Constitution and the principle of separation of powers.

The first round began as soon as the investigators learned that the tapes existed. Senator Ervin, for the committee, wrote to the president on July 17, 1973, and asked for five of them and other relevant White House documents. When the president flatly refused to comply, the committee voted unanimously on July 23 to issue subpoenas for the tapes and other materials. On the same day Special Prosecutor Cox issued a subpoena for nine of the tapes. The White House rejected these subpoenas on July 26. Thereupon, both the committee and the special prosecutor went to District Judge John J. Sirica, whose dissatisfaction with the Watergate trial had helped breach the cover-up, for a ruling to force the White House to relinquish the tapes. The president's counsel hastened to present a counterargument.

All three branches of government had now entered the fray. The special prosecutor—though technically under the attorney general and therefore a member of the executive branch—occupied an ambiguous fourth position of apparent independence of the person who held the ultimate executive authority.

The contest raised several constitutional issues. To justify his refusal to

---

[14]The revelation about the tapes was as big a surprise to most of Nixon's former staff as it was to the public. The only people who had known about them, besides Butterfield and the specialists who had installed them, were Nixon, Haldeman, and one of Haldeman's assistants.

surrender the tapes, Nixon advanced sweeping claims of "executive privilege." He tied the doctrine of executive privilege to that of separation of powers, arguing that the presidency would be fatally compromised, and national security endangered, if either congressional subpoenas or court orders could compel the chief executive to disclose privileged information. The only way that a president could be legally required to do this was through the process of impeachment.

This argument could not be lightly dismissed, and Judge Sirica pondered deeply and proceeded with caution. Separation of powers, for example, was a basic constitutional principle, and the judge, not wishing to violate it, deferred taking jurisdiction over the Ervin committee's suit and ultimately rejected it. Executive privilege was a murkier issue. Legal experts had been sharply critical of the president's virtually limitless construction of the term, but they had not destroyed the concept of executive privilege as an *implied* power, and Sirica was not prepared to rule that there could be *no* privileged information in the material being sought from the White House.

Sirica finally, on August 29, rejected Nixon's argument and ordered release of the tapes; he also stipulated that they come to him first so that he could listen for and excise any privileged sections before turning them over to a special grand jury, which Cox had requested. The case then went to the court of appeals, where the special prosecutor and the president's counsel renewed their legal arguments on September 11. The court's first response was to urge a compromise. The judges feared a constitutional crisis—the president's brief hinted strongly that he might not comply with an adverse decision—and wanted to avoid a confrontation with the executive branch. The opposing lawyers strove to find an acceptable compromise but reported a few days later that they had failed. The court, after pondering the case for three weeks, upheld Sirica's order by a vote of 5–2 on October 12. The judges repeated their hope that president and prosecutor could yet reach a compromise, but they ended on an unequivocal note. The president, they concluded, "is not above the law's commands." The court set October 19 as the deadline for compliance with its ruling, explicitly granting a one-week extension in order to permit an appeal to the Supreme Court.

5. *Spiro Agnew*

Meanwhile, the same summer and autumn witnessed the unfolding of a new scandal, unconnected with Watergate, that involved Vice-President Agnew. The United States attorney's office in Baltimore, which for some months had been investigating political corruption in Baltimore County, informed Attorney General Richardson in June 1973 that it had found evidence implicating the vice-president.

As one of the fastest growing suburban areas in the country after mid-century, Baltimore County had spawned the usual proliferation of highways, housing and apartment developments, bridges, sewer systems, and shopping centers, all of which involved round upon round of real-estate purchases, zoning ordinances, and engineering and construction contracts. Opportunities for profit were large. Not surprisingly, this activity had been accompanied by a tangled web of deals between assorted developers and contractors on the one hand, and various county and state officials on the other. The deals had frequently extended to collusion, kickbacks, and extortion. By late 1972, the resident United States attorney had found enough evidence of misdeeds to impanel a grand jury, subpoena documents, and begin a process known as "dealing up." He would confront lesser figures with the incriminating evidence against them, offer immunity in return for information that would help to convict more important figures, and would repeat the maneuver as far up the ladder as it could be taken.

The attorney's staff learned that Agnew had been receiving kickbacks in return for favorable contracts since the early 1960s. Moreover, the payments and the favors had continued through his term as governor of Maryland, 1967-1969, and also through his first term as vice-president of the United States. By August 1, 1973, the attorney's office had built a strong enough case to present Agnew with formal written notice that he was under investigation for bribery, extortion, conspiracy, and tax evasion.

The story broke a few days later amid a flurry of rumors. Agnew fought back hard. He assured Nixon of his innocence and then called a huge press conference in which he denounced the charges as "damned lies," pledged full cooperation with the prosecutors, and insisted that he had "nothing to hide." During much of August and September he continued to affirm his innocence in public while waging a desperate battle to survive.

Agnew was battling a formidable coalition, and the odds against him were greatly increased by the attitude of two important figures who, for reasons of state and politics, began to put pressure upon him to resign. One of these was Attorney General Richardson, who regarded the case as open and shut and wanted a less disastrous line of succession in case the president did not finish out his term. The other was President Nixon himself. The Agnew scandal put him in a quandary. The vice-president was popular among conservatives and the "silent majority," and the president, fighting for his own survival, was reluctant to offend this constituency. Yet by early September the White House had concluded that Agnew was a liability it could no longer afford. Presidential aides made it clear to the vice-president that his resignation was desired.

Agnew still proclaimed his innocence and responded with several bold ploys and another counteroffensive. These tactics drew applause from conservative audiences, but the legal and political forces that had been set in motion against him were too strong. Speaker Carl Albert denied his request for an investigation by the House of Representatives.[15] In answer to Agnew's claim that a vice-president was not indictable, the Justice Department filed a legal brief that distinguished between the offices of president and vice-president. It held that the former could not be indicted while in office, but that the latter could. And the White House sent blunt private warnings to Agnew to cease his attacks on Justice Department officials.

Agnew threw in the towel in early October. His overriding concern throughout had been to stay out of prison. It was Richardson, bent on Agnew's resignation at almost any price, who devised the formula acceptable to all parties: if Agnew would agree to resign and plead no contest to a single count of income-tax evasion, the other, more serious charges against him would be dropped. Richardson also stipulated that the detailed charges against Agnew be released for publication after he had resigned, so that people could know the legal substance of the case against him. The vice-president agreed, but insisted in turn upon a prior commitment with regard to his sentence: he would not go to prison. Richardson reluctantly consented.

A subdued vice-president appeared in the federal district court in Baltimore on October 10, 1973, and announced his intention to resign. (His official resignation, effective immediately, had just been delivered to the secretary of state.) Agnew pleaded no contest on a single count of income-tax evasion for 1967. He was fined $10,000 and sentenced to three years of "unsupervised probation." The Justice Department then released a forty-page memorandum of the charges against him. Agnew declared a few days later that he was the victim of "scurrilous and inaccurate reports" and had resigned merely to "still the raging storm," but the substance of the memorandum was sufficient to resolve most people's doubts. The case, according to legal experts, would have amounted to a fifty-count indictment. Therewith ended the political career of the man who had won national fame and enthusiastic applause for his outspoken attacks on the permissive liberals who had undermined America's respect for the law.

6. Saturday Night Massacre, October 1973

The Agnew scandal was only one among many crises that beset Richard Nixon in October. On Yom Kippur, four days before Agnew's resignation, Egypt and Syria had launched a massive invasion of Israel. The first few

---

[15] Upon learning of this request, the attorney general called Albert and pointed out that Agnew faced a mountain of incriminating evidence and certain indictment by the grand jury. Even without this reminder, Albert could only regard a House investigation as a political thicket to avoid. If investigation led to impeachment, and impeachment led to removal, and the presidency also became vacant, the Speaker of the House was next in the line of succession—as everyone would know throughout the proceedings. Albert wanted no part of such a situation.

days of fighting cost the Israelis so heavily in armor and air power that only a quick, large-scale infusion of American military aid could enable them to survive. The decision to supply such aid found its way to the president's desk as a question of the first magnitude on October 12 (see p. 1000). On that evening, after two days of canvassing and pondering, he was scheduled to meet with cabinet members, congressional leaders, and other Washington dignitaries at a White House gathering to announce his choice as Agnew's successor, House Minority Leader Gerald R. Ford of Michigan. And, on that same evening, the court of appeals handed down its decision upholding Sirica's order to turn over the Watergate tapes.

The decision of the court of appeals gave Nixon a week in which to exercise his options—to comply with the order, to appeal to the Supreme Court, or to seek a compromise with the special prosecutor. From Nixon's uneasy vantage point these were not attractive options. Cox had already shown no disposition to compromise. Nixon's advisers were now predicting that the Supreme Court would probably uphold the lower tribunals. If Nixon appealed and the Supreme Court ordered him to relinquish the tapes he hardly dared refuse to comply. Yet to hand over those tapes, as the president knew far better than even his close advisers, was to invite disaster.[16]

There was a fourth option, which the president had been contemplating for some time. It was to protect the tapes by firing Cox, the person who was demanding them.

Cox had assumed from the start that he was a truly independent prosecutor, empowered and entitled in his search for evidence to go wherever the trail might lead. The president, in contrast, had originally seen the special prosecutor as an orchestrator and buffer who would keep the White House informed and the regular prosecutors under control.

This initial misunderstanding deepened and widened as Cox went about his task. Cox soon realized that, despite Nixon's public promise of full cooperation, the White House was systematically stalling, evading, or ignoring his requests for documents and files, and his frustration grew as these tactics persisted. "I have been very patient—perhaps too patient—in seeking voluntary cooperation," Cox finally wrote. Hereafter he would insist upon a "prompt, categorical response" to each of his requests.

For his part, the president grew increasingly annoyed and at times outraged by the prosecutor's determination to probe into any and every matter. "Cox wasn't containable," a White House aide recalled later. "He was

---

[16]Nixon had had to assemble virtually a brand-new White House staff in the wake of the Watergate resignations in the spring of 1973. The new men, unlike their predecessors, were totally untainted by Watergate. They were able and dedicated public servants, and they worked zealously to defend their commander-in-chief, convinced of his innocence. The one thing none of them knew until the very last was that he had lied to them as unblinkingly as he had lied to the American public.

constantly expanding." And as summer turned into autumn, he began recording successes in the same process of dealing up that had nailed Spiro Agnew. By early October, Cox was negotiating with none other than John Dean. Nixon pondered his options and decided upon a bold measure that would regain the initiative, keep the tapes in his custody, and, as he put it, "get rid of Cox."

The president accordingly summoned Attorney General Richardson to the White House on October 15. The new chief of staff, General Alexander M. Haig, Jr., informed Richardson that, instead of releasing the tapes or appealing to the Supreme Court, Nixon intended to prepare his own "summary" of the tapes for Judge Sirica and then dispose of the subpoena problem by firing Cox.

Richardson, who as Cox's direct superior was expected to do the actual firing, said that he could not comply. He had promised the Senate, during his confirmation hearings, that he would neither interfere with the special prosecutor in any way nor remove him from office except for "extraordinary improprieties." Cox had committed none, Richardson said, and if he were ordered to dismiss Cox he would have to resign.

Nixon could ill afford to lose Elliot Richardson, whose formidable reputation for integrity and competence had just been enhanced by his handling of the Agnew crisis. Haig proposed a compromise and persuaded first Nixon and then Richardson to give it a try. It was to have a third party authenticate the tapes and prepare a summary for the court, excising all privileged and irrelevant matters. For this task the White House suggested Senator John C. Stennis of Mississippi, a respected elder statesman. Richardson, eager for a satisfactory compromise, agreed to try to win Cox's approval of the plan.

Intricate negotiations followed, but even Haig and Richardson, most skillful of compromisers, soon saw that the gap between president and prosecutor was too wide to be bridged. Nixon and his advisers were determined to safeguard the tapes, provide the court with only an edited transcript, yield no further tapes or documents beyond those already under subpoena, and bring Cox into line or else remove him. The special prosecutor, in turn, although he wanted to avoid a head-on collision with the president and could accept the idea of third-party verification, was firmly committed to two propositions: his continuing right to demand and obtain any and all materials that might prove relevant in a trial court, and such a court's absolute, unequivocal right to examine the actual tapes rather than transcripts.

Both parties were on a collision course, and Nixon steered toward it knowingly and boldly. By Friday, October 19—the deadline for complying with the court order or appealing it—he had determined to adopt the Stennis plan. Stennis duly agreed to participate, provided that Senators Ervin and Baker, for the Watergate committee, also approved. They accepted and agreed to recommend the plan to the committee.[17] Nixon now made the Stennis plan public in a national press release that evening. He portrayed it as a statesmanlike compromise that would resolve the great crisis and announced that Senator Stennis had consented to verify White House summaries of the tapes and that Ervin and Baker had accepted the plan. Nixon then passed the point of no return by adding an important rider which, he knew, Cox had already pronounced unacceptable. With regard to the special prosecutor, Nixon said, "I have felt it necessary to direct him, as an employee of the executive branch, to make no further attempts by judicial process to obtain tapes, notes, or memoranda of Presidential conversations." By this time, Richardson was in receipt of a letter from the president that explicitly instructed him to order Cox to seek no more White House documents of any kind.

Cox responded in the early afternoon of October 20 in a televised public statement. He quietly explained his inability to obey the president's directive and pointed out that Nixon was now in a position of noncompliance with the court order. He also maintained that only the attorney general, who had appointed him, could give him any instructions that he had any legal obligation to obey.

The pivot for the next few hours was Elliot Richardson, who had been striving for compromise and readying himself for this eventuality all week. Although he still believed that the president was innocent of criminal or impeachable offenses, Richardson still felt bound to his commitment not to dismiss Cox for anything except "extraordinary improprieties." Hence Richardson's decision, once the White House's order to dismiss Cox came, was predetermined. He refused and asked to see the president so that he could resign in person. Nixon made one final attempt to persuade his attorney general to stay on, but he refused to budge, made his resignation official, and left.

The events that would be known in history as the Saturday Night Massacre were now irrevocably in motion. Next to be ordered to fire Cox was Deputy Attorney General William D. Ruckelshaus. Ruckelshaus, in agreement with his chief about Cox, also elected to resign rather than carry out the order. It remained for the third-ranking official, Solicitor General Robert Bork, to perform the actual act. He did so only to prevent the decimation of the Justice Department by mass resignations.

---

[17]The three senators were less than fully informed about the situation. Stennis was under the impression that he was to verify the tapes for the Watergate committee rather than for the court, which, he later said, had a right to ask for anything it wanted. Ervin and Baker were pleased because Sirica had just dismissed the committee's suit for the tapes, and the Stennis transcripts appeared to be the best that they could get. Most important, none of the three men knew about Cox's objections to the plan or the collision between prosecutor and White House that would ensue if the plan was adopted.

7. *Firestorm, October–December 1973*

Public reaction was instantaneous, explosive, nonpartisan, and overwhelmingly hostile. Ninety-minute TV specials devoted to the affair later that evening touched off an avalanche of telegrams: more than 150,000 within three days, 300,000 more during the following week. Pulpit and press, including many publications that had supported Nixon in 1972, resounded with angry criticism. College students rallied and denounced. Mail poured into Congress—"as if a dam had broken," one awed member said; another reported that fewer than 10 of his 1,150 messages had supported the president. This was probably a fair gauge. Never before, in a long political career marked by keen sensitivity to grass-roots sentiment, had Richard Nixon so totally miscalculated a public reaction. The deans of several major law schools sent a petition asking Congress to "consider the necessity" of impeachment.

That word was being used now, not as a remote, abstract possibility or in the heat of partisan wrangling, but as something that might have to be resorted to. Demands for impeachment were too numerous to ignore, but Democratic leaders in Congress, wanting to avoid partisanship and hasty action in an emotional atmosphere, proceeded with care. Instead of creating a special committee, they placed the matter in the regular channels of the House of Representatives, where it could move at measured pace while passions cooled.[18] Speaker Albert turned the impeachment petitions over to the House Judiciary Committee with instructions to begin an "inquiry" as to whether impeachment proceedings might be in order. The machinery was now in motion.

Nixon's reputation was now in tatters. His approval rating in the opinion polls had dropped below 30 percent and, like a barometer before a storm, was still dropping. To make matters worse for him, several other unsavory items had come to light during the summer and autumn of 1973. The president was under fire for questionable financial arrangements in connection with his private real-estate holdings in California and Florida.[19]

[18]Congress was quite aware of the drastic, last-resort nature of impeachment as a remedy, equally aware that the only other time it had been used against an American president—Andrew Johnson, in 1868—the procedure had been emotional, highly partisan, and often unfair, and had left such a bad taste in everyone's mouth that most people had since regarded impeachment as a cure worse than the disease.

[19]The president's estates in Key Biscayne, Florida, and San Clemente, California—the so-called southern and western White Houses—had been acquired early in his first term in ways that raised questions about both the sources and the methods of his financing. It came out that several million dollars of public funds had been spent to improve these estates and to adapt them to presidential use. The General Accounting Office decided, after careful scrutiny, that government-financed improvements had greatly enhanced the value of the properties. And it was later ruled that some $90,000 of this public money had been spent on items that had nothing to do with security or official use and should have been charged to Nixon himself.

There were indications that he had been guilty of substantial income-tax evasion during his first four years in office.[20] He was still being criticized for his Cambodian policy, aspects of which had come to light for the first time in the summer of 1973. Testimony before the Watergate committee had disclosed that Nixon had ordered the bombing of Cambodia without congressional consent in early 1969. He had also continued the raids in secret for months, and had kept them secret by means of elaborately falsified reports from the Pentagon and deceptive statements and denials from the National Security Council, the State Department, and the White House.

But the main focus of public dissatisfaction was still Watergate. The disclosures themselves, and the nature of the president's response as investigators tried to piece the story together, had placed him under a cloud of suspicion that grew heavier with each passing month. This suspicion could be dissipated only by forthright and convincing actions by Nixon himself. For a time, he seemed to make the effort. He notified Sirica on October 23 that he would indeed turn over the tapes in compliance with the judge's order. A few days later, the White House announced the appointment of a new special prosecutor who would have "independence" and "total cooperation from the executive branch." He was Leon Jaworski, a conservative corporation lawyer from Texas who bore almost no resemblance to his predecessor save in the qualities of competence and determination to discover the truth.

The president also launched a public-relations campaign, called "Operation Candor," in an attempt to restore his standing and quiet the charges that he was concealing or withholding information. He promised the nation that he did not intend to resign and would continue working "16 to 18 hours a day" at the job he had been elected to do. Haig assured Republican leaders that the tapes would exculpate the president.[21] Groups of representatives and senators were invited to White House breakfasts or evening cocktails. In one week, Nixon saw more than half the total membership of Congress and gave earnest assurances of his innocence. He did the same in public on a barnstorming tour before carefully selected audiences.

In December, Nixon released a detailed financial statement—audits, tax returns, and other documents—designed to lay to rest the suspicions about his personal finances. He announced that he would donate his San Cle-

---

[20] The president had resorted to loopholes and dubious logic to avoid paying taxes in California; he had also reduced his federal tax payments almost to zero by taking enormous deductions for various gifts and donations. Some of these were proper enough, but a detailed IRS investigation of his tax returns later resulted in disallowing many of the deductions, including a gift of his vice-presidential papers that had been back-dated in order to evade a change in the tax laws. The IRS finally concluded that the president owed a total of some $467,000 in back taxes, including interest, for the period 1969-1972. The president agreed to pay the entire amount.

[21] A key point in this assurance was the claim that the president had not learned about the cover-up until late March 1973, when it began collapsing. It should be remembered that neither Haig nor anyone else on the post-Watergate White House staff had actually heard any of the tapes at this time. Haig's assurances to Republican leaders were based on the president's assurances to him.

mente property to the nation after he and Mrs. Nixon died, and that he would let one or two questions about deductions and capital gains on his tax returns be decided by the Joint Committee on Internal Revenue Taxation. In early January 1974 he released statements about his role in the milk price rise and the ITT suit (see pp. 943–944).[22]

Operation Candor was too little, too late. The public, the news media, and Congress, outside of a shrinking hard core of support, remained skeptical, at times carpingly suspicious. The Joint Committee on Internal Revenue Taxation infuriated the president by going beyond the points he had specified and conducting a thorough investigation of *all* of his tax deductions. If some members of Congress were impressed by his displays of sincerity and fighting spirit at those friendly White House gatherings, others were critical. The House majority leader, in a pointed reference to the impeachment inquiry, frankly rebuked him for attempting to "curry favor with his prospective grand jurors." And Senator Goldwater, whose political support was crucial, deflated the White House sessions with characteristic bluntness.[23] The information Nixon released was neither conclusive nor reassuring, and much of it simply confirmed the growing public impression that their president had been operating, at best, on the borders of ethical conduct. The main trouble was that outside of vague reassurances—"I am not a crook!" he told one audience—Operation Candor did not really deal with Watergate at all. Yet it was here that skepticism and doubt were strongest.

Moreover, the whole elaborate parade of frankness was outweighed in the public mind by the impact of two "bombshells" that pertained all too directly to Watergate. The first exploded at the end of October, before Operation Candor had even begun, when the public learned that two of the nine subpoenaed tapes, covering two of the most important sets of White House conversations, did not exist. Court hearings were unable to solve the mystery of how, or by whose hand, these tapes had disappeared, but the White House explanations were neither consistent nor satisfying. Even worse, a few weeks later the White House had to reveal that an eighteen-minute segment of a crucial conversation between Nixon and Haldeman in June 1972 had been erased from the tape.[24] Disbelief, suspicion, and disgust grew apace; calls for impeachment or resignation became louder.

---

[22] The president admitted that "traditional political considerations" played a role in the administration's decision to raise price supports for milk, but denied that the milk producers' pledge of $2 million to his campaign was a bribe. His intervention in the ITT suit, he said, had had nothing to do with the $400,000 convention offer, but was based instead on his disagreement with the "bigness is bad" approach of the antitrust division.

[23] "The only time you get us down here," Goldwater said, "is when you get your ass in a crack and want us to get it out for you."Quoted in Lukas, *Nightmare*, p. 451.

[24] Exactly how this happened or who was responsible will probably never be known. After much careful examination, a panel of experts (jointly chosen by the prosecutor and the White House) concluded that at least five, possibly as many as nine, separate erasures had created the eighteen-minute gap, and that they were probably, but by no means certainly, deliberate acts.

8. *Battle Lines Drawn, January–April 1974*

The opening weeks of 1974 marked the staking out of positions that largely determined how the Watergate affair would run the rest of its course. Nixon, stung by the failure of Operation Candor and the mounting tide of criticism, swung into an increasingly defiant posture. He canceled a plan to issue summaries of the subpoenaed tapes and release various documents in support of his recent public statements. In early January he persuaded James St. Clair, a highly successful Boston attorney, to be his special Watergate counselor, obviously in anticipation of an all-out legal contest. Most important, he became steadily less cooperative with the new special prosecutor. After acceding to some of Jaworski's early requests for new tapes and other materials, he began resorting to the same "stonewall" tactics that had frustrated Archibald Cox.

The president set forth his position in his State of the Union message on January 30, 1974. He was confident, he said, that he had already given the special prosecutor "all the material that he needs to conclude his investigation and to proceed to prosecute the guilty and to clear the innocent." Then he went on in a ringing affirmation of executive privilege.[25] He would cooperate with the investigators, but, he added: "I will follow the precedent that has been followed by and defended by every President from George Washington to Lyndon B. Johnson of never doing anything that weakens the office of the Presidency of the United States." A few days later St. Clair told Jaworski that his pending requests for tapes and documents had been rejected, whereupon Jaworski began to issue subpoenas and prepared to do battle in court.

By this time, there were two new developments in the situation. One was the evidence gathered by the grand jury, which on March 1 reported indictments of seven key figures involved in the cover-up—including Haldeman, Ehrlichman, and former Attorney General Mitchell—on charges of conspiracy, lying, and obstruction of justice. The grand jury would also have indicted Nixon himself on the basis of what it knew had Jaworski not advised them that a "sitting president" was not indictable. (The grand jury did name Nixon as an "unindicted co-conspirator," which meant that his conversations could be used as evidence in the forthcoming trial of his former assistants.) And, again upon Jaworski's recommendation, the big briefcase full of evidence, which the grand jury had collected in support of its case against Nixon, was handed over to Judge Sirica. This was a legal

[25] Judge Sirica, in reviewing the seven tapes before turning them over to the special prosecutor, had provided some support for this doctrine by concluding, in mid-December, that large portions of three of the tapes did indeed contain privileged material and would not be passed along to Jaworski.

sidestep, designed to get around the rule that grand jury proceedings had to be kept secret.

The second new development came when the House Judiciary Committee addressed itself to the question of impeachment. At the outset, this thirty-eight-person committee—twenty-one Democrats, seventeen Republicans—moved with what struck partisans on both sides as maddening slowness. However, the committee's leaders, acutely conscious both of the gravity of their assignment and of the dangers that lurked in it, were determined to proceed with caution. The chairman was Peter Rodino, a New Jersey Democrat; the chief counsel of the committee's legal staff was John Doar, a tenacious lawyer who had performed with distinction and courage in the Justice Department's civil rights division in the 1960s. Under the skillful leadership of these two men, the House Judiciary Committee did in fact grind slowly, but like the mills of God, it would grind exceeding small.

The committee's first substantive task was to define an impeachable offense. The Constitution mentions two—treason and bribery—that were precise but irrelevant to the case at hand. The third offense, "high crimes and misdemeanors," obviously fitted Nixon if he was guilty.

However, there was much legal disputation about the meaning of this phrase. The president and his defenders took the strict view that "high crimes" meant actual criminal acts; if specific criminality could not be proved, no impeachable offense had occurred. Doar set forth the broad interpretation in a report to the committee in late February 1974. After reviewing the history of impeachment in England and America, Doar argued that presidential misconduct, in order to be impeachable, had to be "substantial" but not explicitly criminal. Impeachment was a remedy for "serious offenses," and the true measure was not the conduct itself but the effects of that conduct. Among these Doar specified "undermining the integrity of office, disregard of constitutional duties and oath of office, arrogation of power, abuse of the governmental process, adverse impact on the system of government." And it was clear that these effects could be brought about in ways not anticipated by the criminal law. "Impeachment was evolved . . . to cope with both the inadequacy of criminal standards and the impotence of courts to deal with the conduct of great public figures."

The House of Representatives voted, 410–4, in early February to empower the Judiciary Committee to subpoena anything and anyone, including the president. The inquiry was now fairly in motion. Doar's staff began to compile evidence and organize it meticulously. In March they received permission to acquire copies of the White House tapes and documents already obtained by the special prosecutor. Later that same month, the court of appeals upheld Sirica's ruling that the briefcase full of grand-jury evidence about Nixon could be made available to the Judiciary Committee.[26]

But Doar wanted still more, and in late February he asked the White House for some forty other tapes in addition to the ones it had given Jaworski. Now the committee began to encounter the same resistance Cox and Jaworski had met. For the next few weeks, the White House ignored the request and ridiculed the committee in public for the unreasonableness of its demands.[27]

Matters came to a head in April, when both the special prosecutor and the committee moved to obtain the material they wanted. On April 18 a federal marshal delivered Jaworski's subpoena for tapes containing sixty-four specific conversations between Nixon and his chief aides. Earlier that month, having waited thirty-eight days for a reply to his requests, Rodino warned the president that he had only five days more in which to deliver the tapes. "We have been respectfully patient," the chairman said. "The House has been patient. The people have been patient for a long, long time. But the patience of this committee is wearing thin." When St. Clair stalled again, the committee, on April 11, voted 33-3 to subpoena the tapes and gave the president two weeks in which to comply. Eight days later, it made a further request, this time for tapes containing more than 140 presidential conversations on a whole range of topics. The White House on April 23 asked for one more five-day extension on the earlier batch of tapes, and the committee voted to grant him what Rodino pointedly called "this one last request."

9. The April Transcripts

The vise was closing on Nixon as April ended. He faced subpoenas from both the special prosecutor and the Judiciary Committee. Time had about run out on the tactic of delays, stalls, and requests for extensions. Outright refusal to comply—"stonewalling," in Watergate slang—was no longer viable. Yet total compliance threatened disaster, because two or three of the tapes that Jaworski wanted were extremely damaging and one—con-

[26]The cover-up defendants had sued to block this transfer of evidence on the ground that the resulting publicity could prejudice their forthcoming trials. The president himself, though worried about the contents of that briefcase, had avoided trying such a move, knowing how the suspicious public would interpret it. Sirica was thus able to buttress his ruling in favor of the transfer by pointing out that "the person on whom the report focuses, the President of the United States, had not objected to its release to the committee."

[27]"The mere fact of an impeachment inquiry," one White House spokesman said, "does not give Congress the right to back up a truck and haul off White House files." For some weeks this was typical of the presidential attitude toward the committee's requests for more information.

taining a conversation between the president and Haldeman on June 23, 1972, six days after the break-in—could prove fatal.

The president decided upon another of those bold counterstrokes that he loved to employ. He would release edited transcripts of the tapes being sought, so that the American people as well as the Judiciary Committee could read what had been said in the Oval Office. It was a calculated risk, since the conversations included material that reflected badly upon the president. But the White House reasoned that the risk was worth taking.

Thus Nixon went on the air on April 29, 1974, and told the public what he had decided to do. Looking distinguished, earnest, and magisterially calm, he put on an impressive performance. Clearly visible beside him was a table piled high with handsomely bound blue folders, each replete with presidential seal. They contained, he said, over 1,200 pages of transcripts of forty-six presidential conversations that had taken place between September 1972 and April 1973, and they were about to be released to the public as well as to the House Judiciary Committee. "Everything that is relevant is included," he said, "the rough as well as the smooth, the strategy sessions, the exploration of alternatives." And, "as far as what the President personally knew and did . . . , these materials, together with those already made available, will tell it all."

The transcripts, released the next day, were reprinted in full by most major newspapers and hurried into paperback editions by two publishers. Public reaction was thunderously negative. The transcripts backfired for several reasons. The Judiciary Committee, which had the actual tapes of a few of the published conversations, hastened to make detailed comparisons. It discovered some discrepancies, in nearly all of which the White House version reflected less poorly on the president than the tapes did. It also noted that the transcripts had omitted large sections of certain conversations without indicating that anything had been left out—yet the omitted sections were both relevant and damaging. Many people were bothered by the inordinate number of gaps labeled "inaudible" or "unintelligible"—nearly 1,800 of them, or about three for every two pages. Analysts pointed out that nearly two-thirds of these breaks occurred in the president's own remarks, and occurred with greatest frequency in his talks with Haldeman and Ehrlichman.

What the transcripts left out was bothersome, but most people found them even more damning for what they contained. Nixon had admitted that certain sections might cause him embarrassment. What he utterly failed to appreciate was the overall impression that the transcripts conveyed—of shoddy, petty, backroom wheeling and dealing in the highest office in the land. "If this is what he thought he *could* release," one Democrat said, "I'd like to hear what else is on those tapes." The clergy was naturally shocked: Billy Graham, long a Nixon favorite, "could not but deplore the moral tone"; a prominent rabbi noted "the stench of moral decay." Conservatives were as dismayed as liberals. To one newspaper publisher, Nixon was revealed as "a man totally absorbed in the cheapest and sleaziest kind of conniving." The Senate minority leader, Hugh Scott of Pennsylvania, hitherto one of Nixon's defenders, called the contents "deplorable, disgusting, shabby, immoral." The chorus that clamored for resignation or impeachment swelled appreciably in volume.

10. *The White House Under Siege,* *May–July 1974*

While Nixon's remaining support steadily eroded, he continued to face demands for additional tapes and documents. With the release of the transcripts, he became unalterably committed to the line of defense he had been staking out all along: the investigators had everything that they needed; no more material would be forthcoming. The special prosecutor and the Judiciary Committee deployed against this position from different directions and in different ways, like two allied armies besieging a fortified area. With each measured advance of the attacking forces, Nixon's defensive lines shrank further in upon themselves.

Jaworski attacked through the courts. He had subpoenaed sixty-four tapes on April 18; Nixon responded on May 1 by filing a motion in Sirica's court to quash the subpoena. Before Sirica could rule on the motion, Jaworski went to Haig and St. Clair and proposed a compromise. If the White House would give him thirty-eight of the tapes, he would drop his request for the others. Furthermore, since this would be settling out of court, he would not have to reveal that the grand jury had named Nixon an "unindicted co-conspirator" in the cover-up. Nixon listened to some of the tapes that Jaworski wanted and turned down the compromise offer. He told St. Clair that he preferred to fight it out in court.

After a closed hearing on the president's motion, Sirica upheld Jaworski on May 20 and ordered Nixon to turn over the sixty-four tapes. When the White House announced that it would go to the court of appeals, Jaworski asked the Supreme Court to rule, and it agreed on May 31 to hear the case immediately. Formal opposing arguments before the court began on July 8. The central issue was crystal clear: who had final authority—the chief executive or the judiciary—to decide whether a president should obey a subpoena? St. Clair contended that forcing the president to comply would make him an "85 percent," rather than a "100 percent," executive. Although the president is not above the law, he went on, "the law can be applied to him in only one way, and that is by impeachment." The nation's form of government "is in serious jeopardy," Jaworski warned in rebuttal, "if the President, any President, is to say that the Constitution means what he says it does. . . . If he is wrong, who is there to tell him so?"

The president was now staking everything on two chances—that the Supreme Court would uphold his contention about impeachment as the only means of holding him to account, and that he would not be removed from office even if impeached. This invited attention to that other besieging army—the House Judiciary Committee—which had been slowly extending its lines toward the White House. Nixon's release of the transcripts had not satisfied the committee. While Democratic colleagues fumed and sputtered, Rodino released a statement in which his irritation was under control but evident: "We did not subpoena an edited White House version of partial transcripts of portions of Presidential conversations. We did not subpoena a Presidential interpretation of what is necessary or relevant to our inquiry. And we did not subpoena a lawyer's argument presented before we have heard any of the evidence."

Once again, however, the chairman resisted suggestions from angry Democrats that they institute contempt proceedings against the president. Going to court, he and Doar reminded them, would only trap them in a procedural thicket. ("How can we enforce a subpoena?" one member admitted. "He has a bigger army than we do.") The committee voted instead to send Nixon a letter on May 1 rejecting the transcripts and reprimanding him for not complying with their subpoena.

For the next six weeks the two sides lobbed shells back and forth that carried heavier charges with each exchange. The White House answered the committee's reprimand with the announcement that it was releasing no further Watergate materials. The committee responded on May 15 by issuing two new subpoenas for various White House documents, including eleven additional tapes. The president, in turn, said that he would comply neither with these subpoenas nor with "such further subpoenas that may hereafter be issued." The committee answered on May 30 with a blunt warning: continued defiance of its subpoenas might itself be grounds for impeachment, and continued withholding of evidence might justify the committee in drawing "adverse inferences" about what the material contained. The committee further stepped up the pace by subpoenaing forty-five more tapes and met the president's refusal to comply (on June 10) by issuing four new subpoenas covering another forty-nine tapes. With these subpoenas, Rodino and Doar abandoned legal remedies. The most important development, meanwhile, was the ebbing of partisanship in the committee; a substantial minority of the Republican delegation was now sufficiently exasperated to threaten the president with impeachment.

Partisanship, however, remained a problem. As a bulwark against impeachment it could not be bypassed (as the committee had bypassed the bulwark of a court fight), and if it could not be breached the whole assault upon the president's defensive lines might fail. Impeachment in form resembles the legal process—the House as grand jury, studying the evidence to see whether an indictment should be handed up; the Senate as trial court, deciding upon conviction or acquittal if the House indicts. But impeachment is inescapably a political process as well. Congress is a political institution, composed of political creatures whose careers depend, in various ways, both upon their loyalty to a party that supports them and upon their responsiveness to a constituency that elects them.

Rodino's task was fairly clear. In late June, he and his colleagues completed their review of the written evidence and began taking testimony from witnesses. At this point the committee seemed to be heading toward a recommendation for impeachment. To be effective, however, it would have to pass with at least a measure of bipartisan support. The House might vote not to impeach, and the Senate would almost assuredly vote to acquit, if the twenty-one Democrats alone backed the recommendation. (Rodino had to be careful even here, for the three southern Democratic members were uncommitted and wavering.) So the chairman's strategy was to avoid displays of partisanship and extremism, tread softly, and hope that the southerners and a few moderate Republicans—at least four, to be meaningful—would support an impeachment resolution.

Meanwhile, Nixon tried once again to bolster his sagging defenses. With the lines closing in, he fought back with every weapon at his command— patriotic speeches in the South, where his dwindling support was strongest; trips abroad, to the Mideast and to Russia, to emphasize his achievements in foreign policy and to bask in favorable television coverage before cheering crowds in Cairo or friendly consultation with Leonid Brezhnev in Moscow.

Nixon also tried to drive a wedge into Rodino's nascent bipartisan coalition. The White House, sniping constantly at the committee, accused it of engaging in a partisan witch hunt and a malicious campaign of innuendo and selective leaks. In late June, when the Democrats and Republicans fell into a savage quarrel over several matters, bipartisanship seemed destroyed. The White House redoubled its efforts, castigating the committee as a "kangaroo court" and a "partisan lynch mob." (The president's men, not for the first time, overplayed their hand here. Though Republican members were momentarily angry at their colleagues, they were basically proud of the way the committee had gone about its work and the way Rodino had led it, and many of them resented this intemperate criticism from without.)

11. Downfall of a President

The president's defenses gave way completely during the final week in July, when both the Supreme Court and the Judiciary Committee reached decisions that destroyed his last hopes of remaining in office. Chief Justice Burger, on July 24, read the decision in Jaworski's suit to obtain the sixty-four subpoenaed tapes. This was climax, as the very names on the docket attested: *United States of America* v. *Richard Nixon, President of the United States.* The Court ruled against the president unanimously, 8-0. Burger conceded that executive privilege had a legitimate constitutional basis; however, the evidence being sought did not enjoy such protection. Moreover, the chief justice added, executive privilege could not "prevail over the fundamental demands of due process of law in the fair administration of criminal justice." Burger ordered the president to give the tapes to Sirica "forthwith."

On the same day, the Judiciary Committee began its formal public debate before a nationwide television audience. The members had a few specific articles of impeachment before them for consideration, and they were well prepared. A few days earlier they had concluded their review of the evidence and listened to arguments in summation by both sides. St. Clair had once more presented the White House view: none of the evidence showed positive proof that the president had taken part in the cover-up or committed a specific criminal act. Doar had then submitted a 300-page review that included twenty-nine proposed articles of impeachment. What was at issue, Doar argued, was not a single criminal act but a "pattern of conduct." He concluded that "reasonable men acting reasonably would find the president guilty." The committee's minority counsel had presented a new argument; it was that the basic question was not guilt or innocence, but "whether the public interest would be served or disserved" by removing the president from office. This was Nixon's last line of defense.

Now the committee was ready to debate and decide, while the nation watched. The discussion as a whole was marked by dignity and occasional high eloquence; each member's seriousness of purpose, agony, and sincerity were clearly evident. By July 30, after thirty-five hours of debate, the committee had voted to send three articles of impeachment to the House of Representatives. The first two were the important ones: Article I charged the president with obstruction of justice; Article II charged him with abuse of power.[28]

The most telling aspect of this historic event was the achievement of substantial bipartisan support for Articles I and II. The vote on Article I was 27-11, with six Republicans joining the Democrats; on Article II, a seventh Republican defected and made the vote 28-10. Impeachment was now before the House, and the hope that it could be derailed by strict partisan alignment was all but gone.

What the president's defenders did not yet know was that their other hope of defeating impeachment—the absence of the "smoking gun" that

---

[28]Specifically, Article I indicted Nixon for obstruction of justice—through lies, deceit, withholding of evidence, and so on—in the cover-up. Article II indicted him for abuse of power, subversion of the Constitution, and so forth. Article III, which passed by a narrower margin and was not as important, indicted the president for refusal to heed the committee's subpoenas. The committee rejected two other articles relating to the bombing of Cambodia and income-tax evasion.

would prove a specific criminal act—had been dashed by the Supreme Court on July 24. One of the tapes that the court had ordered Nixon to turn over contained a conversation with Haldeman on June 23, 1972, in which the president had explicitly instructed his assistant to have the CIA fabricate a "national security" operation and keep the FBI away from Watergate. Here was incontrovertible proof that the president had ordered the cover-up, six days after the break-in, and had sought to subvert one government agency in order to prevent another one from investigating a crime. It would be difficult to conceive of a presidential directive that offered more specific evidence of obstruction of justice and abuse of power.

Nixon was in San Clemente when the court handed down its momentous decision. His immediate reaction was a resentful outburst against the three justices he had appointed—Burger, Blackmun, and Powell. However, there was no way out in the face of a unanimous court decision. Thus the president—knowing, as no one else yet knew, that compliance would almost certainly insure impeachment and conviction—reluctantly permitted St. Clair to announce that the White House would hand over the tapes as ordered. Then Nixon asked one of his aides to review the fatal June 23 tape to see if it was as bad as he feared it was. Within the next few days, while the Judiciary Committee wound up its debate and passed its resolutions, Haig and St. Clair also learned about the incriminating conversation. All of them were stunned. They had labored beyond the call of duty in Nixon's defense; they had believed in his innocence, yet he had been actively involved in the cover-up from the start. And he had lied about it—to his advisers, to the public, to Congress, even to his family—for over two years.

12. *Resignation*

While Nixon himself wavered and agonized, unwilling to surrender, Haig quietly set about to convince him that resignation was the only solution. In early August, Haig conveyed the news of the "smoking gun" tape to Vice-President Ford, cabinet members, Nixon loyalists on the Judiciary Committee, Republican leaders in House and Senate, and the rest of the White House staff. Nearly everyone felt betrayed; Nixon's remaining support, outside of a tiny corporal's guard of fanatics, simply vanished.

Meanwhile, the president was still undecided. He agreed that an accurate transcript of the damning conversation should be made public; in fact, he published it on August 5. But he accompanied it with an explanatory statement that suggested that he was not giving up. The June 23 conversation, he admitted, was "at variance" with certain of his previous statements; he had neglected to inform his counsel or anyone else about it. He regretted this "act of omission" and conceded the likelihood of impeachment. However, he urged the Senate to look at events "in perspective" and proclaimed his confidence "that the record, in its entirety," did not justify "the extreme step of impeachment and removal of a President."

The appeal, of course, was useless. The mind of the Senate—and the country—was already made up. Haig, determined to avoid actually recommending that the president resign, now deftly arranged to have the hopelessness of the situation brought home to Nixon from a source he could not ignore. Senator Goldwater, indignant beyond measure at this last, conclusive evidence of Nixon's culpability, was already seeking to convey a demand for resignation to the White House from a group of senior Republican senators. Haig and Goldwater conferred, and, on the afternoon of August 7, the senator from Arizona, accompanied by the Republican minority leaders, Senator Scott and Congressman John Rhodes of Arizona, had a final meeting with the president. Without urging resignation—Haig had cautioned them against this, fearing that it might make Nixon dig in and fight—the three Republican leaders quietly went over the prospects. Rhodes estimated that Nixon had no more than ten votes remaining in the House; Goldwater and Scott agreed that there were no more than ten or fifteen supporters left in the Senate.

In short, impeachment and removal were inevitable. Now even the president could see the futility of further resistance. He decided to resign. The careful Haig already had a writer at work drafting a resignation speech. Vice-President Ford met with the president for a thorough briefing session on Thursday, August 8.

It was all over, now, except for the formalities. The resignation speech, delivered from the White House to a huge national television audience at 9:00 P.M. on August 8, was quietly eloquent, the delivery calm and controlled. Nixon admitted that he had made some mistakes in judgment and expressed regret for any harm he might have done to others. But those mistakes, he insisted, had been made in what he believed at the time "to be in the best interests of the nation." Much of the speech was devoted to reviewing his accomplishments and voicing his hopes for the future of America. At no time did he admit wrongdoing or guilt. He was essentially announcing a political defeat, saying that he had decided to resign because his "political base" in Congress had shrunk to the point where he could no longer effectively lead. He was resigning, as he had always tried to govern, "in the interest of America."

On the following morning, again before a national audience, Nixon bade his staff good-by. He visibly controlled his emotions, and the ceremony was restrained and informal. The high drama and tension had gone before. Richard Nixon, his battle ended, now simply took his leave. He strolled with his wife and the Fords in friendly fashion across the White House lawn to the helicopter that would take him to his plane. In accordance with specified procedure Nixon had written to the secretary of state, formally announcing his resignation in a single sentence. It became effective at noon on August 9, with his plane high over middle America on its way to the Pacific coast.

The national disillusionment and sense of tragedy that had grown along with the dimensions of the scandal during the last eighteen months of his presidency were all too real, but the final days were quietly reassuring. The American constitutional system had worked, slowly but implacably. The transition occurred without a tremor. Gerald Ford took the oath of office on schedule at noon and announced, while the nation breathed a collective sigh of relief: "Our long national nightmare is over."

13. Epilogue: Why Watergate?

Over, but not forgotten. Americans were painfully aware that they had undergone a unique experience and had had a narrow escape. It was not merely that most people's ethical standards and sense of decency had been violated. The corruption of the Nixon administration had amounted to much more (Agnew aside) than an infestation of common felons and petty criminals in high office.[29] It had been a powerful force that sought to replace the American system of government with something very different—a force guided, moreover, by the man to whom citizens had given the largest popular vote and the greatest margin of victory ever accorded an American president. What had happened?

History provides answers that are always incomplete and never final. Even so, the search for them is both obligatory and rewarding, and Watergate is a subject that cries out for answers and lessons to be learned.

Watergate reflected and grew out of a paranoid state of mind. This is best understood by looking once again at the man who embodied it, transmitted it, and made it a powerful moving force—Richard M. Nixon himself. We have already described some of the attitudes and traits of character that helped to shape his political career (see pp. 892–893). These same attitudes and traits contributed strongly to the state of mind that took the president, his White House, and his country down the Watergate trail.

One cause of the paranoia was Nixon's kind of patriotism. Nixon loved his country deeply; he desired to safeguard American interests and do what he thought best for the United States. This was probably his strongest motive. National security, then, had a sacred priority in his mind. Since he, as president, was the guardian of that security, the nation's enemies were his enemies. Nixon's paranoia, moreover, made him reverse

---

[29] Among those who eventually pleaded guilty or were convicted on one or more charges in connection with Watergate were three former Cabinet members (Attorney Generals Kleindienst and Mitchell and Secretary of Commerce Stans); the president's top aides (John Ehrlichman and H. R. Haldeman); several others with important White House positions (including John Dean and Charles Colson); and a host of individuals who had held middle- and lower-echelon appointments in the Nixon administration.

this equation and see his own enemies as the nation's. (He was not the first patriot to fuse—and confuse—these categories.) He saw the most enemies, and the worst ones, at home. And they turned out to be everywhere.

First, there was the violent enemy. America had not been a very peaceful or orderly country during the four or five years before Nixon reached the White House, and it remained turbulent for a year or two after he got there: urban riots, campus riots, unruly mass demonstrations, bombings and arson, the militant destructiveness being preached and occasionally practiced by radical groups, and the counterculture's ostentatious flouting of moral standards (see pp. 616-620, 639-642, 860-863). Nixon and many of his countrymen were badly frightened by all of this and saw it as subversive of law, order, internal security, and civilized values.

Nixon's patriotism demanded an orderly, safe, domestic society. It was bound up equally with his vision of a secure and prosperous nation in a peaceful and stable international order. "World peace" was on his lips as frequently as "national security"; the two phrases dovetailed to form an image of what he hoped to achieve as president. Foreign affairs had always been his primary interest. World peace meant reducing international tensions, which in turn required intricate, patient, skillful diplomacy. He conducted several of these negotiations during his first term. All were difficult, all were important, and all—peace in Vietnam, Mideast accord, détente and arms agreement with the Soviet Union, rapprochement with China—depended in a measure upon confidentiality. But here again, maddeningly, "enemies" were at work—in this case the disloyal bureaucrats and unscrupulous reporters who leaked and published confidential information that could jeopardize delicate negotiations and thereby set back the cause of world peace.

This brought several other overlapping categories of "enemies" into Nixon's perception. One was the federal bureaucracy, which to the men who inherited it in 1969 seemed slow and unresponsive—because (in their view) it was staffed by inefficient paper shufflers and, even worse, by Democrats and liberals now devoted to subverting and sabotaging the policies of a Republican president. Another category was the so-called Liberal Establishment that Nixon had long resented.[30] A third group of

[30]Loosely defined, the Establishment embraced that network of self-assured, Ivy League–educated patricians and intellectuals who held most of the important positions in the interconnected worlds of government, finance, foundations, law, universities, and publishing based along the nation's northeastern corridor.

For a long time, Nixon and his conservative assistants believed that the whole Watergate furor stemmed from the hostility of the Liberal Establishment and their desire to "get" the president. "Our adversaries," one ardent speech writer maintained in July 1973, "do not simply wish to show Nixon's involvement [in Watergate], they wish to castrate the President, to strangle the New Majority in its crib, to reverse the democratic verdict at the polls in November. The Left has an enormous stake in Watergate; they have really nothing else."

Nixon himself summed it up in a talk with Dean in early March 1973, when the White House was still confident of being able to ride out the storm. The clamor, Nixon said, was only a crisis "among the upper intellectual types, the ass holes, you know, the soft heads . . . Basically it's the media, uh, I mean, it's the Establishment. . . . They're trying to use this to smear [us]."

enemies were the leaders of the news media, especially in the influential eastern journals and major television networks. Finally, there was Congress, with its Democratic majorities and its core of hostile liberals.

With the nation and its president encompassed about by so great a cloud of enemies, it was little wonder that the Nixon White House displayed a "siege mentality" long before the Watergate investigations made the siege a reality. From the very beginning Nixon and his close associates—most of them, like himself, from outside the Establishment and sharing his view of it—felt outnumbered, surrounded, hemmed in. They brought with them an atmosphere of suspicion, secrecy, and distrust. Not even their triumphs of the next four years would dissipate or diminish it.

To achieve his goals—peace and stability at home and abroad—Nixon needed to overcome or render harmless these enemies. This, in turn, meant bringing the bureaucracy, the administration, the news leaks, the street violence, and events in general under his *control*. All of this required power—a tremendous consolidation and expansion of presidential power. The instrumentality was the White House staff, the Praetorian Guard. Nixon strove to recruit bright young men who could get things done by working around or through the recalcitrant bureaucracy and the hostile Democratic Congress. Almost none of Nixon's staff had held office or experienced its responsibilities. They brought with them the campaign worker's habit of corner-cutting, a burning ambition, and a fierce, blind loyalty to their chief. They believed that the president was the indispensable man—a Saint George who, if loyally served, could slay all dragons. The president's men were not as bright as he (or they themselves) thought they were, but they were energetic, imaginative, unscrupulous, and determined. Overzealous in their efforts to do what they thought he wanted, they were frequently unable to distinguish between an outright directive and a petulant aside; both were apt to find their way into staff memos and become policy. To these men, the end justified the means. Results were what counted. The president's will was law, and no other law counted as heavily—not even the law of the land. Thus it was appropriate to strike at enemies by any means at hand—wiretapping, surveillance, sabotage, burglary, intimidation, falsehood, subversion, or obstruction of justice.

The nation was fortunate in that so many of the president's men were bunglers. An abler group might have succeeded in a subtle but systematic assault upon the American constitutional system and basic civil liberties. This statement is, of course, speculative. All that one can say is that during the direst constitutional crisis in American history, the instrumentalities created by the Founding Fathers to prevent tyranny worked. First, a free press sounded the danger alarm and set the process of investigation in motion. If, as is true, leadership was given by a few courageous reporters and newspapers, then this fact was all the greater testimony to the power of truth and to the utter necessity for a free press. Second, the oldest American constitutional principle—the separation of powers—worked to turn back this ambitious grab for executive power. The courts, while confirming the principle of legitimate executive privilege, never flinched in asserting that no person, least of all the president of the United States, is above the law. The House Judiciary Committee (and Congress, generally, once the facts were known) proved to be a bulwark against executive usurpation. Finally, the American people, slowly but inexorably, recognized the threat and rallied to the defense of their liberties. All these forces combined to drive a president from office.

It had never happened before. Perhaps it will never happen again. Perhaps future presidents with imperial ambitions will remember the lesson of Watergate—that, given the built-in mechanisms in the American constitutional system against the aggrandizement of power by one branch of the federal government, a counterreaction is inevitable, and that, so long as the American democracy survives in all its resiliency and power, it will ever be *"Sic semper tyrannis!"*

34

The Troubled Seventies

Watergate ushered in a period of uncertainty, frustration, and public distrust. Wherever one looked, faltering leadership and divided counsel were beset by problems of growing complexity and magnitude. Nothing seemed to be working right or going right.

In foreign affairs, the nation's capacity to influence or control events appeared doubtful, and troubles loomed on every hand. Another Mideastern conflict, the Yom Kippur War, broke out in the autumn of 1973, and yet another precarious cease-fire followed. Debacle and engulfment overtook the government of South Vietnam in 1975, and Communist regimes took over all of Indochina. World peace was threatened by protracted civil wars in Cyprus and Lebanon, by assorted guerrilla and border wars in Africa, and by chronic unrest and instability on every continent. Late in the decade, a revolution in Iran unseated a pro-Western ruler and upset a network of military, political, and economic considerations. A shift in the intricate triangular relationship among the United States, the USSR, and the Chinese People's Republic in 1978 merely added to the general uncertainty.

The root problems of the 1970s, certainly the most difficult ones, were economic. And at the root of the economic problems was the question of energy, most notably oil. The Yom Kippur War of 1973 prompted the major oil-producing countries to curtail shipments and drastically raise prices, which in turn subjected the United States and many other nations to fuel shortages, high inflation, and the worst economic slump since the 1930s. A long era of cheap and abundant energy had suddenly ended. The slump was over by 1976, but fuel prices continued to climb. For the United States—and, in differing degree, for most other countries—these were years of worsening inflation, sluggish or spotty economic growth, and nagging unemployment.

The post-Watergate years were also marked by a sense that political leadership was proving inadequate to the tasks at hand. President Nixon was virtually hamstrung by Watergate during his final year in office. Neither Republican Gerald R. Ford, who acceded to the presidency in August 1974, nor Democrat Jimmy Carter, who narrowly defeated Ford in the election of 1976, seemed able to bring the nation's economic problems under control, devise effective policies, or provide a sense of direction and restore public confidence.

Actually, the record of the seventies was far from unmitigatedly bad; setback and tribulation were accompanied by progress and achievement, especially in foreign affairs. But the problems and uncertainties were what weighed most heavily upon people's minds. Americans viewed the future with more misgivings than confidence as this difficult decade ended.

1. The President from Michigan

Both change and continuity marked Gerald R. Ford's accession to power in August 1974. Although at first glance the changes seemed striking, historians will probably give greater emphasis to the continuities. These could be observed in both foreign and domestic policies, and, despite the glaring fissure of Watergate, they give the administrations of Richard M. Nixon and his successor an underlying unity.

The change derived in large part from differences in temperament and personality. Nixon had been a loner; Ford was an affable, gregarious man, with a smile that came from within. Everyone, even his political opponents, liked him personally. Approachable and unpretentious, he radiated openness, candor, and a kind of rugged integrity. The new president underscored the differences and won further acclaim by promising that his administration would be an open one, featuring "communication, conciliation, compromise, and cooperation." Still anguished by Watergate, Americans were hugely appreciative. They also liked the modest, no-nonsense way in which their new leader got down to business.

The change in atmosphere was palpable and refreshing, yet the Ford administration proceeded essentially along the lines its predecessor had laid down. To begin with, neither Ford's background nor his outlook made a change in direction likely. Born in Omaha, Nebraska, on July 14, 1913, Ford grew up in Grand Rapids, Michigan. In 1935 he graduated from the University of Michigan, where he was a star football player, and he went on to work his way through Yale Law School. He obtained his law degree in 1941, returned to Grand Rapids to enter private practice, and enlisted in the navy after Pearl Harbor. Emerging a lieutenant commander after four years of service, he resumed his legal career. In 1948, with the backing of Senator Arthur Vandenberg, he ran for Congress from Michigan's Fifth District and proceeded to make the district his own, winning thirteen consecutive terms from 1948 to 1972. His career in Congress was marked by hard work, party loyalty, service on several important committees, and a steady advance into the upper ranks of the GOP, culminating in his selection as House Minority Leader in 1965.

On domestic issues, Ford was a conservative, perfectly reflecting majority sentiment in and around Grand Rapids; in foreign affairs he followed Vandenberg's example and became an internationalist. These positions made him doubly attractive to Nixon when the vice-presidency opened up in October 1973. A devoted GOP regular, widely respected and popular, the rugged, honest, firm-jawed congressman from Michigan seemed an ideal choice to succeed Agnew and, if need be, to take over as president. But when this happened, the very four-square qualities that endeared him to his constituents and his colleagues made for a predictable kind of leadership. Ford was not the man to break with tradition or attempt bold changes in American policy.

In any case, Ford inherited a situation that militated against new policies. Two problems insured continuity and lack of action in domestic affairs. One was an ongoing deadlock between a Republican president and a Democratic Congress, which stemmed partly from philosophical differences and partly from the rebellious, angry mood that Nixon and Watergate had engendered on Capitol Hill. The second problem was a troubled economy for which no satisfactory or readily agreed-upon solutions existed. Continuity in foreign affairs was provided chiefly by the indefatigable Henry Kissinger, who served both presidents as secretary of state from 1973 to 1977.

2. From Nixon to Ford: Legacy of Mistrust

Congress had been up in arms against the White House during most of Nixon's last eighteen months in office, and resentment of Watergate was the principal but by no means the only factor. Everyone wanted to bring the guilty parties to justice, to be sure, and the scandal had convinced most members of Congress that campaign financing stood in dire need of reform. But many members had become equally incensed by Nixon's calculated policy of impounding funds already appropriated by Congress (see pp. 949–950), and by the revelations of his unilateral acts of war in Cambodia (see pp. 949, 964).

Congress took action in each of these areas. Both houses passed a campaign finance bill before Nixon left office, and Ford signed the measure in October 1974.[1] In the matter of impoundment, several lower-court decisions in 1973–1974 ruled against specific presidential acts of withholding funds, but no one regarded the issue as settled until a ruling could be had from the Supreme Court. This came in *Train* v. *New York*, 1975, when the justices held that Nixon had lacked the authority to impound $9 billion appropriated by Congress for sewage treatment plants. Meanwhile Congress had moved to close the impoundment loopholes and tighten its control over federal spending by passing the Budget Reform Act in 1974.[2]

With regard to war making, Congress first tried to force an end to the bombing of Cambodia by denying the use of funds for that purpose. This effort resulted in a compromise whereby the air attacks were halted in August 1973 (see p. 949, n. 2). But the larger issue of the president's right to engage in acts of war remained, and Congress moved doggedly to limit his authority. It was no easy task. Nixon's determination to prevent any erosion of his powers was not limited to Watergate matters, and he successfully vetoed several bills in 1973 that he saw as weakening presidential authority. But as Watergate disclosures alienated more and more members of Congress, the majority who opposed him became large enough by November 1973 to pass the War Powers Act over his veto. The measure required the president, within forty-eight hours of any commitment of U.S. forces to hostile action overseas, to report all circumstances and details of such action to Congress, and to cease the operation within sixty days unless Congress approved it.

Although Ford began his term in an atmosphere of harmony and good will, his "honeymoon" with Congress was short. Watergate and the Nixon presidency had bequeathed a host of unsolved problems and a murky

---

[1] The Federal Elections Campaign Amendments of 1974 set limits on the amount of money that could be contributed and spent in political campaigns. Limits of $1,000 per individual and $5,000 per organization were placed on contributions to all primary, runoff, and general election campaigns, and neither individuals nor groups could contribute more than $25,000 per year to all candidates for federal office. The law also set limits upon unsolicited contributions, a candidate's own spending, and the amounts that could be spent on presidential primaries, nominating conventions, Senate and House races, and by political parties. It provided for optional public financing of presidential elections, set disclosure and reporting dates, and created an eight-member bipartisan supervisory board to oversee and enforce its complex provisions.

[2] The Budget Reform Act was a long-deferred move in the direction of reforming and improving the complex procedures by which funds were appropriated and allocated. It was an intricate piece of legislation that had great potential, but its success depended entirely on the will and resolve of each succeeding Congress to make the system work and keep the budgetary loopholes closed.

cloud of suspicions and resentments, and, for all his candor and integrity, Ford proved unable to escape this legacy. He startled the nation on September 8, 1974, with the announcement that he was granting Richard Nixon a "full, free and absolute pardon" for any crimes that the former president "committed or may have committed" during his term of office. The White House also announced an agreement giving Nixon custody of his presidential papers—including the notorious tapes, which were to be destroyed after his death. In short, Nixon would never have to stand trial or face the agony of possible conviction and a jail sentence, and the decision to disclose further information from the tapes would remain in his hands.

This news, coming a bare month after Nixon's resignation, sparked a national uproar and cost Ford a great deal of support. The new president undoubtedly acted with the best of intentions. He had real compassion for the ousted Nixon, who was broken in spirit and seriously ill.[3] The agreement that gave him possession of his papers was in keeping with a tradition as old as the republic.

Many Americans were highly indignant. Despite Ford's insistence that there had been no advance bargain or deal between himself and Nixon about the pardon, Watergate had created an atmosphere in which suspicions were bound to arise. Many believed that if Nixon had broken the law he should be tried and sentenced like any other private citizen. They regarded it as unfair that Nixon's subordinates were being tried and frequently sent to jail for their part in Watergate, while the man in whose service (and upon whose orders) they had acted was allowed to go free. The tapes agreement touched off another storm of criticism, which reflected a fear that the whole truth about Watergate might never be learned. Congress passed a law in December 1974 that undid the agreement and kept the papers and tapes under governmental control.[4]

The hue and cry subsided in time, but Ford never regained the bipartisan support that he had enjoyed before the pardon. Criticism and controversy increasingly dogged his heels. He was attacked from both sides for a

[3]Nixon had been suffering for months from recurrent phlebitis in his left leg, a condition that formed blood clots, and finally required major surgery. He was hospitalized in September and operated on in October, after which he went into shock and nearly died. He then began a slow recovery, but a panel of court-appointed physicians examined him in late 1974 and pronounced him in no condition to testify at the Watergate defendants' trial then in process. Certainly he would have been unable to undergo the rigors of his own trial for perhaps another year, but his recovery was eventually complete.

[4]Congress also created a national commission to study and report on the general question, which Watergate had elevated to importance for the first time, of who should own and have access to the official papers of departing public servants. The report, finally submitted to President Carter in 1977, concluded that "job related" papers of presidents, judges, and members of Congress should (under carefully defined conditions) become public property.

Nixon meanwhile had challenged the 1974 law. He sued the government to regain custody of the material, contending that it was his personal property. In Nixon v. Administrator of General Services, 1977, the Supreme Court, in a 7-2 decision, upheld the act and affirmed governmental custody of the Nixon documents.

related attempt to "bind up the nation's wounds" in September 1974 with a program of clemency for the thousands of men who had dodged the draft or deserted the army during the Vietnam War.[5] He drew a steady rumble of criticism for not moving fast enough to replace Nixon appointees in his administration and for some of the new appointments that he did make.

Another tempest grew out of Ford's nomination of Governor Nelson Rockefeller of New York as the next vice-president. The idea of adding this experienced GOP leader to the new administration won general acclaim at first, but Rockefeller's confirmation hearings soon disclosed that in previous years he had advanced a total of some $2 million, as gifts or forgiven loans, to a number of friends and associates who were also prominent public figures, including Secretary of State Kissinger. And, during the campaign of 1970 for governor of New York, Rockefeller had financed a derogatory biography of his Democratic opponent, former Justice Arthur Goldberg. It took Congress nearly four months to confirm the nomination. Rockefeller was finally sworn in on December 19, 1974, but public confidence in the appointment had dwindled and the Ford administration had been damaged. For the first time in its history, the United States had both a president and a vice-president who had not been chosen by the electoral process.

It was in this mood of suspicion and distrust that the nation entered the midterm elections of 1974. Although Ford campaigned hard for his party, the Democrats scored impressive victories at all levels. They gained 43 new seats in the House and 4 in the Senate, enlarging their majorities to 291-144 and 61-38 respectively. Democrats even elected a senator from Vermont, for the first time in the state's history. They made a net gain of 4 governorships, including California and New York, and added to their strength in many state legislatures. Voter turnout was low (38 percent), even for a midterm canvass, and suggested disillusionment with government and elected officials. Widespread independent voting and ticket splitting reinforced a long trend away from party regularity.

The new Congress was more liberal than the old one, as several conservatives in both parties retired or went down to defeat while moderates and liberals won handsomely.[6] It was also the youngest Congress to be

[5]The plan set up a clemency board to review cases of men already convicted. Those who had gone into exile to avoid arrest could obtain clemency by taking an oath of allegiance and doing up to two years of public service. Many of the men in question, joined by other opponents of the war, called the program punitive and claimed that accepting its conditions was tantamount to admitting their guilt. Veterans' organizations, on the other hand, condemned the plan as too lenient. The dispute made an interesting counterpoint to the pardon of Nixon, since many who criticized Ford for being too lenient in one case were themselves inclined toward leniency in the other.

[6]The number of blacks in the new House increased from 15 to 16, and the number of women, in spite of 4 retirements, increased from 16 to 18. Representative Ella Grasso resigned her seat in order to run for governor of Connecticut. Her victory made her the first woman to win such an office without succeeding her husband.

elected since the Second World War. More than ever, obviously, voters wanted new blood and a legislature less tainted by connection with recent events. This younger, more liberal Congress, with its sharp-eyed newcomers, was widely expected to raise ethical standards and improve the political tone in Washington.

Unfortunately, it was the high expectations rather than the Watergate legacy that began to evaporate. Two sets of revelations during 1975 and 1976 jolted public confidence anew. People began to hear new evidence of widespread past misconduct and abuse of power by the federal intelligence agencies,[7] and they discovered that political corruption and immorality had infiltrated Congress as well as the presidency and involved Democrats as well as Republicans. If one positive result of these continuing disclosures was a heightened awareness of the need to improve ethical standards in all branches of government, the chief effect was to add to a growing public cynicism about the whole political process. None of this made the task of devising and implementing new programs any easier.

3. Economic Troubles and Energy Crisis

Ford's other domestic inheritance was a worsening economy. Prices, after holding fairly steady during 1972, had risen sharply as soon as Nixon removed controls under Phase Three of his economic program (see pp. 915, 948–949). While labor leaders complained that "voluntary compliance" with the new wage-price guidelines was resulting in runaway prices and profits at the expense of wages, inflation became so bad during the spring of 1973 that Nixon ordered a sixty-day freeze of consumer prices in June and followed this by the imposition of Phase Four a month later. The price freeze was lifted in favor of a system of "phased" or modified controls that tied price increases to cost increases and retained a flexible 5.5-percent guideline for wage increases. Inflation continued anyway, and Congress let the system lapse in April 1974.

[7]Persistent news stories prompted both president and Congress to launch full-scale inquires in early 1975. The main focus of the new round of disclosures was the CIA, which was found to have been engaging in large-scale domestic spying and burglary, plots to overthrow undesirable foreign leaders, "mind control" experiments, and a variety of other dubious actions. Similar violations, chiefly in the realms of surveillance, breaking and entering, intimidation, and the compiling of dossiers on suspected political dissidents, had been occurring in the FBI, the IRS, the NSA, and army intelligence units. Although the scope and scale of these activities had reached a peak during the Nixon administration, many dated back to the fifties and sixties.

The Justice Department issued new rules in 1976 to bring the FBI under tighter rein, and its new director, Clarence Kelley, issued a public apology on behalf of the bureau. President Ford, in that same year, gave the National Security Council direct authority over covert operations and appointed an independent advisory board to review all intelligence-gathering activities.

These inflationary pressures stemmed from a variety of causes. The return of soaring prosperity in 1972, after the mild recession of 1970–1971, was one factor; swelling consumer demand followed by the sudden removal of controls in early 1973 were in themselves enough to drive prices upward. But the problem went deeper than that. The attempt to reduce America's balance-of-payments deficit and ease pressure on the dollar by successive devaluations in 1971 and 1973 (see p. 917) had reduced the trade deficit by stimulating American exports, only to create another problem. Foreign buyers equipped with great swatches of bargain-rate dollars engaged in a competitive scramble for American goods and created scarcities that drove domestic prices up faster than ever in 1973 and 1974.

All of this might have been manageable had it not been for the sudden injection of a deadly new factor in late 1973. This was the energy crisis, which dealt a staggering blow to the economies and future prospects of industrial and developing nations alike. Herein lay the problem of the epoch. It was, and remains, an issue of transcendent significance, and a few words of explanation and background are in order.

The energy crisis appeared after a decision in October 1973 by the Arab members of the Organization of Petroleum Exporting Countries (OPEC) to cut back on their oil production and place an embargo on shipments to the Netherlands and the United States. The cutbacks were partly aimed at reminding the industrial nations where their interests lay in the Mideastern conflict, and the embargoes were a response to America's massive military support for Israel in the Yom Kippur War and to what Arab leaders regarded as the Netherlands's pro-Israeli policies.[8]

Every industrial nation experienced dislocations and shortages. The Dutch took all manner of austerity measures, including a ban on Sunday driving, and Japan had to declare a state of emergency. The Western governments experimented variously with rationing, allocation of scarce supplies, a shorter work week (in Britain), and other restrictions aimed at conserving energy. The United States, which had large oil supplies of its own and continued to receive shipments from non-Arab producers, suffered less than its allies did. But the jolt was severe, and the inconveniences and discomforts were real: shortages of heating oil, "brownouts" resulting from voltage reductions by hard-hit power companies, industrial layoffs, and a gasoline scarcity that forced filling stations to close on Sundays and dole out dwindling supplies to long lines of impatient motorists on weekdays.

It was another OPEC action, however, that had the most lethal effect. The energy crisis became a chronic, damaging, and potentially disastrous

---

[8]Later in the year, in order to strengthen their ties with black Africa, the Arab producers extended the embargo to South Africa, Rhodesia, and Portugal, which was still trying to suppress nationalist independence movements in its African colonies. The ban on shipments to Holland hurt all northern Europe because of the importance of Rotterdam as a refining and transshipment center.

feature of economic life after 1973, in America and elsewhere, not because oil producers declared embargoes or reduced their output, but because they raised their prices—repeatedly and hugely. By January 1974, within a space of less than three months, the price of oil had quadrupled. It would not come back down; far from representing a temporary upsurge, the new price was maintained for months and then began a series of additional rises at measured intervals for the balance of the decade. Not since the early 1930s had so many of the world's economies faced so cataclysmic a change.

The market price of crude oil had jumped after the Second World War, then held remarkably steady at reasonable levels during the great period of industrial growth in Japan and the West after midcentury. Indeed, the seemingly endless abundance of oil at stable prices, in the face of a mounting worldwide demand, had done much to make that growth possible.[9] But this state of affairs could not continue indefinitely, and by the late sixties various forces making for change had begun to surface.

In the immediate postwar years the United States was the world's largest oil producer. The great Mideastern fields, though they had been important since the 1920s, were operating at a fraction of capacity until European and other Old World markets began their postwar recovery. While American oil production doubled between 1947 and 1970, Mideastern production increased steadily at a rate of 50 percent every five years, began increasing even faster around 1960, and first equaled the North American output in 1965. At this point the two areas together accounted for about half of total world output. By 1972 the Middle East was producing more than one-third of the world's oil, the United States about one-fifth.

Meanwhile, several turning points had been reached in the late fifties. By 1955, Mideastern oil was being brought from the ground so cheaply that more and more independent American refining companies began investing in Mideastern fields and importing oil that could stand the transportation charges and still undersell domestic oil in the American market. American oil imports rose from 14 percent of total domestic consumption in 1954 to 19 percent in 1957, and price stability was threatened. Since this development coincided with the Suez crisis and the closing of the canal (see pp. 804–806), Washington began to worry about the nation's increasing use of foreign oil, especially from so vulnerable and unstable a

---

[9]Despite the great increase in demand during these years, oil was so plentiful that prices could have been even lower than they were—with unpredictably disruptive effects upon the entire industry—had it not been for the powers and policies of the major oil companies. These companies controlled a sufficient proportion of the world's productive, refining, and marketing facilities to keep the rate of oil production in the fifties and sixties from rising faster than demand, thus keeping prices (and a satisfactory level of profits) stable.

region as the Middle East, and placed a quota on imports in 1959. Four years later this quota was fixed at 12.2 percent of domestic production.[10]

The import quota had two consequences. First, it induced American refiners to utilize domestic reserves at a faster rate in order to satisfy the booming home market. Significantly, this began happening just as the country's reserve supply leveled off. For the next few years, while production mounted, the volume of proved reserves remained constant and then started an ominous decline in the late sixties. Second, the companies that could no longer flood the American market with cheap Mideastern oil began selling it at competitive cut-rate prices to Europe and Japan.

Falling prices for their product on the world market led the oil-producing nations, in their turn, to take countermeasures. These nations had originally granted concessions to the Western companies and consortiums that sought to extract oil from their territories, in return for a small fixed royalty of a few cents per barrel. In the early fifties they had demanded, and obtained, new agreements that divided oil revenues with the companies on a fifty-fifty basis, and thus gained a share in the higher price levels of that period. And in 1960 the major producing countries—Saudi Arabia, Iraq, Iran, Kuwait, and Venezuela—created OPEC in an effort to restore prices by a coordinated policy of controlling and prorating production. OPEC managed to keep prices from falling any further during the sixties but could not bring about a rise, and its efforts to limit and control production were not overly successful. The member states were, however, steadily learning more about the complex workings of the world oil trade. After 1970, OPEC having expanded to include most other major producing countries, they became convinced of the need to obtain higher revenues from their rich petroleum deposits.[11]

Two moves thus came to a head at about the same time. One was a series of agreements exacted by OPEC from the oil companies in the years 1968-1971, whereby the producing nations obtained higher prices and larger shares of the revenues through increased taxes and part ownership (at times amounting to outright nationalization) of many of the companies.

[10]National security was, of course, an issue, but John M. Blair, in *The Control of Oil* (New York, 1976), argues convincingly that the real impetus behind the import quota was the desire on the part of the major oil companies (whose rates of return on sales in the United States were dropping) to protect the domestic price from foreign competition. The quota certainly worked that way. Domestic prices were stabilized, at a cost to the American consumer of several billion dollars over the next decade. In economic terms it was an affordable cost, but the reckoning in terms of energy supplies would come in the 1970s.

[11]By the early seventies OPEC consisted of the original five nations plus Libya, Nigeria, Algeria, Indonesia, Ecuador, and the Persian Gulf sheikdoms—every major non-Communist producer outside of the United States and Canada.

Some of the nations, such as Libya, had begun to worry about the finite nature of their oil deposits and wanted to earn more money while the resource lasted. All the producers, moreover, wanted more revenue to cover the increased prices of food and industrial products that they were importing, and to pay for their own industrial development.

OPEC members, encouraged by the success of this policy, which raised the world market price of crude oil in slow stages by some two-thirds between 1970 and the fall of 1973, were soon contemplating further increases.

The second move began with a realization by the American oil companies that domestic reserves were not only dwindling but were becoming progressively more expensive to obtain. Faced simultaneously with controlled prices, growing demand, and mounting production costs after 1970, the oil companies responded predictably: they began to cut back on production. Domestic output leveled off in 1971 and then started to decline, even though the rate of domestic consumption continued to rise on a curve that ascended more steeply every year.

What kept the effects from becoming noticeable immediately was a sharp increase in imports after 1970. This was made possible by the fact that so-called residual oils, used largely by utility companies to generate electricity, had been exempted from the import quota. For a time, therefore, the American oil companies devoted nearly all of their reduced output to gasoline and the lighter and middle distillates (for diesel fuel, heating oil, and petrochemicals) and sold imported residuals to the utility companies. But by early 1973 the insatiable national demand was running sufficiently ahead of supply to become a problem. While American farmers, truckers, manufacturers, and motorists fumed at chronic fuel shortages, domestic output did not increase, and oil imports reached an all-time high, amounting to over one-third of domestic production. OPEC, which dealt extensively with American oil companies, took due note.

Everything, in short, pointed to the sudden onset of an energy crisis in the fall of 1973. The warnings—shortages, brownouts, reports of declining American reserves and growing dependence on foreign oil—had all been evident for months. But hardly anyone outside the oil industry had paid much attention, and the succession of embargoes, cutbacks, and price increases levied by OPEC caught the United States and other major oil users almost completely unaware.

The Yom Kippur War triggered, but did not cause, the energy crisis, which had been long in the making and would have occurred anyway.[12] Nor is it necessary to search for an evil conspiracy among the OPEC nations and the major oil companies. They did cooperate, to be sure, and the new high prices after January 1974 were maintained because the companies supported OPEC by utilizing the elaborate control mechanisms

[12] Although the embargoes and cutbacks in October 1973 were proclaimed by OPEC's Arab members, the drastic price hikes between October and January—the real source of the energy crisis—were made by the entire OPEC group, which included such important non-Arab producers as Nigeria, Venezuela, and Indonesia. A desire to obtain higher prices rather than anti-Israeli sentiment underlay this action; the war merely afforded a pretext.

that they had perfected over the years to keep world production geared to world demand.[13]

The point is that it was in the interest of both OPEC and the oil companies to obtain higher prices. Their product was a nonrenewable fossil fuel that existed in finite quantities. The United States and many other regions had already entered a period of declining reserves, and even the incredibly rich Mideastern field would run out someday. Oilmen first became conscious of these facts of life during the 1960s, and the decision by OPEC and corporate directors to control output and raise prices was merely an act of prudence.

The real fault, if fault must be found, lay instead with the great industrial nations, whose leaders and citizens were acting as though cheap fuel would last forever. This was particularly true of the United States, where habits of energy consumption had reached an extreme of mindless profligacy. The brutal fact at the center of the energy crisis for this country, as President Nixon soberly pointed out in the fall of 1973, was that the United States had 6 percent of the world's population and used 33 percent of its energy.

The actual shortages were brief and temporary. The Arab nations had lifted their embargo by the spring of 1974, and fuel supplies were back to normal. What really hurt was the rise in price, which turned out to be permanent. There seemed to be no end to the ill effects. When oil prices shot up through the ceiling, all other prices sooner or later had to increase with them, and virtually every calculation by which bankers, manufacturers, utility and transportation companies, governments, investors, farmers, and consumers throughout the non-Communist world made their decisions and charted their courses had to be recast.

For oil had seeped its way into the very core of the world's economy. It was the essential ingredient for air, truck, auto, rail, and water traffic and for most major industries. It had become a prime factor in each of humanity's basic needs—shelter, clothing, food. Oil heated millions of homes directly and millions of others by fueling generators at power plants; oil in the form of petrochemicals was indispensable to the manufacture of synthetic fibers and plastics and to the output of pesticides and fertilizers, upon which modern agriculture had become totally dependent. While the prices of all these vital commodities climbed remorselessly after 1974, other countries producing raw materials that were in worldwide demand—coffee, cocoa, bauxite, cobalt, and so on—raised their prices in order to help pay for their oil; these prices, too, were passed along to

---

[13]Along with cooperation from the oil companies, OPEC's ability to cut back production rather than reduce prices when world demand fell off stemmed from two sets of realities in the oil-producing states. Those with smaller reserves, such as Libya, were willing to curtail production so as to make their supply last longer; those with the greatest reserves, such as Saudi Arabia, were willing to cut back because they had more money from oil revenues than they could readily absorb.

MEDIAN FAMILY and PER CAPITA INCOME
1975

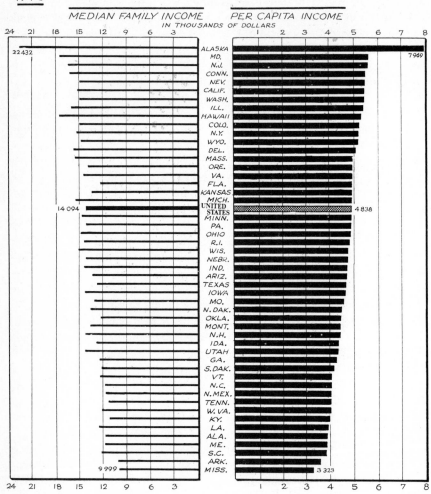

MEDIAN FAMILY INCOME   PER CAPITA INCOME

IN THOUSANDS OF DOLLARS

consumers everywhere. Inflation, already a problem in many Western countries, became global—and grew worse.[14]

Financial difficulties also mounted. The sudden quadrupling of the price of oil deranged trade balances by adding billions of dollars to the cost of imports. The transfer of these billions to the credit of the oil-producing states put a huge burden upon the international banking system. It had to find ways of handling the enormous flow of debits and credits and to recycle the oil money back to the debtor nations in the form of purchases, investments, and loans by OPEC's oil-rich governments.

And for the United States, galloping inflation in 1974—the first year of a "double digit" rate—was accompanied by a recession in the final quarter. Shortages and rising prices of gasoline led to a slump in the automobile industry, which experienced a decline in sales for the first time in years. Real wages in 1974 were 5 percent lower than in 1972. Capital outlays for business expansion started to decline as inventories crept up and retail sales fell off. Housing underwent a pronounced lag in 1974, off some 33 percent from the 1972 high, as mortgage interest rates soared in reaction against inflation. Unemployment, which had been under 5 percent in 1973, rose to 6.5 percent by November 1974 and rose even faster in 1975.

Indeed, during most of 1975 the country was mired in the worst recession of the postwar era. Many key industries, notably automobiles, steel, and construction, experienced lean times. Unemployment reached 9.2 percent in May, the highest rate since the 1930s; the level was even higher among industrial workers, minorities, and young people. Although there were signs of recovery by the year's end, the economy was still wobbly from the effects of the rise of oil prices. The return of prosperity in 1976 was accompanied by higher inflation and a realization that the recovery was both fragile and incomplete.

4. Republican Response

The Nixon and Ford administrations had nearly four years between them in which to cope with the energy crisis and its by-products. They were hampered by a deep public skepticism about governmental pronouncements, sharp disagreements between the White House and congressional majorities, and a lack of consensus about remedies and indeed about the problem.

[14]Developing nations suffered even more than the industrial countries. They desperately needed oil for both their infant industries and, in petrochemical form, as fertilizer to increase agricultural output, which usually ran behind the rate of population growth. Unlike the industrial states, the developing countries often lacked the means to pay for the higher-priced oil, and they faced the grim alternatives of going ruinously into debt or doing without.

Nixon took several steps during 1973 to deal with the energy situation. He attacked the first shortages by lifting the oil import quota. He created a Federal Energy Office to formulate and direct national policies, and an office of energy conservation to promote ways of saving fuel. He announced a five-year energy research and development program to begin in 1975. In September 1973 he submitted a legislative program calling for new offshore facilities for giant oil tankers, an Alaskan oil pipeline to tap the large reserves in that state, and an easing of strip-mining standards to permit more surface coal production.

When October brought the embargo and the first major price hikes, Nixon said that what had been a problem was now a crisis, and he made some stronger proposals. He did not get all the emergency authority that he asked for, but several steps were taken. In addition to authorizing the 800-mile Trans-Alaska pipeline, Congress passed the Emergency Petroleum Allocation Act in December 1973. It sought to stimulate production by raising the controlled price of domestic oil to $5.25 a barrel (a $1 increase) and by providing that oil produced from new wells, or from existing wells in excess of the 1972 volume, would not be subject to controls. The act also empowered the new energy office (soon to be transformed into a full-fledged agency, the Federal Energy Administration) to allocate scarce fuel supplies. The new energy director promptly ordered a cutback in jet-fuel production, directed refineries to make more heating oil and less gasoline for the coming winter months, and allotted as much fuel as possible to industry in an effort to prevent factory shutdowns and layoffs. The maximum speed limit was set at fifty-five miles per hour.

Nixon looked further ahead and introduced a plan in November 1973 called "Project Independence," whereby the country would strive to achieve self-sufficiency in energy by 1980. It was an ambitious program, which he likened to the Manhattan Project of the Second World War and the Apollo Space Program of the 1960s. Project Independence called for an increase in domestic oil production by tapping the Alaskan field and drilling for offshore deposits, an increase in the output of natural gas, a greatly increased use of coal and nuclear power, the conversion of coal to synthetic oil and natural gas, the extraction of oil from shale, and the development of renewable sources like solar and geothermal energy and the wind and tides. Experts called the target date of 1980 totally unrealistic but pronounced the goal laudable. To undertake the search for new sources Congress created the Energy Research and Development Administration (ERDA) in 1974.[15]

All of this marked a creditable beginning. Unfortunately, the initial momentum could not be sustained, and the effort to come to grips with the energy problem was soon reduced to a lot of noisy wheel spinning. By the

[15]The ERDA supplanted the old AEC, taking over that agency's research and development functions as part of its overall program to develop new agency sources. The AEC's regulatory functions were transferred to another new agency, the Nuclear Regulatory Commission.

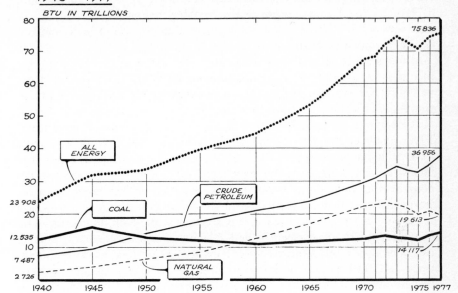

ENERGY CONSUMPTION, *TOTAL*
1940 – 1977

BTU IN TRILLIONS

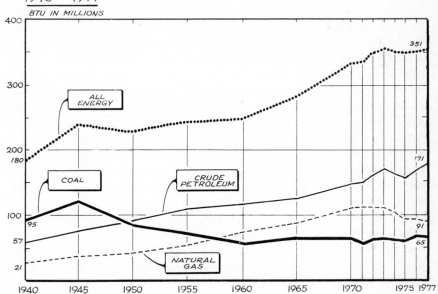

ENERGY CONSUMPTION, *PER CAPITA*
1940 – 1977

BTU IN MILLIONS

time that Ford became president the sense of urgency had vanished, and this proved to be a fatal setback. With supplies back to normal by mid-1974, most Americans ceased to worry about the problem. They reset their thermostats, filled their tanks, ignored the new speed limit, and resumed buying large cars.

In the absence of a sense of crisis, the debate over policy degenerated into theoretical disputes and wrangling among interest groups. Environmentalists opposed the new energy plans because they saw menace in the proposals for offshore drilling, increased strip mining, greater use of coal, and efforts to extract oil from coal and shale. Plans to build more nuclear power plants and to develop so-called fast breeder reactors stirred a new wave of antinuclear protest. Resentment of the huge profits that oil companies were making from the new high prices created a movement in Congress for tying energy measures to a "windfall profits" tax that would recapture what many regarded as ill-gotten gains. Oil-state senators opposed such a tax and occasionally teamed up with environmentalists—in what Senator Henry Jackson called "the most unusual coalition I have ever seen"—to vote against energy legislation. In a related matter, both Nixon and Ford ran into prolonged opposition when they sought to deregulate the prices of domestic oil and natural gas. While the White House maintained that deregulation would encourage conservation and stimulate production of these commodities by allowing their price to rise to the world market level, Democrats held that such a policy would add to inflationary pressures and bear most heavily upon low-income families.

Deregulation, windfall profits, environment—in one way or another these issues got in the way of every attempt to pass energy legislation during the next few years. Nixon vetoed an energy act in March 1974 because Congress added a windfall-profits tax to the items he had originally requested, and Ford found himself at odds with a congressional majority from the very start. Ford's energy program, which he advocated in vain throughout 1975, stressed voluntary conservation. It also called for stiff fees on foreign oil to reduce imports, deregulation of domestic oil and natural gas, production of oil from the naval reserve lands, and an easing of environmental restrictions to encourage greater use of coal. Congress saw all of this as spurring inflation and aiding business at the expense of consumers, and refused to enact any of it. Democrats advocated financing energy development by an increase in the federal gasoline tax and an excess-profits tax on the oil companies. They also urged continuation of price controls and tax incentives to encourage the manufacture and use of fuel-efficient automobiles. But they could not put this together into a measure that commanded enough support to override a veto, and the result was stalemate.

After much effort, Congress and the president finally agreed on a compromise bill that Ford signed in December 1975. Key provisions of the Energy Policy and Conservation Act included (1) authorizing the FEA to order utility companies to switch from oil or natural gas to coal; (2) increasing the president's authority over supplies, allocation, and production of energy; (3) giving the president standby authority to impose gas rationing and conservation measures; (4) creating a billion-barrel strategic petroleum reserve; (5) setting mandatory fuel economy standards for post-1977 automobiles, looking toward a 26-mpg average by 1985; and (6) extending oil price controls into 1979 and rolling back the average market price of domestic oil by about one dollar per barrel. No one cared much for the new law, which contained some useful features but constituted little more than a modest step along the road to Project Independence. Yet the government took no further action on energy for the balance of Ford's term.

Comparable difficulties and disagreements hampered the quest for other economic action. The great dilemma of the 1970s was to experience both inflation and recession at the same time. Since the nation's economic problems were closely interrelated, every attempt to alleviate one difficulty threatened to make another one worse. Moreover, each proposal was supported by some interest groups and bitterly opposed by others. Even as energy measures had run afoul of inflationary considerations, so the battle against inflation impeded energy reform and slowed economic recovery, while efforts to stimulate the economy made inflation worse. Lack of progress was virtually insured by opposing philosophies. Nixon and Ford were more worried about inflation and worked toward balanced budgets, reduced spending, and monetary policies aimed at decreasing the inflation rate. Democratic majorities were more worried about unemployment; they tended to favor tax cuts and public-works legislation, and feared that budget cutting would jeopardize welfare and poverty programs.

The lines were drawn early and stayed firm. Since Ford's campaign against inflation stopped short of anything resembling wage and price controls, which he detested, his anti-inflation policy relied heavily upon appeals for voluntary action, tight fiscal and monetary policies, and the veto. He publicly avowed his determination to fight all legislation that he regarded as inflationary and vetoed some fifty bills during his twenty-nine months in office. Nixon, too, had used the veto for this purpose, and although Democrats were able to override on a few occasions, especially after the elections of 1974, for the most part Congress either sustained the vetoes or settled for scaled-down compromises that the White House could accept. At the same time, the majority repeatedly ignored or emasculated presidential proposals, and the lack of rapport between the two branches was almost as pronounced during Ford's term as it had been during Nixon's last two years.

The government still managed to enact a tolerable amount of legislation in the period 1973-1976. Preoccupation with Watergate, war powers, and impoundment in 1973 kept other legislative activity to a minimum, but Congress did pass a Federal Aid Highway Act, which, for the first time, authorized the use of the $6-billion Highway Trust Fund for urban mass transit. Congress also approved an increase in social security benefits and limited home rule for the District of Columbia, and extended governmental price supports for wheat, feed grains, dairy products, and cotton.

The record in 1974 was more impressive. In addition to budget and campaign reforms, which we have noted, Congress enacted important school-aid and housing legislation[16] and established federal standards and an insurance program for private pension plans. A new $12-billion appropriation to support mass transit set a precedent by permitting aid for operating as well as construction costs. In other actions, Congress gave the president broad authority to negotiate for the reduction of trade barriers, passed a phased minimum wage increase to $2.30 per hour by 1976 and extended coverage to another 7 million workers. Despite presidential opposition, lawmakers attacked the recession by appropriating more than $3 billion for public service jobs and an extension of unemployment compensation.

Little happened during 1975. Firmly on guard against inflationary action, the president vetoed no fewer than seventeen bills; only four were overridden. Congress and president finally agreed upon a compromise energy bill, as we have seen, and reached comparable agreement on a temporary tax cut (desired by Democrats) in return for a congressional pledge to restrain budgetary outlays (desired by Ford) in the coming fiscal year. The most important action was a seven-year extension of the Voting Rights Act of 1965 and its expansion to include Hispanics, Indians, Asian Americans, and Alaskan natives, as well as blacks.

Although the session of 1976 fell short of Democratic expectations, Congress won a few victories. It passed a $4-billion public-works bill over Ford's veto, extended and expanded a public service jobs program first enacted as a temporary measure three years earlier, and extended federal programs to aid higher education. At Ford's urging the lawmakers continued the revenue-sharing program. They also passed a tax-reform law that tightened the restrictions on tax-shelter investments, increased the taxes on high incomes, continued the personal and corporate cuts of 1975, and simplified and shortened the tax code.

---

[16]The Elementary and Secondary Education Act of 1965 was amended and extended, with a four-year, $25-billion appropriation that consolidated several grant programs and altered and extended several others, including aid to the handicapped and compensatory education for the disadvantaged. The most controversial feature of this complex measure was a busing provision that represented a compromise between pro- and antibusing factions. The new law prohibited busing children beyond the school next closest to their homes but permitted exceptions where courts ruled that a longer ride was necessary to guarantee a student's right to attend an integrated school.

The new housing law set up a three-year, $8.6-billion program of so-called block grants (as opposed to categorical grants, which were specifically earmarked) for community development. It also established a rental-assistance program for people with low and moderate incomes and reactivated some subsidy programs that the Nixon administration had suspended in 1973.

These were not, all in all, years of striking legislative accomplishment. National health insurance, a gun law, stronger energy proposals, a consumer protection agency, welfare revision, strip-mining legislation, and a revised Clean Air Standards Act were among the many measures that failed to pass during 1976. Democrats resented the Ford vetoes and hoped to make a campaign issue out of them, but there were indications that the public had grown leery of too much spending and was pessimistic about the efficacy of reform legislation.

5. GOP Foreign Policy: Shuttle Diplomacy and Congressional Power

The dominant figure in American foreign policy during the mid-1970s was Henry A. Kissinger, who had been Nixon's national security adviser since 1969. He retained this post when Nixon appointed him secretary of state in August 1973, and he served in that dual capacity for the remainder of Nixon's term and most of Ford's.[17] Kissinger brought a wide range of experience to his Washington assignments. A former professor of government and international affairs at Harvard, author of respected books and articles on foreign policy, and holder of several directorships, consultantships, and advisory positions, Kissinger had a well-articulated philosophy of international affairs and an intense desire to exert influence in foreign policy.

Kissinger was a political realist. His goal in world affairs was a continually adjusting balance of power that all nations would have an interest in maintaining. He stressed the importance of flexibility, practicality, phased negotiations, a careful analysis of available options, and personal diplomacy. Not since the era of Dean Acheson and John Foster Dulles at mid-century had so influential a figure headed the State Department. Like those illustrious predecessors, Henry Kissinger was a controversial figure whose achievements were marred, in the eyes of critics, by excessive ambition, love of power, and a streak of ruthlessness.[18] Whatever evaluation future historians may make, there can be no denying the importance of his role during the Nixon-Ford years.

[17]Kissinger served as secretary of state throughout Ford's term, but Ford appointed a new national security adviser in November 1975.

[18]Opponents saw him as an unscrupulous and Machiavellian operator whose concern for success at any price fitted well with the shoddy moral tone of the Nixon administration. Kissinger was implicated, in ways that are still murky, in some of the early wiretapping incidents in Nixon's first term, and his drive for power included some maneuvering and corner cutting.

His conduct of foreign affairs also alarmed some observers. For a devastating indictment of his policies and actions in Indochina, see William Shawcross, *Sideshow: Kissinger, Nixon, and the Destruction of Cambodia* (New York, 1979).

The major problem area in foreign affairs during 1973 was the Middle East, where, as we have seen (pp. 959–960), the fourth Arab-Israeli conflict in twenty-five years began on October 6. A concerted invasion by Syrian and Egyptian forces caught Israel in a rare offguard moment. The Arabs fought much more effectively than in earlier contests and recorded several initial gains on both the Golan Heights (Syrian) and Suez (Egyptian) fronts. Determined Israeli counterattacks launched first against Syria and then against Egypt were terribly costly in men and equipment and could not have been sustained without massive United States aid. The Soviets were equally busy replenishing the Arab armies, which were also being supported by 18,000 Iraqis and units from Morocco and Saudi Arabia. Jordan sent troops to fight alongside Syrians on the Golan Heights but did not open a third front.

Within a week the Israelis had pushed the Syrian invaders back across the 1967 boundaries and were rolling their tanks toward Damascus. A few days later, although they had lost some 400 square miles of Sinai desert to the Egyptians, they were able to establish a bridgehead on the west side of the Suez Canal and enlarge it with a sizable force. Material losses on both sides were heavy.

The UN, supported by both superpowers, had been hard at work upon a cease-fire proposal. A Security Council resolution, embodying a formula agreed upon in Moscow by Brezhnev and Kissinger, was approved on October 22 and tentatively accepted by the three warring states. In the absence of a policing mechanism, however, Israel decided to strengthen her bargaining position and quickly fanned troops and armor out from the Suez bridgehead; they advanced toward Cairo and trapped an Egyptian army on the west bank of the canal. On the Syrian front Israeli units pressed closer to Damascus.

For a time everything, including world peace, seemed to hang in the balance. With the deterioration of Egypt's position, President Anwar el-Sadat on October 24 invited the United States and the USSR to send a joint task force to police the cease-fire. Moscow immediately accepted, but Washington, which preferred a UN truce force and did not want to see Russian troops in the Middle East, refused. This brought the two great powers into a brief but dangerous confrontation. The Kremlin threatened a unilateral airlift of Soviet troops. This, together with reports of Russian military movements, induced the American government, at about midnight on October 24, to place its forces on worldwide alert.

Whether or not this was, as Nixon later called it, "the most difficult crisis we've had since the Cuban confrontation of 1962," it resolved itself quickly. The Security Council passed a resolution calling for a 7,000-man peace-keeping force that would not include troops from any of the major powers, and Russia concurred. Kissinger went to the Middle East and persuaded Israel and Egypt to accept a six-point cease-fire, which their representatives signed on November 11.[19]

This was the first in a series of triumphs for Kissinger's "shuttle diplomacy." Largely because of his initiative, Israel and Egypt consented to begin disengagement talks with representatives of four other powers in Geneva. With Kissinger's help they concluded an agreement in January 1974 that called for an Israeli pullback to a line a few miles east of the canal, a buffer zone along this line to be patrolled by UN troops, and a thinning out of Egyptian and Israeli forces for some miles on either side of the zone. This made possible the clearing of the canal, which had been closed since 1967. Kissinger, in May, also engineered a disengagement between Israel and Syria; Israel withdrew from territory captured in 1973 but only relinquished a portion of the strategic Golan Heights.

While a smaller UN force patrolled this cease-fire line, Kissinger's diplomacy began to bear fruit. The Arabs lifted the oil embargo; Egypt, Syria, and Algeria restored diplomatic relations with the United States; and Nixon made a successful visit to the Middle East in June 1974, where he conferred with heads of state in Syria, Egypt, Israel, and Jordan. The Geneva peace talks, which looked toward an overall settlement, made little progress, chiefly because no one could agree upon the role to be played by the Palestinians. But the atmosphere had improved.

Kissinger worked his way through a succession of setbacks and finally achieved an important new Sinai agreement between Israel and Egypt in September 1975. The UN force was to be retained, and an elaborate "early warning system" was to be set up on either side of the line to guard against surprise attacks. The United States also agreed upon aid programs to both countries, while Egypt and Israel pledged not to resolve their differences by the use or threat of force or blockade. The Sinai accord was a genuine achievement. Moreover, throughout the strenuous diplomacy that followed the Yom Kippur War, President Sadat had greatly enhanced his reputation both among his own people and abroad, as a patient, courageous, flexible leader of integrity and good will. To be sure, many problems remained. But Egypt and Israel, at least, had gone beyond cease-fire to the threshold of more lasting agreements.

Progress in the world's other cockpit of trouble and violence—Southeast Asia—was of a different sort. The cease-fire agreements of January 1973 (pp. 935–936) that permitted the United States to withdraw its last troops, recover its prisoners of war, and close down its involvement brought relief to America's agony of spirit but little or none to the embattled people of Indochina. North and South Vietnam continued to grapple

---

[19]The two sides agreed upon discussions to settle an armistice line, UN enforcement, an exchange of prisoners, a corridor for sending nonmilitary supplies to the besieged Egyptian Third Army, an end to the Arab blockade of the Red Sea, and eventual negotiations for an overall settlement.

and maneuver for advantage in violation of the cease-fire. Although the regime of Presiden Nguyen Van Thieu did what it could to consolidate its power in South Vietnam, time was running out for the American client state. Its hold upon the people had always been tenuous because of corruption, favoritism, an angry dismissal of legitimate opposition as Communist-inspired, and a refusal to undertake meaningful reforms. Its military capacities had improved after years of fighting, but it relied too much upon American equipment, training, and support. Now the support was gone, and Congress greatly reduced the flow of aid and equipment after the cease-fire. The military situation was in a condition of seeming stalemate in 1974, but South Vietnam's economic and political situation weakened steadily.

Hopes that stalemate and economic exhaustion might lead the two sides closer to accommodation were dashed in 1975 when disaster overtook the Thieu regime. North Vietnam mounted a new offensive in January. Thieu first announced a "strategic withdrawal" from the northern and then the central regions of South Vietnam, but the retreat suddenly became a wholesale rout. South Vietnamese army units abandoned some $5-billion worth of American equipment, ceased their resistance, and joined the masses of refugees that clogged every road in a headlong flight from the advancing enemy. Thieu stepped down on April 21; a dissident general surrendered to North Vietnam on April 30. In the same month, the Khmer Rouge triumphed over Lon Nol's Western-backed regime in Cambodia, and a Communist faction peaceably supplanted the neutralist government of Laos.

The long war that had devastated Vietnam and had taken an estimated 1.3 million Vietnamese lives was finally over, but the quality of peace was uncertain. Although no bloodbath took place, Hanoi reunified the country with a heavy hand and subjected hundreds of thousands of southerners to prolonged detention in "reeducation" camps. Moreover, the Hanoi government displayed aggressive tendencies in its hour of triumph. It kept troops in Laos and Cambodia, and created a suspicion that it sought hegemony over all of Indochina.

Congress, meanwhile, continued to assert itself in foreign affairs as part of the reaction against the imperial Johnson and Nixon presidencies. Turkey invaded Cyprus in 1974 to protect the rights of the Turkish Cypriots, and Congress voted a ban on military aid to Turkey in February 1975. Ford and Kissinger protested that this action threatened NATO and American security, and Ankara bore them out by taking over U.S. surveillance installations on Turkish soil and threatening to close them. Congress was finally persuaded to ease the arms embargo in October, and the Turks let the NATO bases stay functional, but relations remained in disarray.

Congress also interposed itself against administration policy in Africa. The group that overthrew Portugal's dictatorship in 1974 promptly granted independence to the African colonies, where nationalist elements had long been waging guerrilla warfare against the old regime. Three rival factions, each backed by outside powers, contended for supremacy in Angola, which became independent in 1975. A faction supported by Soviet arms and a few thousand Cuban troops won control of the Angolan government in early 1976. The Cuban presence in Africa irritated the United States, but Ford's request for military assistance for the American-backed group in Angola was rejected by Congress. It wanted no part in an incipient African Vietnam.

In Central America, efforts to renegotiate the status of the Panama Canal, intermittently under way since the early sixties, ran into congressional opposition in 1975. Panama wanted to replace the old treaty of 1903 with a new one that would limit the period of American occupation, recognize Panama's sovereignty over the Canal Zone, and bring about a phased transfer of responsibility for operating the canal. When Washington agreed in principle with these points, the House voted against appropriating funds for continued negotiations, and one-third of the Senate—enough to block ratification of a new treaty—supported a resolution that opposed any changes in the existing treaty.

6. GOP Foreign Policy: The Quest for Arms Control and Détente

American leaders worked earnestly to achieve better relations with the two major Communist powers, but made little more than token progress during Nixon's final months and Ford's brief tenure. With regard to China, Washington and Peking created liaison missions in May 1973 and agreed to expand them when Kissinger visited Mao Tse-tung in November. The Chinese bought quantities of American grain and other agricultural products, and relations between the two countries, after cooling in 1974, improved again in 1975 as first Kissinger and then Ford visited the People's Republic and conferred with Chinese leaders. Peking, while anxious to keep the new American connection alive, made it clear that America's support of Taiwan stood in the way of closer ties.

China was passing through an uncertain transition during this period as its two great leaders, Chairman Mao and Premier Chou En-lai, became feebler with advancing years. Both before and after they passed from the scene, the Chinese hierarchy was shaken and shuffled by rivalries between moderate and radical factions, the latter headed by Mao's forceful wife, Chiang Ch'ing. This jockeying for position was well demonstrated by the ups and downs in the fortunes of Teng Hsiao-ping. Purged as a revisionist during the Cultural Revolution of the sixties, Teng returned to power in 1973 and rose to the position of first deputy premier in 1975, only to be ousted a few months later. All was in flux with the death of Chou in January 1976 and of Mao in the following September, but the scramble for power finally resulted in the triumph of a pragmatic moderate faction.

The man who succeeded Chou as premier in April 1976 and later also became Mao's successor as party chairman was Hua Kuo-feng, about whom Westerners knew little. Hua moved promptly against the radicals, arrested the four top leftist leaders (including Mao's widow), and used the army to maintain control in provinces where radical support was strong. The fallen but respected Teng Hsiao-ping was reinstated in early 1977 as deputy premier and became one of what was in effect a ruling triumvirate along with Hua and Defense Minister Yeh Chien-ying.

A similar blend of uncertainty and cautious cordiality marked the Soviet-American relationship. The two countries strove for a new strategic arms accord, but progress toward a second SALT treaty was limited to statements of intent and agreements "in principle." These were forthcoming on several occasions, but SALT negotiators could never translate highsounding declarations into a new draft treaty. The two sides remained at odds over a host of details and technical points in what was becoming a greater labyrinth of technicalities each year. Advances in modern weapons technology kept outstripping attempts to apply meaningful limitations and controls.

Hopes for peace were also being menaced by the spread of nuclear technology, which both superpowers wished to prevent. Although they continued to persuade more countries to adhere to the Nuclear Nonproliferation Treaty of 1969 (see pp. 875, 918), the signs were not promising. India in 1974 became the sixth nation (along with the United States, the USSR, Britain, France, and China) to explode a nuclear device. Israel was on the verge of nuclear capability, and several other nations were approaching it. Yet some of these states had not become parties to the Nonproliferation Treaty.[20]

In the absence of tangible accomplishments, hopes for stronger East-West accord rested primarily upon continuing close contact between Washington and Moscow. The Russians liked and respected Kissinger, whose efforts to enlarge the basis for Soviet-American détente employed a judicious blend of firmness and flexibility. Both Nixon and Ford were on good personal terms with the bluff, good-natured Brezhnev, who, for all his steely devotion to his nation's interests, was proving the most stable and approachable of the Soviet's postwar leaders.

---

[20]The proliferation problem was exacerbated by the fact that the energy crisis was spurring increased worldwide interest in nuclear reactors to generate electricity. But a major by-product that can be chemically extracted from nuclear waste is plutonium, a prime ingredient of nuclear bombs. International control of plutonium reprocessing plants and their deadly product was under discussion in the 1970s, but experts were gloomy about the prospects of keeping nuclear weapons out of irresponsible hands as more and more countries built reactors and enlarged their nuclear technology.

The troubles were at least being discussed, though not resolved. Attempts to achieve a balanced reduction of forces in central Europe were unsuccessful. Russia objected to American criticism of its emigration policies and repudiated a trade agreement in 1975 because Congress had tied trade concessions to an easing of Soviet restrictions on Jewish emigration. Ford met Brezhnev in Helsinki in July 1975 at a thirty-five-nation conference on European security and cooperation, and the two leaders joined other statesmen in signing an agreement that pledged acceptance of the territorial status quo, mutual respect for sovereignty and borders, and freer movement of people, ideas, and commerce between the East and the West. However, Soviet "adventurism" in strategic areas, particularly in the Indian Ocean, remained a sore spot.[21]

America's other diplomatic troubles were nagging but not crucial. A thaw in relations with Cuba was halted by Castro's use of troops to aid African nationalist movements. Relations with Western Europe were marred by the kind of friendly bickering that had always been a feature of the Atlantic alliance. Everyone, as usual, wanted things both ways. Europe tended to chafe under American military leadership and then to criticize Washington for not providing more of it. The United States, in turn, wanted its allies to show more initiative and to make larger contributions to NATO and yet remain in line behind American leadership. The most disruptive problems were economic: how to reconcile military and political with trade and financial considerations, and—after the crisis of 1973—how to coordinate energy policies in the face of OPEC actions. Europe regarded American attempts to control inflation and conserve energy as inadequate, while the United States was critical of the way in which most European nations rushed to accommodate and appease the Arab states in order to guarantee their oil supplies.

7. The Election of 1976

The campaign of 1976 saw the Democrats retain an unusual degree of party harmony and the Republicans stage an unusually close-fought battle for the presidential nomination, and it ended with a narrow victory for Democrat Jimmy Carter over the Republican incumbent, Gerald Ford. It offered a few surprises, several predictable features, and no very clear mandate from the voters.

[21] The Russians also meddled in the Horn of Africa, scene of tribal, civil, and border disputes that involved Ethiopia and Somalia. Reports of a Russian base under construction in Somalia prompted the United States to begin construction of naval facilities on the island of Diego Garcia, 1,000 miles south of India.

The biggest surprise lay in the whirlwind emergence of Jimmy Carter as Democratic front runner and decisive winner in the contest for his party's nomination. Carter came out of almost total obscurity beyond his native Georgia, where he had been governor from 1971 to 1975. He rose to national prominence in 1976 by simply outrunning and outcampaigning his rivals—Senators Henry Jackson of Washington and Frank Church of Idaho, Governors George Wallace of Alabama and Jerry Brown of California, and Representative Morris Udall of Arizona. Carter had laid his plans well in advance. He announced his candidacy as early as December 1974, but people were still saying " Jimmy Who?" when he entered the New Hampshire primary in January 1976. He finished first in a field of nine candidates, with nearly 30 percent of the vote to runner-up Udall's 24 percent.

This victory established Carter's credentials; his surprising victory in March over the partially paralyzed but still formidable George Wallace in Florida gave him a momentum that he never really lost. He was a tireless and effective campaigner. His approach was earnest, low-keyed, and folksy; his major theme was the need for a leader untainted by Washington who could restore morality and integrity to government. People found both the man and his message appealing. He went on to win handsomely in Illinois and North Carolina, narrowly in Wisconsin, and decisively in Pennsylvania, disproving Jackson's claim that Carter could not carry a big industrial state.

Wallace and Jackson soon dropped out of the contest, and the Georgian became an odds-on favorite. His string of primary triumphs was briefly halted in May when Church, a late entry, defeated him in three western states and Governor Brown won in Nevada and his native California. But Carter continued to capture delegates faster than anyone else, and his big victory in Ohio on June 8 provided a clincher; Mayor Daley of Chicago endorsed him, and both Wallace and Jackson proclaimed their support. By this time he had shown enough strength to eliminate all of his rivals and block any prospect that the convention, in the absence of a clear front runner, might turn to the party's popular elder statesman, Hubert Humphrey. Carter had acquired enough delegates to insure the nomination well before the Democrats assembled in New York on July 12.

The Democratic convention was pleasant, smooth, almost cut and dried. All of the issues that had caused bitter quarrels in past years—credentials, rules, representation, platform—had been ironed out in advance. Carter won easily on the first ballot and chose the popular liberal senator from Minnesota, Walter F. Mondale, as his running mate. Unity was the Democratic watchword, and they made much of it, stressing that they had not only healed party rifts but nominated a man from the deep South for the first time since before the Civil War. "We stand together as a nation, reunited at long last, Georgia and Minnesota, one," Senator Mondale proclaimed, while the crowd roared its approval. There were no disgruntled rivals or alienated factions, and the party high command had fallen readily into line behind its candidate. The platform contained the usual sweeping pledges, touched every base, and affirmed traditional Democratic values.[22]

In his quietly confident acceptance speech Carter called for a "time of healing" to replace the recent "time of torment" and promised an efficient government and new efforts to end race and sex discrimination. He sounded a populist note, saying: "Too many have had to suffer at the hands of a political and economic elite who have shaped decisions and never had to account for mistakes." He praised the American character and the strength of American ideals, and foresaw a nation "on the move again, united . . . entering our third century with pride and confidence." Democrats left New York in a cheerful mood.

The Republicans arrived at their ticket by a markedly different route. Ford's decision in 1975 to seek a full term in his own right came as no surprise, and it was widely assumed that he would win the nomination without difficulty. His only important rival was ex-Governor Ronald Reagan of California, the outspoken ultraconservative who had long been the favorite of the GOP's powerful right wing. Vice-President Rockefeller eased Ford's problems in November 1975 by announcing that he would not be a candidate for the vice-presidency. Ford strategists reasoned that Reagan's extremism would be unacceptable to a majority of voters, and the president sought to project the image of a moderate leader who was healing America's wounds, presiding over economic recovery, and keeping the nation at peace. It seemed to be working. He beat Reagan decisively in the first three Republican primaries in early 1976, and his backers began urging the Californian to withdraw in the interest of party unity.

But Reagan refused to give up. He scored an upset victory over Ford in North Carolina in March and suddenly surged back into contention with a string of triumphs in Sun Belt states, where his conservative constituency was strong. Ford fell behind in the delegate count in May but stayed close with a big home-state triumph and strong performances in two border states. He regained a slight lead by persuading uncommitted supporters in New York and Pennsylvania to declare for him; he then rounded out the primaries in June with victories in New Jersey and Ohio, while Reagan took California by a landslide. Overall primary results had left the two candidates so close that everything depended on who could capture a majority of the uncommitted delegates.

The GOP convention assembled in Kansas City on August 16 with the issue still in doubt. Ford had a slight lead, and Reagan hurt his own candi-

[22]It called for full employment, balanced growth, economic justice, price stability, an anti-inflation policy based on increased productivity, and competent and responsive government. It condemned Republican mismanagement, promised to improve the environment, endorsed the equal rights amendment, and proclaimed a need for welfare and tax reform, national health insurance, new housing and urban development plans, and a strengthening of education and social services. Its defense plank promised the usual combination of savings and strength; its foreign plank envisioned progress in all areas and denounced the wasteful, deceptive, manipulative diplomacy of the Nixon-Kissinger era.

dacy with the surprise announcement that he had chosen Senator Richard S. Schweiker of Pennsylvania, a liberal, as his running mate; this belated bid for broader support only succeeded in alienating several uncommitted conservative delegates. But some of Ford's support was shaky, and Reagan could not be counted out. Along with devoted hard-core backing from the far right, Reagan had kindled enthusiasm among many rank-and-file Republicans, who liked his crisp, hard-hitting oratory and felt that his magnetism and forcefulness made him a stronger candidate than the rather colorless Ford. He had already demonstrated his strength by forcing the president to adopt an increasingly conservative stance. Reagan often criticized the administration as though it were Democratic; Ford often seemed to be agreeing with him, as though the administration were not his own.[23] The staunchly conservative platform was as much a Reagan as a Ford document.[24]

Ford was able to hold his ranks intact and won the nomination on the first ballot on August 18 by a vote of 1,187 to 1,070. Not since Eisenhower fought Robert Taft in 1952 had the GOP witnessed this kind of a contest for the nomination; not since Theodore Roosevelt fought Robert Taft's father in 1912 had an incumbent president come so close to losing his party's endorsement for a new term.

Ford's choice of a running mate was Senator Robert Dole of Kansas, a sharp-tongued conservative. Reagan expressed support for the ticket cheerfully enough, but many of his ardent backers were bitterly disappointed, and it seemed apparent that the party had barely avoided a disastrous split without exactly achieving solidarity. Ford's acceptance speech was effective. With restrained eloquence, he praised the state of the nation as "sound," "secure," and "on the march to full economic recovery and a better quality of life for all Americans." He pledged continuing fights against inflation and unemployment, called for reduced taxes, and spoke of his record as "one of performance, not promises."

The rest of the campaign—until election night—was rather dull. The polls showed Carter to be substantially ahead in July, but the gap nar-

[23] Reagan's favorite issue was the Panama Canal, which he advocated keeping in America's possession with a vehemence that would have delighted Theodore Roosevelt. "We bought it, we paid for it, we built it and we intend to keep it," he would snap. Yet Ford, whose long negotiations with Panama looked toward eventual relinquishment, seemed at times almost to be disavowing this policy in response to Reagan's attacks.

[24] The platform praised the administration record in foreign affairs but included a "morality" plank that criticized certain Ford-Kissinger actions, notably their adherence to the Helsinki Declaration and their refusal (in the interest of détente) to invite the anti-Communist author Aleksandr Solzhenitsyn to the White House when he emigrated from Russia to the United States.

The rest of the platform was a ringing affirmation of Republican virtues—a balanced budget, reduced taxes, less bureaucracy, smaller government, decontrol of oil and natural gas, support for small business, free enterprise, the free market, the family, the neighborhood school. It had an antiabortion plank, and its firm stance against discrimination was qualified by an indirect criticism of busing and a direct criticism of racial quotas in hiring. It sounded an enduring campaign note by lambasting the Democrats as irresponsible spenders, regulators, and advocates of big government.

rowed steadily in ensuing weeks—less because the Republican candidate picked up speed than because the Democratic candidate slowed down. Neither man seemed as well organized or in command as he had been during the primaries, and neither was able to strike many sparks from a curious but cautious electorate. Both tended to deal in generalities: Ford alternately praised his own record and criticized the Democrats as inflationary spenders; Carter proclaimed his lack of Washington connections and promised to do better than the Republicans in all areas. Some interest was generated when Ford challenged Carter to a series of TV debates, but the results were inconclusive. (Polls had Ford "winning" the first debate, Carter the second and third. In a fourth debate, this time between the two vice-presidential candidates, Mondale did much better. Mondale was, in fact, a great asset to his ticket throughout the campaign.)

Carter's early lead had about vanished by October, and pollsters were terming the election "too close to call." The results bore out this prediction. Nearly 82,000,000 Americans went to the polls on November 2, and it was not until the next morning that Carter could be declared a winner. He received 40,827,000 popular votes (51 percent) to Ford's 39,146,000 (48 percent). He carried the District of Columbia and twenty-three states to Ford's twenty-seven, and his electoral margin of 297 to 241 was the smallest since 1916.[25]

Carter's triumph was based essentially upon the same East-South axis that had been a mainstay of Democratic success in John Kennedy's time, in Franklin Roosevelt's, and, indeed, in Thomas Jefferson's. Carter carried New York, Pennsylvania, and all but one state in the Old South; these, together with victories in Massachusetts and Rhode Island, accounted for more than two-thirds of his total. He also ran well in the border states, capturing Delaware, Maryland, the District of Columbia, West Virginia, Kentucky, and Missouri. He won three midwestern states (Ohio, Wisconsin, Minnesota) and lost everything out West except Hawaii.

Carter had proved, as Kennedy in 1960 had proved for Catholics, that a person from the Deep South was no longer barred from seeking and obtaining the nation's highest office. (There was an ironic twist here, in that southern black voters, newly enfranchised since the sixties, voted overwhelmingly Democratic and gave Carter his margin of victory in most, if not all, of the ex-Confederate states—and indeed in the election.) Urban, labor, Jewish, academic, liberal, and other traditionally Democratic voters

[25]Ford's total was reduced to 240 when a Washington elector defected and cast his vote for Reagan. Had Ohio (which Carter carried by a bare 8,000 votes) and Hawaii (which he won by 7,000) gone the other way, Ford would have been elected.

On the other hand, Carter's margin would have been larger had it not been for the candidacy of former Democratic Senator Eugene McCarthy. McCarthy won only 1 percent of the popular vote, but his total in each of four states (Iowa, Maine, Oklahoma, Oregon) was larger than Ford's tiny winning margin, and Carter would probably have carried all four if McCarthy had not been on the ballot.

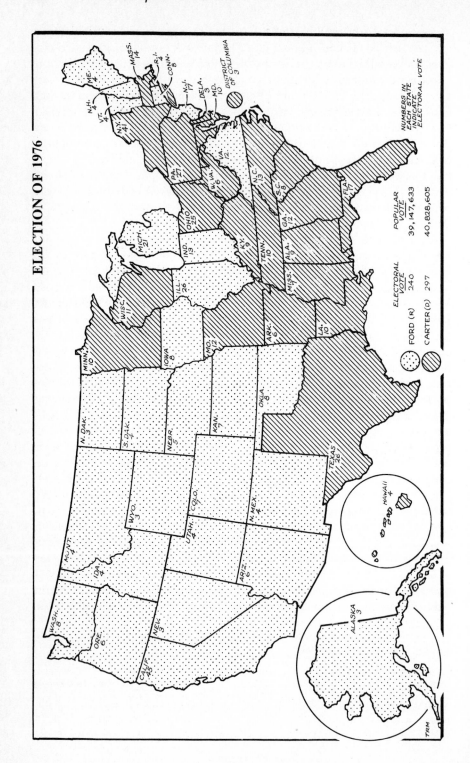

ELECTION OF 1976

NUMBERS IN EACH STATE INDICATE ELECTORAL VOTE

	ELECTORAL VOTE	POPULAR VOTE
FORD (R)	240	39,147,633
CARTER (D)	297	40,828,605

also supported him, and he ran well among midwestern and eastern farmers, who liked his rural origins.

Ford himself had made a close race out of it, but his party had suffered a disastrous defeat. Notwithstanding peace, returning prosperity, and voter dislike of government spending, which many identified with Democrats, the GOP had failed to dent the top-heavy Democratic majorities in Congress or enlarge its small minority of governorships. The Democrats gained one seat in the House, making their margin 292–143, and retained their 62–38 edge in the Senate. The general political complexion of the two houses remained about as it had been.

8. The President from Georgia

What sort of man had the country chosen to be its thirty-ninth president? James Earl Carter, Jr., invariably referred to as Jimmy, had entered presidential politics from an atypical background. He was born near the village of Plains in southwestern Georgia on October 1, 1924, and grew up on a farm that had belonged to the family since colonial times. It was an environment where toil and hardship outnumbered comforts during the depression years of Carter's boyhood, and he did his share of 4:00 A.M. farm chores and sold boiled peanuts in town for pocket money. Upon graduation from high school during wartime, he spent a year in the navy ROTC program at Georgia Tech, then received an appointment to the United States Naval Academy. He was graduated from Annapolis in 1946 in the upper tenth of his class and served in the navy for seven years; he rose to the rank of lieutenant and worked in Admiral Hyman Rickover's nuclear submarine program. He did a year of graduate work in nuclear physics at Union College and looked forward to a naval career, but he decided to leave the service and return to the family farm upon his father's death in 1953.

From this combination of naval experience superimposed upon a modest rural background, Jimmy Carter emerged with traits of personality and character that were there to stay—superquotas of energy and driving ambition, a quiet but unshakable self-confidence, a devotion to home and family, a capacity for hard work, and an engineer's concern to make things function efficiently. He was a devout Baptist who liked to call himself a "born again" Christian.

Back in Plains in the fifties, Carter took over the modest family peanut farm and expanded it into a many-sided and ultimately prosperous operation that included a shelling plant, a seed and fertilizer business, and a farm supply outfit. He also acquired more land, and by the 1970s he was able to list total assets of nearly $1 million. Meanwhile, he had entered Georgia Democratic politics, served two terms in the state senate from 1963 to 1966, tried unsuccessfully for the gubernatorial nomination in 1966, and won election to that office for a four-year term in 1970.

His gubernatorial campaign included some words of praise for segregationists Lester Maddox and George Wallace and a declaration against busing and federally imposed integration—all of which made his first acts as governor startling and dramatic. "I say to you quite frankly," he announced in his inaugural address, "the time for racial discrimination is over." He proceeded to hang portraits of Martin Luther King, Jr., and other black leaders in the state capitol and brought about a marked increase in the number of blacks in state employment. From then on, blacks liked and respected him, down to and including their massive support for his candidacy in 1976.

His record as governor was creditable but hardly outstanding. Its principal elements included governmental reorganization, improved budget procedures and state services, prison reform, and some modest welfare enactments. He proved to be a diligent, persuasive leader—stubborn yet able to compromise, budget-conscious yet concerned for human needs.

These, then, were some of the qualities and attitudes that Jimmy Carter brought to the presidency in January 1977. Deep religious conviction, compassion, love of country, and desire for reform were in some kind of balance with ambition, a craving for managerial efficiency, and a salesman's interest in marketing his product. His blue eyes could sometimes take on a steely glint and offset the toothy grin that became his trademark during the campaign.

His start was effective and in character. His inaugural address proclaimed "a new beginning, a new dedication within our government, a new spirit within us all." He spoke of the need for caution and restraint in attacking problems and thanked his predecessor "for all he has done to heal our land." He took pains to humanize the presidency, remove much of the pomp that surrounded it, and bring it closer to the people. He and his family walked down Pennsylvania Avenue on Inauguration Day. He discouraged the traditional fanfare of playing "Hail to the Chief" and stopped the limousine service for White House aides. He answered questions on a two-hour radio call-in show and met with local citizens at televised "town meetings" in Massachusetts and Mississippi. He expressed his concern for energy conservation by turning down White House thermostats.

Carter's major appointments combined a manager's search for competence, a politician's search for balance, and a newcomer's desire to surround himself with a few trusted friends. His secretary of state was Cyrus R. Vance, a New York attorney who had been a diplomat and deputy defense secretary under Lyndon Johnson. For the Treasury Department, Carter chose W. Michael Blumenthal, head of the Bendix corporation and a Kennedy tariff negotiator. Harold Brown, a physicist who had been Johnson's secretary of the air force and later president of the California Institute of Technology, became secretary of defense. Griffin B. Bell, a friend and fellow Georgian whose legal career had led to a federal judgeship, headed the Justice Department. Governor Cecil D. Andrus of Idaho, respected by both environmentalists and business interests, became secretary of the interior. Congressman Robert S. Bergland of Minnesota, expert on farm problems, was the new secretary of agriculture. One of Carter's two female cabinet appointees was Secretary of Commerce Juanita M. Kreps, professor of economics and vice-president of Duke University and a director of the New York Stock Exchange. The new secretary of labor was F. Ray Marshall, labor economist at the University of Texas. Joseph A. Califano, Jr., a New York lawyer who had served Kennedy in the Defense Department and Johnson in forming Great Society programs, took over HEW. For the Housing and Urban Development Department Carter chose Patricia R. Harris, a distinguished black woman with varied experience as diplomat, corporate board member, and professor of law. Former Congressman Brock Adams became secretary of transportation.

The new national security adviser was Zbigniew Brzezinski, professor of foreign affairs at Columbia. For UN ambassador Carter chose his friend Andrew Young, Jr., the outspoken black congressman from Georgia. Other Georgians in the new administration included Bert Lance, banker and long-time friend, who became OMB director; and a cluster of young men on the White House staff: Hamilton Jordan, former campaign strategist who became a top aide and political adviser; Jody Powell, the president's press secretary; and special assistant Stuart Eisenstat.

No survey of the new administration would be complete without some mention of the president's wife, Rosalynn, who repeatedly proved herself one of his greatest assets. Mrs. Carter was a charming, attractive woman with skills, intelligence, energy, and ambition fully on a par with her husband's; the dynamic First Lady went well beyond the functions of goodwill ambassador and ornament to serve as one of her husband's major advisers, critics, and spokesmen. Not since Eleanor Roosevelt had a president's wife played so active a political role.

9. Toward New Accords: Panama and Middle East

The Carter administration worked hard to bring a new emphasis to the conduct of foreign affairs. The president talked of substituting open diplomacy, accommodation, and principle for the amoral *Realpolitik* that he said had characterized Nixon-Kissinger diplomacy. He proclaimed a "new

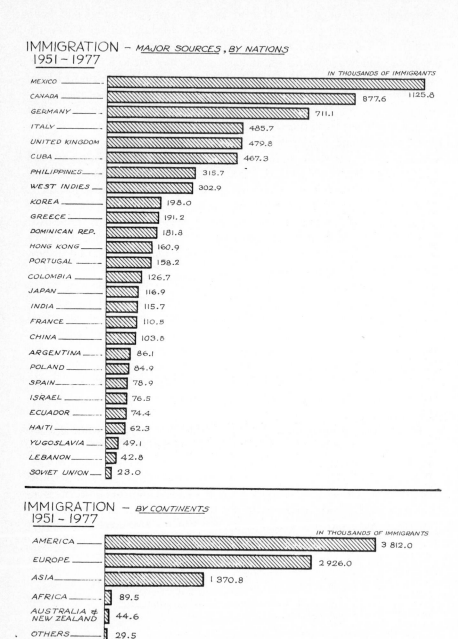

IMMIGRATION – *MAJOR SOURCES*, *BY NATIONS*
1951 – 1977

IN THOUSANDS OF IMMIGRANTS

MEXICO	1125.8
CANADA	877.6
GERMANY	711.1
ITALY	485.7
UNITED KINGDOM	479.8
CUBA	467.3
PHILIPPINES	315.7
WEST INDIES	302.9
KOREA	198.0
GREECE	191.2
DOMINICAN REP.	181.8
HONG KONG	160.9
PORTUGAL	158.2
COLOMBIA	126.7
JAPAN	116.9
INDIA	115.7
FRANCE	110.5
CHINA	103.8
ARGENTINA	86.1
POLAND	84.9
SPAIN	78.9
ISRAEL	76.5
ECUADOR	74.4
HAITI	62.3
YUGOSLAVIA	49.1
LEBANON	42.8
SOVIET UNION	23.0

IMMIGRATION – *BY CONTINENTS*
1951 – 1977

IN THOUSANDS OF IMMIGRANTS

AMERICA	3 812.0
EUROPE	2 926.0
ASIA	1 370.8
AFRICA	89.5
AUSTRALIA & NEW ZEALAND	44.6
OTHERS	29.5

REFUGEES ADMITTED, *MAJOR SOURCES, BY NATIONS*
1954 – 1977

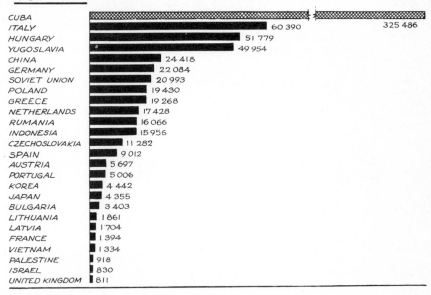

CUBA	325 486
ITALY	60 390
HUNGARY	51 779
YUGOSLAVIA	49 954
CHINA	24 418
GERMANY	22 084
SOVIET UNION	20 993
POLAND	19 430
GREECE	19 268
NETHERLANDS	17 428
RUMANIA	16 066
INDONESIA	15 956
CZECHOSLOVAKIA	11 282
SPAIN	9 012
AUSTRIA	5 697
PORTUGAL	5 006
KOREA	4 442
JAPAN	4 355
BULGARIA	3 403
LITHUANIA	1 861
LATVIA	1 704
FRANCE	1 394
VIETNAM	1 334
PALESTINE	918
ISRAEL	830
UNITED KINGDOM	811

REFUGEES ADMITTED, *BY CONTINENTS*
1954 – 1977

	TOTAL NORTH AMERICA — 327 238
NORTH AMERICA	
EUROPE	324 775
ASIA	70 870
AFRICA	8 757
SOUTH AMERICA	754
OTHERS	157

1752, OTHER THAN CUBAN

REFUGEES ADMITTED, *MAJOR SOURCES*
1977 ONLY

CUBA	67 985
SOVIET UNION	3 972
VIETNAM	1 319
CHINA	975
RUMANIA	722
SPAIN	602
POLAND	504
HUNGARY	271
CZECHOSLOVAKIA	138

foreign policy" that was "democratic . . . based upon fundamental values." At the center of this new foreign policy was a concern for human rights, which Carter sought to dramatize in several ways: by signing an Inter-American Convention on Human Rights, by asking the Senate to approve the UN Human Rights Covenants of 1966, by urging that such international machinery be strengthened, by withholding assistance from nations that did not meet legislated standards in this area, and by expanding American refugee and asylum programs.

The same emphasis upon openness and accommodation could be seen in the economic sphere, where Carter opposed restrictive import quotas (preferring to help American producers through marketing agreements or government aid) and took the lead in supporting a freer world trading system at a Western summit conference in London in May 1977. The United States contributed heavily to the International Development Association, added to its support for UN development programs, and joined in the creation of a new international fund for agricultural development.

While the Carter administration sought to alter the tone of American policy and engage in productive dialogue upon the whole broad spectrum of international issues, it worked hardest upon four specific areas of American concern: the Panama Canal, the Middle East, relations with China, and an arms treaty with the Soviet Union.

Success in the Panama negotiations came in two stages. The United States and Panama concluded thirteen years of effort by agreeing upon a pair of treaties in September 1977. One provided for American operation and defense of the canal until the year 2000, an increase in Panama's share of canal revenues, a slow phasing down of U.S. employees in the Canal Zone, the immediate abolition of the zone itself, and a return to Panama of all lands unconnected with the operation of the canal. The second document—a neutrality treaty—designated the canal as an international waterway to be permanently neutral in war and peace, and open to peaceful passage by ships of all nations equally. American and Panamanian warships would have priority of passage in times of war and emergency. Although Panama would maintain defense sites and military installations after 2000, the United States would retain a permanent right to act along with Panama in defending the canal's neutral status. Panamanians approved the treaties by a 2–1 margin in a plebiscite in October 1977.

The canal negotiations touched off a loud controversy in the United States, and it took a considerable amount of skill, maneuvering, and persuasive logic by Senate supporters and administration leaders to get the treaties approved. Opposition was vocal and strong. Conservatives denounced the agreements, and bitter American residents in the Canal Zone demonstrated angrily against them. Part of the opposition was simply emotional and reflected pride in the canal as a great American achievement and patriotic objection to the idea of giving up a prized possession. But there were substantive fears as well. Many persons felt that the treaties jeopardized American interests and did not provide adequately for the security and defense of the canal once the United States had relinquished control.

To allay these fears, the Senate attached an amendment clarifying and strengthening the priority to be accorded U.S. warships seeking transit in times of war or emergency. Senators also added a reservation that specified America's right to take independent action, including the use of force, to reopen or secure safe operation of the canal if it were closed or interfered with. When Panama objected to this latter point, the Senate modified it by stipulating that American rights to take unilateral action did not extend to intervening in or impugning Panama's independence. The Panamanian head of state, Brigadier General Omar Torrijos, soon reported that his country found the amendments and reservations acceptable.

Proponents had some effective arguments. They answered fears of terrorist attacks by pointing out that sabotage would be much more likely to occur if the treaties were rejected. Bipartisan support and ultimate success owed much to the work of Republicans Howard Baker of Tennessee and Jacob Javits of New York. President Carter assured the nation that American security and trade opportunities would actually be stronger under the new treaties. Ratification, he concluded, would greatly strengthen America's image: "We will demonstrate that as a large and powerful country we are able to deal fairly and honorably with a proud but smaller sovereign nation." The Senate approved one treaty on March 16 and the other on April 18, 1978, by identical votes of 68–32—only one more than the necessary two-thirds. President Carter and General Torrijos met in Panama City in June and exchanged the instruments of ratification.

Carter also recorded a dramatic achievement in the Middle East. Kissinger, after engineering the Sinai agreement of 1975, had failed to make further headway, and Carter and Secretary Vance conducted talks with Arab and Israeli leaders in an effort to restore momentum to the negotiations. The first sign of a breakthrough came in November 1977, when the new Israeli premier, Menahem Begin, electrified the world by inviting Egyptian President Sadat to visit Israel and explore the pathway toward permanent peace by means of direct talks. Sadat accepted.

Never before had an Arab and an Israeli head of state talked face to face. It was a stirring moment, witnessed by millions on international television: Sadat stepping off his plane at Tel Aviv to be greeted by the Israeli premier and an honor guard and a twenty-one-gun salute; the two leaders standing side by side while a band played both national anthems. Sadat later addressed the Israeli parliament and spoke soberly of the need to break down the "psychological wall . . . that constitutes 70 percent of the problem" between Arab and Jew. Then, in a thrilling passage, Sadat tore down part of the wall. "I proclaim to the whole world: we accept living with you in a just and lasting peace. . . . Israel has become an established fact." He added that "peace cannot be realized without the Palestinians," a key point to which Begin did not respond directly. But the Israeli premier offered normal relations and peaceable traffic across open borders, and the two leaders came away from their talks with respect and a liking for each other. Notwithstanding fears and reservations, public sentiment in both countries was eloquently, tumultuously in favor of the effort. Begin paid a return visit to Sadat in Cairo at the end of the year, and hopes continued to thrive.

Negotiations proceeded fitfully during 1978, with the United States playing an important role as mediator. Efforts to win support among other Arab states for Israeli-Egyptian accord got nowhere. Though sincerely desiring a settlement, Sadat and Begin were tough-minded men who drove a hard bargain, and progress was painfully slow. By early summer it had ceased altogether.

Credit for breaking the impasse belonged to President Carter, who invited both leaders to Camp David for a summit conference in September and kept them there for a fortnight while the three heads of state and their advisers slugged things out. On September 17, an exhausted but triumphant president announced that two accords had been reached: a "Framework for Peace in the Middle East" and a "Framework for the Conclusion of a Peace Treaty Between Egypt and Israel."

It was a momentous accomplishment. Israel and Egypt had agreed to negotiate a treaty within three months. Sadat had agreed to a separate peace with Israel rather than insisting upon inclusion of the Palestinians and other Arab states, and Begin had agreed to relinquish control of the Sinai. The "Framework for Peace" spoke in deliberately vague terms of "self-governing authorities" in the West Bank and the Gaza Strip, "freely elected" by the inhabitants—an indirect reference to the explosive Palestinian question. The status of the West Bank and Gaza was to be settled by negotiations among Israeli, Egyptian, Jordanian, and local authorities over a five-year period.

Agreement to negotiate a treaty was one thing; successful negotiation was another. The euphoric glow of the Camp David meeting soon subsided. Follow-up talks raised touchy questions of detail and implementation which the broadly phrased "frameworks" had been able to skirt, and the two nations could not come to terms within the three-month deadline. Indeed, by early 1979 it looked as though the talks might fail altogether. Sadat began to demand that the peace treaty be linked to an agreement about the exact status of the Palestinians; Israel resented this request for linkage because it had not been part of the Camp David accords. In turn, Begin angered Egypt by continuing to plant new Israeli settlements in the West Bank, even though this seemed at direct odds with the notion of eventual Palestinian autonomy for the region. The rest of the Arab world, including the Palestinian Liberation Organization (PLO), the largest of several refugee groups, kept up a drumfire of criticism against the whole idea of a treaty with Israel. Patience on both sides became thinner, and the talks seemed permanently stalled.

But Carter, who had staked much of his own prestige upon a Mideastern treaty, renewed the earnest personal diplomacy that had worked so well at Camp David. After strenuous new discussions, capped by a presidential visit to Tel Aviv and Cairo in March for marathon sessions, the pieces suddenly fell into place. A weary, smiling president arrived home with the surprise announcement that Israel and Egypt had agreed upon terms.

Sadat and Begin signed the peace treaty in Washington on March 26, 1979, while the man primarily responsible for engineering it looked happily on. Israel pledged to withdraw its military forces and remove its civilian settlements from the Sinai over a three-year period, with two-thirds of the territory to be relinquished within nine months of ratification. At this point, Egypt and Israel were to establish normal friendly relations and exchange ambassadors. UN forces were to be deployed in border areas to monitor the agreement. The United States, which had pledged some $5 billion in military and economic aid to both countries as part of the bargain, was to assist in security arrangements by conducting surveillance flights. Egypt was to end its economic boycott of Israel, whose ships and cargoes were granted free right of passage through the Suez Canal. Israel could purchase oil from the Sinai fields that it was about to return to Egypt. And the two countries agreed to begin negotiating the question of Palestinian autonomy within a month after ratification, which took place almost immediately in both capitals. The first Sinai evacuation began the day after the treaty was signed; the second phase took place on schedule in the early summer.

The treaty launched a precarious but hopeful new era in the Middle East. Optimism was necessarily at a discount; the forces that menaced the Israeli-Egyptian peace were numerous and powerful. Egypt had become a pariah in the Arab world, isolated diplomatically and economically, condemned by moderate regimes and openly threatened by radical ones. Discussions of the Palestinian question began on schedule and got nowhere. The two sides were far apart on the exact meaning of "autonomy," and the PLO and other groups were implacably opposed to any settlement that excluded them from the negotiations and did not provide for a fully independent Palestinian state. Tel Aviv refused to concede such a possibility or deal with organizations (such as the PLO) that were committed to Israel's destruction.

The Palestinian issue was compounded by a murderous civil war in Lebanon. The war, which blazed intermittently from 1975 on, grew largely out of disagreement between Christian and Moslem factions over the Palestinian guerrilla and refugee camps in the southern part of the country, bases for terrorist raids and targets of Israeli retaliation. Syrian troops occupied parts of Lebanon in 1976 in an effort to quell the civil war, but neither this occupation nor attempts to mediate by other Arab nations brought peace to the country or solved the two-way flow of violence across its border with Israel.

The balance of power in the Middle East was gravely altered in early 1979 by a revolution in Iran that forced the Shah into exile and replaced him with a reactionary, unstable regime headed by a revered Moslem zealot, the Ayatollah Ruhollah Khomeini. The Shah's drive to convert Iran into a modern industrial state had created diverse and growing opposition: devout Moslems who deplored the erosion of traditional values; Kurdish citizens who sought greater autonomy; and secular groups who chafed under the repression, corruption, and favoritism that characterized the Shah's government. The revolution cost the United States a strong military ally and valuable surveillance equipment along the Iranian-Soviet border. It also disrupted Iranian oil production and touched off a new round of shortages and price increases to bedevil the world's economy. And it replaced a pro-Israeli leader with a militant pan-Islamic government that joined the more radical Arab states in heaping condemnation upon Israel and Egypt.

The Iranian upheaval underscored Israel's growing sense of isolation. Opinion in the UN was highly critical of Israel's refusal to deal with the Palestinians or cease its raids into Lebanon, and the Israelis came to believe that the Western nations were swinging toward a pro-Arab view out of a desire for oil. Israel even began making this accusation against the United States in 1979. Washington sharply denied the charge but did add its voice to the chorus of criticism of Israeli intransigence about the West Bank.

Hanging like a dark cloud over the troubled Middle East was the specter of Soviet aggrandizement. On one flank, internal disorder and economic difficulties had brought Turkey to the brink of collapse, with attendant threats to NATO defenses. On the other flank, a Soviet-backed Communist element overthrew the government of Afghanistan in 1978. A Soviet presence in Ethiopia cast its shadow across the Arabian Sea. Nonaligned observers were worried. "I fear," a Pakistani official commented, "that historians will look back at 1978 as a watershed year when the balance of power shifted against the western world."

Not even this array of trouble could altogether dispel the belief that Carter, Egypt, and Israel had made a permanent breakthrough. The strategic situation improved. While conditions in Turkey remained unstable, American relations with its troubled ally were eased when Carter persuaded Congress in 1978 to lift the partial arms embargo it had imposed on Turkey since 1975; in return, the Turks reaffirmed their NATO commitment and reopened the electronic surveillance bases. The new Communist regime in Afghanistan was itself threatened with overthrow in 1979 by a rebellious movement of disaffected Moslem and tribal elements. Arab states, though bitterly opposed to the Egyptian-Israeli treaty, were also distrustful of Soviet intentions and pursued a cautious policy. If the Palestinian problem remained a rock upon which the treaty—and indeed the entire peace—could founder, there were grounds for believing that Egypt and Israel had staked themselves to friendship and would keep it alive.

10. Toward New Accords: China and Russia

President Carter recorded two other diplomatic achievements that were, like his Mideastern treaty, at once momentous and fragile, hopeful and incomplete, subjects of acclaim and controversy. One was the sudden announcement that the United States and the People's Republic of China had agreed to establish full diplomatic relations; the other was the signing of a new strategic arms limitation treaty with the Soviet Union. Both demonstrated the continuity of American foreign policy in the 1970s; Carter's steps toward closer relations with the two Communist powers were, like the Israeli-Egyptian treaty, advances along lines that his predecessors had laid down.

The agreement with China followed months of secret negotiations. The result was a joint communiqué issued by the two powers on December 15, 1978, which announced that normal relations would be established on January 1 and ambassadors exchanged by March 1, 1979. Teng Hsiao-ping would travel to the United States in late January for talks with President Carter and a cross-country tour—the first official visit by a top Chinese leader since the establishment of the People's Republic thirty years earlier.

For China, the new American relationship was part of the Great Leap Outward that Teng had proclaimed early in 1978—an ambitious program aimed at modernizing the Chinese economy by increasing foreign trade, forging closer economic ties with other nations, and importing needed technology. In a repudiation of some of the late Chairman Mao's socialist formulas, Teng proposed to employ elements of capitalism in achieving this economic growth. Chinese policy was altered to permit foreign loans, joint manufacturing ventures, and investments. The People's Republic signed a treaty of peace and friendship with Japan in August 1978. The two nations had already concluded a $20-billion trade agreement that featured an exchange of Chinese coal and oil for Japanese factories and technology. Trade was also expanded with the United States, and Teng spoke expansively of the great new commercial and investment opportunities that he foresaw for American firms in China.

The price that the United States had to pay for this new Chinese connection was, in effect, an end to the old one—a severing of its official relations with Taiwan. The United States agreed to recognize Peking's longstanding claim that Taiwan was part of China, to end diplomatic relations with Taiwan in January 1979, to withdraw its troops from that island, and to abrogate its mutual defense treaty with Taiwan by January 1980. The United States could, however, retain cultural and trade relations with its former ally and continue to provide defensive weapons. In return, China spoke of "unification" rather than the familiar "liberation."

Although American opinion was generally favorable, the section pertaining to Taiwan infuriated many conservatives, who had championed the cause of the island regime ever since the late Chiang Kai-shek had fled there from the mainland in 1949. Resentful noises came from conservatives in the Senate, where Barry Goldwater was so incensed that he talked of bringing suit against the president to prevent cancellation of the Taiwan treaty. But the president seemed to be on firm constitutional grounds; Senate approval is necessary in order to ratify a treaty but not in order to cancel one, and Carter went ahead in spite of senatorial protests. Administration leaders were able to meet most Senate objections by insisting that the United States would continue to have a stake and an interest in Taiwan's defense, and the Senate went on record in early 1979 by announcing American determination to take whatever steps might be necessary in the event of an attack upon Taiwan from the mainland.

Teng Hsiao-ping's visit to the United States was a great success. The deputy premier disarmed many critics by his talk about China's new economic program and peaceful intentions. Conservatives could not help but applaud Teng's anti-Soviet attitude, which he expressed with an uncompromising vehemence that would have pleased the late John Foster Dulles. Indeed, the administration had to be careful in its exchange of views and toasts with Teng lest the Soviets take offense or regard the Peking-Washington agreement as an alliance against them. Americans who felt uncomfortable with the new Chinese relationship were at least partially reassured by Teng's fears of Russia, and the business community was pleased by the prospect of new opportunities in the vast Chinese market.

An indication of the complexity that would characterize relations among the three great powers was immediately forthcoming. In February 1979 the People's Republic climaxed weeks of angry exchanges and border incidents by launching an invasion of the Socialist Republic of Vietnam, its ally during the recent war with the United States. The Hanoi regime, which had a defensive alliance with the USSR, had irritated Peking since 1977 by its hostility toward the Chinese-backed Communists in Cambodia. This hostility had turned into open warfare in 1978, and Vietnam invaded Cambodia with the frank intention of overthrowing the repressive Pol Pot government. For American observers it was a bizarre spectacle: one Indochinese Communist nation making war upon another while the two major Communist powers supported opposite sides. Hanoi's success in ousting Pol Pot, occupying most of Cambodia, and establishing a puppet regime was what finally triggered the Chinese attack, which was avowedly designed not to conquer Vietnamese territory but to "teach Vietnam a lesson."

There was uneasiness lest this border war broaden into full-scale conflict between Russia and China. But the Soviets showed no disposition to become involved beyond warning Peking to pull back "before it was too late," and the Chinese did in fact withdraw after a few weeks of brisk action inside the Vietnamese border. Both sides sustained casualties, and just what lesson had been taught or learned was unclear. About all that Americans could be sure of was that their policies toward the two Communist giants would have to be conducted with great care.

The new accord with China might or might not have contributed to delays in reaching agreement with Russia. Washington and Moscow had been negotiating earnestly for months, and President Carter had hoped to announce the conclusion of a new SALT treaty at the end of 1978 as a companion triumph to the Chinese-American communiqué. But it was not until June 1979 that Carter was able to meet with an ailing, aging, but still capable Leonid Brezhnev in Vienna and tuck all the loose ends into place. It became obvious during their talks that Brezhnev felt as strongly as Carter did about the importance of reaching accord. "God will never forgive us if we fail," the Soviet leader remarked. They succeeded.

The treaty, signed by the two leaders on June 18, was similar in general terms to the agreement that both Ford and Carter had been working toward since 1975. It set a limit of 2,400 long-range missiles and bombers for each side at the time of signing, to be reduced to 2,250 by 1981. It limited the total number of nuclear warheads to 10,000 for each country and the number of MIRVs to 1,320, and placed a limit of 10 upon the number of warheads that a single ICBM could carry. The American cruise missile was included in the limitation while the Soviet backfire bomber was not, but Brezhnev did pledge to limit production of these medium-range aircraft to the present rate of 30 a year.[26] The two leaders also agreed that SALT III talks would concentrate upon *reducing* nuclear stockpiles.

Carter solemnly assured a joint session of Congress on June 18 that the treaty represented a real gain and provided more than adequately for American safety and security, but controversy over the merits of SALT II began immediately. The hearings and debates over ratification promised to be lengthy, perhaps lasting until well into 1980. Three shades of Senate opinion emerged: a conservative group fearful that the treaty conceded

[26]Both sides had made concessions. The United States allowed the Soviets to have more than 300 of their deadly SS-18 ICBMs, in return for which Russia agreed not to deploy its new mobile missile, the SS-16, during the life of the treaty. The Russians also conceded on equal aggregates, on the 10-warhead-per-launcher limit, and on a limit for submarine-launched MIRVs. America's forward-based systems in Europe were excluded. The United States was permitted to proceed with development of the MX, a mobile ICBM that would be harder to destroy than the present Minutemen and Titans deployed in fixed locations.

too much to the Soviets and endangered American security, a liberal group of supporters, and a moderate element who had reservations but might be persuaded to vote in favor.

The treaty was far from a breakthrough, and its approval by the Senate without crippling amendments was not certain. Nevertheless, the debate was being conducted in sane and informed fashion. There seemed to be consensus that continued efforts to reach accord in this vital area were both possible and necessary, and that even limited and imperfect agreements were preferable to a resumption of cold war rivalries.

11. Energy and the Economy: Democratic Response

The same economic problems that had plagued Richard Nixon and Gerald Ford were still present, in full panoply, to plague Jimmy Carter—energy, unemployment, inflation. The problems and circumstances were such, moreover, that not even the return of one-party control over both the White House and Congress could produce decisive action or end the stalemate of recent years.

For the Carter administration, at least during its first three years, domestic policy began and ended with energy. On Inauguration Day the president ordered his staff to prepare a national energy plan, and on April 18 he unveiled it. Efforts to solve the energy problem, he said, borrowing a phrase from William James, would be "the moral equivalent of war." Dwindling domestic supplies of oil and natural gas, which together accounted for 75 percent of the nation's energy, had created a growing, ruinously expensive, and potentially fatal dependence on foreign oil. (The statistics were sobering. American oil imports, after climbing to a record 40 percent of total consumption in 1974, had been increasing steadily ever since; in 1977 about half of the country's oil came from abroad. The cost of it had grown from $8.4 billion in 1973 to nearly $40 billion in 1977.)

Carter presented his plan to a joint session of Congress two days later. It called for a massive conservation program designed to reduce the growth rate in overall energy use, reduce gasoline consumption by 10 percent, and cut oil imports virtually in half by 1985. It recommended more nuclear power plants and a two-thirds increase in coal production. But the major emphasis was upon conservation—specifically, reduced consumption of oil and natural gas.

Although better insulation of homes and buildings and greater use of solar energy would accomplish part of this objective, the core of Carter's conservation plan was an elaborate system of taxes, tax incentives, and tax rebates and credits. There would be a heavier tax on gasoline. There would be punitive taxes upon gas-guzzling cars and rebates for buyers of fuel-efficient cars. Similar "carrot and stick" taxes were designed to encourage factories and power plants to switch from oil and natural gas to coal. Most important, domestic crude oil and newly discovered natural gas would be allowed to reach the open market price; presumably people would use fuel less wastefully when it became sufficiently expensive. The burden on families of moderate and low incomes would be eased by tax rebates and credits. Greater use of coal and nuclear power would be accompanied by adequate environmental standards and safety precautions.

Congress spent eighteen months debating the president's energy plan before it could pass a bill, and the bill that it passed bore scant resemblance to Carter's proposal, pleased almost no one, and left the energy situation about where it had been before. The House of Representatives responded quickly. It passed the energy bill in August with no important changes—at a cost, critics noted, of rushing through some complex provisions without adequate study, adequate debate, or adequate consideration of whether the bill could accomplish its purpose. Then the Senate proceeded to dismember the proposal and passed so different a measure that it took the conference committee nearly a year to produce a workable compromise. Congress did manage to agree, in 1977, to combine several existing agencies into a new Department of Energy.

The item chiefly responsible for stalling Carter's energy bill was natural-gas deregulation. Natural gas sold in interstate commerce had been subject to federal regulation since 1938, on the theory that homes and industries that use gas are at the mercy of a single supplier and need price protection. Intrastate gas, on the other hand, was not subject to regulation. When shortages and rising prices first became a problem in the seventies, gas producers sold most of their output on the unregulated market, where they could charge higher prices. As a result, gas became plentiful in producing states like Texas and Louisiana and in short supply in regions dependent on interstate shipments.

Proponents of deregulation argued that the only way to correct this imbalance and make gas equally available to all was to let producers charge the market price everywhere. Deregulation was supposed to have the further advantage of stimulating the search for new natural-gas deposits and financing the increased costs of getting at them. (The identical argument was being used as a reason for deregulating so-called "old" oil— the product of pre-1973 wells—which had been subject to price controls since the Nixon years.) Opponents of deregulation insisted that the rise in prices would add to inflation and bear most heavily upon low-income families.

Congress staged a three-cornered battle over this issue. Democratic liberals argued for retaining controls; Carter wanted higher prices as a deterrent to consumption, and would achieve this by a wellhead tax; oil-state senators wanted higher prices for the producer as an incentive to increased output, and would achieve this by deregulation. The result was a compromise that the deregulators liked best: a series of annual phased increases that would bring natural-gas prices up to the open market level by 1985, at which time controls would cease altogether.

An exhausted Congress finally reached agreement in October 1978 and passed the National Energy Act. The president, desperate for tangible results after he had risked much of his political standing on energy legislation for so long, hailed it as a victory, but the lawmakers had either eliminated or watered down most of his original requests. The wellhead tax on crude oil, which he had called the "cornerstone" of the program, was gone. So were the gasoline tax and the rebate for buyers of gas-saving automobiles. The tax on gas-guzzling cars was much reduced, as were the rebates and credits designed to encourage the use of coal in power plants and insulation and solar energy in homes. The authority to order utilities to convert to coal was retained, but the penalty tax for not complying was eliminated, and companies were given until 1990 to make the switch. The president's request for a wellhead tax on natural gas had been replaced by deregulation. Neither the energy situation nor the president's prestige had been much helped by the new law.

Carter got off to a better start in other areas of domestic policy, but he was destined for trouble there as well. Of the twin bugaboos of unemployment and inflation, the former appeared to be the greater problem as his presidency began. The inflation rate, although it began to rise near the end of 1976, had been at a relatively manageable 5.5 percent for the year—a marked improvement over the 7 to 8 percent of 1975 and the double-digit disaster of 1974. Unemployment, on the other hand, had hovered persistently near the 8-percent level during 1976 and showed no signs of improving at year's end.

Aside from energy, therefore, most of Carter's legislative proposals were aimed at stimulating the economy and reducing unemployment. In this effort, his big Democratic majorities were largely in accord with him, and the major enactments of 1977 were standard Democratic fare: $6 billion in federal grants for local public works; $7.9 billion for more public service jobs; a three-year, $34-billion tax cut that included incentives for employers who hired more workers and grants to state and local governments to prevent reductions in public services; increased farm supports; and a phased increase in the minimum wage from $2.30 to $3.35 per hour by 1981. Further economic stimulus was offered by extending to 1980 the deadlines on new automobile-emission standards and on compliance with clean-air standards by coal-converting industries. Congress also responded to Carter's requests by taking action to put the social security system on a sounder financial basis, which included substantial increases in the payroll tax over ensuing decades. Whether in spite or because of these new laws,

EMPLOYMENT AND UNEMPLOYMENT
IN THE UNITED STATES
1950 – 1977

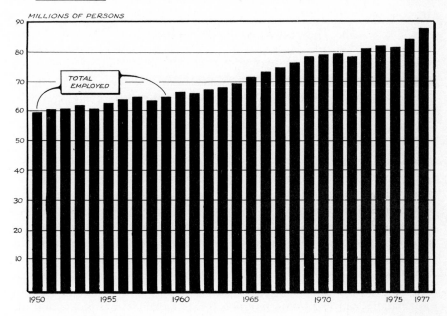

MILLIONS OF PERSONS

TOTAL
EMPLOYED

1950   1955   1960   1965   1970   1975 1977

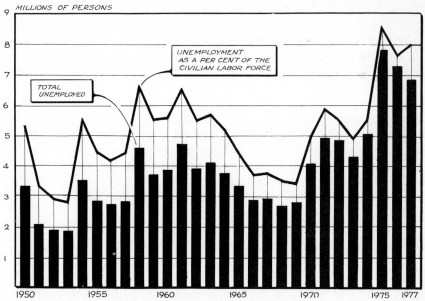

MILLIONS OF PERSONS

UNEMPLOYMENT
AS A PER CENT OF THE
CIVILIAN LABOR FORCE

TOTAL
UNEMPLOYED

1950   1955   1960   1965   1970   1975 1977

unemployment dropped from 7.9 percent in December 1976 to 6.4 percent a year later and fell almost another percentage point in 1978.

12. *The Battle Against Inflation*

Unfortunately, inflation got steadily worse, rising to 7 percent in 1977 and to a painful 9.6 percent in 1978. As signs of public distress mounted, the administration concluded that inflation was the nation's biggest enemy and would have to be brought under control.

What are the principal causes of this complex and intractable phenomenon? Each of the following, in varying degree, has played a role in recent years. The effect of Democratic legislation in 1977—a higher minimum wage, higher farm supports, tax cuts, public works programs—must be mentioned, since nearly all of it put upward pressure on wages, prices, consumer spending, and budget deficits. Government regulations and restrictions, particularly in the areas of transportation and environmental protection, frequently had the effect of making rates and prices higher. Mention should also be made of the ability of certain large corporations to keep prices artificially high. Something was contributed by high consumer expectations and lavish consumption habits induced by a generation of almost unbroken expansion in the output of goods and services.

After a point, too, inflation feeds itself. Imports become more expensive because foreign sellers, knowing each dollar is worth less, demand more for their products—and domestic manufacturers faithfully mark up their own goods to keep pace. Even worse, awareness of inflation induces rapid, almost feverish consumer buying and borrowing on the theory that tomorrow's prices will be even higher and today's loan can be paid back next year in cheaper dollars.

Pivotal responsibility, of course, must be assigned to skyrocketing energy costs after 1973. Not only did they pull nearly all other prices up with them, as we have seen; they also acted with lethal effect upon the so-called wage-price spiral. Because rising fuel and heating costs were so large a percentage of workers' budgets, they felt compelled to demand higher compensatory wage boosts.

A new and disturbing factor that economists first began to notice in the mid-seventies was a declining rate of increase in output per man-hour—a rough but useful guide to industrial productivity. This index had increased at a healthy average rate of 3 percent a year through most of the fifties and sixties. This continuing rise in productivity helped to keep inflation within bounds by enabling employers to grant wage increases without raising prices, since higher payrolls were offset by larger output. But output per man-hour did not resume its normal upward tendency after the recession

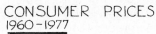

CONSUMER PRICES
1960-1977

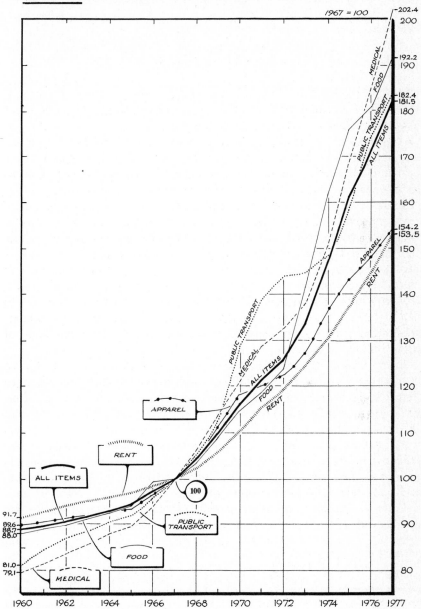

of 1974–1975; instead, after a brief spurt in 1976 it registered a bare 1.6-percent increase in 1977 and an abysmal 0.4 percent in 1978. With productivity so flat, all wage increases must be reflected in price increases—the wage-price spiral, with a vengeance. Chief causes included stricter environmental regulations, an inadequate rate of investment since 1973 in new labor-saving and cost-cutting machinery, reduced expenditures on research and development, a younger and less experienced work force, and (once again) rising energy costs, which made new machinery more expensive to operate. Whatever the causes, the productivity lag had added a worrisome new pressure to the inflationary impulse.

And inflation, whatever *its* causes, was inflicting the kind of material and psychological damage that no government could ignore. Carter's concern manifested itself in several ways. Like Ford, he was strongly opposed to mandatory controls, and his first anti-inflation programs relied essentially on voluntarism: earnest appeals, sober admonitions, "jawboning," cajolery, even threats. And again like Ford, Carter made no discernible headway with the voluntary approach. Impatient observers drew a parallel between the efficacy of persuasion and remonstrance as anti-inflationary weapons and King Canute's success in ordering back the tides.

Carter began moving more forcefully in 1978. In April he announced a 5.5-percent limit upon governmental pay increases and froze the salaries of top-level White House staff members and federal officials. In May he reduced his tax-cut proposal by more than 20 percent—from $25 billion to $19.4 billion—and pushed back its effective date by three months; Congress cut another $700 million from the measure before approving it. (The only justification for any kind of cut was a desire to offset the impact of higher social security taxes.) On guard against inflationary measures, Carter vetoed a $36.9-billion defense appropriation because it contained $2 billion for a nuclear carrier that he regarded as unnecessary, and he vetoed a $10.2-billion public-works bill because it excluded his requests for cutbacks on dams and other water projects. Congress failed to override either veto. Indeed, the legislative roster in 1978 was much shorter than in 1977, and fewer of the new laws were inflationary.[27]

Later in the year, as inflationary alarms in the financial community touched off declines in the stock market and new assaults on the dollar,

---

[27]The two major enactments of 1978 dealt with full employment and civil service reform. The Humphrey-Hawkins Full Employment Act, a watered-down version of a bill pushed by champions of more employment opportunities for blacks and other minorities, committed the government to reduce the unemployment rate to 4 percent by 1983. Its advocates regarded the final version as fatally weakened by the removal of a provision requiring the government to act directly to provide jobs. The Civil Service Reform Act replaced the Civil Service Commission with two new agencies: an Office of Personnel Management and a bipartisan Merit System Protection Board. The law included provisions creating a new level of senior-executive positions and a new system of merit pay increases, a new framework for labor relations governing federal employees, a tighter administrative structure, and somewhat more freedom for officials in dealing with incompetent employees. The president called the law "a long overdue reform" that would bring greater efficiency and accountability to the federal bureaucracy.

Carter tried even stronger action. He proclaimed a new anti-inflationary program in October which established voluntary guidelines aimed at limiting wage increases to 7 percent and keeping price increases at 6 to 6.5 percent. Exceptions were made for low-wage jobs and for raises that were demonstrably offset by higher productivity. The president tried to strengthen the proposal by listing incentives and pressures (such as awarding or withholding government contracts) that could be used to secure compliance with the guidelines, and he asked Congress to authorize a tax rebate for workers whose living costs went up more than 7 percent. He accompanied this with solemn assurances that the government would tighten its own belt. "We are going to hold down government spending, reduce the budget deficit, and eliminate government waste," he promised. "We will slash federal hiring and cut the federal work force. We will eliminate needless regulations."

The program had no impact. While Democratic liberals fumed that Carter's new budgetary policy made him sound exactly like Gerald Ford, the stock and money markets continued to reflect financial uneasiness. AFL–CIO leaders rejected the new wage-price guidelines and said that they preferred mandatory controls. Congress refused to act on Carter's request for a tax-rebate incentive.

The declining value of the dollar assumed crisis proportions in October 1978, and the administration took strong emergency action on November 1. The Federal Reserve Board raised the rediscount rate to a record 9.5 percent and further tightened credit by making regulatory changes that reduced the amount of lendable funds by some $3 billion. In cooperation with its trading partners, the United States acquired $30 billion in foreign currencies and used them to buy dollars in order to sustain the price against speculative sales. The government also began to sell gold in order to end speculative buying.

It was the boldest action that Carter had yet taken, and the reaction at home and abroad was prompt and gratifying. The dollar rose sharply in value against the strongest currencies—the mark, the yen, and the Swiss franc—and the price of gold (which had been rising in market value for years as investors lost confidence in the dollar) dropped $23 per ounce in a single day's trading. The stock market rallied with a thirty-point gain as brokers struggled to keep up with a sudden rush of purchase orders.

The government's actions had averted a financial panic and restored enough confidence to stabilize the dollar and the stock market, but no one regarded the problem as solved or felt much optimism about long-range prospects. The elections of 1978, which took place at this point, reflected voter concerns over inflation. Politically, the results were indecisive. The Republicans made net gains of 3 seats in the Senate and 12 in the House, reducing Democratic majorities to 59-41 and 276-157 respectively. The Republicans also raised their total of governorships from 12 to 18. But these gains were below average for a midterm canvass in a troubled year,

and the expected nationwide surge of support for conservative candidates
was hardly in evidence. Voters on the whole were expressing increased
caution rather than increased conservatism, and moderates in both parties
scored the most victories.

If one political principle emerged victorious in 1978 it was that of budgetary restraint, reduced governmental expenditures, and a ceiling on
taxes. The most striking example of this new demand, which was exagger-
atedly hailed as a "taxpayer revolt," came in California in June, when
nearly two-thirds of the voters approved an amendment to the state constitution that reduced the property tax rate and put a ceiling on annual
property tax increases. Similar proposals were on the ballot in other states
and won considerable support, but voters were cautious here as well.
They tended to be against governmental waste and inefficiency but not
against essential services, and they did not support sweeping tax-cut proposals as widely as conservatives had hoped. The electorate did seem to
be signaling, however, that spending would have to be curtailed at all
levels while the inflationary spiral continued.

13. The Crisis of 1979

The year 1979 brought nothing but more grief. Revolution in Iran stifled
that country's oil production and had disruptive ripple effects everywhere.
OPEC announced a new series of increases which amounted to a 50-
percent rise and brought the world market price of oil to between $18 and
$23 a barrel by midyear. The results were comparable to those of 1973:
shortages, dislocations, and terrible new inflationary pressures. Prices shot
up faster than ever; each month confirmed the prediction that 1979 would
be a worse double-digit year than 1974. By late spring, with interest rates
at record highs in the battle against inflation, signs of a new recession were
appearing—declining labor productivity, layoffs in factories, and sharp
drops in automobile sales and housing starts.

As oil supplies once again ran low, a dramatic warning flashed from
another sector of the energy front. A pump failure in March at the nuclear
power plant on Three Mile Island, near Harrisburg, Pennsylvania, led to a
breakdown in the cooling system and threatened several catastrophes: a
possible meltdown of the reactor core, a possible explosion of the big
hydrogen bubble that formed at the top of the reactor, a possible emission
of great quantities of radioactive gas into the atmosphere. The disasters
were averted; the core eventually cooled down, and the hydrogen bubble
was reduced and conditions were stabilized. But the escape had been
narrow, and the accident—traceable to a variety of human failures and

errors—cast grave new doubts upon the feasibility of too much reliance upon nuclear power.

Meanwhile, shortages in May and June brought distress to American consumers—gasoline prices exceeding $1 a gallon, predictions of a winter scarcity of heating oil, and rumblings against OPEC, the oil companies, and the government. Although gasoline supplies were back near normal in most places by midsummer, tourism fell off, and the shadows of recession grew longer.

As cries of protest and anguish mounted, a worried president scheduled a nationwide energy speech for early July, mystified everyone by abruptly canceling it, and then—after days of thought and high-level consultations at Camp David—went on the air on the evening of July 15, 1979, to tell the nation where he stood and what he proposed to do with regard to the energy problem. The suspense of waiting some ten days for this speech after the earlier cancellation undoubtedly swelled the size of his audience: an estimated 100 million people saw and heard their president on that warm July night.

In what was by far the most eloquent and forceful of his presidential speeches, Jimmy Carter proclaimed a "crisis of confidence" in the American spirit and unveiled an ambitious new energy proposal. Voicing his belief that the crisis had struck "at the very heart, soul and spirit of our national will," the president said that America's security was at stake and predicted that a successful war "upon the battlefield of energy" could restore national confidence and bring about a "rebirth of the American spirit." He frankly admitted his own mistakes and said that he had not provided enough leadership. He pledged to do better, called for the people's help and cooperation, and assured them that he would lead the fight and would act.

The second half of the address set forth a new energy plan in detail. Carter set a goal of cutting oil imports to half their current level by 1990. As a beginning, he announced a freeze on imports in 1979 and 1980 at a level not to exceed 8.5 million barrels a day. Although conservation measures designed to save half a million barrels a day formed an important part of the plan,[28] its major emphasis was upon increased domestic production to take up the slack of reduced imports. This would be achieved in part by building more nuclear power plants under stricter safeguards, in part by a $100-million "solar energy bank" that would use its resources to support low-interest loans for solar-power installations in homes and commercial buildings, and in larger part by decontrolling oil and natural-gas prices.

---

[28]Specifically, Carter asked for $10 billion for public transportation during the eighties. He requested a new law requiring utilities to cut oil consumption by 50 percent by 1990, both by switching to coal and by reforming rate structures to charge more for heavy "peaktime" users. He asked for another law requiring utility companies to provide long-term loans to residential and commercial users to finance such conservation measures as better insulation.

The major component in the enlarged supplies of energy was to be from synthetic fuels. These included methane and other hydrocarbons obtained from organic matter but consisted chiefly of oil and natural gas derived from coal and oil extracted from shale—all totaling 2.5 million daily barrels by 1990. Since the synthetic fuels obtained from coal and shale were too expensive to be produced commercially, Carter proposed to bring them into production by means of an Energy Security Corporation. It would be authorized to conduct joint ventures with private industry, build and operate its own facilities, guarantee governmental purchases and prices, and sell off its assets and patents and go out of business after twenty-five years—by which time, it was hoped, synthetic-fuel technologies would have progressed far enough to enable private industry to take over. Carter also wanted standby gas-rationing authority, continued federal control over allocation and pricing of gasoline, and an energy mobilization board patterned after the War Production Board of 1942-1945 to coordinate and speed action by cutting red tape.

The new energy corporation would raise some of its money by selling government-guaranteed bonds to the public, but the principal source for the huge sums required to finance this program—Carter suggested $140 billion—would come from a tax upon the oil industry's "windfall profits" from decontrolled prices.

The response to this important address was symptomatic. The call for regeneration, renewed confidence, and firm leadership touched a responsive chord; the energy program ran into trouble right away. Experts found fault with nearly all of it; they saw too much cost, too much government, misplaced emphasis, and threats to the environment. The nuclear argument was already irreconcilable: many persons believed that America's energy requirements made more nuclear power a necessity; others, that the hazards made it a price America dared not pay. Congress began to treat specific aspects of the plan (decontrol, gas rationing, windfall profits) with the same carping assertiveness that had marked most of its relations with the executive since Watergate. Despite Carter's plea for a quick and united response, the lawmakers adjourned for the August recess without taking action, even though many components of the plan had already come before them as separate measures.

Whether his plan would pass in anything like the form that Carter had requested, or accomplish the goals he had set forth if it did, was much in doubt. Yet it was here—in the area of conserving and developing energy, and in strengthening an economy that the energy crisis was again pushing into double-digit inflation and recession—that Carter's political future (and perhaps the country's) would be determined.

35

America in 1980:

Dilemmas and Prospects

As the United States moved into the final two decades of the twentieth century, there seemed to be general agreement on three related propositions: (1) the country was not in good shape economically; (2) people were indeed suffering from something like the crisis of confidence that Carter had mentioned; and (3) leadership had failed to come to effective grips with the problems. The three went together, and fed one another. Progress in any single area would necessarily involve greater understanding of the other two. Economists are in full, if inherently discordant, cry after the first point. This concluding chapter will focus mainly upon the second and third points, on the theory that in the kingdom's present condition one-eyed men are apt to show up almost anywhere.

1. The Question of Leadership

If there has in fact been a failure of leadership, how should responsibility be apportioned?

A large majority apparently believed that Jimmy Carter deserved much of the blame. His rating in the opinion polls declined fairly steadily after a robust early start; by mid-1979, despite brief upward surges occasioned by his diplomatic triumphs, the percentage that approved of his presidential capacities had fallen to a near-record low, comparable to Nixon's at the climax of Watergate.

A case can be made. Candidate Carter had made too many promises, voiced too much confidence, and raised too many expectations. His oft-proclaimed integrity and freedom from Washington's corrupting taint were badly compromised in 1977 by the charges of financial irregularity that surrounded and finally engulfed Bert Lance, his close friend and budget director. As so often happened, Lance waited too long to resign, and Carter defended him well past the point of political prudence. In addition, the cocky, inexperienced young Georgians on the White House staff contributed to the problem by guarding their chief too closely, failing to keep in proper touch with Congress, and stepping on too many Washington toes.

Washington's toes were abnormally sensitive, but Carter sometimes seemed to go out of his way to step on them. He had made much of his "outsider" status during the campaign and proceeded to remain an outsider long after he moved to the capital in 1977—continuing to blast Washington as though he were not himself a part of it, criticizing the bureaucracy as though he were not its leader. His relations with Congress suffered for the same reason. Interested in results and what he liked to call competence, Carter the outsider was also too much the engineer; one disillusioned Democratic critic likened him to Herbert Hoover. He was impatient with the kind of sustained politicking on and about Capitol Hill that was expected (and often necessary) in order to get bills passed and policies supported. Many persons felt that this refusal to play the Washington game was to his credit, but it cost him needed votes.

By his own admission, Carter had managed the government instead of trying to lead the people. He had become too involved in details and had spread himself too thinly over too many projects to concentrate long enough on the strategy of gaining the objectives that mattered most or mobilizing the support that would help to gain them. He was not generally a rousing speaker before large groups. He often explained or defended his positions with a combination of stupefyingly undramatic delivery and sanctimonious piety that seldom moved his audiences. He too often projected an image of indecisiveness, hesitancy, and an unwillingness to offend anyone or back up his pious rhetoric with hard action.

In part Jimmy Carter projected such an image and in part it was thrust upon him. No assignment of responsibility for the current malaise would be complete if it did not make some mention of the nation's image makers—the ubiquitous pollsters, who presented their samplings as though they were America's opinion; the pundits of television and press, who had a way of showing snide contempt for styles and accents different from an unspoken norm; the world of political Washington, an insider's club, jealous, insecure, thriving on rumor, eager to cut heroes down to size, and doubly hostile to outsiders lacking their own kind of glamor. Carter never had much chance with this combination. Those who were not downright unfair tended to be patronizing or hypercritical, subjecting every intonation and hesitation and gaffe to the icy spotlight of Olympian scrutiny. The extent to which President Carter deserved the verdict of America's instant judgment seat will be judged by later historians.

Then there was Congress, whose cooperation and approval were necessary in order to translate program and policy into law and reality. Public disillusionment with government was a central fact of life during this period. Government richly deserved it, but the sentiment made concerted action hard to achieve. Perhaps the most enduring and harmful legacy of Watergate was the distrust of executive power that Nixon's excesses had created. The result was similar to Reconstruction a century earlier: a period of reaction in which Congress sought to dominate. But congressional leadership was by definition hydra-headed, seldom capable of speaking with one clear voice or formulating coherent policy. So public disillusionment, being susceptible and impatient, quickly spread to encompass the legislative as well as the executive. It grew impatient with the former while retaining its distrust of the latter. Hence, mobilizing support for *any* policy became correspondingly harder.

The problem of the mobilization of public opinion was aggravated by Carter's style, which was a blend of preacher and efficiency expert and seldom made room for the political leader. But circumstances had ganged up on him. He was the first president since Eisenhower to come to the presidency without prior service in Congress. The four intervening executives had had a good deal of such service, and it had made them aware, as Carter and his aides were seldom aware, of what made Congress tick and how legislators expected to be treated. Eisenhower's enormous prestige and the combination of crises abroad and prosperity at home had made kid-glove handling of Congress unnecessary. With Carter the situation was in effect reversed, and he never wore the kid gloves properly. He expended too much of his supply of credit on Capitol Hill in winning acceptance of his foreign policy, which (unlike Eisenhower's) offered jolts to tradition and assurances that had to be taken on faith—Panama, China, SALT. There was virtually no leverage left for domestic programs that made even greater demands. Unlike Eisenhower, Carter was forced by conviction and circumstance to advocate unpalatable measures and deal with problems for which no acceptable remedy existed.

Carter came up with remedies; whatever their faults, or his faults as advocate, they often failed because the instrument for lining up a majority had dulled. The only means that America had devised for refining several hundred congressional voices into a viably small number of distinct positions was that of the political party; and independent voting, independent thinking, and the pressure of other loyalties had eroded party discipline to a point where it was no longer reliable. In the case of Carter and the Democrats, discipline was further weakened by the president's decision sometime during 1978 to give balanced budgets and reduced expenditures priority over domestic programs dear to the hearts of organized labor, blacks, and other key Democratic constituencies; by 1979, liberals in Congress regarded the president as little better than a Republican. Others, liberal or conservative, were annoyed by his rigorous cutting of funds for dams and other projects greatly desired in someone's home district. So Congress, unable to lead, refused to follow, and the only voices that were heeded under such conditions were those of special interests.

2. *The People and Their Heritage*

This brings the question of assigning responsibility for failed leadership to its proper location in a democratic society—to the people themselves. It was the great misfortune of both Carter and Congress to be confronted with problems that simply could not be solved without inflicting pain and demanding sacrifice. And if president and Congress seemed unwilling to inflict the one or demand the other, the reason for their reluctance can be located. This was not a generation that reacted well, initially, to prospects of pain and sacrifice.

As regards energy, the public attitude was not helpful. Few people had learned a lesson from the brief crisis of 1973–1974. When supplies went back to normal, most Americans resumed their ingrained habits of wasteful consumption and tended to disbelieve or disregard Carter's talk of energy as America's greatest problem. They either doubted (in the absence of shortages) that there was a problem at all, or they blamed existing difficulties on governmental mismanagement, profiteering by the oil companies, or OPEC greed. The main reason for the abject failure of energy policy in the seventies was a public unwillingness to see the issue as their leaders saw it or to bring pressure upon Congress for action.

But pressure was brought. One overriding public sentiment during these difficult years would appear to be a fear and resentment of big government. The fear is healthy at all times, and the resentment in the wake of recent developments was understandable. Yet a closer examination of just what was being resented leads to a conclusion that is neither surprising nor escapable. When people called for reducing governmental size and cost and cutting expenditures, they were talking about every aspect of government activity except the ones that benefited them. Hence proposals that sought to cut back or eliminate an appropriation or program or bureau quickly alienated some vocal group. It brought pressure. By a process of reverse logrolling, this usually led to no meaningful action at all.

Another conclusion flows from this one. Real though they are, the faults of government do no more than reflect—as faithfully and cruelly as a mirror—the faults of society. And in a way, American society had become just what disillusioned old progressives saw it becoming fifty years ago, only on a far larger scale: a heterogeneous, overlapping collection of special interests, each eager to promote its own welfare and feather its own nest.

This has not been good for government. It has meant that the array of organizations, pressure groups, lobbyists, consultants, congressional subcommittees, governmental agencies, legal counsel, and war chests by which each of these special interests seeks to get what it wants and keep what it has—that this formidable apparatus for the obtaining and doing of favors has totally eclipsed the national interest. This became more noticeable in the 1970s, when sudden scarcity came like a thunderclap in the clear blue sky of prosperity and galvanized each interest group into defensive action.

Why not? The seventies were dominated by the so-called "me" generation, conditioned by a quarter century of expansion to seek instant gratification (buy now, pay later) and pursue material comfort; after all, this was the economy of abundance, the throw-away society, impatient of appeals to principle or sacrifice. It is a familiar indictment. It has been made familiar by the unmistakable mountain of supporting evidence that prosecutors can always cite.

This much is true, but not the whole truth. America is large and contains multitudes, and the arraignment of special interests and private greed is not necessarily where the case rests. The querulous, angry voices on the fringe were most often heard, and the ugly incidents most often reported. But Americans were, taken altogether, more than a chorus of fearful or angry voices, more than statistics of violence or repeated examples of greed. The image is contradictory and easy to misread: it had more than 220 million components in a society that proclaimed each component a sovereign and defended his or her right to act and speak.

They were acting and speaking, yet they had much on their minds besides the urge to acquire and consume. They demonstrated this eloquently during the Bicentennial celebrations of 1976, when millions enjoyed the imaginative community displays and recreations and pageants, or thrilled to the spectacular visit of the world's fleet of square riggers—the tall ships—or admired the exhibits in the Freedom Train, or listened to its steam locomotive wail a long salute through the night to the nation's past glories. There was something irrepressible and good-natured about America's prolonged celebration of its two-hundredth birthday, something that bespoke the existence of great reservoirs of good will, commitment, hope, pride, vigor, and continuing devotion to the American dream.

All of this was present too, and it stood in some kind of uneasy equipoise against the forces of blind greed and special interest and doomsday fears. America was neither damned nor saved so much as it was waiting, still undecided, still trying to think through its response to forces little more than half understood. The signals were mixed. They would not be read clearly for a while.

3. Race Relations

Race relations, too, displayed mixed and contradictory signs. Much depended on whether one regarded the bottle as half full or half empty; the evidence warrants neither complacency nor despair. On the one hand, the number of blacks elected to state and local office continued to grow, as did black college enrollment. Black middle and professional classes were generally able to hold their own in terms of jobs and incomes. On the other hand, there were indications that black employment and median income, in relation to figures for whites, had suffered more and recovered less from the recession of 1974-1975 and that fewer poor blacks were rising to the middle class. Certainly the unemployment rate among black youths in the seventies was appallingly high, at times approaching 40 percent. De facto segregation in most northern and western cities remained the rule, reinforced by "white flight" to the suburbs and soaring real estate costs that restricted housing opportunities for moderate-income black families.

Racial busing continued to be denounced in many areas and to work satisfactorily in others. Moves in Congress to prohibit it by constitutional amendment were frequent, yet a majority voted down an antibusing amendment in the spring of 1979. South Boston experienced tension and racial violence when its schools were integrated in the mid-seventies, yet the ugly incidents that made headlines had a way of obscuring quiet evidence of interracial harmony and coexistence in this and other troubled areas.[1]

The controversial effort to aid minorities by using racial quotas in employment and college admissions was similarly on dead center. When a white youth charged that the medical school of the University of California at Davis had discriminated against him by rejecting his application in

[1] The Supreme Court considered each busing plan on its individual merits. The Detroit case of 1974, in which the justices overturned a plan to achieve integration by busing students across school district lines, was offset by decisions in 1979 that upheld such integration in Dayton and Columbus, Ohio. The majority held that busing across school district lines was warranted if, and only if, there was evidence that such lines had been drawn with the *intent* to produce or maintain segregation. The court found such evidence in Dayton and Columbus but not in Detroit.

favor of less qualified minority applicants, the court upheld his contention in *Regents of the University of California* v. *Bakke*, 1978. The 5–4 decision ordered Bakke's admission, but kept the affirmative-action principle alive by ruling that schools could consider race along with other factors in their legitimate search for a diversified student body.[2]

Leadership in the black community—as in the nation—was more fractured and less respected than it had been in the days of King, A. Philip Randolph, and other prominent figures of the fifties and sixties. Black militancy had lost its cutting edge; the urban ghettos festered with unsolved problems and blighted hopes. Yet the record-breaking audiences for the TV series "Roots" in 1977, derived from the award-winning semifictional study by black writer Alex Haley—a moving depiction of the black experience in Africa and America—suggested that a durable bridge across the racial chasm had in fact been securely emplaced.

Other groups, too, were experiencing a mixed bag of gains and setbacks. The Equal Rights Amendment was stalled, yet consciousness in the area of women's rights had undoubtedly risen. Hispanic Americans were gaining in their drive for bilingual education and other recognition, yet they were plagued with the same problems of high unemployment and low income that affected many blacks. Indians were better organized and more active than ever, yet they remained the most depressed and deprived of the nation's minorities.

The record, in short, left much to be desired, and progress had slowed in the troubled seventies. Yet the doors had by no means been closed. It seems fair to observe that renewed advance toward the goals of equal opportunity and a better life for underprivileged groups was merely awaiting another change in the atmosphere. For victims of discrimination the wait seemed unconscionably long, but the gains that had been recorded since midcentury offered grounds for the belief that America would not forget its unfinished business.

4. The Prospect

It all came back, as always, to the American people—in all their varying shades of political opinion, skin color, and attitude. The flaws were there, as we have tried to suggest. And so was the potential, in such a diverse crazy quilt of ways: a nation of backyard tinkerers eagerly testing the

[2]And in the 5–4 *Weber* decision of 1979, the court denied Brian Weber's claim that the Kaiser Aluminum Company had violated his civil rights by accepting black applicants with less seniority than he had. Holding that the Kaiser affirmative-action plan was voluntary and involved no federal or state action, the court majority refused to rule between permissible and impermissible plans but called the Kaiser plan in keeping with the spirit of the Civil Rights Act of 1964.

possible technologies that would make energy in some unlikely looking new vehicle or gadget or machine once again workably available; a nation of believers who were not afraid of hard work or sacrifice or attempting the impossible; a nation of thoughtful God-fearing folk who would think before they jumped, who would not move impetuously or heed the crackpot single-solution doctrines or single-issue zealots; a nation of idealists who would still respond, when the right word was spoken, in the right way. They were waiting, unsure of themselves, not of one mind, never of one mind.

But there were signs that more and more of them were coming to agree with President Carter's view that the crisis was really one of spirit. This was a message that religious leaders, writers, scholars, and other social critics had been sounding for years—indeed, an injunction at least as old as the Gospel according to Saint Matthew.[3] What was dawning, perhaps, was a realization that material well-being and the riches of this world are not, in and of themselves, productive of happiness.

It would naturally take a while for this motorized, electrified, gadget-cluttered, power-driven society of consumers to reach consensus on such a point. The deprived could hardly be expected to understand it; they had never really shared in what they were now being told was perhaps not the American dream after all. The comfortably situated might take even longer, since it is about as hard to give up a luxury as to give up the thought of acquiring one.

Yet Jesus's injunction gave off the uncompromising glitter of truth. And in the realization and acceptance of this truth by a committed majority of Americans might lie the answer. Thomas Jefferson had staked America to the pursuit of happiness, and this was a dream that had fired his own and every succeeding generation. Now, two hundred years later, it was necessary only to redefine happiness in terms that he had had in mind all along. A less extravagant way of life and a less materialistic set of values held out the hope—and there were few others—of salvation, not merely for the nation's economy, but for its soul.

[3] Matthew 16:26: "What is a man profited, if he shall gain the whole world, and lose his own soul?"

Suggested Additional Reading

1. FROM THE SECOND WORLD WAR TO THE COLD WAR: GENERAL
   ASPECTS OF FOREIGN AND DOMESTIC POLICY

A few worthwhile attempts to evaluate the postwar era have already been made. Among the best, to date, are Herbert Agar, *The Price of Power: America Since 1945* (1957); Eric F. Goldman, *The Crucial Decade and After, 1945-1960* (1961); Everett Ladd, Jr., and Charles D. Hadley, *Transformations of the American Party System: Party Coalitions from the New Deal to the 1970s* (1975); Herbert S. Parmet, *The Democrats: The Years After FDR* (1976); and Robert D. Marcus and David Burner (eds.), *America Since 1945* (1972), which includes both historical essays and documents. The indispensable work on foreign affairs is the Council on Foreign Relations, *The United States in World Affairs, 1945-1967, 1970* (24 vols., 1947-1972). See also Arthur M. Schlesinger, Jr. (ed.), *The Dynamics of World Power: A Documentary History of United States Foreign Policy 1945-1972* (5 vols., 1972). The best historical overviews of postwar foreign policy are Seyom Brown, *The Faces of Power: Constancy and Change in United States Foreign Policy from Truman to Johnson* (1968); John W. Spanier, *American Foreign Policy Since World War II* (1965); and Paul Y. Hammond, *Cold War and Détente: The American Foreign Policy Process Since 1945* (1975). The best general survey of twentieth-century foreign policy is Richard W. Leopold, *The Growth of American Foreign Policy* (1962). A valuable documentary collection dealing with all important phases of national policy during the period is National Archives and Records Service, *Public Papers of the Presidents of the United States;* volumes covering all the presidents since 1945 have been published annually. The fourth volume of Arthur M. Schlesinger, Jr., Fred L. Israel, and William P. Hassen (eds.), *History of American Presidential Elections* (4 vols., 1971), covers the elections from 1940 through 1968 and includes interpretative essays, documents, and statistics for each canvass. Excellent brief résumés of recent social, political, economic, and international developments are contained in the yearbooks published by the *Encyclopedia Americana* and the *Encyclopaedia Britannica*. Radical and reactionary political viewpoints in the postwar era are respectively placed in historical context by Christopher Lasch, *The Agony of the American Left* (1969), and Seymour M. Lipset and Earl Raab, *The Politics of Unreason: Right-Wing Extremism in America, 1790–1977* (1978). The best general survey of recent southern history is Charles P. Roland, *The Improbable Era: The South Since World War II* (1975). Otis L. Graham, Jr., *Toward a Planned Society: From Roosevelt to Nixon* (1976), is the best study of that subject.

2. AMERICAN POLITICS SINCE THE SECOND WORLD WAR

A. *The Home Front During the Second World War*

We now have an excellent general study of domestic politics during this period: John M. Blum, *V Was for Victory: Politics and American Culture During World War II* (1976). Geoffrey Perrett, *Days of Sadness, Years of Triumph: The American People, 1939–1945* (1973), is another interesting survey. Jack Goodman (ed.), *While You Were Gone: A Report on Wartime Life in the United States* (1946), contains some good essays. Alan S. Milward, *War, Economy and Society, 1939–1945* (1977), surveys the impact of the war on the American economy in a worldwide setting. Donald M. Nelson, *Arsenal of Democracy* (1946), is an "official" history of industrial mobilization, while Eliot Janeway, *The Struggle for Survival* (1951), is extremely critical of the administration. Frederick C. Lane et al., *Ships for Victory* (1951), is excellent for the shipbuilding program; E. R. Stettinius, Jr., *Lend-Lease, Weapon of Victory* (1944), is good for the export of war materials; James P. Baxter III, *Scientists Against Time* (1946), is a superb account of American scientific achievement during wartime; and Leslie R. Groves, *Now It Can Be Told* (1962), is the story of the Manhattan Project as told by its director. Walter W. Wilcox, *The Farmer in the Second World War* (1947), is excellent, while Randolph E. Paul, *Taxation for Prosperity* (1947), recounts wartime tax struggles with commendable objectivity. Herman M. Somers, *Presidential Agency OWMR* (1950), is especially good on plans for the reconversion of the wartime economy. Davis R. B. Ross, *Preparing for Ulysses: Politics and Veterans During World War II* (1969), is a significant contribution. Dorothy S. Thomas et al., *The Spoilage* (1946), and Roger Daniels, *Concentration Camps, U. S. A., Japanese Americans and World War II* (1972), are scholarly studies of the treatment of Japanese Americans. For Roosevelt's third-term nomination and campaign, see Bernard F. Donahoe, *Private Plans and Public Dangers: The Story of FDR's Third Nomination*

(1965), and Herbert S. Parmet and Marie B. Hecht, *Never Again: A President Runs for a Third Term* (1968).

B. *The Truman Era, 1945-1952*

The historical literature on the Truman years has become voluminous, and grows at an accelerating rate. The Goldman, Agar, Ladd and Hadley, Parmet, and Marcus and Burner studies, cited above, provide useful introductory backgrounds. Richard S. Kirkendall (ed.), *The Truman Period as a Research Field* (1967), is now supplemented by his *The Truman Period as a Research Field: A Reappraisal* (1974). The best general accounts are Cabell Phillips, *The Truman Presidency: The History of a Triumphant Succession* (1966); Alonzo L. Hamby, *Beyond the New Deal: Harry S Truman and American Liberalism* (1973); Robert J. Donovan, *Conflict and Crisis: The Presidency of Harry S Truman, 1945-1948* (1977); and Bert Cochran, *Harry Truman and the Crisis Presidency* (1973). For an interesting, if not always persuasive, radical critique of New Deal and Fair Deal reform, see the relevant essays in Barton J. Bernstein (ed.), *Towards a New Past: Dissenting Essays in American History* (1968).

There is, of course, no definitive biography of Truman as yet. Harry S Truman, *Memoirs by Harry S Truman* (2 vols., 1955-1956), and Merle Miller, *Plain Speaking: An Oral Biography of Harry S Truman* (1974), are invaluable sources. William Hillman (ed.), *Mr. President* (1952), includes brief excerpts from Truman's diaries and letters. See also Morris B. Schnapper (ed.), *The Truman Program* (1949), a collection of the president's speeches on major Fair Deal policies. Jonathan Daniels, *The Man of Independence* (1951), is a good biography that carries the story as far as 1949. Margaret Truman, *Harry S Truman* (1973), is a fascinating personal reminiscence by the late president's daughter, which includes excerpts from many candid Truman letters. Donald R. McCoy and Richard T. Ruetten, *Quest and Response: Minority Rights and the Truman Administration* (1973), is an excellent overall study of the administration's policies in this realm.

American politics during this turbulent era has been the subject of several important studies. Samuel Lubell, *The Future of American Politics* (1965), is a penetrating analysis of shifting political alignments. See also Louis L. Gerson, *The Hyphenate in Recent American Politics and Diplomacy* (1964), and Jack Redding, *Inside the Democratic Party* (1958). The background of the changing political outlook in the South is superbly treated in V. O. Key, Jr., *Southern Politics in State and Nation* (1949). The story is carried forward in George B. Tindall, *The Disruption of the Solid South* (1972). Other general surveys of postwar southern politics include Jack Bass and Walter DeVries, *The Transformation of Southern Politics: Social Change and Political Consequence Since 1945* (1976); Numan V. Bartley and Hugh D. Graham, *Southern Politics and the Second Reconstruction* (1975); and Steven F. Lawson, *Black Ballots: Voting Rights in the South, 1944-1969* (1976). For more specialized studies, see J. Harvie Wilkinson III, *Harry Byrd and the Changing Face of Virginia Politics, 1945-1966* (1968); Andrew Buni, *The Negro in Virginia Politics, 1902-1965* (1967); and Numan V. Bartley, *From Thurmond to Wallace: Political Tendencies in Georgia, 1948-1968* (1970).

For the campaign of 1948, in addition to many of the items already cited, see Irwin Ross, *The Loneliest Campaign: The Truman Victory of 1948* (1968); Jules Abels, *Out of the Jaws of Victory* (1959); and Robert A. Divine, "The Cold War and the Election of 1948," *Journal of American History*, 59 (June 1972), 90–110, which argues, in contrast to most earlier analyses, that foreign rather than domestic considerations were of decisive importance in Truman's upset victory. A careful recent study of the principal domestic controversies that preceded the election of 1948 is Susan Hartmann, *Truman and the Eightieth Congress* (1971).

Arthur M. Schlesinger, Jr., *The Vital Center* (1949), is a liberal Democrat's thoughtful contemporary analysis of Fair Deal liberalism and contrasting political pressures from Right and Left. For developments on the Left, the best accounts are Karl M. Schmidt, *Henry A. Wallace, Quixotic Crusader* (1960), and Norman D. Markowitz, *The Rise and Fall of the People's Century: Henry A. Wallace and American Liberalism, 1941–1948* (1973). See also Edward L. and Frederick H. Schapsmeier, *Prophet in Politics: Henry A. Wallace and the War Years, 1940–1965* (1971). Two excellent studies by Christopher Lasch provide historical contexts for postwar left wing politics: *The Agony of the American Left*, already cited, and *The New Radicalism in America, 1889–1963: The Intellectual as a Social Type* (1965).

Truman's critics and opponents on the Right, being far more numerous and important politically, have received more attention from historians. The president's major GOP antagonist is the subject of James T. Patterson, *Mr. Republican: A Biography of Robert A. Taft* (1972), and the earlier William S. White, *The Taft Story* (1954). Authur H. Vandenberg, Jr., (ed.), *The Private Papers of Senator Vandenberg* (1952), deals mainly with foreign affairs but reveals the tensions that divided the Republican party. Several competent studies have pointed up the close connection between foreign policy issues and domestic politics during the Truman years. Among the best of these are H. Bradford Westerfield, *Foreign Policy and Party Politics: Pearl Harbor to Korea* (1955); Ronald J. Caridi, *The Korean War and American Politics: The Republican Party as a Case Study* (1968); John W. Spanier, *The Truman-MacArthur Controversy and the Korean War* (1965); and Athan G. Theoharis, *The Yalta Myths: An Issue in U. S. Politics, 1945–1955* (1970). Alan D. Harper, *The Politics of Loyalty: The White House and the Communist Issue, 1946–1952* (1969), argues that the Truman administration was victimized by an irresistible climate of anti-Communist opinion. In sharp contrast is Richard M. Freeland, *The Truman Doctrine and the Origins of McCarthyism: Foreign Policy, Domestic Politics, and Internal Security, 1946–1948* (1972), which maintains that postwar anticommunism grew directly out of the Truman administration's purposeful strategy of rousing public opinion in support of the Marshall Plan and other cold-war policies. Also critical of Truman's policies toward radical opposition is Michael R. Belknap, *Cold War Political Justice: The Smith Act, the Communist Party, and American Civil Liberties* (1977).

The most virulent phase of postwar anti-Communist sentiment, McCarthyism, has been the subject of much analysis and conflicting interpretation. Goldman's *Crucial Decade and After*, cited above, includes a penetrating sketch and judgment of the Wisconsin demagogue. The best biography is Richard H. Rovere, *Senator Joe McCarthy* (1959), hostile but judicious. The best case for the senator is made by William F. Buckley, Jr., and L. B. Bozell, *McCarthy and His Enemies, the Record and Its Meaning* (1954). The prevailing intellectual view during the 1950s—that McCarthyism was a kind of mass populist movement fed by antiestablishment "status envy"—has been provocatively challenged by two recent authors who see McCarthyism as a direct extension and outgrowth of GOP partisanship and conventional right wing sentiment: Robert Griffith, *The Politics of Fear: Joseph R. McCarthy and the Senate* (1970), and Michael P. Rogin, *The Intellectuals and McCarthy: The Radical Specter* (1967). On the other hand, Lipset and Raab's *Politics of Unreason*, already cited, suggests that McCarthyism was not a right wing extremist movement but simply a "tendency of the times" and "more a hysteria than a political movement." For more specialized studies of the results of the McCarthy terror, see David M. Oshinsky, *Senator Joseph McCarthy and the American Labor Movement* (1976), the best work on that subject, and E. J. Kahn, Jr., *The China Hands: America's Foreign Service Officers and What Befell Them* (1975).

Closely related to the above works is a substantial literature on communism and civil liberties. David A. Shannon, *The Decline of American Communism* (1959), is the best general work, but see also John P. Diggins, *The American Left in the Twentieth Century* (1973); Joseph R. Starobin, *American Communism in Crisis, 1943-1957* (1972); Wilson Record, *The Negro and the Communist Party* (1951); and three volumes in the superb Communism in American Life series: Ralph L. Roy, *Communism and the Churches* (1960); Robert W. Iverson, *The Communists and the Schools* (1959); and Daniel Aaron, *Writers on the Left* (1961). While Allen Weinstein, *Perjury: The Hiss-Chambers Case* (1978), seems to be definitive on the controversy surrounding Alger Hiss, Alistair Cooke, *A Generation on Trial* (1950), is a balanced analysis of the Hiss trials and their consequences, and Robert E. Cushman, *Civil Liberties in the United States* (1956), is a dispassionate survey. R. K. Carr, *The House Committee on Un-American Activities, 1945-1950* (1952); Clair Wilcox (ed.), *Civil Liberties Under Attack* (1951); and John W. Caughey, *In Clear and Present Danger* (1958), condemn the excessive fear of internal communism and call for a reaffirmation of faith in democracy. A highly polemical but stimulating indictment of anti-Communist attitudes in the twentieth century is Michael Parenti, *The Anti-Communist Impulse* (1969).

On the civil rights controversy, see the President's Committee on Civil Rights, *To Secure These Rights* (1947); Robert K. Carr, *Federal Protection of Civil Rights* (1947); Milton R. Konvitz, *The Constitution and Civil Rights* (1947); and Morroe Berger, *Equality by Statute* (1952), all of which highlight the postwar drive for an FEPC, antilynching laws, and other civil rights measures. Two important recent studies are William C. Berman, *The Politics of Civil Rights in the Truman Administration* (1970), and Richard M. Dalfiume, *Desegregation of the U. S. Armed Forces: Fighting on Two Fronts, 1939-1953* (1969). See also many of the titles listed below under "Race Relations."

Various other important issues of the era are respectively treated in Allen J. Matusow, *Farm Policies and Politics in the Truman Years* (1967); Richard O. Davies, *Housing Reform During the Truman Administration* (1966); and Arthur F. McClure, *The Truman Administration and the Problems of Postwar Labor, 1945-1948* (1969). Walter Millis and E. S. Duffield (eds.), *The Forrestal Diaries* (1951), is especially revealing on military and naval policies.

For economic issues in the postwar era, the best single volume is George A. Steiner, *Government's Role in Economic Life* (1953). Lester V. Chandler, *Inflation in the United States, 1940-1948* (1950), is comprehensive and clearly written. On the Employment Act of 1946, see especially Edward S. Flash, Jr., *Economic Advice and Presidential Leadership: The Council of Economic Advisers* (1965). But see also Stephen K. Bailey, *Congress Makes a Law* (1957); Edwin G. Nourse, *The*

1950s Come First (1951) and *Economics in the Public Service* (1953); and Seymour E. Harris, *Economic Planning* (1949). For the mobilization following the outbreak of the Korean War, see L. V. Chandler and D. H. Wallace (eds.), *Economic Mobilization and Stabilization* (1951); Seymour E. Harris, *The Economics of Mobilization and Inflation* (1951); and Steiner, *Government's Role in Economic Life*, just cited.

Charles W. Tobey, *The Return to Morality* (1952); Paul H. Douglas, *Ethics in Government* (1952); Blair Bolles, *How to Get Rich in Washington* (1952); H. Hubert Wilson, *Congress: Corruption and Compromise* (1951); and Karl Schriftgiesser, *The Lobbyists* (1951), describe the causes and consequences of corruption during the Truman era.

C. *The Eisenhower Years*

Historical literature on the politics of the Eisenhower era is just beginning to emerge. In addition to the relevant *Public Papers* volumes, important documents are contained in Robert L. Branyan and Lawrence H. Larsen, *The Eisenhower Administration, 1953–1961: A Documentary History* (2 vols., 1971). The president's own view is capably set forth in Dwight D. Eisenhower, *The White House Years: Mandate for Change* (1963) and *The White House Years: Waging Peace, 1956–1961* (1965). The best histories of the period are Herbert S. Parmet, *Eisenhower and the American Crusades* (1972), and Charles C. Alexander, *Holding the Line: The Eisenhower Era, 1952–1961* (1975). Many of the political studies of the Truman period cited above also bear upon the Eisenhower years. An excellent analysis of the shifting political attitudes that underlay the election of 1952 is Samuel Lubell, *The Revolt of the Moderates* (1956). Emmet John Hughes, *The Ordeal of Power: A Political Memoir of the Eisenhower Years* (1963), is candid and critical. Three contemporary studies contain useful information about the first term: Merlo J. Pusey, *Eisenhower the President* (1956); Robert J. Donovan, *Eisenhower: The Inside Story* (1956); and Richard H. Rovere, *Affairs of State: The Eisenhower Years* (1956). Richard M. Nixon, *Six Crises* (1962), is an interesting performance; it may be read most profitably in conjunction with Garry Wills, *Nixon Agonistes* (1971), which makes a strong case for Eisenhower as a shrewd and competent political leader. Douglas Kinnard, *President Eisenhower and Strategy Management: A Study in Defense Policies* (1977), presents a more scholarly interpretation of Eisenhower as a strong and active president.

Aaron Wildavsky, *Dixon-Yates: A Study in Power Politics* (1962), covers a major controversy of the period; while Foster R. Dulles, *The Civil Rights Commission, 1957–1965* (1968), is a good analysis of the commission's early years. William J. Miller, *Henry Cabot Lodge* (1967); Joseph B. Gorman, *Kefauver: A Political Biography* (1971); James T. Patterson, *Mr. Republican: A Biography of Robert A. Taft* (1972); and John Bartlow Martin, *Adlai Stevenson of Illinois* (1976) and *Adlai Stevenson and the World* (1977), are informative and readable. See also several of the studies of desegregation and southern resistance cited below.

D. *From Kennedy to Carter*

It is too early for more than tentative, participatory, or journalistic studies of American politics during the sixties and seventies, although several excellent works of this sort have appeared. The best introduction to presidential politics during these decades is contained in the four penetrating studies by Theodore H. White: *The Making of the President, 1960* (1961); *The Making of the President, 1964* (1965); *The Making of the President, 1968* (1969); and *The Making of the President, 1972* (1973). These should be supplemented by the works on southern politics by Tindall, Wilkinson, and Bartley, cited above, and also by Richard M. Scammon and Ben J. Wattenberg, *The Real Majority* (1970). Several of the works cited under "Race Relations," below, are also relevant.

On the Kennedy years, good introductions are Donald C. Lord, *John F. Kennedy: The Politics of Confrontation and Conciliation* (1977); Henry Fairlie, *The Kennedy Promise: The Politics of Expectation* (1973); and James T. Crown, *The Kennedy Literature: A Bibliographical Essay on John F. Kennedy* (1968). Interesting evaluations of Kennedy's leadership are contained in Carl M. Brauer, *John F. Kennedy and the Second Reconstruction* (1977); Aida deP. Donald (ed.), *John F. Kennedy and the New Frontier* (1967); and a new essay in Richard E. Neustadt, *Presidential Power: The Politics of Leadership* (1969). Two excellent, detailed, highly favorable accounts by men who worked closely with President Kennedy are Arthur M. Schlesinger, Jr., *A Thousand Days: John F. Kennedy in the White House* (1965), and Theodore C. Sorenson, *Kennedy* (1965).

A significant legislative study is Richard Harris, *The Real Voice* (1964), dealing with the background of the drug industry bill. Jim F. Heath, *John F. Kennedy and the Business Community* (1969), is a penetrating and judicious study by a historian. An important area of domestic policy is well covered in Vernon W. Ruttan et al., *Agricultural Policy in an Affluent Society* (1969), and somewhat more broadly in Robert J. Morgan, *Governing Soil Conservation: Thirty Years of the New Decentralization* (1966), and R. Burnell Held and Marion Clawson, *Soil Conservation in Perspective* (1965).

Tom Wicker, *JFK & LBJ: The Influence of Personality upon Politics* (1969), is an incisive comparison of the two Democratic presidents. A personal memoir by Kennedy's White House secretary, Evelyn Lincoln, *Kennedy and Johnson* (1968), includes some perceptive observations. Michael Davie, *LBJ: A Foreign Observer's Viewpoint* (1966), and Rowland Evans and Robert Novak, *Lyndon B. Johnson: The Exercise of Power* (1966), contain useful insights. But Doris Kearns, *Lyndon Johnson and the American Dream* (1976), is as close as possible to an authorized biography. See also Eric F. Goldman, *The Tragedy of Lyndon Johnson: A Historian's Personal Interpretation* (1969). These may be supplemented by the interesting first-person observations contained in Lyndon B. Johnson, *The Vantage Point: Perspectives of the Presidency, 1963-1969* (1971); Lady Bird Johnson, *A White House Diary* (1970); and Jack Valenti, *A Very Human President* (1975).

The election of 1972 is the subject of much exciting literature, particularly on the McGovern campaign. The best studies of the Democratic plight are Gordon L. Weil, *The Long Shot: George McGovern Runs for President* (1973); Gary Warren Hart, *Right from the Start: A Chronicle of the McGovern Campaign* (1973); and Richard Dougherty, *Good-bye, Mr. Christian* (1973). For a humorous, cynical account of Democratic foibles, see Hunter S. Thompson, *Fear and Loathing on the Campaign Trail '72* (1973).

The best studies of the Nixon presidency are Jonathan Schell, *The Time of Illusion* (1976), and Arthur M. Schlesinger, Jr., *The Imperial Presidency* (1973). Garry Wills, *Nixon Agonistes*, already cited, reviews the life and career of Richard

Nixon through the election of 1968 and into the early months of his presidency. Robert E. Osgood et al., *Retreat from Empire? The First Nixon Administration* (1973), carries the story forward to 1972. Bruce Mazlish, *In Search of Nixon: A Psychohistorical Inquiry* (1972), is an attempt at a psychobiography. The rise of H. R. Haldeman and John Ehrlichman to positions of great power within the administration is the subject of Dan Rather and Gary Paul Gates, *The Palace Guard* (1974). Surveys of individual initiatives undertaken by the administration are illustrated in Daniel P. Moynihan, *The Politics of a Guaranteed Income: The Nixon Administration and the Family Assistance Plan* (1973), and Vincent Burke and Vee Burke, *Nixon's Good Deed: Welfare Reform* (1974). An excellent study on the four Nixon Supreme Court appointees and their effect on the court's swing toward conservatism is Leonard W. Levy, *Against the Law: The Nixon Court and Criminal Justice* (1974).

The literature on the post-Nixon years is sparse, of course. Gerald Ford, *A Time to Heal: An Autobiography* (1979), reflects upon his truncated presidential term. The campaign of 1976 is explored in Jules Witcover, *Marathon: The Pursuit of the Presidency, 1972-1976* (1977), and Elizabeth Drew, *American Journal: The Events of 1976* (1977). Jimmy Carter is the subject of several new studies. Among the best are James T. Wooten, *Dasher: The Roots and the Rising of Jimmy Carter* (1978), and William Lee Miller, *Yankee from Georgia: The Emergence of Jimmy Carter* (1978). Seymour Martin Lipset (ed.), *Emerging Coalitions in American Politics* (1978), studies the recent political shifts which help to explain recent election outcomes.

There are several outstanding biographies of and autobiographies by important political leaders of the 1960s and 1970s who never made it to the White House: Arthur M. Schlesinger, Jr., *Robert Kennedy and His Times* (1978); Hubert H. Humphrey, *The Education of a Public Man* (1976); George McGovern, *Grassroots: The Autobiography of George McGovern* (1977); James MacGregor Burns, *Edward Kennedy and the Camelot Legacy* (1976); Theo Lippman, Jr., *Senator Ted Kennedy: The Career Behind the Image* (1976); and Marshall Frady, *Wallace* (1968), on Governor George C. Wallace of Alabama.

E. *The Watergate Scandal*

Literature dealing with the Watergate affair is rich and lively. Theodore H. White, *Breach of Faith: The Fall of Richard Nixon* (1975); Barry Sussman, *The Great Coverup: Nixon and the Scandal of Watergate* (1974); and J. Anthony Lukas, *Nightmare: The Underside of the Nixon Years* (1976), are excellent general surveys. Carl Bernstein and Bob Woodward, *All the President's Men* (1974), describes the initial investigation by two diligent reporters from the *Washington Post*. Jimmy Breslin, *How the Good Guys Finally Won: Notes from an Impeachment Summer* (1975), and Frank Mankiewicz, *U. S. v. Richard Nixon: The Final Crisis* (1975), offer thoughtful reflections on particular aspects of Nixon's judicial troubles. Other surveys of interest are New York Times, *The End of a Presidency* (1974), and Washington Post, *The Fall of a President* (1974).

The writing of memoirs by participants in the scandal has become a profitable enterprise. The best is John Dean, *Blind Ambition: The White House Years* (1976). See also H. R. Haldeman, *The Ends of Power* (1978); Jeb Stuart Magruder, *An American Life: One Man's Road to Watergate* (1974); and James W. McCord, Jr.,

A Piece of Tape: The Watergate Story, Fact and Fiction (1974). Richard Nixon, *RN, The Memoirs of Richard Nixon* (1978), concedes nothing to any allegations of the former president's culpability in the affair.

For a superb account of the scandal from a judicial perspective see John J. Sirica, *To Set the Record Straight: The Break-in, the Tapes, the Conspirators, the Pardon* (1979). James Doyle, *Not Above the Law: The Battles of Watergate Pros-ecutors Cox and Jaworski, a Behind-the-Scenes Account* (1977), is a history of the special prosecutor's role in the investigation. Leon Jaworski, *The Right and the Power* (1976), gives an account of his own particular role. Fred D. Thompson, *At That Point in Time: The Inside Story of the Senate Watergate Committee* (1975), tells the story of the Senate's investigation, while Samuel Dash, *Chief Counsel: Inside the Ervin Committee—the Untold Story of Watergate* (1976), gives an in-side glimpse. Philip B. Kurland, *Watergate and the Constitution* (1978), discusses the judicial implications of the scandal. For a vivid description of Nixon's last weeks in office, see Bob Woodward and Carl Bernstein, *The Final Days* (1976).

F. *The Supreme Court Since 1940*

Among the best studies of the Supreme Court and the Constitution are Alpheus T. Mason, *The Supreme Court from Taft to Warren* (1958); Paul L. Murphy, *The Constitution in Crisis Times, 1918-1969* (1972); and Robert G. McCloskey, *The Modern Supreme Court* (1972), which includes material on the Stone (1940-1946), Vinson (1946-1953), and Warren (1954-1965) courts. See also Kathryn Griffith, *Judge Learned Hand and the Role of the Federal Judiciary* (1973); C. H. Pritchett, *Civil Liberties and the Vinson Court* (1954); Arthur J. Goldberg, *Equal Justice: The Warren Era of the Supreme Court* (1972); and Archibald Cox, *The Warren Court: Constitutional Decision as an Instrument of Reform* (1968). Walter F. Mur-phy, *Congress and the Court* (1962), is an important analysis of congressional opposition in the late 1950s. Important studies of specific legal subjects and themes include Richard C. Cortner, *The Apportionment Cases* (1970); Charles A. Miller, *The Supreme Court and the Uses of History* (1969); Richard Claude, *The Supreme Court and the Electoral Process* (1970); and Raoul Berger, *Government by Judiciary: The Transformation of the Fourteenth Amendment* (1977). A recent court controversy is the subject of Robert Shogan, *A Question of Judgment: The Fortas Case and the Struggle for the Supreme Court* (1972).

3. THE UNITED STATES AND ITS WORLD RELATIONS SINCE 1938

A. *The Second Road to War, 1937-1941*

The body of literature on the background of American participation in the Second World War is immense. The two outstanding works on the subject are William L. Langer and S. E. Gleason, *The Challenge to Isolation, 1937-1940* (1952) and *The Undeclared War, 1940-1941* (1953), which rank among the finest products of American historical scholarship. Other fine general works are Robert Dallek, *Franklin D. Roosevelt and American Foreign Policy, 1932-1945* (1979); James M. Burns, *Roosevelt: The Soldier of Freedom* (1970); Robert A. Divine, *The Reluctant*

Belligerent: American Entry into World War II (1965); T. R. Fehrenbach, *F. D. R's Undeclared War, 1939 to 1941.* (1967); and James V. Compton, *The Swastika and the Eagle: Hitler, the United States, and the Origins of World War II* (1967). Robert E. Sherwood, *Roosevelt and Hopkins* (1948), and Winston S. Churchill, *The Gathering Storm* (1948) and *Their Finest Hour* (1949), are invaluable sources. See also Charles A. Beard, *American Foreign Policy in the Making, 1932-1940* (1946) and *President Roosevelt and the Coming of the War, 1941* (1948), critical studies deserving of serious consideration. Particular works relating to the United States and Europe from 1938 to 1941 are Alton Frye, *Germany and the American Hemisphere, 1933-1941* (1967); John M. Haight, *American Aid to France, 1938-1940* (1970); Philip Goodhart, *Fifty Ships That Saved the World* (1965); Warren F. Kimball, *The Most Unsordid Act: Lend-Lease, 1939-1941* (1969); and Theodore A. Wilson, *The First Summit: Roosevelt and Churchill at Placentia Bay, 1941* (1969).

Relations with Japan during the 1930s to 1941 are traced by Whitney Griswold, *The Far Eastern Policy of the United States* (1938); Dorothy Borg, *The United States and the Far Eastern Crisis of 1933-1938* (1964); Waldo H. Heinrichs, Jr., *American Ambassador: Joseph C. Grew and the Development of the United States Diplomatic Tradition* (1966); and Joseph C. Grew, *Turbulent Era, a Diplomatic Record of Forty Years, 1904-1945* (2 vols., 1952). The Langer and Gleason volumes contain the best account of events leading to the rupture in Japanese-American relations, but see also Manny T. Koginos, *The Panay Incident: Prelude to War* (1967); John Toland, *The Rising Sun: The Decline and Fall of the Japanese Empire, 1936-1945* (1970); Herbert Feis, *The Road to Pearl Harbor* (1950); Paul W. Schroeder, *The Axis Alliance and Japanese-American Relations, 1941* (1958); Robert J. C. Butow, *Tojo and the Coming of the War* (1961); and Roberta Wohlstetter, *Pearl Harbor: Warning and Decision* (1962). Insightful essays on various aspects of Japanese and American foreign policies are contained in Dorothy Borg and Shumpei Okamoto (eds.), *Pearl Harbor as History* (1973).

For the great debate over American policies toward the belligerents, we now have adequate studies for both the internationalists and the isolationists: Walter Johnson, *The Battle Against Isolation* (1944); Mark L. Chadwin, *The Hawks of World War II* (1968); Donald J. Friedman, *The Road from Isolation: The Campaign of the American Committee for Non-Participation in Japanese Aggression, 1938-1941* (1968); Wayne S. Cole, *America First, the Battle Against Intervention, 1940-1941* (1953); and Manfred Jonas, *Isolationism in America, 1935-1941* (1966).

B. *The Diplomacy and Conduct of the Second World War*

Robert Dallek, *Franklin D. Roosevelt and American Foreign Policy, 1932-1945* (1979); James M. Burns, *Roosevelt: Soldier of Freedom* (1970); and Herbert Feis, *Churchill, Roosevelt, Stalin* (1957), are the best one-volume accounts. But see also Churchill's magisterial *The Grand Alliance* (1950), *The Hinge of Fate* (1950), *Closing the Ring* (1951), and *Triumph and Tragedy* (1953); Robert E. Sherwood, *Roosevelt and Hopkins* (1948); and W. Averell Harriman and Elie Abel, *Special Envoy to Churchill and Stalin, 1941-1946* (1975). Other general studies are Robert A. Divine, *Roosevelt and World War II* (1969); Christopher Thorne, *Allies of a Kind: The United States, Britain, and the War Against Japan* (1978); and Gaddis Smith, *American Diplomacy During the Second World War* (1965). William Roger Louis,

Imperialism at Bay: The United States and the Decolonization of the British Empire, 1941-1945 (1978), is a monumental study. For more particular works, see Mark A. Stoler, *The Politics of the Second Front: American Military Planning and Diplomacy in Coalition Warfare, 1941-1943* (1977); Herbert Feis, *The China Triangle* (1953); Paul A. Varg, *The Closing of the Door: Sino-American Relations, 1936-1946* (1973); E. J. Kahn, Jr., *The China Hands: America's Foreign Service Officers and What Befell Them* (1975); John L. Snell (ed.), *The Meaning of Yalta* (1956); Stephen E. Ambrose, *Eisenhower and Berlin: The Decision to Halt at the Elbe* (1967); Robert A. Divine, *Second Chance: The Triumph of Internationalism in America During World War II* (1967); Herbert Feis, *Between War and Peace: The Potsdam Conference* (1960), *Japan Subdued* (1961), and *From Trust to Terror: The Onset of the Cold War, 1945-1950* (1971); Frank D. McCann, Jr., *The Brazilian-American Alliance, 1937-1945* (1973); Robert J. C. Butow, *Japan's Decision to Surrender* (1954); and William L. Neumann, *After Victory: Churchill, Roosevelt, Stalin and the Making of the Peace* (1969). Gabriel Kolko, *The Politics of War: The World and United States Foreign Policy, 1943-1945* (1969), challenges, not always successfully and rarely without bias in favor of Russia, many traditional assumptions about relations between the Western Allies and the Soviet Union and about Russian policies.

The sad story of the Roosevelt administration's failure to do much to help European Jews in danger of extermination is related in David S. Wyman, *Paper Walls: America and the Refugee Crisis, 1938-1941* (1968); Henry L. Feingold, *The Politics of Rescue: The Roosevelt Administration and the Holocaust, 1938-1945* (1970); Arthur D. Morse, *While Six Million Died* (1968); and Saul S. Friedman, *No Haven for the Oppressed: United States Policy Toward Jewish Refugees, 1938-1945* (1973).

Winston S. Churchill, *The Grand Alliance* (1950), *The Hinge of Fate* (1950), *Closing the Ring* (1951), and *Triumph and Tragedy* (1953), include brilliant summaries of all major military operations. The best single-volume history is Martha Byrd Hoyle, *A World in Flames: The History of World War II* (1970). But see also A. Russell Buchanan, *The United States and World War II* (2 vols., 1964); Chester Wilmot, *The Struggle for Europe* (1952); and Charles B. MacDonald, *The Mighty Endeavor: American Armed Forces in the European Theater in World War II* (1969). The Department of the Army's Office of Military History has published numerous volumes in its large and generally excellent series U. S. Army in World War II. Samuel E. Morison, *History of United States Naval Operations in World War II* (15 vols., 1947-1962), is definitive, but see Walter Lord, *Incredible Victory* (1967), on the Battle of Midway. Kent Roberts Greenfield (ed.), *Command Decisions* (1959), contains a number of brilliant analyses of crucial military events and also reveals how considerations of military strategy affected diplomacy. Kent Roberts Greenfield, *American Strategy in World War II: A Reconsideration* (1963), is a provocative assessment. For a British perspective on Anglo-American strategic planning, see Michael Howard, *The Mediterranean Strategy in the Second World War* (1966).

For American military and naval leaders, see Alfred D. Chandler, Jr., Stephen E. Ambrose, and Louis Galambos (eds.), *The Papers of Dwight David Eisenhower: The War Years* (9 vols., 1970-1978); Stephen E. Ambrose, *The Supreme Commander: The War Years of General Dwight D. Eisenhower* (1970); Dwight D. Eisenhower, *Crusade in Europe* (1948); Forrest C. Pogue, *George C. Marshall* (3 vols., 1962–1973); William Raymond Manchester, *American Caesar, Douglas MacArthur, 1880–1964* (1978); Gavin Long, *MacArthur as Military Commander* (1969); D. Clayton James, *The Years of MacArthur*, Vol. I (1970); Douglas MacArthur, *Reminiscences* (1964); H. Essame, *Patton: A Study in Command* (1976); E. B. Potter, *Nimitz* (1976); Henry H. Arnold, *Global Mission* (1949); Omar N. Bradley, *A Soldier's Story* (1951); Ernest J. King and W. M. Whitehill, *Fleet Admiral King* (1952); and William D. Leahy, *I Was There* (1950). Richard F. Haynes, *The Awesome Power: Harry S. Truman as Commander in Chief* (1973), is a significant study of the military power contained in the office of the presidency.

C. *The Cold War Revisited*

Special attention must be given to a rash of studies in the 1960s and 1970s by so-called New Left or revisionist historians, who challenged prevailing American assumptions about the origins and causes of the cold war. Although these revisionists disagree considerably among themselves on matters of detail and emphasis, they tend to share a conviction that—to put it as briefly as possible—American imperialistic drives and aims, rather than Soviet or Communist aggression, were primarily responsible for the breakup of the Grand Alliance and the outbreak of the cold war in the late 1940s. Although the reasoning behind many of these works is often unpardonably simplistic and uncritically hostile to the United States, the best of them are based upon careful and thorough scholarship and a laudable insistence upon reexamining the evidence. They have not proved their point, but they have raised serious and provocative questions concerning America's intent and role after 1945. They have broadened scholarly horizons and helped to clear the scholarly air, and other historians of the period—regardless of how far one may agree or disagree with revisionist conclusions and viewpoints—are in their debt.

The following are among the best or most interesting of these revisionist studies: D. F. Fleming, *The Cold War and Its Origins, 1917–1960* (2 vols., 1961), the pioneering study; Gar Alperovitz, *Atomic Diplomacy: Hiroshima and Potsdam* (1966), which argues that the United States consciously used the atomic bomb as a diplomatic weapon in its negotiations with the USSR in 1945; Diane S. Clemens, *Yalta* (1970); George C. Herring, "Lend-Lease to Russia and the Origins of the Cold War," *Journal of American History*, 56 (June 1969), 93–114; Thomas G. Patterson, "The Abortive American Loan to Russia and the Origins of the Cold War, 1943–1946," *Journal of American History*, 56 (June 1969), 70–92; Bruce Kuklick, *American Policy and the Division of Germany: The Clash with Russia over Reparations* (1972); Lloyd C. Gardner, *Architects of Illusion: Men and Ideas in American Foreign Policy 1941–1949* (1970); Barton J. Bernstein (ed.), *Politics and Problems of the Truman Administration* (1970); David Horowitz, *From Yalta to Vietnam* (1967); D. Horowitz (ed.), *Containment and Revolution* (1967); and Walter La Feber, *America, Russia, and the Cold War, 1945–1966* (1967), which presents a balanced view of two expanding societies and aggressive ideologies clashing in the postwar era. The most extensive case for revisionism has been made by Gabriel Kolko in three studies: *The Politics of War: The World and United States Foreign Policy, 1943–1945* (1968); *The Roots of American Foreign Policy: An Analysis of Power and Purpose* (1969), an examination of American relations with the Third World; and (with Joyce Kolko), *The Limits of Power: The World and United States Foreign Policy, 1945-1954* (1972).

Revisionist historiography has been directly or indirectly responsible for the writing of several penetrating studies that seek either to refute its contentions or reexamine the documents in the light of its claims. Revisionist findings are unfairly reviewed in Robert J. Maddox, *The New Left and the Origins of the Cold War* (1973), and harshly attacked in Robert W. Tucker, *The Radical Left and American Foreign Policy* (1971). Lloyd C. Gardner, Arthur M. Schlesinger, Jr., and Hans J. Morgenthau, *The Origins of the Cold War* (1970), present three forceful conflicting essays in which the basic revisionist and nonrevisionist interpretations may be compared and contrasted. Martin F. Herz, *The Beginnings of the Cold War* (1966), and Paul Seabury, *The Rise and Decline of the Cold War* (1967), reflect but partially transcend revisionist influence. Robert Hunter, *Security in Europe* (1969), argues that the conflict was more a consequence of lack of understanding or agreed guidelines than of real clash of interest. William L. Neumann, *After Victory: Churchill, Roosevelt, Stalin and the Making of the Peace* (1969), suggests that wartime realities and exigencies were instrumental in determining the nature of the peace; while Louis J. Halle, *The Cold War as History* (1967), sees high probability, if not inevitability, of conflict between two emerging superpowers with incompatible aims and assumptions.

Balanced, realistic correctives to the revisionist views are presented by Adam B. Ulam, *Expansion and Coexistence: The History of Soviet Foreign Policy, 1917-1967* (1968), and George S. Herring, Jr., *Aid to Russia, 1941-1946: Strategy, Diplomacy, the Origins of the Cold War* (1973). Herbert Feis, *Contest over Japan* (1967), counters revisionist claims by stressing an unbroken American desire to create a democratized and independent postwar Japan rather than a bastion against Communist expansion in Asia. See also the same author's *From Trust to Terror: The Onset of the Cold War, 1945-1950* (1970). The best recent assessment of Russian responsibility for the cold war is Vojtech Mastny, *Russia's Road to the Cold War* (1979). Raymond Aron, *The Imperial Republic: The United States and the World, 1945-1973* (1974), is an eloquent defense of American foreign policy during the period.

The best and most judicious studies of the entire problem are John Gaddis, *The United States and the Origins of the Cold War, 1941-1947* (1972) and *Russia, the Soviet Union, and the United States: An Interpretive History* (1978); Thomas G. Patterson, *Soviet-American Confrontation: Postwar Reconstruction and the Origins of the Cold War* (1974); and Daniel Yergin, *Shattered Peace: The Origins of the Cold War and the National Security State* (1977).

D. *The Diplomacy of the Truman Era*

The relevant volumes in the *United States in World Affairs* and *Dynamics of World Power* series and the works by Seyom Brown, John Spanier, and Richard Leopold, previously cited, are indispensable. Richard L. Walker and George Curry, *E. R. Stettinius, Jr.-James F. Byrnes* (1965); Robert H. Ferrell, *George C. Marshall* (1966); and Gaddis Smith, *Dean Acheson* (1972), study Truman's secretaries of state. Of crucial importance here is Dean Acheson, *Present at the Creation: My Years in the State Department* (1969), memoirs covering the period

1941-1953. See also McGeorge Bundy (ed.), *The Pattern of Responsibility* (1952), a collection of Acheson's major speeches. Arnold Wolfers, *Alliance Policy in the Cold War* (1959); George Liska, *The New Statecraft: Foreign Aid in American Policy* (1960); and the volumes by Westerfield and Caridi, already cited, are valuable for aspects of diplomacy at midcentury.

For the United Nations and American international economic policies in the immediate postwar period, see Leland M. Goodrich, *The United Nations* (1959); Abraham H. Feller, *United Nations and World Community* (1952); Raymond F. Mikesell, *United States Economic Policy and International Relations* (1952); Brian Tew, *International Monetary Cooperation, 1945-1952* (1952); Clair Wilcox, *A Charter for World Trade* (1949); and Alfred E. Eckes, Jr., *A Search for Solvency: Bretton Woods and the International Monetary System, 1941-1971* (1975).

Hajo Holborn, *American Military Government* (1947), and Eugene Davidson, *The Death and Life of Germany: An Account of the American Occupation* (1959), are useful for American occupation policies in Germany. See Robert H. Jackson, *The Case Against the Nazi War Criminals* (1946) and the *The Nuremberg Case* (1947), for a justification of the proceedings. For a recent study of American opinion on the subject, see William J. Bosch, *Judgement on Nuremberg: American Attitudes Toward the Major German War-Crime Trials* (1970). For a highly critical view of the postwar trials in Japan, see Robert Minear, *Victors' Justice: The Tokyo War Crimes Trial* (1971). See also Frederick S. Dunn, *Peace-Making and the Settlement with Japan* (1963); Hugh Borton et al., *The Far East, 1942-1946* (1955); and Kazuo Kawai, *Japan's American Interlude* (1960), for broader studies of the American experiment in Japan.

The causes of the disruption of the Grand Alliance have been told many times. One of the best early studies is William H. McNeill, *America, Britain, and Russia: Their Co-operation and Conflict, 1941-1946* (1953); other good accounts are contained in Winston Churchill, *Triumph and Tragedy* (1953); Robert E. Sherwood, *Roosevelt and Hopkins* (1948); Chester Wilmot, *The Struggle for Europe* (1952); and two excellent studies by Herbert Feis: *Churchill, Roosevelt, and Stalin* (1957) and *Between War and Peace: The Potsdam Conference* (1960). John L. Snell (ed.), *The Meaning of Yalta* (1956), is the best introduction to that controversial conference. For related developments in the Far East, see Herbert Feis, *The China Triangle* (1953) and *Japan Subdued* (1961), together with R. J. C. Butow, *Japan's Decision to Surrender* (1954). James F. Byrnes, *Speaking Frankly* (1947), relates his futile struggle for understanding and friendship with the USSR. There are a few glimpses of Truman's private views in Hillman (ed.), *Mr. President*, and Margaret Truman, *Harry S. Truman*, and detailed discussions of the growing tensions in Mills and Duffield (eds.), *The Forrestal Diaries*, and Vandenberg (ed.), *Private Papers of Senator Vandenberg*, all cited previously. Truman's *Memoirs* are indispensable. George F. Kennan, *American Diplomacy, 1900-1950* (1951), contains an incisive chapter on the Truman Doctrine and Kennan's own influential "Mr. X" article on containment. Penetrating comments on Soviet interests and attitudes are set forth in G. F. Kennan, *Memoirs* (2 vols., 1968-1972), and Charles E. Bohlen, *Witness to History* (1973). For the first Berlin crisis see Lucius D. Clay, *Decision in Germany* (1950), and W. Phillips Davison, *The Berlin Blockade* (1958).

Early studies include Joseph M. Jones, *The Fifteen Weeks* (1955), which analyzes the change in opinion during the development of the Greek-Turkish aid program and the Marshall Plan; Harry B. Price, *The Marshall Plan and Its Meaning* (1955); and Theodore H. White, *Fire in the Ashes* (1953), a moving record of American success in western Europe at midcentury. Halford L. Hoskins, *The Atlantic Pact* (1949), and Drew Middleton, *Defense of Western Europe* (1952), recount the movement toward Atlantic unity and mutual defense. See also Wolfers, *Alliance Policy in the Cold War*, already cited. Truman's *Memoirs* and other previously cited studies of postwar diplomacy are also useful. And, of course, most of the works discussed in the previous section relate to this period.

Questions of atomic weapons, the arms race, and disarmament are capably treated in Martin J. Sherwin, *A World Destroyed: The Atomic Bomb and the Grand Alliance* (1975); Chalmers M. Roberts, *The Nuclear Years: The Arms Race and Arms Control, 1945-1970* (1970); UN Secretariat, *The United Nations and Disarmament, 1945-1965* (1967); and Richard G. Hewlett and Francis Duncan, *A History of the United States Atomic Energy Commission, Vol. I: The New World, 1939-1946* (1972) and *Vol. II: Atomic Shield, 1947-1957* (1972). Excellent sources for this and related subjects are David E. Lilienthal, *The Journals of David E. Lilienthal: The Atomic Energy Years, 1945-1950* (1965), and Harland B. Moulton, *From Superiority to Parity: The United States and the Strategic Arms Race, 1961-1971* (1973). See also Joseph I. Lieberman, *The Scorpion and the Tarantula: The Struggle to Control Atomic Weapons, 1945-1949* (1970). An interesting pioneer study of a basic related question is Eugene B. Skolnikoff, *Science, Technology, and American Foreign Policy* (1967).

American policies in the Middle East after 1945 are discussed by W. H. McNeill, *The Greek Dilemma* (1947); Ephraim A Speiser, *The United States and the Near East* (1947); L. V. Thomas and R. N. Frye, *The United States and Turkey and Iran* (1951); and James G. McDonald, *My Mission in Israel, 1948-1951* (1951).

The debate over the failure of American policy in China has stimulated the printing of most of the basic documents and the writing of some first-rate scholarly studies on American policy in the Far East. Department of State, *United States Relations with China* (1949), is the White Paper that presents the official version and the documents. Feis, *The China Triangle*, cited above, goes through the end of the Marshall mission, while Tang Tsou's excellent *America's Failure in China, 1941-1950* (1963), carries the story to the outbreak of the Korean War. Foster Rhea Dulles, *American Policy Toward Communist China 1949-1969* (1972), is the best general survey of Chinese-American relations during this period.

The best general work on the Korean War is David Rees, *Korea: The Limited War* (1964), but see especially Spanier's *Truman-MacArthur Controversy*, cited above, for the recall of General MacArthur. The general's side of the story is presented in Douglas MacArthur, *Reminiscences* (1964), and William R. Manchester, *American Caesar, Douglas MacArthur* (1978). Mark W. Clark, *From the Danube to the Yalu* (1954), recounts events of the last months of the war and the armistice negotiations. An interesting personal assessment by another important participant is Matthew B. Ridgway, *The Korean War* (1967), by another high-ranking military figure. J. Lawton Collins, *War in Peacetime: The History and Lessons of Korea* (1969), adds little to what was already known. Glenn D. Paige, *The Korean Decision* (1968), is a detailed account of the American decision (June 24-30, 1950) to intervene. Allen S. Whiting, *China Crosses the Yalu* (1960), treats the question of Chinese intervention; while Robert E. Osgood, *Limited War* (1957), considers important strategic discussions and decisions.

E. *Diplomacy Since Eisenhower*

Again, see the *United States in World Affairs* and the *Dynamics of World Power* volumes and the studies by Seyom Brown and John Spanier, already cited. W. W. Rostow, *The Diffusion of Power, 1957–1972* (1972), is an interpretative study by an important witness to the making of American foreign policy. An interesting new study is Justus D. Doeneck, *Not to the Swift: The Old Isolationists in the Cold War Era* (1979). The basic sources for the Eisenhower years are Eisenhower, *Mandate for Change* and *Waging Peace*, cited above. Townsend Hoopes, *The Devil and John Foster Dulles* (1973), and Roscoe Drummond and G. Coblentz, *Duel at the Brink: John Foster Dulles' Command of American Power* (1960), are appraisals of Eisenhower's secretary of state; while Andrew H. T. Berding, *Dulles on Diplomacy* (1965), recounts conversations with the secretary. These may be supplemented by Louis L. Gerson, *John Foster Dulles* (1967), a biography that is longer on summary than on evaluation or analysis. Robert R. Randle, *Geneva 1954: The Settlement of the Indochinese War* (1969), praises Dulles's astuteness. Eisenhower's other secretary of state is the subject of G. Bernard Noble, *Christian A. Herter* (1970). Keith Eubank, *The Summit Conferences, 1919–1960* (1966), includes useful summaries of Eisenhower's Geneva and Paris meetings, as well as the three wartime conferences.

Schlesinger, *A Thousand Days*, and Sorenson, *Kennedy*, both cited above, contain good "inside" accounts of New Frontier diplomacy. A specific episode is the subject of Robert F. Kennedy's fascinating *Thirteen Days: A Memoir of the Cuban Missile Crisis* (1971). For more critical accounts of Kennedy's behavior during this confrontation, see Peter Wyden, *Bay of the Pigs: The Untold Story* (1979), and Herbert S. Dinerstein, *The Making of a Missile Crisis: October 1962* (1976). For two highly critical evaluations of Kennedy's foreign policy as a whole, along the revisionist lines discussed above, see Richard J. Walton, *Cold War and Counterrevolution: The Foreign Policy of John F. Kennedy* (1972), and Louise FitzSimons, *The Kennedy Doctrine* (1972).

Various issues and areas of cold-war diplomacy are respectively treated in Jack M. Schick, *The Berlin Crisis, 1958–1962* (1971); Henry A. Kissinger, *The Troubled Partnership: A Reappraisal of the Atlantic Alliance* (1965); John Newhouse, *De Gaulle and the Anglo-Saxons* (1970); Carl H. Amme, Jr., *NATO Without France: A Strategic Appraisal* (1967); the essay by Lawrence Kaplan in John Braeman, Robert H. Bremner, and David Brody (eds.), *Twentieth-Century American Foreign Policy* (1971), which reviews NATO's first two decades; Robert S. Walters, *American and Soviet Aid: A Comparative Analysis* (1970); R. H. Dekmejian, *Egypt Under Nasser: A Study in Political Dynamics* (1971); and Stephen R. Weissman, *American Foreign Policy in the Congo, 1960–1964* (1974). For Latin America, see William D. Rogers, *The Twilight Struggle: The Alliance for Progress and the Politics of Development in Latin America* (1967); R. Harrison Wagner, *United States Policy Toward Latin America: A Study in Domestic and International Politics* (1970); Lynn Darrell Bender, *The Politics of Hostility: Castro's Revolution and United States Policy* (1975); Jerome Slater, *Intervention and Negotiation: The United States and the Dominican Revolution* (1970); and Abraham F. Lowenthal,

The Dominican Intervention (1972). On the arms race in the 1960s, see Roberts, *The Nuclear Years*, and UN Secretariat, *The United Nations and Disarmament*, both previously cited; Harland B. Moulton, *From Superiority to Parity: The United States and the Strategic Arms Race, 1961–1971* (1972); and John Newhouse, *Cold Dawn: The Story of SALT* (1973). An interesting collection of essays on recent diplomacy is Lloyd C. Gardner (ed.), *The Great Nixon Turnaround: America's New Foreign Policy in the Post-Liberal Era* (1973). General studies on Henry Kissinger, America's major diplomatic strategist in the 1970s, are beginning to appear. See John G. Stoessinger, *Henry Kissinger: The Anguish of Power* (1976); David Landau, *Kissinger: The Uses of Power* (1972); and Stephen R. Graubard, *Kissinger: Portrait of a Mind* (1973). Henry Kissinger, *The White House Years* (1979), is rich in new information but naturally self-serving.

Recurrent crises of the cold-war years have called increasing attention to the way in which high-level governmental decisions are made. Several recent studies suggest that such decisions are affected and at times controlled by internal bureaucratic power plays and maneuvers as much as by statesmen's careful intellectual appraisal. Among the best of these works are Richard E. Neustadt, *Alliance Politics* (1970), discussing the role of bureaucratic politics in Anglo-American diplomacy during the Suez and Skybolt missile discussions; Graham T. Allison, *Essence of Decision: Explaining the Cuban Missile Crisis* (1971); and I. M. Destler, *Presidents, Bureaucrats, and Foreign Policy: The Politics of Organizational Reform* (1972), which reviews this problem under Kennedy, Johnson, and Nixon.

F. Vietnam and the Far East

The basic sources on foreign affairs, previously cited, discuss the developments leading to America's involvement in Vietnam. Many of the recent studies of the cold war, both revisionist and nonrevisionist, also include material on the conflict in Southeast Asia. A few first-rate studies of the war and its background have already appeared. Among these are Bernard Fall, *Two Viet Nams: A Political and Military Analysis* (1967), *Vietnam Witness, 1953–1966* (1968), and *Last Reflections on a War* (1972); David Halberstam, *The Best and the Brightest* (1972), undocumented, rambling, and brimful of devastating insights; Don Oberdorfer, *Tet* (1971); and Frances Fitzgerald, *Fire in the Lake: The Vietnamese and the Americans in Vietnam* (1972). William Shawcross, *Sideshow: Kissinger, Nixon, and the Destruction of Cambodia* (1979), is devastating. Leslie L. Gelb and R. K. Betts, *The Irony of Vietnam: The System Worked* (1979), is a balanced study of American decision making during the Vietnam war.

Valuable excerpts from Daniel Ellsberg's celebrated revelation are contained in *The Pentagon Papers as Published by the New York Times* (1971), and the much longer Senator Gravel edition, *The Pentagon Papers: The Defense Department History of the United States Decision-Making on Vietnam* (4 vols., 1971). See also Townsend Hoopes, *The Limits of Intervention: An Inside Account of How the Johnson Policy of Escalation in Vietnam Was Reversed* (1969); John Galloway, *The Gulf of Tonkin Resolution* (1970); and Henry F. Graff, *The Tuesday Cabinet: Deliberation and Decision on Peace and War Under Lyndon B. Johnson* (1970). Merlo J. Pusey, *The Way We Go to War* (1969), studies the Vietnam crisis as the latest example of a long-standing tendency for the executive to encroach upon congressional warmaking powers. Herbert Y. Schandler, *The Unmaking of a Pres-*

ident: Lyndon Johnson and Vietnam (1977), is superb. William C. Westmoreland, *A Soldier Reports* (1976), is a firsthand account of the American military involvement. See also Townsend Hoopes and Maxwell D. Taylor, *Swords and Plowshares* (1972). Guenter Lewy, *America in Vietnam* (1978), is comprehensive on the moral and legal issues of American involvement.

For background, see Robert Randle's *Geneva 1954*, already cited; King C. Chen, *Vietnam and China, 1938-1954* (1969); Chae-Jin Lee, *Communist China's Policy Toward Laos: A Case Study, 1954-1967* (1970); and Peter Van Ness, *Revolution and Chinese Foreign Policy: Peking's Support for Wars of National Liberation* (1970), which concentrates on examples in the year 1965.

A few recent studies of China provide useful background for the current change in Sino-American relations: John K. Fairbank, *China: The People's Middle Kingdom and the U. S. A.* (1967), by a sensitive and thoughtful China scholar; James Chieh Hsiung, *Ideology and Practice: The Evolution of Chinese Communism* (1970); John W. Lewis (ed.), *Party Leadership and Revolutionary Power in China* (1970); and Frank H. Trager and William Henderson (eds.), *Communist China 1949-1969: A Twenty Year Assessment* (1970).

4. THE AMERICAN PEOPLE AND THEIR ECONOMIC INSTITUTIONS SINCE 1940

A. *Demographic Changes and Economic Development*

The handiest reference for general economic and social data is the *American Almanac* (formerly *Statistical Abstract of the United States*), published annually. The best sources for demographic changes are the summary volumes of the Census. For two specific case studies of postwar demographic change, see Jean Gottmann, *Megalopolis: The Urbanized Northeastern Seaboard of the United States* (1961), and David Lavender, *California: Land of New Beginnings* (1972).

For discussions of American economic development in the postwar period, see W. Elliot Brownlee, *Dynamics of Ascent: A History of the American Economy* (1979); Harold G. Vatter, *The U. S. Economy in the 1950s: An Economic History* (1963); and Ralph E. Freeman (ed.), *Postwar Economic Trends in the United States* (1960). Milton Friedman and Anna Jacobson Schwartz, *A Monetary History of the United States, 1867-1960* (1963), is a monumental study. It should be supplemented by Margaret G. Myers, *A Financial History of the United States* (1970), and Herman E. Krooss and Martin R. Blyn, *A History of Financial Intermediaries* (1971), an important study of the various financial institutions that now control over half of the nation's wealth. For the regulation of one of the nation's most important industries, see Ari and Olive Hoogenboom, *A History of the ICC* (1976). Robert Sobel, *Amex: A History of the American Stock Exchange, 1921-1971* (1972), is a definitive study of this basic economic institution. John W. Kendrick, *Postwar Productivity Trends in the United States, 1948-1969* (1973), is invaluable. For changing patterns of income distribution in the twentieth century, see Simon Kuznets, *Shares of Upper Income Groups in Income and Savings* (1953), and Robert J. Lampman, *The Share of Top Wealth-holders in National Wealth,*

1922-1956 (1962). Simon Kuznets, *Capital in the American Economy* (1961), and Raymond W. Goldsmith, *The National Wealth of the United States* (1962), are more general studies.

The most valuable analytic overview of recent economic development is Thomas C. Cochran, *American Business in the Twentieth Century* (1972). Other thoughtful interpretative insights are provided by John K. Galbraith in *American Capitalism* (1952), *The New Industrial State* (1967), *The Affluent Society* (1969), and *Economics and the Public Purpose* (1973); and by Adolf A. Berle, Jr., in *The Twentieth-Century Capitalist Revolution* (1954) and *Power Without Property: A New Development in American Political Economy* (1959). Robert L. Heilbroner, *The Limits of American Capitalism* (1965), is an outstanding brief assessment of present trends in American economic development. John W. Oliver, *History of American Technology* (1956); Leonard S. Silk, *The Research Revolution* (1960); and Elting E. Morison, *From Know-How to Nowhere: The Development of American Technology* (1974), are good surveys of the technological revolution.

On concentration in American industry, see Willard F. Mueller, *A Primer on Monopoly and Competition* (1970); Ralph L. Nelson, *Merger Movements in American Industry, 1895-1956* (1959); and the more specialized Federal Trade Commission, *The Merger Movement* (1948), *Interlocking Directorates* (1951), and *The Concentration of Productive Facilities* (1949). See also Wassily W. Leontief, *Studies in the Structure of the American Economy* (1953). A more recent analysis is Robert Sobel, *The Age of Giant Corporations: A Microeconomic History of American Business, 1914-1970* (1972). Morton Mintz and Jerry S. Cohen, *America, Inc.* (1971), is one of the best of several recent popular studies claiming that more and more of American wealth and economic power is being concentrated in a few giant corporate hands. The underlying conflicts between economic and environmental interests are polemically but trenchantly examined in Walter J. Hickel, *Who Owns America?* (1971), and Gene Marine, *America the Raped* (1969). For recent studies of the aerospace industry, see William Sims Bainbridge, *The Spaceflight Revolution* (1976).

B. *American Labor*

Philip Taft, *Organized Labor in American History* (1964), and Henry Pelling, *American Labor* (1960), have chapters on the postwar labor movement. See also Joel I. Seidman, *American Labor from Defense to Reconversion* (1953). John Hutchinson, *The Imperfect Union: A History of Corruption in American Trade Unions* (1970); Walter Sheridan, *The Fall and Rise of Jimmy Hoffa* (1972); and Robert F. Kennedy, *The Enemy Within* (1960), analyze labor racketeering; while C. Wright Mills, *The New Men of Power* (1948), and Eli Ginzberg, *The Labor Leader* (1948), are sociological studies of the rise of a new labor leadership since the Wagner Act. For postwar labor policies state, and federal, see Charles C. Killingsworth, *State Labor Relations Acts* (1948); Harry A. Millis and E. C. Brown, *From the Wagner Act to Taft-Hartley* (1950); Emily C. Brown, *National Labor Policy* (1950); and John L. Blackman, Jr., *Presidential Seizure in Labor Disputes* (1967). McClure's *Truman Administration and the Problems of Postwar Labor*, already cited, is also pertinent.

5. SOCIAL AND INTELLECTUAL MAIN CURRENTS SINCE 1940

A. *Social Trends*

Most of the important social developments in the postwar era are examined in William O'Neill (ed.), *American Society Since 1945* (1969), and William Manchester, *The Glory and the Dream: A Narrative History of America, 1932–1972* (1973). Daniel J. Boorstin, *The Americans: The Democratic Experience* (1973), is a fascinating discussion of many recent social changes placed within the larger context of the period since the Civil War. Three penetrating analyses of modern technology and social change and its impact, from an international perspective, are Alvin Toffler, *Future Shock* (1970); Philip G. Altbach and Robert S. Laufer (eds.), *The New Pilgrims: Youth Protest in Transition* (1972); and Peter Drucker, *The Age of Discontinuity* (1968). William O'Neill, *Coming Apart: An Informal History of America in the 1960s* (1971), is uneven, opinionated, full of thoughtful insights, and especially valuable on the counterculture and related social changes. Joseph F. Kett, *Rites of Passage: Adolescence in America 1970 to the Present* (1977), is excellent on this subject. See also Fred M. Hechinger and Grace Hechinger, *Growing Up in America* (1975).

Francis E. Merrill, *Social Problems on the Home Front* (1948), is an excellent analysis of social tensions and changes during the Second World War. The postwar American character is perceptively analyzed in David Riesman, *The Lonely Crowd: A Study of the Changing American Character* (1950); William S. Whyte, *The Organization Man* (1956); and Christopher Lasch, *The Culture of Narcissism* (1978). Irwin Unger, *The Movement: A History of the American New Left 1959–1972* (1974), is a reflective study. From a more favorable point of view, see Edward J. Bacciocco, Jr., *The New Left in America: Reform to Revolution, 1956–1970* (1974). For urban and suburban influences, see Sam B. Warner, Jr., *The Urban Wilderness: A History of the American City* (1972); Zane L. Miller, *The Urbanization of Modern America* (1973); Gottmann, *Megalopolis*, already cited; and Robert C. Wood, *Suburbia: Its People and Their Politics* (1959). John B. Rae, *The Road and the Car in American Life* (1971), is a balanced and thoughtful study that assumes continued dominance by the auto. For outspoken contrasting verdicts, see Ronald A. Buel, *Dead End: The Automobile in Mass Transportation* (1972); Helen Leavitt, *Superhighway-Superhoax* (1970); A. Q. Mowbray, *Road to Ruin* (1969); and especially John Jerome, *The Death of the Automobile* (1972), all including much social as well as technological history. The history of women in American history is a rich new field. Among the more important works are Peter Gabriel Filene, *Him/Her/Self: Sex Roles in Modern America* (1975), and William H. Chafe, *Women and Equality: Changing Patterns in American Culture* (1977). The best study of the problem of crime in modern America is Humber S. Nelli, *The Business of Crime: Italians and Syndicate Crime in the United States* (1976).

B. *The Media*

The effect of the media on American politics and the public has recently aroused much interest. A marvelous study of the power of major news media is David Halberstam, *The Powers That Be* (1979). For ways in which the media manipulate public opinion, see Edward Jay Epstein, *News from Nowhere: Television and the News* (1973). For an in-depth study of one particular instance, see Peter Braestrup, *Big Story: How the American Press and Television Reported and Interpreted the Crisis of Tet 1968 in Vietnam and Washington* (2 vols., 1977). Hunter S. Thompson, *Fear and Loathing on the Campaign Trail '72* (1973), and Timothy Crouse, *The Boys on the Bus* (1972), provide colorful accounts of political reporting from two gutsy insiders.

C. *American Thought*

Merle Curti, *The Growth of American Thought* (1964); Ralph Gabriel, *The Course of American Democratic Thought* (1958); and Henry S. Commager, *The American Mind* (1950), discuss important developments in the twentieth century. Morton White, *Social Thought in America* (1949), is indispensable if specialized. There are no adequate works covering the postwar period as a whole, although the two previously cited studies by Lasch, *Agony of the American Left* and *The New Radicalism in America*, examine one important strand of postwar thought. For its opposite number, see Daniel Bell (ed.), *The New American Right* (1955).

D. *Education*

The best general account of recent educational developments at all levels is Charles E. Silberman, *Crisis in the Classroom: The Remaking of American Education* (1970). See also Edgar W. Knight, *Education in the United States* (1951). Lawrence A. Cremin, *The Transformation of the School: Progressivism in American Education, 1876-1957* (1961), is excellent social history. See also the parallel, but more specialized, Patricia A. Graham, *Progressive Education: From Anarchy to Academe; A History of the Progressive Education Association, 1919-1955* (1967). Lawrence A. Cremin, *The Genius of American Education* (1965), is a thoughtful, brief analysis. The following studies highlight the immediate postwar crises: Benjamin Fine, *Our Children Are Cheated: The Crisis in American Education* (1947); James B. Conant, *The American High School Today* (1959) and *The Education of American Teachers* (1963); Arthur E. Bestor, Jr., *Educational Wastelands* (1953) and *The Restoration of Learning* (1955); and Albert Lynd, *Quackery in the Public Schools* (1953). One of the gravest problems is examined in James B. Conant, *Slums and Suburbs: A Commentary on Schools in Metropolitan Areas* (1961). See also a few of the pertinent items listed under "Race Relations," below. The turbulence of the college campus in the 1960s is treated in Nathan Glazer, *Remembering the Answers: Essays on the American Student Revolt* (1970), and more specifically in James A. Michener, *Kent State* (1971). The opening of educational opportunities by the ending of Jewish quotas and affirmative action on behalf of minority groups is related in Marcia G. Synnott, *The Half-Opened Door: Discrimination and Admissions at Harvard, Yale, and Princeton, 1900-1970* (1979).

E. *Religious Institutions and Thought*

Sydney E. Ahlstrom, *A Religious History of the American People* (1972), and James W. Smith and A. Leland Jamison (eds.), *Religion in American Life* (4 vols., 1961), are the best introductions. Another recent survey is Winthrop S. Hudson,

Religion in America (1973). Clifton E. Olmstead, *History of Religion in the United States* (1960), includes material on the 1940s and 1950s. More detailed, for the immediate postwar years, is Herbert W. Schneider, *Religion in Twentieth-Century America* (1952). Social and religious history are provocatively blended in Will Herberg, *Protestant-Catholic-Jew: An Essay in Religious Sociology* (1960). Excellent general surveys include John T. Ellis, *American Catholicism* (1969); David J. O'Brien, *The Renewal of American Catholicism* (1972); Andrew M. Greeley, *The American Catholic* (1977); Nathan Glazer, *American Judaism* (1972); Joseph L. Blau, *Judaism in America* (1976); Melvin I. Urofsky, *American Zionism from Herzl to the Holocaust* (1976); Naomi W. Cohen, *American Jews and the Zionist Idea* (1975); Winthrop S. Hudson, *American Protestantism* (1961); Kenneth K. Bailey, *Southern White Protestantism in the Twentieth Century* (1964); and Martin E. Marty, *Righteous Empire: The Protestant Experience in America* (1970), a stimulating and highly critical account of the past two hundred years. Martin E. Marty, *The New Shape of American Religion* (1959), and Arthur R. Eckhardt, *The Surge of Piety in America* (1958), raise some important questions about the so-called return to religion in the 1950s. William G. McLoughlin, Jr., *Modern Revivalism: Charles Grandison Finney to Billy Graham* (1959), places modern revivalism in historical perspective. W. G. McLoughlin, Jr., *Billy Graham: Revivalist in a Secular Age* (1960), and Marshall Frady, *Billy Graham: A Parable of American Righteousness* (1979), are excellent for the most influential Protestant religious leader since the Second World War. For the most recent movement in American religion, see David Edwin Harrell, Jr., *All Things Are Possible: The Healing and Charismatic Revivals in Modern America* (1975).

F. American Literature

The basic general history of American literature is Robert E. Spiller et al., *Literary History of the United States* (3 vols., 1963), which contains discussions of virtually every American writer worthy of mention, lengthy essays on the major writers, and a good general bibliography. See also Leon Howard, *Literature and the American Tradition* (1960); Willard Thorp, *American Writing in the Twentieth Century* (1960); and Frederick J. Hoffman, *The Modern Novel in America, 1900–1950* (1951). Walter B. Rideout, *The Radical Novel in the United States, 1900–1954* (1956), is useful for the literature of protest. The best study of postwar fiction is Alfred Kazin, *Bright Book of Life: American Novelists and Story Tellers from Hemingway to Mailer* (1973). Biographical data and excerpts from critical comments about modern writers, including poets and dramatists, are contained in the semiannual series *Contemporary Authors;* see especially Barbara Harte and Caroline Riley (eds.), *Two Hundred Contemporary Authors* (1969), derived from that series.

G. Race Relations

The literature on most aspects of this complex subject is voluminous and rewarding. General histories of the Negro abound, but the best is John Hope Franklin, *From Slavery to Freedom: A History of Negro Americans* (1974). Indispensable background is provided by Gunnar Myrdal, *An American Dilemma* (2 vols., 1944), a massive, penetrating study of all phases of the race question. Arnold M. Rose,

The Negro in America (1948), is an abridgment of Myrdal's volumes. See also August Meier and Elliott M. Rudwick, *From Plantation to Ghetto: An Interpretative History of American Negroes* (1976) and *Along the Color Line: Explorations in the Black Experience* (1976), and Lawrence W. Levine, *Black Culture and Black Consciousness: Afro-American Folk Thought from Slavery to Freedom* (1977). A recent eloquent statement is John Hope Franklin, *Racial Equality in America* (1976).

For developments in the 1940s and 1950s see Arnold M. Rose, *The Negro in Postwar America* (1950); Bucklin Moon, *The High Cost of Prejudice* (1947); Walter B. Weare, *Black Business in the New South: A Social History of the North Carolina Mutual Life Insurance Company* (1973); Frank S. Loescher, *The Protestant Church and the Negro* (1948); Dwight W. Culver, *Negro Segregation in the Methodist Church* (1953); J. Saunders Redding, *On Being Negro in America* (1951); Carl T. Rowan, *South of Freedom* (1952); E. Franklin Frazier, *Black Bourgeoisie* (1957) and *The Negro Church in America* (1973); Jack Greenberg, *Race Relations and American Law* (1959); Margaret Price, *The Negro and the Ballot in the South* (1959); C. E. Lincoln, *The Black Muslims in America* (1973); E. U. Essien-Udom, *Black Nationalism* (1962); and two previously cited works: Berman, *Politics of Civil Rights in the Truman Administration,* and Dalfiume, *Desegregation of the U. S. Armed Forces.* See also Daniel O. Price, *Changing Characteristics of the Negro Population* (1969), a 1960 Census monograph.

The best of the more recent studies of black aspirations and problems include Louis E. Lomax, *The Negro Revolt* (1962); William Brink and Louis Harris, *The Negro Revolution in America* (1964); Charles E. Silberman, *Crisis in Black and White* (1964); Leonard Broom and Norval D. Glenn, *Transformation of the Negro American* (1965); Kenneth B. Clark, *Dark Ghetto: Dilemmas of Social Power* (1965); Nat Hentoff, *Our Children Are Dying* (1966); Robert Conot, *Rivers of Blood, Years of Darkness* (1968), a study of the Watts riot; Joe R. Feagin and Harlan Hahn, *Ghetto Riots: The Politics of Violence in American Cities* (1973); Jerome Skolnick, *The Politics of Protest* (1969); John H. Bracey, Jr., August Meier, and Elliott Rudwick (eds.), *The Rise of the Ghetto* (1971); and John Hall Fish, *Black Power/White Control: The Struggle of the Woodlawn Organization in Chicago* (1973). For recent black participation in politics, see Leonard A. Cole, *Blacks in Power* (1976).

The thoughts and actions of black leaders are variously examined in Jervis Anderson, *A. Philip Randolph* (1973); David L. Lewis, *King: A Critical Biography* (1978); Peter Goldman, *The Death and Life of Malcolm X* (1973); George Brietman (ed.), *Malcolm X Speaks* (1965); S. P. Fullinwider, *The Mind and Mood of Black America: Twentieth Century Thought* (1969); and August Meier and Elliott Rudwick, *CORE: A Study in the Civil Rights Movement, 1942-1968* (1973). White responses, including the backlash, are analyzed in William Brink and Louis Harris, *Black and White: A Study of U. S. Racial Attitudes Today* (1967), and Louise K. Howe (ed.), *The White Majority: Between Poverty and Affluence* (1970).

Good introductions to the segregation controversy are Richard Kluger, *Simple Justice: The History of Brown v. Board of Education and Black America's Struggle for Equality* (1976); Henry A. Bullock, *A History of Negro Education in the South: From 1619 to the Present* (1967); Bernard H. Nelson, *The Fourteenth Amendment and the Negro Since 1920* (1946); C. H. Pritchett, *The Roosevelt Court* (1948) and *Civil Liberties and the Vinson Court,* cited above; Robert J. Harris, *The Quest for*

Equality (1960); Harry S. Ashmore, *The Negro and the Schools* (1954); and Benjamin Muse, *Ten Years of Prelude: The Story of Integration Since the Supreme Court's 1954 Decision* (1964). For various aspects of the controversy following the schools decision of 1954, see John B. Martin, *The Deep South Says "Never"* (1957); Benjamin Muse, *Virginia's Massive Resistance* (1961); H. S. Ashmore, *The Other Side of Jordan* (1960); J. W. Peltason, *Fifty-eight Lonely Men* (1961), on southern federal district judges and desegregation; James W. Silver, *Mississippi: The Closed Society* (1964); Russell H. Barrett, *Integration at Ole Miss* (1965); I. A. Newby, *Challenge to the Court: Social Scientists and the Defense of Segregation, 1955–1966* (1967); Earl Black, *Southern Governors and Civil Rights: Racial Segregation as a Campaign Issue in the Second Reconstruction* (1976); Numan V. Bartley, *The Rise of Massive Resistance: Race and Politics in the South During the 1950s* (1969); Neil R. McMillen, *The Citizens Council: Organized Resistance to the Second Reconstruction, 1954–1964* (1971); and Gary Orfield, *The Reconstruction of Southern Education: The Schools and the 1964 Civil Rights Act* (1969).

The new self-awareness and assertiveness on the part of American Indians are well set forth in Vine Deloria, Jr., *Custer Died for Your Sins: An Indian Manifesto* (1969), and Alvin M. Josephy, *Red Power: The American Indians' Fight for Freedom* (1972).

New studies of Mexicans in the United States have been written recently. The best of them are Matt S. Meier and Feliciano Rivera, *The Chicanos: A History of Mexican Americans* (1972); Peter N. Kirstein, *Anglo over Bracero: A History of the Mexican Worker in the United States from Roosevelt to Nixon* (1977); and Peter Matthiessen, *Sal Si Puedes: Cesar Chavez and the New American Revolution* (1973).

Index

Abernathy, Ralph, 863
abortion ruling, 904
Acheson, Dean, 771; as secretary of
    state, 694, 700–714
Adoula, Cyrille, 812
aerospace industry, 582
affluent society, 607–615
Afghanistan, 1020
AFL-CIO, 593–594, 600–601
Africa, 810–813
Agnew, Spiro, 887, 898, 940, 944,
    957–959
Agriculture Acts, 666, 744, 745
Agricultural Trade Development and
    Assistance Act, 747
agriculture, 575, 583; in WWII,
    511–512; Eisenhower policies,
    744–747
air force, see military
airplane industry, 500, 582
Alaska, oil pipeline, 994
Albee, Edward, 628
Albert, Carl, 959, 963
Aldrin, Edwin, 909
Algeria, 811
Algren, Nelson, 625–626
aliens, rulings on, 754
Alliance for Progress, 826, 920
Aluminum Co. of America, 587
America First Committee, 467
American Federation of Labor, see
    AFL-CIO
American Independent Party, 887
Americans for Democratic Action, 662
American Tobacco Co., 587–588
Andrus, Cecil, 1013
Angola, 1003
Anti-Inflation Act, 505
antitrust, 587–589
Appalachian Regional Development Act,
    852
appliance industry, 581–582

Arab League, 809
Arbenz, Jacabo, 814, 815
Area Redevelopment Act, 829
Argentina: pre-WWII, 459–460; post-
    WWII, 688–690
Armstrong, Neil, 908, 909
army, see military
arts, in 1960, 621
Arvey, Jacob, 662
Askew, Reubin, 939
assassination: of John Kennedy, 843–844;
    of Martin Luther King, Jr., 863; of
    Robert Kennedy, 885
Aswan Dam, 804, 810
Atlantic Conference, 477–479
atomic energy, 656, 742–743
Atomic Energy Acts, 656, 742–743, 788
Atomic Energy Commission, 656, 729,
    741–743
atomic weapons, see nuclear weapons
Attlee, Clement, 559–680
Austria, 458, 554
automation, and labor, 596
automobile industry, 577–580, 590

Baghdad Pact, 803, 810
Baker, Howard, 955, 961–962, 1017
Bakke decision, 1040–1041
Balaguer, Joaquin, 871
Baldwin, James, 861–862
Ballistic Missile Early Warning System
    (BMEWS), 769
banking, concentration in, 585–586
Barkley, Alben, 503, 662
Barnett, Ross, 833
Barth, Karl, 645
Baruch, Bernard, 498, 500, 681
Batista, Fulgencio, 815–816
Bay of Pigs, 834–835
Beard, Dita, 952
Beatles, 621

Begin, Menahem, 1017–1019
Belgium, and Congo, 811–812
Bell, Griffin, 1013
Bellow, Saul, 626, 627
Benson, Ezra Taft, 738, 739, 744–745
Bergland, Robert, 1013
Beria, Lavrenti, 773
Berlin, *see* Germany
Berryman, John, 630
Bestor, Arthur, 633
Betancourt, Romulo, 817
Bevin, Ernest, 700
birthrate, 1940–1970, 561–562
Black, Hugo, 754, 901, 905
Blackmun, Harry, 901, 904
Black Muslims, 764–765, 861
Black Panther party, 861, 862
blacks: in WWII, 515–516; post-WWII,
    564, 572–573; in 1950s, 751–753,
    757–765; in 1960s, 616, 641, 831–834,
    849–850, 857–866; in 1970s,
    1040–1041
Blake, Eugene Carson, 646
Blough, Robert, 828
Blount, Winton, 893–894
Blumenthal, W. Michael, 1012–1013
Bohlen, Charles E., 728
Bohr, Niels, 496
Bonhoeffer, Dietrich, 646
Borah, William, 462
Borguiba, Habib, 810, 811
Bork, Robert, 962
Bosch, Juan, 870–871
Boun Oum, Prince, 801, 802, 840
Braden, Spruille, 689
Bradley, Omar, 553, 712, 713
Brannen Plan, 666
Brennan, William, 901
Brezhnev, Leonid, 875, 921, 1004, 1005,
    1023
Bricker, John, 543, 737, 743
Brooke, Edward, 863
Brown, H. Rap, 861
Brown, Harold, 1013
Brown, Jerry, 1006
Brown, Prentiss, 505–506
Brownell, Herbert, Jr., 738
Brown v. Board of Education of Topeka,
    752, 760–761
Brzezinski, Zbigniew, 1013
Buber, Martin, 645
Budget Reform Act, 983
Bulganin, Nikolai, 773, 774, 785, 806
Burger, Warren, and Supreme Court,
    900–907, 972–974
Burke-Wadsworth bill, 468
buses, desegregation of, 762–763, 832
Bush, Vannevar, 495
busing, school, 897–898, 902–903, 1040
Butterfield, Alexander, 956

Byrne, William Matthew, Jr., 954
Byrnes, James F., 499, 505, 543–544,
    660, 680–681

Cabral, Donald Reid, 871
Cairo Declaration, 684
Califano, Joseph, 1013
California: student rebellion, 639–640;
    taxpayers' revolt, 1032
Calley, William, 933
Cambodia, 794, 928–934, 950, 1002,
    1022–1023
campaign financing, reform, 941, 983
Canada, 869
capital punishment, 906
Carmichael, Stokely, 861
Carson, Rachel, 911
Carswell, G. Harrold, 901
Carter, Jimmy: and election of 1976,
    1005–1011; profile, 1011–1012; for-
    eign policy, 1013–1024; domestic poli-
    cies, 1024–1034; leadership,
    1035–1038
Carter, Rosalynn, 1013
Casablanca meeting, 527–528
Castro, Fidel, 815–817, 834–835
casualties: WWII, 494–495, 557, 558;
    Korea, 715; Vietnam, 880–881, 936
Celler-Kefauver Act, 588, 589
Central Intelligence Agency, 657, 641,
    815, 817, 834–835, 952, 955, 974
Central Treaty Organization, 810
Chamberlain, Neville, 458, 460, 461, 463
Chambers, Whittaker, 669–670
Chapultepec, Act of, 689
Chavez, Cesar, 602
chemical industry, 580–581
Chiang Ch'ing, 1003
Chiang Kai-shek, 484, 537, 550*n*, 559,
    683–688, 794, 798, 1022
Chicago, convention violence, 1968, 886
China: communist takeover, 683–689; in
    1950s, 703, 709–715, 793–795,
    798–801; and Soviet Union, 875; in
    1970s, 925–928, 1003–1004,
    1021–1023; *see also* World War II
Chisholm, Shirley, 864, 937
Chou En-lai, 688, 793, 798, 926, 927,
    1003–1004
Church, Frank, 932, 1006
Churchill, Winston, 680, 691, 773–774;
    see also World War II
cities: in 1950s, 732; in 1960s, 853–854,
    860–861, 863
civil liberties, 512–515, 755
civil rights, 667, 750–753, 897–898; *see
    also* blacks
Civil Rights Acts, 750, 751, 847, 858,
    864, 865–866

Civil Rights Commission, 750
Civil Service Commission, 669
Clark, Kenneth, 758
Clark, Mark, 535, 715
Clay, Lucius, 836
Clayton Act, 588, 589
Cleaver, Eldridge, 861
coal industry, 590
Collins, Michael, 909
colonialism, end of, 785–786, 810–812
Comecon, 793
Committee on National Goals, 615
Committee to Defend America,
465–466, 467
Common Market, 790–793, 827,
869–870, 924
communes, 619
communism: post-WWII, 613, 638, 662,
667–672; in 1950s, 707–709, 720,
726–730
competition, in economy, 583–589
Compton, Arthur H., 497
computers, 581–582
concentration, in economy, 583–589
conglomerates, 586–587
Congo, 811–812
Congress: and taxes, WWII, 501–504;
658–661, 665–667, 671–672; and Mc-
Carthyism, 727–730; and Kennedy,
826–831; in 1970s, 893–900, 996–999,
1037–1038; *see also* Watergate
Congress of Industrial Organizations,
593–594
Congress of Racial Equality, 759, 763
Connally, John, 843
Connor, Eugene, 833
conscription, 477, 654
conservation, 740, 854–855, 910–913
conservatism, 738–743
Constitutional Amendments: 5th, 754;
14th, 752, 866, 868; 22d, 658; 26th,
941; Equal Rights, 1041
consumer movement, 854, 910–913
Consumer Product Safety Act, 911
Cooper, John Sherman, 919, 932
Coplon, Judith, 670
corporation mergers, 584–585
corruption: in unions, 594, 600–601; in
government, 716, 943–944, 957–959;
see also Watergate
Council of Economic Advisers, 655–656
counterculture, 618–619
Cox, Archibald, and Watergate, 954–962
Cox, Harvey, 646
Cozzens, James Gould, 624–625
Cramer, Anthony, 514
crimes: organized, 613–614; and due
process, 866–867, 905–906; and Nixon, 898

Cuba, 1005; Castro takeover, 815–817;
Bay of Pigs invasion, 834–835; missile
crisis, 837–838; African presence,
1003
Cushing, Richard, 844
Cyprus, 1002
Czechoslovakia, 458–460; communist
takeover, 695, 699, 875

Daladier, Edouard, 458, 461
Daley, Richard J., 886, 941, 1006
dams, 741, 804, 810
Daniel, Aubrey, 933
Darlan, Jean, 527–528
Davis, Angela, 862
Day, J. Edward, 825
Dean, John, 954, 956, 961
death rate, 1940–1970, 562–564
debates, on TV, 821, 1010
Defense Dept., 657
Defense Early Warning (DEW) Line,
769
Defense Production Act, 592, 707
de Gaulle, Charles, 528–529, 776, 789,
811, 869
demobilization, WWII, 653–654
Democratic party: in 1950s, 731–733;
see also Congress; elections
Demonstration Cities and Metropolitan
Area Redevelopment Act, 853–854
Denmark, and WWII, 463, 476
desegregation, 763–764, 752–753,
760–764
Development Loan Fund, 826
Dewey, Thomas E., 468, 543–546, 661,
663–664, 717, 718, 720
DeWitt, John L., 514
Diem, Ngo Dinh, 797, 802, 840–843
Dienhienphu, 795
Dillon, C. Douglas, 825, 827–828
disarmament, *see* nuclear weapons
Displaced Persons bill, 666
District of Columbia, home rule, 855,
998
Dixon, Edgar H., 741–742
Doar, John, and Watergate, 967–973
Doenitz, Karl, 554
Dole, Robert, 1008
Dominican Republic, 817, 870–871
Doolittle, James, 525
Dos Passos, John, 624
Douglas, William, 754, 901n, 902
Douglas-Kennedy-Ives Act, 595
Dow Chemical Co., 641
drama, post-WWII, 627–629
Drucker, Peter, 605
drugs, in 1960s, 619
Drummond, Roscoe, 860
Dubcek, Alexander, 875

Dulles, John Foster, 714, 719, 738,
767-769; and foreign policy, 781,
793-800, 803-805
Dumbarton Oaks, 674
Dunkirk, 463
Du Pont Co.,589
Durkin, Martin, 738, 739
Dylan, Bob, 621

Educational Testing Service, 636
Education Amendments, 894
Egypt: in 1950s, 787, 803-805, 809; in
1960s, 871-874; in 1970s, 924-925,
1000-1001, 1017-1019
Ehrlichman, John, 894, 954, 966, 969
Einstein, Albert, 496
Eastern Orthodoxy, 645n, 648, 649
Eastland, James, 834
Economic Development Act, 946
Economic Opportunity Act, 848
economic policy, and inflation,
1028-1032
economy: and WWII, 497-507; and industry, 566-589; mixed, 603-605; in
1950s, 740; in 1960s, 827-828; in early 1970s, 913-914, 986-992, 997-998,
1025-1034; *see also* taxes
Eden, Anthony, 519, 533, 536, 547, 774,
781, 795, 804, 805
education: changes in, 631-642; in
1950s, 749-753, 760-762; in 1960s,
829, 852-853, 859, 897-898, 901
Eisenhower, Dwight, 523, 527-528, 661,
662, 671, 707, 711; and WWII, 535,
539-540; and labor, 597-598; elected
in 1952, 718-722, profile, 724-726;
domestic policies, 726-728, 738-751;
reelected in 1956, 734-735; foreign
policies, 766-778, 794, 795, 806, 808;
and election of 1960, 820-821, 822
Eisenhower Doctrine, 808
Eisenstat, Stuart, 1013
elections: of 1940, 467-471; of 1942,
542; of 1944, 542-546; of 1946,
659-660; of 1948, 661-665; of 1950,
707-709; of 1952, 717-722, 733; of
1954, 733-734; of 1956, 734-737; of
1958, 737; of 1960, 818-822; of 1962,
830; of 1964, 848-850; of 1968,
883-891; of 1970, 898-899; of 1972,
936-947; of 1974, 985-986; of 1976,
1005-1011; of 1978, 1031-1032
electric power, 581-582, 741-743
Elementary and Secondary Education
Act, 634, 853
Ellison, Ralph, 627
Ellsberg, Daniel, 907, 934, 952, 954
Emergency Petroleum Allocation Act,
994

Employment Act, 655-656
energy, 582-583, 656
energy crisis, 987-997, 1024-1025,
1032-1034, 1038, 1041-1042
Energy Dept., 1025
Energy Policy and Conservation Act,
996-997
Energy Research and Development Ad-
ministration, 994
Energy Security Corp., 1034
Environmental Protection Agency, 912
Ervin, Sam, and Watergate, 953, 956,
961-962
Espionage Act, 513
Ethiopia, 1020
European Defense Community, 781
European Economic Community, *see*
Common Market
European Free Trade Association, 791,
870
European Recovery Program, 694-697,
700
Evers, Charles, 859, 864
Evers, Medgar, 859
Export-Import Bank, 587, 678

Fair Deal, 665-667
Fair Employment Practices Committee,
510
Fair Labor Standards Act, 666, 749
family assistance plan, 895-896
farmers, 569-570, 731-732
Farmers Home Administration, 745
farm workers, 602
Farrell, Edelmiro, 688, 689
fashion, 1960s, 619, 620-621
Faubus, Orval, 762
Faulkner, William, 623
Faure, Edgar, 774
Federal Aid Highway Acts, 748,
997-998
Federal Bureau of Investigation, 668,
669, 952, 955, 974
Federal Council of Churches of Christ,
647-648
Federal Election Campaign Act, 941,
950-951
Federal Energy Administration, 994,
996-997
Federal Trade Commission, 588, 589
Federal Water Pollution Control Act,
829
Finch, Robert, 894
Finland, and WWII, 462-463, 476, 533,
542
fiscal policy, in 1950s, 740
Fitzgerald, F. Scott, 623
Flynn, Edward, 662
Flanders, Ralph, 730

Ford, Gerald, 960, 974–976; profile, 981–982; as President, 982–986, 996–999, 1002–1011
foreign aid: post-WWII, 677, 692–697, 700; in 1960s, 826–827
foreign relations: post-WWII, 674–690; 697–704; in 1950s, 704–715, 766–776; Europe, 780–793; Far East, 793–802; Mideast, 802–813; Latin America, 813–817; in 1960s, 834–843, 868–875; in 1970s, 925–928, 999–1005, 1013–1023; *see also* nuclear weapons
Forrestal, James, 657, 691
Fortas, Abe, 900–901
Four Powers Declaration, 536
France: post-WWII, 694–701, 774–776; in 1950s, 781, 788–789, 794–795, 802–807, 811; in 1960s, 868–870; *see also* World War II
Franco, Francisco, 784
Frankfurter, Felix, 754
freedom rides, 831–832
Freeman, Orville, 825
Frost, Robert, 629
Fulbright, J. William, 835, 877, 881, 919

Gagarin, Yuri, 908
Galbraith, John K., 605, 857
García Godoy, Héctor, 871
Garner, John Nance, 460
Garvey, Marcus, 764
General Electric Co., 601–602
German Americans, in WWII, 513–514
Germany: post WWII, 678–679, 681, 699–701; in 1950s, 785, 789–790; in 1960s, 836–837; in 1970s, 922–923; *see also* WWII
Ghana, 811, 812
Ghormley, Robert, 527
G.I. Bill of Rights, 654
Giraud, Henri H., 528n, 529
Glenn, John, 908
gold, and monetary crisis, 915–917
Goldberg, Arthur, 825, 828, 985
Goldwater, Barry, 820, 848–850, 965, 975, 1022
Gomulka, Wladyslaw, 786–787
Gore, Albert, 734
government: post-WWII, 587, 657–667; employees, 602–603, 668–669
Graham, Billy, 643, 647, 969
Graham, Frank, 709
Great Britain, post-WWII, 692, 694, 695, 697–701; in 1950s, 774–789, 794, 795, 802–807, 809; and Common Market, 793, 924; in 1960s, 868–870; *see also* World War II
Greece, 692–694, 869
Green, William, 593

Greenland, in WWII, 463, 475, 476
Grew, Joseph, 486, 487–488
Gromyko, Andrei, 773, 837
gross national product, 566–569
Guadalcanal, battle for, 527
Guatamala, 814–815
Guinea, 811

Haig, Alexander, 961, 974, 975
Haldeman, H. R., 894, 951, 954, 966, 969
Haley, Alex, 1041
Halsey, William, 531
Hammarskjöld, Dag, 809
Hand, Learned, 587
Hannegan, Robert, 544
Hardin, Clifford, 894
Harlan, John, 867, 901
Harriman, Averell, 680, 691, 734–839
Harrington, Michael, 605
Harris, Arthur, 538
Harris, Patricia, 1013
Harrison, George, 719
Hatfield, Mark, 932
Haynsworth, Clement, 901
Head Start, 634
Heberg, Wil, 644
Heilbroner, Robert, 605
Hemingway, Ernest, 623
Henderson, Leon, 504, 505
Hickel, Walter, 894
Highway Beautification Act, 854
Hillman, Sidney, 498, 543–544
Hiroshima, 559
Hispanics, 1041
Hiss, Alger, 669–670
Ho Chi Minh, 797, 840
Hodges, Luther, 825
Hoffa, James, 594
holding company, 586
Honduras, 814–815
Hoover, Herbert, 658, 711
Hoover, J. Edgar, 756, 952
Hopkins, Harry, 468–471, 477–479, 523, 680
House Un-American Activities Committee, 669–670
housing, 748, 862, 864
Housing Act, 666, 829
Housing and Urban Development Act, 852
Hua Kuo-feng, 1004
Hull, Cordell, 459–461, 468–469, 484–490, 536, 674, 675
human rights, 1016
Humphrey, George, 738, 739, 740, 747, 772
Humphrey, Hubert, 662, 665, 734, 819, 847, 849, 1006; and election of 1968, 884–891; and election of 1972, 936–939

Hungary, rebellion, 787
Hurley, Patrick, 684, 685
Hussein, King, 808, 810, 872
Hutchins, Robert, 633, 638
hydrogen bomb, 704, 771, 778

Iceland, WWII, 463, 475, 477
Ickes, Harold, 660
immigration, 564, 672
Immunity Act, 754
impeachment, of Nixon, 963, 967,
    973-975
income, 1940-1970, 503-504, 566-573
India, 1950s, 798-800
Indochina, and WWII, 482, 485, 488,
    489; *see also* Vietnam; Vietnam war
industry, 1940-1970, 497-500, 566-573,
    577-583, 655
inflation, *see* economy
Inge, William, 627-628
Inter-American Development Bank, 815
Inter-American Treaty of Reciprocal As-
    sistance, 690
Internal Revenue Service, 716
Internal Security Act, 754
International Brotherhood of Teamsters,
    594, 601
International Longshoremen's Assoc.,
    594
International Telephone & Telegraph
    Co., 586, 943-944, 952
Iran, 692, 1020, 1032
Iraq, 809, 810
Israel, conflicts, 803-806; 871-874,
    1000-1001; in 1970s, 924-925,
    1017-1021
Italy, 694-701; *see also* World War II

Jackson, Henry, 921, 937, 996, 1006
Jaffe, Philip, 669
Japan, 679, 704, 714, 800, 926, 928,
    1021
Japanese-Americans, in WWII, 514-515
Japenese-American treaties, 480
Javits, Jacob, 1017
Jaworski, Leon, and Watergate, 964-971
Jeffers, William, 500
Jefferson, Thomas, 1042
Jenner, William, 720, 727, 737
Jessup, Philip, 671
Jews, 459, 642-646
John XXIII, Pope, 648
Johnson, Frank, 858
Johnson, Lady Bird, 854
Johnson, Louis, 654
Johnson, Lyndon, 738, 819-820, 822,
    833, 947; and Vietnam, 842, 878-880;
    becomes President, 846-848; elected

in 1964, 848-850; domestic policy,
    850-858; foreign policy, 870-871, 874,
    875; and election of 1968, 884, 889
Joint Chiefs of Staff, 657, 770
Jones, LeRoi, 861
Jordan, Hamilton, 1013
Jordan, 808-810, 872-874, 1000, 1001
Justice Dept., 588-589, 955, 962
juvenile delinquency, 614-615

Kalmbach, Herbert, 954
Kasavubu, Joseph, 811-812
Kassim, Abdel Karim al-, 809
Kefauver, Estes, 613, 716, 718-719,
    734-735
Kennan, George, 680, 691-692, 694
Kennedy, David, 893
Kennedy, Edward, 919, 937, 939
Kennedy, John, 598, 599, 602, 616,
    734-735, 846, 847; elected in 1960,
    818-822; profile, 824-825; domestic
    policy, 826-834; foreign policy,
    834-844, 869, 908
Kennedy, Joseph, 824
Kennedy, Robert, 614, 825, 832, 849,
    884, 885
Kerner, Otto, 863
Khomeini, Ayatollah Ruhollah, 1020
Khrushchev, Nikita, 773, 775-776, 800,
    809, 874-875; and Kennedy, 834-838
Kimmel, Husband, 490
King, Ernest, 523
King, Martin Luther, Jr., 762-763, 832,
    858, 862, 863, 865
Kinkaid, Thomas C., 555
Kissinger, Henry, 771, 894, 931, 935,
    982, 985; and foreign policy, 926-927,
    999-1004
Kleindienst, Richard, 954
Knowland, William, 737
Knox, Frank, 462, 465
Knudsen, William, 498
Koiso, Kuniaki, 558
Kong Le, 801
Konoye, Fumimaro, 482, 483-484, 486,
    487-488
Korean War, 704-715, 717
Kosygin, Aleksei, 874, 875
Kreps, Juanita, 1013
Kuchel, Thomas, 847
Ku Klux Klan, 761
Kurusu, Saburu, 488, 489, 490
Ky, Nguyen Cao, 878

labor, in WWII, 508-511, 515-516;
    post-WWII, 590-603, 611; in 1950s, 732
Laird, Melvin, 893, 919
Lance, Bert, 1013, 1036
Land and Water Conservation Act, 855

Landrum-Griffin Act, 595, 601
Laos, 794, 800-801, 840, 929-930, 934, 950, 1002
Latin America: pre-WWII, 459-460; and WWII, 468-469; post-WWII, 688-690, 813-817, 826, 920
Lattimore, Owen, 670-671
League of Revolutionary Black Workers, 862
Leahy, William, 651, 691
Lebanon, 809-810, 1019-1020
Lend-Lease, 471-476, 470, 529n, 680, 683
Levittown, 607-609
Lewis, John L., 506-507, 510, 590, 659
Lewis, Sinclair, 623
Libya, 810-811
Liebman, Joshua, 643
Lindsay, John, 937
Lippman, Walter, 633
literature, post-WWII, 622-627
Litvinov, Maxim, 519
Lodge, Henry Cabot, Jr., 718, 821, 848
Lon Nol, 929, 1002
Lost Generation, 623-624
Lowell, Robert, 630
Lumumba, Patrice, 811-812
lynching, 515
Lynd, Albert, 633

MacArthur, Douglas, 520, 531, 555, 557; 560, 679; and Korean War, 705-713
MacLeish, Archibald, 910
MacMahon, Brien, 656
Macmillan, Harold, 776, 869
Maddox, Lester, 859
Magsaysay, Ramon, 800
Mailer, Norman, 625
Malamud, Bernard, 626, 627
Malcolm X, 861
Malenkov, Georgi, 773
Malik, Jacob, 559, 714
Malinovsky, Rodion, 773
Manchuria, 549, 685, 686, 687
Manpower Development and Retraining Act, 598
Mansfield, Mike, 869, 881, 919
manufacturing, concentration in, 583-585
Mao Tse-tung, 688, 793, 795, 927, 1003-1004
Maritain, Jacques, 645n
Marshall, F. Ray, 1013
Marshall, George, 469, 477, 523, 528, 537, 671, 681, 686-687, 688, 692
Marshall, Thurgood, 752, 863, 901, 904
Marshall Plan, 694-697, 700
Martin, Joseph, 712
Matsuoka, Yosuke, 482, 483, 484

McCarran Act, 672
McCarran-Walter bill, 672
McCarthy, Eugene, 881, 883-885, 937
McCarthy, Joseph, 670-671, 703, 720, 726-730
McClellan, John, 594, 613
McGovern, George, 881, 919, 932, 950; and election of 1972, 937-947
McGranery, James, 716
McGrath, Howard, 716
McKay, Douglas, 738
McNamara, Robert, 825
McNutt, Paul, 509
Meany, George, 593-594
media, and Pentagon Papers, 907
Medicare, 830, 852
Meredith, James, 833
mergers, 584-586
Merhige, Robert, 903
Middle East, in 1950s, 802-810; in 1960s, 871-874; in 1970s, 924-925, 1000-1001, 1017-1019
migration, 564-566, 607, 610, 860
Mikoyan, Anastas, 773, 790
military: pre-WWII, 464; in WWII, 469, 477, 479, 493-497, 538-539; 653-657; in 1950s, 729, 769-772; in 1960s, 826; *see also* nuclear weapons; Vietnam war
Miller, Arthur, 628
Miller, William, 849
missiles, 770-772, 837-838; and SALT, 918-922, 1023-1024
Mitchell, James, 598
Mitchell, John, 893, 898, 906, 944, 966
Mollet, Guy, 791
Molotov, Vyacheslav, 461, 476, 519, 523-524, 536, 548, 674, 684, 773
Mondale, Walter, 1006
money crises, 1970s, 915-917, 1031
Monroe Doctrine, 463, 689, 816
Montgomery, Bernard, 528, 535, 551, 553
Morgenthau, Henry, 546n
Morocco, 810-811
Morse, Wayne, 722, 877
Moscow Conference, 536-537
Motor Vehicle Safety Standards, 580
Mountbatten, Louis, 537
Moynihan, Daniel, 894
Muhammad, Elijah, 764
Munich Pact, 459
Murray, James, 655
music, in 1960s, 621
Muskie, Edmund, 886, 936-939
Mutual Defense Assistance Act, 701
Mutual Security Agency, 696
My Lai, 933-934

Nader, Ralph, 570-580, 641, 911
Nagasaki, 560
Nasser, Gamal Abdel, 802-805, 809,
    871-872, 924
National Advisory Commission on Civil
    Disorders, 863
National Adronautics and Space Admin-
    istration, 770
National Air Quality Standards Act, 911
National Association for the Advance-
    ment of Colored People, 752, 760,
    861
National Council of the Churches of
    Christ, 648
National Crime Commission, 614
National Defense Education Acts, 750,
    831
National Defense Research Committee,
    495, 496, 575
National Energy Act, 1026
National Labor Relations Board, 593
National Security Act, 657
National Teachers Corps, 853
National Urban League, 759
National Wilderness Preservation Act,
    855
natural gas, 1025-1026
navy, *see* military
Nehru, Jawaharlal, 715, 798
Netherlands, 987
Neutrality Acts, 460, 462, 471, 479
Newark, riot, 860
New Deal, and blacks, 757-758
Nicaragua, 814-815
Niebuhr, Reinhold, 645
Nimitz, Chester, 525, 527, 531, 555
Nixon, Richard, 598, 602, 709, 718,
    734-735, 815, 820-822; elected in
    1968, 886-891; profile, 891-893; do-
    mestic policy, 893-902, 913-917; for-
    eign policy, 918-928, 999, 1003, 1004;
    and Vietnam war, 928-936; reelected
    in 1972, 936, 940-950; resignation,
    974-976; legacy, 982-984; and energy
    crisis, 992-996; *see also* Watergate
Nixon Doctrine, 920
Nomura, Kichisaburo, 484, 488-489, 490
Nonaggression Pact, 467
North Atlantic Treaty, 700-701
North Atlantic Treaty Organization, 707,
    710, 780-784, 787-789, 869, 1002,
    1020
nuclear energy, Three Mile Island acci-
    dent, 1032-1033
Nuclear Nonproliferation Treaties, 918,
    1004
nuclear weapons, 496-497, 559-560,
    704, 771; post-WWII, 681-682; in
    1950s, 776-779, 787-789, 839; in

1960s, 868-869, 875; and SALT,
    918-925, 1004, 1023-1924
nylon, 580

O'Brien, Lawrence, 950
Office of Defense Mobilization, 710
Office of Economic Opportunity, 848,
    946
Office of Price Administration, 504-507,
    659
Office of Scientific Research and Devel-
    opment, 495, 496, 497, 575
Office of Strategic Services, 668
oil, tidelands controversy, 741; *see also*
    energy crisis
O'Neill, Eugene, 627
Oppenheimer, Robert, 497, 704, 729
Organization for Economic Cooperation
    and Development, 826-827
Organization of Afro-American Unity,
    861
Organization of American States, 690,
    814-815, 817, 871
Organization of Petroleum Exporting
    Countries, 987-992, 1032, 1033
Oswald, Lee Harvey, 843-844

Palestine Liberation Organization, 1018
Panama, 815, 870, 1003, 1016-1017;
    Declaration of, 462
Patton, George, 535, 540, 554
Peace Corps, 827
Peale, Norman Vincent, 643
Pearl Harbor, 487-491
Pendergast, Tom, 651
Pentagon Papers, 907, 934
Pepper, Claude, 709
Perón, Juan, 689-690
Peru, 815
Petain, Henri-Philippe, 464, 527
petroleum, *see* energy crisis
Philippines, 555-557, 800
Phoui Sananikone, 801
Phoumi Nosavan, 801, 840
Pittman, Key, 460, 462
Pleven, René, 781
poetry, post-WWII, 629-631
Poland, 680, 786-787; *see also* World
    War II
pollution, 580, 829, 854
Pol Pot, 1022
Poor People's Campaign, 863
population, 561-566
Portugal, colonies, 785
Potsdam Declaration, 559
poverty, 571-572, 612, 857
Powell, Adam Clayton, 749
Powell, Jody, 1013
Powell, Lewis, 901-907

Presidential Succession Act, 658
productivity, and inflation, 1028–1030
Progressive Education Association, 633
Progressives, 651–653, 662, 665–667
Protestants, 642–649
public opinion, in WWII, 512–515

Quemoy and Matsu, 798, 800–801
quotas, racial, 1040–1041

Radford, Arthur, 769, 795
railroads, 590–591, 598–599
Randolph, A. Philip, 516
Rapacki, Adam, 785
Rayburn, Sam, 738
Reagan, Ronald, 886, 940, 1007–1008
recessions, 740, 827–828, 914–915,
    997–998
Reconstruction Finance Corp., 587, 716,
    739
reconversion, 654–656
red scare, post-WWII, 667–672
Rehnquist, William, 901
religion, 638, 642–649, 759
reparations, WWII, 547
Republican party: post-WWII, 703–704;
    in 1950s, 711, 731–733; *see also* Con-
    gress; elections
research, industrial, 575
Resource Recovery Act, 912
Reston, James, 926
Reuther, Walter, 593–594, 719
Revenue Acts, 501–502, 829–830
revenue sharing, 896
revivalism, 643, 647
Rhee, Syngman, 705, 715
Rhodes, John, 975
Ribicoff, Abraham, 579
Richardson, Elliott, and Watergate,
    954–962
Ridgway, Matthew, 714, 771
riots, 850, 860–861, 863
roads and highways, 748
Rockefeller, Nelson, 820–821, 848, 985,
    1007
Rodino, Peter, and Watergate, 967–972
Rogers, William, 893
Roman Catholics, 642–649, 819, 822
Rommel, Erwin, 523, 527, 540
Romney, George, 886
Roosevelt, Franklin: and Munich crisis,
    458–460; reelected 1940, 467–471;
    negotiations with Japan, 480–487;
    fourth term, 542–546, 554, 651, 674,
    675, 679–680, 684; *see also* World
    War II
ROTC, 641
Roth, Philip, 626

Roth, Stephen, 903
rubber industry, WWII, 500
Ruckelshaus, William, 912, 962
Rumania, 461, 476, 542, 680
Rundstedt, Kark von, 540, 551
Rural Development Program, 745–746
Rural Electrification Administration, 745
Rusk, Dean, 825
Russell, Richard, 713, 847
Russo-Japanese War, 549

Sadat, Anwar el-, 924, 1000, 1001,
    1017–1019
St. Clair, James, and Watergate,
    966–974
St. Lawrence Seaway, 747
Salinger, J. D., 624, 625
San Francisco Conference, 674, 680
Sato, Eisaku, 928
Saud, King, 809
Schine, G. David, 729
Schumacher, Kurt, 934
Schweiker, Richard, 1008
science, in WWII, 495–497
Scott, Hugh, 970, 975
Scranton, William, 849
Seabed Treaty, 922
Seale, Bobby, 861
Selective Service, 654
Selective Service Act, 477
Servicemen's Readjustment Act, 654
Shah of Iran, 1020
Sheen, Fulton J., 643
Shepard, Alan, 908
Sherman Act, 587, 588, 589
Shigemitsu, Mamoru, 560
shipping, WWII, 475–476, 500, 529–531
Short, Walter, 490
Shriver, Sargent, 848, 942–944
Shultz, George, 894
Sihanouk, Norodom, 929
Simon, Paul, 621
Sirhan, Sirhan, 885
Sirica, John, and Watergate, 956–957,
    961–970
sit-ins, 763
Smith, Gerald, 515
Smith Act, 476, 512, 671, 672, 756
Smith-Connally Act, 510
social security, 830, 894
Social Security Act, 666, 748, 853
solar energy, 1033
Souphanouvong, Prince, 840
South: in WWII, 515; in 1950s,
    732–733, 760–764; in 1960s, 831–834,
    857–860
Southeast Asia Treaty Organization, 797
Southern Regional Council, 759, 861
Souvanna Phouma, 801, 802, 840

Soviet Union: pact with Hiter, 461; invades Finland, 462–463; post-WWII, 674–675, 679–687; 691–701; in 1950s, 704–706, 714–715, 769–776, 786–790, 802–812; in 1960s, 815–817, 834–839, 874–875, 908; and Mideast, 1000–1001; in 1970s, 1000–1001, 1004–1005, 1022–1023; *see also* nuclear weapons; World War II
space: missile gap, 771–772; moon landing, 908–910
Spain, 784
Sparkman, John, 719
Spruance, Raymond, 531
Stabilization Act, 510
Stalin, Joseph, 461, 478, 479, 677, 680, 681, 684, 691, 773, 786; and WWII, 536–551
Stans, Maurice, 894
Stark, Harold, 469
Stassen, Harold, 661
State and Local Assistance Act, 896
State Department, 669–670, 728
States' Rights Democratic party, 662–663
steel industry, 590, 596–598, 828
Steinbeck, John, 623–624
Stennis, John, 961–962
Stettinius, Edward, Jr., 498, 547
Stevens, Robert, 729
Stevens, Wallace, 629–630
Stevenson, Adlai, 665, 719–722, 734–735, 771, 819, 825, 843
Stewart, Potter, 901
Stilwell, Joseph, 537, 685
Stimson, Henry, 465, 475
Strategic Air Command, 770
strategic arms limitation talks (SALT), 919–923, 1004
Strauss, Lewis, 729
strikes, 506–507, 510, 590–592, 596–598, 601–603
student activism, 639–642
Student Non-Violent Coordinating Committee, 861
submarines, 475–476, 479, 529–531; 769
Submerged Lands Act, 741
suburbs, 607–610, 860
Subversive Activities Control Board, 672
Suez Canal, 804–805
Summerfield, Arthur, 738
Supreme Court: and civil liberties, 513–515, 751–757; in 1950s, 587–588, 589, 592, 671–672; in 1960s, 865–868; in 1970s, 900–907, 972–974, 1040–1041
Suzuki, Kantaro, 558, 559, 560
Symington, Stuart, 772, 819
Syria, 808, 809, 872–874, 1000–1001

Taft, Robert, 468, 593, 660, 661, 703, 706, 709, 711, 717, 718, 720, 727
Taft-Hartley Act, 593, 595, 660, 855
Taiwan, 703, 705, 711–712; and China, 793–801, 926–928, 1021–1022
Tanaka, Kakuei, 928
taxes: WWII, 500–504; post-WWII, 655, 660–661; in 1960s, 829–830, 831; in 1970s, 903–904, 964–965, 998, 1024–1025, 1032
Tax Reform Act, 894–895
Taylor, Glen, 662
Taylor, Maxwell, 771, 876
teachers, 632–633
technology, 573–575
Teheran Declaration, 538
television industry, 581, 617
Teller, Edward, 704
Teng Hsiao-ping, 1003–1004, 1021, 1022
Tennessee Valley Authority, 741–742
Tet offensive, 880, 883–884
Thieu, Nguyen Van, 878, 1002
Tho, Le Duc, 931, 935
Three Mile Island, 1032–1033
Thurmund, Strom, 662-663, 887
Thuy, Xuan, 931
Tibet, 800
Tillich, Paul, 645
Tito, Marshal, 786
Titov, Gherman, 908
Toffler, Alvin, 605
Togo, Shibenori, 488, 489
Tojo, Hideki, 482
Tonkin Gulf Resolution, 876–877, 932
Torrijos, Omar, 1017
Toyada, Teijiro, 484
trade, 678, 915–917, 923
Trade Expansion Act, 827
transportation, 580, 854, 857, 997–998
Transportation Department, 854
Tripartite Agreement, 482, 483, 486
Triple Alliance, 517–519
Trujillo, Rafael, 817, 870
Truman, Harry, 499, 544, 947; as President, 554, 559–560, 590–592; elected 1948, 661–665; domestic policies, 664–672; foreign policy, 674, 679–682, 689–713; discontent with, 716–717; and election of 1952, 718–719
Truman Doctrine, 691–694
Truth-in-Lending Act, 854
Truth-in-Packaging Act, 854
Tshombe, Moise, 811–812
Tunisia, 810–811
Turkey, 692–694, 808, 869, 1002, 1020
Tydings, Millard, 670, 671, 708–709

Udall, Morris, 1006
Udall, Stewart, 825

unemployment, 570, 573n; in 1970s, 914, 1026-1028
United Arab Republic, 809
United Mine Workers, 590, 601
United Nations, 548-549, 666-677; and China, 925; and Korea, 705-707, 709, 714-715; and Mideast, 806-812, 872, 1000-1001, 1019
Updike, John, 625
Urban League, 861
U Thant, 838
U-2 incident, 775-776

Vance, Cyrus, 1012
Vandenberg, Arthur, 468, 656, 693, 695, 703
Vandenberg Resolution, 700-701
Venezuela, 815, 817
veterans, of WWII, 654-655
Veterans Administration, 654-655
Victor Emmanuel, King, 535
Vietnam, 794-797, 802, 840-843; communist takeover, 1001-1002; war with Cambodia, 1022-1023
Vietnam war, 875-881; opposition to, 640-641; and election of 1968, 883-884, 889; winding down, 928-936; clemency for evaders, 985
Vinson, Fred, 499, 671, 751, 753
Voice of America, 728
Volpe, John, 894
voting, 751, 858, 867-868, 941
Voting Rights Act, 998

wage, minimum, 829, 998, 1026
wage-price controls, 914-915, 986-987, 1030, 1031
Wagner Act, 593
Wainwright, Jonathan, 520
Wallace, George, 849-850, 858, 1006; and election of 1968, 887-889; and election of 1972, 937-941
Wallace, Henry, 468, 543, 655, 660-663
War Brides Act, 564
Waring, J. Waites, 751
War Labor Board, 509-510
War on Poverty, 857
War Powers Act, 983
Warren, Earl, 661, 751-757, 844, 868, 900, 905
Warsaw Pact, 785

Watergate: break-in, 944; background, 950-952; cover-up, 953-955; tapes, 955-957; firings, 959-962; public outcry over, 963-965; battle lines over, 966-968; transcripts, 968-970; Nixon under siege, 970-972; Nixon's downfall, 972-974; Nixon resigns, 974-976; reasons for, 976-979; political legacy, 982-986
Water Quality Improvement Act, 911
wealth, 1940-1970, 566-573
Weaver, Robert, 832, 852, 863
Wedemeyer, Albert, 685, 686, 687
welfare, 748, 895-896
Welles, Sumner, 460, 488
Westmoreland, William, 876, 880
Wherry, Kenneth, 703, 711
White, Byron, 901
White, William Allen, 465
White Citizens Councils, 761
Williams, Tennessee, 628
Willkie, Wendell, 468, 543
Wilson, Charles, 738, 739
wiretapping, 906-907; *see also* Watergate
women: working, 611; in 1970s, 904-905, 1041
work rules, 596, 598
World Council of Churches, 648
World War II: and election of 1940, 467-471; in 1941, 471-487; Pearl Harbor, 487-491; mobilization for, 493-500; on home front, 500-516; Triple Alliance, 517-519; Axis progress, 520-525; Allied progress, 525-542; victory, 550-560; *see also* Yalta agreements
Wright, Fielding, 662-663
Wright, James, 631

Yalta agreements, 546-550, 551, 553n, 674, 680, 767
Yarborough, Ralph, 843
Yates, Eugene, 741-742
Yeh Chien-ying, 1004
Yonai, Mitsumasa, 480, 558
Young, Andrew, Jr., 1013
youth, 1960s rebellion, 619-620
Yugoslavia, 786

Zhukov, Georgi, 554
Zwicker, Ralph, 729

About the Authors

ARTHUR S. LINK, who received his B.A. and Ph.D. from the University of North Carolina, is the George Henry Davis '86 Professor of American History at Princeton University and Director and Editor of *The Papers of Woodrow Wilson*. He has held Rockefeller, Guggenheim, and Rosenwald fellowships, in addition to memberships at the Instutute for Advanced Study. He has been the Harmsworth Professor of American History at Oxford University and has lectured in South America, Japan, Western Europe, and Poland. Two of his many books have been awarded The Bancroft Prize, and he has received six honorary degrees. He is a member of and has been an officer of many professional societies and is a past president of the Southern Historical Association and the Association for Documentary Editing.

WILLIAM B. CATTON received his A.B. and M.A. from the University of Maryland and his Ph.D. from Northwestern University. He has taught, at Northwestern University, the University of Maryland, Princeton University, and, since 1964, at Middlebury College, where he has been Charles A. Dana Professor of American History and Chairman of the Division of the Social Sciences. Currently he is Professor Emeritus and Historian in Residence. He is coauthor, with Bruce Catton, of *Two Roads to Sumter* and *The Bold and Magnificent Dream: America's Founding Years 1492-1815*.

A Note on the Type

The text of this book is set in CALEDONIA, a Linotype face designed by W. A. Dwiggins. It belongs to the family of printing types called "modern face" by printers—a term used to mark the change in style of typeletters that occurred about 1800. Caledonia borders on the general design of Scotch Modern, but is more freely drawn than that letter.

This version of Caledonia was set by a computerdriven cathode ray tube by Lehigh/Rocappi from input provided by Random House/Alfred A. Knopf, Inc.

Printed and bound by R.R. Donnelley & Sons.